ecstasy
reconsidered

by

Nicholas Saunders

with bibliography by

Alexander Shulgin

Contributors

My sincere thanks to these major contributors

Peta McGee (layout and general assistance); Alexander Shulgin (Bibliography); Desmond Banks (Law); Leon van Aerts (Toxicology); Karl Jansen (Adverse psychological effects); Mary Anna Wright (Sociological effects); Chris Jones (Treatment); Russell Newcombe (Deaths); Jim Carey (Alcohol versus ecstasy); Alex Bellos (Media); Marian O'Brien (editing); Josh Portway (cover artwork); Richard Ross-Langley and Christine (proof reading); the London policeman for his tips and the providers of test results who wish to remain anonymous.

Sincere thanks also to the many additional generous people who have contributed to produce this book by helping me with my research, sending me information and providing their personal accounts.

Ecstasy Reconsidered by Nicholas Saunders
published by Nicholas Saunders, distributed by Turnaround
(details inside back cover)

©Nicholas Saunders 1997
Printed by BPC Wheatons, Exeter, England.
ISBN 0 9530065 0 6

How to use this book

This book is all about ecstasy, and includes everything from funny stories to serious academic research. How you use it depends on what you are looking for.

Those who are simply curious about ecstasy should start by reading the Personal Accounts, a selection of descriptions by all sorts of people.

Because of widespread concern, much of this book is taken up with the risk and dangers of ecstasy use. The subject is treated in depth, and includes four chapters written by specialists, the first reviews evidence for long term damage or neurotoxicity, the second deals with psychological problems and how to treat them, the third examines ecstasy death reports and the last covers emergency treatment. The subject is complex and experts disagree, so I have included a summary under Dangers and interviews with researchers under Research.

For ecstasy users, the results of recently tested pills are included, while Dance Drugs describes other drugs found on the dance scene. Many lesser-known uses for ecstasy are described from psychotherapy to spiritual enlightenment. For those unfortunate enough to be arrested, there is advice from a solicitor and a policeman.

I hope that you find this book useful as well as interesting and amusing. If you want further information, or would like to contribute yourself, please visit my Internet site. You can also email me from there.

Nicholas Saunders, April 1997

Introduction

M y interest in the drug ecstasy was aroused in 1988. I had taken LSD in the sixties which I believe altered the course of my life in a positive direction. The experience was profound and gave me an expanded view of my existence, but it was difficult to assimilate because it was hard to recall and impossible to describe in words.

Ecstasy does not provide a psychedelic experience. You remain grounded and aware in the same state of consciousness as normal, yet with some extra awareness. It removes the fear which normally inhibits our behaviour and allows us to open up. It allows us to indulge in pleasure, or to look deep into ourselves. Later, the experience can be recalled and insights applied to everyday life. It is an excellent teacher.

My own first experience was not only extremely pleasurable but provided a valuable insight into my life. It gave me a taste of letting go and being unusually 'normal', playing and laughing more freely than I had for years. I questioned what was different to normal and could clearly see that I had been tormenting myself by holding a resentment against someone – for several years. Perversely, like a mourner tearing out his hair, I had been punishing myself instead of him. But having seen that, I was able to let go and enjoy life once more. I experienced the sheer joy of living, and laughed with the realisation that simply breathing and stretching gave me more pleasure than I had had for years.

The experience got me out of a rut and convinced me that this was a drug with enormous potential for improving the quality of our lives. The special character of Neal's Yard, a courtyard in central London which I had established in the seventies with some idealistically run businesses, was being eroded by 'straight' businesses moving in. For years I watched gloomily as my ideas were discarded and the buildings were bought up by developers, but after my ecstasy experience I stopped moping about the loss of 'the good old days'. Instead, I enthusiastically competed by borrowing money to redevelop two buildings and start more businesses in my own style.

My experience of ecstasy fascinated me and led me to find out more. I quickly discovered that researchers already knew much about the drug which the media and the ravers were ignorant of. The press portrayed ecstasy as a killer drug forced on to innocent teenagers by ruthless pushers, while users' folk wisdom was equally lacking in factual information. Someone really had to write a book about it. For the next three years I was committed to my building project, but when that was finished learned all I could about the drug from academic research and personal experiences.

While dancing on ecstasy, I enjoyed an extraordinary closeness between myself and everyone around. It was as though we were members of an exclusive tribe celebrating an ancient ritual with our hearts wide open. There was an uplifted spiritual quality, a feeling that our group experience was on a higher plane than normal where openness and honesty replaced superficial behaviour. It was as though we had rid ourselves of corrupt cultural pressures and were allowed to express our true selves.

Publishing *E for Ecstasy* provided me with an introduction to secretive users, including therapists, monks and a rabbi. My research took me to Northern Ireland to investigate stories about ecstasy breaking down barriers between Catholics and Protestants, to Switzerland to interview therapists licensed to use ecstasy and even to Nicaragua where ecstasy was being used to treat soldiers suffering from war trauma. This lead to *Ecstasy and the Dance Culture*.

Since then I have continued to explore every aspect of ecstasy and have visited the main researchers in the USA where I took part in two separate research projects as a volunteer. This book is a compilation of all that I have learned.

Research trip to the USA

First stop was Johns Hopkins Medical Institute in Baltimore, Maryland an enormous research establishment. There I spent a week as a guinea pig, in a trial looking for damage to brain functions resulting from ecstasy use. Previously the researcher, George Ricaurte, found indications that ecstasy damages the brain, yet failed to find evidence that the brain worked less well. This study was not looking for damage inside the brain, but for damage to the way it functioned by comparing ecstasy users with non-users.

I was given an extremely thorough medical examination, at the end of which the nurse said: "Unfortunately your sense of taste is normal." I soon discovered why: the food was a controlled diet without tea, coffee or goodies, and I was not allowed out all week in case I sneaked off to have my fix of coffee or chocolate.

My days were taken up with endless IQ and personality tests on a computer, psychiatric interviews, pain endurance tests and responses to other drugs. For several hours I had to lie still while I was fed drugs through one arm and blood was sampled from the other; I had electrodes glued to my head while I slept; a spinal tap that gave me an alarming twinge in one leg and a slight headache for a couple of days... but nothing was as bad as the food. I also interviewed Dr. Ricaurte, but my questions were not very incisive as my appointment turned out to be shortly after being injected with morphine.

Rockefeller University

On to New York where I visited James O'Callaghan, a researcher into neurotoxicity who was then working at Rockefeller University. He showed me round and proudly introduced me to his rats which were black with white stripes instead of the usual dozy albinos. His research has lead him to believe that ecstasy is not neurotoxic, in complete contrast to George Ricaurte: I include interviews with both of them in this book in the chapter on Research.

Besides their difference in opinion, it was clear to me that they were very different personalities. Ricaurte is an imposing man who speaks calmly with an authoritative air, describing his work in simple language – the perfect interviewee. By contrast, O'Callaghan is an intensely energetic workaholic who talks nonstop using lots of technical terms. It was hardly surprising that they did not get on personally, and I was left wondering how much this affected their polarised opinions.

Purdue University

Next stop Purdue University where I interviewed Dave Nichols who is doing research into new psychoactive drugs for use as tools for research into how the brain works. One of his inventions was MBDB, which turned up in tests of ecstasy tablets with '$' and Fido Dido logos. Nichols' view is that ecstasy is neurotoxic when taken in very high doses.

Multidisciplinary Association for Psychedelic Studies (MAPS)

From there I flew to North Carolina where I stayed with Rick Doblin who runs MAPS, the organisation campaigning for research into MDMA and psychedelics. There are a few projects in the pipeline, but it's a slow uphill task as each one takes years of planning, lobbying and persuasion. We spent a few days working on the US edition of my book, *Ecstasy: Dance, Trance and Transformation*, which helps to support MAPS.

University of California at Los Angeles(UCLA)

On to LA where I was again a guinea pig, this time for Charles Grob at UCLA. I was not given MDMA, but Grob has tested people while actually on the drug and built up data on a variety of its measurable effects.

First, I had a Magnetic Resonance (MRI) scan. My head was held still by being sticky-taped down and having a barred visor clamped over it. I was then motored back right into a narrow tunnel, but a mirror fixed to the visor enabled me to see my feet and beyond I had a glimpse through a window into the control room. For the next one and a half hours there was a series of loud noises, at first like machine gun fire, then a variety of higher pitched noises that could well be sound effects for a sci fi movie. Afterwards I was showed some views of my scan on screen. Sections were taken across the head and axially; one could zoom in for detail.

Straight afterwards I went to another scanner. I was wedged in, taped down and given a snorkel type device to breath through which turned out to contain a radioactive gas. The scan only lasted a few minutes, but I was then injected with a radioactive marker and was scanned again for half an hour while the machine made a noise and rocked as though a large mass was being swung round my head. Later they would combine the MRI and SPECT scans using software developed by themselves; as each shows different kinds of information.

The results of the trials are still not published, but Grob told me that two of the 18 subjects given MDMA had bad reactions although all were regular users. One had an allergy to cats and had stayed with a friend with a cat the night before, so the bad reaction to MDMA was probably related to his allergy or to the proprietary medication he used. This prompted me to carry out a survey looking for relationships between bad reactions and medications, but none emerged.

The second person had such a bad reaction that he was released from the trial. But when the 'blind' was broken, it was found that he had been given a placebo, yet another demonstration that the effect of a drug can depend very much on the 'set and setting'.

Herbal ecstasy

After the scans I spent the afternoon on Venice Beach. I soon noticed a herbal ecstasy stall, and saw it was the brand with a butterfly logo. I picked up a leaflet and sure enough on the top was "People reported all kinds of effects. Some even saying it was the best ecstasy experience they had ever had. Nicholas Saunders, UK. E for Ecstacy." My words had been deliberately edited to sell the product, while in fact I had said it was useless.

Behind were two girls and a man with dark glasses. I said "This is me, and I have been misquoted." The guy with dark glasses replied, "Oh yes, and you misquoted me too. I was really disappointed with that article you wrote, but I've quoted you word for word. And I've sold millions of these." He then suggested that I "take a walk", but I said I was going to take a photo of him instead. "Hey, you can't photograph me!" "Yes I can, I'm in a public place" and got out my camera, but he fled by the time I was ready.

On the way I visited a Benedictine monk who believes that ecstasy brings us back to the uncorrupted state which has been lost through the pressures of civilisation. He believes that although this 'natural' state may not be suitable for life in our society, it is valuable as a way of opening the door to religious experience. In fact, he persuaded me to write a book on the spiritual uses of psychedelics, not just ecstasy.

Since then I have established an Internet site about the drug which has helped me to keep in touch with users throughout the world.

This book is a compilation of all my knowledge, besides containing articles I have commissioned by experts in particular branches of science and medicine.

History

The chemical named ecstasy was invented long ago, yet remained unknown until the seventies and only became a popular dance drug in the nineties.

Ecstasy was first used by Americans as an aid to psychotherapy and personal development. They regarded it as a sacrament which could allow them to be their true, uncorrupted selves in the state that God created mankind before 'the fall', and they named it Adam for that reason.

By the mid–eighties the drug was also known as a 'good time pill' and, being still legal in the US, was openly promoted under the brand name ecstasy. Alarmed US authorities hurriedly banned the drug and put pressure on other countries to follow suit, but that did not stem the drug's popularity.

It was not till the late eighties that people discovered its use as a dance drug, and even the 1989 edition of "Ecstasy the MDMA Story" did not mention that use. Once discovered, the combination of dancing and the effect of ecstasy took off and developed into the rave scene, particularly in Britain.

The ecstasy dance culture has developed from big events and warehouse parties into mainstream city nightclubs worldwide, and has split into several distinct factions each with their own style of music, dress and behaviour. But, in spite of widely exaggerated scare stories and government campaigns claiming to 'educate' users of the drug's dangers, its use shows no signs of declining.

M DMA was patented in 1912 by the German company Merck. Rumour has it that the drug was sold as a slimming pill along with comic descriptions of its strange side effects. This was almost certainly a myth. MDMA was just one of many new compounds which were patented but never marketed. The next time it came to light was in 1953 when the US army tested a number of drugs to see if they could be used as an agent in psychological warfare.[1]

US Army tests [1]

In the 1950's, MDMA was one of the analogues of MDA that was given to animals by the US army at the Edgwood Arsenal, which was then investigating drugs for use in chemical warfare. There is no evidence in the public domain to indicate that MDMA, which was code named Experimental Agent 1475, was ever given to humans or was tried as a truth serum

---

The father of MDMA – or stepfather as he describes himself – is Alexander Shulgin. After obtaining a PhD in biochemistry from the University of California at Berkeley, Shulgin got a job as a research chemist with Dow Chemicals, where he invented an insecticide. This turned out to be a winner for Dow who rewarded Shulgin with his own lab and an invitation to research whatever interested him.

Having once had a dramatic experience on mescaline, Shulgin used the opportunity to research psychedelic drugs. An accepted test for psychedelic effects was to observe how fighting fish change their behaviour. But there were problems: fish don't say when they are under the influence and, well, have you ever seen a fish that doesn't look stoned? His answer was to 'suck it and see'. Eventually Dow was embarrassed to find themselves holding the patents of some popular street drugs and he was politely given the push.

Shulgin continued testing new compounds on himself and a select group of friends for many years. Thanks to his remarkable ability to maintain friendly contact with people who do not share his controversial views, he earned the respect of influential people and was able to carry on with his research until recently. His approach to psychedelics is similar to that of a botanist: he specialises in the phenethylamines, and delights in recording the subtle differences between each member of that family of drugs.

His experiences are described in his biography jointly written with his wife Ann, *Phenethylamines I Have Known And Loved* or *PIHKAL*[2] . MDMA is but one of nearly 200 psychoactive drugs which he describes in detail, and, although its effects are less dramatic than many, MDMA is perhaps the one which comes closest to fulfilling his ambition of finding a drug with psychotherapeutic potential. The Shulgins are now working on a companion book on the tryptamines to be called *TIHKAL* which should be available before the end of 1997.

> **PIHKAL** [2]
>
> *Shulgin describes himself as the stepfather of MDMA if not the inventor. "I made it in my lab and nibbled. It gave me a pleasant lightness of spirit. That's all. No psychedelic effects whatsoever... Just a distinct lightness of mood. And an indication to get busy and do things that needed doing," he recounts.*
>
> *The book is a delightful combination of autobiography, graphic descriptions of drug effects and detailed instructions for synthesising nearly 200 drugs (including several methods of synthesising MDMA). However, only a well-equipped chemist could follow the instructions. Even the laboratory notes include humorous asides; I particularly liked the comment that many big name drugs have analogues with similar effects that could be made without infringing patents.*

Shulgin first synthesised MDMA in 1965, but it was only after hearing glowing reports in the early seventies from other experimenters who had also synthesised and tried MDMA that he took an interest. He describes how in 1977 he gave some to an old friend who was about to retire from his career of psychotherapy:

He phoned me a few days later to tell me he had abandoned his plans for a quiet retirement. I know none of the details of the increasingly complex network which he proceeded to develop over the following decade, but I do know that he travelled across the country introducing MDMA to other therapists and teaching them how to use it in their therapy. They had all begun, of course, by taking the drug themselves. He believed (as I do) that no therapist has the right to give a psychoactive drug to another person unless and until he is thoroughly familiar with its effects on his own mind. Many of the psychologists and psychiatrists who were instructed developed small groups or enclaves of professionals who had been similarly taught, and the information and techniques he had introduced spread widely and, in time, internationally.

It is impossible to ever know the true breadth of therapeutic MDMA usage achieved during the remaining years of his life, but at his memorial service, I asked an old friend of his whether she had a guess at the number of people he had introduced to this incredible tool, either directly or indirectly. She was silent for a moment, then said, "Well, I've thought about that, and I think probably around four thousand, give or take a few."

The full story is told in a book called *The Secret Chief* (see Information chapter page 252).

Those first psychotherapists to use MDMA were keenly aware that they had found a valuable new tool. As one put it, "MDMA is penicillin for the soul, and you don't give up penicillin once you've seen what it can do".[3, 4] They were equally aware that if MDMA became a popular street drug, it could follow in the footsteps of LSD and be criminalised by the US government. They agreed to do as much informal research as possible without bringing the drug to public attention, and did pretty well – MDMA only gradually became known as a fun drug and it wasn't until 1984 that the bubble burst.

If ecstasy is so wonderful, why hasn't it been marketed by any of the big drug companies? One reason is that the US Food and Drug Administration (FDA) prohibited trials on humans until 1992. But the most significant obstacle to the commercial exploitation of ecstasy is that it has already been patented once and cannot be patented a second time. Before a new drug can be marketed, the company selling it has to show that the safety risks are justified by the drug's benefits *as a medicine*, and this involves long and expensive trials. The normal way of recouping that expense is by obtaining exclusive rights to sell the drug through holding its patent. In fact, the drug companies have a vested interest in preventing the use of ecstasy for psychotherapy, as the therapeutic use involves very few doses as opposed to regular administration of traditional drugs.

A deeply embedded puritan ethic seems to affect the response to drugs in western societies. To use a drug for pleasure is taboo, yet to use a drug to relieve pain is acceptable. In reality there is no sharp distinction: if someone is suffering from depression and a drug makes them feel happy, it is regarded as a medicine and meets with approval. But if they are regarded as normal and take a drug that makes them happy, they are indulging in something socially unacceptable – unless that drug happens to be alcohol.[5]

Those years 1977 to 1985 are looked back on as the golden age of ecstasy or Adam[6] as it was then known. In psychotherapy its use only appealed to a few experimental therapists, since it didn't fit in with the usual 50-minute psychotherapy session, but those who did include some of the most dynamic people in the field, including some who claimed that MDMA could greatly shorten treatment.[7] There was also a select group of explorers who used the drug in a variety of ways, but it was many years before it was used as a dance drug.

By 1984 MDMA was still legal and was being used widely among students in the USA under its new name ecstasy.[6, 8] (Rumour has it that a big-time dealer called it Empathy, but, although the name is more appropriate, he found that ecstasy had more sales appeal). In Dallas and Fort Worth, Texas, ecstasy replaced cocaine as the drug of choice among yuppies and even spread to people who normally kept well clear of drugs; it was even on sale in bars where you could pay by credit card. This public and unashamed use resulted in the drug being outlawed.

Prohibition

During 1985, ecstasy got into the mass media because a small group of people sued the US Drug Enforcement Agency (DEA) in an attempt to prevent them from outlawing the drug. The controversy provided free advertising which made ecstasy spread like wildfire throughout the USA. This was particularly bad timing, following soon after a widely publicised disaster: a batch of China White (a designer drug sold as a legal substitute for heroin) contained a poisonous impurity which caused severe brain damage.[9]

The media made ecstasy into a scare story implying that it was a similar drug, and as a result the US Congress passed a new law allowing the DEA to put an emergency ban on any drug it thought might be a danger to the public. On 1 July 1985 this right was used for the first time to ban MDMA – what is more, MDMA was placed in the most restrictive category of all, reserved for damaging and addictive drugs without medical use.[10] The effect of prohibition was to prevent research into the drug without changing the attitudes of recreational users.[11]

Attitude [11]

A hundred MDMA users were interviewed in depth between 1987 and 1989, i.e. after it was made illegal. The article concludes that making MDMA illegal made no difference to recreational users' attitudes.

Scare stories

MDMA was scheduled in the most dangerous category of drugs because the hearing followed soon after users of another new synthetic (China White) suffered brain damage similar to Parkinson's disease, and the false assumption that MDMA is similar to MDA which had already been scheduled.

Designer drugs

The term was originally used to mean compounds that were designed to have the same effect as illicit drugs without being illicit themselves. However, the term is often used to mean new drugs which have been designed to have a particular effect.

In 1985, under American pressure, the International Convention on Psychotropic Substances asked member nations to place MDMA in Schedule 1 although the chairman of the World Health Organisation (WHO) Expert Committee disagreed with this decision, stating that "At this time, international control is not warranted." A clause was added encouraging member nations to "facilitate research on this interesting substance".[12]

The temporary ban only lasted for a year; meanwhile a hearing was set up to decide what permanent measures should be taken against the drug. The case received much publicity and was accompanied by press reports advancing the kind of scare stories now current in Europe, which added to the pressure to make the ban permanent.

One widely publicised report referred to evidence that another drug, MDA, caused brain damage in rats and concluded that MDMA could cause brain damage in humans.[13] Just as now in Britain, the US media saw this as justification to portray horror scenarios of a generation of children's brains rotting within a few years. On the other side were the psychotherapists who gave evidence of the benefits of the drug – but they had failed to prepare their ground by carrying out scientifically acceptable trials, so their evidence was regarded as anecdotal.

The hearing ended with the judge recommending that MDMA be placed in a less restrictive category, Schedule 3, which would have allowed it to be manufactured, to be used on prescription and to be the subject of research. The recommendation was ignored by the DEA, which refused to back down and instead placed MDMA permanently in Schedule 1. A group of MDMA supporters made a challenge to this decision in the Federal Court of Appeal, but their objections were overturned on 23 March 1988.

The criminalisation of MDMA in America has had wide-ranging consequences. The first was to prevent the drug being used legally by therapists, except in Switzerland where it was allowed between 1988 and 1994. The second was to reduce the quality of the drug as sold on the street, because demand was now met by clandestine laboratories and the drug was distributed through the criminal network. Criminalisation did not prevent the drug's popularity spreading worldwide.

Ecstasy arrives in Europe

E cstasy was brought to Europe by two distinct groups of users in the mid-eighties. Followers of Bhagwan Rajneesh, the Indian guru whose disciples wore orange, brought it with them when they moved out of their ashram in Oregon; they spread its use as a means to self enlightenment.[14] At about the same time, in the winter of 1987-8, ecstasy reached the holiday island of Ibiza where it became a popular party drug.

Returning British holidaymakers started to organise their own parties. Instead of city venues with their restrictive licenses, organisers set up out of town events in empty warehouses or under the stars. They avoided the authorities by being secretive, selling tickets with a phone number but with no address. If the address became known, then the police would obtain court orders allowing them to prohibit people from reaching the site, but once thousands of people were holding a party it was unstoppable. The procedure was to phone the number shortly before midnight when an answering system would give the meeting place such as a motorway service station.

Once a large number of cars had arrived, they would drive in convoy to the site. The police would be there too, of course, but were routinely tricked. The police had to let the convoy move so as to clear the road, but if they went in front, then the leader would divert down side roads; if they followed, then the car in front would lead the police astray. A variation was to give several meeting points on all sides of the site and then the actual location later.

The authorities responded by bringing in a new law in 1990 which meant that party organisers could face up to six months imprisonment and confiscation of profits.

The result was to push ravers into dance clubs. The Hacienda in Manchester led the trend in 1988 and established the now prevalent style: DJs who never spoke, but teased the dancers with their subtle 'scratching' establishing the Manchester sound.[15]

Despite prohibition, anti-drugs propaganda and scare mongering by the media, ecstasy use as a dance drug has progressed from an exclusive elite to a mass dance culture which has spread worldwide, including the USA from where it originated.

Recent history

Over the last ten years the culture has changed. At the beginning, anyone who had experienced dancing on ecstasy felt part of 'one big happy family' without barriers. Mirroring the rise of LSD in the sixties, people were either 'one of us' or not according to whether they had taken ecstasy. There were no barriers of colour, education, sexual orientation or language – the only thing that mattered was whether you had been initiated into the magical open-hearted world of dancing all night on ecstasy.

At the very first parties there was no set behaviour, allowing people to really let go and be themselves. But, imperceptibly, ravers conformed until they had established an acceptable code of conduct which distinguished them from outsiders regardless of their drug experience.

As the movement grew it split into factions. Waving white-gloved hands in the air while dancing to nonstop techno was OK in Scotland, but was looked down on by Southerners who had 'moved on' to new types of music and cooler behaviour. Factions became associated with particular types of people, each with their own variations of acceptable music, behaviour and drugs.

Much has been, and is being, written about the development of the ecstasy-dance scene and will not be repeated in this book. Matthew Collin describes the recent history graphically[16] without pretending – like most club owners and promoters – that ecstasy and other drugs were hardly relevant.

References

1. Report of US Army tests on ecstasy from Rick Doblin president of the Multi-disciplinary Association for Psychedelic Studies in the US.
2. *PIHKAL (Phenethylamines I Have Known And Loved); A Chemical Love Story* , by Alexander and Ann Shulgin. Published by Transform Press (Berkeley USA) at $18.95. Also available from Compendium Bookshop, London. The companion volume *TIHKAL* is due 1997.
3. Meetings at the Edge with Adam: A Man for All Seasons? by Philip Wolfson from *Journal of Psychoactive Drugs* Vol. 18 April 1986 Wolfson introduces himself as an established

psychotherapist passionately involved with people experiencing painful altered states of consciousness. He says that ecstasy opens up new possibilities for treatment of such cases, but there are some hazards to be wary of.
4. Interview with Deborah Harlow, research fellow at the Division on Addictions, Harvard Medical School, October 1993.
5. *Living with Risk*, published by the British Medical Association, 1990. This book contains statistics and evaluations of various risks commonly taken by people in the UK.

6. The Nature of the MDMA Experience by Ralph Metzner and Sophia Adamson in *ReVision*, Spring 1988.

7. Subjective reports of the effects of MDMA in a Clinical Setting by George Greer and Requa Tolbert from *Journal of Psychoactive Drugs* Vol. 18/4 1986.

8. *The Phenomenology of Ecstasy Use*, by Teresa O'Dwyer, Senior Registrar of Adult Psychiatry at St Thomas Hospital, Morpeth, November 1992. This paper is an account of a study of users' experiences on ecstasy and the patterns and circumstances of their use undertaken by the Leeds Addiction Unit between January and September 1992.

9. *Psychedelics Encyclopedia*, by Peter Stafford, 3rd edition published by Ronin, 1992

10. Differences Between the Mechanism of Action of MDMA, MBDB and the Classic Hallucinogens, by David Nichols, from *Journal of Psychoactive Drugs*, Vol. 18 April 1986.

11. Why MDMA Should Not Have Been Made Illegal, by Marsha Rosenbaum and Rick Doblin, from the book *The Drug Legalisation Debate*.

In this article it is argued that with many claims of people benefiting from taking MDMA and few reports of the drug causing damage, its use should not have been outlawed in the US.

12. 22nd report of the Expert Committee on Drug Dependence 1985, published by the World Health Organisation as part of its Technical Report Series #729, para 2.28 Methylenedioxymethamphetamine.

13. Neurotoxicity of MDA and MDMA in *Alcohol and Drug Research*, Volume 7. This paper argues that the dangers associated with MDA should be assumed to apply with MDMA unless it is proved otherwise.

14. *Ecstasy – The Arrival of a Consciousness-Raising Drug*, by Arno Adelaars, published in de Knipscher, 1994. Originally published in 1991 with updates including analysis of Dutch samples in 1993.

15. Manchester RIP, Kaleidoscope, BBC Radio 4, 6 February 1993.

16. *Altered State, The Story of Ecstasy Culture and Acid House* by Matthew Collin published by Serpent's Tail 1997. ISBN: 1 85242 377 3.

Attitudes

*A*ttitudes about the use of illicit drugs have always been polarised, but never so greatly as with ecstasy. An objective look at the evidence would suggest that both the dangers and benefits of ecstasy are in the same league as alcohol, yet hardly anyone would agree. The mass of the population sees ecstasy as an extremely dangerous menace to society without any virtues, while the minority regard the drug as low-risk and even beneficial.

Information about ecstasy is seldom objective. Users rightly distrust the authorities, 'education' programmes and instead have developed their own street wisdom. While this provides useful knowledge on usage, it also includes myths.

Users see the government's division between legal and illegal drugs as hypocrisy, and it is hard to justify their legal status in terms of public health. Further, there is growing evidence that anti-ecstasy propaganda is supported by vested interests in the alcohol industry who view ecstasy as a threat to their profits.

A deeply-embedded puritan ethic seems to affect the response to drugs in Western societies. To use a drug for pleasure is taboo, yet to use a drug to treat illness is acceptable. This was clearly expressed in *The Economist* on 6 of April 1966:

> Society's moral confusion over drugs is neatly illustrated by its differing reactions to Prozac and ecstasy.
>
> Every week, according to the most conservative estimates, half a million Britons take a pill to make them happy. This pill was originally developed as an appetite suppressor. Now it is an adjunct to partying. In America, some five million people regularly take a different sort of pill. This one was developed as an antidepressant. Now it is widely used as a chemical accessory by those who think it is unfair that they should ever feel low.
>
> The British users are breaking their country's law. The Americans are not. Which raises an important question. If it is not acceptable to take MDMA (better known as ecstasy) to make you feel happy when you just want to have fun, why is it acceptable to take the antidepressant fluoxetine (better known as Prozac) to make you feel happy if you are not actually clinically depressed?

Both sides like to justify their arguments by reference to scientific and statistical evidence. But, as with so many political conflicts, opinions depend more on emotional input than logic. In the case of ecstasy, this boils down to those with experience of the drug 'feeling' that it is good and healthy, against those who see it as a threat to social order 'knowing' it is a corrupting influence.

From an ecstasy user's viewpoint, it is sheer hypocrisy to tolerate alcohol and prohibit ecstasy, as expressed by the sociologist Mark Gilman: "The hypocrisy is absolutely astounding. Let's have another look at that. We live in a society that actively promotes the highly addictive drug, tobacco. This is a drug that kills hundreds of thousands of people every single year. But it's a good earner. Then, let's think about those sophisticated television adverts that urge us to drink more alcohol. Alcohol kills a few thousand people every year and a few thousand more get maimed by dangerous drunks. Ah well, never mind, alcohol is OUR drug and WE like it, so get off our case."

Many ecstasy users are dismissive about possible dangers because they are well informed and decide it's worth the risk. However, others continue to use it even though they believe the negative propaganda. Some regular ecstasy users even believe myths such as that the tablets they consume contain heroin or poisons – suggesting that risk is not always such an unattractive quality.

The generation gap is now wider than ever, with a large proportion of young people unable to confide in their parents and distrustful of politicians of all parties. The establishment sees this as a threat, blames ecstasy as the cause, and tries to clamp down on its use by a variety of means. First the government tried scare tactics, but when these failed turned to 'education' in the form of information edited so as to provide a far more negative bias than scientific evidence would suggest.

Even scientific evidence tends to be biased against ecstasy through grants being awarded for research into possible harm but not to benefits, a trend which is further exaggerated through reporting in journals (see under Media). Respected scientists may have vested interests in promoting a particular viewpoint, particularly those who work for pharmaceutical companies, and it is generally against their interests to express positive findings about illicit drugs. One example, which I have on good authority, concerns a researcher who unexpectedly discovered that a supposedly toxic drug did not result in physical damage. He was reluctant to publish his results in case he was branded as 'pro drug' which he believed would prejudice future grant applications.

Among people working professionally in the field of drug abuse, it is those who have close contact with ecstasy users who are least antagonistic. This is significant and supports the idea that prejudice is based on ignorance of the issue. Unfortunately, policies tend to be made by senior people who are out of touch.

World attitudes

Worldwide, there is a wide range of attitudes towards ecstasy. At one extreme is the American establishment view that drugs are evil in themselves: they cause enormous damage to young people and must be stamped out by tough use of the law, using campaigns such as Just Say No. People who uphold this view believe that the reason's people use drugs are due to persuasion and inadequate personality. Drug dealers are seen as ruthless criminals who have no respect for their customers and give the kids free samples to get them addicted while alcohol and cigarettes are not thought of as drugs. Those who support such views tend to be older and isolated from illicit drug users, but they do include some influential people such as senior police officers[12] and many professional people including some in the drug abuse treatment profession.

Australia has been caught up a the grip of anti-ecstasy publicity which mirrors that of Britain, following the death of a 15 year old girl at a rave party. The general perception perpetuated by the media and the government is that ecstasy, which has became a generic name for killer drugs, is a product of the rave culture and that if you stamp out the raves your kids won't take drugs.

As a result the Government is taking a very 'hard-line' anti-rave stance, proposing to introduce a similar law to the British 'Criminal Justice Act', and by making examples of dealers and people caught in possession of ecstasy. They have threatened police charges such as 'attempted murder' for supply resulting in death and jail sentences for possession.

This has created a contradiction in attitudes with the focus of all the anti-drug action almost entirely on the rave scene, while generally overlooking prolific drug use at other music and dance events, where it has become an accepted part of the culture. One example would be the Gay and Lesbian community who hold regular dance parties and an annual Mardi Gras parade, which last year, had a group rolling a giant ecstasy tablet through the streets.

In Europe, Holland has been leading the way towards liberalisation but faces pressure from other European countries to tighten up. Both Dutch and Spanish government committees have submitted reports recommending that MDMA be reclassified to the same class as cannabis, but neither is likely to be implemented.[3]

Myths – spinal fluid

A widely believed myth is that MDMA causes a loss of spinal fluid. This seems to have stemmed from research on ecstasy users where spinal fluid was removed for analysis.

Attitudes to drugs [4]

Almost every psychoactive drug has been regarded by some society as a dire threat to public order and moral standards, while as a source of harmless pleasure by others. Almost every society has one drug whose use is tolerated, while others are regarded with deep suspicion.

The Dutch are followed by the Spanish, Swiss and Danish. Although members of the United Nations and therefore signatories to the Convention on Psychotropic Substances,[4] the Dutch have decided, without actually changing the law, not to prosecute people found in possession of drugs for their own use. Instead of trying to prevent usage, the authorities in Holland give drug users help and information so they can choose for themselves. Subsidised testing facilities are encouraged where users are given immunity from arrest even if they are dealers. The pact gives dealers an opportunity to talk about their side of the trade and to have samples of their wares tested, while it provides the authorities with detailed (although anonymous) information about what is going on.

British attitudes

One might say that Britain is in between. My impression is that the British establishment and police favour the official American view, while workers in the field sympathise more with the Dutch. In researching this book, I have come into contact with a number of people who are paid by the government including social workers, teachers, doctors, psychiatrists and researchers in the field of drug use. Many of them cannot afford to say openly what they believe, but off the record have told me they believe that ecstasy has done more good than harm; several having tried the drug for themselves.

> **Drug chief viewpoint** [1]
>
> *When I suggested that truthful counselling would inform users that MDMA is no more harmful than alcohol, Detective Chief Inspector Todd replied that two wrongs don't make a right. He accepts that young people will take drugs whatever is done, but says that if no action is taken we will end up with a society where drug taking is normal.*
>
> *"I will fight to prevent that," he said passionately.*

It is hardly surprising that Conservative MPs support the establishment viewpoint, but their methods are hardly honourable. At a youth conference in Manchester, the MP Nigel Evans contradicted me, saying that he had seen conclusive new evidence that ecstasy use caused long term damage to humans. My response, that I was not aware of such evidence, played into his hands, but when I later asked for his source, he sent me a cutting from *The Times* which quoted an editorial in the *British Medical Journal* which in fact contained no new evidence, (see Media chapter, page 28). I pointed that out, ending: "I sincerely believe that freedom of information is a fundamental requirement for a democracy, and I see my role as accurately interpreting the available information on this subject for the benefit of consumers. This follows several years spent as director of the Consumers Association. As a representative of the people, I trust that you hold similar principles. True education must provide balanced information, not prejudiced by political motives." He did not reply.

> **Police attitude** [2]
>
> *"It is a myth that ecstasy users are a separate group from those who use addictive drugs. Once a market for a drug is established, users will switch to any other drug." Detective Chief Superintendent White also believes that dealers mix addictive drugs in with MDMA in order to get clients hooked. The best advice, he says, is "just don't do it".*
>
> *White believes police action is misunderstood when it comes to stopping raves, as the use of drugs is a very minor motive. The reasons are, in order of priority, (1) Public safety, (2) Public order, (3) Public Nuisance, (4) Use of drugs. He believes that very little drug dealing goes on at raves, because ecstasy "takes about 4 hours to have its full effect" and so users take it before they arrive. [In fact full effect is felt within one hour.]*
>
> **Students swap drink for E** [5]
>
> *A survey in late 1995 among students at Oxford and Cambridge showed that ecstasy use had doubled compared to the previous year, while alcohol use had halved. Use of cocaine and amphetamine was also up, while cannabis and LSD was about the same.*

Current trends

I n Britain, views have been further polarised recently by the high profile Leah Betts campaign on one hand, and positive comments from well known stars of their ecstasy use including Sting, Brian Harvey, Noel Gallagher and Tony Mortimer.

While the government remains staunchly against ecstasy and the whole culture that goes with it, and has brought in new laws to try to prevent drug use in clubs, the Prime Minister says he is proud of Britain leading world youth culture, apparently unaware of the contradiction.

Informed debate seems as remote as ever among the public, although *The Economist* continues its crusade to legalise drugs on the grounds that prohibition is the root cause of about half of all crime, and that present policies simply do not work[6] – a view also voiced by Commander John Grieve of the Metropolitan Police.[7]

Probibition and crime [7]

"The parallel with the prohibition of alcohol in the US in the twenties and thirties is exact. Slavery apart, no greater mistake was ever made in America's social history... If cigarettes were declared illegal, the story would be the same: soaring prices, pushers at street corners, addicts stealing to feed their habit and so on." Commander John Grieve, head of Criminal Intelligence at the Metropolitan Police called on the Government to examine whether the supply and use of illegal drugs could be licensed.

"Licensing for illegal drugs including ecstasy should be explored, perhaps on the basis of licensed cafés in Amsterdam... Either we go to war with drugs dealers across the globe, or we have to come up with new options."

References

1. Interview with Dectective Chief Superintendent Derek Todd, Drugs Co-ordinator with the No. 9 Regional Crime Squad, at Spring Gardens, London, February 1993.
2. Interview with Dectective Chief Superintendent Tony White, head of drugs and money laudering branch of the National Criminal Intelligence Service, which is under the control of the Home Office, at Spring Gardens London, February 1993.
3. In February 1993, the Netherlands Istitute for Alchol and Drugs in Utrecht recommended that MDMA be reclassified as a 'Soft Drug', but this recommendation was ignored by the Dutch parliament. – A visit to Arno Adelaars, a part-time purchaser of street samples for testing by the Dutch Government.
4. Refer box on page 17.
5. Survey carried out by and reported in *The Independent*, 11 December 1995.
6. *Sunday Times* 9 January 1994.
7. Refer box on page 19.

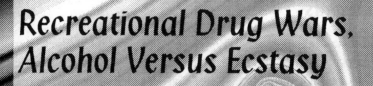

Recreational Drug Wars, Alcohol Versus Ecstasy

I n this article, Jim Carey, a freelance journalist, investigates how the alcohol industry has responded to the threat of competition from ecstasy.

For the second year in succession, Chancellor Kenneth Clarke punctuated his 1996 Budget speech with swigs of malt whisky. For the alcohol industry the event provided multiple cause for celebration. Not only had the Chancellor gifted them with another prime piece of televisual product placement, he had also boosted industry hopes of increased sales by cutting tax on alcoholic spirits.

In the same parliamentary year, the British Government backed a Private Member's Bill giving Local Authorities the power to close dance clubs if police report evidence of drug taking. During the passage of the Public Entertainments (Drug Misuse) Bill, particular and persistent reference was made to ecstasy as the prime target of the new law.

To the alcohol industry, any measures which clamp down on the recreational use of ecstasy are only likely to increase sales of their product. With the recreational effects of E diminished by alcohol consumption, people taking ecstasy tend to drink far less alcohol. This encroachment on the alcohol industry's domination of the market became financially significant in the late eighties, when the exploding rave culture in the UK swung youth preference away from alcohol and pubs, towards ecstasy and communal dancing.

the percentage of 16-24s taking any illegal drug doubled to nearly 30 per cent between 1989 and 1992

A report on *Leisure Futures*, published in 1993 by influential market analysts the Henley Centre for Forecasting, revealed that between 1987 and 1992, pub attendance in the UK fell by 11%, with a projected 20% decrease by 1997. Estimates used in the report suggested the percentage of 16-24s taking any illegal drug doubled to nearly 30 per cent between 1989 and 1992. Using a rather conservative estimate suggesting one million people attend licensed raves each week, the Henley Centre estimated UK ravers were spending £1.8 billion a year on entrance fees, cigarettes and illegal drugs.

The report concludes: "This of course poses a significant threat to spending for such sectors as licensed drinks, retailers and drink companies. Firstly some young people are turning away from alcohol to stimulants; secondly raves are extremely time consuming and displace much of the time and energy which might have been expended on other leisure activities like pubs or drinking at home."[1]

In presenting the Public Entertainments (Drug Misuse) Bill, MP Barry Legg noted that "there was a lot of money involved in the business" and that the new bill would "squeeze every penny of profit from the drug dealers".[2] Indeed, profit levels attainable from the sale of alcohol are the kind which command considerable political lobbying power. Evidence suggests that this power has been regularly employed in a sophisticated marketing war waged between the alcohol industry and rave culture since the late eighties.

In 1989, a new public relations alliance was formed by the UK's leading alcohol companies. Instrumental in setting the ball rolling was Lord Wakeham, a Tory peer and then chairman of the Ministerial Group on Alcohol Issues. According to Anthony Hurse, civil servant at the Department of Health: "Lord Wakeham made it clear to the alcohol industry that he would like the industry's collaboration. He spoke to Peter Mitchell [Director of Strategic Affairs] at Guinness who agreed he'd do what he could."[3] As a consequence of Wakeham's suggestions, the UK's seven leading alcohol companies including Whitbread, Bass and Seagram, launched a new PR organisation from the headquarters of Guinness plc in London's Portman Square. The Portman Group's publicly stated aim is "to promote sensible drinking" However, according to Professor Nick Heather, Director of the Newcastle Centre for Alcohol and Drug Studies, the Group's real agenda is rather different: "The attempt to distance alcohol as a drug from other kinds of drug and to give it a good face is the main activity of groups like the Portman Group."[3]

With over £1 billion being cut from government research funding over the last ten years, scientists have been forced to compete for private funding. The Portman Group is just one of the many corporate interests which have populated this funding vacuum. In late 1994, the Portman Group operated a scheme which offered medical scientists £2,000 pending their agreement to criticise a damning new book on alcohol.

the Portman Group operated a scheme which offered medical scientists £2,000 pending their agreement to criticise a damning new book on alcohol

Published in 1994 in conjunction with the World Health Organisation, *Alcohol and the Public Good* was unequivocal in its emphasis on the connection between alcohol and ill health.[4] According to Professor Griffith Edwards, Emeritus Professor of Psychiatry at the University of London and chairman of the team which compiled the report: "The Portman Group is using sleaze tactics to try to undermine this work. It is the result of an extensive review of scientific research by 17 contributors from nine countries, none of whom has been paid a penny or will receive any royalties. By offering money and anonymity to academics to attack their colleagues, the industry has poisoned the springs of healthy academic debate."[5] Professor Edwards also reports being offered a charitable donation from the Portman Group pending his agreement not to use the phrase "alcohol and other drugs" in future reports.[3]

One of the people helping to facilitate this 'cash for criticism' scheme was Dr. John Duffy, a member of the Edinburgh University Alcohol Research Group. This supposedly independent medical research unit was set up in 1978 with core funding from the Scotch Whisky Association and is now heavily funded by the Portman Group. In a letter to a national newspaper, Dr. John Rae, director of the Portman Group, defended this backing saying: "We fund Edinburgh University because its alcohol research group is the best in the country."[6] However, as Douglas Cameron, a Senior Clinical Lecturer in Substance Abuse at the University of Leicester and former adviser to the Portman Group, recently stated: "I think that the drinks industry have made every attempt to drive the research agenda in the direction it wants it driven."[3] Indeed, the Edinburgh Unit is well known for its scientific support of the tangible health benefits of alcohol.

Perhaps more damning, given the current sociopolitical preoccupation with law and order, is the British Medical Association's (BMA) report on alcohol and crime published once again in the late eighties. This report highlighted alcohol's association with 60-70 per cent of homicides, 75 per cent of stabbings and 50 per cent of domestic assaults.[7] According to an ex-rave music plugger at Virgin records: "There are so many

stories about ecstasy that lie below the surface. Big rave events that I was involved
with in the past had a very low police presence compared to the big rock festivals I've
been involved with where there's
alcohol. They knew people were going
to be loved up and not violent."[8]

Ironically this interviewee asked to
remain anonymous because of his
current connections with the advertising
industry.

Ignoring advice from almost the entire
medical establishment, the Secretary of

*"Big rave events that I was involved
with in the past had a very low police
presence compared to the big rock
festivals I've been involved with where
there's alcohol. They knew people were
going to be loved up and not violent."*

State for Health (Stephen Dorrell) raised his department's officially recommended
weekly limits of alcohol by 33% in 1995. In response, Dr. Maristella Monteiro, a medical
officer for the World Health Organisation, accused the British government of "being
in the pocket of the drinks industry".[9]

The first legislative victory for the alcohol industry in its battle for market control,
came in the form of the Entertainment (Increased Penalties) Act in 1990. This successful
Private Member's Bill was introduced by Conservative MP Graham Bright, who referred
to it as "the acid house party bill". The new law placed fines of up to £20,000 on the
organisers of unlicensed raves and had a highly detrimental affect on an exploding
new culture with its impromptu venues. At the time, Graham Bright was Parliamentary
Private Secretary to Prime Minister John Major, a post he held for four years. Since
1979, Bright had represented Luton as an MP, a town which hosts the headquarters
of one of the UK's leading brewery companies, Whitbread plc.

When the now infamous 'Cash for Questions' scandal broke in the British media in
1994, Tory MP Neil Hamilton's greedy associations with lobbyists, Ian Greer Associates,
took centre stage. In contrast, Graham Bright escaped lightly, despite implicating
associations with both Ian Greer Associates and some of Ian Greer's clients, including
Whitbread. Evidence of Bright's associations with the scandal were exposed in a Cook
Report programme prepared by Central TV. The programme revealed documents
written by Ian Greer Associates, revealing Graham Bright to be one of the lobby firm's
conduits to political influence. Although one of the most eagerly awaited
documentaries of the year, the programme was inexplicably pulled from the
broadcasting schedule by the heads of Carlton TV. Since that date leaked transcripts
of the programme have been used to reconstruct parts of the censored programme
and broadcast on Channel Four.[10]

As the 'Cash for Questions' scandal began breaking in the media in 1994, Graham
Bright was quietly dismissed as PPS to John Major, given a knighthood and sidelined
as one of three vice-chairmen of the Conservative Party. As a result of the scandal, Ian

Greer Associates finally went into liquidation in 1996, but not before they had acted on behalf of Whitbread plc in helping to establish a parliamentary beer club. With its 125 member MPs including Chancellor Kenneth Clarke, it is now the largest industrial group within Parliament. Indeed, Greer's firm sent a proposal to Whitbread in 1993 that read: "Members of the beer club can be encouraged to raise excise duties at Treasury questions but also through, early day motions, adjournment debates and private members business". At the time, Greer's firm was receiving £30,000 a year from Whitbread for their services.

Although the most silent MP in the House of Commons for two years running, Graham Bright certainly knew how to get things done as "private member's business". His 1990 anti-rave legislation was one of a minority of private member's bills that actually became law. Ian Greer also recommended the use of "co-ordinated parliamentary pressure, using the beer club and other friends of Whitbread."[11] Indeed, primary culprit in the 'Cash for Questions' scandal, Neil Hamilton, acted as parliamentary consultant to the Brewers' Society from 1987 to 1989,[12] whilst Conservative MP James Couchman, personal private secretary to the Leader of the House of Commons, is also an adviser to the Gin and Vodka Association. Despite this web of political manipulation, the alcohol industry's involvement in the lobbying scandal received scant attention.

The sophisticated response to the market threat posed by ecstasy has been multimedia in its strategy. When Tory MP, Iain Mills died from 'acute alcohol intoxication' following an excess of dry gin at the beginning of 1997, the newspapers reported the story in terms of his "lonely life": an understated approach when viewed in contrast to the media reaction to one of the rather less frequent ecstasy related deaths. Complicity in the distribution of relative misinformation about these two drugs is commonplace in both national and regional media, when many such media sources have economic interests in maintaining good relations with the alcohol industry. Whitbread alone spends £20 million on marketing and advertising each year.

When Tory MP, Iain Mills died from 'acute alcohol intoxication' following an excess of dry gin at the beginning of 1997, the newspapers reported the story in terms of his "lonely life"

Advertising, described as "the science of influencing public opinion", has borrowed heavily from images taken from rave culture, even though it has been harnessed to usurp that very culture. One recent television advertisement for Holsten Pils shown in the UK, illustrates the point: An actor, clutching a bottle of the aforesaid lager, strolls through a fantastically coloured computer simulated landscape. In the closing shot, a smiley yellow tablet comes zooming out of the sky and, in idiotic voice tones, advises the actor to "get wired man". The actor, replies "Get a life sucker" before pulling on a string to deflate the tablet like a spent balloon. The connotations are obvious.

Meanwhile alcohol companies like Seagram (Absolut Vodka), Holsten, Grolsch and Fosters are blitzing youth culture magazines with specially targeted advertising campaigns designed to re-establish alcohol as a drug of youth preference. Alcoholic soft drinks have exploded onto the market with extraordinary economic success. Within six months of being introduced to Norway, in 1996, Hooper's Hooch alcoholic lemonade had overtaken all foreign beer sales in the country.[13] The company which makes Hooch is one of the UK's largest alcoholic drinks companies, co-sponsors of the Portman Group.

> *a smiley yellow tablet comes zooming out of the sky and, in idiotic voice tones, advises the actor to "get wired man"*

According to Sir Donald Acheson, president of the British Medical Association and ex-Government Chief Medical Officer: "It seems self-evident that alcopops appeal to those who are still drinking soft drinks. They might have a tendency to habituate people to alcohol in childhood."[14] Ironically, the Portman Group issued a press release in 1996 recommending that children should be allowed a certain amount of alcohol, claiming it would help them know how to handle it in later life. So whilst Gordon's try to rejuvenate dry gin's greying image with athletic male models and bubbles, Seagram now operate an Absolut Vodka bar in one of London's most well known and politically connected dance clubs, the Ministry of Sound. "Absolut is hip at the moment in trendy clubs," says Mike Mathieson, founding director of youth marketing and PR company FFI. "There's a bit of a return to alcohol, which seems to be the new ecstasy substitute."[15] Interestingly, FFI are the company which provided the street lingo for one of the most unusual anti-ecstasy advertising campaigns. In the week following Leah Betts' funeral 1,500 billboard poster sites displayed a picture of the teenager lying comatose in hospital. In large lettering next to the photo was the word 'SORTED', and in smaller lettering 'JUST ONE TABLET OF ECSTASY TOOK LEAH BETTS'.

The deluge of anti-ecstasy commentary following Leah's death in 1995 pumped wild and alarming conclusions into the public's perception of E. In fact it was Leah's fourth ecstasy tablet, not her first, and on the night of her death she had also been drinking alcohol.[16] As the nearest person the UK has to an expert on ecstasy, Dr. John Henry, scientific adviser to the National Poisons Unit, was interviewed by just about every national newspaper. His quotes were used as 'authoritative scientific' back up for emphatic media tirades against ecstasy. However, according to Dr. Henry: "There was an over reaction to her death. An awful lot was made of it that I don't think was very scientific at all because the press were jumping on every word. I had things served up to me by journalists. It makes serious discussion very difficult."[17]

When the inquest into Leah's death confirmed she had died from drinking too much water, journalists took less notice. Asked what Leah's death teaches us scientifically, Dr. Henry is less dismissive of the truth: "It teaches us that if you take a lot of fluid suddenly when you've got no reason to do so, it's dangerous." As the vast majority of ecstasy related deaths have thus far been associated with dehydration, a common myth had circulated that water was an antidote to the chemical effects of ecstasy.

Drug education experts argue that Leah's death was likely to have resulted from misinformation and that misinformation is the greatest danger. It was also the greatest criticism levelled at the dramatic but inaccurate Leah Betts/Sorted posters. This poster campaign was unusual because it had been constructed by three advertising companies. Media buyers, Booth Lockett and Makin; advertising agency, Knight Leech and Delaney and youth marketing consultants, FFI. The most remarkable aspect of the campaign was that each of the companies involved in the organisation and design of the project gave their time and work for free; highly unusual in a commercial advertising industry that would normally have netted £1 million in design, consultancy and site fees for such a campaign. Booth, Lockett and Makin even split the costs of printing with Knight Leech and Delaney.

There are many possible motives for this campaign, including prestige, creative design freedom and the personally held beliefs of some of the advertising executives involved. However, one contributory factor which precludes any of the altruistic intent portrayed by the companies themselves can be found by examining their client portfolios. For whilst Booth, Lockett and Makin have Lowenbrau as a major client, both Knight Leech and Delaney and FFI represent the 'energy' soft drink company, Red Bull. "There's a growth in the energy drinks area and it's very competitive," says FFI's Mike Mathieson. "We do PR for Red Bull for example and we do a lot of clubs. It's very popular at the moment because it's a substitute for taking ecstasy."

The 'Sorted' campaign presented obvious commercial benefits to their client's product and therefore also to the advertising company's reputation as successful marketeers

Indeed, Red Bull are the joint most lucrative client on Knight Leech and Delaney's books, providing £5 million worth of business. The 'Sorted' campaign presented obvious commercial benefits to their client's product and therefore also to the advertising company's reputation as successful marketeers. The reverberations went far and wide, with Granada TV even making a programme for schools off the back of the campaign.

The emerging implications of this investigation are not that alcohol is bad and ecstasy good; both drugs have their pros and cons.

But when the Secretary of State for Health increased the officially recommended alcohol limits in 1995, he defended his manoeuvre thus: "Alcohol consumption will always be a major public health issue and it is important for the government to present a balanced view which recognises the risks but also offers soundly based and credible advice on which people can base their own choices."

Were this an approach applied to other recreational drugs, his statement might have been welcomed as a move to a more unfettered debate. Instead its selective application to alcohol is indicative of that industry's deep-seated influence on national politics and culture. One drug has been made socially acceptable whilst the other has not, with the criteria for this selective demonisation having more to do with the pollution of public information by corporate interests than it does with concerns for public safety.

© Jim Carey, March 1997

References

1. *'Leisure Futures'* pub The Henley Centre for Forecasting 1993. Price £374.

2. *Hansard* 17 January 1997 Col 525.

3. Dispatches, Channel Four 12December 1996 produced by Ray Fitzwalter Assoc.

4. *'Alcohol and the Public Good'* by Prof. Griffith Edwards et al. pub Oxford University Press 1994.

5. Letter to *The Independent* 5 December 1994

6. Letter to *The Independent* 7 December 1994.

7. *Guide to Alcohol and Accidents*, British Medical Association 1989.

8. Personal Interview on tape .

9. *The Independent* 13 December 1996.

10. Dispatches, Channel Four 16 January 1997 produced by Fulcrum Prod.

11. *The Observer* 20 October 1996.

12. *Private Eye* No. 910 1 November 1996.

13. *Folket* 15 November 1996.

14. *Daily Telegraph* 6 December 1996.

15. Personal Interview on tape with Mike Mathieson.

16. *Daily Telegraph*, 1 February 1996

17. Personal Interview on tape with Dr John Henry.

Media

*A*n essential part of democracy is for government policies to be questioned and criticised, a function normally undertaken by the media. However, the media tends to support the government view on illicit drug use without question, and in doing so has failed to play this important role.

In this chapter, a journalist looks at the reasons behind newspaper attitudes and suggests that the tide may be turning.

Then I trace how even the most respectable medical journals publish unsubstantiated reports on ecstasy damage, and deliberate misinformation gets repeated in newspapers until it is regarded as fact.

The media and ecstasy

by Alex Bellos

The British have formidable appetites for both newspapers and drugs. We have ten national dailies – a remarkable number compared to other European countries – and, as we know only too well, illicit substances have had major roles to play in most of our significant youth cultures. The two have, however, been uneasy bedfellows. Passing from the reefer madness of the Fifties through the pills 'n' pot scares of the Sixties and Seventies, and then the glue and skag exposé's of the Eighties, newspapers, especially the tabloids, have traditionally demonised drugs and drug-users. They make good targets, and the papers have usually been able to maintain a fairly consistent line. Although the broadsheets had a bit of trouble with the well-reasoned and organised campaigns to legalise dope that flourished a quarter of a decade ago, editors could generally rely on most of their readers not to take drugs, and not to sympathise with people who did. It was easy. E-asy. But recently strange things have happened in the British newspaper offices. Things that suggested this old certainty was, well, not so certain any more.

When Brian Harvey offered his by-now legendary account of his recreational chemistry, you could almost feel the news media's excitement. January is a slow month for news, which means any scare stories that generate a bit of controversy are always welcome. And this one had a celebrity. And not one that your pop pages were going to want interviews from later. The Daily Mirror led the charge, devoting its first seven pages to an Ecstasy Shock Issue: Every Family Must Read This. Strangely, however, the Mirror would also lead the charge back again a fortnight later when Noel Gallagher spoke in defence of Brian Harvey and added for good measure the cheeky soundbite that taking drugs is "like getting up and having a cup of tea in the morning". "Stars and fans blast his words" had been their headline for Harvey – in comparison with which "E's got a point. Stars-back Oasis Noel's outburst on drugs" was an undeniably more reflective sell. Noel's full statement may have been carefully worded – "I've never – condoned the use of drugs. I just slam as hypocrites those politicians who simply condemn drug abuse as a criminal activity and think they are doing something positive. The criminalisation of drug users simply isn't working" – but it was nevertheless significant that a British "family newspaper" did not apparently regard it as sacrilege to compare drugs with tea.

Anyway, there was evidence that other editors were having similar conversions. In the Telegraph, John Casey, a Cambridge don, wrote: "It is no use our screaming with rage when a pop singer says that taking ecstasy is no more dangerous than driving a car. Statistically he may be right. Horrid though it is to admit, it may be necessary to speak candidly about safe drug taking." London's Evening Standard printed a think-piece entitled "Why Noel Is Right About Drugs", arguing for legalisation. The Mirror was on a roll. It opened a telephone poll about whether Noel was right to call for a debate on drugs. The result made their front page: 87 Per Cent Back Noel. Hopefully its leader writers saw the irony in the polemical editorial: "Mirror readers have shown they have a lot more sense than knee-jerk politicians... [Gallagher] has started the debate which needs to go on." More than just backing a celebrity, the paper had decided it was a cause to fight for.

Newspapers don't like appearing hypocritical – it's not good for business – and they will only admit defeat if they think they are totally out of synch with their readers. Which in this instance it was beginning to look as though they were.

You can trace some of the roots of this dilemma back to the Seventies to when Rupert Murdoch bought the Sun and appointed a ground breaking editor called Larry Lamb. Lamb realised that the age of the newspaper was coming to an end, because people were getting their 'news from television as it happened' in its place he created a paper which 'would entertain as much as it would inform', a paper which effectively constituted the blueprint for today's tabloid, affording pop culture the same prominence as news and politics. The Sun has never really looked back. However it, like all other British newspapers, has had to look forward. In the Eighties, with the launch of two new daily titles (Today and the Independent) and a general slip in overall sales, competition began to intensify on Fleet Street. In this climate, nabbing young readers was seen as a vital way to secure a prosperous future, for two reasons. First, because young readers are a long way from dying. Newspaper owners are always concerned with replacing the old readers who are constantly dying off with new recruits (they refer to the "media bath", which has to be topped up at the same rate it empties in order for it not to run dry).

Second, because the young haven't yet made up their minds about what they want to buy. Advertisers love them because of this, but because TV has a generally old and downmarket audience, they find it hard to reach them. Which means that any newspaper or magazine with a young readership can theoretically, make money. For a long time.

Article by Alex Bellos published in *The Face* April 1997.

Misrepresentation

I am often accused by the media of promoting ecstasy and of distorting the facts so as to make the drug appear less dangerous than it really is. However, the evidence I present in this book shows that the opposite is true: from respected medical journals to popular television, the media has consistently misrepresented ecstasy through misreporting and selection of evidence so as to exaggerate its dangers.

In October 1992, *The Scottish Medical Journal* published a paper entitled 'Ecstasy and Intracerebral Haemorrhage', which described how a 20 year old man had died "after his drink had been spiked with ecstasy".[1] Since the symptoms described were unusual for MDMA, I asked the author how much ecstasy and what other drugs were found in the patient. He replied: "Unfortunately, no assays for MDMA or related substances were made."

In spite of this remarkable failure, his paper was reprinted in the *British Medical Journal* and featured by the *Glasgow Herald*'s medical correspondent under the headline 'Highlighting the dangers of ecstasy'. Not only did this article state unequivocally that ecstasy was the cause of death, but elaborated by adding that ecstasy had been shown to cause serious brain damage and that patients were in psychiatric care as a result of the drug. Thus he combined three unrelated reports to produce a credible-sounding theory: research shows that ecstasy damages the brain which is confirmed by this tragic death and has also made many others psychotic.

More recently a case was published in a journal called *Clinical Intensive Care* entitled: *Ecstasy Intoxication – an unusual presentation*.[11] Although the entire paper blamed ecstasy, no evidence was mentioned. In reply to my queries, Dr. Cregg replied from Toronto that:

> *Urinalysis tested positive for traces of amphetamines, opiates and cocaine. In addition friends of this young girl, on questioning, admitted that tablets of 'speckled dove' had been taken at the party that night. An unusual term to us, so we questioned further and discovered the 'content' of these tablets. Unfortunately, no tablets were available to us for analysis.*

In other words, ecstasy was blamed on hearsay, while tests showed she had taken amphetamines, opiates and cocaine... but not MDMA.

In 1996, the *British Medical Journal (BMJ) published* an editorial called 'Ecstasy and Neurodegeneration' which argued that ecstasy was more dangerous than generally realised. It was written by two scientists who are known and respected for their work on serotonin, and cited support from no less than 12 papers published in the scientific literature. To the doctor or medical correspondent on a newspaper, the article provided indisputable evidence that ecstasy is extremely dangerous. However, all the supporting papers were published over a year previously while the recent evidence outlined above was ignored.

As an example of extreme damage that can be caused by illicit drugs, a large part of the article described how another street drug had caused symptoms similar to Parkinson's Disease, giving the impression to the casual reader that ecstasy might also do so, although that possibility was investigated and dismissed in 1986.[2]

As a result, *The Guardian*'s medical correspondent warned that long term ecstasy users may suffer from a kind of Parkinson's Disease. The paper was honest enough to admit their mistake by publishing my letter, but far more readers would have read the original warning than my letter, and be left with a false impression. Many other newspapers here and even in the USA reported the *BMJ* article as providing new evidence that ecstasy is neurotoxic.

On 7 April 1996, The *Sunday Telegraph* ran a prominent story entitled 'Tests prove ecstasy harm is permanent' by Rachel Sylvester claiming that new research had established that ecstasy causes "permanent brain injury", based on an interview with the Californian researcher, Charles Grob. The article claimed that Dr. Grob had found brain damage by using hi-tech brain scans on long term users. Two weeks later, the paper published Dr. Grob's response in which he denounced the article saying: "This is a gross distortion and misrepresentation of our research..."[3] The editor played down the rebuke by heading the letter: "Ecstasy: too soon to judge."

On 12th May 1996, *The Sunday Times* ran a major feature by Olga Craig called E is for Agony: 'How many young people are clubbing themselves to death on ecstasy?' illustrated by photos of teenagers captioned 'Killed by the Drug Culture'. The centre of the page displayed a quote in large type: 'Experiments detected profound effects on the brain, which were confirmed by brain scans in long-term users'.

The text revealed that this was based on the work of Dr. Charles Grob. The same article also claimed that Mary Hartnoll (the senior Scottish social worker widely condemned by the media for saying that the dangers of ecstasy had been exaggerated) 'has now backtracked, now saying she believes the drug is "very risky"'. I wrote to Ms. Hartnoll to ask whether she had changed her mind and if so why, and she replied: "I have not changed my mind and restricted myself to clarifying what I had said".[4]

On 14th June 1996, *The Independent* ran a feature by Glenda Cooper headed 'Ecstasy users risking long term brain damage'. In it she states that "a study in the US, carried out for the Food and Drug Administration, found 'profound' and 'permanent' effects on the brain which were confirmed by brain scans on long term users". She admitted to me that her source was *The Sunday Telegraph*.

I wrote a letter to the editor pointing out the error, but he did not respond. So I took my complaint to the Press Complaints Commission, a supposedly independent arbitrator set up to adjudicate in such cases. Eventually I received their judgement:

> Another study in the US, carried out for the Food and Drug Administration on 18 human volunteers who had taken the drug before, found "profound" and "permanent" effects on the brain which were confirmed by brain scans on long-term users.

The Commission ... did not believe that the short reference to it in an article primarily about the beliefs of other scientists, would mislead readers. We regret that, in the circumstances, we are unable to help you further.

In 1965 the Press Complaints Commission dealt with over 2,500 complaints and upheld 28. It is funded entirely by the press.[5]

The Time Out saga

S urprisingly, *Time Out* has outdone even the shoddiest of scare reporting concerning ecstasy. In 1993, the magazine ran the headline:

Bitter pills

Ecstasy has turned to agony for thousands of E users as dealers spike tablets and capsules with heroin, LSD, rat poison and crushed glass. *Padraic Flanagan* investigates.

T housands of lives are at risk as spiked Ecstasy tablets flood the capital. Drug agency workers believe that adulteration with heroin, LSD and even crushed glass and rat poison will

cling into the market were noticed two years ago when a marked deterioration in quality was reported by regular Ecstasy, or MDMA, users.

Stephen Beard, a worker at the Newham Drugs Advice Project

take drugs they can rely on. I think it is now almost impossible to be certain that what you're taking is Ecstasy, it's become a lottery,' says Beard.

'We know dealers put a touch of

The article 'revealed' that what is sold as ecstasy often contained dangerous contaminants including crushed glass, heroin and rat poison.[6]

The named source, Stephen Beard, refused to tell me who told him or give me supporting evidence of any kind. The National Poisons Unit was unaware of any recent cases of poisoning due to crushed glass or rat poison. Yet *Time Out*'s editor, Dominic Wells, said he trusted his reporter and no correction was necessary.

Three years later (13/11/96),[7] *Time Out* declared that "heroin in ecstasy is an urban myth". But the article contained several other false statements, including that DMT and 2CB are legal, and propagated a new myth that there was a new drug called LSD 27. Once again, the magazine refused to admit the mistakes.

Positive press

T he small proportion of good press about ecstasy has been made up for by its quality.

New Scientist ran an editorial describing the Government's response to ecstasy as a panic reaction. It pointed out that the dangers were small compared to alcohol, tobacco and hobbies such as horse riding:

> *Ecstasy takers know this, and become understandably cynical about warnings issued by those in authority. Trust disappears—another victim of panic. It would be far better to present an honest assessment of the risks and issues, but we have to accept that ecstasy use is widespread and deal with it rationally. Attempts to curtail the supply of the drug have failed. So we must*

learn as much as we can about its effects, and present that information honestly.[8]

The Economist showed up the public hypocrisy by comparing social attitudes towards ecstasy and Prozac:

> *The question is whether a line can be drawn between therapeutic and non-therapeutic use of the drug. And if it can be, should it be?*
>
> *...The other way of answering the question is to admit that Prozac, like ecstasy, is often used recreationally, to enhance pleasure, rather than to treat depression – and, if this is not approved of, to ban its use in these cases. But why ban the recreational use of drugs?*[9]

The surprise in the pack was *The Mail On Sunday* magazine whose cover feature consisted of a double page spread picture of a man fishing captioned "More dangerous than taking ecstasy".[10]

Apart from these, *The Guardian* is the only British national paper to regularly publish well informed articles about ecstasy.

The Internet

Lastly, a new addition to the media in the form of the Internet has provided a truly free source of information and discussion on illicit drug use. A number of newsgroups exist where people can post reports of their experiences and ask questions which others answer. My first book *E for Ecstasy* has been on-line since 1994 where it is consulted over 400 times a day, and my site ecstasy.org is a well known source of information.

Unlike many people, I look forward to the commercialisation of the Net. If it was possible for me to collect small fees, then I could supply services which are in demand but too costly, such as regular testing of ecstasy samples.

References

1. Ecstasy and Intracerebral Haemorrhage by JP Harries and R de Silva, *Scottish Medical Journal* October 1992.
2. Designer drug confusion: a focus on MDMA by J Beck et al, *Journal of Drug Education* 16: 267-82 (1986).
3. Ecstasy: too soon to judge by C Grob, *The Sunday Telegraph* 21 April 1996.
4. Personal communication, 25th June 1996.
5. Personal communications on and subsequent to 16 August 1996.
6. Bitter Pills by P Flanagan, p.12, 27 October 1993.

7. Medicated Followers of Fashion by M Collin, *Time Out*, p. 13 November 1996.
8. Press the Panic Button, *New Scientist* editorial, 25 January 1997.
9. Better than Well, *The Economist*, 6 April 1996.
10. Night and Day magazine pages 4 to 8 published with *The Mail on Sunday*, 3 March 1996.
11. Ecstasy Intoxication – an unusual presentation in Clinical Intensive Care, 1996; 7: 265-266.

More dangerous than taking Ecstasy

BY WILLIAM LEITH

Some facts: if you are prescribed penicillin, you have a one in 200,000 chance of it killing you. And your chances of dying if you take an Ecstasy tablet? One in five million. Last year, five people died because they ate a peanut. Three people, all teenagers, died partying on Ecstasy. Meanwhile, every year 40 Anglers die indulging their passion. What does all this tell us about our fear of E?

Who takes ecstasy?

Because ecstasy is mainly used as a dance drug, users tend to be young. However, the emergence of the rave culture into the mainstream has made ecstasy use more widespread among clubbers in general, including many in their thirties.

The dance culture itself includes diverse social groups and distinct factions, but there are also non-party users, particularly in the USA. These include older people who tend to be more interested in using the drug for personal development. They include psychotherapists, seekers of spirituality, couples working out their relationships, writers looking for inspiration and even monks in a state of prayer.

Estimates of the number of regular users vary widely, and there are conflicting views as to whether ecstasy use is increasing or declining in Britain. However, there is no doubt that a significant proportion of the population who go clubbing are regular users of illicit drugs, and that ecstasy is one of the most popular.

Widespread ecstasy use has spread to most of the richer countries except those in the Far East, with France lagging behind the rest of Europe. This may reflect cultural values, with ecstasy appealing less to people who are reluctant to let go emotionally.

How many people take ecstasy?

Over the years, many estimates have been made of the number of users of ecstasy. The usual basis has been to estimate the number of venues with late night dance music and multiply by the average number of people in each; then multiply by the guessed proportion of people using ecstasy. Obviously there is enormous scope for error.

Such guestimates have ranged from 200,000 to five million uses per week, with one million widely accepted.[1] Equally unreliable evidence is provided by British customs seizures which run at around 500kg per year. Research suggests that customs intercept between 0.3% to 1%[2], in which case the amount imported is enough for 50 to 150 million doses. In addition, amateur production cannot be ignored, since even a domestic kitchen 'factory' can produce a kilo ecstasy per week – enough for 50 million Es a year.

However, in 1996 a British Crime Survey deduced that there were only about 120,000 regular users, defined as those who had taken ecstasy in the previous month. (Another surprise finding was that far more people had tried magic mushrooms than ecstasy.)

What kind of people take ecstasy?

Most users are clubbers, but the term includes many distinct groups, each with their own accepted type of music, dress, behaviour and language. Ecstasy is just one of the popular dance drugs, and although the club promoters and owners deny it, the supply of drugs, and ecstasy in particular, is essential to provide a conducive atmosphere.

Millions of ravers [1]

More than one million young people attend raves per week, spending an average of £35 at each event. This is probably an underestimate, since it only includes legal events.

Customs seizures [2]

A Home Office study by Prof. Alan Maynard et al states that customs rarely achieved the 10% seizures of drugs consistently claimed, and that in fact the figure since 1985 has fallen from 1% to 0.3% in the case of heroin.

Teenagers

Young people are the most receptive to E. Among British schoolchildren, ecstasy is the drug most frequently encountered apart from cannabis, with girls trying it earlier

11-16 year olds [3]

Survey of behaviour of boys and girls aged 11-16 and their activities including drug use.

Illegal drug experience rises to about one third of the sample by the age of 16, with alcohol and tobacco use about twice as high.

Girls drink and smoke more, but boys are more likely to try illicit drugs.

London [5]

35% of schoolchildren have bought or been offered drugs in London area schools. Trends suggest that the majority of kids will have tried drugs before they leave school. Typical starting age for trying drugs is now 14 while 5 years ago it was 17-18. 41% of school users are 14 or under. Drugs use is more prevalent at private fee-paying schools.

Other drugs used [8]

Drug use is generally related to alcohol use; those who drink more also have above average consumption of other drugs. However, those who use ecstasy drink less alcohol than users of the more popular drugs above. 45% of respondents had had sexual experiences. Of these, 25% had been drinking before their last sexual experience.

Of those who had tried ecstasy, nearly all had tried cannabis, 80% had tried LSD, 76% amphetamine, 69% psilocybin mushrooms and 60% nitrites. But only 4% had tried cocaine and 7% heroin.

Influence on life [10]

60% felt E had changed the way they looked at their life. Over half 'felt that while under the influence of ecstasy they could see a new significance in current and past events'.

70% of respondents used ecstasy on weekends only. Half had tried it only once. 31% had never taken more than one E at a time, but 7 at once had been taken by 12%. During the onset of the drug, the apprehension felt by inexperienced users sometimes developed into panic. Many said it was essential to feel very hot to get the full effect of the drug. To this end, a group of friends once drove around in a car with the heater on.

Over half reported losing personal interests including sport and drinking, but a third said they gained new interests, such as music and clothes.

58% of respondents said they had stopped using ecstasy. The most common reasons given were that: it was no longer providing enough pleasure; it had caused problems due to the associated lifestyle of all-night raving; or it caused paranoia or concerns about health. 30% reported social problems such as losing their job or the break-up of a relationship after using E. Most felt that the quality of the drug had deteriorated.

Modifying drug use [11]

An important factor determining extent of drug use was that individuals tended to monitor themselves and their peer group. This implied looking after and advising one another as to how to modify drug use.

than boys.[3,4,5,6] A readership survey in Sky magazine (1995) found that women went clubbing more than men, and were twice as likely to use E.

A survey of school children across the whole of England found that 4.25% of 14 year-olds had tried ecstasy,[7] i.e. 24,000 nationally. Another (regional) survey found that 6% of 14-15 year-olds have taken ecstasy[8] or 70,000 if applied nationally.

Homosexuals

A transvestite dealer called Samantha invited me to come on a tour of the gay clubs in London one Saturday night. He was certainly welcomed and we were ushered in as honoured guests ahead of the queue.

He explained that clubs need to have E easily available to develop a good atmosphere, so they allow favoured dealers to operate and would even encourage them. Samantha was obviously well known and popular among the staff who would point him out to punters looking for E. Meanwhile their security staff put on a show of trying to stop drugs.

There were always a number of dealers in each club who knew each other and were supportive, helping each other out. Each had his own clients and sold on reputation.

Homosexual use survey [9]

Percentages at a Gay Pride day who said they had used these drugs once or more:

	Male	Female
Alcohol	89	95
Tobacco	65	70
Poppers	70	48
Cannabis	67	75
LSD	42	48
Amphetamine	48	39
ecstasy	46	45
Magic Mushrooms	29	46
Cocaine	32	38
Ketamine	13	11
Heroin	6	9
Prozac	8	3
Crack	4	3
Drug cocktails	53	49

Widening social use

There are private clubs which organise parties for particular social groups. I was invited to an event "for more mature ravers, professional people". It was efficiently organised and held in a photographic studio which was more comfortable and better decorated than the usual warehouse venues. It got going at midnight and carried on through the night. I was introduced to an architect, a computer animator, a conference organiser and a lawyer. Most were white, conventionally dressed and aged around 30.

Many took E later "when they feel relaxed after a few drinks". Behaviour was a blend of that associated with alcohol and E – blissed out dancers and huggers were accepted along with chatting up and flirting, but without aggressive behaviour. However, the atmosphere was not conducive to a magic group experience, nor was there any rapport between dancers and DJ.

Country users

For my first book, I interviewed a group of families living in the country who use ecstasy at their private parties which include parents and children. That still goes on with the result that instead of a generation gap, parents and children are extremely close. In fact, ecstasy is probably just as popular in the country as the cities.[12]

> **Country drug use** [12]
>
> *The reason why inner cities usually come top of the list is "because drug squads aren't so likely to operate in rural areas". A government survey in rural East Sussex found that 20% of 14-15 year-olds had tried an illicit drug, about the same proportion as in cities.*

Frequency of use

My impression is that there are two distinct groups of users. One group normally takes at least one E at weekends, while the others are special occasion users. However, the regular weekend users tend to have an occasional break either from ill health or from finding that the use of the drug interferes with their life.[10,11]

Hollywood stars

While in Los Angeles, I interviewed a dealer who supplies famous names in Hollywood. He told me that demand has increased each year because E is spreading to a wider clientele. These tend to be well established people who have never been previous drug users except for cocaine.

As an example of new users, he mentioned a well-known film director whose latest film had been trashed by the media and whose wife had been ousted from a charity she had founded. They were both devastated, but friends had suggested they take some ecstasy. A few days later they phoned him to say that their ecstasy trip had put everything in perspective and restored their self esteem.

Extroverts and introverts

Arno Adelaars, a Dutchman who has written a book about ecstasy,[13] says that extroverts and introverts use the drug differently. The extroverts use it for entertainment, to open up and relate to strangers at parties, while the introverts take it at home with a lover or a few close friends to provide intellectual insights.

Trends

The 1994 figures showed that British school children aged 14-16 increased their consumption of cannabis, LSD and amphetamine but that, for the first time, their ecstasy consumption remained constant.[3] If these young people set the trend, the figures could mean that ecstasy use has peaked and is on the decline.

Over the years the scene has become divided into distinct subgroups – each with their own style of music, clothes and, to a lesser extent, drugs of choice.

Alcohol has made a comeback on the British dance scene. This, along with the use of other drugs was probably due to the worsening reputation of drugs sold as E, and that in turn was due to regular users taking too much to retain the original effect. Besides amphetamine, cocaine and other drugs are now more commonly used with ecstasy.[14,15] Recently, drugs such as crack cocaine and heroin, in the form of the smokeable impure 'Brown' variety, has appeared in some British clubs, while ketamine is popular in New York.

Trends [14]

Article discusses the changing patterns of drug use by ravers in a study based in North-East England.

Researchers report 'stacking' (taking a planned series of drugs) by ravers, a rise in the popularity of alcohol, cocaine and amphetamine besides the use of ketamine.

Race, raving and drugs of choice

There is a racist dimension to raving in the Midlands which could be caricatured by saying blacks use crack, coke and cannabis and listen to 'dark' jungle/reggae; while whites use speed, E and cannabis and listen to 'happy' hardcore/techno/drum & bass/ jungle.

– A sociologist field worker

The atmosphere at events is closely related to the consumption of drugs. This varies widely but in general appears less open-hearted, although there are some non-commercial events in Britain that still create the atmosphere from the good old days. These free parties have injected a boost of energy into the scene, and with the introduction of the Criminal Justice Act in 1994 marked its politicisation. Taking mobile sound systems and a 'keep it fluffy' attitude to a variety of events, their form of nonviolent direct action is used not only to campaign against the draconian new laws, but also to support other forms of protest especially anti-roads activism.

Overall it seems that, like all counter-cultures, a diluted form of raving has become mainstream. Rather than being considered deviant, for many people it is culturally acceptable to go to a club and take E. Some upwardly mobile professionals have absorbed ecstasy and rave-type parties into their lifestyle, dressing much as they would for an office party. Within clubs, the proportion of those on E is now lower while those using other drugs, including alcohol, have increased. Meanwhile, club owners accept the importance of ecstasy being available to create a good atmosphere, so they allow dealers to operate while pretending to exclude them.

The commercialisation of chill out parties and the rise in popularity of ambient music has marked another new trend. Formerly, ravers would invite others back to their homes for impromptu chill out parties. This was very much part of the culture and continues, but now some clubs cater for these needs providing somewhere comfortable to go while coming down off E.

On Ibiza, in London and elsewhere there are 'breakfast clubs' that open early in the morning for this purpose.

In Britain the Criminal Justice Act has made some changes. Some large illegal parties have been replaced by legal events such as the UK Tribal Gathering, but inevitably the atmosphere has suffered. On the other hand, the heavy hand of the law has politicised and united party people more than ever.

Trends in clubs [15]

Regarding trends, the jungle scene is vibrant and buzzing at the moment, as evidenced by the opening of large new clubs. Last year people spoke to me of their personal experiences of 'snidey Es' leading them to choose other dance drugs instead, in particular LSD and speed. More recently, it seems that improved quality has led some to move back to ecstasy as the preferred dance drug. Now, however, a lot of people are sticking to brands they know and trust, especially Doves, rather than the previous trend for wanting to try the latest E on the market.

"A small but growing number are using cocaine, which is increasingly available and at a lower price. Male friends say they quite often get offered a snort in the toilets at venues... There is also a race dimension, with young black men in Wolverhampton more likely to be doing speed, cocaine (crack and coke), cannabis and alcohol in various mixtures rather than E which is definitely still the first choice for young white men.

References

1. *Raves threaten jobs in drinks trade*, article in *The Times*, October 1993.
2. *Independent* 7 March 1994.
3. *Young People in 1992* by John Balding, University of Exeter. Questions were asked of a representative sample of over 20,000 11-15 year olds.
4. *The Ecstasy Study by Lifeline*, 1993 published as part of Sheila Henderson's *Final Report.*
5. London Programme, ITV 27 March1994. Commissioned a survey among school children.
6. *Young people and drug-taking: facts and trends* by John Balding, *Education and Health* 12 April 1994.
7. *Young People in 1992*, by Schools Health Education Unit of Exeter University. Questionnaires were completed by over 20,000 pupils aged 11 to 14 in 132 schools in England in 1992.
8. *The Normalisation of Recreational Drug Use Amongst Young People in North West England* by Fiona Measham, Russell Newcombe & Howard Parker, accepted by *British Journal of Sociology* 12/93. This paper presents findings relating to a first cohort of teenagers in the study. The sample was designed to be representative of gender, class and geographical area.
9. Survey of drug use among homosexuals Carried out at a Gay Pride meeting November 1994 by Project LSD, 136 Kingsland High Street, London E8 2NS (+44 181 806 7353).
10. refer box page 38.
11. *Luvdup and DeElited*, by Sheila Henderson, researcher for Lifeline, a non-statutory drug agency in Manchester. A paper given at South Bank Polytechnic May 1992.
12. *Drug culture grips heart of England* from *The Times*, 14 February 1994.
13. *Ecstasy – The Arrival of a Consciousness-Raising Drug* (book), by Arno Adelaars, published by in de Knipscher, 1994. Originally published in 1991 with updates including analysis of Dutch samples in 1993.
14. *Youth & the Rave Culture, Ecstasy and Health*, by Jacqueline Merchant and Robert MacDonald, *in Youth and Policy; the Journal of Critical Analysis*, Issue 45 summer 1994. The authors conclude that Rave Culture is different from previous subcultures.
15. Letter from Fiona Measham, February 1994.

Effects

The effects of ecstasy can be divided into three categories: physical, mental and emotional.

The physical effect of ecstasy is to stimulate the release of brain chemicals. This causes muscles to relax besides a number of side effects (and the desired emotional effect). It may also cause injury to particular brain cells with possible long-term consequences.

Mental and psychological tests usually show slightly worse results when people are on ecstasy. However, this may be due to problems with focusing attention on the tests.

Pain and discomfort are reduced. This can be dangerous by interrupting the normal feedback mechanism by which we look after ourselves.

The emotional effect is usually dramatic. The drug does not impose a particular mood so much as to allow the user to let go and feel good. It appears to do this by dissolving the fear which normally modifies our behaviour. Users feel both relaxed and stimulated. The state is ideal for indulgence in pleasurable activities.

In a group setting, this state results in empathy and open heartedness towards others. Combined with dancing this can induce an experience of group celebration.

In a therapy setting, the same state can provide insights into one's life and relationships, allowing suppressed memories to emerge and be faced.

The ecstasy state is also conducive to prayer, meditation and spiritual experience.

It is important not to regard ecstasy as a 'happy pill'. Although most people do feel happy when they let go, the effect depends on the person, their feelings at the time and the surroundings.

Finally, the emotional impact greatly diminishes after the first few occasions of use.

Physical effects

When ecstasy is swallowed, it is digested in the stomach and enters the blood stream. Blood carries it to all parts of the body and some of it reaches the brain. The action in the brain is to release serotonin ('5HT') and dopamine. These are called neurotransmitters because they control the messages transmitted between neurons (brain cells). Neurotransmitters influence the flow of information within the brain, so that changing the balance of neurotransmitters changes our mood. In normal life these neurotransmitters alter mood's to suit our particular situation: for instance, the neurotransmitter adrenaline is released to create a mood of excitement in situations where we need to be alert. Similarly, serotonin is released naturally to create the mood for situations such as being in love, and dopamine is released to suppress pain in situations where we are hurt but have to carry on, as in sport.

The effect of ecstasy is to force our brain to change mood by altering the flow of internal information.

Neurotransmitters control other brain functions apart from mood, including the regulation of body temperature. Ecstasy (and amphetamine) cause neurotransmitters to allow us to overheat without discomfort, and it is this quality that is most dangerous.

In fact the brain is not yet fully understood and the way ecstasy works is probably more complicated, since the release of dopamine and serotonin by other drugs does not produce the same effect.

Pain relief [1]

Dr Charles Grob believes that ecstasy raises the pain threshold, probably due to its effect on the neurochemical mechanism of the brain. In addition, it appears that ecstasy enhances the effect of morphine. The second benefit is expected to be emotional: ecstasy generally improves mood, lowers fear and provides patients with a greater sense of being in control.

Metabolism

As blood is circulated, some of the ecstasy is metabolised (broken down) into other chemicals by the liver, mainly into MDA which is itself an active drug. The kidneys then transfer waste products and impurities such as ecstasy to the urine. As a result, the urine of someone who has recently taken ecstasy will contain about two thirds of the ecstasy unchanged plus about 7% of the dose as MDA. [2] It should therefore be possible to recycle the drug in the same way as Siberian tribesmen who drink their urine after eating magic mushrooms.

The half life of ecstasy is about 6 hours, meaning that half is removed after six hours, half of what remains in the next six hours and so on. Even a high dose will therefore reduce to less than 1mg in 48 hours. This is probably too little to show up in blood or urine tests.

Mental and psychological effects

Researchers have attempted to identify the effects of ecstasy by asking psychiatrists to report on its effects in psychological terms.[3] Various trials have shown that judgement is impaired, problems occur with arithmetic and conflicting reports of memory loss.[4, 5]

Effects of ecstasy noted by psychiatrists [3]	
Altered time perception (speeded up or slowed down)	90%
Increased ability to interact with or be open with others	85%
Decreased defensiveness	80%
Decreased fear	65%
Decreased sense of separation or alienation from others	60%
Changes in visual perception	55%
Increased awareness of emotions	50%
Decreased aggression	50%
Speech changes	45%
Aware of previously unconscious memories	40%
Decreased obsessiveness	40%
Cognitive changes	40%

Afterwards one member of a couple "focused on how they were defensive with each other" while the other "saw love underneath" actions which they had thought implied that the other partner didn't care. There was a shift away from materialistic values and toward interpersonal relationships.

Main after effects lasting up to a week (observed by at least two subjects):

Decreased sleep	40%
Decreased appetite	30%
Increased sensitivity to emotions	25%
Decreased ability to perform mental or physical tasks	20%
Decreased desire to perform mental or physical tasks	20%
Increased ability to interact with or be open with others	20%
Decreased defensiveness	20%

Main effects lasting more than a week

Improved social/interpersonal functioning	50%
Changes in religious/spiritual orientation or practice	46%
Changes in values or life priorities	45%
Improved occupational functioning	40%
Increased ability to interact with or be open with others	35%
Decreased defensiveness	30%
Changes in ego boundaries	30%
Decreased desire to use alcohol	25%
Decreased fear	20%

Most effects are similar (but far more intense) to the popular antidepressant Prozac (fluoxetine): users of both feel relaxed, happy, less self-conscious and warm towards others, though ecstasy also enhances the sense of touch.[6] Both drugs lower serotonin levels, though by different means.[7,8]

Ecstasy is unlike most other drugs in that it increases awareness of touch and sound, an effect that has been observed in laboratory rats.[9]

I believe that the drug's various effects can be reduced to two primary effects, one physical and one mental: the relief of muscular tension and the dissolution of fear. People on ecstasy feel able to move and to express themselves more freely, as though temporarily relieved of the restraints we have come to regard as a normal part of life.

...d of early childhood when they looked people in the eye, lived
...d were free of inhibitions.

...Wilhelm Reich, which have greatly influenced modern psychotherapy,
...ant. Reich developed the theory that children in times of trauma brace
...s against pain by tensing their muscles, a reaction which becomes habitual.
As ad...s, this habit develops into what he called body armour, a rigid way of behaviour
which protects against being hurt, but also prevents them from behaving openly
towards others. Reich believed that muscular tensions go hand in hand with emotional
tensions or neuroses – in fact he believed that each neurosis in the mind is matched
by a muscular tension in the body. People who are free of neuroses, he believed, are
also free of bodily tensions, allowing them to move 'orgasmically' – spontaneous
undulations flowing smoothly from head to toe. Such free-flowing movements
sometimes occur on ecstasy, which could be explained in Reichian terms by the drug
temporarily relieving neuroses and the associated body armour. The same effect is
sometimes described as allowing the life force, or chi, to flow freely.[10]

Therapeutically, ecstasy is useful in allowing traumatic memories, suppressed for
years because they are too painful to face, to be looked at without terror. Insights
into what is really happening in life can also occur. Pain may be reduced,[7, 11] especially
if it is based on fear. The fear of death among terminal patients is a prime example.[12]

Emotional effects

Ecstasy produces a unique effect among recreational drugs: empathy. It provides
pleasure through increasing open-hearted communication, making it a sociable
drug suited to group experience.[13] It is not normally used by one person alone.

The most predictable feelings experienced are empathy, openness, peace and
caring.[14,15] However, what people experience can vary from paranoia[16] to sleep,
depending greatly on other factors called 'set and setting' which include their cultural
beliefs, expectations and state of mind at the time. Even your genetic make up may
affect your experience,[17] while larger doses produce more alertness and less empathy.[18]

Some people explain all the effects by saying that we are normally inhibited from
expressing love, moving freely and enjoying ourselves because of fear, and that the
fundamental effect of ecstasy is to remove fear; hence the saying 'love is letting go of
fear'. Another way of looking at the effects is as a drug that opens the heart and allows
love to flow.

Spiritual effects

Some people use ecstasy to help them in their spiritual growth, while others report
mystical experiences on ecstasy without seeking them. There have been various

claims that ecstasy facilitates spiritual practices including meditation, yoga, tai chi, guided imagery, psychosynthesis, shamanic journey work and rebirthing. "The detached yet compassionate attitude required for meditation is easy to attain, providing the foundation for deeper states...".[14]

A healer claimed that she saw a client's aura brightened by ecstasy,[20] and there are reports of people becoming more spiritually aware.[21,3]

The effects of ecstasy vary greatly according to the intention of the user and external stimulation during the trip. In my experience, minimum stimulation (such as lying on the floor wearing a blind and ear plugs) in secure surroundings produces the most inward-looking experience, while the type of experience (whether emotional or spiritual), can be controlled depending on one's intention.

Consistent effects [4]

Subjects' short-term memory was unchanged, but half the subjects had difficulty multiplying numbers, apparently because of difficulty in focusing on the task. Nearly half the subjects' judgement was impaired, implying that decision-making should be postponed or decisions should be re-evaluated after taking ecstasy.

Finger-to-nose testing was impaired in 2 subjects. Gait and co-ordination were affected in a third subject, suggesting driving could be dangerous.

"Ecstasy has remarkably consistent and predictable psychological effects that are transient and free of clinically-apparent major toxicity".

Memory loss [5]

Mental status examinations did not reveal any clinical impairments in cognitive function.

Performance in the Wechsler Memory Scale was subtly impaired in several subjects.

The overall result was that heavy ecstasy users probably had slightly worse short-term memories, but were not depressed nor did they show any other problems that might affect their lives.

Multiple Sclerosis

I have MS, and last year was at the stage of being able to get around using sticks with difficulty due to poor coordination, when I was invited to a party. I took ecstasy and amazed my myself and friends by dancing all night! I had complete relief and there was no come down, but the next day I was back to my sorry state. Next time I tried E also relieved me of symptoms, but on the third occasion I felt slightly worse and have not dared to try again.

-A reader in London

Group experience [13]

Some New Agers relate the ecstasy experience to 'morphic resonance', a term coined by Rupert Sheldrake, as though the E allows them to tap into a field of cumulative collective experience. The forerunners of raves were Grateful Dead concerts that have been going ever since 1965, where a large number of people take drugs and feel a group-mind experience.

Fear of death [1]

When people know or believe they are terminally ill, the fear of death results in emotional pain and also makes physical pain harder to bear. Anecdotal reports suggest that ecstasy allows people to accept their inevitable mortality and that this acceptance removes a burden.

Potential [10]

Perhaps MDMA's greatest potential in therapy is nonverbal. It could aid body therapies that utilize the attention, the breath, sound and hand pressure to open up and remove blocks that prevent contact with the life force within and hinder the elan vital from flowing.

Judgement [11]

A client's judgment can be interfered with by their heightened sense of excitement under ecstasy.

Effects of ecstasy [15]

But I did try it, and ... well, this is going to sound ridiculous. What happens is, the drug takes away all your neuroses. It takes away your fear response. You feel open, clear, loving. I can't imagine anyone being angry under its influence, or feeling selfish or mean or even defensive. You have a lot of insights into yourself, real insights that stay with you after the experience is over. It doesn't give you anything that isn't already there. It's not a trip. You don't lose touch with the world. You could pick up the phone, call your mother, and she'd never know.

From a description by a 'straight' middle aged man on the Internet

Laing on ecstasy [19]

"It's my opinion that government agencies, instead of slapping a total ban on this drug should explore it like they do others ... There's definitely a place for it. It's a pity to see it being cut out like that". Asked to explain why there is a need for drugs such as ecstasy, he said: "Most of us live within a sort of crypto-delusional structure as to our needs; we haven't quite got it right about love and loving and what other people feel about us ... which is part of the popularity of this drug. It changes your feeling. But this can also be a danger ... Under its influence it would be unwise to make [important] decisions there and then ... as it would over a bottle of whisky".

Telepathy

In an experiment where people tried to guess whether they were being stared at from behind, most subjects scored no better than chance but one man was extremely successful. He said afterwards that he was on ecstasy and felt heightened sensitivity.[22]

Many people feel telepathic on ecstasy, or as one reader remarked, "Where does empathy end and telepathy begin?" Although there are supporting anecdotes,[23] I received no response when I asked readers to test their telepathic abilities by trying to communicate with friends in another room.

The rave experience

The combination of the drug with music and dancing can produce an exhilarating trancelike state, perhaps similar to that experienced in tribal rituals or religious ceremonies.[24,25,26,27] It seems to dissolve the internal dialogue and with it self consciousness, allowing the music and movements to blend and producing an exhilarating feeling of group celebration. The experience is remarkably different to when taken quietly with friends, possibly partly due to increased oxygen intake. Release of negative feelings is rare, perhaps due to the party atmosphere.

Many claim that regular raving and/or use of ecstasy has improved their general mental state and their relationships with others. An archive of personal accounts called The Spirit of Raving can be found on the Internet at http://hyperreal.com/raves/spirit/

A trend has been for more people to describe the experience as spiritual. This may be due to the term becoming more accepted, but I have been to some events where the spiritual aspect was quite intentionally emphasised. One took place in a disused church in which an altar had been set up with Goddess figurines, carefully lit by strobes. That provided a focus while the DJs were hidden behind, and seemed to me to provide a missing element 'to dance to'. Another took place in an active Christian church, with approval of the vicar.

Aura change [20]

David came to his last session looking very different. His aura was twice as bright and much larger than usual. The cocoon had opened. I asked what had happened to him. He said that he had taken a drug called ecstasy over the weekend. On closer inspection, I could see that the ecstasy had opened the left side of the pineal gland. The mucus from the third eye that had been placed there partially from doing pot and LSD was cleared away on the right side. There was still work to be done, but the overall change in David's field was amazing... I asked Heyoan [her spirit guide] about it. He said, 'That depends on who takes it, and what their field configuration is at the time of taking it' Drugs ... do not cure disease; they assist the individual to cure himself.

Nirvana

The circuits of the brain which mediate alarm, fear, fright, fight, lust, and territorial paranoia are temporarily disconnected. You see everything with total clarity, undistorted by animalistic urges. You have reached a state which the ancients have called nirvana, all seeing bliss.

- Thomas Pynchon (American novelist) on ecstasy

Spiritual opening

I took a pill of E about six years ago. All I know is that for one night, the world was filled with my brethren, I was joyous just to be a part of the wondrous human experience! And still, I was able to carry on a conversation without any obvious impairments.

That one dose of changed my entire perspective. I considered things in new ways that night... and later realized that I could do that day to day. Now I am open to all possibilities for enlightenment and spiritual health. Meditation is a large part of my life, and I am more open minded about the possibility of chemical and natural remedies for the body and spirit.

- 28 year old American man

Self love

Before I took E I was probably the most unconfident guy I knew. When it came to voicing my opinions or meeting new people, I was terrible...

My experiences with E have been to allow me to come to accept and love myself. This has had a profound effect on my interaction with other people. I have met new friends, old friends have grown closer and all in all my life is so much better.

- South African reader

Spiritual practices [14]

Various practices may be greatly facilitated by ecstasy and the effects amplified. This is best done on low doses (50-100mg) or towards the latter half of a session.

'Main reason for living' [27]

"It would be no exaggeration to say that raving is now one of the main reasons for living for a huge group of socially diverse people aged between 15 and 35 years."

Less safe sex

Andrew Thomson's study showed that some 80% of those interviewed had practised sex on ecstasy, while 18% claimed that ecstasy use did impair their decision to have safe sex.

Unpleasant effects

Ecstasy is not always enjoyable. The very same qualities that make it rewarding can be very uncomfortable in certain situations. Although users nearly always blame the quality of the drug, bad experiences can also occur with pure ecstasy. Normally people find the drug liberating and enjoy letting go, but in some situations they may feel uncomfortable without their normal defences. Lowered defences may provide a wonderful feeling of liberation in a warm supportive environment, but may be extremely unpleasant in other circumstances. Users may come to bitterly regret having revealed their insecurity or longings when under the influence of ecstasy and some insights can be painful, such as realising that your partner never loved you or that your dreams are not attainable. To remember a traumatic situation without support can be devastating. When someone is just managing to keep life together, such situations may result in a nervous breakdown. Fortunately such bad reactions are rare: a more common problem is being unable to let go. Resisting the effect of the drug is uncomfortable, often manifesting in a headache and nausea.

A survey conducted in Sydney[31] found that seven percent of those who tried Ecstasy did not enjoy it while 80% did (13% found it neutral). Three-quarters of regular users in Manchester said they usually enjoyed ecstasy and most said it was here to stay in their lives, although 18% enjoyed it less than they used to.[30] Much of the effect depends on the setting – if you feel relaxed anyway you are almost certain to enjoy it; although many tense people use the drug to help them relax, not everyone can yield to its effects. Those using ecstasy in psychotherapy tend to enjoy their first experience but to get absorbed in their problems on subsequent ecstasy sessions.[31]

Ecstasy can upset people's lives. There are many examples of young people squandering ridiculous amounts of money on E and only living for their next binge. One known personally to me was a 23-year-old art student who used to live for the weekends when she and her friends took ecstasy, and spent the rest of the time in a state of depression. This lasted for about a year until eventually she was thrown out of college, which made her even more depressed. However, two years later she emerged again as her former vibrant self, and looking back saw that her problems had resulted as much from her parents' divorce as from taking ecstasy through which, she says, she made good friends.

It is important to realise that bad effects are not due to the drug alone, but to a combination of the effects of the drug and the situation at the time. A guide who has introduced ecstasy to many people over the past 18 years assures me that none of them has ever had a bad experience, even though some were difficult cases. He attributes this to him being able to give whatever support was needed.[32]

Motives for raving [26]

Drugs were the primary reason given for involvement in the rave scene by only 6%. Another 6% were involved in the culture without taking drugs other than cannabis. 75% had used cannabis before getting involved, but only 2% had previously tried ecstasy. 90% of a sample of women had been through periods of weekly use, frequently following their first experience.

Early in the study, alcohol drinkers were looked down on and referred to as "beer monsters", but drinking is now accepted.

Belonging to a wide family and feeling secure is an important attraction of raving. "The first time I took E, I was with this bloke and I just looked at him and I thought 'Oh I can't, don't wanna be with him any more' and that was it. 'Cos there were so many other people and I just felt so confident and you could tell them what you want and be/do anything."

Wide social circle

Before becoming a regular user of ecstasy I believed that I was a completely fulfilled and happy person, content to live day in and day out with the same group of snobbish friends. I felt that because I was with the popular crowd my life couldn't be better. Then I took a Rhubarb and Custard at a rave and it had the most profound effect on me. I could not help but share the feelings I was having, something I would not normally even think of doing. I talked to people of all races and backgrounds. I don't think I stopped talking all night.

After taking it a few more times I began to feel a lot more positive about myself. I felt I had developed and matured mentally and didn't feel such a fickle and shallow person any more. Things like how much money and what kind of job didn't matter any more. I became more interested in developing genuine friendships rather than the meaningless ones I'd had. Previous friends noticed I had changed, particularly in my opinions and values. I have found for myself that when used in moderation ecstasy can be good for the mind as well as the body (especially the hips!)

My favourite part of taking E is not only when you're 'buzzing' but also the come down. You'll find yourself chilling with other people you have a common bond with, knowing that they have felt and experienced what you have, physically, mentally and spiritually. I can honestly say that I am a better person from having taken ecstasy, I firmly believe it's a drug with insight and maturity.

– A reader

Contagious effect

On E you can make the best of a bad night. I've been to a dreadful party with a friend where no-one is dancing and everyone looks on edge. We've taken an E and it's turned out to be a brilliant night. We've been dancing, arms in the air and smiling with no inhibitions. The effect is contagious and everyone else begins to relax just watching us and soon most people start dancing.

–A reader

Side effects

These can be uncomfortable, but few users find that side effects spoil the experience. Dry mouth and loss of appetite are almost universal, and various muscular reactions are common, as though some muscles resist the drug's demand to let go. These include holding the jaw tightly clenched, eyes flickering from side to side (nystagmus), twitches, nausea and cramp, especially as the drug first takes effect. Generally these soon pass. Side effects are more pronounced with higher doses and frequent use.

A long-term side effect experienced by ravers is weight loss[34] which is sometimes a motive for using the drug.[35] Weight reduction is presumably caused by the combination of exercise and loss of appetite. Some women find their periods become irregular when using ecstasy,[25] which may often be due to poor and irregular diet.[35] Urinary tract infections are sometimes reported, but the cause is uncertain. Sleep may also be affected.[36]

Some people are concerned that a long term side effect may be to alter personality in negative ways, although the changes so far identified could be considered improvements.[37]

After effects

People often feel exhausted after taking ecstasy, although others may feel an afterglow[38]. This hangover is hardly surprising considering that the mind, and usually the body, have been so much more active than normal, and is similar to that experienced by users of LSD and amphetamine.[29]

Hangovers can be reduced by avoiding other drugs such as alcohol and amphetamine and getting a good night's sleep afterwards.

Depression,[33] weight loss[35], inability to sleep[36] and paranoia[35] sometimes occur, particularly among heavy users. Pain in the lower back may be due to muscle ache or dehydration of the kidneys.[35]

Effects on animals

A laboratory researcher believes that animals do not enjoy any psychoactive drugs but feel confused, and that this is accentuated in higher animals like monkeys.[39] However, researchers studying toxicity in dogs noticed that they became more friendly on low doses, while a man who took E and gave his German Shepherd dog half a tablet was convinced that the dog liked it and became more sensitive, remaining as affectionate as ever without its usual clumsiness.

Utopian idealism [27]

Mary Anna Wright sees the rave culture as part of the movement towards ecological and spiritual awareness. She examines the lyrics from more commercial rave music as an indication of underlying attitude of the scene as a whole. Wright comments: "Songs heard in the rave-scene have changed with time. Early songs had frequent reference to the use of ecstasy".

"Ecological messages within rave records tend to be more implicit. The overall theme tends to be of utopian idealism with an indication to my view of the metaphorical significance of rave as a guide for metanoia. There are exceptions, Gaia is sometimes used to embody the idea of unity with our environment."

Obsessive behaviour

Every time I have taken E I experience what can only be called an obsessive nature. Once I was hardly able to stay out of the toilets; another time I felt compelled to make milky sugary tea for everyone every half hour, and most recently I became obsessed with hanging upside down off chairs. It is this mad urge to do things with complete seriousness that I love about E. Apart from making me laugh afterwards, these fetishes have deepened friendships with whoever I share the experience with, and it helps me to see another dimension to myself.

–A reader

Key to liberation

Ecstasy is so often condemned and vilified yet it is such a positive drug. It is a joyous celebration of life.

Those who fear ecstasy should realise that users have found a way to enhance their lives and look on the bright side. It is inspirational and also places things in perspective.

Ecstasy is precious as it holds the key to happiness and liberation in a world that often seems gloomy. It seems crazy that something so therapeutic is deemed a social problem.

More often than not, it opens hearts and minds and makes people feel glad to be alive.

– Letter from a 21-year old reader written under the influence

Unrepeatable effect

I am completely convinced, in what I heard from others and from my own findings, that with repeated exposure to ecstasy, the extraordinary impact which is its particular signature is lost after the first few uses. I have no idea if this is due to physical changes in the brain making the unique magic no longer expressible, or to psychological learning that makes it no longer needed. The ecstasy experience continues to be rich and useful, but that special something seems gone. It is remembered, but not re-experienced.

Dr Alexander Shulgin

A reader told me that he uses ecstasy to relax wild animals. He believes that nervousness makes them ill or prevents them from getting well, especially when being handled by humans as when he tries to put a splint on a broken leg. I have also heard rumours of horses being doped with ecstasy before races to help them relax, and of the effect on killer whales.[40]

Sex

Although the media portray ecstasy as an aphrodisiac, the drug tends to inhibit erections in men (and male rats[41]). Many users never become sexually aroused on ecstasy and find the state incompatible with lust,[25,42] while others find that they can continue on a sexual energy level if they are feeling sexy as the drug takes effect.[43,44,35]

On E, women are more likely to become sexually aroused than men, but both find orgasm suppressed. Couples who have had sex on E say that it is unusually nice even without orgasm; they feel more loving than passionate and unusually sensitive to each other. It seems that a universal effect of the drug is to remove male sexual aggression, or as one woman put it, "to bring out the feminine qualities in men". People on ecstasy become more sensual and less lustful.[45, 46]

Behaviour at raves during the first few years, where nearly everyone was on E, was very different to that at alcohol-based clubs, and seemed to follow from the lack of male sexual aggression. Hugging and even caressing strangers was acceptable on a sensual level without implying a sexual advance.[25]

Sheila Henderson, a researcher studying the way young women use ecstasy and author of papers entitled *Women, Sexuality and Ecstasy Use*[25]and *Luvdup and DeElited*[42], wrote in 1992: "Most men have the opposite to an erection: a shrinking penis". Women can enjoy kissing at raves because it is safe – not a prelude to having sex. They are less likely to have casual sex following a night raving than after going to an alcohol-based club. As one girl put it, "you don't go to a rave to cop". In fact, sexual safety was an attraction at raves in contrast with alcohol-based clubs which were seen as a cattle market.[25] However, by 1994 ecstasy was not the predominant drug used in most venues and a more sexual vibe was evident.[47]

Other sociologists have noted that sexual behaviour at raves is less than at other social activities,[24] and that, although some found sex enhanced by the drug, "thoughts about sex when on E were not always matched by desire".[33] A study of the girlfriends of working class men in the north revealed that ecstasy had a reputation for "long, slow sex" on comedown.[25] An American pamphlet claimed that: "Sexual experience only occurs when it is appropriate on a heart level for both of you... Know that whatever you choose to create will be a perfect and appropriate choice".[48]

Menstruation [25]

A quarter of the women who used ecstasy weekly for over six months reported lighter or less frequent periods, sometimes none at all for several months. This is likely to be the result of indirect effects – suppressed appetite, sweating and all night exercise.

Becoming ill

Me and my closest friends take E almost every weekend and we discuss the positive and negative effects, such as midweek depression and tendency to mood swings. I feel the reason regular users become ill is due to the appetite depressing qualities. After not eating for 24 hours our stomach shrinks so we eat less. Another factor is the cost of food against ecstasy. Positive aspects include letting people really open up to each other, and tuning in to a more positive side. By dancing for a night on ecstasy, a feeling of absolute bliss, contentment and utter fulfilment is achieved. Of course the downside to this is that nothing else beats that feeling, thus reality can seem boring.

– A reader

Paranoia

After nearly four years of using E every weekend, I got paranoid walking down the street, thinking that everyone was looking at me. I work as a bank clerk, and sometimes felt that all the customers I served were planted to test me, like I was under investigation.

– A reader.

Uglys

Once the onset of ecstasy kicks in I feel absolutely terrified and all I can think is that I need it out of my body and I need to be home and safe (I'm covered in sweat and feel I need to isolate myself). This passes quickly but during the 30 minutes of the "come up" it can return in short bursts. Exactly the same for "the uglys" when diving... all one wants is to be back on the boat and one's SCUBA equipment advertised for sale! but then it suddenly goes away and the dive is enjoyed.

32 year old Australian

Depression and weight loss [33]

A depressed mood was reported by most users as the after effect of taking E and this sometimes lasted for a couple of days. Paranoia was reported by 85%. "For many, this began as an awareness of being admired by others. Gradually as the weeks passed, this admiring regard changed to critical scrutiny and ridicule. Increased sensitivity to comments and a tendency to interpret situations in a threatening way was described by some," – Teresa O'Dwyer

Most people experienced a hangover lasting from 12 to 24 hours, but for some this lasted for up to a week.

76% of respondents had lost weight averaging one stone through taking E.

This sensual-rather-than-sexual aspect of the drug gives rise to nonsexual orgies at some parties, referred to as feely-feely or snake slithering.[49] People indulge in group sensual delights through caressing and slithering over one another, though I've only heard of this in Australia and California.

The question whether ecstasy's effect increases risk factors concerning sexual behaviour is being examined in depth by Andrew Thomson. Preliminary results show that over three quarters of those interviewed who regularly used ecstasy in clubs had practised sex while under its influence, and that one in six of these said that the effect of ecstasy made it less likely that they would practice safe sex.[43] Two other studies have indicated that injecting polydrug users who take ecstasy have more sex than those who don't; but that amphetamine users who took E were less at risk of catching HIV because they were more likely to use condoms.[50]

The Swiss psychotherapists tell me that, in hundreds of sessions they have never come across a participant becoming sexually aroused while on ecstasy. They say that sexual longings are sometimes expressed, but not the immediate desire for sex.

However, a survey of users in the San Francisco area conducted in 1985[51] found that only half of the men who responded said it was more difficult to have an erection on ecstasy, though, of those who said they had had sex on the drug, two thirds said they had problems in achieving an orgasm. The survey found that ecstasy did not make users initiate sex although they were slightly more receptive.

Respondents to an Australian survey[31] described the effects of ecstasy as sensual rather than sexual.

I believe the explanation is that the effect varies considerably according to the user's expectations. Surveys may also produce results which are biased towards those who are more potent on the drug (or said they were), while those who felt that the questionnaire might reveal them to be inadequate may be under-represented. Suggestion may also be involved: the Swiss men who were treated with ecstasy may have been influenced by their therapists' belief that men cannot have erections on the drug. I also suspect that many people do not make a clear distinction between sensuality and sexuality.

Reduced effect with use

The technical term for a drug that has less effect with use is 'tolerance'. Ecstasy shows tolerance, but in a rather extreme and unusual way.

With most drugs, increased dosage is needed to maintain the same effect. But with ecstasy, increased dosage produces a more speedy and less empathic effect. In fact, frequent heavy users often give up and take amphetamine instead as it provides a similar effect for less money.

Mood for sex [35]

Some people can get turned on sexually while on E, but the important point is that the mood that existed when taking E continues and becomes exaggerated – "just like alcohol". But ecstasy does lower inhibitions to some degree. It also depends on the social context in the widest sense, including the atmosphere and expectancy of the situation where it is used. Quite apart from the use of ecstasy, sexual arousal is common at clubs but not at raves. Some women described getting randy on E in clubs and one stopped taking it in clubs so as to keep in control.

Sleep [36]

23 ecstasy users were compared to matched non users. Ecstasy users averaged 19 minutes less sleep and 23 minutes less non-REM [non rapid eye movement] sleep than controls.

The only significant reduction was of 37 minutes in stage 2 sleep.

Telepathic whales [40]

I believe that E has allowed me to get closer, or work more effectively with killer whales at work. The training philosophy is based on the concept of "positive reinforcement" and the development of relationships with the animals over time. (The positive reinforcement history is the foundation of this relationship.) On a couple of occasions (I have been training for several years), I have come to work after a night of Xing. Although the peak of the E trip had long since ended, there were definitely residual effects. These effects seemed to allow me to take my relationship with a certain whale to new heights. I thought nothing of it until several months ago when two of my colleagues and I went out and took some E. I had the next day off, but one of the other guys did not. When I called my friend-colleague at work he said it was the best day he's had with that same whale. The interactions with her he said were unbelievable. He implied that they were almost telepathic. When I read about E and telepathy, as well as effects on animals, I decided to send you this information.

Animal sex [41]

Sexual activity was suppressed in most animals while on ecstasy, but returned to normal after a week "despite a marked depletion of 5-HT content in the striatum and hippocampus".

In addition, for those rats who did copulate on ecstasy, "ejaculation latency and postejaculatory interval were dramatically lengthened".

Effects of Ecstasy on Human Sexual Function by Zvi Zemishlany et al, Tel Aviv University, Israel. [46]

Sexual function was evaluated in 20 men and 15 women aged 21-48 following consumption of ecstasy. Although erection was impaired in 40% of the men, over 90% reported greater desire and satisfaction. Orgasm was delayed but perceived as more intense.

There is another unusual effect that applies even to moderate users: the euphoric quality is nearly always limited to the first few occasions. Later experiences lack the first wonder, and it may never be experienced again even after a long break.

Experts disagree about the cause. Some people have suggested that this is an indication of permanent injury, but others believe it is purely emotional and point to similarities with other experiences. I notice the effect myself, but then I also noticed it with repeated parachute jumps.

Sexual pressure [42]

Girls don't feel threatened at raves and therefore are free to respond. "I used to go to Indie clubs which are alcohol based ... there was a definite pressure to cop off with men at this type of club. At house clubs it's much more just getting to know people".

Snake slithering [49]

I went into the chillout room to discuss something with a friend. Gradually I noticed a girl, semi-prone beside me, was moving her hand up my leg. She was also being massaged by someone else. She had shorts. I immediately went for her legs, and it gradually turned into a nonverbal multi-peopled sensual groping, squeezing, massaging, hugging kind of thing. Nearly all strangers to me. I thought (not too much) isn't it great to feel free to do something like this.

This is the therapeutic aspect of these events which needs to be more fully recognised as such. Medicines and therapy for the ills begot by egoic barriers and repressive social conventions. This sort of spontaneous, sensuous body contact is, in my mind, the sign of a good X party. In Marin we call them 'puppy piles'. I've seen flyers with special rooms set aside for this aspect of the X experience called 'feely feely' rooms or 'petting zoo' or 'snake slithering'.

Sex on E

"I actually prefer sex without E for my own pleasure. I find that my sensations are dulled, and that my nipples and clitoris are far less sensitive to being touched, which is perhaps why I can never reach orgasm on E. What I find is better is touching my partner and sharing his pleasure of being touched".

- Woman reader aged 35.

Pleasurable side effect

My experience is that ecstasy in the first couple of hours reduces sex-drive to a near-zero point. However, after a couple of hours, it comes back with a vengeance. Not only is it highly pleasurable, but stamina is way up, and we can go on for hours. I don't orgasm until I want to, which has proven a very pleasurable side effect of ecstasy.

- Internet news group alt.raves

San Francisco survey [45]

70% of users had engaged in sexual activity while on ecstasy. Of these, 88% of the women and 74% of the men said that the sensuality of the sexual experience was enhanced. They indulged in less, but the same type of, sexual activities on ecstasy, with the exception of more heavy petting. 81% of users said that the sensuality of the experience was enhanced and several commented that ecstasy was a sensual, not a sexual, drug. Half the men said it was more difficult to have an erection and 62% said they had difficulty achieving orgasm, but, among women, as many found it easier to have an orgasm on ecstasy as found it harder. 76% of users said ecstasy had not caused health or emotional problems. Complaints included urinary tract infections, tiredness, colds, headaches and mild depression next day.

While 85% of users said ecstasy had no effect on their sexual desires, the rest felt like doing things, such as having group sex, that implied being free of inhibitions. No increase in users' willingness to initiate sexual activity was reported, but they became slightly more receptive.* A third of users thought ecstasy had helped them overcome inhibitions, and made comments like "cleared pelvic blocks," "lessening of resistance," "better sensual communication" and "more relaxed". All the women and 87% of the men thought ecstasy increased emotional closeness, and two thirds said this did not depend on the dose.

*The researchers conclude that ecstasy is not an aphrodisiac, but enhances the sensual aspects of sex. They note that, while half the men and a third of the women felt more receptive to sex on ecstasy, "it is curious that a drug which can increase emotional closeness, enhance receptivity to being sexual and would be chosen as a sexual enhancer, does not increase the desire to initiate sex".

References

1. Interview with Dr Charles Grob in Los Angeles at UCLA in 10/93 on his proposed trial for using MDMA in the treatment of terminal cancer patients.

2. Entry in *Micromedex*, vol. 75, a hospital database printout from the National Poisons Unit at Guy's Hospital, London.

3. Phenomenology and Sequelae of MDMA use by Dr Mitchell Liester, Dr Charles Grob et al., *Journal of Nervous and Mental Disease*, 180/6 1992.

4. The Psychological and Physiological Effects of MDMA on Normal Volunteers, by Joseph Downing, from *Journal of Psychoactive Drugs*, Vol. 18/4 1986.

5. *Chronic MDMA use: Effects on Mood and Neuropsychological Function* by George Ricaurte et al. in *American Journal of Drug and Alcohol Abuse* 18/3, 1992.

6. *Sunday Times* 13/2/94.

7. Visit to Dr John Henry at the National Poisons Unit at Guy's Hospital, London, 12/92.

8. Fluoxetine, from Martindale Pharmacopeia. Fluoxetine is an antidepressant which selectively inhibits the re-uptake of serotonin.

9. *Effects of [MDMA] on acoustic and tactile startle reflexes in rats* by Kehne et al. in. *J Pharmacol Exp Ther* 1/92. Startle response to noise and touch was increased by MDMA in proportion to the dose given. This was prevented by fluoxetine.

10. Neurotoxicity of MDA and MDMA in *Alcohol and Drug Research*, Volume 7. This paper argues that the dangers associated with MDA should be assumed to apply with MDMA unless it is proved otherwise.

11. Meetings at the Edge with Adam: A Man for All Seasons? by Philip Wolfson from *Journal of Psychoactive Drugs* Vol. 18/4 1986. Wolfson introduces himself as an established psychotherapist passionately involved with people experiencing painful altered states of consciousness. He says that MDMA opens up new possibilities for treatment of such cases, but their are some hazards to be wary of.

12. Meeting with Dr Charles Grob in Los Angeles, 10/93.

13. *The Pursuit of Ecstasy – the MDMA Experience* by Gerome Beck and Marsha Rosenbaum published 2/94 by State University of New York Press at $14.95.

14. The Nature of the MDMA Experience by Ralph Metzner and Sophia Adamson in *ReVision*, Spring 1988.

15. *This world*, 23/6/95.

16. *Chronic paranoid psychosis after Ecstasy* by McGuire *BMJ* 3/91.

17. *Metabolism of 'ecstasy' by CYP2D6)* by Tucker et al. published in abstract form in *Br. J. Clin. Pharmacol.* 36:144P, 1993. This paper suggests that about 8% of Caucasians are genetically deficient in a particular enzyme which helps metabolize MDMA.

18. *Ecstasy: the clinical, pharmacological and neurotoxicological effects of the drug MDMA* (book), edited by Stephen Peroutka, published by Kluwer Academic Publishers 1990.

19. Laing on Ecstasy by Peter Naysmith *International Journal on Drug Policy* 1/3.

20. *Hands of Light* (book), by Barbara Ann Brennan, Bantam, 1988.

21. Subjective reports of the Effects of MDMA in a Clinical Setting by George Greer and Requa Tolbert from *Journal of Psychoactive Drugs* Vol. 18/4 1986.

22. *Seven Experiments that could Change the World* (book) by Rupert Sheldrake, 1994.

23. Personal communications from Rick Doblin of MAPS.

24. *The Use of Ecstasy and Dance Drugs at Rave Parties and Clubs: Some Problems and Solutions*, by Dr Russell Newcombe, paper presented at a symposium on Ecstasy, Leeds, 11/92.

25. *Women, sexuality and Ecstasy Use – The Final Report* 1993, by Sheila Henderson, published by Lifeline, 101 Oldham St, Manchester M4 1LW.

26. *Dancing and rave drugs*, by Dr Russell Newcombe, 1991. Newcombe suggests that clubs are safer than illegal raves because of fire and other health precautions.

27. *The Rave Scene in Britain – A Metaphor for Metanoia* by Mary Anna Wright, MSc dissertation, Centre for Human Ecology, University of Edinburgh, 1993. This 100-page document was researched through participant observation at a number of raves and events, particularly Castlemorton Festival 5/92.

29. Recreational MDMA use in Sydney: a profile of Ecstasy users and their experiences with the drug, by Nadia Solowij et al., in the *British Journal of Addiction*, 1992.

30. New Age Seekers: MDMA use as an adjunct to spiritual pursuit by Watson and Beck, *Journal of Psychoactive Drugs* 23/3.

31. Group theraphy session. I attended a group theraphy session in 3/94.

33. Subjective reports of the Effects of MDMA in a Clinical Setting by George Greer and Requa Tolbert from *Journal of Psychoactive Drugs* Vol. 18/4 1986.

34. Fit for anything, by Sarah Champion, *The Guardian*, 12/4/93.

35. The Phenomenology of Ecstasy Use, by Teresa O'Dwyer, Senior Registrar of Adult Psychiatry at St Thomas' Hospital, Morpeth, 11/92. This paper is an account of a study of users' experiences on Ecstasy and the patterns and circumstances of their use undertaken by the Leeds Addiction Unit between January and September 1992.

36. *Effects of MDMA on sleep* by Allen et al. in *Sleep* 9/93.

37. *Serotonin Neurotoxicity after MDMA: A Controlled Study in Humans* by George Ricaurte et al. 1994 *Neuropsychopharmacology* .

38. *The Pursuit of Ecstasy – the MDMA Experience* by Gerome Beck and Marsha Rosenbaum published 2/94 by State University of New York Press at $14.95.

39. Visit from Stuart Frescas, a chemist working as part of Dr David Nichols' team at Purdue University, 1/94.

40. Refer box page 60.

41. *Effect of MDMA on sexual behaviour of male rats* by Dornan et al. in *Pharmacol Biochem Behav* 7/91.

42. *Luvdup and DeElited*, by Sheila Henderson, researcher for Lifeline, a non-statutory drug agency in Manchester. A paper given at South Bank Polytechnic 5/92.

43. *'E'sy sex: a cultural myth in perspective* paper by Andrew Thomson presented at Medical Sociology Conference, York University 1993.

44. *The Essential Psychedelic Guide*, by D. M. Turner.

45. MDMA and Human Sexual Function, by John Buffum and Charles Moser, from *Journal of Psychoactive Drugs*, Vol. 18/4 1986. This paper gives the findings of a survey carried out by distributing an anonymous questionnaire around the San Francisco area in 1985-6. Of 300 distributed, 76 were returned.

46. Refer box page 60.

47. Letter from Sheila Henderson, 2/94.

48. *The Adam Experience, a guide for first-time users*, by Starfire, 1985.

49. Visit to and subsequent communications from Clive, part time dealer in California, who attends many events.

50. *An analysis of the potential for HIV transmission among stimulant-using ravers* by Drs Hilary Klee and Julie Morris, Manchester Metropolitan University, 6/93.

51. MDMA and Human Sexual Function, by John Buffum and Charles Moser, from *Journal of Psychoactive Drugs*, Vol. 18/4 1986. This paper gives the findings of a survey carried out by distributing an anonymous questionnaire around the San Francisco area in 1985-6. Of 300 distributed, 76 were returned.

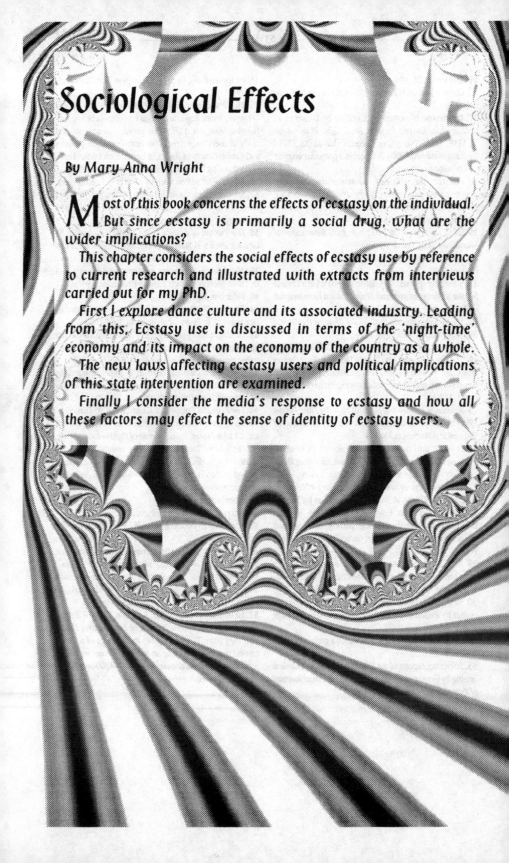

Sociological Effects

By Mary Anna Wright

Most of this book concerns the effects of ecstasy on the individual. But since ecstasy is primarily a social drug, what are the wider implications?

This chapter considers the social effects of ecstasy use by reference to current research and illustrated with extracts from interviews carried out for my PhD.

First I explore dance culture and its associated industry. Leading from this, Ecstasy use is discussed in terms of the 'night-time' economy and its impact on the economy of the country as a whole.

The new laws affecting ecstasy users and political implications of this state intervention are examined.

Finally I consider the media's response to ecstasy and how all these factors may effect the sense of identity of ecstasy users.

Ecstasy as part of the dance culture

Ecstasy's effects have blasted an imprint into British culture. Over the past years ecstasy seizures have increased by around 50% each year. The main reason for this increase in ecstasy use is its popularity on the dance scene. MINTEL predict the nightclub market will continue to grow, doubling from its current £2 billion value by the year 2000. The huge expansion is primarily due to midweek openings catering for evolving tastes and a proliferation in genres of dance music. As this doesn't include outdoor events and illegal parties, the growth of dance culture as a whole must be even greater.[1]

Some writers gloss over the use of drugs within the dance scene and are highly critical of those who believe that drugs have a major impact. While there is no doubt that other factors like the music itself are hugely important, ignoring how ecstasy's effects have moulded the scene is naive. Matthew Collin, on the other hand, uses the phrase ecstasy culture for what he calls an ultimate entertainment, a combination of musical, chemical and computer technologies.[2] According to Lee Fawcett of Scottish Drugs Forum:

> Rather than discussing ecstasy's impact it's maybe better to look at the impact of dance culture. For many it was a package; music, atmosphere, like-minded people and drugs. E was just part of that package and is increasingly only one of a whole range of drugs now in common use.[3]

Ecstasy and dance culture have attracted the attention of academics. Opinions are divided about their social impact. For some, the importance is as an escape into a void of meaning. They feel other sub-cultures were in opposition to the dominant culture, but dance culture is not. Hillegonda Rietveld, for example, writes "when one escapes instead of opposes, no alternative moral values are proposed at all".[4] Other writers suggest that clubbers somehow find themselves after their individual identities have been dissolved by the music, the crowd and the drugs.[5]

My research has involved interviewing punters, promoters, press, DJs and free party people within all genres, to determine if an alternate moral value is proposed. What 'finding themselves' really means, and how this affects the rest of society. It seems that despite differences in taste and background most members of dance culture share similar ideals. This is often related to their ecstasy experiences.

For some, this 'E-thos' simply means they are less judgmental, or they are closer to their friends. Among people taking ecstasy, women may feel more comfortable to dress and act as they please without getting the sexual advances they often endure among drunken men.[6] This situation is not so cut and dried now, with a pinch of 'post-modern' irony there has been an emergence of new ladism and in some clubs it seems expected that women will 'act the babe' in order to fit in.[7]

George McKay discusses ideas of resistance within dance culture and compares it with the full frontal opposition displayed by subcultures like the punks.[8] There is nothing wrong with escapism or with pleasure for pleasure's sake, but if the state clamps down, some elements are prompted into more visible action. Gibby from campaign group Justice? explains:

> When you start meeting like spirited souls you discover there is a different way of doing things and competitiveness is not essential and selfishness isn't essential. The protest scene has taken in and politicised a lot of the E generation. These people have crossed an invisible legal boundary, so they've empathy with anyone under attack. A gulf has opened and created a very healthy atmosphere of questioning authority.

Across the world pockets of resistance have been formed around the ecstasy/dance experience, examples of what Hakim Bey calls 'temporary autonomous zones'.[9] Some are found in a nightclub on a Saturday night, others hold more permanent claims on space. One example, the Exodus collective, know first hand how other industries feel threatened by dance culture. When their parties started in 1992 the local pubs experienced a 40% drop in trade.

Allegations abound of council pressure prompting police harassment and encouraging bad publicity in the local press.

Mark Gilman agrees with other researchers that "for many, ecstasy is now just part of a whole repertoire of drugs used". In 1990 his research showed how football fans' attitudes to opposing team's supporters changed as they stopped drinking alcohol in favour of taking ecstasy. Recently he watched the Tyson v Holyfield boxing match with the same group. The ritual seemed to have gone from their ecstasy use. After the room emptied he saw the floor was covered in empty beer cans, it seemed like they just took E because it was too tricky chopping out cocaine. Using a drug associated with warmth and empathy to watch a fight seemed really ironic.

This polydrug use makes it difficult to make a priori statements on the social effects of ecstasy. Could football stadium disasters like Hillsborough or police surveillance have changed supporters' behaviour? Could the community feelings of the dance floor be an antidote to Government ideals? Even Jarvis Cocker sings "is this the way they say the future's meant to feel? Or just 20,000 people standing in a field?".[10]

Night time economy

The importance of the industries built around the dance scene is unquestionable. One cause of dance culture's longevity is that its creative force comes from within. By continually being reinvented, it avoids the gross commercialisation of other subcultures. Fashion outlets and record shops are filled with items aimed at clubbers made by clubbers. As Sheila Henderson, a research fellow at the University of Essex says:

Ecstasy culture has had a huge impact on popular culture in general. Even if you don't go to clubs you are wearing it; the look is everywhere. It has crossed generations and become part of both the adult world and the young world. It has spread right out from the cities so rural kids are really urbanised in their heads; drug slang is part of normal conversation. They are also urbanised in their bodies by the clothes they wear. (pers. comm 1997)

Journalists and photographers from within dance culture have set up numerous niche publications and fanzines. Dance magazines' importance within the whole music press market is now attracting big name publishers. There are difficulties facing all of these magazines as Billy Graham from M8 explained: "It's a balancing act. We need to give our readers safety information, but can't appear to promote drug use".

This new productivity comes from smaller more flexible industries than the old corporate structures. Richard Smith and Tim Maughan consider the dance music industry to be a good example of a "post-Fordist economy" and describe it as a "high technology cottage industry". They found capital investment for this music production often comes from the 'night-time' economy; DJing, illegal parties and drug dealing.[11]

Micro labels

According to BPI statistics, dance music album sales are increasing faster than other genres, with compilations proving particularly lucrative[12]. If Smith and Maughan are correct, the BPI will have vastly under estimated the sales from independent record labels. They feel dance music is characterised by:

> ... the use of new technology which reduces the costs of production, a cultural aesthetic that embraces this diversity and the sounds that can be made from the technology, plus an underground DJ culture which generates space for micro-labels and restricts the domination of the major music corporations.

They conclude that members of dance culture do indeed 'find themselves', but this is not through an ephemeral trance dance ecstatic experience, but by becoming the producers of their own culture.

Only small record shops can cope with the rapid turnover, diversity and proliferation of dance music. This reinforces the separation from the major labels and high street stores favoured by the record industry. Writers like Jeremy Gilbert consider Britpop as a reaction against dance culture,[13] Britpop has a repackaged corporate rock aesthetic of guitars, live shows and 'meaningful' lyrics. There is now a move by the major labels to sign DJs and producers from the dance scene and to buy up some of the micro-labels that are associated with this kind of music.

The most influential areas of cultural productivity, writes Andy Lovatt, are in "the unseen rhizomic impulses of popular culture".[14] He considers Manchester's night life, with the 'Madchester' dance explosion of the early 90s, had a greater impact on the city's economy than its Olympic bid, international concert halls and other 'high' cultural investments. Student applications to Manchester institutions rose by 30% in this period (reflected later in Liverpool following the rise of the superclub Cream).

Drew Hemment has written about the illegal raves around the town of Blackburn at the tail end of the '80s. He tells an anecdote of its renaming as Boomtown which he feels was: "Paying homage to the anti-Thatcher dream at the same time as marking its emergent illicit economic power".[15] We are now told London is swinging again, with magazines like Newsweek featuring the capital's better known clubs. With most visitors aged under 34, subcultural tourism is big business. Tourists hold importance for the night-time as well as the regulated economy.

DJ Rap, a respected name on the Drum and Bass circuit feels productivity should be encouraged:

> We were all ravers who just got into a style of music we liked, we all became DJs and the DJs now own labels. You've got to hand it to the people in this industry for how passionate they are about what they do to have done it for so long without any money. People don't look at the positive side of it, how it's bonded the youth of today, and the money and jobs it's generated, the sheer raw talent it's generated.

Further creative activity comes as an explosion of fiction influenced by drugs and dance culture. Such work holds far more relevance to lifestyles of most young people than bodice-ripping classics, block busters or aga sagas. Set in the future, in Ibiza, in suburbia, in the inner city, the list is growing as fast as the respect for the writers themselves.

Introducing her collection of stories from authors like Irvine Welsh and Jeff Noon, Sarah Champion stresses the importance and tradition of such contemporary writing. She asks "how can you capture the madness of the last decade in facts and figures?".[16] I think the two go hand in hand; facts support fiction which is inspired by facts.

Does all this mean that Ecstasy makes you more creative? It may do, users often describe feeling motivated and confident, but other factors are at work too. High unemployment and more part time workers mean people have more free time. Short term contracts mean the traditional job for life doesn't exist any more. People have time to cut that record, write that novel, take a chance and start designing clothes. As Lee Fawcett says:

> Leisure is now a major industry in Britain. Some people work hard and play hard, others have no choice but to have too much free time. We have also become accustomed to a culture of instant gratification; fast food, TV, cheaper, bigger, better thrills. Put this together with a largely alienated and demoralised generation and it's not really surprising that this culture of drugs and dance and living for the moment has exploded in this way.

We are being bombarded from all sides with images and music from dance culture. TV and radio music researchers are hot to give credibility to their channel. On one hand dance culture is derided by the press, on the other it forms the links for

Grandstand. Television advertising frequently uses a symbolic drug experience to sell products. Eat Aero chocolate and float away to a blissful utopia. Look through a bottle of Smirnoff vodka and the world becomes part of a psychedelic experience.

Successions of lurid visuals and the use of drug slang with a break-beat rhythm are taken from the dance scene, repackaged and sold back. Since the dance culture has positive associations for millions, advertisers make use of its imagery to enhance their product's image.

Media

The news media has not been so open to dance culture's influence. Much of the news coverage is based on emotion at the expense of the truth, creating a drug hysteria. When East 17 singer Brian Harvey made some puerile comments about drugs, radio stations banned the group's records and he was sacked. In their spoof documentary Brass Eye, Channel 4 satirised this hysteria and the readiness of prominent people to join the war on drugs. They pretended that there was a new drug called 'cake' and provoked politicians and celebrities to air their fears of this totally fabricated drug problem. One MP even raised the question of 'cake' in Parliament.

Ecstasy users distrust the news media because they find the sensationalised accounts of drugs don't reflect their own experience. This disbelief can extend to the political system, and may be a significant reason why fewer young people vote. There seems to be no voice representing the views of the chemical generation. None of the major parties have seriously considered what affects their young constituents. Being soft on drugs has always been a vote loser, but now ignoring the issue may be a voter loser.

New laws

The 1994 Criminal Justice Act caused a union of party people and activists in a movement of broad interests.[17] Legislation presently under consideration could end the party for good. The Police Bill contains measures to counter crime, particularly that involving drugs, giving police extra powers of surveillance. In its definition of serious crime it includes "behaviour by a large number of people in pursuit of a common purpose". This means rave organisers could legally have their homes bugged. Being caught with drugs could now ruin your career with clause 100 enabling your employers to ask you for a conviction certificate.

For those who thought only dealers or free parties were under threat there is another Bill. Proposed by Barry Legg MP, the Public Entertainments (Drugs Misuse) Bill gives police power to close clubs on suspicion of a serious drugs problem. The Bill doesn't define what this means; is it a couple of people having a quiet smoke? People jacking up at the bar? It also makes a huge assumption that closing clubs stops drug dealing. What next? Will they ban birthday parties? As Hardcore DJ Vibes said "You can stop the parties but you can't stop the culture".

The outcome of Legg's Bill will depend on the attitudes of police in different regions. It may be devastating for dance culture, and if MINTEL is correct, the whole British economy. Dance culture is slow to respond with only a few articles in the dance press and a couple of small opposition groups. Legg's Bill will affect the other extreme of dance culture to the Criminal Justice Act; clubbers more than ravers. It will be interesting to see how any campaigns compare to the anti-Criminal Justice Act ones; whether invested capital will talk or whether the direct action veterans will use their skills. If capital and activism were combined it may make Legg's Bill unenforceable.

Transitory tribes

What of the social identity of the ecstasy user? Ben Malbon has reworked French sociologist Maffesoli's writing of tribal formations. He includes loose temporary and spatial variations incorporating clubbers and ravers in what he calls transitory tribes (pers.comm 1997). People elect which transitory tribes to join as they lack the rigid kinship structures of traditional tribes. Based on shared experience they provide a strong sense of identification, even if membership only lasts for a weekend.

Has the social effect of ecstasy been to split society into a 'have done E' and 'have not done E' division? It seems to unite those sharing ephemeral experiences of drug use or clubbing regardless of their class and age. Ecstasy users are bonded by their willingness to cross a legal boundary, no matter how conventional the rest of their lives.

As more ecstasy users become parents, solicitors, teachers, politicians the chemical generation's influence must increase. When the proto-ravers are in their old people's home singing House anthems and hugging each other over their zimmer frames, will Britain's attitude to drugs and to pleasure have changed? For increasing numbers of young people the ecstatic experience is already significant in their initiation into adulthood.

Ecstasy plays an important role in two economies; the regulated and the illicit 'night-time' economy. Two sets of moral codes; one bound by state legislation, one by an E-thos found in the vision of drug euphoria. When sheer numbers of users can no longer go unheard its influence will be concreted. The full social impact of ecstasy will become clear only when it is allowed to.

©**Mary Anna Wright 1997**

References

1. MINTEL. (Sept. 1996). *Nightclubs and Discotheques*. MINTEL International Group Ltd., London.
2. Collin, M. (1997). *Altered State: The Story of Ecstasy Culture and Acid House*. Serpent's Tail, London.
3. Lee Fawcett, National Development Officer (recreational drugs). Scottish Drugs Forum. Meeting 10 March 1997.
4. Rietveld, H. (1993) Living the dream. In, Redhead, S. (1993) (ed.). *Rave Off: Politics and Deviance in Contemporary Youth Culture*. Avebury, Aldershot. pp 41-78.
5. Malbon, B. (1997). *Clubbing: Consumption, Identity and the Spatial Practices of every-Night life*. In, Valentine, G. & T. Skelton (eds). Youth in the West. (forthcoming). Routledge, London.
6. McRobbie, A. (1994). *Shut up and Dance: Youth Culture and the Changing Modes of Femininity*. In, McRobbie, A. (1994). Postmodernism and Popular culture. Routledge, London.
7. Henderson, S. (1997). *Ecstasy: Case Unsolved*. Pandora Soap Box, London.
8. McKay, G. (1996). *Senseless Acts of Beauty*. Verso, London.
9. Bey, H. (1991). T.A.Z. *The Temporary Autonomous Zone, Ontological Anarchy, Poetic Terrorism*. Autonomedia, New York.
10. Pulp (October, 1995). Sorted For E's and Wizz. Island Records, London.
11. Smith, R & T. Maughan (1996). *Youth Culture and the Making of the Post-Fordist Economy: Dance Music in Contemporary Britain*. Working paper, Dept. of Social Policy and Social Science, Royal Holloway College, University of London, Egham, Surrey.
12. BPI Statistics 1996. British Phonographic Industry Ltd, London.
13. Gilbert, J (1997). *Soundtrack for an Uncivil Society: the CJA and the politics of Modernity*. In, New Formations (summer edition).
14. Lovatt, A. (1996). *The City Goes Soft: Regeneration and the Night-time Economy*. In, Wynne, D & J. O'Connor (1996) (eds). From The Margins to the Centre. Arena, Aldershot. pp 141-168.
15. Hemment, D (1997) *E is for ekstasis*. In, New Formations (summer edition).
16. Champion, S. (1997), (ed.). *Disco Biscuits*. Sceptre, London.
17. Wright, M.A (1994). *Freedom to Party: An investigation of the British Rave/Dance scene and the Implications of the Criminal Justice Act*. In, Yearbook for the Study of Ethnomedicine and Consciousness. (3) pp 343-351.

Social Effects

This chapter explores how ecstasy changes the ways people relate in everyday life.

The ecstasy generation may not claim to herald the dawn of a New Age like the sixties LSD generation and most clubbers may declare their only intention is to have a good time. but their accepted way of relating is less aggressive and superficial compared to previous generations.

In previous books, I included accounts of some particular groups of people and how this aspect of their lives changed after using ecstasy. Shorter versions of these are included here.

Country families

E cstasy transformed relationships among a group of families living in the countryside. Here is an excerpt:

> Between parties, people would meet more often than before and communicate more wholeheartedly. "Although we had known each other for so long, it took ecstasy to break through the very British taboo about hugging one another," Daniel said. But the new closeness also caused crises in couples' relationships. "We became more open and truthful. If couples had stayed together through habit, then it came out". Life was taken more seriously and heartfelt: honest expression was valued more than easy, superficial encounters.

> Social life was never the same. People who had known each other as neighbours for ten or twenty years felt suddenly bonded in a far deeper way through the weekend raves.

Football hooligans

I also included an account from a sociologist, Mark Gilman, who was recording the change in behaviour and values of a group of teenagers as they grew up in Manchester. They included football hooligans who liked to get drunk and fight the opposing team's supporters. By chance, ecstasy arrived on the scene during the study, so Mark was able to observe and record the change, which was dramatic. They immediately gave up their macho, aggressive behaviour, replacing it with dancing on ecstasy – even when their previous enemies were in the same club.

This did coincide with a nationwide reduction in football violence which has never returned to its previous level, even when these particular supporters left ecstasy in favour of speed. Perhaps even the temporary lull in violent behaviour due to ecstasy was enough to make a permanent change, but there are always other factors involved so its not possible to be sure.

Less hooliganism[1]

"Soccer hooliganism fell last year to its lowest level for five years.

Home office figures showed the number of fans arrested and ejected from grounds in 1991-2 dropped to 8,556 while attendances rose to 20,487,192".

Northern Ireland

I n *Ecstasy and the Dance Culture*, I wrote about my research trip to Northern Ireland where I was following up rumours that ecstasy had eased the tension between

Catholic and Protestant youths. I went to two parties on a weekend, one in a Catholic and the other in a Protestant area. When it became known what I was there for, people came up to me hand in hand with friends of the opposite sect, if not sex, who they had met under the influence of ecstasy. They nearly all told me they never would have become friends without ecstasy.

My conclusion was that there was probably some truth in it, although simply going to the same large parties where the sects had fun together – instead of going out to separate clubs – may have had the same result. Again, you can't be sure.

Meeting ground [2]

At the warehouse doors, no-one asks your religion... The raves are the last meeting ground for the children of Catholic and Protestant violence. ". . We've never known anything but hatred... It's always the same: them over on one side, you on the other, except at raves.

Survey

In a survey of readers which I carried out and published, I asked 24 questions related to changes noticed in normal life since their first use of ecstasy, not while under the influence. About 135 responses were received.

In order, the highest six scores were:

1. Increased enjoyment of dancing
2. Improved quality of life
3. Greater ease of self expression
4. More caring for other people
5. Increased spiritual awareness
6. Greater happiness

Surprisingly, just as many people reported decreases in depression and paranoia as increases. As always, it is not possible to draw general conclusions since those who responded were not representative of users as a whole.

Letters

I get a large number of personal stories from people who declare that ecstasy has made a positive change to their social lives. Those who write to me, and particularly use E-mail, are again not representative and their stories are not checked. However, they do support the idea that ecstasy users have turned away from macho behaviour, materialism and superficiality towards a more tolerant and caring attitude, without rigid barriers between social groups. Such values do fit neatly with the effects of ecstasy.

Sociosexual behaviour

There has been a radical change in socially acceptable behaviour coinciding with the change from alcohol to ecstasy at dance events. Traditional alcohol-based events always had an undertone of trying to score sexually through flirting and small talk. This was consciously rejected by the rave culture where women found it a relief to be able to have fun without being hassled by men and could also be attributed to the direct effect of MDMA as a sexual suppressant.

Although many young people in the dance scene do not take ecstasy, superficial chat-up and sexual aggression is still out of fashion. Many clubbers are too young to have known anything else.

Social interaction [3]

All respondents described an increase in social interaction under MDMA, an increased ability to approach and relate to strangers, and an enhanced ability to express affection.

World views [4]

A lot of people's world views have been changed by their ecstasy experiences. Comparisons with the sixties are in order here.

A teenage girl's changed attitude to sex

About two months ago I took my first E with friends at a club in Vauxhall.

Before knowing these wonderful friends, I had been obsessed with pulling men and sleeping with them, which I now know was to prove to myself and to others that I was attractive, which I know is a very insecure way to behave and did my self esteem no good at all. That night was the first time I had gone out to a club with friends and not only not thought about sex all night, but come home and sat up talking – really talking about important things – all night with my boyfriend and not felt the need to "give" him sex so that he would still like me.

We are still happily living together, and do a couple of pills when we go out (about twice a month) – but the E made us realise what each of us was like as a person, not just in terms of sex. It was great. I won't do it every day or even every weekend because I don't need to.

- E-mail from a London reader.

References

1. *The Independent*, August 1992.
2. *Ulster, San Francisco Chronicle* 26 October 1994.
3. Subjective reports of the Effects of MDMA in a Clinical

Setting by George Greer and Requa Tolbert from Journal of Psychoactive Drugs Vol. 18/4 1986.
4. Mark Gilman, interviewed in Manchester, 1992

Dangers

The underlying danger of ecstasy is often overlooked; it makes you feel so good that you don't notice discomfort. It's as though your body's warning systems have been turned off, allowing you to happily carry on regardless in conditions that would normally be unbearable. This factor is probably responsible for all deaths due to ecstasy, although not the specific cause.

The most researched danger is neurotoxicity or brain damage. This has been detected in animals and most researchers believe the same applies to humans. On the other hand, a minority of equally eminent researchers believe that even high doses cause no permanent damage to humans. Since this is a major concern, I include a specially commissioned review paper by a toxicologist in the chapter called Toxicity. I have also included interviews with two of the main researchers concerned who hold opposing views in the chapter on Research.

The major cause of death is allowing body temperature to rise. This can lead to a cascade of problems, and has caused most deaths. Liver and kidney damage has also been associated with ecstasy use. Medical dangers such as these are covered in this chapter and also in How to Deal with Problems.

Lastly, psychological dangers are covered in another paper written for this book by a specialist psychiatrist in a chapter called Adverse Psychological Effects, page 112.

This is all a lot to absorb, so I have also written my own conclusion at the end of this chapter.

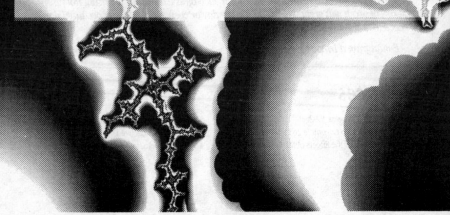

Neurotoxicity

What follows is a summary of the detailed information is the chapters called Toxicity and Research.

It sounds as though it should be easy to tell whether ecstasy is neurotoxic in humans, but in fact the main researchers have come to different opinions in spite of spending years, and millions of dollars, trying to find out.

One problem is that techniques used to identify damage give conflicting results. Another point of disagreement is how much animal research applies to humans. Then there is the question of whether neurotoxicity implies visible damage to brain cells, or whether it includes long term reductions in brain chemicals, or whether it implies that the brain functions less well.

Animal trials

Most experiments have been done on rats, although mice, dogs and primates have also been used. After the animal has been given the drug, it is killed and its brain sliced into sections for examination. Because there are so many brain cells and they are very small, damage may not only be difficult to see but the shear scale of the task makes it impractical. The researchers have therefore used indirect methods to indicate whether and where damage has occurred.

Most animal trials indicate that ecstasy damages some brain cells. The most basic indication is a lowered level of a brain chemical that controls mood called serotonin. The worry is that a person with lowered serotonin might become depressed. However, this has not been found in psychological trials so far, and it is disputed whether lowered serotonin indicates damage at all.

More sophisticated methods of testing indicate physical damage to parts of brain cells called axons. These are long tentacles which make contact with other cells in order to transfer information. It is believed that these wither, and that if they regrow, then they do not grow back quite the same. This has been reported in the media as 'rewiring the brain'. However, other techniques show no damage at all, even at fairly high doses, and some researchers believe that no damage in fact occurs.

Neurotoxicity evidence comes from examining the brains of animals. This gives rise to a further dispute, especially as tests indicate that damage varies from one species to another. The strongest evidence that humans are affected in the same way as monkeys comes from examining their spinal fluid. A researcher found that monkeys whose brains were damaged (according to his test) had more of a particular chemical in their spinal fluid, and that ecstasy users had more of this chemical than non users.[1]

Having found a link implying neurotoxicity in humans, the researchers looked for

Neurotoxicity is not neuronal degeneration

Chronic high level users could deplete their serotonin to a degree that would render the effects of ecstasy to zero; but where is the data that shows that such subject don't regain efficacy over time? Indeed, with fenfluramine, you have to continue to use it for it to be effective, therefore, even high level long-term users must show some release of serotonin for the drug to continue to work as an appetite suppressant (which it does). It has to be admitted, however, that drugs like ecstasy and fenfluramine are capable of quite long-term depletions of 5-HT (like a year) after withdrawal of the drug. I have no argument with people who call this neurotoxicity, but it's not neuronal degeneration.

Dr James O'Callaghan

Neurotoxicity research [2]

Dr. O'Callaghan had a 3-year $750,000 research contract to establish a method of assessing neurotoxicity. He took this to mean physical damage to the brain affecting its function. He compared various methods and chose Reactive Gliosis as the most sensitive, since it responded to all kinds of known damage from air pollution, stab wounds, disease and even old age degeneration. However, MDMA, MDA and d fenfluramine did not show damage.

Effect of cages on ecstasy toxicity [3]

Laboratory rats are normally kept in either plastic or metal cages. The two types differ greatly in the way rats are able to dissipate heat. With all other factors identical when given MDMA, Aluminium floors enabled rats to regulate their core temperature when they were unable to do so on acrylic floors. This may invalidate previous research where cage type was assumed to make no difference.

Fenfluramine approval [4]

In May 1996, the US Food and Drug Administration approved fenfluramine for daily use to treat obesity on the usual grounds that the benefits were considered to outweigh the risks, although it was known to cause a rare but sometimes fatal reaction called Primary Pulmonary Hypertension. (This is not a known danger of ecstasy.)

Human trial on the effects of ecstasy by Dr. George Ricaurte [5]

30 ecstasy users and 28 matched controls were compared. On average, users had taken 170 mg doses of MDMA weekly on 95 occasions over 5 years. Results showed that ecstasy users had lower levels of 5-HIAA, implying that their serotonin levels were lower. Personality measurements showed statistically significant differences between ecstasy users and controls: ecstasy users were less impulsively aggressive. This was unexpected, since it had previously been assumed that lower serotonin levels corresponded to increased impulsive aggressive behaviour.

impaired brain functions. They gave users and non-users a set of standard psychological tests, but they found that the users' brains worked just as well.[5] However, they did find that users had milder personalities and regarded this as supporting the damage theory. Critics argue that the type of people who like to use ecstasy may have more of the chemical in their spinal fluid and milder personalities anyway.

A further trial is under way in which I took part and interviewed the researcher, see page 242.

The non-toxic argument

The view that ecstasy is neurotoxic went largely unchallenged until a pharmaceutical company wanted to market a drug called fenfluramine in the USA. Opposition came from researchers whose tests indicated that fenfluramine was almost identically toxic to ecstasy, while the researchers who believed that ecstasy is not neurotoxic supported approval. After listening to the evidence on both sides the US Food and Drug Administration approved fenfluramine in May 1996 for lifetime daily use. Some say that this only shows that a drug company can obtain a licence to kill, but the company is confident that the drug is safe, and by implication, so is ecstasy.

The argument for ecstasy being non toxic is given by James O'Callaghan on page 247. Briefly, he has developed tests for neurotoxicity which he believes are more accurate, and he believes that there is a flaw in other tests for neurotoxicity. Meanwhile, other researchers believe that his test is too specific and does not cover all aspects of neurotoxicity.

Human trials

Amazing as it seems, no one has yet done research on people before and after they have taken ecstasy to see what changes may have occurred. Instead, research on humans has consisted of comparing ecstasy users to 'matched controls', that is non-users who are similar. But its impossible to match people perfectly, allowing plenty of room for doubt. There is always the 'chicken and egg' problem: how do you know if the difference was caused by ecstasy, or if it was that type who were attracted to the drug?

The best known research has been carried out by Drs Ricaurte and McCann at Johns Hopkins and National Institute of Health in the USA, two of the world's largest medical research centres.

Guinea pig

I took part as a guinea pig in one of Ricaurte's trials in 1965. This involved spending a week in a hospital and being given an incredible number of tests. At least twice a day, I had to do a series of computer tests for short term memory, reaction time, recognition and associations. I had to provide a sample of spinal fluid via a spinal tap; I was wired up to electrodes glued to my head for two nights to record my brainwaves; my tolerance to pain was tested with and without morphine... At one time I had to keep still for several hours with a catheter in each arm, one pouring in various drugs and the other taking samples while I was given psychological tests.

The purpose of the trial was to look for effects of ecstasy by comparing users to non-users. In a previous trial, users scored significantly better in psychological tests.[5] The idea of this trial was to look more carefully for evidence of possible damage in users. (Results are still not available.)

Optimists and pessimists

Optimists point out that some areas of the brain can be damaged or even totally destroyed without harming brain function. Since the observed functional changes caused by ecstasy appear to be more therapeutic than harmful, they do not regard the change as damage or neurotoxicity.[6]

Pessimists fear that cells damaged by ecstasy may be involved in some kind of subtle function that doesn't show up in tests, or may result in depression due to lower serotonin release. Or that the cells which are damaged may be needed after other cells have died off, resulting in mental problems in old age. They believe the reason why such problems have not yet been seen is because it is only recently that large doses have become common.

How to reduce the risk of neurotoxicity

Animal trials and theory suggest that neurotoxicity depends on dose. Risk is greatest when large amounts are in the body (either through taking a lot at once or topping up). A single large dose is far more toxic than the same quantity spread out over several separate occasions.

Medical dangers

Ecstasy raises heart rate and blood pressure, and this can be dangerous for some people.[7] It also puts an extra load on the liver which can cause jaundice in people whose livers have been damaged by hepatitis. But the most dangerous effect is on body temperature: ecstasy interferes with the body's thermostat, allowing users to overheat.

Heatstroke

Nearly all the deaths due to ecstasy have resulted from heatstroke. This occurs when people exercise for hours on end in hot, humid conditions without drinking sufficient water. Without ecstasy, dancers would not be able to carry on when so exhausted, hot and thirsty, so they would have to stop, cool off and drink some water. But on ecstasy they can carry on because they don't feel the discomfort.

The relative lack of rave deaths in the US implies that deaths in Britain are due to the conditions in which the drug is used: dancing in hot venues without drinking enough water. Those who die may be especially vulnerable.

Heatstroke is a well-known cause of death, but in other situations it only affects people who are pushing themselves to the limit[8] or are unable to escape from the heat. What is peculiar about ecstasy-related deaths is that the victims appear to make no real attempt to cool down. This has been explained by ravers being in a trancelike state due to the music, but experiments with rats and mice show that it may be a direct effect of the drug.

Researchers have examined the way rats respond to ecstasy in very hot conditions. Without ecstasy, the rats did their best to cool down by moving less and losing heat through their tails (the rat equivalent to sweating). But on ecstasy they became more active and did not attempt to lose heat - as though they had lost the sense of being too hot - until they died of heatstroke.[9] Meanwhile, experiments on mice show that ecstasy is five times more toxic in crowded conditions.

Fortunately most dancers are now aware of this danger, yet there are still deaths from overheating. There is also evidence that other forms of toxicity is greatly increased at higher temperatures.

Too much water

Recently, there have been several reports of death from drinking too much water. One raver was reported to have drunk 26 pints, but another girl died after drinking only about 6 pints who was with friends at home.[10] The mechanism is believed to be that the blood becomes diluted which causes tissue cells to swell by osmosis. This is harmless to most organs, but because the skull does not allow the brain to swell, pressure builds up and presses down on the brain stem which can be fatal.

This can be avoided by drinking 'isotonic' sports drinks, or eating a little salt such as in a pack of nuts or crisps. Even sweet drinks are better than plain water.

It has also been suggested that ecstasy may effect the kidneys of some people so that they do not get rid of water but only salts; this would be indicated by small amounts of dark urine even after drinking a lot.

Death by water [10]

The danger is drinking too fast rather than too much. Therefore it could be dangerous to gulp down two or three pints of water straight down in one go, while safe to drink several times as much during a night out – providing that as much water is lost as urine and sweat.

Does change imply damage?

Extrapolating the animal data to the human neurotoxicity question is problematic. Even aside from the species differentiation issue, at this point in time we do not fully understand the implications of the findings of axonal degeneration. Calling it neurotoxic implies clear injurious outcome, and prematurely forecloses further dialogue and exploration of alternative interpretations. It is important to also examine questions concerning the lack of perceptible adverse behavioural sequelae in experimental animals given large amounts of ecstasy as well as the failure of appreciable numbers of human casualties to materialize despite the fact that millions of individuals have taken the drug over the last two decades.

Although there is no doubt that humans may potentially experience highly adverse outcomes, the numbers remain small and are usually associated with a variety of extenuating circumstances. And we cannot altogether disregard the frequent reports of positive change.

– Dr. Charles Grob

Is pleasure toxic?

Recent research suggests that dopamine release, rather than serotonin release, is the cause of neurotoxicity. The theory is that excess dopamine is metabolised into a substance that releases 'free radicals'. Large amounts may damage the neuron terminals on re-uptake and contribute to fatigue and mental dysfunction often associated with sustained amphetamine abuse.

But other researchers believe that dopamine is released whenever we experience extreme pleasure such as having an orgasm, leading to the bizarre conclusion that 'having too much fun is bad for you'!

Heatstroke at marathons[8]

"Heatstroke is becoming a problem in long distance running events ... In Canada, 1% are admitted to hospital during and after mass-participation runs [marathons]".

Rats die of heatstroke [9]

I spoke to the researcher, Dr. Gordon, on the phone and learned that he is a specialist in temperature control mechanisms. He has a long chamber which is kept hot one end and cool the other, so that animals inside can choose whatever temperature they prefer.

At higher ambient temperatures rats lost water through evaporation far more rapidly, increased their metabolic rate and did not show any attempt to cool down. Their core body temperature increased rapidly until they died. This was assumed to be a direct effect of ecstasy on the part of the brain that controls body temperature.

The point to remember is that water is needed to replenish what is lost. You will lose lots of water if you are dancing vigorously in hot conditions, but not much if you are sitting around with friends at home.

Toxicity separable from desired effects

An animal study has shown that ecstasy toxicity as recorded by Ricaurte and others can be eliminated by taking Prozac at the same time or even up to 4 hours afterwards.[11,12] Some people assume this also applies to humans and take 20mg Prozac with E. A survey showed that most report the effect is unchanged, and nearly all report less hangover.

Liver and kidney damage

The British medical press have reported hepatitis or jaundice (both diseases of the liver) among people who had taken ecstasy several times and kidney damage has also been suggested.[13,7] In the USA, damage to liver and kidneys has not been reported, nor has it been found in animal trials. Some people believe that a contaminant in British street ecstasy may be responsible.[13] Yet others believe that it is the combination of drugs used in Britain.[12,13]

In 1996, researchers in Britain made intensive examinations of the organs of seven people who had died after taking ecstasy, and found damage to all of their livers and kidneys. Dr. Forrester, one of the British researchers, told me:

> The problem is why doesn't everyone get liver, brain and heart rot from ecstasy use if that is the mechanism. Catastrophes from ecstasy use are so rare, perhaps as common as being struck by lightning, that there must be something else going on. My thoughts have been a combination of events including metabolic abnormalities and maybe amphetamine use all coming together to cause catastrophe in very rare cases.

Contaminants

Another danger is that what you bought as E is mixed with a poison of some kind. Although this is a possibility, it doesn't appear to happen.[16,17]
Dr. John Henry of the National Poisons Unit looks for poisons in the blood and urine of people who have died or are seriously ill after taking drugs, but has not come across such cases,[17] although he has found Paracetamol, Codeine, Amphetamine, MDA, MDEA, Ketamine, Tiletamine and LSD.[17] Similarly, Dr. Les King at the Aldermaston Forensic Laboratory has never come across (or even heard of) poisonous additives to ecstasy, although he does not specifically test for them.[19] Likewise my own tests and the hundreds of tests in Holland and Germany have failed to find poisonous contaminants.[20]

Chinese medical view

A reader wrote quoting her acupuncturist: "In Chinese medical terms, ecstasy attacks the heart and heart protector organs, so reducing the ability of the heart to store 'shen' in the future." A Chinese herbal practitioner whom I consulted commented: "If ecstasy is expansive, then it probably does attack the heart store 'shen' (spirit of the heart) but not the heart itself."

Toxicity separable from desired effects [11]

Subjective trials show that the psychoactive effects of MDMA are not affected by taking fluoxetine [Prozac] first. Serotonin re-uptake inhibitors block MDMA neurotoxicity. Since fluoxetine is a serotonin re-uptake inhibitor, this implies that the desired effect of ecstasy may be enjoyed without its neurotoxic effects.

Three of the subjects were experienced ecstasy users who took 20mg fluoxetine 40-60 minutes before large doses of ecstasy, 300-450mg including booster doses. The sense of euphoria and closeness was unaffected. There was a greater sense of calmness but less increase in energy. Side effects normally felt such as jaw clench were less than normal, though nausea was worse. Two found it easier to sleep afterwards. Next-day fatigue was considerably less than normal, even for the one who found sleep as difficult as usual.

The fourth was a woman who had been taking 20 mg fluoxetine for the previous 10 days. It was her first ecstasy experience and her description of it was typical, implying that fluoxetine did not affect it.

The paper concludes that these cases "argue against the view that serotonin release is the basis for MDMA's psychoactive action", since this is prevented by pretreatment with fluoxetine. This is supported by the fact that drugs such as fenfluramine do not produce similar psychoactive effects to ecstasy.

Prozac blocks neurotoxicity [12]

Rats were given four doses of MDMA at 12-hourly intervals. Doses varied from 25 to 150mg/kg. The brains were then frozen, sectioned, silver stained and examined. The staining showed up where damage was caused, which was to particular parts of the brain.

Fluoxetine at 5mg/kg did not produce staining on its own. When given 30 minutes before MDMA, fluoxetine reduced by about half the volume of tissue stained "and dramatically reduced the intensity of staining throughout the affected regions".

Purity and toxicity [18]

Reports from the USA suggest that ecstasy is only mildly toxic. The main causes of death were cardiac arrhythmia, rhabdomyomas and disseminated intravascular coagulation (DIC). Most cases the authors were consulted about had mild symptoms. There was a clear pattern of toxicity in the most severe cases. Death was probably due to heatstroke "in which severe hyperthermia was accompanied by DIC". There was no evidence of drug impurity being responsible for toxicity.

Heroin in E

Many people are convinced that ecstasy sometimes contains heroin but it has not been found in analysed samples, even those tested by a Swiss magazine that were all reputed to be laced with heroin.

Taken orally by someone not used to it, heroin produces drowsiness, feeling of well being, nausea, itchiness (particularly around the nose) constricted pupils and constipation. If a pill consisted of half heroin and half ecstasy, the effects of that quantity of heroin would be weak compared to the ecstasy and may be masked altogether.

But perhaps the most convincing argument is economic: it does not make economic sense to sell a more expensive drug as ecstasy.

Getting run down

It's often said that taking ecstasy affects your immune system. I have not found any evidence to support this, but it is common medical knowledge that you are more vulnerable to disease when you are exhausted, and that a hot sweaty environment is ideal for transmitting viral infections. Added to this, many people make skin contact while on ecstasy, and its use drains one's reserve of energy which may indirectly make you more susceptible to colds and other infections.

Chest and back pain

Both of these are widely reported and are sometimes rumoured to be a direct effect of ecstasy. A far more probable explanation is stretched muscles and anxiety, possibly combined with dehydration of the kidneys and physical exhaustion.

Back pain

During his 50 in-depth interviews, Andrew Thomson has included questions about fluids consumed and lower back pain after use. Those who consume large amounts of nonalcoholic drinks do not have back pain, and people who normally have pain can prevent it by drinking water. He suspects that lower back pain is due to the effect of dehydration on the kidneys.

Incompatible medical conditions

Taking ecstasy increases metabolic rate: it drives the body harder thus putting extra strain on the organs. In particular, this will tax the heart and liver, while the increased blood pressure and pulse makes strokes more likely. If you are not fit you may also strain muscles.[18] Animal research suggests that ecstasy does not harm the offspring of users,[29] but it is advisable to avoid any stimulant while pregnant.

Chest pain

Three normally fit teenagers came to the emergency department of a hospital complaining of severe chest pain. Had all danced for some hours. All discharged themselves after learning that their pain was not cardiac.

Contaminants [16]

According to the drugs squad house magazine, none of the seizures of "Ecstasy" contained poisonous or addictive substances.

Contaminants [17]

We at the National Poisons Unit are not so interested in the non-pharmacological constituents, but have heard of fishbowl preservative tablets, camden tablets etc. being sold. These are not particularly dangerous.

Pregnant rats [22]

Groups of pregnant rats were administered varying doses of MDMA on alternate gestational days. Gestational duration, litter size, birth weights and physical appearance were unaffected. Behaviour and intelligence of the offspring were unaffected, except for subtle behavioural changes such as enhanced olfactory discrimination.

Asthma, diabetes and epilepsy

Asthma: There is no pharmacological reason why asthma should be made any worse by E.

Diabetes: There is no known effect on blood sugar, but if you take E you are likely to be more energetic. If you are diabetic, you should adjust your sugar intake or insulin dose to allow for increased physical activity.

Epilepsy: E can cause epileptic fits if taken in overdose. If you suffer from epilepsy and take E you are more likely to have fits.

Overdose story

I was fed up with the quality of E, so went to Holland and bought 200, packed them in condoms and swallowed them. I looked out of the plane window and saw the wing melt and the next thing I remember was waking up in hospital with the police looking down at me. When the condoms came out, 50 pills were missing.

- Letter from a reader in prison

Vitamins to avoid fatigue

It has been suggested that the effects of free radicals could be avoided by taking antioxidant supplements. Suggested dose for prevention is 2-4gm vitamin c; 1,000 IU vitamin E; 5mg ß-carotene; 2gm bioflavanoids; 1gm L-cartinine; 2gm N-acetylcysteine and 25mcg selenium. For treatment, three times this dose is recommended.

Incompatible medicines

MAOIs (monoamine oxidase inhibitors) are antidepressants that work by inhibiting MAO from metabolising serotonin and dopamine thus increasing their level in the brain. Combining MAOIs with drugs such as ecstasy, amphetamines and ephedrine may cause a hypertensive crisis.

There is also potential for problems when ecstasy is taken at the same time as some over-the-counter drugs. These include paracetamol and stimulants which could add to the speedy effect and lead to a 'hypertensive crisis' – when the heart races and blood pressure soars. Medicines that contain stimulants are: Actifed, Sudafed, Contac 400, Day nurse, Mu-Cron, Sinutab tablets etc – even Lemsip.

Overdosing

The effect of taking several Es at once is to produce a more amphetamine-like effect. Some users take ecstasy specifically to achieve this. It is likely that taking large and frequent doses is neurotoxic,[21] although deaths have not been blamed on overdoses.[18]

Social dangers

There are several social pitfalls to ecstasy use. Unlike alcohol, where people recognize the symptoms of drunkenness and make allowances for it, people not used to ecstasy may be upset by the behaviour of those taking it. Someone on E expressing warmth may appear false and prompt people to respond in an antagonistic way, or simply cause embarrassment. Acting on impulse may be bitterly regretted.[23]

Taking ecstasy with a lover can be a wonderful way of bonding the relationship, but this can be disastrous with the wrong person.[24,25] A more profound danger has been suggested which is that ecstasy allows love and intimacy to flow too freely straight away, so that there is no room for further development.

Addiction

Although not addictive in the same sense as opiates, many people find ecstasy very difficult to give up and a few are certainly addicted in the psychological sense. However, like cigarette smokers, many people have used ecstasy occasionally over many years and are not addicted. Before the rave scene, ecstasy was considered non-addictive because it fails to deliver the empathic effect after frequent use, but people often say that they are addicted to dancing on drugs, not ecstasy itself.

Conclusions from a user's perspective

The question we all want answered is: "Will it do me any harm to take ecstasy?" Research has provided some clues.

The first lesson is the importance of keeping cool, as most problems start with high temperature. Bingeing is far more dangerous than taking the same amount spread over a few weeks. Taking ecstasy on its own is less dangerous than with some other drugs, particularly speedy ones.

There is a real risk that heavy use will cause long term damage, but the risk is unknown, if it exists at all. But alcohol and tobacco are also neurotoxic and are known to cause long term damage to people who take too much. It is likely that ecstasy is much the same, and that heavy users are likely to suffer damage while light users are not. How much is unknown, and probably varies from one person to the next.

References

1. Phone call from Dr George Ricaurte, March 1995.

2. *Assessing Neurotoxicity of Drugs of Abuse*, by Dr James O'Callaghan, NIDA monograph 1993.

3. *Metabolic and Thermoregulatory Responses of the Rat maintained in acrylic or wire screen cages: Implications for Pharmacological Studies* by Christopher Gordon *Physiology and Behaviour* 1994.

4. *The Neurotoxicity of MDMA and Related Compounds*, by Dr Molliver, in *The Neuropharmacology of Serotonin*, published in *Annals of the New York Academy of Sciences*, 1990. A paper comparing the action of ecstasy with fenfluramine.

5. Serotonin Neurotoxicity after MDMA: A Controlled Study in Humans by George Ricaurte et al. Neuropsychopharmacology 1994

6. *Seven Experiments that could Change the World* (book) by Rupert Sheldrake, 1994.

7. Meeting with Dr John Merrill of NW Regional Health Authority, August 1992.

8. *Living with Risk* (book), published by the British Medical Association, 1990. This book contains statistics and evaluations of various risks commonly taken.

9. *Effects of ecstasy on Autonomic Thermoregulatory Responses of the Rat*, by Christopher Gordon et al., 1990.

10. Refer box page 81.

11. Reinforcing Subjective Effects of MDMA May seperable from it's Neurotoxic Actions by McCann and Ricaute, J. Clinical Psychopharmacology 6/93.

12. A Quantitative Analysis of Neural Degeneration Induced by MDMA by Karl Jansen 1993. In Asessing Neurotoxicity

of Drugs Abuse, NIDA monograph 136:133-149.

14. Visit to Dr John Henry at the National Poisons Unit at Guy's Hospital, London, 12/92.

15. Meeting with Dr Charles Grob in Los Angeles, October 1993.

16. *Drugs Arena*, National Criminal Intelligence Service, 1990.

17. Letter from Dr John Henry of the National Poisons Unit, December 1993.

18. Toxicity and deaths from ecstasy from *The Lancet* by John Henry et al. August 1992. A report of toxicity and fatalities related to ecstasy use during 1990 and 1991.

19. Conversations with Dr Les King, team leader of the drugs intelligence laboratory at the Forensic Science Laboratory at Aldermaston, part of the Forensic Science Service, a Government agency, 12/92, 3/94 and 1/95.

20. A visit to Arno Adelaars, a part-time purchaser of street samples of drugs for testing Amsterdam, October 1992.

21. Refer Toxicity chapter page 90.

22. Behavourial and Neurochemical effects of prenatal MDMA exposure in rats. by St Omer et al in Neurotoxicol Teratol.

23. *The Psychological and Physiological Effects of MDMA on Normal Volunteers*, by Joseph Downing, from *Journal of Psychoactive Drugs*, Vol. 18 April 1986.

24. *The Adam Experience, a guide for first-time users*, by Starfire, 1985.

25. *Through the Gateway of the Heart* (book) published by Four Trees Publications, San Francisco 1985

Alexander Shulgin at his home laboratory, where he reinvented MDMA in 1965.

Toxicity

By Leon van Aerts, Ph.D

In the ecstasy consuming community the view that MDMA is a relatively safe drug prevails. However, knowledge of the toxicity of MDMA and of the risks involved with the use of ecstasy is scarce amongst those consuming it. In this chapter the existent scientific knowledge on the toxicity of MDMA is reviewed, and based on the available animal data, the dose-effects relationships of MDMA use in humans are estimated.

Two areas of toxicity are of concern. These are the acute systemic toxicity and the neurotoxicity of MDMA. Acute systemic toxicity refers to the acute severe reactions that occur occasionally, and that may lead to hospitalization or even can be fatal.

It is now well recognized that a greatly increased body temperature plays a pivotal role. Control of body temperature is therefore the most important means in preventing the severe reactions to MDMA. Recently, concerns have also been raised about a possible idiosyncratic liver toxicity.

Most of the animal research has concentrated on the neurotoxicity of MDMA. Of main concern are the long term effects of MDMA on the serotonergic system. High doses or repeated administration of MDMA cause serotonin nerve terminal degeneration and serotonin axonal degeneration in animals. Lower doses result in changes, usually decreases, of serotonin neuronal markers, amongst which reduced serotonin brain tissue levels, reduced density of the serotonin reuptake transporter protein, and reduced activity of tryptophan hydroxylase. It is unclear if the changes that are observed after administration of low doses of MDMA are of a neuromodulatory nature, or if these are a reflection of neurodegenerative processes, or if it is a combination of these two possibilities.

Although studies with a retrospective study design cannot establish a causal relationship, the observation that MDMA users had lower levels of a serotonin metabolite in their cerobrospinal fluid is an indication that changes in their serotonergic system may have occurred. Extrapolation of the available animal data to humans *implies that neuromodulatory events in the serotonergic system of the brain will occur at recreational doses, and that nerve terminal degeneration is likely to occur at high doses. It is therefore advisable to refrain from the use of high doses, boosters or bingeing on ecstasy, as these will increase the likelihood of neurodegenerative processes.*

Introduction

In this chapter information will be given on the toxicology of MDMA. It is a reflection of a study of the available scientific literature on this subject. It is not my purpose to add to the prevailing media scare around ecstasy, nor is my purpose to play down the potential dangers that are related with the use of ecstasy. The sole intention is to present the current knowledge on an intrinsic property of MDMA, namely its toxicity and, based on this knowledge, to make an estimation of health risks concerning the human use of ecstasy.

The plea is made by the drug consuming community that the user himself should be free to decide which drugs he uses, so that, the user becomes his own risk manager in this matter. In order to make sound decisions on the risks that will or will not be taken, the risk manager must be provided with a solid risk assessment. A simplified presentation of such a risk assessment is given by presenting estimates of the effects that may be expected with the use of various doses of MDMA.

Toxicity of MDMA

Toxicity is an intrinsic property of a substance, namely its ability to disturb the physiological balance of an organism to such an extent that the organism no longer can be considered healthy. In other words it becomes ill (Koeman, 1996). The Environmental Protection Agency (EPA) of the US considers the effects of substances as toxic or adverse when there is functional deterioration or pathological damage that affects the functioning of the whole organism or that reduces the ability of the organism to react to additional hazards.

Concerning the toxicity of MDMA there are two main areas that deserve attention: acute systemic toxicity and neurotoxicity. The effect of the acute systemic toxicity on the health of the organism is obvious. In the case of neurotoxicity no immediate effect on the health of the animal or human is observed. Nevertheless, the deterioration of very specific parts of the nervous system, as observed in animals, must be considered to be potentially toxic, since such a deterioration may eventually affect the health of the animal or human, or reduce its capacity to cope with additional hazards.

Acute systemic toxicity of MDMA

The first studies on the acute toxicity of MDMA were performed in 1953 and 1954 at Michigan University, supported by the US Army, declassified in 1969 and published by Hardman et al. (1973). They showed that the LD50 (dose at which 50% of the animals die) varied from 14 mg/kg, intravenously (i.v.) in the mongrel dog to 98 mg/kg, intraperitoneally (i.p.) in the guinea pig. In the monkey (Macaca mulatta) it was 22 mg/kg, i.v.. Compared to mescaline, MDMA was, depending on species, two to almost six times as toxic. Noteworthy is that 3,4-methylenedioxyamphetamine (MDA) was even more toxic with a LD50 in the monkey of 6 mg/kg, i.v., approximately four times the human recreational dose.

At high doses MDMA caused a number of effects in the dog (5-50 mg/kg, i.v.) and monkey (10-75 mg/kg, i.v.) as a result of its action on the nervous system, including: lack of movement control, convulsions, muscle rigidity and tremors, vomiting and difficulties with breathing. Pathology was not performed. In a subchronic study (28 days) rats and beagle dogs were given MDMA orally at dose ranges of 0-100 mg/kg and 0-15 mg/kg, respectively.[1] Besides clinical manifestations as mentioned above, the testicles of one out of three dogs in the 9 mg/kg group and one out of three in the 15 mg/kg group were reduced in size and two out of three dogs in the 15 mg/kg group had enlarged prostatic glands. Rats showed no gross lesions at necropsy. Some haematological parameters were slightly changed at the higher doses, but these changes were statistically not significant.

Noteworthy is that no neuropathological effects were observed. However, the histological methods that were used were not properly described and may not have been appropriate to detect MDMA-induced lesions.

Unfortunately, the acute toxicity of MDMA has also become apparent in humans. With the rise of rave culture in the UK reports of severe reactions, including fatalities after the use of 'ecstasy' appeared in the medical literature. They were reviewed by Henry et al. (1992). The predominant toxicity patterns that emerge from these reports are fulminant hyperthermia, convulsions, disseminated intravascular coagulation (DIC) (blood clotting in the blood vessels), rhabdomyolysis (dissolution of skeletal muscle), and acute renal (kidney) failure. DIC and rhabdomyolysis may be brought about by the hyperthermic condition, and rhabdomyolysis can also be caused by acute renal failure. Acute liver failure is another serious complication reported in association with the use of MDMA and can also precipitate from a hyperthermic condition.[2]

It is now well recognized that hyperthermia plays a central role in these events, and body temperature control is therefore an important means in preventing the serious conditions above. Providing the body with enough fluid is one way in achieving this, however it should be stressed that excessive drinking of water may lower the ionic strength (salt concentration) of the body fluids, cause tissues to swell – a problem for the brains – and can eventually lead to death. One fatality postmortemly examined by Milroy et al. (1996) was a case of water intoxication after the taking of ecstasy, and Matthai et al. (1996) described two cases, that were shown to have developed mild cerebral oedema (abnormal accumulation of fluid in brain tissue) due to unrestricted water intake. When very thirsty it is therefore wiser to drink isotonic fluids instead of solely water.

Although raving for hours in a warm environment may aggravate the onset of a hyperthermic condition, it should be noted that MDMA by its pharmacologic action may lead to a rise in body temperature by itself. Severe reactions like hyperthermia, DIC and rhabdomyolysis were rare at the time it was used only in more relaxed settings in the 80s in the US. However, observations of this type were reported.[3]

Cardiac arrhythmia (irregularities in the heart rhythm) are often also noted in emergencies that are brought in and are probably another way by which death may precipitate, especially in those that are predisposed by having cardiac abnormalities. The increase in blood pressure and rise in heart rate caused by MDMA may be deleterious in people with heart problems.[4]

Besides acute liver failure as part of the above mentioned syndrome there is concern MDMA causes damage to the liver, resulting in acute hepatitis.[5] The mechanism here is probably different and might be caused by the accumulation of a toxic metabolite from MDMA.[6] There are only a few reports of acute hepatitis related to the use of ecstasy until now. Toxicological examinations were not performed, but the subjects admitted the use of ecstasy.

Therefore, if there is a causal relationship, it is not clear whether the liver toxicity was caused by MDMA, or by another psychoactive compound that was contained in the "ecstasy" tablet, by a contaminant or by the consumption of another drug. If it is MDMA that causes the observed liver toxicity, than this phenomenon is clearly idiosyncratic (inherent to an individual's (genetic) condition), and the exact relation and mechanism are unresolved. Nevertheless it may be prudent to be cautious with the combination of ecstasy and substances which are known to put an extra burden on the liver, like alcohol and acetaminophen (Paracetamol). Furthermore, people having liver problems may be more sensitive to a possible toxic response of the liver.

Additionally there are a few rare cases in which the use of ecstasy was mentioned. Amongst these were several in which there were vascular problems.[7] However a clear causal relation with the use of ecstasy could not be established and the cause could be an undetected pre-morbid condition or the simultaneous use of amphetamine. In two reports the occurrence of pneumomediastinum (accumulation of air in the space between the lungs as a result of rupture of marginal alveoli in the lung, associated with the sudden onset of central chest pain) was reported.[8] The first report mentioned vomiting as a possible cause and in the second the authors could only speculate that retching might have caused the problems in one case and presumed severe physical exercise in another. All cases of pneumomediastinum recovered in a few days. In one report two cases of aplastic anaemia (blood abnormality) were found after the use of MDMA.[9] Since all of the cases mentioned in this paragraph are seldom found in association with the use of MDMA it is questionable whether there is a causal relationship.

Mild unpleasant side effects are common with the use of MDMA. These include loss of appetite, trismus (jaw clenching), bruxism (teeth grinding), nausea, muscle aches, stiffness, ataxia (impairment of motor control), blurred vision, increased sweating, anxiety, tachycardia (increased heart rate), insomnia (sleeplessness) and fatigue.[10] Most of these side effects subside within 24 hours, however complaints of muscle tension in the jaw continued for two days to six weeks, blurred vision up to three days and psychological effects like insomnia, depression and anxiety up to eight days.[11]

Psychiatric disorders like depression, anxiety disorder and psychosis associated with the use of MDMA are dealt with under Adverse Psychological Effects, page 112.

Neurotoxicity of MDMA

Neurobiology

Brain cells communicate with each other by sending chemicals (neurotransmitters) to each other. The neurotransmitter is released from nerve terminals which are located at the end of an axon, a long fibre from the neuronal cell body to the effector region. After diffusing across the synapse, the gap which separates neurons, the neurotransmitter binds a receptor located on the surface of the receiving cell. Binding of the transmitter to some receptors induces, inhibits, or modulates currents of electrically charged particles (ions) across the cell membrane. Other receptors regulate the levels of "second messengers", small molecules which produce biochemical changes within the cell. There are also receptors which regulate gene expression, and still others which catalyse chemical modifications to themselves or other proteins (e.g. phosphorylation).

Amongst the many neurotransmitters present in the brain, *serotonin* (5-hydroxytryptamine, 5-HT), and dopamine (both so-called monoamines), are the ones that are of utmost importance in both the pharmacologic and the toxicologic action of MDMA. Serotonin is synthesized within the nerve cell from the amino acid tryptophan, and *tryptophan hydroxylase* (TPH) is the rate-limiting enzyme in this synthesis. When serotonin is synthesized it can be stored within so-called presynaptic or membrane vesicles within the nerve terminal. *5-hydroxyindoleacetic acid* (5-HIAA) is a metabolite of serotonin.

The serotonin signal is limited in space and time through a process called reuptake. Most of the released neurotransmitter is reabsorbed by the nerve terminal for repackaging and reuse. The *(re-)uptake site (carrier, transporter)*, a specialized proteinaceous structure located in the nerve terminal membrane, is responsible for this process.

To investigate if the serotonergic system in the brain is affected by MDMA, the above mentioned *serotonin neuronal markers* can be measured by appropriate methods. Serotonin and 5-HIAA can be assayed by analytical chemistry, TPH can assessed with an enzyme assay, 5-HT uptake sites can be quantified by either measuring the rate of the uptake itself, or by binding of radioactively labelled ligands that bind specifically to the uptake carrier, and subsequently measuring the radioactivity or visualize the sites by autoradiography (exposing photographic material).

A recently developed method uses 5-HT-uptake ligands that can be visualized in the living brain with positron emission tomography (PET). Furthermore, functionality can be tested by artificially stimulating the serotonin neurons electrically or challenging them chemically with a serotonin releasing agent. The ultimate proof of neuronal damage however is cutting the brain into very thin slices and observing them under the microscope (histology). Specific staining techniques have been developed, either to show neuronal damage (Fink-Heimer silver staining), or to mark serotonergic neurons with the use of specific antibodies (immunohistochemical staining).

Alternatively, indirect evidence of neuronal damage can be assessed. For example, an increase in the volume of glial cells (a supporting and nourishing type of brain cell) (=gliosis) or an increase in glial fibrillary acidic protein (GFAP) are associated with neuronal damage and can be used as markers. Finally behavioural tests can be performed in animals or humans, however, as we know very little of how the various aspects of the serotonin system influence behaviour, such tests are difficult to interpret.

Effects of MDMA on the serotonergic system in animals

M any of the above mentioned methods to investigate the effect of MDMA on the brain serotonergic system have been applied to a variety of mammals, including rats, guinea pigs, mice, and squirrel and rhesus monkeys. Here the evidence of MDMA-induced neurotoxicity in animals will be reviewed briefly. However, it should be noted, as will be discussed in the paragraph on up- and down-regulation, that the decreases in serotonin neuronal markers do not necessarily reflect neurodegenerative processes under all circumstances, as these markers are also under genetic control and may be affected by regulatory processes.

Tissue 5-hydroxyindoles levels

The most acute effect of MDMA is a rapid release of serotonin and dopamine from the presynaptic vesicles.[12] Although in mice the effect is predominantly on the dopaminergic system,[13] in most species the serotonergic system is in the long run more affected. The process of serotonin release is thought to be mediated by an interaction of MDMA with the serotonin uptake carrier leading to a reversal of the serotonin flow.[14]

Within 24 hours after a single injection of a high dose in rats the greatly reduced levels of serotonin and dopamine have been restored to control level, however thereafter there is a progressive decline of tissue levels of serotonin and its metabolite 5-HIAA.[15] These deficits can persist for weeks to more than a year after multiple doses of MDMA depending on which brain area and species are tested, with the (non-human) primate (squirrel and rhesus monkey) being the most sensitive with respect to the size of the dose that induces the protracted serotonin depletion as a well as to the extent and the duration of depletion.[16]

Tryptophan hydroxylase activity and serotonin uptake sites

TPH activity is also greatly reduced after repeated doses of MDMA in the rat.[17] The acute inactivation of this enzyme involves the oxidation of sensitive sites of this enzyme, whereas the prolonged decreased activity after repeated injections with high doses of MDMA may reflect loss of serotonin nerve terminals.[18] Loss of serotonin nerve terminals is also suggested by the reduction in the density of the serotonin uptake carriers as indicated by a reduced serotonin uptake capacity[19] and decreased binding of specific serotonin uptake ligands.[20]

Immunohistochemistry

Further evidence, suggestive of reduced serotonergic innervation, was provided by immunohistochemical staining. This method demonstrated that MDMA reduced the number of serotonin antibody positive nerve fibres, and that it was the fine fibre type axons ascending from the dorsal raphe nucleus (an area of serotonin neurons in the brain stem) that were specifically vulnerable to the action of MDMA.[21]

Morphological observations

Evidence of neuronal damage was revealed by the application of silver staining techniques, which showed degenerating axons and nerve terminals in the rat (lowest dose single oral 40 mg/kg).[22] In the rhesus monkey injected subcutaneously with 5 mg/kg MDMA (twice daily for four days), abnormal inclusions within the cell bodies of dorsal raphe nucleus cells were found, which were not seen in the cell bodies of the median raphe nucleus or in non-serotonergic nuclei such as the substantia nigra or the locus ceruleus.[23] The authors interpreted these inclusions as cytopathological changes. The nature and the meaning of these inclusions, however, remain unclear. Remaining fine fibre serotonergic axons visualized with immunostaining were often swollen and fragmented, providing further evidence of axonal degeneration (rat: eight doses of 20 mg/kg; monkey: eight doses of 5 mg/kg).[24]

Axon regeneration

Loss of axons while the cell body stays intact leaves the possibility of axon regeneration. That this indeed happens has been shown in both the rat[25] and the squirrel monkey.[26] The recovery is region and time dependent. In the rat (exposed to repeated doses of 20 mg/kg) recovery of serotonin neuronal markers progresses in a rostral-caudal way (from the front to the back of the brain), with only partial recovery after 52 weeks in the occipital, temporal, and part of the frontal-parietal neocortex.[27] In the monkey (exposed to repeated doses of 5 mg/kg) there is an initial but partial recovery of serotonin markers by 10 weeks, however after 18 months levels have dropped to the low of two weeks after treatment.[28] In the squirrel monkey the pattern of reinnervation is different from what it was before treatment: Regions closer to the brain stem, where the damaged axons originate, appear to be hyperinnervated with serotonergic fibres, whereas the more distant parts remain poorly innervated after 18 months. Furthermore, the extent of regional redistribution of serotonin neuronal markers differed between animals, both in rats and in squirrel monkeys.[29]

Functional and behavioural effects

Besides neurochemical and morphological approaches, investigation of the functionality of the serotonergic system may help to assess the functional implications of the neurochemical and morphological changes observed after exposure to MDMA. Gartside et al. (1996) exposed rats to a neurotoxic dose-regimen of MDMA (eight doses 20 mg/kg). Two weeks later they observed that the firing activity of the dorsal raphe neurons had not diminished, nor were the basal extracellular serotonin levels in both the hippocampus and the frontal cortex (brain areas innervated by axons originating from the dorsal raphe nucleus) reduced, although the extracellular 5-HIAA levels were reduced by 50%. Moreover, no change was observed in the amount of serotonin released in the hippocampus in response to electrical stimulation (5 Hz) of either the dorsal or median raphe nucleus, but a marked reduction in the amount of serotonin released was observed in the frontal cortex after electrical stimulation of the dorsal raphe nucleus. It has also been reported that basal extracellular serotonin levels in the rat striatum could be maintained until tissue levels of serotonin are depleted by more than 95%.[30]

More evidence that basal cortical extracellular serotonin levels can be maintained after a MDMA-induced lesion, but that the maximal release is reduced was provided by Series et al. (1994), who challenged the serotonin system chemically with the serotonin releasing agent fenfluramine. Complex brain functions in the rhesus monkey that are first affected acutely by MDMA are related to behavioural tasks involving time estimation, motivation to work for food (which is not surprising considering the known appetite suppressing response to MDMA) and learning.[31] It was shown that after chronic exposure of these monkeys to MDMA (daily for four months, doses escalating from 0.1 mg/kg to 20 mg/kg) baseline performance in the behavioural tests returned to the levels obtained before the exposure.

However, the acute decrease in performance observed when the monkeys were given MDMA again five, twelve and nineteen months after the end of the chronic exposure period, was increasingly less pronounced, which disclosed the existence of a residual tolerance. It was suggested that in effect, the serotonergic system may be able to compensate for the loss of a majority of its central innervation during non-stressful or normal conditions. However, when challenged, the remaining components of the serotonergic system no longer have the capability of responding to the same degree as the fully intact system would.[32] The reduction of maximal response has been demonstrated in the laboratory by electrical and chemical stimulation. Whether there are physiological conditions under which the serotonergic system is stressed to this extent is not known.

Dose, route, regimen, and other variables

Many variables, including dose, route of administration, and regimen, determine the extent to which toxic or neuromodulatory effects will be observed. Many studies show that the effects of MDMA are dose-related.[33] It has also become clear that repeated administration is more potent than single administration. Administering 10 mg/kg subcutaneously in the rat, Battaglia et al. (1988) showed that the reduction of serotonin neuronal markers was greatest when the number of doses was increased from two to eight (injections every twelve hours). Administering four times 10 mg/kg subcutaneously to the rat produced effects comparable to those seen after administering eight times 5 mg/kg.[34] This suggests that dose and frequency of administration are additive, at least when within the near linear middle part of the dose-response curve.

Scarce data on route dependency are available. In the squirrel monkey subcutaneous administration was, depending on the brain region examined, two to three times more effective than intragastric administration.[35] However, in the rhesus monkey intragastric administration was twice as potent compared to the subcutaneous route, as assessed by the maximal serotonin uptake capacity of hippocampal synaptosomes and serotonin concentrations in cortical and hippocampal brain regions.[36] Finnegan et al. (1988) compared intragastric with subcutaneous administration in the rat and found similar dose-related reductions in serotonin levels in the hippocampus two weeks after administration.

A number of variables may affect the toxicity of MDMA. Besides the already mentioned species differences and dose, route, and regimen dependency, differences in sensitivity have been observed between different strains within one species.[37] Gender differences have also been observed.[38] This is a common phenomenon in the rat, but rarely seen in larger animals.[39] The stage of development may also influence the long-term effects, as Broening et al. (1994, 1995) showed that newly born rats (ten days old) quickly replenished their cortical serotonin tissue levels and showed no reductions in serotonin uptake sites one week after an oral administration of MDMA (40 mg/kg), whereas young adult rats (ten weeks) did not recover the loss in serotonin levels and showed a progressive decline in serotonin uptake sites during the following week.

In both rats and mice it has been shown that increased body temperature facilitates the neurotoxic action of MDMA, and that neurotoxicity can be diminished by reducing the ambient temperature, by co-administering drugs that decrease the body temperature, or by restraining the animals.[40]

Up- and down-regulation of serotonin neuronal markers

If serotonergic neurons would stop producing serotonin, but otherwise would be intact, this could result in a lowering of serotonin and 5-HIAA levels, reduction of TPH activity and disappearance of serotonin antibody reactive staining of serotonergic nerve fibres. It has therefore been argued that reduction of these neuronal markers after exposure to MDMA does not necessarily mean that the axons and nerve terminals have degenerated, but that a long lasting pharmacological action of MDMA may account for the observed effects.[41] O'Callaghan and Miller (1993) observed in the Long-Evans rat no increase in GFAP at doses (10-30 mg/kg twice daily for seven days) where there was a marked decrease in serotonin levels.

Intraventricular injection of the well-known serotonergic neurotoxicant 5,7-dihydroxytryptamine produced similar reductions in tissue serotonin levels in the presence of an increase of GFAP, which shows that the GFAP marker can be used to demonstrate serotonergic neuronal damage. These findings contrast with those of Slikker et al. (1988). The latter showed that a single oral administration of 40 mg/kg MDMA in the Sprague-Dawley rat increased the number of silver stained nerve terminals by 90%, indicating nerve terminal degeneration. Also Jensen et al. (1993), using a cupric silver stain, observed increased silver staining in the neocortex of the rat after administration of 25 mg/kg MDMA twice daily for two days.

However, it should be noted that the affected neurons were not serotonergic. Commins et al. (1987), who also observed silver stained non-serotonergic neocortical neurones after the administration of MDMA, speculated that these neurons could be affected by 5,6-dihydroxytryptamine, a neurotoxicant produced by serotonergic afferents. These conflicting results suggest that the reduction in serotonin levels after administration of repeated doses of 10-30 mg/kg MDMA is largely caused by a lower concentration of serotonin in the remaining nerve terminals, while the extent of nerve terminal degeneration is too little to be detected by the GFAP marker.

An alternative explanation for the absence of an increase in GFAP after administration of 10-30 mg/kg MDMA twice daily for seven days could be that MDMA directly or indirectly affects the glial cells in such a way that the GFAP response is inhibited with these doses. It has been shown that serotonin inhibits the expression of GFAP in cultured astrocytes (Le Prince et al., 1990). Furthermore, MDMA-induced prolonged activity of glial glycogen phosphorylase may compromise the energy state of the astrocytes (Poblete and Azmitia, 1995). Nevertheless, when the dose was increased to 75 mg/kg (twice daily for two days) an increase in GFAP could be observed.[42]

Reduction of another serotonin marker, the density of serotonin uptake sites, also does not necessarily reflect a reduction of serotonin nerve terminals, as it has been shown that acute serotonin depletion by administration of the tryptophan hydroxylase inhibitor para-chlorophenylalanine down-regulates the messenger RNA (mRNA) template for the transporter protein shortly after the treatment.[43] However the density of the transporter protein was not reduced at early time-points, but was reduced 14 days after treatment,[44] while the level of mRNA for the transporter was increased seven days after treatment. These results show that changes in serotonin transporter mRNA are not temporally related to changes in serotonin transporter protein levels.[45] Chronic administration of the serotonin re-uptake inhibiting antidepressants imipramine and fluoxetine also reduced the expression of serotonin transporter mRNA in the rat brain.[46]

An experiment by Ali et al. (1993) showed that at an exposure level of 1.25 mg/kg (administered orally twice daily for four days), rhesus monkeys had an increased serotonin level in the caudate 30 days later. This result suggests that the first long-lasting effect of MDMA exposure above the NOAEL is an up-regulation of the serotonin system in some brain areas.

A related discussion affects the putative neurotoxicity of the psychostimulant methamphetamine. It had been reported that high doses of this substance caused long-lasting reductions in dopamine concentrations and other dopamine nerve terminal markers in the striatum of non-human primates.[47] Postmortem examination of 12 chronic human methamphetamine users revealed that three dopamine nerve terminal markers (dopamine, tyrosine hydroxylase, and the dopamine transporter protein) were reduced. However, two other markers (DOPA decarboxylase and the vesicular transporter protein) were not reduced.[48]

Since the latter two markers are also reduced in Parkinson's disease, the authors concluded that at the doses taken by the subjects no permanent loss of striatal dopamine nerve terminals occurred. However, in Parkinson's disease the dopaminergic neurons are destroyed, whereas the alleged neurotoxicity of methamphetamine involves only the nerve terminals of the dopaminergic neurons. Unfortunately, only concentrations of these markers were measured and no immunohistochemistry was applied. This leaves open the possibility that the unchanged markers were located at a higher concentration in fewer nerve terminals.

Considering the morphological evidence cited in previous paragraphs, the view that the loss of neuronal markers after repeated 20 mg/kg doses in the rat or repeated 5 mg/kg doses in the squirrel monkey is solely caused by a pharmacological action of MDMA becomes difficult to interpret. At lower doses it may be possible that regulatory mechanisms influence the levels of serotonin neuronal markers observed, or that both degenerative and regulatory processes result in a reduction of serotonin neuronal markers.

The fenfluramine issue

Dexfenfluramine is a substituted amphetamine used as an appetite suppressant. Although it, like MDMA, is a serotonin releasing agent, its psychoactive effect is different. A number of studies in animals, both rats and primates, have shown that fenfluramine administration, like MDMA, produces acute and long-lasting reductions in serotonin neuronal markers,[49] decreases serotonin neuronal function[50] and affects the regulation of the serotonin transporter.[51]

However, MDMA and fenfluramine seem to affect the dopaminergic system in different ways. MDMA depleted striatal dopamine and increased GFAP in the mouse, whereas fenfluramine had no effect.[52] Moreover, chlormethiazole, a GABA agonist that reduces dopaminergic function, reduces MDMA-induced serotonergic toxicity in rats, whereas fenfluramine-induced neurotoxicity was not affected by chlormethiazole co-administration.[53] Therefore, the precise mechanisms by which MDMA and fenfluramine reduce the serotonin neuronal markers may be different, although functional consequences may be the same.

The decision of the FDA to approve the use of dexfenfluramine as an anorectic drug is often mentioned in the discussion of the neurotoxicity of MDMA, since indications of neurotoxicity are very similar. However, it should be noted that doses of dexfenfluramine taken by humans (approximately 0.3 mg/kg) are much lower than those used in the animal experiments and are lower than the doses of MDMA that are taken by humans, whereas the neurotoxic potential of both substances are very similar, dexfenfluramine being slightly more potent with respect to the serotonin neuronal markers. Still, when extrapolating the animal data to the human, the dose range of dexfenfluramine at which reduced, but reversible, brain serotonin concentrations can be expected in the human is close to or overlaps the dose range taken by humans. However, the doses at which neuronal damage may be expected that can be detected by experimental techniques independent of serotonin content, or where irreversible reductions of serotonin neuronal markers are to be expected are higher than the doses taken by humans.

Effects of MDMA on the serotonergic system in humans

M any experiments are done in animals which may be impossible to do in humans. Therefore indirect approaches must be made to assess the effects of MDMA on the serotonergic system in humans. However, such indirect ways of assessing the integrity and function of the serotonin system in humans are often difficult to interpret. Furthermore, due to the complexity of neural systems, knowledge of all elements, how they work and how they interact is incomplete. This too makes it difficult to understand what the meaning is of a change in a parameter if such changes are observed. This must be born in mind when looking at the effects of MDMA on the serotonin system in humans.

In a small scale study by Peroutka et al. (1987) cerobrospinal fluid (CSF) 5-HIAA levels of five MDMA users were compared to literature controls. In this study no differences were observed. In a larger and internally controlled study, levels of 5-HIAA in CSF of 30 MDMA users was measured and appeared to be reduced by 32% as compared to levels in 30 controls.[54] In a previous study[55] squirrel monkeys were administered 5 mg/kg MDMA subcutaneously twice daily for four days. In this study the monkeys showed, two weeks later, 73-94% depletions of serotonin and 5-HIAA in brain, 42-45% depletions of serotonin and 5-HIAA in spinal cord and 60% reductions in CSF 5-HIAA. McCann et al. (1994a) therefore concluded that the observed reduction in CSF 5-HIAA in human MDMA users may have reflected a partial depletion of the subjects brain serotonin levels, and therefore could be interpreted as a sign of MDMA-induced neurotoxicity.

A common problem with retrospective studies of this kind is that they cannot establish a causal relationship, as the difference in CSF-5-HIAA levels may have been pre-existing. For example, differences in personality related to serotonin levels and pre-disposing to MDMA use could be a confounding factor that cannot be excluded. To see if the implicated reduction in brain serotonin levels caused any change in functionality of the serotonin system in the same subjects, they were submitted to a tryptophan challenge. This is a test in which tryptophan is given intravenously and prolactin levels in blood are measured. Tryptophan, which is a serotonin precursor, will increase serotonin release, which then elicits an increase in prolactin levels (Charney et al., 1982). If serotonin system functionality is reduced this increase in prolactin is expected to be smaller.

However, in the study of McCann et al. (1994a) MDMA users showed an increase in blood prolactin levels similar to those in control subjects. Previously, Price et al. (1989) had found a blunted response to the tryptophan challenge on prolactin release in nine MDMA users, that were pre-selected from the McCann study (1994a) for their low CSF 5-HIAA level, as compared to nine healthy controls. However, this decrease was statistically not significant.

If the lower average CSF 5-HIAA level in MDMA users observed by McCann et al. (1994a) was not pre-existing, then it indicates that a change in the serotonin system had occurred, but the nature of this change is unclear. It could be a reflection of neurotoxicity, but regulatory events leading to different metabolism and disposition of serotonin and its metabolite 5-HIAA may just as well have been the cause. The lack of a change in the tryptophan challenge suggests several possibilities: 1) that the serotonin system, at least as far as this neuroendocrine response is concerned, is still intact, 2) the system has only deteriorated to a degree where there is no loss in neuroendocrine functionality, or 3) that the prolactin release system itself has become sensitized and is maintaining release at lower than normal serotonin levels.

In the study by McCann et al. (1994a) personality assessments were made as well. It was found that MDMA users had greater harm avoidance behaviour, showed less hostility and were less impulsive than controls. No significant changes in pain sensitivity, pain endurance and pain tolerance between MDMA users and controls were observed. In another study on sleep performance it was found that MDMA users had less stage 2 sleep compared to controls.[56] In a study of nine individuals Krystal et al. (1992) did not find any indication of depressive mood or affective disorder, however MDMA users scored slightly lower in memory tests in the absence of any clinical signs of cognitive impairment. However, the subjects were compared with literature controls, not matched controls. Furthermore, 7 grams of tryptophan was administered minimally three hours before the testing. Although neuroendocrine response was observed to be returned to baseline, a residual effect on neuropsychological performance cannot be excluded.

The role of the serotonin system in human behaviour is complex and it has been implicated in the regulation of sleep, mood, anxiety, pain, aggression, memory and appetite.[57] The findings mentioned above therefore suggest that some change in the serotonin system may have occurred. However, these data cannot answer whether or not structural changes of the serotonin system have ensued from the MDMA exposure.

It is clear from the neurochemical, neuroendocrine and neuropsychological data discussed above that the evidence for MDMA-induced neurotoxicity in humans is far from conclusive. In ongoing studies at John's Hopkins University newly developed positron emission tomography (PET) techniques are employed to further investigate the effects of MDMA use in humans on the brain serotonin system.[58] This method is based on ligand binding to the serotonin uptake transporter.

However, even if reductions in ligand binding are found, it will be difficult to interpret such reductions, as they may be caused by either reduction in nerve terminals as a result of degeneration, or by down-regulation of the uptake transporter. In the end it will be necessary to do postmortem neuropathological examinations in order to produce more conclusive evidence. Such examinations should include immunostaining of brain sections, making use of antibodies to serotonin, different parts of the serotonin uptake carrier[59] and the vesicular monoamine transporter protein. Measuring the concentrations of these components alone may produce inconclusive evidence, as was the case with postmortem evaluation of chronic methamphetamine users.[60]

Protection against neurotoxicity and dangerous interactions with other drugs

It has been shown that selective serotonin re-uptake inhibitors (SSRIs) reduce the neurotoxicity of MDMA in animals,[61] SSRIs like fluoxetine (Prozac®) are used as antidepressants. As the uptake site facilitates the MDMA-induced release of serotonin,[62] and the serotonin release is thought to be important for the psychoactive response to MDMA, it may be anticipated that fluoxetine reduces this response to MDMA.

However, a report from McCann and Ricaurte (1993) describes the experience of four subjects that have experimented with the combination of MDMA and fluoxetine. The subjects claim that some side effects, notably nausea and vomiting increased with some of them, but also that fewer after effects like fatigue occurred. The entactogenic properties of MDMA remained, however doses of MDMA taken (totals 450, 450, 300 and 125 mg) were rather high.

In ongoing research by Katherine Bonson at the National Institute of Health in the US (personal communication) additional reports on the combination of fluoxetine (either acute or chronically) and MDMA have been collected. Although some subjects reported no change in response to MDMA after fluoxetine, other case reports suggest an increase as well as a decrease in response to MDMA following fluoxetine use. However, when sertraline, another SSRI, was taken chronically, it reduced the psychoactive responses to MDMA in seven of eight individuals.

It should also be emphasized that the combination of MDMA with an MAO inhibitor has been known to induce a hypertensive crisis and could lead to death. Thus, ayahuasca and other cocktails that contain MAO inhibitors (e.g. harmaline) should therefore also not be combined with MDMA. To report experiences with combinations of MDMA or other psychoactive drugs and prescription or other drugs, contact Dr. Bonson at kbonson@codon.nih.gov.

Gudelsky (1996) recently showed that large quantities of reducing agents (vitamin C, cysteine) had a protective effect with respect to the neurotoxicity of MDMA in rats. These experiments add to the accumulating evidence that at some point in the toxic mechanism of MDMA oxidative processes are involved. High concentrations of antioxidants may reduce the oxidative stress.

However, the concentrations that were applied in the experiment of Gudelsky (1996) were extremely high and a human would have to take about 15 grams of vitamin C applying the same weight-to-body weight ratio. It is questionable if such large quantities are still to be considered healthy. However, taking into account the increased clearance and other pharmacokinetic parameters that likewise change as a result of the lower body mass of the rat, it is conceivable that a quantity of 1-2 gram of vitamin C may afford some protection in humans. However, if such a protective effect can be generalized to the primate, should be investigated by primate studies. Also some more dose finding experiments should be done.

Because oxidative mechanisms may play a role in the neurotoxicity of MDMA, and perhaps also in the suspected liver toxicity, it may be wise to refrain from combining MDMA with drugs that also result in oxidative stress, for example, the widely used analgesic acetaminophen (Paracetamol).

From animal experiments it has become clear that high body temperature enhances the neurotoxicity of MDMA (see above). Therefore control of body temperature is not only of importance in preventing acute severe toxicity of MDMA, but in minimizing the risk of neurotoxicity as well. Besides reducing the ambient temperature, facilitating cooling of the body by light clothing, and reducing physical activity, the availability of drinking water is of importance.[63]

However, to avoid water intoxication one should not drink water alone, but should also maintain electrolyte and carbohydrate intake.

At what level does MDMA become toxic in humans?

An exact level of exposure below which there is no toxicity and above which all individuals will react to exposure with a toxic response cannot be determined. In general, toxicity of a chemical substance is observed as a gradual increase of the severity of the response with an increasing dose. Furthermore people differ amongst each other. Therefore more susceptible individuals will show signs of toxicity at lower doses than less susceptible individuals. Nevertheless, when sufficient data are available, an average response of humans can be predicted by extrapolating the average response as observed in experimental animals.

Concerning the acute toxicity, no level of exposure can be given at which severe effects occur. In animal experiments lethality is only observed after injection with very high doses of MDMA. However, severe reactions with a fatal outcome in humans have occurred after taking a normal dose. The event of severe acute reactions in humans therefore appears not to be dose-related and hence is unpredictable. A risk assessment concerning the acute toxicity should accordingly be based on epidemiologic data. Unfortunately, precise figures on the number of human MDMA consumers, the frequency of use, and the amounts used at each occasion are lacking. Although the number of fatal reactions is fairly accurately known, the number of severe reactions without a fatal outcome are unknown. Therefore risk estimates concerning acute severe reactions to MDMA are hypothetical. Nevertheless, an attempt will be made elsewhere in this book.

The neurotoxicity of MDMA in humans has not been established, therefore, based on human data, a level of exposure at which MDMA becomes neurotoxic cannot be determined. However, the phenomenon of neurotoxicity has been investigated extensively in animals, and appears to be dose-related. This makes it possible to estimate at which levels of exposure adverse effects may occur in humans.

To make a prediction of the effects that might occur in humans, the animal data have to be modified by applying extrapolation factors to the dose at which a specific effect occurred in the animal. Animal-to-human extrapolation factors are, based on pharmocokinetic considerations, related to body weight.[64] Here the equation (body weight human) $^{0.4}$ / (body weight animal) $^{0.4}$ = extrapolation factor, will be used. This gives for the rat an extrapolation factor of 10, for the squirrel monkey an extrapolation factor of 6, and for the rhesus monkey an extrapolation factor of 2. It should be noted that this is a rough approximation and that physiologically based pharmocokinetic models may provide more precise extrapolation factors.

Nevertheless, the observations that hyperthermia in the rat is dose-related increased in the rat with doses from 5 to 20 mg/kg[65] and that in humans such an effect occurs at doses approximately 10 times lower, indicate that a rat-to-human extrapolation factor of 10 is a good approximation. Furthermore, differences in toxicity depend on the route of administration. The extrapolation factors for the route of administration can be based on the data mentioned in a previous section.

To start at the lower end, the first level of exposure that is of interest, is the highest level of exposure at which no adverse effects are observed. This is known as the No Observed Adverse Effect Level (NOAEL). Unfortunately, most of the studies cited above are designed by researchers interested in the toxic effects per se, and therefore only doses at which an effect can be expected have been administered. Consequently most of these studies do not provide a NOAEL. However, a few studies did find a NOAEL.

In one study, squirrel monkeys were given 2.5 mg/kg MDMA twice monthly for four months by the intragastric route.[66] No changes in serotonin or 5-HIAA levels were observed in eight brain regions that were examined. In rats, brain serotonin levels and serotonin uptake site densities were not reduced after a single oral administration of 10 mg/kg[67] or single subcutaneous administration of 5 or 10 mg/kg.[68] However, Schmidt (1986) and Stone et al. (1987) found reduced brain serotonin levels in the rat one or two weeks after a single subcutaneous injection of 10 mg/kg MDMA in the rat. Applying the extrapolation factors to the squirrel monkey and rat data gives 0.4 and 1.0 mg/kg, respectively, as the predicted NOAEL in humans for the oral route.

As noted previously, the first long-lasting effects of MDMA exposure above the NOAEL are an up-regulation of the serotonin system in some brain areas. An experiment by Ali et al. (1993) showed that at an exposure level of 1.25 mg/kg (administered orally twice daily for four days), rhesus monkeys had an increased serotonin level in the caudate 30 days later. Broening et al. (1994) did not find any change in caudate, cortical or hippocampal serotonin levels in the rat when 10 mg/kg MDMA was given orally. A single oral dose of 5 mg/kg administered to the squirrel monkey only reduced the serotonin levels of the thalamus and the hypothalamus two weeks later.[69] From these data it may be predicted that at exposure levels around 1 mg/kg in humans some protracted neuromodulatory effects may occur that may include up-regulation of components of the serotonin system.

When the dose is increased, reduced levels of brain serotonin and 5-HIAA, and reduced densities of serotonin uptake sites are observed. When administering 2.5 mg/kg twice daily for four days by the intragastric route in the rhesus monkey, 5-HIAA levels in the cortex were increased, but the serotonin level in the hippocampus was decreased 30 days later.[70] Administering 20 mg/kg to the rat decreases the density of serotonin uptake sites.[71] Rat cortical, hippocampal and caudate serotonin levels were also decreased when 20 mg/kg MDMA was administered by the intragastric route to the rat.[72] Thus, when extrapolating these data, it seems that at a dose of 2 mg/kg, neuromodulatory events may occur in humans, and that more elements of the serotonin system may respond by down-regulation.

When administering 40 mg/kg orally to the rat, Slikker et al. (1988) observed an increase of 90% of silver stained nerve terminals. However, O'Callaghan and Miller (1993), when administering MDMA to the rat in a similar dose range, did not find an increase in GFAP, indicating that the extent of the nerve terminal degeneration with these doses is limited. When these data are extrapolated to the human, this would suggest that with a dose of 4 mg/kg nerve terminal degeneration may occur. In experiments in which axonal degeneration could be observed by histology, animals were given multiple doses of MDMA.[73]

These data, when extrapolated, suggest that at total doses of 10 mg/kg or above, taken within a few days, axonal degeneration could be expected in humans.

Table 1: animal-based estimates of dose-effect relationships of MDMA in humans

DOSE[a] (mg/kg)	EFFECT	NEUROTOXICITY
0 – 0.4	No observable Effect.	No.
1.0	Some changes of serotonin neuronal markers, amongst which increases of serotonin.	No, probably neuromodulatiry effects, amongst which up-regulation of serotonin system components
2.0	More long term changes in serotonin neuronal markers, predominantly decreases.	Disputed. Either neuromodulatory effects, predominantly down-regulation of serotonin system components, or, as some claim, the observed reductions reflect nerve terminal degeneration.
4.0	Increased silver staining.	Yes, nerve terminal degeneration.[b]
10.0	Disappearance of serotonergic fibres and swollen and fragmented axons.	Yes, axonal degeneration.

a. Total dose taken during one day or night.
b. It is disputed whether the affected nerve terminals are serotonergic or non-serotonergic.

Comment by Dr O'Callaghan on axonal degeneration at 10 mg/kg:

This is not evidence of terminal or axonal degeneration. It is simply a loss of serotonin staining (and is accompanied by long-term, but reversible, decreases in serotonin levels). This is the example of the water in the pipe analogy I use. Serotonin is the water. If you drain the pipe you won't see staining, but that doesn't mean the pipe is not still there and functioning. I still maintain (and so would Ricaurte and Molliver) that the d-fen story is relevant to the MDMA story. I argue that this supports the lack of evidence of neurotoxicity, although Ricaurte and Molliver will say they all produce damage.

Comment on the above comment by Leon van Aerts:

Besides this point of lack of serotonin antibody staining observed by Wilson et al. (1989),

Ricaurte et al. (1988b) and O'Hearn et al. (1988), these researchers found that axons were swollen and fragmented. These are clear-cut signs of neurodegenerative processes. I therefore do not see how such signs cannot be regarded as signs of axonal degeneration. Furthermore, the reversibility of the effects is only partial after such high doses, as was observed by Fisher et al. (1995), Lew et al. (1996), Sabol et al. (1996) and Ricaurte et al. (1992).

The estimates that are produced by these extrapolations are summarized in Table 1. However, it should be noted that, for several reasons, the levels of exposure associated with certain events are only rough estimates. One reason is that for the interspecies extrapolation, standard extrapolation factors related to body weight have been used. However, when new data on the pharmacokinetics of MDMA in animal and human emerge, more precise extrapolation factors can be derived, so that the exposure levels associated with certain events may be adjusted up or downward.

Furthermore, average responses in animals were extrapolated to the human. However, the sensitivity of both animals and humans varies between individuals. Therefore, susceptible individuals may exhibit nerve terminal degeneration at lower levels of exposure than the average. Finally, the more severe effects were observed in animals that were exposed to repeated high doses of MDMA. No attempt was made to investigate these effects at lower doses. It is reasonable to expect that at somewhat lower doses these effects also would have occurred, albeit to a lesser extent.

Also, the occurrence of reduced serotonin and 5-HIAA levels, as well as reduced densities of serotonin uptake sites observed long after the administration of MDMA, are interpreted by some investigators as signs of nerve terminal degeneration, and therefore as signs of neurotoxicity, whereas others claim that these effects are only of a modulatory nature.

In any case, when looking at an undisputed marker of neural damage – increased silver staining – it seems reasonable to suppose that at a total dose of 4 mg/kg MDMA neurotoxicity in the form of nerve terminal degeneration may occur in humans. This is a dose that is frequently consumed by the more heavy users during a day or night.

It may be argued that if serotonergic damage has occurred in more heavy users it is strange that so little clinical evidence has emerged. A possible explanation for this could be the apparent redundancy of the serotonergic system. Even when a large proportion of the serotonergic nerve terminals has been destroyed basal functionality may be preserved. Kirby et al. (1995) showed that more than 95% of tissue serotonin levels had to be depleted before extracellular levels were reduced. How much the serotonergic system in humans can be depleted before a loss of function is observed, or under which circumstances a reduced capacity would become apparent, is unknown.

Until now neural damage as a result of MDMA use has not been shown in humans. Also is it unclear what the functional consequences would be when serotonergic brain damage would occur in humans. Nevertheless the animal data do give reason for concern. Therefore, for the time being, it may be advisable to refrain from the use of high doses, boosters or bingeing of Ecstasy.

© **L.A.G.J.M. van Aerts. Correspondence by E-mail: leonva@telebyte.nl**
I would like to thank Dr. Nicholas V. Cozzi for critically reviewing the manuscript. Also many thanks to Chris and Karen for correcting the text and Socorro for being patient.

References

1. Frith et al., 1987.
2. Henry et al., 1992; Milroy et al., 1996.
3. Hayner and McKinney, 1986.
4. Dowling et al, 1987; Suarez and Reimersma, 1985.
5. Milroy et al., 1996; Fidler et al. 1996; Henry et al., 1992.
6. De Man, 1994.
7. Harries and De Silva, 1992; Manchanda and Connolly, 1993; Rothwell and Grant, 1993; Hughes et al., 1993.
8. Levine et al., 1993; Rezvani et al., 1996).
9. Marsh et al., 1994.
10. Greer and Tolbert, 1991; Siegel, 1986.
11. Siegel, 1986.
12. White et al., 1996.
13. Logan et al, 1988; Miller and O'Callaghan, 1995.
14. Hekmatpanah and Peroutka, 1990; Gudelsky and Nash, 1996; Rudnick and Wall, 1992.
15. Schmidt, 1986; Stone et al., 1987.
16. Commins et al., 1987; Fisher et al., 1995; Insel et al., 1989; Sabol et al., 1996; Ricaurte et al., 1988a, 1992; Stone et al., 1986, 1987.
17. Stone et al., 1987.
18. Stone et al., 1989.
19. Commins et al., 1987; Sabol et al., 1996; Schmidt, 1986.
20. Battaglia et al., 1987, 1988; Fisher et al., 1995; Insel et al., 1989; Lew et al., 1996; Ricaurte et al., 1992.
21. Fisher et al., 1995; O'Hearn et al., 1988; Wilson et al., 1989.
22. Commins et al., 1987; Slikker et al., 1988.
23. Ricaurte et al., 1988b.
24. O'Hearn et al., 1988; Ricaurte et al., 1988b; Wilson et al., 1989.
25. Battaglia et al., 1988; Lew et al., 1996; Scanzello et al., 1993; Sabol et al., 1996.
26. Fisher et al., 1995; Ricaurte et al., 1992.
27. Lew et al., 1996; Sabol et al., 1996.

28. Ricaurte et al., 1992.
29. Fisher et al., 1995.
30. Kirby et al., 1995.
31. Frederick et al., 1994, 1995.
32. Frederick et al., 1995; Slikker et al., 1995.
33. Ali et al., 1993; Battaglia et al., 1988.
34. Battaglia et al., 1988.
35. Ricaurte et al., 1988a.
36. Kleven et al., 1989.
37. Zheng and Laverty, 1993 [cf. Miller and O'Callaghan].
38. Colado et al., 1995; Fitzgerald et al., 1989.
39. Campbell, 1995.
40. Broening et al., 1995; Farfel and Seiden, 1995; Miller and O'Callaghan, 1995.
41. O'Callaghan and Miller, 1993.
42. O'Callaghan and Miller, 1993.
43. Yu et al., 1995; Linnet et al., 1995; Rattray et al., 1996.
44. Yu et al., 1995; Rattray et al., 1996.
45. Rattray et al., 1996.
46. Lesch et al., 1993.
47. cf. Wilson et al. 1996.
48. Wilson et al., 1996.
49. Appel et al., 1989; Colado et al., 1993; Kleven and Seiden, 1989; McCann et al., 1994b; Ricaurte et al., 1991; Scheffel et al., 1996.
50. Series et al., 1994)
51. Gobbi et al., 1996; Rattray et al., 1994, 1996; Semple-Rowland et al., 1996.
52. Miller and O'Callaghan, 1995.
53. Colado et al., 1993.
54. McCann et al., 1994a.
55. Ricaurte et al., 1988c.
56. Allen et al., 1993.
57. cf. Allen et al., 1993.
58. Szabo et al., 1995.

59. Zhou et al., 1996.
60. Wilson et al., 1996.
61. Battaglia et al., 1988; Schmidt, 1987.
62. Gudelsky and Nash, 1996; Hekmatpanah and Peroutka, 1990; Wichems et al., 1995.
63. Dafters, 1995.
64. Campbell, 1995.
65. Colado et al., 1995; Dafters, 1995.
66. G. Ricaurte, unpublished observations.

67. Broening et al., 1994.
68. Kate Chapman, personal communication.
69. Ricaurte et al., 1988a.
70. Ali et al., 1993.
71. Schmidt, 1986; Broening et al. 1995; Kate Chapman, personal communication.
72. Broening et al. 1994, 1995.
73. Commins et al, 1987; O'Hearn et al., 1988; Ricaurte et al., 1988b; Wilson et al., 1989.

Adverse Psychological Effects

By Dr. Karl Jansen

Ecstasy was initially perceived as a drug with few adverse effects, as amphetamine had been until the mid-1960's. As with amphetamine, however, widespread use resulted in reports of confusion, anxiety, panic attacks, depression, sleeping difficulties, depersonalisation, derealisation, hallucinations, flashbacks, paranoia, psychosis, tolerance and dependency syndromes, and subsequent addiction to sedatives. However, many of these reports are based on single case studies or short, uncontrolled series, in which no evidence is provided that the pill taken was in fact ecstasy, that other drug use was not significant and that urine samples were free of other drugs and their metabolites, that the condition would not have occurred by chance, that the person was not predisposed to the condition and other factors. Animal studies have shown that large quantities of ecstasy can result in persistently low serotonin levels. Attempts to relate these chemical changes to adverse effects ignore the role of psychological changes due to the emotional effects of ecstasy, which can upset the balance of the mind by releasing disturbing material from the unconscious. Although this effect can be used as an aid to psychotherapy, the same release may result in anxiety, depression, insomnia and nightmares. Psychological explanations must be considered along with chemical changes as many, although by no means all, of the adverse effects appear to follow just one or two doses rather than chronic dosing. Heavy weekend users tend to have midweek problems such as low mood and irritability and may develop a dependency syndrome. This chapter also contains the first comprehensive discussion of treatment options for ecstasy-related problems.

Introduction

Like other potent mind-altering drugs, the use of ecstasy has been associated with impaired mental health and impaired judgement. While under the influence of the drug, users may sometimes experience confusion, disorientation, anxiety, panic attacks, depression, insomnia, depersonalisation, derealisation, perceptual disorders and hallucinations, paranoia and psychotic phenomena. It is possible that some of these effects may continue for a period after cessation of the drug.[1]

The term 'ecstasy' has now widened its meaning to embrace a class of drugs which includes MDMA, MBDB, MDE, MDA, MDEA and 2CB, amongst others. These drugs differ from each other in their various effects and thus, unless otherwise stated, the term 'ecstasy' where used in this review refers to MDMA only. This review is intended for non-specialists and specific references are only given for controversial issues. This review is not a list of all known reports: additional reports may be found in the annotated bibliography.

There was little interest in ecstasy until the mid-1970s when the chemist Alexander Shulgin introduced ecstasy to those with an interest in drug-assisted psychotherapy. The psychotherapists considered the drug to be moderate in its effects, which were principally characterised by feelings of empathic understanding for others and a release of emotions. They generally reported that the drug had potential for overcoming 'blocks' in psychotherapy and enhancing insights, particularly insights concerning relationships.[2]

By the early 1980s, ecstasy had moved off the couch and out into the wider community. The 1990s has seen the widespread use of ecstasy as a recreational drug, resulting in increasing reports of an apparent association between ecstasy use and a diverse range of psychological symptoms and psychiatric disorders.[3,4] It was also reported that large doses of MDMA repeatedly injected into laboratory animals lowered the levels of a chemical messenger in the brain called serotonin, and to a lesser extent dopamine, and damaged the nerve terminals from which serotonin was released.[5,6,7] These effects were dose related and recovery was incomplete.[6] There is some limited evidence of serotonin deficits in human ecstasy users. The relevance of these studies to humans taking one or two ecstasy tablets occasionally has been questioned [8,9], but the animal studies do suggest that persons taking large quantities of ecstasy for several days may be at some risk of persistently low serotonin. As low serotonin has been linked to depression and anxiety, it has been suggested that heavy users of ecstasy may be at increased risk of developing psychological problems of this nature.

Many investigators consider animal studies to have relevance to human use: 'The loss of 5-HT (serotonin) axons in monkeys is greater than that in rats that were given a fourfold higher dose of MDMA and, therefore, MDMA is far more toxic in the primate than in the rat... in view of the extensive destruction of 5-HT terminals at doses that are approximately twice that commonly used for recreational purposes by humans, MDMA may have a relatively small margin of safety, and it would be prudent to consider this drug potentially hazardous for human use..'.[10] Molliver et al. (1989) remark on the similarity between serotonergic axons damaged by ecstasy and those seen in Alzheimer's disease, where the most consistent receptor change is often loss of presynaptic serotonergic receptors[11], although the greatest biochemical change is loss of acetylcholine.

In terms of explaining adverse reactions to ecstasy the focus has been to a very large extent upon possible brain chemical changes as described above. There has been a tendency to ignore the fact that ecstasy releases emotions and can have marked effects upon the psychodynamic balance of the mind. A core concept in psychodynamics is that anxiety provoking material 'unacceptable' to waking consciousness is repressed into the unconscious, from where it may make itself known via dreams and other methods. 'Defences' are erected against this material. Some psychotherapies may involve bringing such material to the surface so that it can be 'worked through' and discharged. In this context it is valuable to recall that ecstasy was used in psychotherapy to remove 'blocks' and defences.[12]

What happens if these defences against disturbing material in the psyche are removed in a non-psychotherapeutic context? There may be little possibility for working through the material or containing it. A possible consequence may be the range of symptoms associated with the neuroses: anxiety, depression, insomnia and nightmares for example, and these are of course precisely the symptoms most commonly associated with ecstasy use. The observation that duration and dosage are not currently linked to the probability of developing such symptoms (e.g. Wodarz and Boning, 1993) tends to support an examination of psychological causes, and suggests that the current focus upon neurotransmitter changes may be misguided, particularly in view of the remarkable lack of change in the behaviour of animals following chronic, high dose injection of ecstasy. Many of the communications received from persons who have had adverse psychiatric sequelae in association with the use of ecstasy describe only taking a few doses. Nevertheless, it is still possible that large and rigorous studies will eventually demonstrate a link between at least some adverse effects and dosage/duration of ecstasy use.

The relevance of the amphetamine literature

The empathogenic effects of ecstasy have led to the suggestion that it is a member of a new class of psychoactive compounds, which have been labelled 'entactogens' or 'empathogens'.[12,13] While formulation of a new class of compounds may be warranted the psychological effects, MDMA is nevertheless a partial derivative of amphetamine and has many physical effects in common with the amphetamine group (see later), which leads to the suggestion that susceptible persons may be at risk of the same adverse effects as have been reported for amphetamine, in both a physical and a psychiatric sense. [14] This is likely as both types of drug have similar effects on dopamine, and these effects are believed to play a role in the development of psychosis for example. [15,16,17,18,19]

While the possible range may be similar, clearly the probabilities will be different. In other words, it would not be correct to say that ecstasy is as likely to cause certain adverse effects as amphetamine, and vice versa.

This chapter will consider the pros and cons of some of the arguments set out in this introduction. Much of the information we have about adverse reactions to MDMA is in the form of single case studies and short, uncontrolled series. There are several key issues to bear in mind when considering publications of this nature:

Was the drug taken actually MDMA?

A uthors who allege that a person took MDMA should attempt to present toxicological proof to support this claim (tests of the tablets taken or at least a urine test) as many pills sold as 'ecstasy' have been shown to contain other drugs instead, sometimes in dangerous combinations. Other drugs commonly found instead of MDMA are MDEA, MDA, MBDB, MDE, 2CB, Ketamine, amphetamine, LSD, pseudoephedrine and pharmaceutical agents. [20] Some pills contain no psychoactive substances at all. MDEA (MDE) has a shorter duration of action (2 hours) and is more amphetamine-like, having less emotional effects. MBDB is quite similar to MDMA but is described by some as less intense with a greater 'cognitive' component as distinct from 'empathogenic/emotional', MDA is far more psychedelic (LSD-like) and is considered to be more toxic. 2CB is more psychedelic than MDMA but less so than MDA. [21] Amphetamine is a very common additive, and the links between amphetamine use and paranoid psychosis, for example, are well established. [22] MDEA is also very common in the UK [20], is closer to amphetamine in its effects than MDMA, and may possibly show a more similar profile to amphetamine in terms of adverse effects. Ketamine has been given to experimental subjects to produce a 'model schizophrenia' and can be profoundly hallucinogenic. [23]

It is thus clear that some of the adverse effects which have been attributed to ecstasy may be due to 'dodgy E' rather than pure MDMA.

The role of poly drug use

T he 'pure' ecstasy user is a very rare entity. The overwhelming majority of persons who take ecstasy also use other drugs, and some of these drugs are clearly identified with a risk of mental health consequences. This point is rarely emphasised in the case reports attributing a psychiatric disorder to ecstasy use, where other drugs use is often dismissed in a few lines. The concurrent use of large amounts of cannabis, LSD, alcohol and/or amphetamine, for example, is often pushed into the background. A very large number of habitual, weekend ecstasy users are also daily or near daily users of cannabis, which makes the 'come down' and mood cycle less apparent. This is an important factor to bear in mind when conducting research in this area. The use of cannabis has been linked to relapse in schizophrenia.[24,25,26,27] There has been increasing attention given to ketamine in the media recently,[28,29] and it will be of interest to observe whether eventually case reports will appear associating mental illness with ketamine use, while ecstasy is relegated to the 'other drugs taken' list, warranting no further discussion. For example, there is a case report of persisting depersonalisation syndrome after ingesting ecstasy only once.[30] It was subsequently pointed out that this patient had a history of daily alcohol and cannabis use, and serious doubt was cast upon the role of ecstasy in the case.[31]

The importance of poly drug use has been confirmed by a study of drugs taken at raves.[32] The OPCS Psychiatric Morbidity Survey [33] surveyed 10,500 UK households. 504 people used one of the listed illicit drugs in the preceding year, and had used that drug more than five times in total. 10% had used ecstasy and polydrug use was the norm amongst persons who preferentially chose ecstasy. The preferred other drugs were cannabis, hallucinogens, amphetamines and hypnotics. Alcohol was not included in the study. McMiller and Plant (1996) have recently reported on a major study of drug taking in 15 and 16 year old school children, pupils born in 1979, from 70 schools across the United Kingdom. The percentage reporting use of 'Ecstasy (MDMA)' was 7.3% (293 persons out of 3999) of girls and 9.2% of boys (326/3555), less than the LSD figures which were about 12% and 17% in girls and boys respectively. This comparison with the LSD figures is of interest when we consider the similarities between the media generated 'LSD hysteria' of the 1960s and the media generated 'ecstasy hysteria' of the 1990s. Although LSD is a more popular drug now than ever, it appears to no longer be seen as a major threat to the mental health of the nation by the media, and has largely disappeared from the pages of psychiatric journals and tabloid newspapers. This suggests that the way in which the media deal with drug issues sometimes has little rational basis. This seems particularly likely when we ponder the fact that over one million people in the UK have died of smoking related illness in the last 10 years, at least 400,000 have died of alcohol related illness, at least 2,500 from heroin and related opiates, and at least 1200 from sniffing solvents, while the number of people who have died in association with taking the 'killer drug' ecstasy numbers a modest 60.[34]

The role of set and setting

This term 'set' refers to the personality, past experiences (including previous drug experiences) mood, motivations, attitudes and expectations of the subject while 'setting' refers to conditions of use, including the physical environment and the 'set' of other people present. A pleasant set and setting are more likely to have a positive outcome, while an unpleasant set and setting are more likely to have a negative outcome. However, ecstasy effects are less susceptible to the influence of set and setting than psychedelic drugs such as LSD. Thus ecstasy is a more predictable drug.

Although ecstasy appears to energise the taker in a nightclub setting where fast music is played, in this context it is also likely that the drug consumed is not actually a full dose of pure MDMA, but rather a combination in which amphetamine features prominently, or where amphetamine has been taken deliberately together with MDMA. It is also possible that the drug is actually MDEA. Persons who have taken a substantial dose of pure MDMA in these settings may often be seen either standing on the sidelines or sitting in the quieter areas, possibly engaged in emotional conversations with others. Enthusiastic dancers sometimes avoid the emotional effects of MDMA by only taking small, stimulant doses at regular intervals – for example, half a tablet periodically through the night. Careful examination of what actually takes place at raves, and who is taking what, generally indicates that pure MDMA in the 120mg dose range is quite consistent in its effects, producing similar results in the gardens of California as it does at the 25,000 person Tribal Gathering rave in the UK. Nevertheless, expectations do play an important part in all drug effects, and there are many who wish to dance because they have been conditioned to associate this with ecstasy, irrespective of the actual content of the pill they have swallowed, just as many will declare their love to the others present for the same reason.

These issues are important because a large percentage of the 'bad reactions' to LSD, psilocybin and mescaline may be attributed to a 'bad' set and setting,[35,36] but this is less likely to be true for ecstasy. However, the role of expectations is significant, as discussed above. Expectations can also have a negative outcome. For example, from a statistical perspective, serious physical effects from ecstasy are relatively rare. Nevertheless, a perception on the part of the consumer that they are experiencing such effects has increased considerably in the wake of fear spread by the media, as a result of which there has been an increase in the number of persons presenting with the false belief that they are in physical extremis. The real diagnosis is more likely to be panic which can be treated with a quiet room, the passage of time, reassurance and possibly lorazepam (a fast acting relative of Valium). Many of these 'cases' recover while waiting to see the doctor.

What are the risks in numerical terms?

At the present time, the actual risk of developing a serious psychiatric condition following use of ecstasy is unknown. The degree of publicity which accompanies a possibility such as depression obviously has no scientific relevance in determining the actual risk, although it may lead to a tremendous distortion in the minds of the public as to what that risk may be, as has now been seen with respect to the risk of death. The relative risk of any particular outcome should be determined by dividing the total number of outcomes of that type by the total number of doses consumed (risk exposures). A guide to estimating the total number of doses consumed between 1985 and the present may be found elsewhere in this book. Many case reports make no attempt whatsoever to provide a statistical perspective, but it is necessary to tolerate this deficiency as such estimates are very difficult to provide. We do not know how many cases of ecstasy associated psychiatric disturbance are treated by the medical community but never reported, and even more inaccessible are those which occur but are never treated at all.

Another method of gaining perspective on the general importance of ecstasy-induced mental disorder is to spend several weekends in the casualty (emergency room) departments of a large inner city hospital, and also the emergency clinic of a psychiatric hospital. This pragmatic investigation will produce a clear conclusion: the drug which is principally associated with suicidal depression, homicide, cognitive deficits and psychosis in this society is alcohol, by an enormous margin. It is likely to be several weeks before a single case associated with consumption of toxicologically proven ecstasy is seen, and even longer before a case is seen which does not involve other drugs and a personal or family history of pre-existing psychiatric disorder.

Nevertheless, one study of self-reported immediate and long-term effects (months or years after ingestion) in 500 people resulted in high levels of reported adverse psychological effects [37]: immediate effects: paranoia, 20%; anxiety 16%, depression 12% long-term/recurring effects: depersonalisation (defined later) 54%; insomnia 38%; depression 38%; flashbacks 27%. Two double-blind, placebo controlled assessments of MDEA users (n=14) with non-using controls reported one case of toxic psychosis, a severe dysphoric reaction and one anxiety disorder.[38] It must be noted this study involved MDEA, and not MDMA.

Other confounding variables: The issue of causality

Many of the published reports draw cause and effect conclusions which are not justified by the data presented, i.e. they conclude that ecstasy consumption caused the symptoms rather than being associated with the symptoms. In general, it is useful to consider whether the criteria suggested by Strassman (1984) and Poole and Brabbins (1996) are met for research of this nature before concluding that ecstasy did in fact cause the mental disorders described. Strassman's review does not include ecstasy, but is focused on LSD. Nevertheless, the core principles are the same: 'there is a tendency for people with poorer premorbid adjustment, a history of psychiatric illness and/or treatment, a greater number of exposures to psychedelic drugs, drug-taking in an unsupervised setting, a history of poly drug abuse, and self-therapeutic and/or peer-pressure-submission motive for drug use, to suffer these complications'.[36]

We have already considered the use of other drugs in addition to ecstasy, that the pill swallowed was not ecstasy at all, and variations in the set and setting of use as possible confounding variables, i.e. possible explanations for an association. Other such variables are: the probability of a chance association. 'It is important to recognise that, among the large group of drug users within the general population, a proportion will become mentally ill regardless of any supposed psychotomimetic properties of drugs'.[39] Depression and anxiety are common conditions in the general population. It is a statistical certainty that a substantial percentage of persons who take ecstasy will develop depression regardless of whether they took ecstasy or not. The one year incidence of major depression in the general population is 80-200 per 100,000 for men and 240-600 per 100,000 for women.[40] It is interesting to note a comment by Gelder et al.: 'it is not certain why consistently higher figures are reported for women: possible reasons are (a) women's greater readiness to report symptoms and (b) the abuse of alcohol by some depressed men which may lead to a diagnosis of alcoholism rather than depressive disorder.' Thus drug use influences the determination of incidence levels of psychiatric conditions, and vice versa. This statement also suggests how difficult it can be to accurately estimate the incidence of depression itself in a population.

Anxiety, panic attacks and all of the other symptoms associated with ecstasy use also have an incidence, sometimes substantial, in the non-ecstasy using population.

o   Poor pre-morbid adjustment: a poor adjustment to circumstances and life in general is associated with an increased likelihood of drug use, and a worse prognosis when major mental illness develops. Drug use may be a symptom of impending or actual mental illness as a result of 'self-medication' of distress, or impaired judgement.

o   Preexisting mental illness and a family history of mental illness: such a history is common in persons who develop psychiatric illness in apparent association with drug use.

o   Preexisting neurochemical, genetic and personality differences: Each year brings new reports linking genes to receptor subtypes, and subsequently to behavioural patterns. It is possible that persons who take large quantities of psychostimulants may have preexisting, genetically determined 'under-functioning' of serotonergic and/ or dopaminergic systems, and this 'under-functioning' increases the likelihood of depression and anxiety, and creates an inner drive towards becoming over-involved with drugs which provide temporary relief from the problem. Thus retrospective studies of serotonergic parameters in high dose, chronic ecstasy users, in comparison with non-using controls, may be confounded by preexisting differences between the two groups. The present state of knowledge is that duration and dosage of ecstasy use do not appear to predict the probability of developing most psychological difficulties.[30] This may change with further research. However, if true then this would tend to argue against such difficulties being due to structural damage to serotonergic nerve terminals.

The adverse psychological effects of MDMA

A review of adverse reactions due to ecstasy has been presented by McCann et al. (1996). As noted in the introduction, current research evidence is sparse and retrospective, generally uncontrolled, generally lacks toxicological confirmation of the drugs taken, lacks data on course and outcome, rarely relates mental state to toxicological results, and depends heavily on single case studies but nevertheless frequently concludes cause and effect relationships from what may be chance associations, although it is also possible that the cause and effect relationship is true.

Psychotic phenomena

With respect to serious mental illness such as prolonged psychosis, there is currently a dearth of accurate statistics. Ecstasy may rarely produce a state of intoxication which mimics a psychosis, such as paranoia,[4,41] but this does not usually last for more than a few days, and appears to be relatively rare. Although ecstasy is not a hallucinogen in most people, it can cause hallucinations on occasion, especially in higher doses. I have myself seen a person in a state of toxic delirium after taking no more than 200mg of pure MDMA and no other drugs (toxicologically confirmed). She was completely disoriented, had marked difficulty walking (she collapsed several times injuring herself), and spent several hours trying to pick up nonexistent objects from the floor and talking to people who were not present. There was no history of psychosis, although her mother had suffered from depersonalisation disorder (see below). She was an experienced ecstasy user with no previous phenomena of this nature. She experienced depersonalisation on a single dose of fluoxetine ('Prozac').

The use of ecstasy may sometimes alter the clinical picture in a pre-existing psychosis such as schizophrenia. This is referred to as a pathoplastic effect. Some people with schizophrenia or manic-depression will also take ecstasy, especially as the peak age of onset of schizophrenia is 20-30. It has not been clearly established whether or not ecstasy can specifically induce a relapse of preexisting schizophrenia or manic-depression, beyond the increased risk of relapse attached to any substantial emotional stressor. Ecstasy experiences are typically emotional events, and for this reason alone one would expect to see an association with increased risk of relapse in serious mental illness. Ecstasy releases dopamine in a similar manner to amphetamine and cocaine [13] and as such might be expected to increase the risk of psychotic illness in a similar manner to other psychostimulants, although possibly not to the same extent. Some investigators report that they have repeatedly observed clear links between the onset of psychotic symptoms and the use of ecstasy.[42] This latter study is based on two cases, other substances were involved, and there was no toxicological confirmation of pill content. However, there are several other reports[41,43,44,45,46] and taken together the evidence is indicative of a risk. The size of that risk is unknown at the present time, but is likely to be relatively small.

Can ecstasy cause a true 'drug-induced psychosis'? As distinct from the categories above, Poole and Brabbins (1996) have argued that this term should be restricted to psychotic symptoms arising in the context of drug intoxication but persisting beyond elimination of the drug and its metabolites from the body. Such a psychosis should only recur on re-exposure to the drug, and must have a different course and outcome from the major functional psychoses (i.e. schizophrenia, manic-depression et al.). The drugs for which there is at least some scientific evidence of such a syndrome are amphetamines, cocaine and cannabis. Ecstasy may eventually be included in this group.

Anxiety disorders and panic attacks

As stated previously, we are currently limited to a handful of case reports.[1,3,4,38,47,48,49] However, the majority of communications from persons who have suffered adverse effects in association with taking ecstasy suggests that the leading theme may be anxiety disorders rather than depression, and this impression is confirmed by the published clinical reports in which forms of anxiety disorder appear to be more common than depression. It is possible that the serotonergic terminals involved in anxiety control are a distinct subset from those principally involved in mood control, and that ecstasy may preferentially affect the former. However, it is more likely that the real explanation lies in the psychological effects of ecstasy in terms of impairing psychic defences against anxiety generating material in the unconscious as discussed previously.

Depersonalisation and derealisation

Depersonalisation refers to the feeling that one is not 'real', and that one is detached and unable to feel emotion.[40] It is very unpleasant. Sufferers may feel that they are separated from the world by a glass wall. Derealisation is where the environment appears to be unreal and devoid of the usual emotional component. People may be described as 'cardboard-like'. Although these phenomena have been reported in association with ecstasy use,[30] they may be due to fatigue and may be seen as symptoms in a wide range of disorders, including depression, anxiety, schizophrenia and temporal lobe epilepsy. Depersonalisation and derealisation disorder may also occur spontaneously, so once again care is necessary in drawing a cause and effect conclusion from an association which may be accidental.

Depression

A brief period of low mood associated with the 'come-down' is common, although experienced users will tend to avoid this by taking other drugs. Chronic ecstasy use is also sometimes followed by a longer lasting depression.[50] However, it is unclear whether the chronic use of ecstasy might not have been a form of self-medication of a pre-existing depression, or latent depression, rather than actually causative of depression.

Depression may be predicted on theoretical grounds due to links between mood and serotonin. However, rats and monkeys with extensively damaged cortical serotonergic nerve terminals generally show little difference, or only very modest differences, in their behaviour relative to control animals. It is possible that this is because ecstasy appears to preferentially alter one type of serotonin terminal, and not those of a second system in the brain.[10] One conclusion from the data so far is that it is probably this second system which controls mood, appetite, sleep, and sex drive. Serotonin levels are low for a week in this second system, but the structural changes are generally not seen.[10] This matches the weekly cycle of what has actually been observed in humans. It is clear that further studies are required.

Cognitive deficits
(Impaired memory, attention and concentration)

Research into drug-induced cognitive deficits is difficult to do well. The number of possible confounding variables is high. For example, it is essential to control for the use of other drugs, particularly regular cannabis smoking, and for the effects of any mood disorder upon cognition. If subjects have been told to abstain from all drugs for several weeks, a withdrawal syndrome may result which could confound tests conducted during this period. All claims of cognitive deficits should be accompanied by evidence that the urine tests of the subjects were clear of drugs and their metabolites, particularly cannabis metabolites which can take at least 4 weeks to disappear from urine. Reports of subtle memory deficits which not accompanied by urine test data may be due to cannabis use.

A report of subtle memory deficits in association with ecstasy use has been made by Krystal and Price, 1992.

The pandora's box syndrome (pbs); busy head syndrome

Persons who have taken large quantities of drugs such as LSD, ecstasy and ketamine for a prolonged period may develop a mental state which involves a high level of internal, 'mental' imagery but no perceptual disorder. It is as if perforations have been made in the defences which usually separate conscious from unconscious processes, resulting in material percolating through the conscious mind where it would not normally be found. I have named this syndrome after the legend of Pandora's box: once opened it proved impossible to push back in all that flew out. The condition is not serious. It does not prevent the afflicted person from going to work or going about the normal business of life. However, attention and concentration are impaired, which may lead to an apparently poor memory due to failure to attend to new information. The person may be said to have 'lost their edge' or 'lack focus'. The imagery is intensified by the same factors as intensify flashbacks, principally anxiety generating situations. This is consistent with a psychodynamic explanation.

Flashbacks

Flashbacks have been described by ecstasy users.[51] Some flashbacks may be a form of post-traumatic stress disorder (PTSD), which is a psychological condition in which flashbacks and sleep disturbance result from severe psychological trauma. Flashbacks appear to be more likely following very traumatic drug experiences, which adds weight to the suggestion that some flashbacks are in fact PTSD, or at least anxiety related. One of the three cases cited by Creighton et al. (1991) involved a woman who had been abducted and raped while under the influence of MDMA. The other two cases involved heavy daily cannabis use and LSD-like features which Creighton et al. suggest may have been due to such substances in the pills. This once again demonstrates the importance of polydrug use in these limited series reports.

The Tenth International Classification of Diseases [53] classifies PTSD as 'a delayed or protracted response to a stressful event or situation (ICD-10) of an exceptionally threatening or catastrophic nature'. A small number of ecstasy experiences may be very stressful and perceived as catastrophic by the consumer. ICD-10 notes that pre-existing personality traits such as being compulsive or a past history of neurosis increases the probability of subsequent development of PTSD and aggravates its course. 'Typical symptoms include episodes of repeated reliving of the trauma in intrusive memories ('flashbacks') or dreams... there is usually a state of autonomic hyperarousal' (ICD 10). Other flashbacks may be a form of psychological 'conversion disorder', where anxiety with a neurotic basis is 'converted' into psychological symptoms, just as it may be converted into physical symptoms such as a 'paralysed' arm.

The likelihood that flashbacks are in fact due to persisting changes in the brain is considerably reduced by the observation that a wide array of drugs, with radically different mechanisms of action in the brain (e.g. LSD and ketamine), have also been linked to flashbacks. Ketamine use is as likely to result in flashbacks as LSD use.[36,54,55] It is also noteworthy that persons who have never taken any illicit drugs but who are prone to severe anxiety and panic attacks may describe visual and other phenomena which bear a marked resemblance to the flashbacks described by some drug users. The similarity of the conditions which provoke such flashbacks also indicates a psychological rather than a neurochemical origin.

In conclusion, the currently available evidence suggests that flashbacks are probably not the result of 'brain damage' or the improbable theory that there are 'lingering drug quantities' in the brain. Flashbacks are most usefully understood as PTSD and a form of neurosis of the dissociative conversion/anxiety disorder type.

Sleep disturbance

Insomnia for several days after taking ecstasy is relatively common, but in a few cases this has persisted for months with excessive dreaming and sometimes nightmares.[1] A persistent reduction in stage 2 sleep has been verified in a sleep laboratory, although the subjects in this investigation were not considered to be suffering from sleep disorders.[56]

Ecstasy – a stepping stone to other drugs?

The use of ecstasy is associated with the use of other drugs to modify the unpleasant 'come-down'. Temazepam has become very popular for this purpose recently, and was rescheduled as a controlled drug. Temazepam belongs to the 'Valium class', although it is much shorter acting. Tolerance and dependence can develop relatively quickly. Of much greater concern is the spread of heroin smoking through the dance culture. Heroin addiction is rapidly increasing in the U.K. There is also a link between taking ecstasy and a desire to smoke excessively, which may be related to the effect of these drugs upon dopamine pleasure systems in the brain. Respiratory illnesses are a common result when the smoker is moving from a hot dance environment to the cold night outside.

Tolerance, dependence and withdrawal

The use of almost any substance may become compulsive and excessive in some individuals and there are certainly those who have taken ecstasy on a daily basis, regardless of tolerance effects, for prolonged periods.[23,29,42] It is far more common, however, for 'problematic' ecstasy use to involve consumption of the drug in 48 hour weekend binges with 4-5 days in between. The experience of the 'love effect' from ecstasy rapidly fades with repeated use, and the effects become increasingly like those of amphetamine.[57,1] This may partially explain some of the escalation in dose levels seen in recent years, as some users will be vainly attempting to recover the mental state which they experienced initially – now impossible due to neurochemical and psychological changes in the brain and mind resulting from repeated use. Other reasons for escalating dose levels are the substantial drop in price, and an observation from animal research that under-functioning of serotonergic nerve terminals results in increased use of amphetamine-like substances for pharmacological reasons which lie beyond the scope of the present discussion.[58,59]

The day after taking ecstasy, if they have had a reasonable amount of sleep, not consumed large quantities of cannabis, and not gone clubbing, a substantial number of users feel quite elevated in spirits. However, this cheerful mood has generally started to crumble by the second day, and by the third day low mood, which may be quite severe, and irritability are common. This continues into the fourth day, with relative recovery of mood occurring on the fifth. The cycle frequently repeats itself with ecstasy use on the 6th and 7th days. Thus some persons may be said to be continually affected by the drug, even if they only take it in the weekends. With repeated use, the effects of ecstasy come to increasingly resemble those of amphetamine, and the patterns of use may begin to have the appearance of a dependency problem, particularly in persons who are taking 25 pills Thursday to Monday month after month. It is not necessary to take a drug every day before a dependency syndrome can be identified, nor is physical withdrawal essential to the diagnosis.[53,60,61] The possibility that ecstasy may be associated with tolerance, dependence and withdrawal syndromes will surprise those 'Apollonian' users who only take the drug occasionally in controlled circumstances (as distinct from the Dionysian, 3 day party, 'neck em', stack em' and go' group).

In this context it is valuable to recall the history of amphetamine itself. In the late 1930s, the American Medical Association approved the use of amphetamine for a wide range of disorders, and the pharmaceutical company Smith, Kline & French reassured physicians that 'no serious reactions had been observed'. Between 1932 and 1946, the pharmaceutical industry found 39 licensed uses for amphetamine, including the treatment of schizophrenia and tobacco smoking.[62] It was not until the late 1960s, after numerous case reports, that it was officially accepted that amphetamines were addictive and that amphetamine-associated paranoid psychosis was relatively common among heavy users.[53,60,61]

This picture took decades to form. With respect to ecstasy, deleterious effects upon serotonin were found in 1985, and it is really the 1990s which has seen an increasing frequency of reported psychiatric complications.[4]

As noted above, the concept that a 'withdrawal syndrome' requires clear-cut 'physical' manifestations of dependence has been largely discarded, although some controversy in the area continues. The extreme fatigue, excessive sleeping and then anxiety, insomnia and depression which follow cessation of chronic amphetamine use are regarded as a bona fide withdrawal syndrome. Which aspects of this picture chronic, high dose ecstasy users may share has not yet become apparent.

Ecstasy has an effect on dopaminergic systems which is similar to that of stimulants associated with dependency, and activates dopamine-based pleasure systems in a manner resembling amphetamine and cocaine.[13] It was once believed that ecstasy would be free of any dependency risk because of the rapid loss of the empathogenic 'loved up' effect with repeated use.[57] However, while loss of this effect may lead to declining use in an older group who take ecstasy for its empathogenic properties, younger users in the dance culture may come to appreciate the more amphetamine-like qualities, and have different expectations. This group rarely take pure compounds and may have been conditioned from the outset to expect amphetamine-like effects from a 'pill', as many pills are in fact amphetamine or MDEA, rather than MDMA,[20] and also because polydrug use is very common,[33] with many of those who party throughout the weekend deliberately taking amphetamine and other drugs in addition to ecstasy, a milieu in which the particular effects which distinguish ecstasy from other pleasurable stimulants are diminished. The animal evidence suggests dependency potential, and presumed changes in serotonergic nerve terminals do not result in reduced frequency of MDMA self-injecting behaviour in monkeys.[63] In fact, impaired serotonergic function has been linked to increased self administration of amphetamine because of a complex interaction between serotonergic systems and dopamine pleasure systems in the brain's pleasure centres.

A questionnaire investigation of 100 ecstasy users in Sydney found that 2% of the sample considered themselves to be 'dependent'.[65] The value of such a self-report is questionable however. 47% of respondents in the study expressed the belief that it was possible to become dependent on ecstasy.

Treatment of psychological and psychiatric adverse effects

A multi-levelled, individually tailored, dogma-free approach is generally the best, combining biological, psychological and social methods. There is virtually no literature which specifically deals with the treatment of psychological and psychiatric adverse effects due to ecstasy.[29] Accordingly, many of the references are to methods originally developed for amphetamine and cocaine dependence. Nevertheless, the principles are similar across the 'psychostimulant group'.

An initial assessment is followed by a decision about which of the available services is most suitable.[66] Apart from those with severe psychiatric and physical complications, ecstasy users are most likely to remain in the community. The management of disorders which can be classified and treated as would be normal were they not drug-induced will not be considered further here. The reader is referred to standard works on adult general psychiatry (e.g. Gelder, Gath & Mayou 1995).

When carrying out an assessment, it is important to bear in mind that a 'drug induced psychosis' should not be diagnosed simply because a patient with a psychosis has also been using drugs. Incorrect attribution of psychotic symptoms to the use of ecstasy may result in persons with schizophrenia or affective disorder not receiving proper care and education about their illness. They are not prescribed depot medications or lithium, are not adequately engaged with services, and their families are not appropriately educated. The result is a very high relapse rate. It is thus important to take a careful history, speak with relatives, and avoid jumping to hasty conclusions to ensure that there is not an underlying psychiatric disorder which is associated with drug use by chance. Urinanalysis is essential when psychotic symptoms occur in association with drug use. It is also important to note that the overwhelming majority of ecstasy users are polydrug consumers, and care must be taken not to attribute symptoms to the wrong drug.

Counselling, psychotherapy and cognitive/behavioural therapy

A non-judgmental attitude may be helpful at the outset to create a trusting relationship, as some of the clients have difficulties with authority figures.[67,68,69] However, Rogerian-style unconditional positive regard and empathy are typical effects of ecstasy, and it is reasonable to suppose that some users may occasionally respond better to firm limit setting and reality orientation.

Denial is an important defence mechanism: 'Everyone knows E's and Whiz aren't addictive, I can stop anytime'. Denial can be dealt with using facts from the person's life rather than research findings, e.g. 'Lets examine the effect that taking 10 E's every weekend is having on your studies... on your finances... on the way you feel by Wednesday afternoon... on your life in general now that you have been arrested and charged with intent to supply because you bought a big bag of pills to save money... on your having a relationship with a violent nightclub bouncer... on your increasing tendency to smoke "brown" (heroin) for the comedown...' This approach may be more effective than discussions about serotonergic terminals.

There is a general account of problems which may be encountered in Zweben, 1989.

The cognitive-behavioural approach focuses on problem behaviours, as distinct from nondirective therapies which concentrate on feelings and relationships. Cognitive aspects include explaining the causes of relapse and the conditioning mechanisms which lead to the sudden appearance of craving in some situations. The place, people and objects associated with the primary "reward" can become conditioned stimuli for drug use by classical conditioning. Therapy may attempt to change the "behaviour eliciting" properties of key stimuli.[70,71]

Motivational interviewing can be a very valuable technique (see Miller & Rollnick, 1991), and relapse prevention is important.[72,73]

Psychodynamic psychotherapy

This approach may be suitable for persons whose symptoms have a strongly neurotic character, and who are not too seriously impaired. The approach involves a gradual exploration of the unconscious, and a 'working through' of difficult material. The focus is not usually upon the drug taking behaviour itself. Persons with a clear history of childhood trauma may do well. There is a valuable account of psychodynamic, 'object relations' based approaches to treating the stimulant dependent in Wallace, 1991.[74,75,76]

Meditation, relaxation and martial arts

Relaxation exercises may be useful for persons with anxiety problems. Tapes are widely available. Meditation involves learning to attend to a single stimulus without allowing the attention to wander. This is useful for a range of disorders, particularly 'busy head syndrome'. Some people are deterred from meditation by the association of this discipline with quasi-religious groups. It is not necessary to join a group to meditate effectively, nor is teaching required or any form of religious affiliation. Lawrence LeShan's brief account 'How to Meditate' [77] is all that is required. See also Gorski, 1990.

Martial arts are also useful for strengthening the 'signal over noise' ratio, and improving attention and concentration. They are demanding, and require a complete change of lifestyle from weekend long raving. They can also meet high stimulus needs, provide an 'endorphin rush', and encourage self-control. Okinawan Goju-Ryu karate is particularly suitable, providing high intensity, little physical contact, high stimulation training environments. In fact, most forms of physical exercise and gym work can be valuable in persons who wish to stop the regular use of psychostimulants.

Medication

The client may be self-medicating an underlying disorder which should be treated separately, such as depression, an anxiety disorder, a personality disorder or an incipient psychosis. If such a condition is identified or suspected, treatment should be as for the underlying condition (antidepressants, antipsychotics, lithium, carbamazepine etc.)

Antidepressants

Antidepressants such as fluoxetine ('Prozac') may be useful. Serotonin reuptake inhibitors such as fluoxetine will prevent the neurotoxicity of MDMA in animal studies if taken within 3 hours of the MDMA dose. 50% of the depletion is blocked at 6 hours, but there is no protective effect at 12 hours.[5] However, these studies generally involve massive doses of fluoxetine. Fluoxetine after MDMA has been reported as able to reduce sleep disorders and restlessness.

Antioxidants and Food Supplements: Tryptophan and Tyrosine

Some ecstasy users also take high doses of antioxidants such as vitamin C and vitamin E. There is some evidence that free radicals may be involved in the neurotoxicity process. Tyrosine and tryptophan may elevate levels of serotonin,[78] but the use of tryptophan is severely restricted in the UK and other countries due to a contaminated batch. It may only be prescribed by a medical practitioner on a named patient basis. Bananas and chocolate are rich sources of tryptophan, and it is a valid suggestion that persons taking ecstasy may profit by eating these foods. It is also possible to obtain a product called '5-HTP Serotonic'. 5-HT is another term for serotonin, and 5-HTP is actually one step closer to serotonin in the biochemical pathway than tryptophan. This product may be obtained from Life Enhancement Products, P.O. Box 751390, Petaluma, California CA 94975-1390.

Benzodiazepines (Lorazepam, Temazepam, Diazepam ('Valium')

Insomnia may be treated with a short course of temazepam. Panic attacks are often treated with lorazepam. Severe chronic anxiety may be treated with intermittent courses of diazepam. All of these drugs are potentially addictive. Accordingly, they are best not used for more than a few weeks at a time. Antidepressants such as fluoxetine and sertraline are also useful for treating anxiety. If the person can not tolerate these, clomipramine is a good alternative. The brain's anxiety mechanisms may play a specific role in the neurobiology of stimulants, which suggests that benzodiazepines may be useful in the early stages of withdrawal.[79,80]

Haloperidol and other antipsychotics

Antipsychotic drugs such as haloperidol and chlorpromazine are not a good first choice in ecstasy-associated anxiety and psychosis. In general, such symptoms associated with ecstasy use are short-lived. It is thus better practice to administer benzodiazepines for at least the first few days, as the antipsychotic effect of dopamine antagonists such as haloperidol usually takes several weeks to become manifest, by which time symptoms will have resolved in most cases. Haloperidol and chlorpromazine have numerous serious and unpleasant side-effects, and the neuroleptic malignant syndrome may be linked to the hyperthermic syndromes associated with several ecstasy-related deaths.[81]

Complementary therapies

It is sometimes worth considering acupuncture,[82] homeopathy, massage and other types of bodywork, and aromatherapy.

Conclusions

It is clear that large-scale, rigorous, well designed studies are required to establish the true levels of serious adverse psychological effects from taking ecstasy. The results from animal neurotoxicity studies, in combination with the tendency to use higher doses of the drug, suggest that there are grounds for concern. However, current indications are that many of the disorders which have been reported may be related to psychological events rather than neurotoxicity. The cause and effect conclusions often drawn by single case studies must be viewed with caution, but this does not necessarily mean that they are incorrect or that these studies should be disregarded. There is still a widespread tendency to diagnose persons as suffering from conditions induced by illicit drug taking when they are in fact suffering from conditions such as schizophrenia and manic-depression. This tendency is strengthened by the natural inclination on the part of the sufferer to seek an explanation for their condition 'external' to themselves, over which they have some control. Our understanding of the actual relative risk from this drug is at an early stage.

©**Dr. Karl L. R. Jansen MB.ChB., M.Med.Sci., D. Phil. (Oxon), MRCPsych 1997.**

Dr. Karl Jansen is currently writing a book about ketamine. If you would like to share your ketamine experience/knowledge/opinion, write to: Dr. Karl Jansen, 63-65 Denmark Hill, London SE5 8AZ e-mail: K@BTInternet.com

Please cite as: Jansen, K.L.R. (1997) Adverse Psychological Effects Associated With the use of Ecstasy (MDMA), and Their Treatment. In: Saunders, N. Ecstasy Reconsidered

Panic attack account

I have been taking ecstasy for over two years, but my last experience was a nightmare. I had returned from an all night party when I took another E and smoked a couple of joints, thinking I would relax to some music. Suddenly was lying there and could feel my chest slowly tightening and began to breathe faster. I felt I was slipping into a trance and began to panic.

I felt pins and needles spreading up from my toes and fingers. I was sweating and taking in huge gulps of air, and when I tried to breath normally the pins and needles got worse and I saw flashes of light across my vision. After a couple of hours my whole body was numb. I doused myself with cold water and rubbed my arms, but could not get out of the trance. After 4 hours I even wrote a 'goodbye' letter and by 5 hours my whole body was shaking.

Since then I get twitches and feel panic attacks, and feel really weird some days.

– Edited from a reader's letter to his doctor

References

1. McCann, U. D. & G. S. Ricaurte (1991) Lasting neuropsychiatric sequelae of 3,4 methylenedioxymethamphet-amine (MDMA) J. Clin. Psychpharmacol. 11: 302-305. McCann, U. D., Shiyoko, O. S. and G. S. by Dr. Karl Jansen Ricaurte (1996) (USA) Adverse reactions with 3,4-methylenedioxymethamphet-amine (MDMA; Ecstasy) Drug Safety 1996 Aug. 15 (2) 107 – 115.

2. Greer, G. and Tolbert, R. (1990) *The therapeutic use of MDMA* In: Ecstasy: the clinical, pharmacological and neurotoxicological effects of the drug MDMA. (Ed. S.J. Peroutka)., pp21-37

3. McGuire, P. , Cope, H. & Fahy, T.(1994) Diversity of psychopathology associated with the use of 3,4-methylenedioxy-methamphetamine (Ecstasy) *British J Psychiatry* 165, 391-395.

4. Kemmerling, K., Haller, R. & Hinterhuber, H. (1996) das neuropsychiatrische Risiko von 3,4 methylenedioxy-methamphetamine (Ecatsy). Neuropsychiatrie 10: 94 – 102.

5. Schmidt, C. J.. (1989) Acute and long-term neurochemical effects of methylenedioxymeth-amphetamine in the rat In: Ecstasy: the clinical, pharmacological and neurotoxicological effects of the drug MDMA. (Ed. S.J. Peroutka)., *Kluwer Academic Publishers*, Massachusetts, pp179-195

6. Battaglia, G., & E.B. De Souza (1989) Pharmacologic profile of amphetamine derivatives at various brain recognition sites: selective effects on serotonergic systems. In: *Pharmacology and Toxicology of Amphetamine and Related Designer Drugs*, ED.s K. Asghar, E De Souza, NIDA Research Monograph 94, Maryland, pp240-258. Battaglia, G., Yeh, S. Y.. & E.B. De Souza (1988) MDMA-induced neurotoxicity: parameters of degeneration and recovery of brain serotonin neurons. Pharm, Biochem and Behaviour 29, 269-274.

7. Insel, T. R. et al. (1989): 3,4 methylenedioxymetham-phetamine selectively destroys brain serotonin terminals in rhesus monkeys. J. Pharmacol. Exp. Ther. 249, 713 – 720.

8. Grob, C., Bravo, G. & Walsh, R. (1990) Second Thoughts on 3,4-Methylenedioxy-methamphetamine Neurotoxicity. Archives of General Psychiatry 47, 288.

9. Liester, M.B., Grob, C. S., Bravo, G. L. and Walsh, R. N. (1992) Phenomenology and sequaelae of 3,4-methylenedioxy methamphetamine use. Journal of Nervous and Mental Disease 180, 345-352.

10. Molliver, M. E., mamounas, L.A. and M. A. Wilson (1989) Effects of neurotoxic amphetamines on serotonergic neurons: immunocytochemical studies In: Pharmacology and Toxicology of Amphetamine and Related Designer Drugs, ED.s K. Asghar, E De souza, NIDA Research Monograph 94, Maryland, . pp270-304.

11. Jansen, K. L. R., Faull, R. L. M. et al (1990) Alzheimer's disease: Changes in hippocampal NMDA, quisqualate, neurotensin, adenosine, benzodiazepine, serotonin and opioid receptors: an autoradiographic study. Neuroscience 39, 613-617.

12. Nichols, D.E. (1986) Differences between the mechanisms of action of MDMA, MBDB and the classical hallucinogens. Identification of a new therapeutic class: Entactogens. Journal of Psychoactive Drugs 8, 305-313.

13. Nichols, D.E. and Oberlander,R. (1989) Srcture-activity relationships of MDMA-like substances. In: Pharmacology and Toxicology of Amphetamine and Related Designer Drugs, ED.s K. Asghar, E De souza, NIDA Monograph 94, Maryland, pp01-29.

14. Hall, W., Hando, J., Darke, S. and Ross, J. (1996) Psychological morbidity and route of administration among amphetamine users in Sydney. Addiction, 91, 81-87.

15. Johnson, M. P.; Hoffman, A. J. and Nichols, D. E. (1986) Effects of the enantiomers of MDA, MDMA and realed analogs on [3H]serotonin and [3H]dopamine release from superfused rat brain slices. European Journal of Pharmacology 132, 269-276.

16. Kamien, J. B., Johanson, C.E.; Schuster, C.R. and Woolverton, W. L.(1986) The effects of (+)-methylenedioxymethamphetamine and (+)-methylenedioxyamphetamine, in monkeys trained to discriminate (+)-amphetamine from saline. Drug and Alcohol Dependence 18, 139-147.

17. Koob, G. F. and Goeders, N. (1989) Neuroanatomical substrates of drug self-administration. In Neuropharm-acological Basis of Reward: J. M. Liebman & S. J. Cooper, Ed.s: 214-263. Elsevier Science Publishing Co., New York.

18. Stone, D., Stahl, D., Hanson, G. and J. Gibb (1986) The effects of 3,4-methylenedioxy-methamphetamine (MDMA) and 3,4-methylenedioxyamphetamine (MDA) on momonaminerguc systems in the rat brain. Eur. J. Pharmacol. 128, 41-48.

19. Yamomoto, B.K. and Spanos, L. J. (1988) The acute effects of methylenedioxy-methamphetamine on dopamine release in the awake-behaving rat. European Journal of Pharmacology 148, 195-203..

20. Saunders, N.E. (1995) Ecstasy and the Dance Culture. London: 14 Neal's Yard WC2H 9DP

21. Shulgin, A. and Shulgin, A. (1992) PIHKAL: A Chemical Love Story. Transform Press, Berkeley, California.

22. Connell, P. H. (1958) (UK) Amphetamine psychosis. Institute of Psychiatry Maudsley Monographs Number 5, Oxford University Press.

Bell, D. S. (1965) Comparison of amphetamine psychosis and schizophrenia. British J of Psychiatry 111, 701-707.

23. Jansen, K. L. R. (1996a) Neuroscience, ketamine and the near-death experience: the role of glutamate and the NMDA receptor. Chapter 17 In: The Near-Death Experience: A Reader (Eds. Lee J. Bailey and Jenny Yates) Routledge, New York and London, pp265-282. JANSEN, K. L. R. (1996b) Using ketamine to induce the near-death experience: mechanism of action and therapeutic potential. Yearbook for Ethnomedicine and the Study of Consciousness (Jahrbuch furr Ethnomedizin und Bewubtseinsforschung) Issue 4, 1995 (Ed.s C. Ratsch; J. R. Baker); VWB, Berlin, pp55-81.

24. Knudsen, P. & Vilmar, T. (1984) Cannabis and neuroleptic agents in schizophrenia. Acta Psychiatrica Scandinavica 69, 162-174.

25. Mathers, D. C. & Ghodse, A. H. (1992) Cannabis and psychotic illness. Brit. J. Psychiatry 161, 648-653.

26. Negrete, J. C. (1989) Cannabis and schizophrenia. British Journal of Addiction 84, 349-351.

27. Treffert, D. A. (1978) Marijuana use in schizophrenia: a clear hazard. Am. J. Psychiatry 3135, 1213-1215.

28. Jansen, K. L. R. (1993) Non-medical Use of Ketamine. British Medical Journal 298, 4708-4709.

29. Jansen, K.L.R., Griffiths, P., Fahy, T., Farrell, M. (1997) Treatment Approaches to Amphetamine and Other Psychostimulant Use. Geneva 12-15 November. The WHO Meeting on Amphetamines, MDMA and other Psychostimulants, 12-15 Novemeber 1996. Meeting Proceedings WHO (in press).

30. Wodarz, N. and Boning, J. (1993) Ecstasy-induziertes psychotisches Depersonalisation sysndrom. Nervenartz 64: 478-480.

31. Gouzoulis, E. And Hermle, L. (1994) Die Gefarhen von Ecstasy. Nervenartz 64: 478-480.

32. Brown, E. R.S., Jarvie, D.R. and Simpson, D. (1995) Use of Drugs at 'Raves' Scottish Medical Journal 40,168-171

33. Meltzer, H., Baljit, G. and M. Pettigrew (1994) The prevalence of psychiatric morbidity among adults aged 16-64, living in private households, in Great Britain. OPCS Surveys of Psychiatric Morbidity in GB, Bulletin 1.

34. Shapiro, H. (1996) (UK) Drug Deaths. Druglink Factsheet 19, ISDD, Waterbridge House, 32 Loman Street, London SE10EE.

35. Grinspoon, L. & Bakalar, J. B. (1981) *Psychedelic Drugs Reconsidered*. Basic Books, New York.

36. Strassman, R.J. (1984) Adverse reactions to psychedelic drugs. A review of the literature. Journal of Nervous and Mental Disease 172, pp577-595.

37. Cohen, R.S. (1995) Subjective reports on the effects of the MDMA (Ecstasy) experience in humans. Prog. Psychopharmacol. Biol. Psychiat. 19, 1137-1145.

38. Hermle, L., Spitzer, M., Borchardt, D., Kovar, K. A. and Gouzoulis, E. (1993) Psychological effects of MDE in normal subjects. Neuropsychopharmacology 8: 171-176

39. Brabbins, C, & Poole, R. (1996) Drug induced psychosis. British Journal of Psychiatry 168, 135-138.

40. Gelder, M. Gath, D. and Mayou, R. (1995) Concise Oxford Texbook of Psychiatry, Oxford Univeristy Press, Oxford, pp149-150.

41. Williams, H., Meager, D. and Galligan, P. (1993) MDMA (Ecstasy). A case of possible drug induced psychosis. Ir. J. Psychol. Med. 162: 43 – 44.

42. McGuire, P. and Fahy, T.(1991) Chronic paranoid psychosis after misuse of MDMA (Ecstasy,) British Medical Journal 302, 697.

43. Schifano, F. (1991) Chronic atypical psychosis associated with MDMA (Ecstasy) abuse. Lancet 338: 1335

44. Schifano, F. & Magni, G. (1994) Ecstasy abuse: Psycho-pathological features and craving for chocolate: A case series. Biological Psychiatry vol. 36, no. 11, pp. 763-767

45. Winstock, A. R. (1991) Chronic paranoid psychosis after misuse of 3,4 methylenedioxymethamphetamine. Brit. Med. J. 302, 1150-1151.

46. Nunez-dominguiez, LA (1994) Psychosis because of ecstasy Addicciones, vol. 6, no. 3, pp. 301-307

47. Greer, G. and Tolbert, R. (1986) Subjective Reports of the Effects of MDMA in a clinical setting. J. Psychoactive Drugs 18, 319-327.

48. Whitaker-azmitia, P.m. & Aronson, T.A. (1989) Ecstasy (MDMA)-Induced Panic. Am. J. Psychiat. 146: 119.

49. Pallanti, S. & Mazzi, D. (1992) MDMA (Ecstasy) Precipitation of panic disorder. Biol Psychiatry 32, 91-95.

50. Benazzi, I. & Mazzoli, M. (1991) Psychiatric illness associated with ecstasy. Lancet 338, 1520.

51. Creighton, F.j., Black, D.l. and Hyde, C.e. (1991) Ecstasy

Psychosis and Flashbacks. Brit J Psychiatry 159, 713-715.

52. McGuire, P. and Fahy, T.(1992) Flashbacks following MDMA British J Psychiatry 160, 276.

53. World Health Organisation (1992) The ICD-10 classification of mental and behavioral disorders: clinical descriptions and diagnostic guidelines. World Health Organisation, Switzerland, pp70-83.

54. Jansen, K. L. R. (1990c)Ketamine: can chronic use impair memory? International J of Addiction 25, 133-139.

55. Alarcon, R.d., Dickinson, W. A.,& Dohn, H.h. (1982) Flashback phenomena: Clinical and diagnostic dilemmas. Journal of Nervous and Mental Disease 170, 217-23.

56. Allen, R, McCann, U. & Ricuarte, G. A. (1993) Persistent effects of MDMA on Human Sleep. Sleep 16, 560-564

57. Peroutka, S. J. (1990) Recreational use of MDMA. In: Ecstasy: the clinical, pharmacological and neurotoxi-cological effects of the drug MDMA. (Ed. S.J. Peroutka)., Kluwer Academic Publishers, Massachusetts, pp53-63.

58. Gately, P. F., Poon, S. L., Segal, D. S. & Geyer, M. A. (1985) Depletion of brain serotonin by 5,7-dihhdroxytryptamine alters the response to amphetamine and the habituation of locomotor activity in rats. Psychopharmacology 87, 400-405.

59. Lyness, W. H.& K.E. Moore (1983) Increased self-administration of d-amphetamine by rats pretreated with metergoline. Pharm Biochem and Behaviour 18, 721-724.

60. Leith, N. J. & Barrett, R. J. (1976) Amphetamine and the reward system: evidence for tolerance and post-drug depression. Psychopharmacology 46, 19-25.

61. Watson, R., Hartmann, E. and Schildkraut, J. J. (1972) Amphetamine withdrawal: affective state, sleep patterns and MHPG exvcretion. Am. J. Psychiat. 129, 263-269.

62. Lukas, S.E. (1985) Amphetamines: Danger in the fast lane. The Encylopaedia of Psychoactive Drugs. Chelsea House Publishers, New York.

63. Beardsley, P.m.; Balster, R. L & Harris, L.s. (1986) Self-administration of methlenedioxy-methamphetamine (MDMA) by Rhesus monkeys. Drug Alcohol Dependence 18, 149-157.

64. Krystal, J. H. and Price, L. H. (1992) Chroni 3,4 methylenedioxymethamphetamine (MDMA) use: effects on mood and neurophysiological function? Am. J. Drug Alcohol Abuse 18, 331-341.

65. Solowij, SH, Faillace, L & N Lee (1992) Recreational MDMA use in Sydney: a profile of Ecsatsy users and their experiences with drugs. Brit. J. Addict. 87, 1161-1172.

66. Glass, I.B., Farrell, M and Hejek P. (1991) Tell me about the client: history taking and formulating the case, in Glass, I.B (ed). The international handbook of addiction behaviour , pp. 216-224; London, Routledge.

67. Drummond, C.(1991) Individual therapy with drug takers, in: GLASS, I. B. (Ed.) The International Handbook of Addiction Behaviour, pp.85-89 (London, Routledge).

68. Kertzner, R. M. (1987) Individual psychotherapy of cocaine abuse. In H. I. Spitz and J. S. Rosecan (Eds) Cocaine abuse: new directions in treatment and research. New York: Brunner/Mazel.

69. Rogers, C. R. (1957) The necessary and sufficient conditions of therapeutic personality change, Journal of Consulting Psychology 21, 95-103.

70. Childress, A. R., Ehrman, R., Mclellan And O'Brien, C. P. (1988) Conditioned craving and arousal in cocaine addiction. Problems of Drug Dependence, NIDA Monograph Series, DHSS pub. n. (ADM)88-1564, pp74-80.

71. O'Brien, C. P. & Childress, A. R. (1991) Behaviour Therapy of drug Dependence, in: GLASS, I. B. (Ed.) The International Handbook of Addiction Behaviour, pp.230-235; London, Routledge). O'Brien, C. P., Hildress, A. R., A. T. McLellan & R. Erhrman (1990) The use of cue exposure as an aid in the prevention of relapse to cocaine or heroin dependence. Addict. Behav. 15, 355-365. O'Brien, C. P., Hildress, A. R., A. T. Mclellan, R. Erhman (1992) Classical conditioning in drug-dependent humans. IN: Kalivas, P. H. And Samson, H. H,.The Neurobiology of Drug and Alcohol Addiction, Annals of the New York Academy of Sciences 654, 400-415.

72. Marlatt, G. A. (1982) 'relapse prevention: a self-control program for the treatment of addictive behaviours, in: Stuart, R. B. (Ed) Adherence, Compliance and Generalis-ation in Behavioral Medicine (New York, Bruner/Mazel).

73. Marlatt, G. A. & Gordon, J. R. (1985) (Eds.) Relapse prevention. New York: Guildford.

74. Kernberg, O. (1976) Object relations theory and clinical psychoanalysis. New York: Jason Aronson

75. Kohut, H. (1971) The Analysis of the self: a systematic approach to the psychodynamic treatment of narcisstic personality disturbance. New York: International Universities Press. KOHUT , H. (1977) The restoration of the self. New York: International Universities Press.

76. Wurmser, L. (1985) denial and split identity: timely issues in the psychoanalytic psychotherapy of compulsive drug users. J of Substance Abuse Treatment 2, 89-96.

77. LeShan, L. (1974) How to Meditate. Bantam, New York. Levin, J. D. (1987) Treatment of alcoholism and other addictions: a self-psychology approach.New York: Jason Aaronson

78. Smith, F. L. , D.S.YU, D.G.smith, A.P.Leceese and W.H. Lyness (1986) Dietary tryptophan supplements attentuate amphetamine self-administartion in the rat. Pharmacology, Biochemistry and Behaviour 25, 849-855.

79. Piazza, P.v., S. Maccari, J.m., M. Le Moal & H. Simon (1991) Corticosterone levels determine individual vulnerability to amphetamine self-administration. (1991) Corticosterone levels determine individual vulnerability to amphetamine self-administration. Proc. Natl. Acad. Sci.. usa 88, 2088-2092.

80. Goeders, N. E. (1992) Potential involvement of anxiety in the neurobiology of cocaine. In: Kalivas, P. H. and Samson, H. H,.The Neurobiology of Drug and Alcohol Addiction, Annal of the New York Academy of Sciences 654, 357-367..

81. Ames, D. & Wirshing, W.c. (1993) Ecstasy, the serotonin syndrome and the neuroleptic malignant syndrome – a possible link. J. American Medical Association 269, 869.

82. Lipton, D.s., Brewington, V. and M. Smith (1994) Acupuncture for crack-cocaine detoxification: experimental evaluation of efficacy. Journal of Substance Abuse Treatment 11, 205-215.

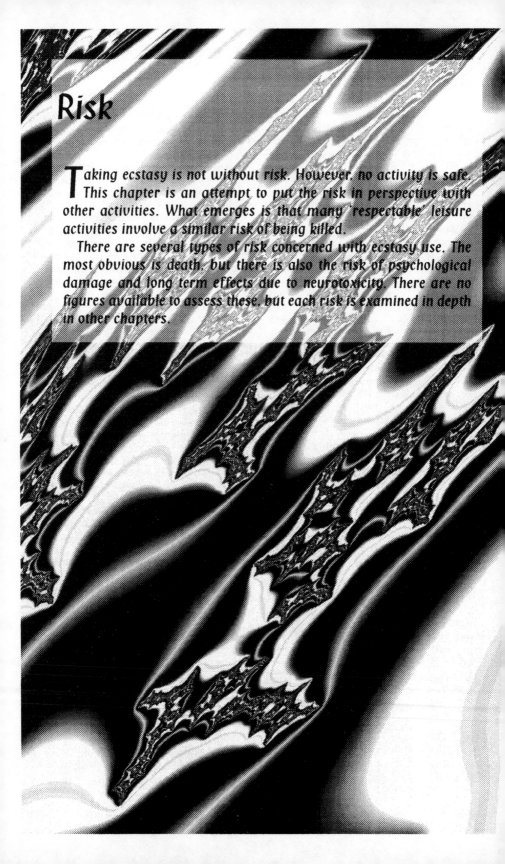

Risk

Taking ecstasy is not without risk. However, no activity is safe. This chapter is an attempt to put the risk in perspective with other activities. What emerges is that many 'respectable' leisure activities involve a similar risk of being killed.

There are several types of risk concerned with ecstasy use. The most obvious is death, but there is also the risk of psychological damage and long term effects due to neurotoxicity. There are no figures available to assess these, but each risk is examined in depth in other chapters.

Risk of death

The risk of death from taking a dose of ecstasy equals the number of deaths due to taking the drug divided by the number of times it is consumed. Unfortunately, these numbers are arguable.

Number of deaths

Official statistics put the number of deaths in the UK per year due to ecstasy as low as six, while the media attribute about 12 (see Ecstasy Deaths report). The true number may be higher due to people dying of an indirect effect when the drug was not implicated, or lower due to ecstasy being wrongly blamed. When several drugs are used at the same time, it may not be possible to say which was responsible.

I will assume the true figure lies between 6 and 20.

Drug Misuse Declared: results of the British Crime Survey for the Home Office, 1996 [1]

This survey covered a representative sample of 10,000 people aged 16-59 in England and Wales. The statistics were obtained by respondents sitting in front of laptops, where their answers could not be seen by others. A bogus drug name was included to catch out over reporting, and only one person claimed to be a user of it. The survey team believe that slight under reporting is probable as this is the case with alcohol use.

Two surprising facts emerge. The use of Ecstasy is lower than generally estimated, and the use of magic mushrooms is higher. More than twice as many people (nearly two million) had tried magic mushrooms than Ecstasy, and nearly as many regular mushroom users (as many young men users, but fewer young women).

The results show that the regular* use of Ecstasy is 1% of those under 30 and less than half a percent of older people. Overall, 2% had tried Ecstasy but were not regular users.

Applying these percentages to the population, this implies:

121,000 are regular users and 728,000 more have tried it. The report says the margins of error are such that the maximum number of users is 177,000 regular and 848,000 ever.

For LSD:

152,000 are regular users and 1,334,000 more have tried it. The report says the margins of error are such that the maximum number of users is 212,000 regular and 1,492,000 ever.

For Amphetamine:

303,000 are regular users and 2,486,000 more have tried it. The report says the margins of error are such that the maximum number if users is 385,000 regular and 2,696,000 ever.

*Those who said they had used ecstasy in the past month were regarded as regular users.

Number of uses

This has been estimated at one to two million per week. However, in 1966 the British Crime Survey[1] estimated 121,000 people had used ecstasy in the previous month. If half of those take it an average of once per week and the other half once a month, this comes to 363,000. This number is approximate: twice a weekend users would make it higher, and once fortnightly users lower.

These figures work out to 18,876,000 and 104,000,000 per year. I will assume the actual figure is between 20 and 100 million occasions of use per year.

Risk calculation

Dividing the highest number of users with the lowest number of deaths gives the lowest risk of one in 17 million; while the highest risk works out at one in a million.

Comparative risks

Such a risk is comparable with other leisure activities such as horse riding[2] (one in 3.3 million) or even fishing[2] (one in 4.5 million), while a skiing holiday is at least twice as risky at two in a million.[3] If your hobby is parachuting, the chance of being killed is one in 82,500 jumps: between ten and 170 times higher than taking an E.[4]

Like other activities, risk of can be reduced by taking adequate precautions. However, switching from ecstasy to a more respectable activity is not necessarily safer.

Fishing and Horse Riding [2]

People go fishing on 45 million occasions a year in the UK resulting in 10 deaths; people ride horses on 40 million occasions a year and 12 are killed as a direct result, many of them women under 25.

Drinking dangers [5]

"The impact that drugs have on the young has received huge publicity. What is not so widely recognised is that alcohol causes ten times as much damage [to the same age group, 16 to 25] as drugs." If that is true and there is more than one illicit drug user to every ten drinkers under 25 in the UK, then turning people away from drugs may result in them doing more harm.

Risk of needing medical treatment

A British study has put the risk of ending up in the emergency room of a hospital at 230 per million rave attendances. The majority of the sample studied discharged themselves after being given treatment for a racing heart. None of those who had taken ecstasy alone needed further treatment, the rest having taken a variety of other drugs at the same time.[6]

Dr Russell Newcombe tells me that out of a total of 17,000 attendances at a club where ecstasy was very widely used, 4 were taken to hospital with heatstroke (all recovered). This works out at a very similar figure of 235 per million. By comparison, the risk of injury while on a skiing holiday in Switzerland is three percent or 30,000 per million – a thousand times higher.[3] In fact every sport carries a far higher risk of injury: horse riding accounts for 16,000 injuries per million occasions; soccer 65,000 and even keeping fit 8,000.[8]

Medical treatment [6]

An examination of the frequency and nature of presentations to West Lothian hospitals in 1991 and 1992 following the ingestion of drugs in the context of rave parties, by means of retrospective analysis of case notes.

Dr Freeland found a total of seven cases; six having said they took ecstasy and at least two having taken other drugs in combination with ecstasy. Six were aged between 18 and 21 and the seventh was 27. Five were male. The invariable clinical finding was tachycardia – a racing heart. Complaints on admission included "buzzing sensations", anxiety and collapse.

One patient admitted taking ecstasy, Temazepam, cannabis and a cocaine-related drug in combination. He had a high temperature (39.5℃) and developed acute renal failure and coagulopathy – kidney failure and blood clotting. He recovered and was discharged after 18 days.

Another had taken ecstasy, amphetamine and cannabis and complained of palpitations and a buzzing sensation. He was discharged the next day.

In addition, one patient had severe muscle spasms: this patient did not admit to taking any drug, but amphetamine was found in his blood (MDMA was not looked for).

The other patients, including all those who admitted to taking ecstasy, discharged themselves. There were no fatalities.

The minimum hospitalisation rate is calculated to be 23 per 100,000 rave attendances, based on venue capacities.

Dr Freeland concludes: "Although the study aimed to look particularly at MDMA, the high prevalence of multiple drug use and the absence of specific toxicological results on these cases make it impossible to pass any judgement on MDMA per se."

British government risk classification

Sir Kenneth Calman, Government Chief Medical Officer, has instituted a government directive on how to explain risks to the public in a consistent way, intended for patients with a choice of treatments. They argued that statistics are confusing to normal people, and so they want to establish consistent use of terms so that the 'man in the street' can compare one type of risk with another.

Risk of dying in any one year as a result of exposure to the various dangers:[9]

Moderate risk = < 1:100 but > 1:1,000, eg Smoking 10 cigarettes a day, parachuting

Low risk = < 1:1,000 but > 1:10,000, eg Influenza, road accident

Very Low risk = < 1:10,000 but > 1:100,000, eg leukaemia, playing soccer, accident at work, murder

Minimal risk = < 1:100,000 but > 1:1,000,000, eg railway accident, horse riding, fishing

Negligible risk = < 1:1,000,000, eg. hit by lightning or radiation leak from nuclear power station

---

The figures [9] refer to the risk for people exposed to these dangers in any one year, not the number of times they were exposed (it's the number of people who play soccer, regardless of how often). Thus we need the number of people who used ecstasy, even once, in the past year: this is not known but is probably between one and two million. This has to be divided by the number of them who died as a result, which we have taken as between 6 and 20.

If we assume the top figure of 20 deaths per year and only one million users, this works out at 1:50,000, implying the risk is 'Very Low'. If we assume two million users and six deaths per year, this works out at 1:330,000, implying the risk is 'Minimal'. The risk is therefore comparable with people who go horse riding or play soccer as a leisure activity.

I have tried to be fair, but even if ecstasy was five times as dangerous, it would still be come into the 'Very Low' category.

A data gathering system called DAWN (Drug Abuse Warning Network, part of the National Institute of Drug Abuse) collects reports of illicit drug use from hospital emergency rooms all over the United States.[10] Whenever someone turns up at an emergency room and a drug is involved, either found on the person or in their blood or urine, or even if a patient comes in with a problem and mentions that it is drug-related, a report is sent to DAWN besides reports from postmortem examinations when drugs have been detected. These reports are analysed and figures are published each year. In 1992 ecstasy had 236 mentions compared to cocaine with 119,843, marijuana with 23,997 and LSD with 3,498. DAWN publishes a separate list of drugs that have caused more than 10 deaths but ecstasy is not included. The figures imply that there is no general medical cause for concern over ecstasy use in the USA: though there are mishaps, these are rare. Indeed, there were 129 other drugs that caused more problems.

Comparison of deaths in Britain resulting from legal and illegal drug use

100,000 people die each year out of 12,000,000 smokers, i.e. 8,300 per million

25,000 people die each year out of 40 million alcohol drinkers, i.e. 625 per million

120 people die each year out of 500,000 solvent sniffers, i.e. 240 per million

7 people die each year out of 1,000,000 ecstasy users, i.e. 7 per million

---

References

1. Refer box page 135.
2. Government statistics in OPCS Monitor DH4 92.
3. Skiing Dangers, *Sunday Times*, 24/1/93.
4. British Parachute Association.
5. Alcohol and the Young, published by The Royal College of Physicians 1965. The author, Professor Turnberg, was quoted in The Times: "Alcohol causes ten times as much damage [to the same age group, 16 to 25] as drugs."
6. Rave & Ecstasy related admissions in West Lothian 1991-1992; a review by Dr. P. Freeland submitted for publication to *The Annals of Emergency Admission*.
7.
8. Keeping fit: Shiela Henderson quoted in Fit for Anything, *The Guardian*, 12 April 1993.
9. *The Times*, 26 September 1996 on "On the State of the Public Health", published by HMSO 1995.
10. Drug Abuse Warning Network (DAWN) figures, published by *The U.S. National Institute on drug Abuse*, 1992 (published 1994)

The Law

In the seventies, there was concern about a new group of drugs called hallucinogenic amphetamines such as MDA and MDMA, which had not yet reached Britain. With a tradition of being more prohibitive than other countries, the British government tried to forestall trouble by classifying the entire chemical family as Class A drugs: the most restrictive category carrying the highest penalties. This was effected through the Misuse of Drugs Act 1971 (Modification) Order 1977 (SI Number 1243). So, although prohibition dates from 1977, MDMA is a controlled drug under Class A of the Misuse of Drugs Act 1971. Class A includes all compounds structurally derived from an N-alkyl-a-methylphenethylamine by substitution in the ring with an alkylenedioxy substituent, and this includes MDMA and its salts. Parliament may move drugs to other classes after consultation with or on the recommendation of the Advisory Council on the Misuse of Drugs, whose purpose is to keep under review the situation in the United Kingdom.

The British government is a signatory to the International Convention on Psychotropic Substances which requires member nations to make laws to control specified drugs. In spite of objections from the chairman of the Expert Committee, the Convention issued a directive to outlaw MDMA in 1985, but urged countries to use the provisions of article 7 of the Convention on Psychotropic Substances to facilitate research on this interesting substance. Although the English law against MDMA was made before this, the Act does allow for Class A drugs to be used for research.[1]

Penalties

The maximum penalties that may be passed by any court for drugs offences are set through legislation. Courts have a wide discretion on what penalty to impose provided that they do not exceed the maximum. They must act judiciously and not arbitrarily, and they must take note of the Court of Appeal's guidelines. It may be possible in practice to persuade a court to pass a lighter sentence for an offence involving MDMA than the court would have passed had a quantity of heroin of an equivalent weight been involved, but the Court of Appeal has always held that no distinction should be drawn between the various types of Class A drug, it being for Parliament (as advised by the Advisory Council on the Misuse of Drugs) and not the courts to classify drugs.

For offences involving Class A drugs, the maximum penalties are as follows:

1. For production, supply, offering to supply and possessing with intent to supply: life imprisonment and confiscation of assets (except for assets proved not to have been acquired as a result of drug trafficking)

2. For allowing premises to be used for producing or for unlawful prescribing: fourteen years' imprisonment

3. For possession: seven years' imprisonment.

For any of these offences, the Crown Court has the power to impose an unlimited fine in addition to or as well as imprisonment. If a magistrates' court hears the case, the maximum is six months' imprisonment and/or a fine of up to £5,000 for any offence in relation to Class A drugs.

All courts have the power to impose sentences such as community service or probation instead.

The Court of Appeal's guidelines for a Class A drug (as laid down in the Aramah, Bilinski and Arganuran cases) for offences other than simple possession are, briefly:

1. Fourteen years for importation of more than the equivalent of 5 kg of the drug at 100 per cent purity

2. Ten years for importation of 500 g to 5 kg

3. Four years for the importation of any appreciable amount

4. Three or more years' imprisonment for supply

5. There may be a considerable reduction in penalty if there is a confession of guilt coupled with considerable assistance to the police.

Precursors (chemicals that may be used to make MDMA) are controlled under section 12 of the Criminal Justice (International Co-operation) Act 1990 which was enacted following the signing of the Vienna Convention Against Illicit Traffic in Narcotic and Psychotropic Substances. This makes it an offence to manufacture or supply such a substance, knowing or suspecting it to be used in the unlawful production of a controlled drug. The maximum penalty for this offence is 14 years' imprisonment.

How the law is applied

The way you will be treated for a drug offence depends on whether you are considered to be a dealer or to have drugs for your own use. Dealers are charged with supply or with possession with intent to supply while users are charged with possession.

However, you will be considered to be a trafficker and charged with supply, if you pass on drugs to other people. It makes no difference whether you have made a profit, or if other people asked you to obtain the drugs for them. Even a gift to a friend of a single tab of ecstasy makes you guilty of supply. The fact that MDMA is a Class A drug means that a person convicted of an ecstasy offence can expect to be given a higher sentence than for one concerning a Class B drug (such as amphetamine) particularly if accused of supply.

Once the police have decided that they have clear evidence of a suspect's guilt, they must then consider what to do next and in particular whether or not to offer a caution. They will almost always prosecute for supply or intent to supply although they might offer a caution for the supply of a small amount of a controlled drug such as ecstasy to a partner for personal use.

A person found in possession of ecstasy is not always prosecuted. Police guidelines suggest prosecution is appropriate when a large amount of ecstasy is involved or if other crimes have been committed to pay for it, but not when the person concerned is undergoing treatment for their addiction or is willing to have treatment or another form of help.

Possession

If you are caught by the police in Britain with one or two pills, what happens to you depends very much on chance. The luckiest outcome will be if the police happen to be overloaded or concentrating on arresting a gang, when they may just confiscate the drugs and let you go. Normally they will arrest you and take you to the police station. Most of those arrested for possession are simply cautioned and let go, and this is more likely to happen in a big city, particularly London.

You may feel relieved if the police offer you a caution, but it is not always wise to accept. If you do accept a caution, you will have to admit the offence and (although it is not actually a conviction) the caution will be recorded on your criminal record just like a conviction. If you do not admit the offence and the police take no further action, then there is no formal record. So you should think carefully about it, and perhaps take advice from a solicitor.

If the police decide that you should be prosecuted, you will have to appear first in a magistrates' court. A typical penalty on conviction for a first offence of possession of a few tabs of ecstasy for own use might be a fine of £100 to £200.

In Scotland cautions are seldom given, but, if found guilty of possession of a small amount and you have no previous convictions, you stand a good chance of admonishment – no penalty on that occasion, but more severe penalties on a further offence.

Supply

B uying for your friends and even giving away drugs is defined as supply. If you are charged with supply, your case will almost certainly be heard at a Crown Court. Imprisonment is the usual penalty on conviction, unless your advocate persuades the court that you are not a dealer but simply supplying friends on a non-commercial basis. Sentences vary from 6 months to 5 years in most cases; again, chance plays a big part. Besides the quantity, being found with several different kinds of drug or a lot of cash will go against you, so will evidence that you were seen trying to sell drugs or that someone suffered as a result. Image counts too; if the court sees your trade as part of an organised operation rather than that of a naive individual, then you are in trouble.

What to do if you are arrested

D o not resist, make notes of exactly what happens including the police officers' numbers and what they say. *Ask for a solicitor*, or ask to phone Release who can advise you how to get one (0171 603 8654). If you cannot make notes on paper, then memorise events as best you can until you have the chance to write down what happened.

The reason for making notes is that the police quite often make mistakes in procedure which can sometimes be used to your advantage by your solicitor. Resistance may be interpreted as implying guilt, and could result in you being charged with another offence. Assistance from a solicitor is free to suspects held by the police, but you may have to wait in a cell, sometimes for a long time.

Legal advice may be particularly useful if the police are trying to strike a deal with you. This is quite common. A typical offer might run: "You confess that the pills are ecstasy, and I'll ask my supervisor to caution you and that will be the end of it." The pledge will usually be kept, but it has been known for suspects to be double-crossed. Once you have confessed, the policeman may come back and say, "Sorry, but my boss has decided to charge you all the same". The underlying reason for this is that if you confess to possessing ecstasy the police need not have the drug analysed, which can take up to 3 months and is not cheap.

Warrants

If the police arrive with a warrant, read it, ask for a copy and note what they do on your premises. Don't resist, the only way you can help yourself is to co-operate but object to any incorrect procedure later.

Searches

The police must have reasonable cause to search you – the mere fact you were in a place where drugs were on sale is not sufficient. Ask what their reason is for searching you and note what they reply. If the reason is not good enough, then the evidence so obtained should not be used against you.

Searches may include a strip search. Under section 55 of the Police and Criminal Evidence Act 1984 a senior police officer may authorise an intimate search of someone in detention whom he or she believes to be in possession of a class A drug. Ecstasy is Class A. An intimate search is now defined as a "search which consists of the physical examination of a person's body orifices other than the mouth". The mouth is excluded from this definition because there are fewer restrictions on the power of police to search a suspect's mouth, even to the extent of holding a suspect's jaw and nose to get him to gag and spit out something concealed in the mouth.

Intimate search is not allowed on people who are suspected of possession but not detained by the police. An unlawful intimate search by the police would be an assault, or indecent assault if the police search the genitals or anus. Intimate search means looking inside any part of the body, including the ears.

Blood and urine tests

You cannot be compelled to give samples except in traffic cases. However, the fact you have refused to give a sample may be used as evidence against you. See under Drug tests page 224.

The Criminal Justice Act

The Criminal Justice and Public Order Act 1994 introduced far-reaching changes in the law that makes it very difficult for suspects to know what to say and how to react after being arrested. The right to silence has been severely undermined, but there is still no obligation to answer police questions and the best advice will often still be not to answer them. What is new is that failure to mention something when questioned under caution by the police can count against you if the court decides you should reasonably have mentioned it then. It is now more important than ever to insist on your right to have a solicitor present when questioned and to talk to him or her in private before being interviewed. If there is something that may be important that you are holding back, it may be necessary in the interview to tell the police why. For example, it may be that you are in too much of a state of shock to think straight, you do not want to get someone else in trouble, or that the police have not given good enough reason for requiring you to answer the question. If your solicitor advises you not to answer questions he or she ought to tell the police this while the interview is being tape-recorded, giving your reasons if possible.

It is too early to say if the change in the law will achieve the Conservative government's declared aim of securing more convictions of guilty people, particularly professional criminals. If it does result in more convictions, these are more likely to be of innocent people than guilty, for criminals can plan their alibis and defences in advance, whereas the innocent cannot plan anything. What is certain is that police and court procedures will take much longer and will cost much more in police and court time and legal aid.

It is outrageous that the innocent now have to answer police questions and account for themselves or risk being convicted of something they have not done. We all have secrets but under the Act we keep them from the police at our peril and what we say will be private no more, for the police cannot always be trusted to keep confidences and in many circumstances do not have the power to do so.

The attack on the right to silence is not the only change made by the 1994 Act that may affect actual or suspected ecstasy users. If you are found with a pill or in a place where one is found and you refuse to account for its presence when asked, this could be held against you in court. In much the same way, if you are arrested and refuse to say why you were in the place where you were found, the court may be allowed to draw a sinister inference from your refusal. This could be relevant if you were arrested somewhere that drugs were sold.

Raves

The Criminal Justice and Public Order Act 1994 introduced new powers for the control of raves. The term "rave" is even used in the headings in the Act. As defined in the Act, a rave is a "gathering on land in the open air (including a place partly open to the air) of 100 or more persons (whether or not trespassers) at which amplified music is played during the night (with or without intermissions) and such as, by reasons of its loudness and duration at the time at which it is played, is likely to cause serious distress to the inhabitants of the locality". Music is described as "sounds wholly or predominantly characterised by the emission of a succession of repetitive beats". If there is an entertainment licence the definition of rave does not apply.

A senior police officer now has the power to require people preparing the rave, or waiting for it to take place, to leave. If they do not do so, they commit an offence. If are not removed, the police can remove vehicles and sound equipment. Police can stop people within five miles of a rave from travelling there and the courts have the power to confiscate sound equipment.

Night is not defined in the Act; presumably it begins at sunset. It does not matter if the event is commercial or not. A loud private party held in a marquee partly open to the air could be a rave under the 1994 Act, so perhaps we will see the police stopping guests on their way to wedding parties and arresting them if they disobey.

by Desmond Banks, a London solicitor

Clubs

The Public Entertainments Licensing (drugs misuse) Act 1997 has recently become law.

It gives the police power to close clubs if they suspect that drugs are being sold or used in or near the premises. The outcome has yet to be seen, but it effectively gives the police powers to close any club at will.

Tips for people charged with drugs offences

A friendly London policeman told me the procedure that the police must follow when someone is found in possession of small quantities of illicit drugs for personal use. This procedure is laid down by and for the Metropolitan Police. Other police forces probably use similar manuals. I have now seen a copy of the "Case Disposal Manual incorporating Specific and General Gravity Factors" and discussed the matter with a solicitor.

The manual lays down a precise procedure that has to be followed when someone is arrested. The aim is fairness, so that someone arrested is not treated differently according to which police station they are taken to or which policeman arrested them. The effect is to remove discretion from individual officers. The manual states that "The main thrust... in respect of drugs related offences is to target drug trafficking". 'Trafficking' means dealing, and does not apply to people found in possession of a 'small amount' for their own use. "The term 'small amount' may differ according to the circumstances surrounding the offence and the offender. A small amount for a first time user may differ greatly to an addict who may possess larger amounts for personal use..." This implies that someone found with a handful of tablets, who would normally be sent to prison for supply, may get off if the police believe they are addicted.

The procedure for dealing with a person arrested for being in possession of small amounts of any drug is first to find out if they have a police record. This will include previous convictions, cautions and formal warnings. Whether the case goes to court will depend on such 'gravity factors', but if the person has no police record, the rules say that they should not be taken to court but instead be Cautioned or given a Formal Warning.

The Custody Officer will usually say that if you confess, he will 'let you off' with a Caution rather than prosecute. The law does give him the authority to decide, but his job is to follow the procedure laid down in the Case Disposal Manual. Before deciding to prosecute, he must also be satisfied that there is enough evidence to win the case and that the cost of the case is justified, otherwise his decision will be overturned by the Crown Prosecution Service. The Custody Officer would have to provide good reasons to his superiors to go against the guidelines.

When the police want to prosecute, they have to prepare a file which is examined by the Director of Public Prosecutions and it is they who decide. They will only take you to court if the police have shown that they have enough evidence to win; that it is in the public interest when the cost of the case is taken into account, and if the local courts have capacity (the most serious cases take priority).

Cautions and Formal Warnings

A Caution can only be given if you have admitted the offence. You will not be charged but you will have a police record, just like a criminal record, which is kept on computer and will be available to any policeman, even in the street. If you are later prosecuted, it can be mentioned in court (although the court will not punish you for the offence it relates to). A Formal Warning is only recorded in the local police station, not on computer, so that if you are stopped again in another police area it will not be known about, and in practice is usually not checked even in the same police area. In practice it is the same as being let off altogether.

Caution

If the police say they will let you off with a Caution and you refuse to accept it, they must either prosecute you or give you a Formal Warning. You may be afraid that they will plant more drugs or invent worse evidence if you don't accept the Caution, but my informant says that, although the police do bluff a lot, they do keep to the rules and are basically honest, "at least on my level as a uniformed policeman or CID officer". If you have not admitted the offence and the police have any doubt at all about winning, then the policeman's advice is to refuse the Caution and be given a Formal Warning instead.

How to behave

Make yourself easy for the police to handle but without incriminating yourself. The most important thing is to insist that any suspect drugs in your possession are for your own consumption as otherwise you will be dealt with as a dealer. Secondly, do not identify what they are. If you have pills with a logo on them, it is fair to say that you do not know what drug they contain and that they may contain none at all. Without your confession they will have to be analysed, increasing the cost of the case and making it more likely to be thrown out by the CPS (see above).

How to avoid arrest

If you don't want your drugs to be found, keep them in your underpants. To carry out an 'intimate search', the police have to take you to a police station and follow a tedious procedure, and they try to avoid that. They have to justify the search to their superiors, such as that friends in the same car were found with drugs. But if all of them had put the drugs in their underpants, then none would be charged. Obviously there is a fair amount of luck involved, but if you do not admit that any substances are illegal drugs then they must be analysed and the extra expense will reduce the chance of a court case.

More tips

If the police stop a car full of people and ask them to get out, and then find some pills on the floor, they do not have not enough evidence to charge anyone unless someone admits it is theirs. They will usually say they will "charge the lot of you" to try to get someone to confess, but this is bluff. However, this would enable them to get a search warrant to search the homes of all the occupants. If pills were found in your car, you are less likely to be tried in court if you do not admit they were yours. If one person in a car tells the police that the drugs found belong to someone else he identifies in the hope of getting off, he could find that instead he is accused of 'conspiracy to supply'.

Court Reports

If you are charged with an offence in certain circumstances, it may be in your best interests to have a lawyer request a Court Report, an expert witness opinion, from an expert in the area. You should not contact the expert yourself. These circumstances include being in an abnormal state of mind at the time, including a state due to drug use, committing an offence because you are addicted to a drug and need treatment; and being charged with intent to supply because you are in possession of a large quantity of a drug for your own use because you are addicted to it.

Expert witnesses follow a strict ethical code, and are bound to tell the truth. If your story is false, bear in mind that the expert may detect this and make their opinion known to the court. It is not the role of the expert to decide on your guilt or innocence, that is entirely the role of the court: usually a jury in drug cases. Thus experts are not always in your best interests. They are a source of accurate information for the court, not part of your defence team. It is best to use expert witnesses only if you are telling the truth, as they can be a two-edged sword.

There are currently only a limited number of recognised expert witnesses who have a comprehensive knowledge of ecstasy use. Your lawyer can check the Law Society Directory of Expert Witnesses. Organisations such as Release can also be helpful in locating expert witnesses. Dr. Karl Jansen, the author of the chapter in this book on adverse psychiatric effects, sometimes acts in this capacity.

Are you in possession of the contents of your stomach?

The law refers to possession, and it has been established in a case where a man admitted to swallowing illegal drugs that he was no longer in possession, even after the police had his stomach pumped and the contents analysed. The judge said that the man was no more in possession of the drug than someone would be in possession of a glass of whisky after they had drunk it.

References

1. Phone conversation with Mike Evans, at the Home Office February 1993.

Ecstasy Deaths

By Dr Russell Newcombe

oral panics about drug use and deviant behaviour among young people have a long history (eg. Cohen 1973; Silver 1979). Since the late 1980s, the British mass media have spent many column inches and sound-bytes warning the public about the dangers of ecstasy/MDMA, a "new" drug taken by young people at dance parties (initially called raves). In particular, the media have given great attention to deaths linked to the use of ecstasy, using headlines such as "Ecstasy and the Dance of Death" and "the Ecstasy and the Agony".

This reached a peak in late 1995 with the case of Leah Betts, who was reported to have died after taking ecstasy for the first time at her 18th birthday party, although it later emerged she had taken ecstasy and other illicit drugs several times before. During 1996 and early 1997, the mass media have continued to highlight "casualties" of ecstasy, attacking almost anyone who made statements which did not condemn the drug.

Is ecstasy use or raving associated with a significant mortality trend among its participants? This short paper attempts to examine this question, by assessing the two main sources of relevant information:

(1) Official statistics and information on drug-related deaths in the UK;

(2) News stories about relevant incidents in the mass media.

Official statistics

First, there are two additive sources of official statistics on drug-related deaths: figures based on death certificates indicating controlled drugs as causal factors in fatal poisonings, and figures based on Coroners' verdicts of death from dependent or non-dependent drug abuse (Home Office 1996). Between 1979 and 1994 there were 48 fatal poisonings involving stimulant amphetamines and/or ecstasy, peaking at 14 in 1994. Separate figures for ecstasy are available for 1993 and 1994 only and show that 12 out of 20 relevant deaths over those two years involved ecstasy. Between 1980 and 1994 there were also 91 drug abuse deaths involving stimulant amphetamines, and 39 involving MDMA/MDA. These peaked at 17 in 1993 for speed, and 19 in 1994 for ecstasy. There is a general upward trend in both types of mortality since 1988, averaging 10 per annum for speed and five or six per annum for ecstasy.

The proportion of annual drug-related fatalities which involved dance drugs peaked in 1994, at 3% for fatal poisonings and 7% for drug abuse deaths (opiates and benzodiazepines are the main culprits). Four in five such deaths involved males, with the peak age range for deaths being 20-24 years, though fatal cases of ecstasy poisoning were more likely to occur across the 16-24 age band, compared with fatal poisonings on speed (which were more common in the 25-44 age band).

Employing prevalence statistics from the 1991 British Crime Survey, the drug-specific mortality rates for users of each drug were estimated. In general, the mortality rate among speed users was higher than that among ecstasy users, though the 1994 rate was twice as low as the rate for ecstasy (three amphetamine-related poisoning deaths per 100,000 speed users, compared with six ecstasy-related deaths per estimated 100,000 ecstasy users). These mortality rates are far lower than those associated with other psychoactive drugs such as opiates and hypnosedatives.

Mass media reports

The second source of information is relevant deaths reported in the mass media, notably the press. Between 1988 and 1996 there were 100 deaths linked to dance drugs or dance parties in the press. The unreliability of many press reports must be kept in mind when interpreting breakdowns of this figure. First, 75 of these deaths were linked to ecstasy – an average of about eight ecstasy-related deaths per year (with a range of zero to 20).

No clear trends are discernible over the nine-year period (1988-96), except that annual numbers of ecstasy-related deaths appear to have peaked around 1992 and 1994. All but three of the ecstasy-linked deaths were known or believed to have involved ecstasy – there was only one reported fatality involving MDEA (1992), and two reported cases involving MDA (1992 and 1993).

A further 15 deaths (15%) were related to other dance drugs (excluding ecstasy), averaging one or two per year. Amphetamines were involved in nine of these deaths, LSD in five cases, and GHB (gamma-hydroxy-butyrate) in one case. Third, 10 cases were reported to involve non-drug deaths at dance parties/clubs (typically homicide). 80% of the deaths involved males, and the peak age-range was 18-20 years. The typical ecstasy-linked death involved use of one tablet/capsule, with no other drug use reported. The estimated mortality rate was between two and five deaths per 100,000 ecstasy users.

Results

The above analyses, combined with the findings of recent research studies, suggest the following picture. That the typical "dance drug death" in Britain involved a young male, who became ill after taking drugs at a dance party or nightclub, and who later died in hospital. Ecstasy was frequently singled out as the main contributory factor in the death by medical or legal professionals (eg doctors, coroners). However, this picture is partly at odds with the official statistics on drug-related deaths which suggest that the stimulant amphetamines are generally involved in significantly more deaths than ecstasy and its chemical cousins.

Indeed, compared with other popular drugs, ecstasy has a relatively low mortality rate. In a factsheet on drug-related deaths issued in September 1996, the Institute for the Study of Drug Dependence (ISDD) compared the annual mortality rates for four different types of drug, estimated on the basis of the available evidence about prevalence, consumption and deaths up to 1994. The reported mortality rates were 1.5% to 3% for opiate users, 0.9% for tobacco users, 0.5% for alcohol users, and 0.0002% for ecstasy users. Although the mortality rates reported for each drug were based on different kinds of source data and estimation procedures, ISDD concluded that "however calculated, it is clear that related to the user-base, deaths associated with ecstasy are rare".

In conclusion, the statistical risk of death from use of ecstasy – or other dance drugs such as LSD, cannabis or amphetamines – appears to be very low, at least in the short to medium term. These low mortality rates are particularly notable when comparisons are made with other popular drugs – such as alcohol, tobacco, opiates and hypnosedatives. Indeed, the statistical risk of death from the use of ecstasy or from attending raves is also lower than the risks associated with many socially acceptable activities and lifestyles – including sports and leisure activities like skiing, mountain climbing, and fairground rides.[4]

The relatively low mortality risks of ecstasy use seem to hold true across Europe, though drug-related death monitoring systems vary widely from one country to another.

> *Despite intense publicity ... it is clear that the risk of death per dose taken is far lower for ecstasy than for injected heroin ... In countries where ecstasy and similar drugs are integral to certain sectors of youth culture, even conservative consumption estimates run into millions of 'doses' taken annually; in this context the risk of death is low but of concern.*
>
> *- Annual Report on the State of the Drugs Problem in the European Union (European Communities 1996, p.14).*

In seeming ignorance of these expert opinions, the British mass media instigated a new tidal wave of hysteria about ecstasy during the first few months of 1997. Although the objective basis for this renewed moral panic reports of a number of ecstasy-linked deaths over the Christmas/New Year holiday period (in fact there were no more than usual), it was fuelled by media reports of "pro-ecstasy" comments made by members of pop groups such as *East 17* and *Oasis*. In particular, the tabloid press raged for revenge on these "youth role-models", with extensive coverage given to the views of the parents of ecstasy "victims" concerning these new "folk devils". Draconian legislation to close down any nightclub at which drugs are sold was already being hurried through Parliament. During this furore, a Labour MP called for additional legislation making it an offence to "incite" people to use drugs by publicly "promoting" them (punishable by up to five years imprisonment). In all this moral heat, the only light thrown on the issue came from an editorial in the *New Scientist* magazine:

> *In the middle of a panic, what's needed is for everyone to calm down. And that's just the treatment Britain requires for the current panic over the drug ecstasy. Following the heart-rending deaths of several teenagers who were apparently trying ecstasy for the first time, it has become impossible to express any sensible opinion on the drug. Either you condemn ecstasy use out of hand, or you risk being seen as in favour of killing children ... The real problem in dealing with ecstasy is the huge gap in the perception of the drug between those who take it and those who do not. And the real scandal is our lack of understanding of its long-term risks.*
>
> *- 25th January 1997.*

Conclusion

The negative consequences of our moral panic about ecstasy include the potential health risks that users are left to face years or decades from now, and the current fashion to find scapegoats among those in the nightclub and pop music business. In addition to carrying out too little relevant research and passing too much unjust legislation, Britain may also be witnessing the start of sinister changes in medical policy toward ecstasy users. On November 27th 1995, Michelle Paul, aged 15 years, took half an ecstasy tablet; she became ill, and was taken to Edinburgh's Royal Infirmary, where she died. The pathologist stated that her liver had shrunk to one third its normal size and that her brain was grossly swollen. Michelle Paul died just two weeks after Leah Betts. While the press hysteria on the Betts case was still raging, Paul's death was hardly reported in the press. In January 1997, the fatal accident inquiry at Aberdeen sheriff court was attended by the mother of Michelle Paul. She claimed that the surgeon who attended her daughter refused to save her life by carrying out a liver transplant, on the moral grounds that the young woman was a drug misuser.

References

Cohen S. (1973). Folk Devils and Moral Panics. Paladin.

Henry J. (1992). ecstasy and the dance of death. *British Medical Journal*, 305, 6-7.

Home Office (1996). Statistics of drug addicts notified to the Home Office, UK, 1995. Croydon: Government Statistical Service.

Milroy C., Clark J. & Forrest A. (1996). Pathology of deaths associated with ecstasy and eve misuse. Journal of Clinical Pathology, 49, 149-53.

Mixmag (1997). Clubbers: the death toll rises. *Mixmag* (dance music/club culture magazine), 2 (69), February 1997 [and previous issues]

Mott J. & Mirrlees-Black C. (1995). Self-reported drug misuse in England & Wales:findings from the 1992 *British Crime Survey*. London: Home Office.

Newcombe, R. (1997). ecstasy deaths and other fatalities related to dance drugs and raving. Liverpool: 3D Research Bureau.

New Scientist (1997). Press the panic button. Editorial, 27th January 1997.

Saunders N. (1996). *ecstasy and Dance Culture*. London: Neals Yard.

Silver G. (ed)(1979). *The Dope Chronicles* 1850-1950. San Francisco: Harper & Row.

Steele T., McCann U. & Ricaurte G. (1994). 3,4-Methylenedioxymethamphetamine (MDMA, ecstasy): pharmacology and toxicology in animals and humans. *Addiction*, 89, 539-551.

Dr. Russell Newcombe, 26/5/57, separated, 2 kids, existentialist, philosphically adrift BA in Social Psychology (Sussex Uni 1979), PhD in Social Psychology (Kent Uni 1986) Main research posts: Drug Misuse in Wirral (1985-87, Liverpool Uni); Director, Drugs & HIV Monitoring Unit (1988-91, Mersey RHA) Research Fellow, Alcohol Drugs & Crime Project (1991-93,Manchester Uni) Director, 3D Research Bureau, 47 Arundel Av, Liverpool L17 3BY; 0151-280-9690 (independent drugs research and consultancy service). Books: Co-author of "Living with Heroin" (OU Books, 1988) Co-editor of "The Reduction of Drug-Related Harm" (Routledge 1992) Writer of "Potology: Dr. Nuke's Guide to the Science of Cannabis and the Sociology of Getting Stoned" (Lifeline Publications, Manchester, 1995) Forthcoming (1997): "Wizology: Dr. Nuke's Guide to the Science of Stimulant Amphetamines and the Sociology of Speeding" Recent publications and reports: "Live and let die: is methadone more likely to kill you than heroin?" Druglink, 11,9-12 (1996) "Staying Alive: how safe is methadone?" Juice (the Methadone Magazine, Issue 1 (1996). "Drug Misuse in Suffolk", Report to Suffolk Health Authority, 1997. "Ecstasy-related deaths and other fatalities related to dance drugs and dance parties", 1997, revised report, 3D Research Bureau, Liverpool. "The behaviour of customers of dance music clubs and parties in Britain between 1988 and

1996: an overview of a series of studies"; 3D Research Bureau, Liverpool, 1997.

After over 10 years as a kind of double-agent on the British drugs scene, I have reached the inescapable conclusion that it is five minutes past midnight in the war on drugs – prohibition has failed. Controlled availability of drugs is the best alternative policy, but given the pervasive mythology about drugs, stupidly perpetuated by the mass media, this may be a long time coming. In the meantime, the best strategy is harm reduction – though this is going out of fashion in mid 1990s Britain. It is presently being insidiously replaced by a stricter law and order approach – though historical analysis suggests that this is a but a sign of the final death throes of drug prohibition.

Uses

Ecstasy is now generally regarded as a dance drug, but it was previously used for many years in other ways – dancing was not even mentioned in the 1989 edition of the book 'Ecstasy, the MDMA Story'. This chapter is about non-dance uses.

The drug is used in situations which require letting go of inhibitions while remaining grounded. It can help people, who are normally blocked by self consciousness, to express themselves as in art. It can also help with problem solving.

Ecstasy can help people to allow suppressed emotional material to come to the surface and be looked at without fear; this can be used as an aid to psychotherapy or for self-development.

The empathic quality of ecstasy helps people relate to one another honestly. This makes it a suitable drug for use in resolving conflicts, for example between family members or work colleagues.

Some people use it to keep fit through dancing as an alternative to the gym. Some sportsmen have also made use of ecstasy in their training.

The use of ecstasy as a spiritual tool and for psychotherapy is dealt with in other chapters.

Artistic expression

Ecstasy can be used as an aid to drawing, writing, playing music,[1] singing[2] or other artistic activities. Very often the effect of the drug is to open up the artist, sometimes uncomfortably, to a broader perspective. There have been creative writing workshops where the participants take a small amount of MDMA, about half a normal dose, and set to work.[3] Some find it good for inspiration, and in particular is useful for overcoming writer's block.[4]

Drawing and painting

Several artists have told me how ecstasy has influenced their work, not always for the better. In Los Angeles, I visited an artist who had earned a comfortable living for many years by painting pictures which, he now says, people liked because they were 'easy on the eye, the kind of stuff chosen by interior designers'.

The third time he took ecstasy was in a house with one of his paintings. He saw it as 'complete crap', and could never paint that way again. His style became more abstract and gutsy, with strong dark lines which he felt expressed his true feelings. The trouble was that they didn't sell.

In 1995 I organised two events where artists tried the effect of E on their work. In the first, they paired up and drew portraits of each other. Then they had a break, took E, and drew the same person's portrait again. My main concern beforehand was that people would become distracted and never finish, but in fact everyone became absorbed in their painting.

The second drawings tended to be less disciplined, and some said they were unable to be precise, although nearly everyone preferred them as being more expressive. The exception, who was professional, simply felt that he had lost his technique and gained nothing.

For the second session, I asked people to use paints if possible, and had them draw a nude model. This was less successful but an interesting lesson: the greater distance from the model (physically and emotionally) meant they had less empathy with their subject, and several felt uncomfortable using paints, especially since the room was carpeted.

In the first case, they sat facing each other and were close enough to become totally absorbed by the other person, so that on E they developed empathy and the freedom to express it.

It seems as though the ideal situation is when artist and model both take E, sit close and draw each other's face using a medium they are completely at ease with in a place where they are not worried about making a mess. It is also helpful if they draw each other before taking E so as to focus their attention on the project.

Creativity [4]

"There are two ways of using MDMA that may help elicit creativity. In the first, the creative task is attempted during the MDMA session. In the second, the MDMA session is used to generate ideas that later may be applied to the creative task". Painting, sculpting, writing and music are suggested for the first, while the second is suggested for overcoming writer's block.

Artist's flavour enhancer [3]

One artist described MDMA as a flavour enhancer. A writer described how ecstasy allowed him to engross himself more in the content, and to allow his descriptive prose to flow more spontaneously.

Poetry and philosophy

I am certain that it is due to ecstasy on a weekly basis that I have developed this intense desire like never before for philosophy, poetry and deep conversation... I feel totally moved and in love with the world of literature.

- A 23 year old woman reader

Drumming [1]

John finds E good for playing drums, as creativity is improved and it allows him to be in touch without the fear that normally censors free expression – "If you are trying, then you're not where it's at". However, 2CB is much better for playing more sophisticated instruments, since the use of ecstasy lacks the necessary discipline.

Jam sessions

I go clubbing every weekend and I also write poetry/songs. I play the mouth organ and sing – often friends come round and we drop, then jam together – it is really creative and "bonding".

- A reader

Poetry

I've been writing poetry since I was a child and I'm also published. Part of my ecstasy usage was to help instigate more creative output. It didn't make me more prolific but it did shine added insights on language uses I'd not explored before.

The greatest asset of E on my creative juices was mainly one of "loosening" the brain muscle and not exerting so much control on the flow (ergo: kicking the proverbial inner editor in the butt).

- A reader

Ecstasy does tend to produce a looser and more expressive style which can be refreshing, but has disadvantages. It reduces the ability for delicate motor control. Second, some people find that it reduces the artistic tension or 'angst'.

A BBC TV programme tried a similar experiment using Prozac. The conclusion was that the drug may reduce angst, but that overall it did not impair creativity.

Another method for overcoming writer's block is to focus on the idea of writing while taking a normal dose, but to leave the actual writing until afterwards.

Some London enthusiasts have put on events involving music, drama and art with both artists and audience on MDMA. Thus not only is the expression of the art made freer, but also its interpretation: "The artistic experience becomes almost religious", says a performer with experience of using MDMA.

Problem solving

This is best done on a normal dose within an hour of the effect coming on, as this is when the effect is strongest. It is useful to write down your problem before you start. For instance, you could decide to look at your relationship with your mother and why you avoid her. Or why you don't enjoy your job. Or to find out whether you really love someone (who is not present). It's a good idea to have a tape recorder handy and record how you see things. Failing this, have pen and paper ready, but you may find that thoughts come so quickly that it is hard to write fast enough, and that you are reluctant to make the effort.[5]

This exercise can provide insights; described by some as an unobstructed view, perhaps the way you might see your situation if you were looking back a year or two later. However, a study indicated that judgement may sometimes be impaired by ecstasy,[6] so any new insights should be evaluated later before they are acted upon.

I have tried MDMA for problem solving, but the first time got completely distracted into having fun – the exercise takes discipline. The second time I took MDMA with an old friend with the specific intention of resolving problems and examining relationships in our lives. We each wrote down a list of subjects that we wanted to explore beforehand, and spent the first hour after the drug came on concentrating on one issue at a time.

I had snapped at an ex-neighbour and this had shocked me as I couldn't see why I had done it. But on ecstasy it seemed clear: I felt threatened by the people who had moved into his flat and he had 'caused' this problem by having moved out. Next I focused my attention on one particular friend whom I had always admired for what he had achieved in the face of enormous difficulties. My image of him was shattered and instead I saw him as a Chinese juggler spinning plates on bamboo sticks, desperately rushing from one to the other to forestall a catastrophe. These didn't seem like revelations, more as though I had known all the time, yet these were viewpoints that I had not seen before. On later reflection, I assessed these insights on MDMA as valid and useful but not the complete picture.

Picturing the future

Several techniques taken from Neuro Linguistic Programming (NLP) and hypnotherapy can be used when on MDMA.

While on MDMA it is possible to address a problem you expect to face in the future using proven techniques. For example, you may have a colleague at work who you don't get on with, but whose point of view you can appreciate on MDMA and with whom you could have a much better working relationship if you could be open and appreciative at work. The technique is, while on E, to visualize your work situation and how you would relate to it, then try to apply the insight to the real life situation.[4]

Another technique is to visualize a situation in the future after you have achieved a goal, such as getting the job you want or marrying the person you desire. Imagine yourself settled in the new job or marriage and look back at how you got there. From this perspective, maybe you can see what was needed more clearly than looking forward, or perhaps you can see other possible ways of achieving your aim.

The third technique is to check whether your goal will really satisfy your needs. Imagine having achieved your goal in the example above and see how it feels. After the initial excitement of the novelty and achievement has waned, are you satisfied? Does it restrict you? What do you look forward to – another goal, or developing this new position? Was it the right goal?

Future pacing [4]

One suggestion for using the MDMA experience for later benefit is called 'future pacing'. Here you conjure up, while in your alternative state, a mental image of people or situations which you would like to experience in an open and empathic way. Then you construct an image, visual, auditory, and/or kinaesthetic, of an experience of being in the MDMA state while with those persons or in that life situation. In the days ahead, your experience of the person or situation focused on might change as a result of this exercise.

Imaginary journeys

This technique can be used purely for fun or to learn more about yourself. Ask a partner to talk you through a journey where you face various difficulties and pleasures. The E state will help you to feel the situations and respond to them emotionally. Your partner notes your responses and discusses them with you afterwards.

I was told about someone who had decided to go travelling to the third world for the first time. A friend who was a veteran traveller took him on a fantasy journey based on some of his real-life experiences, from the exhilaration of visiting an Amazonian tribe to the misery of being ill with malaria. Even though the guide was not on MDMA, he said that he relived his experiences just because he had such a good audience.

Mini vacation

For people with an intense and busy lifestyle, ecstasy can provide as much relaxation in two days as a week on a tropical island. A London acquaintance made the comparison:

> I like to work hard without a break, and then have a holiday. But if I go away for a week I spend the first half of it winding down and the last day getting geared up again, leaving only two days of actual relaxation. But about a year ago I started to take MDMA with a friend who is also a workaholic, and now it's become a three monthly event. We go to his cottage in Kent for a weekend, sometimes with one or two others. On Saturday morning we take the MDMA along with our first cup of tea, and just allow ourselves to slump into a sumptuous state of relaxation, sometimes dancing a bit but mainly just lying around blissed out. We sort of agree that we are not going to talk much or do anything to distract the others during the first few hours, but in the afternoon we usually go for a walk and talk quite a lot about what happened for us, and how we saw each other. By evening we are hungry and go to bed early, and next day get up late and sit around and talk again. It's all very low key, but actually some of my best ideas have occurred to me on those weekends.

There is an American report on similar use in the US, based on interviews with 100 people who have hectic lifestyles.[7] The report describes a very organised approach with much advance preparation and precise doses being matched to the person's weight. Some will rent a house for the weekend and follow a well-worn routine.

Sport

Some sportsmen find that ecstasy can help them to feel relaxed and confident, and that this can make a significant difference to their performance.

Basketball

I play basketball and have seen many talented people who can do practically anything in practice, but seem to lack the confidence in a game situation. I normally just take ecstasy on Saturday nights and never more than one. Its hard to say there's a drastic improvement, but I feel more confident and cocky when playing.

- A reader

Mini vacations [7]

"During the trip there is much warm, affectionate conversation, a feeling of bonding and closeness with friends. Generally, the spirit is positive and euphoric. There is much affirmation of life, of relationships," the report says.

The second day is spent quietly together, regarded as a valuable part of the experience, when the "best interactive work can be done".

International sportsman

I am an international sportsman and at first I was shocked to see other sportsmen taking ecstasy, but eventually I tried it. I now use it regularly and find it has changed my life in small constructive ways. For one, I very rarely drink any more. I keep just as fit with less training: a good night out at a club is like a long gym session. And I feel more confident.

–A reader

Keeping fit

According to Sheila Henderson, who ran a research project on women ecstasy users in Manchester;

> The motivations for raving and keeping fit are similar. They are about pleasure-seeking, socialising, music and body image. The difference is that one's naughty and the other's nice. One makes you feel virtuous, the other you enjoy because it's a bit deviant. The combination of dancing all night and burning up calories is attractive to figure-conscious girls. Lots of women mess themselves up by going on crash diets. Many are now taking ecstasy to slim.[8]

However, she adds that the switch from the gym to the rave is not so much a deliberate act – more that raving fulfils the same role as the gym, and provides an alternative lifestyle with similar benefits.

Massage [9]

Massage benefits can be amplified using low doses. For the masseur, the drug helps tune in to the client; while the recipient's ultra relaxed state allows for much greater appreciation.

Treating addiction

Although there is no study to date, there are anecdotal reports that ecstasy can help cocaine[10] and heroin addicts to break their habit, of which a personal account is included on page 265-6.

Treatment of alcoholism is another possibility.[11] A trial on alcoholic rats showed that they consumed less alcohol and more water when given MDMA.[12]

Alcoholic rats [12]

Alcoholic rats were given free access to food, water and ten per cent alcohol. After being injected with MDMA for three consecutive days, they drank less alcohol and more water from the time of the first dose, with the effect diminishing to nothing three days after the last dose. No behavioural changes were noticed on MDMA, implying that the results are direct effects of the drug. This suggests a possible use in treating alcoholism.

Relationships [13]

Unlike LSD and other drugs, MDMA works in terms of relationships – with oneself, God, nature. It even opens up a common ground with strangers.

Relieving pain

There is growing interest in MDMA's potential as a pain killer. This has been stimulated by observed effects of the drug: that when people injure themselves while they are under its influence they can easily accept the pain[14]; that it appears to enhance the effect of morphine[15] and that it dissolves fear, which can include the fear of death. Dr John Henry of the National Poisons Unit believes that MDMA stimulates opioids, a neurotransmitter that acts like a pain killer. This occurs when people injure themselves at sport.[14]

Russian researchers are also interested in doing research on using MDMA for pain relief, and, with funding from the west, hope to investigate MDMA for the treatment of alcoholism, neurosis and also terminal cancer patients.[11]

Relationships

A unique effect of ecstasy is to increase empathy and this may be used to enhance relationships.[9,13,16] Ecstasy was regularly used in a large community in New Zealand where several hundred people would take it together in order to develop their relationships. This is described under Personal Accounts.

Making friends

At a recent occasion (when artists drew each other) the discussion turned to where they had met their friends. The consensus was that 80 per cent of their friendships had been made while under the influence of ecstasy.

Conflict resolution [9]

MDMA produces predictable feelings including empathy, openness, peace and caring. With the right intention, individuals are able to use the MDMA state to resolve long-standing intrapsychic conflicts or interpersonal problems in relationships.

Deeper friendships

My friends and I continue the same conversations we had on E, and this has resulted in a change from superficial to deep and heartfelt relationships in our daily lives.

- A reader

Depression cured

I had been receiving psychiatric help for chronic depression following the loss of my wife. For nearly two years I had been unable to communicate with my friends, go out socially or have any contact with the opposite sex.

One particularly suicidal night I was dragged out to a pub by an old friend. He put an E in my mouth and I thought – What have I got to lose? What followed was a very bewildering quarter of an hour followed by my first happy evening in two years. My face actually ached next day because it was so unused to smiling. Within a month my depression was all but gone and a revitalised social life led to romance and a new record contract.

I now live with my lover, it's the best relationship ever. We have a pact that we only take the same pills together, so we always share the same experience. It works magnificently, avoiding jealousy and promoting a spiritual bond. I have had my first top 40 success in years, and normally make music the day after an E. My quality of life has spiralled upwards.

- Letter from a musician

Couple relationships

Very often couples become estranged over the years, relating to each other in less open and intimate ways. This may have advantages, such as providing a working relationship that avoids arguments, but it usually goes with an empty emotional life. Taking ecstasy together has been called a marriage saver.[18] The experience can break through barriers built up over many years and, with these removed, restores intimacy to a relationship. One woman described her experience:

We were at each other's throats when Andrew said, 'Look, this is ridiculous, let's take that E we hid away and try to enjoy life like we used to'. I agreed, with some sarcastic comment about not being able to face the situation without drugs, and after taking it we carried on pulling each other to pieces. I remember saying to myself, 'No drug will make him see sense,

I'm going to divorce him.' But as I was preparing my next onslaught I felt my aggression slide away and the intensity of my argument became deflated until I felt a bit silly.

Andrew was not yet hit by the drug but, as he told me later, without my anger it felt like fighting a sponge: he couldn't carry on without opposition. I had felt confused: on one hand I was desperately trying to gear myself up to continue the battle, but the ammunition kept melting. I gave in and laughed, and so did Andrew. Soon I was crying, not out of sorrow for how I'd behaved but because we'd wasted so much of our marriage blaming each other instead of enjoying life. We both went through a lot of pain, but we ended up knowing we belonged together, and even now when we row we can see how petty it really is. I don't think we will ever get so bogged down again.

Ending relationships

Taking ecstasy does not always have an obviously happy ending. Another estranged couple who took MDMA opened their hearts to one another, but while the man expressed love for his wife, she confessed that she did not love him and had never enjoyed making love with him. As a result the marriage broke up. Indeed, some therapists believe that the best use of MDMA among couples is resolving a peaceful end to a relationship.[17]

Ending relationships

In couple therapy using MDMA, Dr Martha Rosenbaum's experience is that MDMA is more useful for making a split than mending relationships, by allowing couples to resolve their differences with compassion for one another. The best use, she believes, is in conflict resolution.

Parents-in-law

A London doctor got married to a woman whom his parents disliked and refused to accept even in their seventies. He desperately wanted to resolve the relationship amicably, especially when his father had cancer and had not long to live, and managed to persuade his parents to take ecstasy with him and his wife. His wife opened up and told his parents how hurt she had been by their rejection and how much their respect mattered to her, and in that open state she was able to be her true self for them to see. His father listened and made eye contact with her for the first time and it seemed like a breakthrough. However, next day he maintained that the drug had had no effect on him and never referred to the event again. His mother was far more open and enjoyed it, although afterwards she said it was a change rather than fun. Outwardly the situation remained the same, but the doctor was convinced that his parents were more understanding.

Parent-child

A woman, whose husband had left her, had become estranged from her 13-year-old daughter. It was a typical teenage rebellion with the girl staying out all night and the mother feeling she had lost control; conversation was limited to hurtful sniping. One day the mother was amazed and delighted to find that her daughter wanted to curl up in bed with her and talk about intimate secrets. Unknown to the daughter, the mother had taken ecstasy the day before – although the main effect had worn off, the residual afterglow must have made her approachable. Hostilities returned, but so did these times of closeness.

Another woman took ecstasy with her 20-year-old daughter at a party. They were on good terms anyway, but the conversations they had under the influence of ecstasy reinforced the deep affection they felt for each other.

Siblings

"Siblings always have a lot of shit together".[1,18] As adults, there are always a number of unresolved issues relating to childhood, such as one bullying the other or receiving more attention from parents. Taking ecstasy together as adults allows long-suppressed resentments to be looked at and resolved, and underlying love for one another to be expressed.

Family reunion

As a Father's day treat, a middle aged man chose to spend a day with his family on ecstasy. The parents and two grown up sons all enjoyed the occasion, and look back on it as one that bonded them together again as a family of adults after a separation caused by teenage rebellion and leaving home.[1]

Brother helps sister [1]

John's sister (in her late 40s) was devastated when her husband left her, having no social life of her own. Although they were not close and she did not do drugs, John persuaded her to spend a day with him on E. It was an amazing day of exchange of heartfelt feelings between them, going back over events in their lives and establishing that they really did care for one another, providing her with the confidence that she was not completely alone.

Understanding parents

I used to hate my parents. One night I went clubbing and took an E as usual, but I wasn't in the mood so I came home early.

My parents arrived home from visiting friends just afterwards, and they were in a good mood (having had a bit to drink) and pleased to see me. Instead of annoying me as usual, I felt really good towards them and saw how they cared for me too. We've been getting on better ever since.

- A reader

References

1. Interview with a musician and visiting dealer in California, November 1993.

2. *Through the Gateway of the Heart* (book) published by Four Trees Publications, San Francisco 1985. This book is a collection of some 60 subjective accounts of positive experiences by users and "guidelines for the sacramental use of empathogenic substances". The accounts are divided into men's, women's and group experiences.

3. *The Pursuit of Ecstasy – the MDMA Experience* by Gerome Beck and Marsha Rosenbaum published 2/94 by State University of New York Press at $14.95.

4. *Ecstasy: The MDMA Story*, by Bruce Eisner published 1994 at $17.95 by Ronin Publishing Inc., PO Box 1035, Berkeley, CA 94701, USA.

5. Letter and manuscript from Myron Stolaroff January 1994.

6. *The Psychological and Physiological Effects of MDMA* on Normal Volunteers, by Joseph Downing, from *Journal of Psychoactive Drugs*, Vol. 18/4 1986.

7. *International Journal on Drug Policy*, Vol. 2 10/89 *Ethnographic Notes on Ecstasy Use Among Professionals* by Rosenbaum, Morgan and Beck.

8. Fit for anything, by Sarah Champion, *The Guardian*, 12 April 1993.

9. *The Nature of the MDMA Experience* by Ralph Metzner and Sophia Adamson in *ReVision*, Spring 1988.

10. Visit to and subsequent communications from Clive, part time dealer in California, who attends many events.

11. *Research in Russia*, from *MAPS* November 1991.

12. *Attenuation of Alcohol Consumption by MDMA in Two Strains of Alcohol-Preferring Rats*, by Amir Rezvani et al., 1991, from *Pharmacology, Biochemistry and Behaviour*, vol. 43.

13. Visit to a Soto Zen monk and teacher.

14. Visit to Dr John Henry at the National Poisons Unit at Guy's Hospital, London, December 1992.

15. Meeting with Dr Charles Grob in Los Angeles, October 1993.

16. *Meetings at the Edge with Adam: A Man for All Seasons?* by Philip Wolfson from *Journal of Psychoactive Drugs* Vol. 18 April1986. Wolfson introduces himself as an established psychotherapist passionately involved with people experiencing painful altered states of consciousness. He says that MDMA opens up new possibilities for treatment of such cases, but their are some hazards to be wary of.

17. Meeting with Jerry Beck and Marsha Rosenbaum in San Francisco, November 1993.

18. *Diversity of Psychopathology Associated with Ecstasy* by McGuire et al *British Journal of Psychiatry* 1994.

Psychotherapy

In the USA, the best known use for ecstasy in the seventies was as an adjunct to psychotherapy. Literally thousands of therapists gave the drug to their patients, quite legally, and it was seen as having enormous potential in the future of psychology. This continued until prohibition, and even continues underground to this day.

Just after the American use was officially ended, a group of Swiss psychiatrists were given government permission to use ecstasy with their clients until 1994. They also trained many others to use the drug, and some of these now do so underground in Europe.

MDMA therapy can be done with groups or individuals. Ecstasy is regarded as a tool to open people up to a deeper level. It is only given to clients who are already undergoing therapy, and even then the great majority of sessions are drug free.

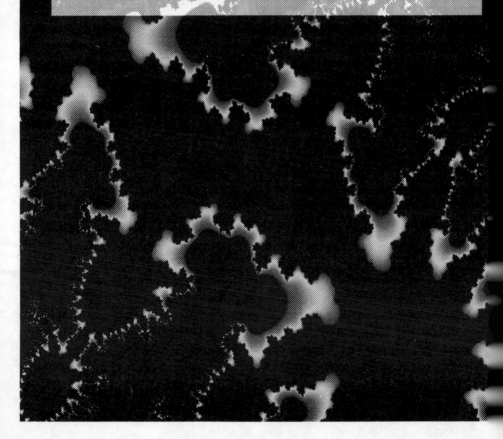

RD Laing on MDMA

What scientists have always been looking for is not a tranquiliser, an upper or a downer but a stabiliser, and in the seventies Alexander Shulgin thought he had found such a drug. In the context of its use among very responsible therapists in America, all direct reports, including my own, were positive.

The tragedy of the psychiatric use of ecstasy is that neither the American nor the Swiss therapists compared the effectiveness of MDMA-assisted therapy with non-assisted therapy in a controlled trial. They simply said it worked, but such evidence is regarded as 'anecdotal' and the drug was classified under the law as 'of no medical use', preventing its use and making it difficult to get permission for research.

The only serious attempt to evaluate the therapeutic effects of MDMA was a paper called *Subjective Reports of the Effects of MDMA in a Clinical Setting* by Dr George Greer and Requa Tolbert.[1]

Of the 29 subjects, "18 reported positive changes in mood after their session; 23 reported improved attitudes, such as towards self and life in general; 28 reported improvement in interpersonal relationships, and three of the five couples reported benefits lasting from a few days to up to two years; nine reported improvements in their working life; 14 reported diminished use of abusable substances (alcohol, marijuana, caffeine, tobacco, cocaine and LSD); 15 reported beneficial changes in their life goals; and all nine subjects with diagnosable psychiatric disorders reported considerable relief from their problems".

Changing relationships [1]

Other benefits claimed ranged from a greater acceptance of others to an appreciation of being alive and feeling they could be more warm and loving. Positive, mostly long-lasting, changes in relationships were reported by most participants and even their partners who did not take part in the sessions. Two couples resolved significant conflicts under MDMA.

Some subjects whose relationships were already in decline reported no improvement: one woman felt "more guilt around men for a while" and proceeded from a separation with her husband to a divorce. Many reported that their feelings were stronger after sessions and some now avoid superficial social meetings such as cocktail parties.

People "who want MDMA to cure their problems" make poor subjects, while those who want to use it to learn about themselves are most suitable.

"The single best use of MDMA is to facilitate more direct communication between people involved in a significant emotional relationship". They also recommend MDMA as an adjunct to insight-orientated psychotherapy, for promoting self-understanding and spiritual and personal growth.

In general, the authors conclude that "the single best use of MDMA is to facilitate more direct communication between people involved in a significant emotional relationship". MDMA was also recommended as an adjunct to insight-orientated psychotherapy, for enhancing self-understanding and was found to be useful in spiritual and personal growth.[2]

According to an article in the *American Journal of Psychotherapy* by Grinspoon and Bakalar,[3] the effects of MDMA – heightened capacity for introspection along with temporary freedom from anxiety and depression – 'should be of interest to Freudian, Rogerian and existential humanist therapists'. It is said to strengthen the therapeutic alliance between therapist and client by inviting self-disclosure and enhancing trust. Clients in MDMA-assisted therapy report that they lose defensive anxiety and feel more emotionally open, making it possible for them to get in touch with feelings and thoughts which are not ordinarily available to them.

Psychotherapeutic use in Switzerland

When the World Health Organisation (WHO) asked members of the United Nations to ban MDMA, it included a clause encouraging member countries to do research into therapeutic use of the drug. Although Switzerland is not a member of the UN, the Swiss government was impressed enough to be guided by its recommendation and licensed a group of psychiatrists to use MDMA from 1988 until 1993.[4]

I interviewed Dr Bloch, one of the Swiss therapists while she was still licensed to use MDMA:

What kind of people do you treat using MDMA?

These are mostly patients who have difficulties with their feelings. So they are mostly people with unusually hard character armour. These are, for instance, women with bulimia, some compulsive characters and depressive patients.

How often do you run an MDMA group?

Twice a year. I don't like to use more drugs than I have to. I also get results with breath work and body work. It is the hard core ones who sometimes need a push with MDMA.

Can you describe how you run an MDMA group?

We meet at eight o'clock in the morning. We all sit around in the circle; say how we are feeling at the moment; if we have any news; how we feel about taking the drug. Then we do some meditation. We sit there in a circle, breathe and go deep into ourselves. It's like Zen. Then they take 125mg MDMA, lie down and close their eyes.

Does the problem come up that you get one or two clients who draw attention to themselves?

When I stay with a patient, I always watch my own feelings, because there are some people who want to draw attention forever. Suddenly I get the feeling it is no longer good for me and I just go. And then the patient has to deal with the loss, not getting enough attention. That's a very important experience.

After people have started opening up, what do you do next?

Then I play music on tapes. Mostly meditative music but also some with bass, rhythmic bass – it stimulates some feelings and activity.

Do you use music to bring up aggression, for instance?

Yes, and some kinds of music to arouse anxiety.

Film music from a thriller?

That's right. But people require different stimuli. It's not only music which stimulates feelings, but also contact. Sometimes it's very important that closeness between a patient and myself brings up a feeling of anxiety, because they are afraid of closeness.

Even on MDMA?

Even more so. I remember an obsessive-compulsive character who was never in touch with her feelings of closeness, and the last time with MDMA she really got in touch by having close body contact and also eye contact. It was the first time she felt her panic by being close.

Is MDMA useful for bringing back memories from childhood, or memories that have been suppressed because of pain, or just generally getting in touch with feelings?

All of those. With one patient it brought back very early memories that as a child he had been sick very often, and he relived it again. Another patient realised for the first time with MDMA "Oh I have a heart, there is my heart beating. I never before could feel my heart beating". It was important for him to feel inside his body, he said "Aaaarrrh! Now I feel inside". It's different for each patient.

What happens towards the end of the session?

After four and a half hours we have some tea and they lie down again for half an hour. Afterwards they all have to draw a mandala, a drawing of their experience. Then we form a circle again and they put their mandala in the middle, and each of them talks about their experience.

In the groups, is the atmosphere happy, or is it mainly feeling pain?

When you take MDMA the first time it's beautiful. You feel "Ah! That's great!" but later on it's much more difficult for the patients because they get into their sadness, into their pain. So I feel the deeper you get, the more difficult it is with MDMA. When this beautiful feeling of happiness goes away, that is when you can work psychotherapeutically.

Do you relate MDMA to energy flow, such as the Chinese Chi or Reich's Orgone Energy?

As a body therapist I work with energy, and I realise that with MDMA there is opening up especially of the block in the chest, then the energy flow is better in the whole body.

Do you think MDMA works by relaxing muscles that store neuroses?

Probably, it just opens up the blocks. When you have a block in the body it is because it is too painful to allow the feelings to flow. MDMA is able to open up the blocks because it also releases the feelings – or releases the feelings and then the blocks open, you can say it either way. But I also use MDMA because of its spiritual value. MDMA is the drug that really opens up the heart, and in normal therapy I also work with opening up the heart. That, for me, is the main goal. For me it's not important that people are totally de-armoured, but that they get in contact with love; love for themselves. That is why I really like to work with MDMA.

After the Swiss therapists lost their licence to use MDMA, a follow up survey on ex-patients was undertaken.

Psycholytic Therapy follow-up [5]

This study was carried out retrospectively on 121 ex-patients treated with LSD and/or MDMA by three practitioners of the Swiss Association for Psycholytic Therapy.[150] Dr Bloch worked with 125mg MDMA alone; Drs Styk and Widmer used 125mg MDMA for the first three or four sessions, then LSD in doses ranging from 100mg to 400mg.

All practitioners used group therapy. Typically, patients saw their therapist once every two weeks over three years. On average, they participated in a drug session every five months following ten non-drug sessions. The most common reasons they undertook therapy were: Personality disorder (38%); Adjustment disorders (26%) and Affective disorders (25%).

The follow-up included a wide range of questions and responses

Patients were asked if they experienced any changes after treatment, and of what quality. 65% reported Good Improvement; 26% Slight Improvement; 4% No Change; 2% Slight Deterioration and 2% fluctuating changes. Thus 91% showed improvement, compared to 62% in a comparative study of patients treated without drugs.

In addition, 84% claimed the treatment had improved their quality of life, with 3% saying it was worsened; 82% claimed more self acceptance against 2% less; 68% more autonomy against 2% less. 74% said they had a better approach to the Divine; 1% less.

During psycholytic therapy, none of the patients committed suicide, were hospitalised in a psychiatric ward or had a psychotic episode longer than 48 hours.

Focusing [6]

A technique called Focusing (from a book called Focusing by Eugene Gendlin) is described as "one of the most effective means I know to contact and release hidden feelings, and particularly to relieve body stress". Having chosen a feeling to examine, the technique is to alternate experiencing the feeling without resisting, with finding an appropriate 'handle' to describe the feeling such as a word or phrase. In the example given, a woman listens to her body and handles suggest themselves such as 'tired', 'unlistened to' and 'pushed around'.

> ### Self disclosure [7]
>
> *MDMA strengthened the therapeutic alliance by inviting self-disclosure and enhancing trust. Psychiatrists suggested it was also helpful for marital counselling and diagnostic interviews. Patients in MDMA-assisted therapy reported that they were released from defensive anxiety and felt more emotionally open, which made it possible for them to get in touch with deeper feelings. It was also easier for them to receive criticisms and compliments.*
>
> *A patient described the major advantage of psychotherapy with MDMA as: "Being safe. Nothing could threaten me".*

Long before the rave scene, ecstasy was used by psychotherapists. One I interviewed was Deborah Harlow:

> I first tried MDMA with another therapeutic intern at a conference at Esalen in 1981. We were amazed at the clear view it gave us of our own psychology, and at how easy it was to express what we saw to each other. We felt that this might be a major breakthrough for psychiatry and psychotherapy and talked enthusiastically about the drug's potential for enhancing insight and motivating therapeutic change.

In later research and practice, she administered MDMA to over 200 individuals without any bad reactions whatsoever, although she did screen out 'borderline' cases, i.e. those without clear boundaries between reality and fantasy.

When prohibition loomed, Harlow conducted a survey among 17 psychiatrists and psychologists who used MDMA in their work. When asked to rate the psychotherapeutic value of MDMA by the progress of patients, 16 replied "Very positive" and one "Positive". MDMA was judged to be most valuable in treating post-traumatic stress syndrome, in the care of terminal patients, and in facilitating insight based psychotherapies and couple counselling. In addition, MDMA was thought to have some value in the treatment of addictions, particularly for cocaine abusers who were motivated to break their dependence.[8] One therapist has estimated that in five hours of an MDMA session, clients could activate and process psychic material that would normally require five months of weekly therapy sessions.[9]

Psychiatrists also suggest MDMA is helpful for marital counselling by making it easier to receive criticisms and compliments. "There's less defensiveness between us and more leeway for diversity", observed an ex-client. Long-lasting increased self-esteem was also reported by clients. Greer says that another use is in working through loss or trauma, because the issue can be faced and accepted instead of being shut away through fear.[10] However, some therapists are doubtful about how permanent changes may be.

No special techniques are necessary, but some are particularly appropriate such as focusing, which helps contact and release hidden feelings.[11]

Another technique Stolaroff describes is to "find a place in the body that feels good, and focus on increasing the good feeling". Later you discover that it doesn't matter what you are focusing on as long as it is worthwhile; holding the mind steadily focused encourages the bliss inside to grow continually.

Current use in psychotherapy

There are a few qualified psychotherapists in the USA, Denmark and Germany who risk losing their licenses by using MDMA. However, more unqualified therapists use MDMA probably because they have less to lose.

Interview with a licensed psychiatrist

Why do you still use MDMA even though it is illegal?

I believe that MDMA is such a valuable tool that I am prepared to take the enormous risk of being informed on and struck off the register. However, I now only use it with clients whom I completely trust and who have no serious problems. I would use MDMA more widely if it were legal as it is an ideal aid to psychotherapy. I sometimes use it for meditation and breath work in low doses, or before the drug has taken full effect. MDMA is also an ideal tool for couples, simply by allowing them to talk.

Does its use shorten therapy?

No. In fact, MDMA often takes the therapy onto a deeper level, so its use may prolong treatment.

Is MDMA treatment suitable for everyone?

Suitable clients should have a strong sense of themselves.

It is not suitable for people who are defensive and do not believe in themselves. For them, it is safer to remain defended – opening up feels alien to them, and is hard to accept. They may even forget or deny the experience as a way of avoiding the threat of being undefended.

How much MDMA do you use?

Dose is important, 2mg per Kg being about right. If the dose is too strong, some people become scared and respond by fighting instead of yielding to the effect, whereas too weak a dose may not overcome defensiveness.

Do you take MDMA yourself with a client?

I prefer to take 6-8mg 2CB [he is average weight], but sometimes I take a light dose of MDMA such as 50mg. This makes it easier to join in and stay with the client.

Can you describe an MDMA session?

I start by asking the client to identify the agenda for the session. I may then begin with evocative music or perhaps simple drumming, and may ask my client to breathe deeply with hand on belly. [The psychotherapist is a neo-Reichian.] Some clients use earplugs and eye shades. I encourage them to tell me what is happening, and remind them if they wander from their agenda without condemning it. Clients tend to go where it is rich for them, to get involved in whatever is their most important issue.

Towards the end of a session, I use an anchoring technique borrowed from Neuro Linguistic Programming. I ask the client to go over what happened and to relive the highlights with the intention of holding onto them, while squeezing together their finger and thumb. The idea is that this physical action will help them to remember the experience at a later date.

Can the E experience sometimes be misleading?

It can sometimes be tunnel vision but it is always true. However, ways of relating on E may not be appropriate in the real world and insights have to be tested to be of any value.

What part does MDMA play?

The primary effect is to lift anxiety. However, anxiety does play an important role in life and can't simply be dismissed. Anxiety is fear neurosis resulting in defensiveness – useful in some situations, but an obstacle in others. So I say "respect your anxieties but ask them to stand aside, ready to be called upon when needed."

What about hangovers?

To reduce fatigue I avoid secondary doses and give 20mg Prozac at the end of a session. I also recommend calcium and magnesium. I encourage clients to eat simple food such as soup, bread and sweet tea. Exhaustion also depends on the amount of emotional work done.

What do you think about self therapy using MDMA?

This only works for people without serious neuroses who are pretty good at self direction, otherwise the session is likely to be wasted. It is also important to establish a clear sense of direction before a self-session, and one way is to use the I Ching. The advantage of a guide is to interact and to bring one back to the issue rather than allowing the mind to wander.

Post-traumatic stress disorder

In 1993 I visited Nicaragua where the military hospital has been using MDMA for the treatment of Post-Traumatic Stress Disorder (PTSD). The chief psychiatrist, Dr Madriz, called in 20 patients – all male soldiers who had previously been diagnosed as having depression or anxiety disorders such as PTSD. They were each given a capsule of MDMA simultaneously. The patients were simply asked to take the pill without being told what it was, and were given a standard warning that they may experience giddiness and blurred vision. There were about eight staff present.

The first evaluation was made one hour later. Half said they felt better and half reported side effects. 15 of the group spontaneously came together and hugged one another, talking emotionally about how they wanted peace and an end to war. They were relaxed and communicative but not euphoric. Some praised the doctors; others said they felt love for everyone, even their enemy. They wanted a lot of attention from the staff, but were easy to deal with. There was no come down; the effects wore off so gradually they didn't notice and felt positive for many days.

However, five separated themselves from the others. Two of them panicked as though they were reliving the trauma and were given tranquillizers while another became paranoid as though he was being tricked. Of these, three were depressed beforehand.

A second evaluation was made five days later. Two had dropped out; 13 were better, of whom seven were regarded as needing no further treatment and were discharged. Five were worse, of whom two were suicidal and given tranquillizers. Dr Madriz and Dr Sandino believed negative symptoms expressed were latent before the MDMA was administered. Of course, such a trial is not ethical by Western standards, but it has led to a proper trial being planned.

Personal therapy experience

As part of my research, I arranged to have a session with a qualified therapist who had much experience of treating clients with MDMA before it was outlawed. I started by trying to get her to tell me what to expect, but she would not say. I got rather tense and withdrawn, and she then said that I had a lot of sadness. I was not sure if this was true, but she persuaded me to lie down, breathe deeply and allow myself to feel it while she put a hand on my belly. Within a very short time, I surprised myself by crying and thrashing about like a baby. This went on for a while, as feelings flushed through my mind from rage to despair, at one point making me vomit. I had had a similar experience over 20 years previously when I was given primal therapy, but the MDMA therapy was easier to accept – previously, I remember a struggle with myself not accepting what was happening.

Group therapy session

A reader invited me to attend a 'journey', an event which he and a few friends made fortnightly on ecstasy. Without having met any of them previously, I turned up at an address in north London one Saturday afternoon.

The participants were old friends in their thirties who had previously been involved in rebirthing. They felt that spiritual paths were often a distraction from coming to know and change oneself. They believed that releasing their internal anger and other negative emotions would result in being able to let these go.

The session started by each person (including myself) taking the 'medicine' in a cosy room with lots of candles and a coal fire. Some took a whole tablet, others three-quarters.

When the drug came on, one member of the group started to talk about the knot he felt in his belly, and the rest of us focused our attention on him, encouraging him to feel it and interpret it. When he seemed to exhaust this route, another person took over the central role. Some would talk and reveal their secrets, others would regress and describe situations they believed were from a previous life. One particular member took on the role of interpreting what was going on, and the others tended to accept his views. For instance, he might say that someone was angry and that person would reply "I don't feel angry", to which he would suggest that this was because they were suppressing anger.

The atmosphere was intense without fun. I found myself identifying intensely with the pain being expressed, but this was exhausting and too much to take after the first couple of hours. I then became more detached and observed, aware of my own doubts about the theory that expressing pain is therapeutic and the dogma that there is no gain without pain.

At the end of the session we all shared a meal, and they considered it an important 'journey'. They planned to meet a couple of days later without E to go over it, which was their normal practice.

The group continues fortnightly and has since grown in size to about a dozen people. In general the work involves less verbal expression and catharsis but more silent personal experiences including past life memories.

Amateur psychotherapy

Unlicensed MDMA therapists

As a result of prohibition, there are a number of amateur or lay therapists using MDMA. This alarms some professionals, while others comment that "Instinct is the most valuable skill, so the helper need not be a qualified psychotherapist".

In California, I interviewed a man who had made a fortune through tough dealing in the commodity market but was unable to have a warm relationship, even after 19 years of psychiatric treatment. Then, after only five MDMA sessions with an unqualified therapist, he felt able to express warmth for the first time in his life – but also found he had lost his ability to make money.

There are also self-help groups who use E, friends who meet regularly and try to sort out their problems. And of course a lot of people who use E at home with friends find themselves expressing deep feelings and resolving conflicts. But just to feel and express may not be enough to be therapeutic: the experience has to be integrated into normal life.

Self therapy

Some people use MDMA alone.[12] They believe it can help you to open up your heart and rid yourself of neuroses without the need for a therapist or guide, and claim that the process is more direct if there is no-one else to take responsibility for the problems except yourself. An enthusiastic Californian therapist is said to have believed in this so strongly that he gave up his practice and became a dealer instructing his clients in self therapy.[13]

Self therapy [13]

A therapist's opinion:

It can work, but a helper is essential. There has to be someone to accept, listen, acknowledge and give the support of unconditional love to the client, but not to control the session. It is easier to empathise if the helper is also on MDMA, but it is not necessary. MDMA can also be used in co-counselling sessions [where two people take turns at being therapist and client].

However, most professional people feel that a guide is essential to give support, unless the person is unusually good at self direction and without neurotic problems, as neurotic people can become exposed to deeper problems on the drug.[13,14]
A man wrote to me how about how he feels E helped him:

> I could see myself so clearly as this pathetic person who always put on an act of being the nice guy to cover up that I was really scared stiff of people. But on E I wasn't scared. I didn't try to be the nice guy and found that the people I was with liked me more as I was. This made quite an impression on me, and gradually I experimented with dropping the 'nice' me in everyday life. A few months later I had some E again and this time got fascinated by what was going on inside myself. I found that it went back to being rejected by my mother who had me adopted: that made me distrust people and look for approval. I can't say it was an instant cure, but I do feel as though I came to terms with the past and now relate to people more honestly.

However, most self-therapists believe that it really helps to have a guide for support, but not necessarily a trained psychotherapist. An experienced self explorer believes that people can go a long way by themselves, but wise guidance can be valuable in some situations. Two experienced American psychotherapists also thought that a wise helper was essential, but this need not be a trained psychotherapist.[13,14]

If you should decide to use ecstasy in this self-help way, there are two approaches, i.e. with or without the guide taking MDMA as well. The advantage of both people taking it is the very close communication made possible; the disadvantage is that it's hard for the guide to remain disciplined and devote him or herself to the task. One solution is for the guide to take a small dose, about a third, as described by Alexander Shulgin.[15]

Rules in therapy:

1. Sexual feelings are allowed but may not be acted out.
2. Feelings of hostility are allowed but may not be acted out.
3. Confidentiality is to be respected.
4. The patient must accept the guide's advice during the session.
5. The session lasts until both therapist and guide agree that it has ended.

Notes for guides

To be a guide is usually a delightful experience, but it is a responsibility that must be taken seriously. Take time beforehand to find out the aims and expectations of the person you are to guide. You should not only ask them whether they are sufficiently fit and free from emotional problems to take ecstasy, but also judge for yourself. It's not a good idea to play the guide to someone who is looking for something to cure them unless you are an experienced therapist. But, however well you vet people, difficulties can still arise and you must be prepared to deal with them. People used to taking ecstasy at raves may react differently when they take it with only their guide for company.[16]

Obviously it is important to make the venue pleasant and free from interruptions, but it is also important to show that you put care into the preparations. As one person remarked, "When I arrived and saw how much care and attention had gone into preparing for my trip I immediately relaxed as I knew I was going to be well looked after". Present yourself as a servant and as a committed supporter.

It is also important that you give the expectation of a wonderful time. If you show signs of worrying, this may make your friend look for something to go wrong with the trip; if you are enthusiastic and expect your friend to have a wonderful experience, you will help to bring this about.

Discuss beforehand what the purpose of the session is. If it is just for fun and to experience the effects of the drug, you can offer to give a guided tour of the effects from looking inside to dancing and perhaps a walk outdoors. But, maybe the person wants to explore something about themselves, in which case the guide's job is to simply be there: to provide security by giving reassurance when appropriate and to be available to talk to, typically as the effects wear off. Side effects very often manifest as a result of emotional problems, and it may be helpful to suggest looking at the underlying cause. People who become stuck can be supported in what they are feeling, and if it is uncomfortable, reminded that they will become unstuck as the drug wears off.

One example of many described in *Through the Gateway of the Heart*[17,] an American collection of positive experiences on ecstasy, is a 32 year-old man who was at a transition point in his life and career. His aim was "to examine this transition and proceed as quickly as possible to the task at hand":

> I gained an important insight into the history and development of my personality and character. My awareness, confidence, and self assurance improved. The session provided me with one of the best opportunities I have ever had for true self-examination. I felt refreshed, vigorous, alert, and happy to an unusual degree...

> I discovered and understood with a positive and profound conviction that my identity and personality were intact. I had feared, I suppose, that I might find that I had been damaged in some irreversible way. I felt tremendous relief and joy when I learned otherwise.

He added that for him, the most beneficial effects of MDMA were greater presence of mind and "being able to talk with clarity."

Another example given in the book is that of a woman who had been raped eight years before she took E. She had the help of two friends/guides. Although LSD was the main drug involved, she was helped by a 65mg dose of MDMA given 2 hours after the LSD:

> My friends asked me to keep silent for ten minutes and to think of and feel what was happening to me. It took a long time before I could do this, always fearing that I would simply go mad. When I finally accepted it and did it, I could feel the pain take over my body so that the suffering was physical as well ...

> I spoke of the rape. For eight years I have kept the most horrible aspects of that day hidden in the back of my mind, and it was only then that I realized that the little details I had wanted to ignore were eating at me like cancer [which she had in remission at that time]. The memories became very vivid in my mind and the suffering became more intense ... I started to feel the horror of that day and started vomiting ... getting rid of pain, of an evil that had been destroying me.

Nine years later one of the helpers told me that "she is doing great these days".

References

1. *Subjective reports of the Effects of MDMA in a Clinical Setting* by George Greer and Requa Tolbert from *Journal of Psychoactive Drugs* Vol 18/4 1986.

2. *New Age Seekers: MDMA use as an adjunct to spiritual pursuit* by Watson and Beck, *Journal of Psychoactive Drugs* 23 March 1997.

3. *Can drugs enhance Psychotherapy?* by Grinspoon and Bakalar, from *American Journal of Psychotherapy*, 1986.

4. Swiss Medical Society for Psycholytic Therapy, Birmannsgasse 39, 4055 Basel.

5. *Reorganisation of ascending 5-HT Axon Projections in Animals Previously Exposed to the Recreational Drug MDMA.* Fischer, Hatzidimitriou, Wios, Katz and Ricaurte in *Neuroscience* August 1995.

6. Letter and manuscript from Myron Stolaroff January 1994.

7. *Can drugs enhance Psychotherapy?* by Grinspoon and Bakalar, from *American Journal of Psychotherapy*, 1986.

8. Survey among therapists with experience of MDMA-assisted therapy by Deborah Harlow.

9. *The Nature of the MDMA Experience* by Ralph Metzner and Sophia Adamson in *ReVision*, Spring 1988.

10. Subjective reports of the Effects of MDMA in a Clinical Setting by George Greer and Requa Tolbert from *Journal of Psychoactive Drugs* Vol. 18/4 1986.

11. Letter and manuscript from Myron Stolaroff January 1994.

12. Interview with a musician and visiting dealer in

California, November 1993.
13. Interview with Deborah Harlow, research fellow at the Division on Addictions, Harvard Medical School October 1993.
14. Visit to a licensed psychotherapist in California, October 1993.
15. *PIHKAL (Phenethylamines I Have Known And Loved); A Chemical Love Story,* by Alexander and Ann Shulgin.

16. A researcher reports from the rave by Russell Newcombe, *Druglink*, January 1992.
17. *Through the Gateway of the Heart* (book) published by Four Trees Publications, San Francisco 1985. This book is a collection of some 60 subjective accounts of positive experiences by users and "guidelines for the sacramental use of empathogenic substances".

Spiritual Uses

Some people regard ecstasy as a catalyst which facilitates spiritual experiences. These cover a wide range from 'feeling in touch with nature' to 'opening a direct line to God'.

Sometimes people going out partying have spiritual experiences without looking for them, while other people try to induce them by organising rituals for the purpose.

Deliberate use of ecstasy for spiritual purposes can consist of meditation or practising martial arts, 'toning' with others or simply listening to an uplifting story with eyes closed.

Rituals have been devised where ecstasy is used, often based on those used by Native Americans, where people make use of the group energy to raise their consciousness.

Most spiritual teachers are strongly against the use of any drug. Some warn that drugs will undo years of hard-earned progress towards enlightenment, while others say that the drug-induced state may appear the same but is on a lower level, and that this can mislead people. A few believe that a true mystical state can be induced by drugs, but that its value is less when a drug is used as a 'short cut'.

However, there are leaders of traditional religion who use MDMA as an aid to prayer or meditation, and there is even a religious movement based on the use of ecstasy.

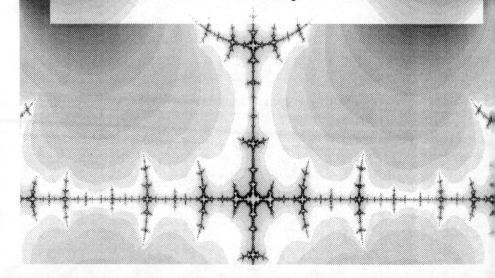

Ecstasy as an entheogen

The word 'entheogen' – from the Greek 'bringing the God within' – is sometimes used for drugs such as ecstasy and psychedelics when they are used for spiritual purposes. Various people have experimented with MDMA as a catalyst for spiritual purposes and there are reports of a Navaho medicine man who is a member of the Native American church using MDMA in place of peyote. An organisation interested in this aspect is The Council On Spiritual Practices (CSP).[1]

Organisation [1]

The Council on Spiritual Practices is a non-profit transdenominational group devoted to the furtherance of primary religious experience. Its purpose is to explore and cultivate practices yielding the benefits that mystical experiences are said to bring to everyday life, such as increased awareness and compassion. The Council's Entheogen Project focuses on the controlled spiritual uses of psychoactive plant and chemical substances. For more information, visit CSP's Internet Web site <http://csp.org/csp/>. CSP is committed to working through lawful means.

Spiritual awakening

I discovered E at 18. When people have used E to its full potential and understand what it has to offer, the chances are that their spiritual journey will have begun. I see it as a substance that starts you off without scaring you off, unlike cocaine which has zero spiritual content. Drugs may not be the ultimate answer, but right now they are the best chance we've got. Those who are ready to grapple with the mystery of existence can be informed of what is on offer.

- A reader

The rave as a religious service

The dance/rave culture, seen as purely hedonistic by outsiders, is frequently regarded as a spiritual event by those involved. Raves are likened to trancelike tribal rituals where ravers celebrate their unity and shared uplifted state, giving and receiving freely from one another. As a reader put it:

> While not being highly entheogenic itself (especially after much usage), ecstasy helps the user to open up to entheogenic altered states "caused" more by the repetitive drumming and dancing found at raves, as well as the group feeling which (at the good raves) gets generated and helps people feel comfortable enough to "let go" and experience the spirit. Ecstasy may be the key, but the rhythm and the group vibe opens the door.

Rave in a church

I attended a dance party in an active Christian church with approval of the parish council. It was described in the church programme as "Trance Dancing, an ancient practice which invites the spirit to embody us and to heal us through external spiritual ecstasy... The spirit knows the moves and once awakened, the spirit takes over..."

The front few rows of pews had been removed to allow room to dance, and some cushions were placed on the floor of a carpeted side chapel as a chill out area. A sound system and mixing desk was set up at one side of the front of the nave, and the pulpit was used to house projectors aimed at the back wall. A nice touch was that the DJs names were displayed on the board designed for listing the hymns to be sung.

It was all rather low key including the volume of sound, but I eventually managed to open up and dance freely. I then saw it as a magnificent and most appropriate venue, and appreciated its beautiful high vaulted roof and resonance which complemented my uplifted feelings. Later, I realised that I had been prejudiced against churches, which I had always seen as sterile monuments.

On another occasion, I went to a large private party in a disused church. The hostess had constructed an altar to the Goddess, with statues cleverly lit by strobes and the DJs hidden behind it. This provided a focal point 'to dance to', and made for a wonderful atmosphere.

Yoga and martial arts

I have had several reports from people who have used ecstasy while practising martial arts. This report is by someone who only uses MDMA while doing kung fu and yoga:

> One of the major aspects that the E shed light on was the use of energy (prana/chi) rather than a focus on muscular strength. My overall impression of the benefits of E usage in Hatha Yoga was that the session had its own distinct harmony and produced a highly balanced mode of perception in which contradictions of body and mind were synthesised into a very pleasant equilibrium. The insights gained from the session have been incorporated into my daily practice, so that now the sensations produced by the E can be reproduced by the yoga – rather like a free trip.

The effect of ecstasy on Kung Fu was to make clear that the user, who was male, was good at the hard or yang movements but had neglected those that were soft or yin. He commented:

> I found that the softer feminine touch counterposed the external, physically athletic male side of kung fu; the balance of the two working in harmony improved the speed, power and insight into a given technique to quite a considerable degree... though I am not sure I would wish to be challenged to a fight under the influence.

> ### Kendo
>
> *I use MDMA for practising Kendo, working with my brother as partner (who is not on MDMA). We find it allows us to anticipate each other's movements and flow together. It's extremely pleasurable, but we think it would be too much for both of us to take it; anyway, it works fine as it is.*
>
> *– A reader*

Rituals

S ome people use MDMA as part of a ritual,[2] either with each individual exploring inwardly and only sharing their experience later, or by interacting as a group, perhaps speaking in turn using a talking-stick.

Among the Personal accounts are two descriptions of ritual use. One, under the title *The Harvard Agape* (page 256) describes a religious ceremony performed by a group of Harvard divinity students. The other, *Centrepoint* (page 267) describes its use in a large residential community.

> ### Ritual use [2]
>
> *I always ritualize the Adam experience, seeing it as a sacred medicine. The room is carefully prepared with mattresses on the floor covered with soft cloth and velvet cushions, candles, music, incense, flowers, and precious objects. Aqua Libra in fine goblets, the Adam on a tray covered with an embroidered cloth. We fast for eight hours beforehand, bathe and dress in clean cotton or silk. There is not enough ritual in our lives at present.*
>
> *We use the half hour after taking it to share, meditate, massage or breathe deeply. I like the first hour 'alone' to go deeply inside when the experience is particularly intense. After that I need contact with others – touching, sharing.*
>
> *The Adam experience removes veils and allows a deeply fulfilling experience. The deep meditative state is far easier to access after experience with the drug. My spiritual life has become much more important. At certain times, with due ritual and awe at approaching the sacred, I take Adam to draw aside the veils, to approach the secret, the inner knowledge.*
>
> *– A reader in Devon*

Lion Path

T he Lion Path[3,4] is a road to enlightenment using MDMA as a tool in combination with astrology. The theory is that throughout history there have been periods of openness to spiritual growth, determined by astrology, and that one of these exists at present. For individuals, suitable days for spiritual growth are astrologically determined, and on such open days followers are asked to meditate in isolation. Until prohibition, they were also instructed to take specific doses of MDMA on these days to increase their openness, a practice that still continues although officially MDMA is no longer recommended.

Before each meditation, participants fast and decide on their intention for the session. They take the drug, close their eyes, lie down and "allow the universal force to penetrate". The intention may consist of a personal aim or acquainting oneself with the character of the ruling astrological power. This sets the pattern for individual spiritual growth "within a cosmic egg". There is no other dogma, and participants do not meet.

One follower told me:

> The sessions are a sacred ceremony of one's own higher growth and regeneration – a form of time surfing. The sessions build up and resonate with preceding and following sessions. All the powers that have been lying dormant within us, become activated and purified. By remaining open to love and trust, we can overcome limitations and receive aid to transform ourselves... The post-session interval then provides the opportunity to fill out and embody this higher destiny.

Use of ecstasy in traditional religion

Buddhism

The Buddhist magazine Tricycle[3] published a special issue on "Psychedelics: help or hindrance?", with articles by well known writers including Jack Kornfield, Rick Fields, Terence McKenna, Ram Dass and ten others. Although ecstasy is not a psychedelic, many of the same arguments apply.

In a readership survey, over 40% said that their interest in Buddhism was sparked by psychedelics; 59% thought that psychedelics and Buddhism do mix, while 41% disagreed; 71% believe that "psychedelics are not a path, but can provide a glimpse of the reality to which Buddhist practice points. Yet 58% said they would consider using a psychedelic drug in a sacred context.

Age made a difference, with more using psychedelics over 50 or under 30: those aged between 30 and 50 were most against the use of drugs.

The articles reflected these views, with the majority believing that the drug induced state is valid and probably equal to that induced in other ways. Other writers saw it as a misleading illusion, or as valid yet also an obstacle to deeper spirituality.

Zen

I interviewed two Zen monks who use ecstasy, a Soto Zen called Pari and a Rinzai Zen monk called Bertrand. I asked Pari how it was that some people say that ecstasy can help meditation, while others that it was a hindrance. He replied:

> There is no contradiction. Drugs disturb acquired patterns of meditation, but while taking MDMA it is easy to meditate. Being still when taking MDMA helps you to know how to sit. It provides you with experiential knowledge.

But is it a good way to learn?

> It is like a medicine. If we look at the state of our own mind and the planet, we should be grateful for any means that can help. However, like any good medicine, it can also be misused.

Both of them believe that they have benefited from the use of MDMA, that it can help produce a valid mystical experience, that it does no harm to the psyche and is a useful tool in teaching students. The reason they do not promote its use is that they have to follow the policies of their religious orders, and these naturally uphold the law.

Visit from a Rinzai Zen monk

In 1994, I was visited by Bertrand, a Zen Buddhist monk and teacher of meditation in his early seventies.

Following a conventional career, Bertrand had an awakening experience on mescaline at the age of 47. This made him re-evaluate his role in life, and after many years of training with a strict Japanese master, he eventually became abbot of a Zen monastery. During the training he once used ecstasy while undertaking a Zen exercise called Koans. During Koans, the master names the task which the student must contemplate, such as the classic: "to understand the sound of one hand clapping". The student has to demonstrate comprehension, normally after a considerable time, and very often after being sent away to try again – but on ecstasy, Bertrand zipped through the Koans with impressive ease.

Since then, Bertrand has taken ecstasy about 25 times over 10 years. He has found it most effective on the second day of a seven day meditation. The first day is spent in preparation for the meditative state, so that he is already fully focused on the task by the time he actually takes the drug, which makes it easier for him to go deeply into the meditative state. He feels that the experience would be of great value to some of his devout but stiff fellow Zen monks, but there is only one who shares his secret.

I asked Bertrand whether the ecstasy experience was of equal value to 'getting there the hard way'. He replied: "Ecstasy simply allows one to focus wholeheartedly on the task in hand, and so the result is in every way as real because it is the same. In fact, ecstasy has allowed me to go further." On two occasions he has felt enlightened, although he is wary of claiming that this was the highest level.

I pressed him for negative aspects, and he told me that he once made the mistake of taking ecstasy just before leading a meditation, which made him see how his students were strained and needy. He told them: "You look like corpses, all lined up in your black shawls". This made them feel worse and afterwards he realised that it was inappropriate, so he did not use ecstasy while teaching again. His mistake lay in not respecting that his students were in a different space. However, Bertrand believes that ecstasy would be an extremely useful tool for teaching if the students were on it too. In fact, he hoped that he would live long enough to be able to use it legally in this way. Pressed again for possible problems, he said: "There are always people who come wanting to be given enlightenment on a plate, and news of a new technique using a drug would be bound to attract the type who expected it to be done for them.

Raving as meditation

I invited Bertrand to a dance party where he took some ecstasy. It was the first time Bertrand had taken the drug except while meditating, and he was surprised at how different the experience was. Beforehand, he said he could hardly stand the noise, but after the drug took effect, he could see the value of the volume in drowning out distractions. As the drug took effect his face changed expression from curious to happy and he exclaimed: "I can see what it's all about, this is like walking meditation. These people are meditating only they don't realise it. They are in the same state. They are completely in the 'here and now', moving spontaneously without thinking about it." Far from being alien to his experience, he saw that everyone was totally aware yet absorbed in their dance without self consciousness or internal dialogue, and that this was the very essence of meditation. He had once been a guest at an American Indian ceremony which provided the feeling of tribal bonding by the use of a drug and monotonous beat, and thought that the rave was comparable, although it missed the Indians' cultural framework and focus.

The next day, he said this may be an important turning point in his life. He had to take time to digest what he had learned, but his immediate response was that he could not continue to be part of the establishment of his school in its present form. He could see that the contractive aspect of the training had been overemphasized in his school, in the belief that westerners were too expansive anyway. In fact, those who sought Zen masters in the West really needed the ability to be expansive – and the rave provided it. A month later, Bertrand rang me to say that he had just given a week's retreat, and that it was lighter and more positive with almost a sense of gaiety. He attributed this to the rave experience affecting him, which in turn affected the participants. Also, he still feels much younger and more flexible. In fact, a back problem that had caused him pain for several years appeared to be completely cured, which made him suspect that back problems in particular are caused by the mind. He described it as "a nourishing experience".

> ### *Meditation*
>
> *When I tried to meditate after taking E I found it immediate and easy, and very quickly got into the profound state I'd only experienced before after a lot of preparation and effort. I felt also that it was imperative that I do what I can to help other people find a way, through Buddhism or meditation, to enlightenment or a release from suffering. I felt that I really experienced the bliss of enlightenment, but that it was vital that I help others to find it too in a lasting way; that there cannot be peace on earth until every being can reach that state.*
>
> *Our delusions and habitual thoughts and attitudes are like clouds across the mind, obscuring the clarity and perception of true reality. In some sense I felt like E cleared away many clouds for me.*

Visit to a Soto Zen monk

Pari first took LSD at university. In fact, he moved into a commune that took LSD at regular weekly rituals, but later this quest for knowledge led him away from drugs and to Yoga, which he practised intensely for several years. He then travelled and got involved with Zen, living in a Soto Zen community for ten years until he was ordained as a monk. He has since been made an abbot by his master; ie given the power to ordain new Zen monks. He now lives in a beautiful quiet Victorian house in the city with his wife and son, where he has a small zendo, except when teaching in his mountain retreat. He divides his time between Buddhism and social/ecological activism. Over the previous five years, Pari had taken ecstasy about 15 times, usually alone or with his wife or intimate friends. It provided him with great clarity and calmness, as after a week-long sitting (seshin), when everything became more clear, more awake. Although eastern teachings are usually strongly anti-drug, his particular tradition was an exception to the rule, and his teacher in Japan had used peyote, LSD and ecstasy.

Pari had once angered the famous Vietnamese Buddhist teacher Thich Nhat Hanh by pointing out that the majority of his Western students had come to seek him as a result of drug experiences, so it was not right for him to take such a strong stand against the use of drugs, especially since he had not tried them himself.

Pari has used ecstasy for teaching with a few students, including one who has since been ordained a monk. This was a man who was extremely keen, and put tremendous effort into trying to succeed in meditation. Ecstasy helped him to see that trying itself was his main obstacle. Another student was a very successful and hard-driving businessman. Ecstasy simply stopped him – he made a dramatic change into a warm, contented person who just wanted to sit quietly in the zendo. When I asked if success through the use of ecstasy was as valid as without, he replied: "It is the experience that matters, not how you get there. Look back at the history of the major religions. Many of their founders and saints had their mystical unions during wound-fever, during which, as we know today, the body produces psychedelic substances. A good example would be Ignatius de Loyola, the founder of the Jesuit order."

I asked if Pari thought there may be types of people who would not benefit from ecstasy, or who might be misled by it. "It could be a problem for those who are not sufficiently well grounded, those who have a tendency to float into other worlds rather easily anyway. However, most of us are too earth-bound, too stuck in this particular reality, and a little help from a friend can be of great value. Unlike LSD and other drugs, ecstasy works in terms of relationships – with oneself, God, nature. It even opens up a common ground with other people whom one does not yet know."

I asked Pari whether there was any point in using ecstasy once enlightenment had been achieved. "Enlightenment is a transitory experience for most of us, and it's seldom achieved. After a while, the true experience becomes replaced by a memory of it. We need direct experience to refresh from time to time."

But, I asked, is the drug-induced experience really the same? After some hesitation Pari replied, "Yes, the state of mind is identical, yet there is a subtle difference, perhaps due to the drug's physical effects on the body. Without the drug, there is one less factor. This is simpler, and perhaps this implies it is better. The value of the state is the same: to be able to look back and to see one's 'normal' state of mind with a clear but different perspective."

I asked what is the ideal situation for a beginner. "A trusted, more experienced friend is highly recommended. You must create an environment that you find conducive. Do whatever spiritual practice you have. For some this may be singing, praying, painting, meditating or sitting in a cathedral; for others walking alone in the mountains. Then you must be prepared that not every attempt is positive.

"The spiritual path is like a climber walking in the mountains who is lost in the fog and unable to see the peak he has set out to climb. All of a sudden the fog clears and he experiences the reality of the peak, and gains a sense of direction. Even though the fog moves in again, and it's still a long, hard climb, this glimpse of the goal and direction is usually an enormous help and encouragement. And ecstasy can provide that glimpse."

Christianity

Comments by Brother Steindl-Rast

Brother Steindl-Rast is the Benedictine monk quoted praising the use of ecstasy in *Ecstasy: The MDMA Story*. He rarely replies to letters or gives interviews, but a mutual friend put some questions to him for me. He has tried ecstasy about four times, but does not use it any more. He thinks people tend to expect too much of ecstasy, although he knows of many people who were helped considerably by the drug to overcome their interpersonal barriers.

Learning from ecstasy

I have used E with friends for over three years now and can identify many benefits for myself that are directly related to it. However, it must be recognised for what it is: a chemical that creates an altered state of consciousness. The important point to realise is that the state is temporary but 'relivable'. It's possible to learn an appreciation of what one can achieve; such as engaging in truly loving conversations and genuine spiritual states; then bring this 'new knowledge' back into ordinary lives and make worthwhile changes.

- A reader

Interview with a Benedictine monk

Brother Bartholemew is a monk who has used ecstasy about 25 times over the past 10 years as an aid to prayer. He explained that 'prayer' normally means 'trying to pray', but to succeed implies true communication with God, and this is rarely achieved. Ecstasy can help to remove barriers when one is trying to pray. He has taken ecstasy alone, but usually does so among a small group of like-minded people.

Bartholemew describes the effect of ecstasy as opening a direct link with God. He has also experienced a very deep comprehension of divine compassion while using the drug. He has never lost the clarity of this insight, and it remains as a reservoir upon which he can call. Another benefit of his use of ecstasy has been that the experience of the divine presence comes to him effortlessly. The effect manifests in its elemental form in the breath, the breath of divine God. After the awakening, he began to discover the validity of all other major religious experiences.

He believes ecstasy is a tool which can be used on different levels. "When used appropriately, it is almost sacramental. It has the capacity to put one on the right path to divine union with the emphasis on love, vertical love in the sense of ascending. However, this gain only happens when one is already facing the right direction. It should not be used unless one is really searching for God."

I asked what the ideal situation was: "The place where ecstasy is taken should be quiet and serene. There should be a close emotional bond among those sharing the experience, and there has to be a certain amount of supervision, because the influence of ecstasy produces a tendency for attention to drift off. There is also a danger of squandering the experience by being trapped in euphoric feelings, rather than reaching into a spiritual realm. However, although it can be invaluable, its use should not be necessary, as the need for a drug negates freedom." Asked what he thought about ecstasy use at raves, he felt is was sacrilegious: "The experience is not appropriate for immature hedonists."

I sent Brother Bartholemew a copy of my notes for approval, and he added the following: "One element you might want to add is that of intimacy of voice in conversation. MDMA always propels me into an intimate space in conversation. There is a special quality to this conversation. One feels a heaviness, a sense of the weight of the moment, of something profound, of the seriousness of life itself. It is a space that is inner, without masks, without pretence, utterly open and honest. It is not an erotic intimacy, but a philosophical and mystical intimacy. Does this make any sense? One has the consciousness that this is an inner communication rarely achieved in ordinary discourse. There really are no adequate words to express this state of awareness, only to say, that it is essential in my experience."

Interview with a rabbi

After a talk which touched on the need to prepare for death, I asked the rabbi a question about the value of ecstasy in terminal patients (referring to Dr. Charles Grob's study in Los Angeles.) He replied, with a knowing twinkle in his eye: "Ecstasy may be valuable for the dying as well as at raves, by allowing the feeling of oneness and seeing life from a new aspect. Prohibition is not the best way to deal with substances that can be used in ways that are as sacramental as communion wine. These substances may arouse feelings of awkwardness which may be uncomfortable, but are essential for deeper understanding of our selves." With that, he invited the next question.

After the talk was formally ended, the rabbi beckoned me to come up onto the stage. He took me out to a fire exit staircase, out of earshot of his entourage, and told me that he could not afford to undermine his project by publicly supporting the use of illegal drugs, but that he had my book (which he praised.) He was aware that dancing on MDMA could be a spiritual experience. He believed that MDMA and other psychedelics could be used to immense benefit, not only for personal awareness, but also for the sake of Gaia – the cosmic wellbeing of the planet.

"Nowadays, young people are more likely to have a spiritual experience at a rave than in a church or synagogue. The feeling of oneness and seeing life from a new aspect is an equally valuable experience for ravers. Priests who want to understand young people should take ecstasy for themselves, both in order to understand them, and to see the validity of spiritual experiences produced by drugs." When asked whether drugs produced the same quality of experience, he referred to Abraham Maslow's conclusion concerning 'peak experiences': that taking drugs is like reaching the top of a mountain by cable car instead of the toil of climbing – it can be seen as cheating, but it gets you to the same place. He ended by giving me a big hug and encouraging me in my work.

Conclusion

I found it fascinating to hear how similar these views were from religious leaders who did not know one another, whose religions were very dissimilar, yet how different from most other ecstasy users.

References

1. Refer box page 183.

2. *Through the Gateway of the Heart* (book) published by Four Trees Publications, San Francisco 1985. This book is a collection of some 60 subjective accounts of positive experiences by users and "guidelines for the sacramental use of empathogenic substances". The accounts are divided into men's, women's and group experiences.

3. Tricycle, The Buddhist Review, volume 6 January, 1996. UK distributor phone number is 01803 732 082.

Safety

Safety is relative. Nothing is completely safe, but some activities are safer that others. For each activity there is also a level of safety depending on the way it is carried out.

The chapter on Risk compares taking ecstasy with other activities. This chapter concerns the safety of ecstasy users.

Some authorities have adopted policies which are intended to reduce the harm done by drugs, rather than preventing their use. Such policies are called 'harm reduction', and consist of reducing the dangers associated with drug use. In the case of ecstasy, this includes making rules for clubs to avoid dangerous conditions.

Some aspects of safety also depend on individuals. Other drugs they use can make a difference, and there is even one that may protect against neurotoxicity.

Finally, there is psychological safety to consider. This may vary according to personality, and also depending on the situation where ecstasy is used.

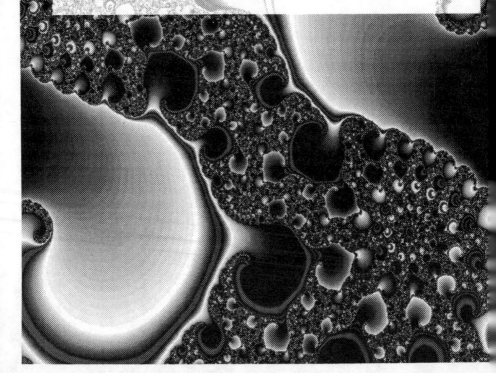

Group safety – Harm reduction

The more enlightened authorities admit that preventing drug use is an unattainable goal, but that it is possible to reduce the harm caused by drug use. Harm reduction policies[1] are based on the idea that harm is largely due to the way in which drugs are used, and that this can be influenced. It was first applied to opiate (heroin) users in response to the AIDS scare by supplying free needles to prevent the HIV virus being spread through sharing a contaminated needle.

Harm reduction [1]

According to Newcombe, the four main components of a harm reduction strategy should be: (1) rationale, (2) content, (3) implementation and (4) evaluation.

(1) It should be acknowledged that people like to get high, and that this is not likely to change. Drug use may be rational, not deviant, Newcombe says. It should be acknowledged that many psychoactive drugs are no more harmful than prescribed drugs. "The message that drugs are unhealthy is akin to warning soldiers in battle that chewing gum can cause indigestion," he says. Harm reduction policies are based on a caring rather than a judgemental approach, and are therefore less likely to drive drug users underground.

(2) The strategy must be based on knowledge. The focus should be on controlling use rather than seeking complete abstinence, which is out of character with modern life. Instructions should be given on suitable quantities, effects, safest methods of administration, obtaining help when needed, avoiding hazards and methods of controlling mental states.

(3) The implementation strategy should draw on knowledge of how to maximise the probability of success.

(4) It will be necessary to do before and after studies and long-term follow-ups using control groups to evaluate the effectiveness of harm reduction strategies.

Harm reduction in relation to ecstasy use has been adopted as a policy by Manchester City Council[1] in the form of The Safer Dancing Campaign. As a result, many club owners are becoming more responsible[2] and some even employ people to look after ravers who have problems associated with drug use.

Dr Russell Newcombe has been one of the main protagonists of this idea.[1] Under the name 3D Research Bureau, he offers a consultancy service to club owners who wish to have their premises monitored.[3]

The code pioneered in Manchester requires clubs to do the following:

1. Monitor air temperature and air quality.
2. Provide adequate "chill out" facilities.

3. Provide free drinking water.

4. Provide information on how to avoid problems and where advice and help can be obtained.

5. Employ outreach workers to operate on site.

6. Train security staff to recognise and look after people with problems.

Safety at clubs

It is important for club-goers to put pressure on clubs to supply free water and chill out areas. Write to dance magazines and report clubs that cut off water in the toilets, have no free drinking water or have no chill-out facilities. Dance magazines are listed in the Information chapter.

Safety at free parties

Harm reduction policies assume that safety can be assured through control of premises. Although some people believe that free parties are a recipe for disaster, in practice casualties have nearly all occurred on licensed premises.[4] Free party organisers say that the profit motive is the root cause of casualties, through selling drinks at inflated prices, overcrowding and restricting people from going outside.

> **Potential for disaster** [4]
>
> *According to Russell Newcombe, illegal raves have a far greater potential for disaster due to poor fire access, factors such as the absence of lighting (apart from strobes) and lethal substances being sold as drugs. Crushing due to panic from an emergency, police raid or a fire could result in a major disaster.*

Individual safety

This section is intended for those who have decided to use the drug in spite of its illegality and potential dangers.

Health and other drugs

Ecstasy puts an extra strain on the body, so illness and tiredness will reduce your body's capacity to cope with the extra load. In particular your heart, liver[5] and kidneys all have to work harder, and, if you are dancing, so will your lungs and muscles.

Other drugs, both legal and illegal, may interact with ecstasy. These are listed under Dance Drugs page 210.

It's probably wise to stay off ecstasy if you are pregnant, although trials show that MDMA does not harm the offspring of rats.[6]

Protection

A nimal trials show , and many people believe, that a single capsule 20mg of the common antidepressant Prozac will protect a human when taken with ecstasy or up to four hours later. However Prozac will not protect against overheating or other immediate dangers.

Personality

Y our mental health is equally important, and rather more difficult to assess: see the chapter Adverse Psychological Effects (page 112). People most at risk are 'borderline personalities' (people without a clear distinction between reality and fantasy), people who are very easily upset and those who are 'unsure of who they are'.

In addition, people who have psychiatric problems which are under control are vulnerable. The drug allows the subconscious to surface, releasing suppressed problems. This may be useful in the right conditions, and this is why the drug was used in psychotherapy, but without the right support it may make matters worse.

Mature people with a strong sense of self are less vulnerable.

Situation

F ind a situation where you feel good.[7] If you enjoy large parties and clubs, that could be ideal especially if you are with friends. The main danger is overheating, so make quite sure that you keep cool enough. Drink enough water to prevent dehydration, either in the form of 'isotonic' drinks or eat a small pinch of salt with each pint, and avoid gulping. Remember that you may feel fine even when you are not, so get friends to look after you.

Taking ecstasy with a lover can be wonderful, but avoid being with people you are not sure of. The ideal home setting for taking ecstasy is a spacious room where you feel secure and can let yourself go without disturbing the neighbours. Outdoors in warm weather can be nice provided it is a place where you can let go without being seen or overheard.

Looking after yourself

If you have any doubts at all, take a very small dose and wait a whole hour before deciding whether to take more. Half a dose is quite enough for many first time users, especially women and small people. Drink plenty of water or fruit juice (except black currant[8]). The ultimate precaution would be to use a forehead thermometer, a plastic strip that changes colour with temperature, sometimes available free (from a chemist or pharmacy) to promote medicines.

After effects

Taking vitamins may help to reduce exhaustion, but getting plenty of sleep is more important. Folklore has it that calcium and magnesium help prevent jaw clench and even toxicity,[9] but this is not supported by medical evidence. Drugs such as L-Tyrosine and L-Tryptophan are also used, but again the effects are not proven.[10, 11]

Home use

Without external stimulation, ecstasy tends to make the user aware of deeper feelings and emotions.

Guide

If you decide to take ecstasy at home, choose a guide to look after you. A lover may be ideal, although that carries the risk of upsetting the relationship. The safest choice is someone familiar with ecstasy whom you trust and do not have to impress. Establish a clear set of rules for the trip, such as confidentiality, no sex and no activity that could be destructive or draw attention from neighbours.

Preparations

Ensure that you will not be disturbed by visitors or by the telephone. Wear loose clothing, line up some favourite music. Bring some personal objects that you are fond of – things to handle and look at, or perhaps some photographs of people you are fond of. A mirror can be fun for looking at yourself. A tape recorder and camera or video camera can be used to help to you relive the experience later; if you don't have access to these, have a pen and paper ready in case you have the urge to make notes. Earplugs and blinds like the ones given away on planes can be useful, too. Finally, make the space comfortable and attractive: have nice things to look at, smell and touch.

Timing

The full effect of the drug only lasts for three or four hours, but if possible you should allow a couple of days so that you have the next day to go over your experiences with your guide.[7]

If you can't take more than one day off, start reasonably early in the morning so that you will have plenty of time with your guide after the trip before getting a full night's sleep.

E and Prozac

Well, it was on New Year's eve and I wanted to bring in the New year ecstatically along with some friends. By this time I had been on Prozac for 16 days and hadn't recognised any differences in my mood. We took the E and the others soon began their journey into wonderland, but after 2 hours I was completely the same. I concluded that the Prozac inhibits the action of E.

Next day I decided that taking Prozac for depression is not as effective as taking E, and have since stopped. E has shown me my essential nature as beautiful, light, serene, loving, wise and joyful.

- A reader

[Anecdotal reports suggest that about a third of users find that Prozac prevents the effect of MDMA, a third that it makes no difference and the rest that it reduces the effect.]

L-Tryptophan [10]

Believed to help replenish serotonin levels and also to produce a mild pleasant buzz.

Restore neurotransmitters [11]

L-Tyrosine and L-Tryptophan have been "postulated to promote biosynthesis and thus to restore neurotransmitter function. Their use in open trials has produced unclear results. No controlled studies document their effectiveness."

Blackcurrant juice [8]

Blackcurrant juice is an MAO inhibitor and could be dangerous with ecstasy. "50 grams concentrated 5.5 times inhibits 92% of MAO action and electroencephalograms show remarkably increased brain activity." The same applies to dried tablets.

References

1. *High Time for Harm Reduction*, by Russell Newcombe, *Druglink*, January 1987.
2. A visit to Lifeline, a non-statutory drug agency in Manchester, August 1992.
3. 3D Research Bureau, 25 Halkyn Avenue, Liverpool L17 2AH (+44 151 733 9550). Dr Russell Newcombe's trade name for research into dance drug use, formerly called Rave Research.
4. Refer box page 196.
5. Visit to Dr John Henry at the National Poisons unit, Guys Hospital, London, December 1992.
6. *Behavioural and neurochemical effects of prenatal MDMA exposure in rats*, by St. Omer et al., in *Neurotoxicol Teratol*, vol. 13.
7. *The Adam Experience, a guide for first-time users*, by Starfire, 1985.
8. *Chemtech*, page 63 June 1993.
9. *Ecstasy: The MDMA Story*, by Bruce Eisner published 1994 at $17.95 by Ronin Publishing Inc., PO Box 1035, Berkeley, CA 94701, USA.
10. Available in 500 mg tablets "for pet animals only" from Cantassium Vitamins, 225 Putney Bridge Road, London SW15 2PY.
11. *Illicit psychostimulant use in Australia* by Dave Burrows et al, monograph, Australian Government Publishing Service, 1993.

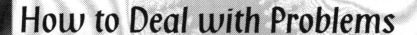

How to Deal with Problems

By Chris Jones, Teacher of Critical Care Courses for Nurses, Edge Hill University College, Liverpool.

This chapter explains the medical nature of deaths and problems caused by ecstasy, particularly overheating.
There are help sections on different levels, from the ordinary person to hospital staff. The first explains what to do if you are out with friends and one gets ill. It tells how you can help someone who has had a fit, or collapses. The next is for those trained in first aid and paramedics. Last, there is a section aimed at staff working in hospital emergency units.

A section for night club owners shows how they can provide support and how to handle casualties.

Is it really ecstasy?

There have been many well publicised cases of young and previously healthy people experiencing some very ugly reactions to tablets containing MDMA (ecstasy). Some others may have experienced adverse reactions to tablets sold as 'ecstasy' when in fact they contain substances other than MDMA. The reactions to ecstasy in this discussion will be confined to those situations where the person has bought genuine ecstasy, and MDMA will be considered as synonymous with ecstasy and E. These reactions to ecstasy can range from panic and the fear of dying, to actually dying in the most depressing circumstances.

The following is an attempt to describe what happens to people who react badly to ecstasy and what current thinking is to prevent and to treat E related problems.

Overheating

It is a cliche to repeat this sentiment, yet it remains a cliche which holds a lot of truth: if one wants to avoid the risks associated with ecstasy or any other type of drug then the best way is to avoid taking it. Nobody dies an ecstasy death without taking ecstasy.

That said, deaths associated with the use of E are relatively rare, compared to the number of doses which are thought to be taken. And compared with say motor cycling or even glue sniffing the number of fatalities is very small.

But that should not obscure the fact that ecstasy related deaths are very grim. The problems associated with E result from overheating (hyperthermia). This does not sound so bad. The problem is that the overheating in a serious E event is so severe that even experienced and case hardened Emergency and Intensive Care workers claim never to have never seen temperatures so high (41-42°C). This level of heat produces a cascade of other problems including unstoppable bleeding due to disturbances in the clotting system, even where unlimited blood transfusions are available, liver and kidney failure and death.

This of course is the absolute worst case scenario which is thankfully relatively rare. Nevertheless its rarity does not detract from its tragedy.

So what causes this sequence of events to commence? Can it be prevented? And what does one do if a friend looks ill? What is the role of the club paramedic? What is one to look out for? What equipment ought night clubs to have at hand? Does anybody know?

Heat stroke

Currently the leading theory is that the deaths associated with E are a form of drug induced heat stroke. This theory has a number of appealing features including the following – E alters the body's thermometer and inclines its user to warm up the core body temperature particularly where the external ambient temperature is high. It is also said to lower temperature if the external temperature is low. A warm temperature seems to enhance the E experience. The overheating effect of ecstasy is exacerbated by the following factors:

- o E users are thought to dance well beyond the point of which a "normal" person would tire and sit down.
- o DJs play seamless sequences of records which keep dancers active, and therefore producing more heat, over long periods of time.
- o The club atmosphere is hot and humid. The evaporation of sweat is an essential body defence mechanism to prevent overheating. Beyond a certain level of ambient humidity skin stops evaporating sweat – you can't unload water as efficiently into an atmosphere which is already damp.

The result of this hyperthermia is that blood starts to clot or coagulate over a widespread or disseminated area of the circulatory system. Elements in blood which are normally there to block holes are activated. The blood coagulation process uses the blood's elements involved in clotting (platelets, fibrinogen and clotting factors) faster than they can be replaced. This leads to an absolute decline in the quantity of these elements. The result of this decline mimics the result of anticoagulation; blood eventually refuses to clot. Bruising takes place. Gums bleed. There is haemorrhage. With an ecstasy death this process takes place very quickly. Hyperthermia leads rapidly to Disseminated Intravascular Coagulation (DIC) and the victim bleeds to death (in the most severe cases).

DIC is a complication of the hyperthermia. Hyperthermia is a complication of the use of the drug and its circumstances of use.

This is a very convincing theory which makes a lot of sense. Before the rave scene, ecstasy was in widespread use in the USA. It was responsible for a number of fatal incidents. But they did not involve bleeding to death. Most fatalities were not the type of death we are familiar with in the UK.

On the other hand, the heat stroke theory is just that – a theory. There is very little empirical evidence to support it. No studies have been done to demonstrate that the night clubs in which there has been a fatality were excessively hot or damp. It has not been demonstrated that victims danced more or less than on other occasions, or drank more or less than on other occasions.

In addition there is a heavy weight of literature suggesting that there are other drugs of the stimulant type which can on occasion cause a syndrome resembling heat stroke. Both amphetamine sulphate and cocaine have been reported to do this even in circumstances where there has been no great physical effort. And conversely, if the cause of these hyperthermic deaths were due to physical activity and ambient temperature then one might expect dancers at night clubs who had ingested cocaine or amphetamine to become hyperthermic through a similar mechanism, but this does not appear to happen.

There are also non stimulant drugs which produce hyperthermic responses. For example some drugs used in psychiatry, and in anaesthesia will produce a fatal hyperthermic reaction on occasion. The point of this discourse is to suggest caution. Maybe E related harm is due to the circumstances in which E is taken; the night club or party environment. Circumstantial evidence suggests this is so; these are the venues which usually produce the admission to hospital.

A more recently reported set of problems seem to be emerging. For a subset of people who are injured by ecstasy there appears to be another sequence of events at play. These are people who, for an improperly understood reason, lose some of the sodium (salt) in their blood. Maybe it is sweated out. Maybe it is urinated out in higher than normal quantities. Maybe ecstasy causes people to become thirsty and they dilute their sodium by drinking too much water. For whatever reason, they lose sodium. Technically, this is called hyponatraemia.

Sodium has the remarkable quality of holding water in the body's veins and arteries. Without it we tend to lose water into the fabric of our body's tissues. We swell. This does not present so much of a problem for most tissues but it presents the brain with real difficulties. The brain, encased as it is by skull, cannot swell a lot. It becomes compressed and puts pressure on the brain stem which controls heart and breathing functions. This can be fatal. 'Isotonic' drinks, unlike pure water, will help replace some minerals like sodium and preserve the balance of fluids in circulation.

So what do I do if I am out and my friend becomes ill?

The first thing to say in that most of the untoward effects of taking an E will be self limiting. A sensation of heat, a sense of the heart going faster, nausea, teeth clenching and visual disturbance may all be regarded as the 'normal' effects of a dose of ecstasy. Not everyone who has taken a tablet will like these effects. Many people will feel they have started something they cannot control and will feel fearful that they cannot stop themselves being carried along by the experience. They will be aware of where they are and what day it is, but they will be anxious and fearful. Get them out of the noise and the bright lights. Stay with them. Be reassuring. Give them a drink to sip but be careful they do not attempt to drown their anxiety in water. If possible try and get them to drink an 'isotonic' or sports type drink. Tell them they will be all right and take them home. Don't leave them alone, just in case they become worse.

Things to watch out for:

- Disorientation in time and place. They can't say where they are or what day it is.
- Drowsiness that comes to be unresponsive to commands like "open your eyes" or "squeeze my hand".
- Anything which looks like fitting.
- Breathlessness or difficulty breathing.

o   They feel abnormally hot to your touch even though they have been in a cool environment for some time.

At this point it is time for professional advice and a trip to hospital. You will be treated in confidence and with respect by the medical and nursing staff.

Collapse and unconsciousness

You are dancing with your friend on the dance floor, they look rather sweaty and out of it, their legs look heavy and clumsy. They fall and appear to faint. They may appear to have a fit.

Do not disregard this turn of events. Do not think they will be all right if they get up and 'dance it off'. Hyperthermia first affects the central nervous system and can cause it to shut down. This could be the prelude to some very serious events and needs a prompt response.

If you are at a night club the security personnel should be alerted and the club paramedic should be summoned (if there is one). A quiet and subdued recovery area should be available to take the person into.

Give as much information as you can about your friend's medical history. Are they epileptic? Are they diabetic? What have they taken? In what combinations?

Make a note of the response of the club staff. If they simply dump your friend out of the club and into the street then this should not be tolerated by the community and should carry consequences for the organisers.

What implications should these casualties have for night club owners?

The organisers of a rave, a large dance event or a night club have special difficulties. In the current climate the balance between organising a relaxed and informal dance event and preventing drug dealing and related problems by adequate security is hard to achieve. A night club which has heavy security atmosphere will find it hard to generate the underground atmosphere that clubbers seem to find appealing.

That said, there are numerous codes of practice in circulation to assist night club owners and dance event organisers to provide minimally decent conditions for their clients. Particular attention is drawn in these documents to the following headings:

o   The prevention of overcrowding. This is obviously of crucial importance in the control of the temperature but also the humidity of the night club or dance.

o   The availability of drinking water. This should be regarded as a basic requirement of decent management. Free water (or rather water as part of the entrance costs) should be available for dancers on request. Chilled soft drinks should also be available, particularly sports drinks which contain sodium.

o   Air conditioning and ventilation. This will control temperature rises in the night club and prevent overheating, which will contribute to the comfort and safety of dancers.

o Provision of 'chill out' areas where people can sit and cool down in a quieter and cooler environment

o Thought on the part of the DJ about giving dancers a rest periodically, by placing breaks in the music or by slowing the tempo down intermittently.

o The provision of first aid or paramedic cover, particularly at large or remote events.

What should be the response of the paramedic?

The definition of what constitutes the term 'paramedic' is subject to various interpretations. In this discussion the rather non technical definition of someone formally trained in first aid (as a minimum) will be used.

For all the services designated to help promote safety in clubs the emphasis should be on prevention of problems. If heat stroke is the cause of the fatalities and overheating can be prevented then lives may well be saved by some simple precautions.

Paramedics are in a position to assist in researching the problem of E related problems – for instance in measuring the temperature and humidity in night clubs. Club owners might consider the measurement of these parameters a wise legal precaution in the event of them being accused of poor public safety provision for their clients. Other priorities for the paramedic might include:

o Keeping notes on the types of problems which occur including the name of the casualty, what formal observations are made (temperature, pulse, level of consciousness etc.).

o Relating problems to the types of E which have been taken : are some "brands" producing more problems than others?

For paramedics in nightclubs there are bound to be a huge range of problems to deal with, mostly non E related, and the paramedics role is likely to be very challenging.

o There will be cuts and sprains.

o There will be alcohol related problems; vomiting , passing out etc.

o There will be non E related drug problems, after all ecstasy is not the only drug used by clubbers.

o There will be general medical conditions, asthma, epilepsy etc. that come on in the club where there are high output smoke machines and stroboscopic light effects.

o There may be the fights with resulting levels of trauma.

o There may be the complex pathology of ecstasy toxicity.

The first essential piece of equipment required by a paramedic is formal paramedic or first aid training by a recognised qualifying organisation e.g. Red Cross or St. John's Ambulance. At large venues in particular, it is simply not enough to have untrained personnel dealing with potential problems of this order of complexity. Basic life support skills are essential. Secondly they ought to be aware of drugs and drug related problems particularly relating to hyperthermia, dehydration and anxiety states.

Considering that fatalities have been associated with overheating, a paramedic facility ought to be equipped with somewhere to lie the casualty down, cold water, maybe some sachets of mineral replacement powders available from pharmacies, a fan or air conditioning device, an electric thermometer, a collection of airways, an ice machine and a non contact artificial respiration mask should be available. There should also be a telephone so that an ambulance can be called if required. Any first aid facility should have enough room to get a stretcher in and out if necessary.

Friends should be asked to reassure and sit with people whose problems amount to little more than anxiety. Also to accompany the victim to hospital if required. They can give an accurate history to medical staff and will be aware of subtle alterations in the patients psychology.

Suggested approach for club paramedics

A person is brought to the paramedic:

- o Is the person conscious? If No, ring ambulance.
- o Is there a normal level of consciousness? (Do they know where they are or what day it is?) If No, ring ambulance.
- o Can you detect any physical problems? eg. Racing pulse (over 120/min over five minutes of quiet and rest), high temperature, abnormal prolonged sweating or breathlessness. If Yes, ring ambulance.
- o Put in recovery position. Sit down, observe for levels of consciousness, heart rate, temperature.
- o Do not give anything by mouth.
- o Keep off dance floor.
- o Check pulse.
- o Do not leave alone.
- o Assess temperature.
- o Remove excess clothing.
- o Commence cooling – fan/water.
- o Observe for unusual bruising/bleeding.

If the problems associated with E are due to overheating then the quicker that heating can be controlled the fewer (theoretically) complications will occur.

Removing hats, woollies, shoes and socks and commencing fanning and sponging down ahead of the arrival of the ambulance might reduce body temperature enough to prevent the worst of the problems.

Do not be tempted to give the victim large volumes to drink. Drinking pint after pint of water can seriously damage the delicate balance of fluids inside a person's body. The result of this can be catastrophic and itself cause unconsciousness and fitting in the victim. Sipping a glass of cold water over an hour will replace lost fluids, and a mineral rich replacement sachet or isotonic sports drink should supplement salts.

If you have to call an ambulance

Get as accurate a story from a witness as possible. Send a friend of the victim if you can – the friend will have an idea about the type of tablets taken and may still posses an example for analysis. This might be extremely useful if a toxic batch has come on to the market.

Advice to staff working in emergency units

M any hospitals in city areas have now seen at least one example of an ecstasy related emergency and most units are now sensitive to this type of drug emergency.

This does not alter the fact however that an ecstasy casualty can produce a confusing clinical picture and may exhibit odd and atypical signs and symptoms. Frequently the patient is not in a position to "own up" to taking drugs due to loss of consciousness and the best source of information are friends who may have come in the ambulance. These friends are not likely to be as forthcoming as they might otherwise be if they fear the response of the accident and emergency staff.

Confidentiality, particularly with parents and police, and an open and non judgmental attitude is not only the basis of an ethical approach to ecstasy related problems, it is of vital clinical importance. The friends are your best source of information if the casualty is unconscious. They must feel confident in you. They must feel safe with you. There must be a relationship of trust.

Taking dance drugs is, after all, a mainstream activity for many thousands of young people every week end. Victims are unlucky or maybe foolish (depending on your point of view) rather than evil.

So what needs to be done?

Firstly the drug induced aspect of the problem needs to be recognised.

- o What is the source of admission? Is it a night club, a concert, a party (high suspicion), or is it somewhere quiet and unlikely to have a rave atmosphere (low suspicion)?
- o What is the time of admission? Is it in the early hours of the morning (high suspicion) or is it in the middle of the afternoon (low suspicion)?
- o What day is the admission? Is it a weekend night (high suspicion) or the

midweek (low suspicion)?

o What does the patient appear like? Are the pupils dilated? Are they writhing and twisted? Are they hot?

o What is the drug? Are they carrying any tablets or what do their friends say?

Formal observations may include temperature which may be elevated, pulse which may be rapid and thready and blood pressure which may be low.

Central to controlling ecstasy related problems is thought to be the control of core temperature and restoration of circulating volume. The patient may be rigid and exhibiting tremor and/or fitting. Cooling the patient, control of muscle spasm (and thereby reducing heat production) are top priority. Intubation, sedation and paralysis may well be considered, though this has been reported to be difficult in circumstances where the jaws are so tightly clamped that an endo tracheal tube is difficult to pass. Transfer to intensive care may be necessary. Active cooling measures may be commenced concurrently. Bathing with water, fanning, removal of clothes may all act to reduce temperature.

Restoring circulating volume is a little more problematic. Heat stroke may require large volume fluid replacement. However low circulating sodium levels may make rapid volume infusion a dangerous course of action to take. Until the level of plasma sodium has been measured care should be taken with fluid replacement. Over rapid fluid replacement in the presence of low sodium can lead to swelling of brain tissue and damage to the brain stem. While waiting for the blood results to come back from the laboratory the insertion of a CVP line may be considered to guide fluid replacement.

Recommended blood investigations

o Urea and electrolytes to investigate the balance of electrolytes, particularly sodium levels.

o Full blood count to measure haemoglobin levels and assess the presence of blood loss.

o Plasma osmolality to measure dehydration and the concentration of plasma. Clotting studies to assess the loss of platelets and fibrinogen and the measurement of clotting times.

o Creatinine Kinase because many ecstasy casualties have developed rapid muscle breakdown (Rhabdomyolysis) and this investigation can quantify cell breakdown products in circulation.

o Blood gases for determination of gas exchange and blood acid/base balance.

o Toxicology assays to pinpoint the likely combinations of drugs.

Recommended urine investigations:

o Osmolality to measure the content of solutes in the urine

o Electrolytes to measure sodium levels of the urine
o Myoglobin to measure muscle breakdown product in the urine
o Toxicology studies

Specific treatment for the minute by minute management of the E casualty should be guided by experts. All drug victims should have their treatment guided by the advice of the regional poisons services who hold extensive databases on adverse drug reactions. All accident and emergency departments carry their phone number.

© **Chris Jones, 1997**

The author would like to thank Dr. Chris Luke, Dr. Euan Shearer and Dr. John Ramsey for their kind advice and support. Also the library staff of the Aintree Complex, in particular Zoe, for kind assistance in gathering data for this paper.

References

Brown C, Osterloh J (1987) Multiple severe complications from recreational ingestion of MDMA (ecstasy) *Journal of the American Medical Association* 258: 780-1

Chadwick IS, Linsley A, Freemont AJ, Doran B, Curry PD (1991) Ecstasy, 3,4 methylenedioxymethamphetamine (MDMA) a fatality associated with coagulopathy and hyperthermia. *Journal of the Royal Society of Medicine* 84;371

Henry J, (1992) Ecstasy and the Dance of Death. *British Medical Journal* 305; 5

Henry J, Jeffreys KJ, Dawling S (1992) Toxicity and Deaths from 3,4, methylenedioxymethamphetamine (Ecstasy). *Lancet.*

Jones C (1993) The doubts surrounding Ecstasy and the response of the emergency nurse. *Accident and Emergency Nursing* 1;193-198

Jones C, Dickinson P (1992) From ecstasy to agony. *Nursing Times* March 25.

Kessel B, (1994) Hyponatraemia after ingestion of "Ecstasy". *British Medical Journal* 308; 414.

Matthai SM, Davidson DC, Sills JA, Alexandrou D, (1996) Cerebral oedema after ingestion of ecstasy. *British Medical Journal* 312; 1359.

Ginsburg M, Hertman M, Schmidt-Nowark WD, (1970), Amphetamine intoxication with coagulopathy, hyperthermia, and reversible remal failure. A syndrome resembling heatstroke *Annals of Internal Medicine* 73:81-85.

Notle KB, (1991), Rhabdomyolysis Associated with Cocaine Abuse, *Human Pathology* 22, (11), 1141-1145.

Welch RD, Todd K, Krause GS, (1991), Incidence of Cocaine-Associated Rhabdom-yolysis, *Annals of Emergency Medicine* 20 (2): 154-157.

Oh T (1990) *Manual of Intensive Care* Chap 74, Butterworth, London.

Hollander JE, Hoffman RS, (1992), Cocaine induced myocardial infarction: an analysis and review of the literature. *The Journal of Emergency Medicine* 10 (2); 169-177.

Institute for the Study of Drug Dependence,(1991), *Drug misuse in Britain*, ISDD, London.

Pollack CV, Biggers DW, Carlton FB, Achord JL, Cranston PE, Eggen JT, Griswold JA, (1992) Two Crack Cocaine Body Stuffers *Annals of Emergency Medicine*, 21:(11) 1372-1380.

Derlett RW, Rice P, Horowitz BZ, Lord RV, (1989), Amphetamine Toxicity: Experience with 127 Cases *The Journal of Emergency Medicine* 7: 157-161.

Merigian KS, Park LJ, Leeper KV, Browning RG, Giometti R, (1994), Adrenergic crisis from crack cocaine ingestion: Report of Five Cases *The Journal of Emergency Medicine* 12:(4) 485-490.

O'Donnell AE, Mappin FG, Sebo TJ, Tazelaar H. (1991) Interstitial pneumonitis associated with "crack" cocaine abuse. *Chest* ; 100: 1155-7

Kloner RA, Hale S, Alker K, Rezlalla S,(1992), The Effects of Acute and Chronic Cocaine Use on The Heart, *Circulation* 85 (2) , 407-419

Lancet 340:384-387

Wake D, 1995, Ecstasy overdose: a case study. *Intensive and Critical Care Nursing* 11 (1): 6-9.

Dance Drugs

Ecstasy is often used to include various drugs besides MDMA. This chapter is about the chemicals referred to as ecstasy and other drugs found on the dance scene – and some which are more often used at home for exploration.

Two other drugs are similar enough to be accepted as MDMA by many people, but some people don't notice the difference even when what is sold as ecstasy is no more than a form of speed. A large part of the effect depends on expectations.

On the other hand, regular users often believe that the quality has gone down, or that they have not been able to get pure MDMA recently, when in fact it is the effect on themselves that has changed.

Most people who take ecstasy choose to 'mix and match' their drugs, so the effect of some popular combinations are described. Then there is a description of each of the more popular drugs.

Lastly, a section about testing; both tests to see if drugs have been used, and tests to see what is in a sample of a drug.

MDMA

The full chemical name is '3,4-Methylenedioxy-N-Methylamphetamine', pronounced 'Three-Four Methylene Dioxy N Methyl Amphetamine'. To a chemist this is a description of the molecule. The word Methyl is sometimes abbreviated to Meth, and the letter N and numbers 3,4 are sometimes omitted, leaving the more usual 'Methylenedioxymethamphetamine'. The 3,4 indicates the way in which parts of the molecule are linked together, as it is possible to produce an *isomer* which has all the same components joined differently. Similarly, the initials are sometimes reduced to MDM (although this is old-fashioned) and of course there are the various popular names such as ecstasy, E, Adam and X.

Many people believe that the name implies a mixture of ingredients but this is wrong – just as water is not a mixture of oxygen and hydrogen although its molecule consists of oxygen and hydrogen atoms. Like water, **MDMA is a compound, not a mixture**. So, although the name contains the word amphetamine and the law refers to MDMA as 'psychedelic amphetamine', **MDMA contains no amphetamine**. However, the amphetamine-like effects are probably due to similar dopamine release due to having a similar molecular structure, although MDMA releases serotonin in preference to dopamine.[1,2]

Physical properties

Pure MDMA is a white crystalline solid that is normally hydrated. When heated any water of crystallization first boils off before it melts at about 148°C.

When the crystals are too small to see it looks like a fine powder which tends to stick to a dry finger but without forming lumps. Crystals are often large enough to sparkle and it is possible to grow giant crystals up to a gram.

MDMA is chemically stable: it does not decompose in air, light or heat so that it has a long shelf life. It dissolves in water and alcohol but does not absorb dampness from the air.

Taste is distinctly bitter. However, this is similar to some other substances and cannot easily be distinguished from amphetamine sulphate.

How MDMA is taken

Ecstasy type drugs are nearly always taken orally, usually in pill form. Powder is usually swallowed in a capsule to avoid the taste, but it can be dissolved in a drink or dabbed into the mouth with a damp finger. However, it can be dissolved in water and taken by injection, when it comes on with a rush, or inserted into the anus, when, according to a reader, it has a smooth rapid effect "if you can work out a good clean way of pumping it in".

Is it really ecstasy?

What is sold as ecstasy in Britain may be a number of different drugs. Of these, MDA (3,4 Methylenedioxyamphetamine) and MDEA[3] (3,4 Methylenedioxyethyl-amphetamine, also called MDE or Eve) are quite similar to MDMA.[1] Some contain only speedy drugs like caffeine, amphetamine and ephedrine, a few contain completely different drugs and of course some are simply fakes with no effect at all.

Varying quality

Since ecstasy first arrived in Britain, the quality has varied widely. At first it was almost entirely pure MDMA, but as it became more popular the quality declined, reaching a low ebb in the winter of 1992. Since then quality has generally improved, with a higher proportion of pills containing MDMA, and average doses 10% higher. The chance of getting pure MDMA in Britain or Holland is about two out of three, and the chance of a pill containing a similar type of drug (MDA or MDEA) is about three out of four.[4]

Eve banned [5]

MDEA was officially banned in Holland on July 27 1993, but a 3-day grace period was granted to allow customers of a 'dial-a-drug' service to hand in their purchases, since producers had exploited a legal loophole by advertising door-to-door deliveries like Pizza.

MDMA, MDA and MDEA [1]

Release of dopamine in rats is greatest with MDA, less with MDMA and least with MDEA. Dopamine release may relate to amphetamine-like side effects.

Clear or stoned

MDMA is clear, MDEA is vaguely stoned, and MDA is quite stoned.

– A reader

How long will E keep?

If MDMA had been hidden away in the pyramids by the Pharaohs of ancient Egypt, it would still be active today.

Alexander Shulgin

Dr. King, of the forensic laboratory at Aldermaston, told me that Snowballs, a notoriously strong brand of ecstasy widely available in the early eighties, consisted of very strong pure MDA[6] which came from a government laboratory in Latvia. After splitting from the Soviet Union, Latvia needed western currency and had the advantage of no drug laws, so they joined up with a German businessman to produce MDA for export as ecstasy. This went well for a couple of years until a consignment of ten million tablets was intercepted in Frankfurt airport, since when MDA has been rare. Similarly, MDEA is less common since it was outlawed in Holland. The result has been a higher proportion of MDMA on the market.

Drugs with similar effects to MDMA

M DEA and MDA are two common drugs similar to MDMA. All three are psychedelic amphetamines with fairly similar effects, although connoisseurs invariably prefer MDMA because of its empathic quality. MDA lasts twice as long (8-12 hours, while MDMA lasts 4-6 hours), is more speedy and has a psychedelic edge to it. MDEA (sometimes sold as Eve), lasts a rather shorter time (3-5 hours) and is nearer to MDMA in effect, but still lacks its communicative qualities.[3]
2CB is occasionally sold as ecstasy. It is more psychedelic and less empathic, but it does not inhibit erection and allows more intellectual thought patterns.

The effects of all these drugs is less after a few successive days' use, a phenomenon known as tolerance. However, there is no cross tolerance between MDA and MDMA: someone who has taken so much MDMA that it has no more effect can still get off on MDA and vice versa.[7]

Why ecstasy may not be as good as it used to be

Although the average quality of ecstasy has improved in Britain over the years, street wisdom declares that ecstasy is not as good today.[4] What are the reasons for this?

The first is tolerance.[8] If you had an unlimited supply of absolutely pure MDMA and took the same dose each day in the same situation, you would find that the most smooth, open, loving experience with the least amphetamine-like effects would be on the first dose. Each subsequent experience would have less of the loving feeling and more speediness until, after five days or so, you might as well be taking amphetamine (speed). You would then have to stop taking MDMA for a time before you could experience the good effects again. After a week without MDMA, its effect will be nearly back to normal, although to get the full effect you may have to abstain for as long as six weeks. Even then, the experience may not be as good as your first one – but that is probably due to being familiar with the effect. Tolerance varies according to the individual.

The second factor is your state of mind. Although this applies less with MDMA than with many other drugs (particularly LSD), the effect is highly responsive to your mood – in fact one of the drug's effects is to liberate suppressed feelings. You may not even notice that you are uncomfortable about something until the drug takes effect. It has also been suggested that dancing may also alter the effect.[9]

Expectation of the effect of a drug also plays a surprisingly large role – people get what they expect. Everyone likes to believe that they won't be fooled, but tests in which LSD and hash were substituted with a placebo show that, with those drugs at least, nearly everyone experiences what they expect.[10] Alexander Shulgin, who wrote a book on the effects of psychedelics,[11] describes how he had an emergency operation on his thumb during the war. Before the operation he was given a glass of orange juice with white powder at the bottom which immediately sent him unconscious – later he was told the powder was sugar.

Placebo effect [10]

A trial using male actors found that LSD subjects experienced maximum loss of control after 30 minutes, and this declined gradually. "After two hours, subjects reported feelings of having acquired new meanings and a more prominent general feeling of disinhibition." The researchers found that those who had taken placebos experienced similar types of symptoms at two, five and eight hours after ingestion, although the symptoms varied from strong to very weak.

With marijuana, some placebos were made by extracting varying amounts of the active ingredient THC (tetrahydrocannabinol). The symptoms reported by most subjects were consistent with strength, but the unexpected result was that chronic users felt stronger reactions from the placebo.

MDMA combined with other drugs

Many party users like to take ecstasy with speed[12] which adds excitement and prolongs the experience at relatively low cost. Some ravers prefer to combine it with LSD (known as candy-flip in the USA) or with psilocybin mushrooms, so combining hallucinogenic qualities with the warmth of ecstasy. This also extends the experience at low cost, as LSD lasts for about twice as long as MDMA. Home users often use this combination, particularly in natural surroundings.

Ecstasy is also used with cannabis and alcohol at dance parties, and cannabis is widely smoked in the chill-out period afterwards. Although drinking has made a comeback,[13] most users feel that alcohol drowns the effect of ecstasy. Alcohol taxes the liver and kidneys, causing dehydration, so taking it in combination with ecstasy is likely to increase the danger of overheating and result in worse after effects.[14,15] Similarly, when taken with amphetamine the toxicity is greater than when each drug is taken on its own.[16]

Home users sometimes refer to MDMA as a 'psychedelic amplifier' or 'catalyst', enhancing the effect of psychedelics without changing their quality. This has been tested with LSD, 2CB, MEM, 2-CT-2 and may apply to all other psychedelics.[17] Others report that LSD loses its usual effect and simply amplifies the effect of the ecstasy.[18] Another use for ecstasy is to avoid bad trips: once a positive mood is established, the course is set for the LSD trip.

A new book due to be published in 1997 called The Secret Chief [19] by Myron Stolaroff describes the effect of various combinations. Myron and his wife Jean experimented and found that LSD, 2CB, MEM, and 2-CT-2 were enhanced when taken an hour or so after MDMA.

> *The aftermath of MDMA was not the same as with established psychedelics such as LSD and mescaline, which most often leave the body quite cleansed and rejuvenated... If one's psyche is relatively clear, the descent is quite euphoric, and the remainder of the day is spent in a very satisfying state of contentment. However, if there is unresolved material in the unconscious that did not get dealt with completely, the drop in the action of the drug seems quite sudden, and one is left physically uncomfortable and somewhat unsettled.*

> *To counteract this we thought, why not supplement with another, more powerful, psychedelic substance. This turned out to be a splendid idea. I particularly liked it, because what made the beginning of my explorations [with true psychedelics such as LSD] uncomfortable was the negative karma I had accumulated, which had to be expiated before I could thoroughly enjoy the experience. Now I could dispose of this with MDMA, which occurred, I felt, automatically and very pleasantly [enabling me] to soar into fresh spaces free of my usual psychic load.*

> *This worked so well that I embarked on a study to prove that every good psychedelic was better if first preceded by MDMA.*

> *from The Secret Chief[19]*

A popular combination among home users is 2CB taken towards the end of an MDMA trip. As the 2CB takes over from the MDMA, the experience is subtly changed towards a more intellectual viewpoint from which some people find it easier to assimilate any insights gained.[20] 2CB also has the reputation of providing the erotic component usually suppressed by ecstasy.[18] Ketamine is also sometimes used while on ecstasy for self exploration.[20]

Dangers of combining ecstasy with other drugs

Marijuana –   No known dangers. Many people enjoy the combination but being stoned reduces the MDMA clarity.

LSD –   No known dangers. Popular combination in low doses.

Amphetamines -   Risk of toxicity, overheating, problems due to high blood pressure, psychological problems and possibility of addiction increased. Popular and cheap way to extra energy for dancing, but reduces the warmth of MDMA.

Cocaine – Risk of toxicity, overheating, problems due to high blood pressure, psychological problems and possibility of addiction increased.

Tobacco – No known added dangers. Some people find E enhances the pleasure of smoking.

Alcohol – Both dehydrate and tax the liver leading to worse hangover and greater risk of overdose. Used by some to relax before taking MDMA, but reduces clarity.

Combinations

2CB can be taken with, before or after the E and can produce deep empathic content and helps ecstasy users to retain and develop their insights. It can also help an E trip to become sexual, but he suggests that the way to make any psychedelic trip sexual is to become sexually involved early on.

LSD and E ('Candyflip') produces a more intense E high rather than an acid high, but deeper and more visual. The author says Ketamine is not enhanced by ecstasy.

Nitrous oxide on E is 'quite enjoyable'. "A blast of nitrous oxide always feels good, especially if you're already high…It can put an additional peak on your peak, and can be used to 'break up' a state of mind so you can switch to something else".

Future ecstasy-type drugs

The conditions are right for a flood of new and interesting drugs coming onto the black market. New techniques and equipment will soon open the way to creating whole new ranges of drugs. It may soon be possible to design a drug to produce a desired effect, then to get a preliminary idea of the effect by means of electrodes implanted in the brains of rats.[16]

The way is now open – and the search is on (illicitly) – to produce something that has the empathic qualities of MDMA without toxicity. One approach is to invent a more potent drug – this could be less toxic, since less would be used and toxicity is related to dose rather than effect.[16]

Future psychoactive drugs may well be tailored according to fashion. As people become bored with the current fashion and move towards a new way of behaviour (such as being more grounded, perhaps) drugs will be created to produce the desired mood.

Non-ecstasy dance drugs
Speedy drugs

Amphetamine (amphetamine sulphate, speed, whizz, billy in UK)

The most widely used dance drug, probably because it is cheaper than ecstasy and its effect is more predictable. Mostly sold in wraps about 10 per cent pure, usually cut with inactive filler but sometimes with other drugs. Provides energy and is often used for dancing, carries the same physical dangers as MDMA but is addictive and may cause amphetamine psychosis. May be responsible for many deaths attributed to ecstasy.[21] Energy gained has to be repaid by exhaustion. Overdose results in feeling irritable and even violent. Lasts up to eight hours, but users often top up by dabbing small amounts onto their gums throughout the night. Can also be snorted, added to a drink or injected.

Amphetamine the real killer?

Dr. Russell Newcombe has analysed Government statistics and shown that among the few reliable reports, more people died as a result of amphetamine than ecstasy. Since amphetamine is more commonly used and also causes heatstroke, it is quite possible that the media blames ecstasy when in fact amphetamine is the actual killer.

Methamphetamine (ice or crystal meth, speed or tweak in US)

A pure form of amphetamine. Very toxic over 25-30mg. Can be smoked, snorted or injected. Lasts up to 24 hours. A white crystalline solid. When heated gives off a vapour which is inhaled. Tendency for 'binge and crash' behaviour and can produce psychosis or paranoia ('sketching').

Dexedrine (dexys)

5mg white scored tablet marked EVANS.DBS. Consists of dexamphetamine sulphate. Effect is similar to speed and causes high blood pressure. Should not be used with MAO inhibitors.

Cocaine (cocaine hydrochloride, coke, charlie, snow)

Similar to amphetamine in effect but gives a characteristic numbness where it touches the mouth or throat. Usually snorted up a nostril using a rolled up banknote. More expensive and less long lasting than amphetamine, which may account for its luxury image and the cocky attitudes of users. Comes on quickly, but only lasts about half an hour. Became more popular as a dance drug (particularly in House and Garage clubs) in 1993 when poor quality ecstasy flooded the market. Can eventually dissolve the division between nostrils.

Crack cocaine (rocks, freebase)

Derived from cocaine. It is smoked and gives a shorter, bigger burst of energy but is more addictive. The high is almost instant, but quickly diminishes and is over in about 10 minutes.

Ephedrine and over-the-counter stimulants

Ephedrine is found in over-the-counter drugs such as Primatine, and pseudoephedrine hydrochloride is sold as Sudafed. About three tablets (60mg each) have a similar effect to caffeine. It is also sometimes sold as ecstasy, and as a constituent of 'herbal ecstasy'.

Ephedrine is a prescription drug with a maximum dose of 60mg. According to the British National Formulary an overdose produces restlessness, muscle spasms, racing heart, dry throat and cold extremities. It is "not recommended and should be avoided whenever possible". Note that the recreational dose is several times the prescription dose, and is potentially dangerous for people with weak hearts. Lasts three to four hours with gentle comedown.

Preparations sold as cold remedies often contain ephedrine, pseudoephedrine, phenylephrine and phenylpropanolamine. When taken in large doses, these produce speedy effects, mood elevation and even euphoria. Side effects are similar to amphetamine, and are increased if used in combination.

However, some medications also contain paracetamol which can damage the liver in large doses. The 'best' products to use are the ones that contain only sympathomimetics such as Sudafed. However, SudafedPlus tablets also contain paracetamol as well as the ephedrine.

Methcathinone (cat, khat or qat)

A herb (Catha Edulis) that is chewed to produce an amphetamine-like effect. Somali immigrants use it as a legal high in the UK, and recently also party goers, although it is illegal in the US and some other countries. It only works when fresh, so avoid if limp or dried up. A drug Cathinone or Methcathinone can be derived from the herb.

Isobutyl nitrate (poppers, liquid gold)

Now illegal in Britain unless prescribed by a doctor. Sniffed or breathed in open mouth.

Gives strong rushes of euphoria for a minute or two, especially while on E. Can cause black out, headache, nausea and even heart attacks. Less common is 'English poppers' (amyl nitrate). Popular among gay men for sex as it relaxes the anus without loss of erection.

Drugs which produce relaxation, 'depressants'

Temazepam

Sold in 10-30mg capsules; also 10-20mg tablets. Muscle relaxant and sleeping pill. Popular in Scotland when coming down after E, and its use is spreading. Normally swallowed, but when melted and injected can solidify and cause circulation problems. In 1994, 50 deaths were linked to Temazepam in the Glasgow area alone.

GHB, (liquid E or GBH)

A drug that reduces anxiety and relaxes muscles in low doses but too much can lead to unrouseable sleep. Normal dose is 2-3 grams and lasts about four hours. An enthusiast says it removes inhibitions much like E but the biggest difference is that it slows you down until you eventually fall asleep. "After a night out on E and Speed, GHB is an alternative to smoking dope on comedown, and if you have sex it's good for a while until you fall asleep."

My one experience was of feeling relaxed in a drunken way but giddy also and nauseous, but I was told this effect is caused by taking too much. It comes in small bottles, looks like water and tastes salty.

Recently there have been a number of reported deaths from its use in the USA, reported addiction among heavy users and warnings not to combine it with alcohol.

DXM (dextromethorphan hydrobromide)

Low dose is similar to alcohol producing carefree clumsiness with a touch of psychedelic and speedy effect. Intense and rhythmic music induces a state of euphoria and dancing becomes fun. On a higher dose imagination can be vividly experienced (not always pleasant), feelings of dissociation from the body can occur and on very high doses "profound alterations in consciousness".

Contained in over-the-counter cough medicines sold as syrups, capsules and sometimes in pill form. Popular sources are Robitussin Maximum Strength Cough and Vicks Formula 44, but Drixoral Cough gelcaps contain 20mg DXM. Cough mixtures listing other active ingredients may have unpleasant effects.

Dose: about 100-200mg for someone weighing 70 kg (150 lbs or 11 stone). Topping up tends to increase duration rather than intensity. Duration: 4-8 hours.

Avoid if you are taking an antidepressant of the MAOI type. Other types such as Prozac may increase the effect.

Drugs which produce altered states of consciousness [18]

Ketamine

Usually sold as Special K, sometimes as ecstasy mixed with other drugs such as ephedrine and caffeine. Low doses produce a floppy relaxed feeling but higher doses produce dissociation (feeling separate from your body), near death experiences and insights. Higher doses may cause more powerful hallucinations than LSD; these can be confused with reality. Since it is used as an anaesthetic in far higher doses, Ketamine is not physically dangerous although its mental effects can be. Ketamine is both chemically and neuropharmacologically related to PCP.

LSD (acid, A, trips and type names such as microdots, windowpane or strawberries)

In low doses can enhance sound and lights, but in higher doses produces strong visual and emotional effects (not always pleasant).[22] Blotters (small bits of paper with a logo) usually contain about 50µg (1µg is a microgram or millionth of a gram). LSD will decompose in warmth, air and light.

---

ecstasy, amphetamine and LSD compared [22]

A survey comparing the subjective effects of amphetamine, ecstasy and LSD. 31 subjects were questioned averaging 24 years old. 21 were men (8 homosexual).

On ecstasy, people reported being far more agreeable than on LSD or speed, besides being more elated and composed. Amphetamine users reported being more energetic, confident and clear headed.

MDMA and amphetamine both had positive effects on five out of six measures of mood, however, ecstasy produced anxiety while amphetamine caused confusion. LSD caused both these negative effects plus loss of confidence, and less positive effects than the others.

Overall, ecstasy scored top closely followed by amphetamine with LSD producing as many negative effects as positive.

The dose normally taken in the sixties was 250µg. This produces a different level of consciousness which provides dramatic new insights but which may prove hard to relate to everyday life. Hallucinations can be powerful, but can be distinguished from reality. The experience may be personal with communication difficult, although in some situations trips are shared as though telepathically.

The very low dose of LSD used (a thousand trips contain less drug than a single E) has the result that purity can be pretty well guaranteed simply because active amounts of other drugs would not fit on a blotter. Psychological dangers do exist, but medically it is harmless.

The LSD experience may seam to be out of control, but in fact depends very much on the situation and can be 'steered'. It is a myth that different varieties of acid having different effects.

Bad trips are often blamed on strychnine (rat poison) in LSD, this is a myth. The amount of strychnine that could fit on a blotter would not be enough to have any effect. Bad trips result from your own fears becoming magnified, so don't do acid where you may not feel completely secure.

Dealing with a bad trip

Always remember that the bad experience is induced by a drug that will wear off. The same chemical can also produce beautiful effects and it really is possible to turn any trip into a good one. Albert Hofmann (inventor of LSD) suggests to keep telling yourself that 'you are immortal': nothing you see because of the trip can hurt you. If you experience something horrible don't try to fight it, but go with it and it will change into something wonderful by itself. Someone on a bad trip may appear impossible to communicate with, but in fact needs attention and reassurance – remind them that the effect will wear off in a few hours. People on bad trips are likely to be in a paranoid state; so that if you are trying to help someone, be prepared for them to distrust you.

Attempts to force a come down by giving other drugs such as tranquillizers are liable to make matters worse; some people have used MDMA to help turn the bad trip into something positive, but this should only be done by people able to give appropriate support.

Bad acid

"There was speed in this acid, I was restless as hell". He was restless all right, but before taking it. It is amazing how people cling to their view that everything bad is coming from the outside.

I never had any crap LSD. It always worked. I saw God regularly, every Saturday afternoon for two years. Then I got bored with him, and decided that the devil had all the best drugs.

Comments posted on the Internet newsgroup alt.drugs

Magic mushrooms (psilocybin, liberty caps, mushies, shrooms)

Effect: similar to LSD with the added attraction of being natural, free and even legal if eaten fresh from the field – processing, which could include handling and drying, makes it a Class A drug.

Appearance: Usually dried and are thin dark brown, but may be powdered. Typical mushroom smell. These are found in pasture in the autumn, but tend to be hidden in the grass. They are among the smallest mushrooms, and are distinguished by being uneven greyish rather than brown; their pointed caps and wiggly stems. The whole cap and stem are active. Can be eaten or stewed and drunk as tea.

Dose: 0.5-3 grams dried or 5-30 small mushrooms. Strength varies.

Cannabis, marijuana (hash, smoke, draw, weed)

Most common illicit drug. Normally smoked either as dried leaves (grass) or the resin (hash), on its own in the US but usually mixed with tobacco in Europe. Can also be eaten but the effect is not immediate so it's hard to judge how much to take. Effects are a flow of imagination, amusement, enhanced sound and colour, but can also produce paranoia and even LSD-like hallucinations in high doses.

Generally regarded as harmless, but when smoked with tobacco is probably more harmful than tobacco in terms of risk of lung cancer due to deep inhalation.

Skunk is a particularly potent variety of marijuana developed in Holland.

Herbal ecstasy

Legal substitutes for ecstasy are becoming popular. They contain various herbs or herbal extracts that are psychoactive and are advertised to have similar effects to ecstasy but are claimed to be legal and safe.[23] In fact, many of them are not safe, and some are illegal because they contain extracts rather than herbs (such as cathinone or ephedrine) which requires a 'use license'.

In fact, none of them cause serotonin and dopamine release which are the keys to the emotional effect of ecstasy; some are dangerous and also illegal in the quantities recommended. Some cause similar physical effects such as tingling skin, raised blood pressure, heart rate and sweating, and it is possible that these physical effects remind us of ecstasy and stimulate our brains to release neurotransmitters, just as happens with 'contact high'.

I sent a list of all the ingredients found in a variety of products and herbs sold as legal highs to a German specialist in psychotropic plants. She reported that most produced only speedy effects except the plant Ephedra or Ma Huang in Chinese, from which the drug ephedrine is extracted. "You feel shivers up and down your spine, especially in the roots of your hair. Ephedra makes you sweat and feel your muscles and skin more intensely. It can act as an aphrodisiac, especially for women. Unlike ecstasy it helps you to concentrate your mind, so that some people find it a good drug to use for mental work. As it's unpleasant to overdose, start with a low dose such as tea made from one teaspoon of dried herb stewed for five minutes and strained."

Ephedra is prescribed in Chinese medicine, but the maximum dose of the herb that may be legally prescribed is 600mg three times a day. See above under Ephedrine for effects and dangers.

Cloud 9 [23]

Cloud 9 is the street name for Ephedra, the active ingredient in the Chinese herb Ma Huang. It's taken in conjunction with two enhancers Nirvana Plus – a mixture of three amino acids, and Yohimbix 8, a liquid based on the hallucinogen Yohimbine, extracted from the bark of an African tree. Newcombe says Yohimbine (which the paper says is in the same class as LSD) may be dangerous when combined with red cheese/red wine and may cause long term psychological damage.

Herbal ecstasy trial

I was given 50 samples of a herbal ecstasy (with a butterfly logo, then called e-line ecstasy) to try out at Glastonbury festival in 1994, complete with instructions:

> *Open your heart and allow yourself to become overwhelmed, because then and only then can you feel the true force of this experience... All six senses may become intensified. Things may seem crisper and clearer. Sounds may sound louder and feel more intense. Touch becomes more enhanced, things just simply feel better to touch, taste, see, smell, and feel. Imagination will flow more rapidly, thoughts may become clearer and new ideas may appear at a more rapid pace.*

I handed out 100 samples as herbal ecstasy on a deposit which was refunded in exchange for a completed questionnaire, but 50 were herbal vitamin pills. Some people compared their pill with others, deduced they had a placebo and reported no effect, but among the rest the results were similar. Experiences reported varied from nothing to the best ever with no hangover – yet as many were wildly enthusiastic about vitamin pills as herbal ecstasy. I asked each user to say how much they would have paid for the pill, and the average for vitamin pills was £4.12 while for herbal ecstasy was £3.98.

The company with the butterfly logo has quoted me out of context to make false claims: "Enjoy Natural Euphoric Sensations From an Herbal Dietary Supplement... People *reported all kinds of effects. Some even saying that it was the best ecstacy experience they'd ever had.* -Nicholas Saunders, U.K.; E for Ecstacy, 1992."

Conclusion

Because something is natural and legal does not mean it is safe. Herbal ecstasy without Ephedra will have no greater direct effect than coffee or caffeine drinks such as Red Bull, while Ephedra may well be more dangerous than MDMA. Remember that poisoned darts are tipped with natural herbal extracts.

A large part of the effect of any drug depends on expectations, and someone who knows and expects the mood produced by ecstasy is likely to experience that, especially when prompted by some familiar physical reaction. Expectations can trigger moods by releasing neurotransmitters in the brain, just as happens when someone takes a drug.

Drug tests

Urine tests

MDMA can be detected in urine tests for two to five days after use. This depends mainly on the size of the last dose taken, as every six hours the amount in your body is halved. So a 128mg dose taken at midnight would reduce to 64mg by 6am; 32mg by midday and so on down to 1mg in less than 48 hours. However, if you take several Es every weekend, it is possible that some may be stored in your body fat and will be released gradually over a couple of weeks. Some tests may indicate amphetamine even when you have taken only MDMA.

The easiest drug to detect is cannabis which is stored in body fat and slowly released. It can be detected up to "five weeks after a single reefer" according to Dr. Henry, although people who drink plenty of water are usually undetectable in two weeks. LSD is hard to detect even after a few hours.[24] Mushrooms are also hard to detect.

There are many rumours about how to pass the piss test, but the best way is to wash yourself out and dilute your urine by drinking lots of water right up to the test.

Hair tests

Drugs in the bloodstream are deposited in hair as it grows, so a length of hair can provide a record of your drug use while it was growing. This test is expensive and not completely reliable at present, but may become so. A company in Scotland has advertised to test samples of children's hair sent in by parents to see if they use drugs.

Swab tests

An American company called Barringer is marketing DrugAlert which they describe as "a low cost weapon in the war against illegal drugs". This costs about $35 or £20 and consists of a swab to wipe surfaces (such as the telephone) touched by someone suspected of using drugs, which is then returned and analysed. They claim to be able to detect amounts as small as a nanogram (a billionth of a gram) of cocaine, heroin, methamphetamine, LSD, PCP, marijuana and derivatives including MDMA. However, they caution that positive results may be caused by traces being accidentally picked up from another person, and provide a follow up kit for retesting at half price. The results cannot be used in court as the sample is destroyed in testing. Phone (+1) 908 665 8200.

Jellinek test results [25]

The Dutch Institute tested 545 samples described as ecstasy in 1994. These were brought in for testing, mostly by small-time dealers, so may not be not typical. 89% were tablets; 10% capsules.

On average, 83% contained ecstasy-type drugs: 63% contained pure MDMA; 15% MDEA, 3% MDA and 2% other phenethylamines. 9% contained caffeine, of which about half were mixed with amphetamine, and another 3% contained only amphetamine. Another 5% contained paracetamol or unknown drugs. The samples that contained phenethylamines did not contain other drugs.

Strength of MDMA tablets varied from 3mg to 222mg, but the average was 107mg.

MDMA powders varied in purity from 33% to 100%, averaging 73%. MDEA tablets averaged 141mg and MDA 32mg. Caffeine tablets averaged 87mg and amphetamine 30mg. (All plus filler.)

Testing ecstasy

It is not possible to identify MDMA without sophisticated equipment. Most people judge by the appearance as some brands have a good reputation, but beware of fakes. Lookalike pills can always be distinguished when compared side by side, but it's hard to be sure later. It's a good idea to examine each pill very carefully and remember features that are hard to copy such as precise details of the design pressed into the pill. Capsules are obviously far more dodgy, as the same ones may contain different powders which may look similar. The only clue then is taste, but this is hard to distinguish from amphetamine.

Samples can be submitted to the following address under a fake name, and they will find out what is in them for $100, or find out how much of each active ingredient for $175: Drug Detection Lab 3117 Fite Circle Street, 104 Sacramento, CA 95827. +1 916 366 3113.

In Holland, a government-funded organisation called Jellinek tests street drugs in a dedicated laboratory and publishes results.[25] Some related agencies charge organisers to set up stalls at parties where people bring pills to find out what they contain. This is done by comparing with tested pills, or if the pill is unknown by using Marquis.[26] There is a safe house project by which licensed people can test drugs and give advice without fear of prosecution.[27] The Dutch government even pays people to buy samples of street drugs and send them in for analysis so that the results can be published.[28]

A laboratory reagent called Marquis (consisting of sulphuric acid and formaldehyde) is the only immediate way of testing drug samples. Marquis shows a dark colour with MDA, MDMA and MDEA, but also turns dark with many prescription drugs and even some paper, so is not reliable. However, regular users claim to be able to acquire the skill to distinguish between several drugs including amphetamine, which shows orange, from MDMA which is nearer to brown/black-purple.[29]

Drug testing kit [29]

A drug testing kit is marketed by British Drug Houses and Merck (product code 321761, price about £35). This consists of 40 ampoules of Marquis; to use it you break off the neck of an ampoule and drop in a tiny bit of the drug. The instructions say that within a minute the Marquis turns violet with opiates and 'yellow/orange/brown' with amphetamines and MDMA-type drugs.

Absence of colour indicates none of these drugs are present, and this is the purpose of the kit – as a quick way to check whether a suspect tablet does not contain an illicit drug.

Poppers now illegal

On January 13 1997, amyl nitrite was reclassified as a prescription only medicine, meaning it is an offence to sell it without the authorisation of a doctor.

2CB

My body for one reacts totally differently to 2CB than ecstasy. It's a completely different feeling. 2C-B is very benign on me, almost transparent physically. No problems during, and no fatigue afterward or any of that. When it ends, it drops off suddenly and completely with no somatic hints that it was ever there. MDMA, of course, leaves me drained-feeling and has side effects lasting a good 24 hours afterward.

An American user

Ecstasy pill test results

These are the results of laboratory analysis of pills sold as ecstasy in Europe. Beware that there is no guarantee that a similar pill has the same ingredients, and that when a pill has a good reputation it is likely to be copied by 'lookalikes' which are usually inferior. Lookalikes can usually be distinguished by comparing the precise dimensions given below, but again, sometimes the same die is used for different ingredients.

Name	thick mm	diam mm	profile	weight mg	active ingredients		date tested
Anchor	4.3	8.1		245	MDMA	11 mg	03/97
light blue pill with anchor logo, score line on reverse. Too weak to be effective							
Angel	4.18	9.15		309	MDMA	149 mg	07/96
greyish/white pill, crumbly texture, with Angel with trumpet logo, score line on reverse							
Apple Menu	4.55	8.10		291	MDEA	97 mg	07/96
white-greyish pill with deeply pressed Apple-Mac logo, slightly shiny, score line on reverse							
Autumn meadow	3.22	8.13		194	MDMA	139 mg	07/96
pill with intense green colour merging into yellow, score line on reverse.							
Batman	3.36	9.09		263	MDMA	75 mg	06/96
light grey pill with yellowish speckles, comic hero Batman logo, score line on reverse							
Two Colour	4.09	10.04		359	MDEA	129 mg	07/96
pill with one side white side with score line, other side speckled violet and domed							
Pound	3.38	10.04		327	MDMA	5 mg	03/97
white/light grey pill with £ logo					MDEA	106 mg	
Buddha	4.48	8.08		242	MDMA	69 mg	03/97
white pill with sitting Buddha logo, score line on reverse							
Butterfly	3.21	8.05		202 mg	MDEA	36 mg	03/97
yellow-brown pill with butterfly logo							

Name	thick mm	diam mm	profile	weight mg	active ingredients		date tested
Chip & Chap	2.36	10.04	▬	222 mg	MDMA	49 mg	05/96
					MDEA	15 mg	
					Caffeine	25 mg	
white/light grey with logo of squirrel, front view, score line on reverse							
Champagne	3.1	10.2	▬	276 mg	MDMA	86 mg	03/97
white/grey with CHAMPAGNE written on one side and champagne bottle logo on reverse							
Champagne	3.19	10.11	▬	290 mg	MDMA	134 mg	06/96
white/grey pill with CHAMPAGNE written on one side and champagne bottle logo on reverse							
Champagne	3.06	10.08	▬	288 mg	MDMA	142 mg	06/96
white/grey pill with CHAMPAGNE written on one side and champagne bottle logo on reverse							
Pink crown	3.58	8.19	▬	245 mg	MDMA	2 mg	03/97
pink pill with crown logo							
Crown	4.1	8.2	▬	228 mg	MDMA	61 mg	02/97
white pill with crown logo, score line on reverse							
Dollar	3.56	10.60	▬	328 mg	MBDB	184 mg	12/95
snow-white pill with dollar sign on one side							
Dollar	3.82	10.14	▬	348 mg	MDEA	97 mg	04/96
white, light grey pill with $ logo, score line on reverse							
Dollar	4.30	9.06	▬	302 mg	MDEA	105 mg	05/96
white pill with broad $ sign, score line on reverse							
Dolphin	4.64	12.1	▬	583 mg	MDMA	111 mg	05/96
yellow pill with side view of dolphin, score line on reverse							
Dolphin	4.57	12.1	▬	592 mg	MDMA	160 mg	06/96
yellow pill with side view of dolphin, score line on reverse							
Donald Duck	4.5	9.1	▬	302 mg	MDMA	59 mg	02/97
white pill with head of Donald Duck, score line on reverse							

Name	thick mm	diam mm	profile	weight mg	active ingredients		date tested
Elephant	3.53	8.54	▬	301 mg	MDMA	78 mg	05/96
snow-white, slightly shiny octagonal pill showing side view of an elephant, score line on reverse							
Heart with arrow	3.73	8.57	▬	228 mg	MDEA	116 mg	01/96
white pill with logo of pierced heart, score line on reverse							
Kangaroo	3.06	10.08	▬	292 mg	MDEA	117 mg	05/96
white pill showing kangaroo, side view, jumping right, score line on reverse							
Kangaroo	3.11	10.07	▬	301 mg	MDEA	109 mg	06/96
slightly shiny white pill showing kangaroo, side view, jumping right, score line on reverse							
Key	3.68	9.04	▬	unknown	MDEA	111 mg	01/97
white pill with key logo							
Lightning	5.25	8.13	▬	383 mg	MDMA MDEA	51 mg 12 mg	03/97
pink pill with zig-zag 'lightning' logo							
Lightning	4.6	8.2	unknown	315 mg	MDMA	71 mg	02/97
light yellowish pill with zig-zag 'lightning' logo							
Lightning	3.9	8.2	unknown	266 mg	MDMA	88 mg	02/97
white/light brown pill with zig-zag 'lightning' logo							
Lion	3.56	9.06	▬	unknown	MDEA MDMA	64 mg 35 mg	01/97
white/grey pill with lion head logo							
Love	3.54	9.10	▬	295 mg	MDMA	114 mg	12/95
white pill with yellow & brown dots, with LO|VE on one side, score line on reverse							
Pink love	3.42	9.04	▬	280 mg	MDMA	97 mg	04/96
pink pill with yellow & brown dots, with LO|VE on one side							
Mushroom	4.04	9.04	▬	275 mg	MDEA	112 mg	05/96
white/yellow-greyish pill with mushroom logo stamped off-centre, score line on reverse							
Mushroom	4.01	9.04	▬	270 mg	MDEA	140 mg	06/96
white/yellow-greyish pill with mushroom logo stamped off-centre, score line on reverse							

Name	thick mm	diam mm	profile	weight mg	active ingredients		date tested
Mushroom	4.04	9.04	▬	275 mg	MDEA	112 mg	05/96
white/yellow-greyish pill with mushroom logo stamped off-centre, score line on reverse							
Mushroom	4.01	9.04	▬	270 mg	MDEA	140 mg	06/96
white/yellow-greyish pill with mushroom logo stamped off-centre, score line on reverse							
Mushroom	3.47	9.07	▬	unknown	MDEA	167 mg	01/97
light grey pill with mushroom logo, score line on reverse **Note high dose**							
Obelix	2.89	10.07	▬	263 mg	MDMA	1 mg	03/97
white pill with head of comic hero, score line on reverse					MDEA	trace	
Pax	4.03	8.62	▬	242 mg	MDEA	50 mg	03/96
dull white pill with PAX on one side, score line on reverse							
Playboy	3.8	9.0	▬	303 mg	MDMA	98 mg	01/96
white pill with playboy logo, score line on reverse							
Playboy	3.5	9.2	▬	293 mg	Caffeine	19.7 mg	03/96
white/yellowish grey pill with playboy logo, score line on reverse					MDEA	14.1 mg	
Playboy	3.36	9.08	▬	287 mg	MDMA	1.7 mg	05/96
shiny light grey pill with rabbit head looking left, score line on reverse					MDEA	108 mg	
Playboy	3.16	9.04	▬	264 mg	MDMA	1.3 mg	06/96
white pill with rabbit head looking to the left, score line on reverse					MDEA	105 mg	
Pinoccio	3.82	8.59	▬	214 mg	MDEA	83 mg	03/96
white shiny pill with head of Pinoccio, score line on reverse							
Road Runner	3.58	9.09	▬	323 mg	MDMA	125 mg	12/95
white pill with yellow-brown dots and comic figure Road Runner, score line on reverse							
Road Runner	3.53	9.12	▬	290 mg	MDMA	100 mg	05/96
grey pill with grey-brown dots and comic figure Road Runner, score line on reverse							

Name	thick mm	diam mm	profile	weight mg	active ingredients		date tested
Road Runner	3.63	9.07		298 mg	MDMA	112 mg	06/96
grey pill with grey-brown dots and comic figure Road Runner, score line on reverse							
S	c3	c8.5		257 mg	MDEA	113 mg	01/96
white pill with large letter S, score line on reverse							
Smiley	3.74	10.07		374 mg	MDEA	91 mg	03/96
white pill with grey speckles, smiley logo (mouth and eyes)					**MDMA**	**8.8 mg**	
Sonic	4.2	9.1		288 mg	MDMA	59 mg	02/97
white pill with comic figure Sonic twice, score line on reverse							
Star Dust	4.60	8.04		226 mg	MDMA	3 mg	03/97
white, crumbly pill with stardust logo, score line on reverse					**MDEA**	**71 mg**	
Sun	3.92	9.04		317 mg	MDMA	132 mg	01/96
white pill with sun logo (no face), score line on reverse							
Supermario	3.01	10.04		286 mg	MDEA	94 mg	05/96
white pill with comic figure Supermario (Nintendo), score line on reverse							
Swallow	3.35	9.20		226 mg	MDMA	48 mg	08/96
white pill with flying swallow, side view							
Swallow	3.28	9.08		238 mg	MDMA	71 mg	09/96
white pill with flying swallow, side view							
Tiger	4.3	10.1		316 mg	MDEA	75 mg	02/97
white/yellowish pill with tiger head					**MDMA**	**20 mg**	
Triple Five	5.75	8.00		315 mg	Caffeine	11 mg	02/96
light green pill with 5 stamped three places 120° apart					**Amphetamine**	**9 mg**	
					MDMA	**17 mg**	
Triple Five	5.88	8.04		265 mg	MDMA	76 mg	04/96
light yellowish pill with 5 stamped three places 120° apart							

Name	thick mm	diam mm	profile	weight mg	active ingredients		date tested
Triple Five white pill with 5 stamped three places 120° apart	**5.23**	**8.04**	▬	**257 mg**	**MDMA**	**110 mg**	**06/96**
Toucan white glossy pill with side view of bird, score line on reverse	**3.56**	**9.07**	▬	**313 mg**	**MDEA** **MDMA**	**118 mg** **8.2 mg**	**03/96**
Venus yellowish white pill with Venus sign, score line on reverse	**c3.2**	**c9.2**	unknown	**239 mg**	**MDEA**	**106 mg**	**01/96**
Woody white pill with head of comic hero Woody Woodpecker, score line on reverse	**3.45**	**9.08**	▬	unknown	**MDMA**	**86 mg**	**01/97**
Ying-Yang white pill with ying-yang sign	**5.32**	**9.23**	▬	**319 mg**	**MDMA**	**75 mg**	**09/96**
Palm white pill with palm tree, score line on reverse	**c4.0**	**c9.0**	unknown	**281 mg**	**caffeine** **amphetamine**	**82 mg** **46 mg**	**03/96**
Harley Davidson white pill with Harley Davidson logo, score line on reverse	**c4.2**	**c9.0**	unknown	**285 mg**	**caffeine** **amphetamine**	**3.4 mg** **59 mg**	**03/96**
Superman white shiny pill with Superman logo (S in triangle)	**5.40**	**9.00**	▬	**273 mg**	**amphetamine**	**60 mg**	**07/96**
Superman shiny pill with Superman logo (S in triangle)	**4.25**	**10.20**	▬	unknown	**amphetamine** **MDMA** **MDEA 7 mg**	**31 mg** **7 mg**	**01/97**
Superman greenish-white pill with Superman-logo without border, score line on reverse	**4.03**	**8.18**	▬	**285 mg**	**amphetamine**	**4mg**	**03/97**
Superman white/light blue speckled pill with Superman logo (S in triangle)	**3.83**	**10.0**	▬	**331 mg**	**amphetamine** **MDMA**	**22 mg** **1 mg**	**03/97**

In addition, a selection of 46 pills sold as ecstasy without logos were tested. All but one contained MDMA or MDEA. 72% contained between 80 and 140 mg MDMA, 12% MDEA. Overall, unbranded pills came out better than the branded ones above.

References

1. Entry in *Micromedex,* vol. 75, a hospital database printout from the National Poisons Unit at Guy's Hospital, London.

2. MDMA-induced dopamine release: effect of dopamine uptake inhibitors by Nash and Brodkin in *J Pharmacol Exp Ther* November 1991.

3. Psychological Effects of MDE in Normal Subjects by Leo Hermle et al. *Neuropsychopharmacology* 8 February1993 .

4. Conversations with Dr Les King, team leader of the drugs intelligence laboratory at the Forensic Science Laboratory at Aldermaston, part of the Forensic Science Service, a Government agency, December 1992, March 1994 and January 1995.

5. Dutch drug makers surrender bucketfuls of Eve from *Reuters,* 29 July 93.

6. Police to stop raves in *The Guardian* February1994..

7. *The Background Chemistry of MDMA,* by Alexander Shulgin, from *Journal of Psychoactive Drugs,* Vol. 18 April1986. According to this paper, MDMA is less toxic than MDA but more so than mescaline. The lethal dose is between 20 and 100 mg per kilo of body weight depending on the species taking it. With mice, it is 5 times more toxic given in crowded conditions.

8. *The Phenomenology of Ecstasy Use,* by Teresa O'Dwyer, Senior Registrar of Adult Psychiatry at St Thomas' Hospital, Morpeth, Nov 1992. This paper is an account of a study of users' experiences on Ecstasy and the patterns and circumstances of their use undertaken by the Leeds Addiction Unit between January and September 1992.

9. A researcher reports from the rave by Russell Newcombe, *Druglink,* January 1992.

10. The Placebo Effect in Healing, by Michael Jospe, 1978.

11. *PIHKAL (Phenethylamines I Have Known And Loved); A Chemical Love Story,* by Alexander and Ann Shulgin. Published by Transform Press (Berkeley USA) at $18.95. Also available from Compendium Bookshop, London.

12. A visit to Lifeline, a non-statutory drug agency in Manchester, August 1992.

13. *Women, sexuality and Ecstasy Use – The Final Report 1993,* by Sheila Henderson, published by *Lifeline,* 101 Oldham St, Manchester M4 1LW.

14. *Ecstasy – The Arrival of a Consciousness-Raising Drug,* by Arno Adelaars, published by in de Knipscher, 1994. Originally published in 1991 with updates including analysis of Dutch samples in 1993.

15. *British Medical Journal* vol. 305 August 1992 letters in reply to Dr Henry's article.

16. Visit from Stuart Frescas, a chemist working as part of Dr David Nichols' team at Purdue University, January 1994.

17. Letter and manuscript from Myron Stolaroff January 1994.

18. *The Essential Psychedelic Guide,* by D. M. Turner.

19. *The Secret Chief* (book) by Myron Stollaroff

20. *Through the Gateway of the Heart* (book) published by Four Trees Publications, San Francisco 1985. This book is a collection of some 60 subjective accounts of positive experiences by users and "guidelines for the sacramental use of empathogenic substances". The accounts are divided into men's, women's and group experiences.

21. *Ecstasy Deaths and other fatalities related to Drugs and Raving* by Dr Russell Newcombe, updated 12/94. This 20-page report has 3 sections covering death from illicit drug use: Official Statistics; Media Reports and Research Papers.

22. Conversation with Ian of Universe, August 1994.

23. Cloud 9 from *Sunday Telegraph,* 20 November 1994.

24. Visit to Dr John Henry at the National Poisons Unit at Guy's Hospital, London, 12/92.

25. Jellinek, 1e Weteringplantsoen 8, 1017 SK, Amsterdam (+31 20 570 23 55; fax 626 72 49). A Dutch drug institute working in the areas of prevention, treatment, probation and harm reduction. Two of their consultants, August de Loors and Jaap Jamin, arrange the testing of samples and use results to identify drugs at dance parties in Holland.

26. A drug testing kit is marketed by British Drug Houses and Merck (product code 321761 price about £35). This consists of about 40 Ampoules of Marquis; to use you break off the neck of the ampoule and drop in a tiny bit of the drug.

27. Visit to August de Loor, Entrepotdok 32A, 1018 AD, Amsterdam.

28. A visit to Arno Adelaars, a part-time purchaser of street samples of drugs for testing by the Dutch government. Amsterdam, 10/92.

29. Conversations with Dr Les King, team leader of the drugs intelligence laboratory at the Forensic Science Laboratory at Aldermaston, part of the Forensic Science Service, a Government agency, December 1992, March 1994 and January 1995.

Manufacture and Distribution

To make ecstasy requires considerable effort and risk, making it more attractive to well organised criminals than amateurs. Western countries have suceeded in clamping down on domestic production but failed to prevent smuggling, with the result that manufacture has moved to eastern Europe and third world countries.

Dealing ecstasy is often done by amateurs at the lowest level, but the main profit is made by gangs who control the supply and use violence to maintain their market. Clubs and larger events are often supplied with drugs by gangs working with security guards.

Very little MDMA is manufactured legally,[1] so that what is sold on the black market is made in clandestine factories.

Most of what is sold as ecstasy in Britain comes from abroad, reputedly eastern countries where the materials and equipment are less controlled and imprisonment can be avoided with bribes. However, the methods are well known[2] and small scale manufacturers are widespread. All you need to make ecstasy is a competent chemist, the right materials and a fully equipped laboratory – but without these it is extremely difficult.

Recipes [2]

The Complete Book of Ecstacy was rated as the best guidebook by these manufacturers. "It's definitely the best of the lot. Good points are that it gives alternatives, so that if you get stuck for some reason you can try another method. It also includes how to make most of the precursors and has a good reference list of other books and papers.

"However, some methods mentioned are extremely dangerous, such as one involving cyanide gas and another the Ritter reaction that caused an explosion with us. Instructions for many of the processes I have used start off well, but later leave out detail. This would make the recipes hard to follow for a novice."

E made in pharmaceutical factory [4]

A Parke Davis pharmaceuticals factory was used to produce ecstasy by two of its staff. They were discovered after three years surveillance

---

In Britain, a factory was discovered in a shed in a garden centre which produced a batch of 20kg – enough for 200,000 tablets – every 24-36 hours.[3] This is a typical of a small factories that can be quickly to avoid detection. Ecstasy is also sometimes made in research labs.[4]

Interview with clandestine manufacturer

In 1994 I interviewed a group of people who manufactured MDMA.

How did you start?

> Three of us spent about 3 years planning – reading up syntheses; finding equipment and buying materials. None of us had any previous laboratory experience apart from my school chemistry.

Where did you get supplies?

> Getting equipment without arousing suspicion was difficult. Laboratory suppliers would not sell us anything more complex than a thermometer for cash over the counter, otherwise they would ask us to open an account and then want bank and trade references. When I tried to open a business bank account, they asked for identification and the precise nature of my

intended business. So we looked for existing companies who had accounts with suppliers, and made personal contacts so that orders could be placed through them – risky, as they might inform the police or blackmail us. We found some pieces of equipment in theatre prop shops and even car boot sales – it was nearly all glassware, as we used laboratory rather than production methods, and we had a lot of breakages.

What about precursors?

Key precursors, such as safrole, had to be bought from black market sources at very high prices. Even solvents were not available without question, and some ingredients required a poisons license, although we found a couple of Indian suppliers who took cash and asked no questions. We spent £4,000 in all.

How did you actually make it?

We rented a basement flat for the purpose. Then we experimented to find the best method. We studied everything we could get hold of including chemistry textbooks; Secrets *of Methamphetamine Manufacture, PIHKAL* by Alexander Shulgin;[2] and even patents in the Patent Office. It was much harder than we expected – even following instructions to the letter, some reactions simply did not happen while others were so violent they that broke the apparatus. All the recipes had small but vital steps missing so we had to piece together a recipe that worked.

How long did it take?

One kilo of MDMA took about two weeks continuous work for three people because some processes could only be done in 50 gram batches. We used 75 litres of solvents which we had no way of recondensing and we had no fume cupboard, so all that was boiled off producing vast amounts of vapour which was heavier than air and would fill up the basement. There were toxic fumes and a lot of spillages because we got overtired. Sometimes we were left coughing and ill from inhaling fumes which hurt our eyes and made us giddy.

We were also worried about explosions which could be sparked off by the vacuum pump motor, so when things got really bad we had to evacuate the basement and the fumes could be seen drifting out of the windows. Once a flask of ether exploded, and during the Ritter reaction hot sulphuric acid and methyl cyanide shot up to the ceiling and dripped down onto us. I think it has permanently damaged my lungs.

How about selling it?

We tried to find a single dealer but were afraid that those who could afford to buy in kilos would be connected to criminals and might turn up with guns. So we ended up selling in smaller amounts which meant that far too many people were into our secret, and even then we could not get more than the usual trade price of £40 per gram even though our product was pure. The whole thing became a bit of a nightmare for me although one of my partners found it exhilarating.

What would you do different if you started again?

I would go for larger scale. I think the risks would be lower because we would be able to pay someone else to obtain the equipment and materials; also we could afford safer premises, better equipment and security.

The manufacturing process produces a raw substance of which between 80% and 95% is MDMA. Incomplete synthesis results in a brownish colour.[5] Pills typically weigh between 200mg and 600mg each, of which only 100mg is MDMA.[6] Sometimes colour is added. Speckled effects are produced by mixing different colours of filler, giving the impression that the pill contains several active ingredients.

Pill-making is done by specialists. The MDMA is mixed with filler to increase the size and help bind into a hard, smooth tablet, then a piston forces the ingredients against a die at high pressure. The die is engraved with a logo or name and can be changed to identify a 'brand'.

When a brand has a good reputation, fake lookalikes are produced; the reputation is lost and new brands emerge – this cycle takes three to six months.[6] An exception is Doves which have been on the market for years in spite of variable quality. Different brands may be produced for export to reduce the risk of being traced.[7]

Proprietary medicines are sometimes rubbed down to remove their markings and sold as fake ecstasy.[8] Ecstasy sold as loose powder or in capsules probably comes from small manufacturers.

Police action to prevent manufacture in Britain follows the principle of encouraging the suppliers to inform the police of suspicious orders. Illicit laboratories raided to date have all been discovered by tip-offs from informants.[3,9]

Distribution

According to the police,[3] the typical drug dealer nowadays is a middle-aged criminal who has been in prison many times and probably committed armed robberies when he was younger. The Mafia and other gangs of organised criminals are not suspected. This view is supported in a book called *Traffickers* by Nicholas Dorn.[10] Dorn says that in Britain there are no drug barons and relatively little corruption.

Wholesalers buy by the kilo for £20,000 or so (£2 per dose) and sell on to middle men who buy a thousand Es at a time for £2 to £3 each and re-sell by the hundred at about £5 per E to the dealers who sell to the public at £8 to £15 each.[11]

Much of the retail trade is conducted by people buying for their friends without making a profit, although usually gaining a few free tablets for their own consumption. Then there are user-dealers who only supply regular clients and cannot afford to provide poor quality.

Another variation is for friends to arrange a meeting place, usually a pub, before going clubbing. One person may buy for everyone which costs less than separately.[11]

Most clubs have regular dealers who are known by regular customers and are accepted by the security staff, who often 'tax' them for the privilege. Since they rely on reputation they tend to be honest. Some employ runners to increase their trade.[12]

Transvestite dealer [12]

Although a well established dealer, Samantha still thought that ecstasy consisted of a mixture of drugs including LSD.

Nowadays Samantha finishes selling before taking E himself and dancing. This is a lesson learned the hard way: once he simply lost his entire stock but was having too much of a good time to care. On another occasion he stuffed a plastic bag full of E down his front while dancing and the sweat ran into the bag turning the pills into an unsaleable mush. To this he added a bit of acid and speed "to make up for it being a mess", bought some capsules of a proprietary brand medicine and replaced the contents with the mixture, then sold them as a 'new E just in'. They were so popular that he had people coming up to him for weeks afterwards asking for more!

Security searches [13]

According to Dr Newcombe, security staff cannot legally strip-search customers, so dealers can easily smuggle drugs in their underwear. Women are sometimes used to carry drugs in as they are less likely to be carefully searched and can carry several hundred tablets in their vaginas.

Dealer's story

I set out like the pied piper and started distributing ecstasy in a very successful manner when it was still legal. I sold millions and personally turned on most of the country's biggest coke dealers... I'm sad to say that the authorities didn't see eye to eye with me and I'm now doing 12 years for conspiracy to supply MDMA.

- A reader writing from a US prison

There is a trend towards a more organised form of supply through retail specialists who co-operate with security staff. Some members go around asking people if they want to buy drugs without carrying stock themselves, while the stock and money is carried by members who are well protected by bodyguards. Lookouts warn of police activity and have contingency plans worked out in case of a surprise raid; for example, members who are free of drugs might cause a fight so as to attract the attention of the police while those carrying drugs and money escape. The police hardly ever attempt to arrest such gangs.[13] Drugs sold this way are generally low quality and are sometimes fake, but nobody complains because the gangs are intimidating.

References

1. Manufacturers of MDMA in Switzerland. Chemische Forschung & Entwicklung, Im Latten Acker 5, 8200 Schaffhausen, Switzerland tel. 053 25 72 72.

2. Refer box page 235.

3. Interview with Detective Chief Superintendent Derek Todd, Drugs Co-ordinator with the No 9 Regional Crime Squad, at Spring Gardens, London, February 1993.

4. *Independent on Sunday*, 11 July 1993.

5. *Psychedelics Encyclopedia*, by Peter Stafford, 3rd edition published by Ronin, 1992. This edition has an added 26-page section on MDMA.

6. Conversations with Dr Les King, team leader of the drugs intelligence laboratory at the Forensic Science Laboratory at Aldermaston, part of the Forensic Science Service, a Government agency, December 1992, March 1994 and January 1995.

7. Visit to August de Loor, Entrepotdok 32A, 1018 AD, Amsterdam.

8. *The Pursuit of Ecstasy – the MDMA Experience* by Gerome Beck and Marsha Rosenbaum published Feb 1994 by State University of New York Press at $14.95.

9. Interview with Detective Chief Superintendent Tony White, head of the drugs and money laundering branch of the National Criminal Intelligence Service, which is under the control of the Home Office. At Spring Gardens, London Feburary 1993.

10. *Traffickers*, (book) by Nicholas Dorn et al., published by Routledge, 1992.

11. A visit to Lifeline, a non-statutory drug agency in Manchester, August 1992.

12. Visit to gay clubs in London, February 1994. I was taken on a tour of gay clubs in London by a transvestite dealer called Samantha.

13. *The Use of Ecstasy and Dance Drugs at Rave Parties and Clubs: Some Problems and Solutions*, by Dr Russell Newcombe, paper presented at a symposium on Ecstasy, Leeds, November 1992.

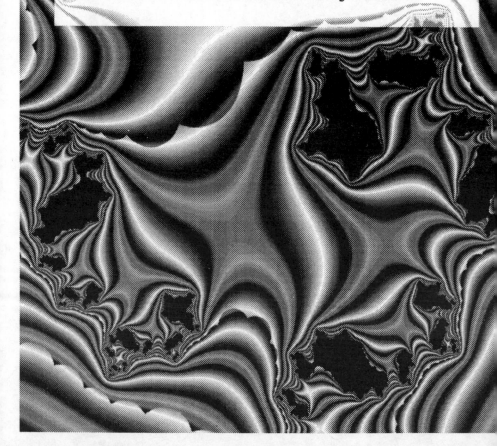

Research

Surprisingly little research is being done into ecstasy that is relevant to those who use the drug. This is because of a 'chicken and egg' situation: MDMA has been put into the most restrictive category which implies that it is highly dangerous to humans and has no medical use, therefore it is extremely difficult to do research involving the effect on humans.

In fact, the reasons are political rather than logical, and a change of political climate may be imminent which would encourage human research.

Anyone contemplating doing research should remind the authorities that, when the World Health Organisation advised member nations outlaw MDMA, they added a clause encouraging them to "facilitate research on this interesting substance".[1]

Human research

There is practically no human research being carried out. The reason usually given is that the drug us too neurotoxic, but those providing evidence for neurotoxicity have far more liberal attitudes. I discussed this with Dr. George Ricaurte and his wife Dr. Una McCann while taking part as a volunteer in their trial. Ricaurte he told me that he thought the political climate had changed and that the time was right to study the positive uses for MDMA, and asked me what I thought would be the most promising use to explore. I suggested the treatment of Post-Traumatic Stress Disorder as a result of my visit to Nicaragua where I talked to doctors who had tried it. Later, McCann told me that Ricaurte had come home that night enthusiastic about her doing such a trial. Her opinion was that the National Institute of Health, where she works, was not yet liberal enough to explore positive uses for 'drugs of abuse'. These conversations demonstrate that researchers quoted in the media in support of rigid anti-drugs policies often have far more open views.

At the 1997 conference of the British Psychological Society, a researcher at London University told how the ethical committee would not give permission for any kind of research which could be seen to encourage use. This was interpreted so strictly that it was not possible to make appointments to test people while on ecstasy. So the researchers had to find people who said they had taken already taken ecstasy, which they managed to do after first getting permission of a club owner. But the ethical committee then decided that people under the influence of ecstasy would not be in a state of mind to be able to give their informed consent for tests to be carried out.

Ecstasy is a popular research subject for students and postgraduates. Because of ethical restrictions and cost, these usually consist of comparing ecstasy users with non users by means of psychological tests or questionnaires.

The problem is that drug users are notoriously untruthful about their use, as has been established by comparing self-reports with urine tests, and most users of ecstasy also take other drugs. So that the effects noticed can only be attributed to the drugs actually tested for, yet this is seldom done.[2]

Short term memory loss?[2]

A research report presented by Dr. Morgan of the University of Swansea at the 1997 conference of the British Psychological Society concluded that ecstasy users had impaired short term memory. However, consumption was based on self reports without tests, so the effect may well have been due to undeclared drug use. Cannabis is very often smoked by ecstasy users and is well known to impair short term memory.

Trials under way

At present Dr. George Ricaurte is undertaking a five year trial at Johns Hopkins, described in my interview with him below. The trial is an extension of his previous work using more elaborate methods, including brain scans, but does not involve giving ecstasy to people or comparing individuals before and after ecstasy use. This will still leave the results open to the possibility that differences between users and non-users existed beforehand instead of being caused by ecstasy.

There is also a much smaller scale trial at University of California at Los Angeles conducted by Dr. Charles Grob, the only researcher presently licensed to administer ecstasy to humans. His work involves combining the images of two types of brain scanner and comparing the images of people's brains with and without ecstasy. This is supposed to be a preliminary trial to establish whether the drug can be given safely for therapeutic purposes, but funding is mainly from private sources and progress is slow. Preliminary results show that there are changes in the brain blood flow which appear to be long term

Planned human trials involving administering ecstasy

USA

Two separate trials are being planned on the use of ecstasy to treat Post-Traumatic Stress Disorder. One it is hoped will take place under the auspices of the Indiana University School of Medicine in collaboration with highly motivated and competent psychologists and psychiatrists.

Russia

Dr. Evgeny Krupitsky in St. Petersburg writes that he has "discussed again the possibilities of MDMA research with Drs. Rzhankova and Dunaevsky from the Leningrad Institute of Oncology, Academy of Medical Sciences of the USSR. They informed me that maybe it will be possible to receive permission for this work from the Pharmacological Committee of the Ministry of Health".

Dr. Krupitsky proposes that the Russian control group receive "logical therapy", much like what we call "cognitive therapy".

England

Dr. Karl Jansen has permission to carry out a study on ecstasy at the London Institute of Psychiatry (Maudsley Hospital).

The study would involve brain scans using Functional Magnetic Resonance Imaging.

A comparison would be made between the brains of people who say they have taken ecstasy over 1,500 times and those who have taken ecstasy less than five times.

Switzerland

Dr. Franz Vollenweider has permission to carry out a psychotherapy study using ecstasy at the Zurich Psychiatric University Hospital. It is hoped to begin in 1988.

Information of the current state of these and other research projects can be obtained from MAPS (see page 253).

Animal research

The combination of the call for more research and restrictions on human research results in a large number of experiments on animals (as can be seen in the bibliography). Although some of these do add weight to evidence of toxicity, other trials have absolutely no practical use.[3]

Useless research [3]

The research involved feeding larvae on the decomposing flesh of rabbits. Some of the rabbits were given 67mg of MDMA (equivalent to about 50 human doses) before they were killed, and it was found that this made the larvae develop more quickly. The paper claims that "The results have implications for determination of time since death." Does that mean feeding larvae off the flesh of dead people who had taken 50 E's to see when they died?

Sent to me "for my amusement" by Alexander Shulgin

Many trials are under way, but one which could have implications for humans is being carried out by Christine Cloak under Dr. Russ Poland at UCLA. It consists of a study of blood plasma levels of MDMA by various routes of administration, and should provide data which will make it easier to translate existing animal data to humans.

Pathology

An paper studied the organs of seven people who had died after taking ecstasy. Four of the deaths were reported to be due to hyperthermia, one from a heart attack, one from liver failure and one from water intoxication. Hyperthermia is known to cause liver damage, but all of them showed damage to their livers. One explanation is that the others also had hyperthermia before they died of other causes.

Otherwise, this is evidence that ecstasy causes liver damage. However, if this is the case, then it applies idiosyncratically, as many regular users do not suffer such damage.

It may possibly be a genetic susceptibility, or it may be the way the drug us used or what other drugs are used with it.[4]

Interview with George Ricaurte [5]

— on his research study into ecstasy neurotoxicity

What is the specific aim of this study?

> The issue as to whether or not MDMA damages serotonin neurons in the human brain is still unresolved. There is some preliminary indication that the serotonin neurotoxicity that was produced in animals may also occur in humans, but we still don't know that for sure. The purpose of the ongoing study is two fold. Firstly, can we obtain further indications as to whether MDMA's serotonin neurotoxic potential generalises to humans. To do that we are going to look not only as CSF and 5HIA as markers of neurotoxicity, but we are also looking at a different neuroendocrine measures of serotonin function in living humans. That's the MCCPT test. Secondly, we are asking the simple question: "If there is any suggestion of serotonin toxicity in humans, is it associated with any functional change?", so along those lines we look for changes in pain perception or sensitivity, changes in sleep, the cognitive functions that are evaluated by the computerised test batteries, and the various behavioural spheres that are assessed with a series of questionnaires. Those are the major things within the human study. Apart from that, we are also trying to look for evidence of possible toxicity in humans with a ligand that selectively labels a serotonin neuron in the human brain.

So its like an extension of the squirrel monkey comparison looking for functional damage?

> That's exactly right. I still strongly believe that in humans we are forced to use indirect measures of serotonin brain functions. What we need to do is to gauge serotonin function in a number of different ways, and hopefully collect data that is consistent and points to the same conclusion. If it doesn't, that's obviously important and raises questions about the validity of the methods we are using.

How was damage seen in squirrel monkeys?

> We look for specific markers for serotonin neurons, and simply determine their presence or absence. We do this long after the drug has been discontinued and we inferred that if all the markers for neurons are missing for a long time after we discontinued the drug, then it seams reasonable to conclude that the drug has produced a loss of the axons that pertain to the serotonin nerve cell.

Can you not look for the axons visually, or are they too small?

> We can look directly at the brain tissue, postmortem, in animals. I think one of the things to do in the future is to look at the brain tissue of people who have died, from whatever cause, who have been MDMA users. That's how we have come to learn about Parkinson's disease. There is no reason why the same strategy should not be used with MDMA users.

Would it be a difficult study to do?

Well, it would require specialised techniques, but it would be feasible.

What do you believe is the reason that you did not come across functional effects of MDMA in your previous study?

We actually did find some functional differences. As a group, the individuals that had prior exposure to MDMA scored lower on hostility and impulsively. In the sleep studies, the MDMA group had less stage 2 time. We didn't note any negative functional consequences. Its a very difficult thing to tap into functional difference. That is a very imperfect science. One of the promising things is that by carefully examining such a group of subjects we may get some direct insight into the functional role. As long as we don't have a clear idea of what it is that serotonin does in the human brain, it is difficult to set up a testing strategy.

Is the damage direct, like that of a bullet, or is it more of a distortion?

I think the latter. Typically the neurotoxic effects of MDMA are extraordinarily selective. That's why MDMA is such a useful tool in research. You can see how, for experimental purposes, MDMA could be such a useful tool. Because damage is generally restricted to just the axon and axon terminals, there is a potential for regrowth. In monkeys, regrowth occurs, but the regrowth is abnormal, i.e. different to that observed in the control. One of the reasons why regrowth can take place is that the MDMA lesion, in contrast to a knife wound, doesn't form a scar, leaving potential to regrow. In monkeys this leads to a rewiring of the serotonin system, and at this point in time we have no idea what the rewiring does to the function of the animal. Those are things that have yet to be addressed.

A commonly expressed concern about MDMA use is that damage may not show up now in tests, but may do so in the future. Can you see any reason why that may be the case?

There are theoretical reasons, at least three that I can think of. If one uses the dopamine system as an example, we know that if you deplete something over 90% of an individual's dopamine, that individual becomes Parkinsonian. We also know that, unless you deplete dopamine by at least 90% behaviour looks entirely normal. We also know from the dopamine system that there are toxins, some related to drugs of abuse, that can damage the system; we also know that there appears to be a decline of dopamine with age; we also know that dopamine neurons can be damaged by various disease processes.

So one can see the scenario that if an individual sustained partial insult during early life, damaging 50% of the dopamine neurons, that individual will be fine as long as he doesn't suffer some other insult but might develop symptoms in conditions that others with normal reserve would not. The same may apply to serotonin systems. One could make the case that an individual that has the normal complement of brain serotonin has a normal risk of developing brain disorders, but the individual who has lower serotonin would be at increased risk of developing diseases associated with depletion of brain serotonin.

Would this also be true for fenfluramine and fluoxetine [Prozac]?

It would certainly apply to fenfluramine. Drugs like fluoxetine actually enhance serotonin transmission. The fundamental difference is that the effect of MDMA is long lasting and related to actual destruction of the nerve axons, whereas fluoxetine just alters the metabolism. When you stop taking fluoxetine, serotonin returns to its normal level. What's unique about drugs like MDMA is that they actually prune the axon field.

How does MDMA compare with fenfluramine in the way they cause damage?

As best I can tell, they are identical. If anything, fenfluramine might be a little more potent as a serotonin toxin.

How about a study on fenfluramine users and the onset of Parkinson's disease?

Given that serotonin is more implicated in things like mood regulation, as opposed to movement which is primarily affected in Parkinson's disease, a nice study would be to see if people exposed to fenfluramine are at a higher risk of developing neuropsychiatric disorders which have been linked, albeit indirectly, to serotonin dysfunction: such as depression, anxiety, sleep disturbances, memory function. Those would be some of the areas I would begin to look at in the fenfluramine cohort to see if humans exposed to high doses of fenfluramine show any evidence of long lasting serotonin dysfunction.

I think you said there is a 3 month limit on prescribing fenfluramine. [That was true before May 1996] Might that mean the doses taken would not be high enough to show effects?

The issue of possible serotonin toxicity secondary to fenfluramine use is, I think, a very, very important one. In every experimental animal tested to date, the dose of fenfluramine required to reduce food intake is virtually identical to the dose that produces serotonin toxicity, or only slightly lower. When humans use fenfluramine, they are told to take it 2 or 3 times a day for long periods. For d-fenfluramine which is presently being evaluated in the US, the manufacturers recommendation are life long use. The suggestion put forth is that obesity should be regarded like diabetes: the obese person may need to take fenfluramine daily for life. When you consider that the use is chronic and the dose is very close to toxic level, then I think you have cause to question the safety of its use.

Going back to present study, how long before you will get preliminary results, and are you involved with other studies?

Its a five year study, and I expect it will be at least a year before we get preliminarily results. The human studies are complemented by animal studies, some directed to consequences, others to mechanisms of toxicity. We are particularly interested in the aberrant reinnervation in monkeys. Without the knowledge we have obtained with monkeys, one might have predicted that in the wake of MDMA use we might expect a blunted response to neuroendocrine challenge with specific pharmacological probes. Now I'm not so sure that hypothesis is correct. Perhaps we should be looking for augmented responses if indeed the regions of the brain that subserve the neuroendocrine response in the long term are hyperinnervated as opposed to hypoinnervated. The animal studies serve an important role in helping direct us as to the proper way to asses humans, and how to appropriately interpret the data. There is a constant interplay in this study between the two.

Does the neuron degradation you have observed with MDMA also occur with alcohol or ageing or in other ways?

It can occur within some diseases, but whether serotonin declines with age has not been determined. The same toxicity occurs with a limited number of other drugs that are close chemical cousins, such as MDA, but not amphetamine sulphate or anti depressants.

Just how harmful is MDMA in comparison to other drugs or alcohol?

Not to be alarmed, but I think that if you compare MDMA to other psychoactive drugs, it is unique precisely because it has the potential to damage serotonin systems at doses close to that taken to produce the required effect. You would have to drink far more than social drinking to produce such damage. So if you consider the problem from that perspective, these drugs have a far higher risk associated with their use.

Interview with Dr James O'Callaghan [6]

Dr James O'Callaghan is a senoir researcher for the US Environmental Protection Agency who I interviewed while he was a guest researcher at Rockefeller University.

I understand that you and your colleagues at the U.S. Environmental Protection Agency were awarded over \$750,000 by the National Institute on Drug Abuse to provide a reliable assessment of the potential neurotoxic effects of MDMA and other drugs of abuse.
Why is it so difficult to determine if a drug is neurotoxic?

The overall problem is that the brain is exceedingly complex. This complexity is reflected in all of the different types and sub types of neurons and glia, the cells that compose the brain. Because there are all these diverse types of cells it is not surprising that there are diverse and unpredictable targets of damage that result from exposure to neurotoxic agents. You can't predict what compound will hit what, because you don't know what would make a given cell type vulnerable to damage, and you don't know anything about the chemical to predict which cell is going to be targeted. You can't do this by computer modelling ; you can't look at the molecule and say "Gee, I know that's going to damage this particular brain cell".

I have seen 'before and after' photographs of the brains of monkeys used as evidence of neurotoxicity by Ricaurte. The 'after MDMA' slide shows far less lines. Is this a fair visual representation of damage caused by MDMA?[7]

NO. This is the water in the pipe issue, not evidence of damage to the pipe. Serotonin immunostaining data does not indicate that neurodegeneration occurred. It is very subjective; in the absence of quantitative data (i.e. levels of 5-HT) to support the photomicrographs, it is difficult if not impossible to claim that what you see is what you get in a representative sense. In other words, if you see one (selected) picture this tells you very little. My point is underlined by the fact that the quantitative data does not support the "representative" photomicrographs in the paper you refer to.

The recently published article by Ricaurte and colleagues [J. Neurosci. 15: 5476-5485, 1995] describes the effects of MDMA on various indices thought to reflect the integrity of serotonergic innervation in the brain. Both the rat and squirrel monkey were examined in this study. The conclusions reached by the authors are that the long term effects of MDMA cause a reorganization of serotonin innervation of the brain, effects which are repeatedly referred to as evidence of "serotonin neurotoxicity." While the actions of MDMA in the rat and primate brain at the high dosages employed in the study (at least 25 times the human dosage) may in fact reflect a toxic effect of this drug on serotonin pathways, other interpretations of the data are possible.

For example, what Ricaurte and others have shown is, at high dosages, MDMA causes prolonged decreases in brain serotonin. This effect, per se, cannot be equated to destruction of serotonergin axons (i.e. bonafide serotonin neurotoxicity) because assessments of serotonin are only indicative of the presence of this transmitter in neurons, not the actual neuronal structures themselves.

In other words, MDMA can decrease the level of serotonin without necessarily destroying serotonergic axons. An analogy would be draining water from a pipe without destroying the plumbing. The prolonged decreases in serotonin seen after high dosages of MDMA have not been associated with the classic evidence of neuronal destruction such as astrogliosis [O'Callaghan and Miller, 1993] or silver degeneration staining [Commins et al., 1987; Jensen et al., 1993]. Moreover, retrograde transport studies, which could be used to assess whether serotonergic axons are still functional even when depleted of serotonin, have yet to be performed following exposure of rats or primates to MDMA.

The brains of squirrel monkeys before and after being given ecstasy. Ricaurte believes the missing lines indicate neurotoxicity, but O'Callaghan does not. See the interviews above.

How, then, do you find damage to the nervous system?

Historically, and to this day, the gold standard for determining whether something damages the nervous system is based on morphology. This means that you rely on histological staining to determine if you see loss of a given cell type or change in staining patterns of specific groups of cells. However, in the brain that doesn't work so well.

Why is that?

The problem is that there are so many myriads of cell types that compose the brain with different structural DNA/RNA make ups that you can't tell one from another, they look kind of the same, but they aren't the same, they perform very different functions, based on their specific molecular components. Obvious damage can be seen if a sufficiently large numbers of cells are lost and such findings would certainly constitute a neurotoxic effect because, once lost, these cells will not likely regenerate. Unfortunately, classical staining procedures (i.e. ones that will tell you if a brain cell is lost) will not allow you to determine if there has been damage to nerve terminals, nerve axons, or damage to a small population of cells. You can't see it even with a systematic survey of the entire brain using classical techniques.

Why is that, can't you get sufficient magnification?

If you could magnify the whole brain so that you could survey every cell type, it would take you two millenniums to sample everything because there are so many different cell types. Sampling at that level just cannot be done, so you have to rely on other ways of detecting damage or, alternatively, you have to start with a hint as to where the target is. The standard techniques only allow you to see a very small percentage of the total population of cells in the brain. Even if those staining techniques only missed one cell out of ten, that might be a very important cell in terms of brain functioning.

So, if the damage can't be assessed visually, how can you measure it?

I have gone into the literature and looked at what is known in terms of general responses of the nervous system to damage, and I include trauma-induced, disease-induced, stroke-induced damage besides chemical-induced damage that is of issue with respect to MDMA. When you get damage to any part of the brain and spinal cord the damaged area responds by an enlargement of a brain cell known as an astrocyte, a star-shaped glial cell. Astrocyte hypertrophy (enlargement) is called gliosis (the response of astrocytes to injury of neurons or glia to injury). This response recently has been associated with a very specific protein, GFAP. Increases in GFAP can be detected by a specific antibody and this is easy to see in sections of brain tissue when the increase in astrocyte size is on the order of 2 to 3-fold.

Is this a classical test, or one developed in your lab?

GFAP staining of tissue sections in not a classical test, but it is one that has gained wide acceptance for assessing, qualitatively, the presence of brain damage. I have extended this analysis to a different level by developing an assay for this GFAP, so that you can actually quantify the degree of increase in this protein in a given brain area. Its analogous to a blood test for the antibody to HIV; its a test for the presence of increased levels of GFAP.

So you have developed a new indirect method for measuring neurotoxicity. But how can you be sure if it gives the correct result?

> The general idea is to develop a profile of broad types of known neurotoxic compounds, that is, compounds that are known to damage the nervous system, and see if you can get an increase in GFAP using the immunoassay I have developed. The test shows positive to a broad class of toxicants – from metals to endogenous compounds like bilirubin that accumulate in blue babies at birth; to toxins that poison muscles, to seaweed poisons; to drugs used as tools to damage specific components of the nervous system. Stab wounds to the brain, extremely advanced age, infections to the brain and damage such as induced by Alzheimer's disease would also show positive, because they increase GFAP. Likewise, the test shows negative with a large number of drugs that we have tried at therapeutic doses. These include barbiturates, anti-psychotics, anti-cholinergics, steroids, anti-inflammatories, blockers of monoamine oxidase – even Ketamine under certain circumstances. These agents do not damage the brain and do not increase GFAP.

How does your test compare with traditional methods?

> For example, with respect to serotonin containing neurons, the toxicant 5, 7-dihydroxy tryptamine (which selectively damages serotonin nerve terminals) has been found to increase GFAP. Thus, damage to serotonin nerve terminals will cause gliosis and this is very useful for determining that damage has occurred because if the brains of animals treated with 5, 7-dihydroxytryptamine were examined by traditional staining methods, the brain would look normal when, in fact there is underlying damage to serotonin neurons.

So you've applied your test to a number of different known and suspected neurotoxic drugs and chemicals and it always works. How about fenfluramine and MDMA?

> Realistically, we don't think fenfluramine, MDMA or even methamphetamine causes any damage in the rodent even at high dosages of these three compounds. The transmitter changes we see are prolonged but they return to control and they are never associated with gliosis (increased GFAP) or evidence of degeneration at the dosages that we have used. In the mouse but not in the rat we have shown clear-cut damage to dopaminergic nerve terminals after very high dosages of methamphetamine, MDA and MDMA. In rats or mice we have not observed damage to serotonin neurons due to methamphetamine, MDA, MDMA or d-fenfluramine, despite the fact that we do see weeks-long decreases in serotonin.

So your test indicates that MDMA is not neurotoxic to serotonin neurons, even at dosages higher than those commonly used in humans. But does this apply at high temperature?

> The temperature data is too complicated to go into but I would say that all of the toxic effects of MDA, MDMA and methamphetamine require sustained temperatures above base line levels throughout the dosing regimen. When I refer to toxic here, I'm referring to systemic toxicity (e.g. cardiovascular collapse) that results from malignant hyperthermia. Its the acute toxic effects, not neurotoxicity, that kills you.

Are there any doubts at all about your methods of testing?

A possible argument that could be raised against the GFAP increase as evidence of serotonergic neurotoxicity could be that the serotonin decrease isn't associated with the increase in GFAP. What we have done here is instead of relying on the so-called serotonergic neurotoxic compounds, that is MDMA, d-fenfluramine or even paracloramphetamine, we have given the most widely characterised neurotoxic compound targeting serotonergic neurons which is 5, 7-dihydroxytryptamine. When we administer this compound to rats, the levels of brain serotonin decrease by 50 to 70% while we see 30 to 100% increases in GFAP over control.

What this means is that damage to the serotonergic nervous system leading to prolonged decreases of serotonin give you prolonged increases of GFAP. In other words, damage to serotonin nerve terminals results in gliosis and, therefore, an increase in GFAP. In contrast, when MDMA or d-fenfluramine are administered to rats a 30-70 % decrease in serotonin also is observed but these decreases are not associated with an increase in GFAP. We interpret these findings as evidence for a lack of a neurotoxic effect of these drugs. Instead, we believe that the decrease in serotonin after MDMA and d-fenfluramine can be explained as neuromodulatory/regulatory phenomena, i.e. protein synthesis inhibition as a natural extension of the pharmacological activity of those compounds.

I understand that a recent postmortem study of the brains of chronic methamphetamine users failed to find the expected neuronal damage. Do you think the same might apply to MDMA users?

Yes. It would be very surprising not to find decreases in serotonin in the brains of high-dose MDMA users. Again, as Kish found for methamphetamine abusers, this does not necessarily mean there is damage to nerve terminals.

References

1. Clause added to The International Convention on Psychotropic Substances 1985 report to the World Health Organisation.

2. Refer box page 241.

3. *Effects of MDMA in decomposing tissues on the development of Parasarcophbagaruficornis* [insect larvae] by Goff et al in *Journal of Forensic Sciences*, 1997 pages 276-280.

4. Pathology of deaths associated with ecstasy misuse by Milroy et al, Journal of Clinical Pathology 1996, 49, 147-153.

5. Face to face interview with Dr George Ricaurte at Johns Hopkins Medical Institute, Baltimore, USA in October 1995 while I was taking part in one of his trials as a volunteer.

6. Face to face interview with Dr James O'Callaghan in October 1985 at Rockefeller University, New York, with revisions by email in April 1997.

7. Ricaurte et al, *J. Neurosci.* 15: 5476-5485, 1995.

Information

Internet

By far the best source of up to date information is the Internet. Public libraries often provide free access. There are two distinct parts: Newsgroups, and Web sites.

Newsgroups are written discussion groups allowing anyone to post comments and anyone else to reply. There is no quality control, but after a while you get to know names of people who write sense, and you can always contact them by email. These are listed on Internet Drug Resources, see below.

Web sites are equivalent to showrooms full of information run by individuals and organisations. Quality varies, but you soon get to know which sites you can trust.

My site is called **ecstasy.org** (http://obsolete.com/ecstasy in Europe and http://ecstasy.org in America). It is regularly updated and has sections for reader's experiences, surveys, student research projects, questions and answers.

Links from my site take you to my 1993 online book E for Ecstasy; **The Lycaeum** for "visionary" drugs; **Hyperreal Drug Archives** for recreational drugs; **XTC information** for ecstasy; **Yahoo Drug Index** for links to particular drugs; **Internet Drug Resources** for newsgroups. Also online zines, event listings, DJ's sites etc.

Publications and mail order bookshops

Ecstasy edited by Stephen Peroutka, published by Kluwer Academic Publishers 1990. The classic serious work on MDMA, out of print but in academic libraries.

Ecstasy – The MDMA Story by Bruce Eisner, $17.95. published by Ronin 1989 revised 1994. Good general book written from American pre-rave viewpoint.

The Pursuit of Ecstasy by Gerome Beck and Marsha Rosenbaum 1994 State University of New York Press $14.95. ISBN: 0-7914-1818-9. Written by two sociologists.

Altered State, by Matthew Collin published 1997 by Serpents' Tail, London £10.99. ISBN: 1 85242 377 3. Detailed history of rave culture, less about the drug.

Through the Gateway of the Heart published in 1985 by Four Trees Publications ISBN: 0-936329-00-9. A collection of personal accounts of ecstasy use.

PIHKAL (Phenethylamines I Have Known And Loved), A Chemical Love Story by Alexander Shulgin, 1991, $18.95 ISBN: 0-9630096-0-5. Personal account of the invention and testing of many new psychedelics including MDMA. Nearly 1,000 pages.

TIHKAL (Tryptamines I Have Known And Loved) by Alexander Shulgin, 1997. Companion volume to PIHKAL covering tryptamines.

Psychedelics Encyclopedia by Peter Stafford, $24.95, published by Ronin, PO Box

1035, Berkeley, CA 94701. ISBN: 0-914171-51-3. Useful general book on psychedelics.
Thanatos to Eros: Thirty-five Years of Psychedelic Exploration by Myron Stolaroff, 1995. A lifetime's exploration and guided use of Ecstasy and psychedelics.
The Secret Chief by Myron Stolaroff, due 1997 published by MAPS (see below). The true story of the therapist who taught therapeutic use of ecstasy (see History chapter).
The Essential Psychedelic Guide by DM Turner, $14.95 from Panther Press, ISBN: 0-9642636-1-0. Valuable personal experience of a psychedelic explorer.
The above books and many more can be obtained from **Mind Books** 321 S Main St #543, Sebastopol, CA, 95472 USA. Phone: +1 707 829 8127. Fax: +1 707 829-8100.
Books on manufacture can be obtained from **Loompanics**, P.O. Box 1197, Port Townsend, WA 98368 USA phone +1 206 385 2230. Both take credit cards.

UK Dance Magazines

To the Core, PO box 63 Wisbech, Cambs, PE13 5HB. Telephone 01945 474040
Eternity, PO Box 4, Robin Hood, Wakefield, WF3 3XB. Telephone 01924 892557.
Mixmag, PO Box 89, London, W2 3GP. Telephone 0171 7068003.
M8, 11 Lynedoch Place, Glasgow, G3 6AV. Telephone 0141 3531118.
DJ, 50 Doughty Street, London WC1N 2NG. Telephone 0171 405 2055

Organisations

Multidisciplinary Association for Psychedelic Studies (MAPS), 1801 Tippah Avenue, Charlotte, NC 28205, USA (Phone +1 704-358 9830, Fax +1 704 358 1650). A charity promoting research into psychedelics, supported by donations. Overseas subscribers pay a minimum of $40 which includes a magazine style quarterly newsletter.
Institute for the Study of Drug Dependence (ISDD) 32 Loman Street, SE1 OEE (0171 928 1211). Good reference library and helpful staff. ISDD publishes *Druglink*.
Lifeline, 101 Oldham Street, Manchester M4 1LW (0161 839 2075; fax 834 5093) Walk-in advice, collaborate in research projects and publish over 50 information leaflets.
3D Research Bureau, 25 Halkyn Avenue, Liverpool L17 2AH (0151 733 9550) Consultancy run by Russell Newcombe who wrote the Deaths section.
Project LSD, Box 9, 136-138 Kingsland High Street, London, E8 2NS. Telephone 0181 – 806 7353. Harm reduction advice for homosexuals.
Flying Squad. Information for club goers on ITV Teletext page 363, or by telephone 0839-600616. To include your club contact 134 Curtain Road, London EC2A 3AR.
The Advance Party PO Box 3290, London, NW2 3UJ. Free party information.
United Systems c/o 19 Thurleby Road, Middlesex, HA8 0HF. Advice on sound systems for free parties.
Justice? Prior House, 6 Tilbury Place, Brighton, BN2 2GY. Telephone 01273685913. DIY advice.
Release (0171 603 8654). Release has an emergency helpline giving 24 hour drug and legal advice, their own solicitors and can recommend solicitors.

Personal Accounts

These are some of many accounts sent to me, selected for interest and to show a wide range of uses and effects.

Although these are overwhelmingly positive, I have not excluded negative accounts. No doubt people who have had a good time are more keen to write about their experiences and are more able to write well.

Does ecstasy mess up your life?

It's not the drugs that mess you up, it's the people

The first time I tried X was about four years ago and I loved it and the way it made me feel. My friends took me out in the woods where they made me feel comfortable and relaxed so I could enjoy my experience. I was very lucky to have them as they knew what to do how to prepare me and how to take care of me. That was the best experience of my life. I took it quite often but when I felt I needed more to get the feeling I stopped going to clubs and taking the drug. I now take it occasionally and am a very functional person. I go to work, I own 2 cars and my husband and I are looking to buy a home.

Many adults scare kids and don't warn them on what kind of precautions to take. That's how they die. It's not the drug that messes up peoples' lives, it's people who mess up their own lives.

- A 20yr old woman living in Florida.

Connected to God

Ecstasy has brought me closer to my family

Close to 1 hour after taking the roll [ecstasy] I felt a very loose feeling in my muscles. Minutes later I was in a complete altered state of consciousness. I felt my life's worries and fears lifted from my soul. The world had opened its doors to me to experience all that it could give. My visual perceptions took a beating as I pulled myself into another dimension. I fell under the influence of the lasers, fog, and darkness of the main room. I was standing at one point staring up at the lasers above my head and thought how wonderful life was and how lucky I was to have been born. I silently thanked my parents and God. I believe this was the first time I felt connected to God.

An hour later I found myself tearing up the dance floor and having one of the best times of my life. I no longer cared how I appeared to other people as long as I was true to myself and put on no "masks". I had found a groove and danced long and hard. Once in a while my guide found me to ask me how I was doing, give me some water, and present new thoughts about how to "control" the roll.

Later I found myself beginning to come down off the roll. I had a half a roll left and set out to find my guide. I felt an odd feeling surge through my body, I was being absorbed into the music and I could feel the "vibes" that other people were giving off in great detail. I found my guide and described my sensations. He told me that it was an effect of slowly coming down. My guide also told me that I could shortly take the other half of my roll.

After another hour or so I was back up to that previous high, although my energy was decreased so much I needed a break and took a breather. I talked with a very good friend who has cerebral-palsy and is confined to a wheelchair. We spoke for quite some time and I felt very close to him. I could feel that he had buried deep inside a want to dance, but had come to the realization that his purpose on this world was to experience the music not through dancing, but listening. I felt very happy to feel such a feeling from him. He makes me very happy to this day.

Over the next few hours I danced and talked with many people, including many strangers whom I have kept in contact with. At the end of the night I saw the sun rising and streaming through cracks in the sheets covering the windows of the building. I felt warmth from the single beam of sunlight hitting me. I didn't want to leave, but knew I would soon have to return to my home. I felt true happiness. I have gained something very positive from that period.

During the next few days, my life changed as I experienced a heightened sense of my surroundings. I was told by my guide that these effects were normal and that I should use them to my advantage. I became a more open and considerate person. I also found myself coming closer to my family. Conversations with my mother became easier and more relaxed. Since then, my relationship with my mother has grown stronger and stronger.

To anyone interested in experimenting with ecstasy, I would offer the following advice: 1. Read as much literature as you can about ecstasy 2. Have someone who has done ecstasy before "guide" you through your roll. 3. Be in a good frame of mind before you take your pill. 4. Lastly, be prepared to explore yourself in as many ways as possible.

18 year old from Atlanta, Georgia USA

The Harvard Agape

A Harvard Divinity School graduating senior led a parting ritual using ecstasy

We agreed to meet a few hours beforehand and share some simple food. Zapapaias and I arrived last. The group was already there; Brother D, being our host and master of ceremonies, Golden Voice, Drummer Boy, Brother Peace, Healer and Rosebearer. The small room where the feast table had been set was warm, cosy, full of pillows and candles, a perfect cradle for the divine to settle in. In a corner people had already offered up their sacred tools. I added mine: an icon of the Magdalene given to me by my mentor, an icon of the Virgin and Child brought back from Brazil by Zapapaias, a picture of my brother and me, Jake the Lizard (being a sweet gift of Rosebearer), two tarot cards from the Rider-Waite deck, namely the lovers and the sun, and a great number of candles.

We began the ceremony at 5pm with the ringing of the bell. Brother D started with a welcome and a Buddhist meditation from the Gandavyuha Sutra about the joy of having found true friends. After the reading, Brother D spoke a little and then we all communicated (took ecstasy). Right afterwards we all took turns, orally or silently, dedicating the Agape. I dedicated it to my brother. Then there was silence ... silence ... silence.

I had imagined 20 minutes would be enough time for the sacrament to reveal its power, so after 30 minutes I decided to end the silent meditation. I could hear Drummer Boy impatiently tapping his little drum pad. Not that I minded. I wanted to tell him it was OK but I couldn't. In order to do that I had to end the meditation and sing the Agape Hymn even though I was far from feeling the effects. I knew my voice would be tighter, not so sharp, not so clear, not the best, but It had to happen. We all knew that the Hymn would mark the beginning of the trip. So I chanted.

The hymn done and the bell rung, the liturgy was open to the group. We discussed for a little bit our situation vis-a-vis the sacrament. Only Brother D and Rosebearer were in the spirit. We waited. Golden Voice had opted out of taking ecstasy, preferring the sacred herb. Soon after the opening of the ceremony (after the Agape Hymn) Golden Voice offered us a most wonderful gift: she sang "Amazing Grace" for us. The spirit was coming down, resting upon my shoulder as her words filled the room and our hearts. I was in communion with everyone else in the room. It was as if, at that moment, all barriers had come down, all suffering had ended, all pain had been relieved, all joys had been known. I forgave the offences I had suffered and was forgiven for my sins.

I thought of that woman and that child that I had hurt. I felt delivered from the agony of guilt. I thought of that man that I would never be able to see. I felt free. I thought of that man that was still grieving, still silently bleeding. I inwardly dared ask for pardon. I thought of the man I was with, of the pain I had suffered. I was healed. I was strengthened. I was redeemed.

It must have been 50 minutes since the ingestion. Wow, Golden Voice's tune was lifting me away into a supernatural dimension and the sacrament was simultaneously making its healing presence known. The song over, we all looked at each other and smiled. We were all "there." Zapapaias sang one of his sacred songs. I sang one of my favourite hymns called "For the fruit of all creation". Later Healer showed us some of the work of her hands, beadwork. Beautiful work requiring a lot of patience. I knew Rosebearer was proud of her work. She also told us how once she was about to commit suicide and that ecstasy saved her life, gave her hope in herself and in the future.

Zapapaias showed me a picture of Inanna his goddess. He was afraid before of showing it to me because he thought I would be jealous. I laughed. Yes, I am jealous. I think my jealousy comes from my fear of abandonment. We put the picture of the goddess on my little altar.

As the sacrament slowly wore off, we quieted down a bit. We all respected each other's space, each other's words, each other's silences. We all took turns sharing something powerful with the group and I believe we all came out of the experience enriched. And surprised too. How easy it is to feel free in such a safe setting. Ecstasy helps tremendously, of course.

We ended the evening around midnight with the Doors playing The End. The lyrics had never made sense to me before. That night they appeared three dimensional. I felt as if I was flying or swimming in the great sky or the great ocean that the music was. The lyrics were like fish or birds moving all around me. I went to bed with blue sharks shaped like the Venus of Milo floating through my mind.

I woke up the next day wondering what had happened. Of course something had happened. After all I was the main liturgist with the title of Priestess, the main theologian behind the liturgy. I had thought about the theory behind the Agape for a long time. We had all shared of ourselves, and shared a deep part of ourselves.

How do I feel as the liturgist? Certain elements have to be met in order to have a liturgy, a cultus. I think they were met that night. Underhill cites four necessary elements of cultus: 1) ritual or liturgical pattern, 2) symbol or significant sacrament, 3) sacrament (not as mere signifier but as a conveyor of invisible realities), and 4) sacrifice or voluntary offering.

Our agape was unusual, unique, out of the ordinary. But the structure was present. The bell was rung to delimit the sacred time. The symbol was the communion/dedication. The outward and visible form of the sacrament was ecstasy; the inward and spiritual grace imparted was manyfold, from healing to the building of community to personal growth. The sacrifice was evident from the gifts offered up on the altar. We shared in the sacrament for and with our brothers and sisters, our parents, our loved ones, our friends, not only the people present but those absent. We offered ourselves up for and to them, as channels of grace, as bearers of gifts later to be shared.

I left Harvard a couple weeks later. I feel that I have left behind true and deep friends, people with whom I shared one of the most meaningful experiences of my life. People I trust. People who have seen a very important and personal part of me. People to whom I am joined in love. I also met another side of the divine. There was no great revelation of God that night, no road to Damascus episode. But there was a peace, a certain sense of comfort, of spiritual truth. Of all the people there, I think I am the most concerned with organised religion. I am an Episcopalian and most of my knowledge and experience of God has been acquired through the Church. A rare thing, I know. But that night I met another aspect of God, the God that dwells in each and everyone of us, in our souls, in our hearts, in our minds. It was a God I had always believed in but never met. In a sense, I regained a bit of lost faith.

Higher states of consciousness

I now have a new outlook on life.

For me a spiritual experience is one that opens you up to the flow of life. An experience that allows your natural state of oneness to be unobstructedly expressed. With all drugs that I take I search for that feeling, that amazing warmth of allowing love to flow through your body like waves. The most profound experience I have ever had has been with ecstasy. My life is a constant journey to achieve that beautiful state without the assistance of psychoactive drugs, however, I am still young and haven't found it yet. Sharing nature with ones that I love has brought me close before though. There is definitely powerful magic in Mother Nature's splendour.

I arrived at my friends house in the country at around 6:30 and immediately took my one tab of ecstasy. Making sure to drink plenty of water, I watched the gorgeous Texas sunset and enjoyed the antics of my friends' many cats. In about an hour I began to feel extremely spontaneous and clear. My body felt cushioned and I had a happy feeling not unlike a nice beer buzz, and at the same time like nothing I had ever experienced before. As the drug really began to take its effect I was suddenly nauseous. This was not really unpleasant and overall made me feel a lot better and did not dampen my experience at all. I was with two very close friends and two strangers, but even though I had never met these people before, I felt equally close with them, and with everyone alive. This experience lasted for roughly four hours.

When I was coming off the drug at first I felt a little sad and for a brief moment extremely paranoid. Looking back now I attribute these side effects to my personal defensive characteristics which had been stripped away and forgotten in my total surrender to the ecstasy. Another possibility could have been the interaction of the marijuana that I had smoked right before I began to come off the drug.

I cannot stress more the importance of this experience to me. I now have a new outlook on life and feel that this has helped me in my journey to enlightenment. This morning I woke up with a smile and felt the sun streaming through the window and knew that my life was headed in a new direction. I am in love with life in a way that I never was before.

— An 18 year old American woman

Life after death

I am changed after a near death experience
I have take ecstasy since I was 15 or 16 to enjoy myself, "be out of my mind", and feel part of the group. But one night something very strange happened that changed my life.

I came home from a party early, before the drug had worn off. When I lay on my bed I started to feel my heart beat faster, then slower until I could hardly feel it. I was frightened by this and thought I was dying.

I felt very light and "saw" that above me everything was good, and below everything was bad, with me in the middle. I knew that if I wanted, I could choose to go up, but I chose not to go, because that would mean death. I chose to stay in the middle and tried to focus my mind on good things. Eventually I started hearing birds singing, and it seemed they were speaking to me, showing me the way to come back.

This experience deeply changed my life. I had never thought about "something after death" before. I don't know if it was heaven and hell, and real life in the middle, I feel stupid saying that, but I'm sure it was something regarding a part of my mind which does not die. From that moment I started to use drugs to explore myself, not only to enjoy myself during parties or raves, and everyone says that I'm really changed.

– Italian woman aged 20

Alone

Taking ecstasy on my own helps me get results
One night here at school some kids were throwing a party but I couldn't really get into it. Then I managed to get a hit from my friend. I took the hit at around midnight and went to a local bar where the kids all hang out. At about one, the E still hadn't kicked in so I went back to my dorm room. I put on a black light, and then put on a CD from Ministry of Sound in London. Another half-hour passed but nothing.

Then for some reason I put on Moby's DJ Mix album and it hit me all at once. It was just me, my room and Moby and I took off. The Moby for some reason was the trigger to the E and it was unbelievable. I sat for about four hours that night becoming one with the bass which was permeating my room. It was if I was being transformed. At times the E hit me so hard that I couldn't even lift my head. I've tripped before on mushrooms, but the sense of being alone on shrooms scared me. But the sense of being on E by myself was so fulfilling that I even locked my door because I didn't want to see anyone while I was on it.

It felt as if I was not on this planet for those hours and at the same time I was searching for my true being. So many things had changed for me this year at school; being a freshman, being away from home, and dealing with new problems, I saw what I would have to do to rectify them. The experience was so overwhelming that I Exd the following night by myself again because I felt so in control while being by myself. It was a feeling of independence and freedom from the problems that were holding me back this year.

After Exing by myself and seeing how important school, family and friends are I have improved my GPA here at school by amazing figures. Since the Ex, I have taken my work more seriously and presently have a 3.3 cum. GPA. Some of my friends won't ever touch E and some of my friends don't understand why and how I would Ex by myself. I feel for anyone who does take E to try it out when they are by themselves and see what it will do. It will open windows and doors to your inner self that you were either to afraid to look at or just didn't know how. I can't wait to do it again by myself and learn more about me and live a richer and fuller life.

Finding my goal

Coming to know myself worked well in combination with E

I am a fan of E, having tried many different drugs, mostly in a concentrated effort to find new "doorways" to understanding myself.

I am a mother of three, my partner and I professional musicians, and responsibilities dictate that I don't get to trip on anything as often as I might otherwise. I have been involved in a very intense Gestalt-type of therapy (only experiential rather than traditional therapist-patient) with some friends of mine for about a year and a half, with the principle aim being "making the subconscious conscious" and raising actual intelligence/creativity in the process. I found that much of the very hard work I was doing in working through my insecurities and coming to know myself worked very well in combination with E.

Sort of like: in "the work" I struggle towards a goal I am only dimly aware of. I take E, and am inside the goal, but without a road map of how to get there "for real". After a time I was able to sustain the clarity of experience for as long as a week (after the same minimal dose, only once a week). My supply dried up, and I am only a little closer to my goal (still moving, albeit at a frustrating crawl). I am very interested in the glimpse I get of the outcome-state in this process, which is one of great clarity and uninhibited creativity.

– American woman

Losing old friends

I have noticed a drastic change in my personality and lost my best friend

Two weeks ago today I tried E for the first time. It was the most beautiful, religious, spiritual experience I have ever encountered. Since then, I have tried other drugs as well, but nothing "hard" such as heroin or cocaine. I had never tried drugs at all before.

I was touched when a friend, who really didn't know me that well at the time invited me to a Rave. I am in the position to really mess up his life as for as his career goes. I felt that if he could trust me, I could trust him and give it a shot. I think the fact that I was lonely played a huge part in my decision as well. I wanted to be part of the "family" my friend had told me so much about.

I am however, very concerned about what it may do to me in the long run. I have already noticed a drastic change in my personality. It wasn't until my best friend visited that I noticed these changes. We had never been in an argument before, but we didn't get along the whole weekend. He just seemed totally different to me. I had never noticed he was such a nervous person. He would just go off on a particular subject and would try to get me to argue with him. I would express my desire to just have a good time (it was a Saturday night) and he got very mad because I didn't want to argue. He said things like you can't just float around and act like nothing matters.

I guess that is what I have been doing. I mean, things, however unpleasant still do matter or don't they? I am so confused and a bit scared. I don't want to lose the "family" I have just been adopted into, but I don't want to become a "slave to the vibe" either.

– American man

Addiction to the ecstasy-induced state?

I am addicted to ecstasy in order to feel at peace

The drug itself has awakened in me such beautiful visions which I had only glimpses of while being sober, and it has changed my life in dynamic ways. I have not had the opportunity to use this drug for maybe four months now, and in this time I have seen my mother die and my entire world fall apart.

I feel disillusioned again, but this time it pierces me on a much deeper level than it ever has. I am not sure if this is due to my facing death, or the loss of ecstasy in my system. I have reason to believe the latter, for I have been able to cope with death all of my life, at times preferring what I know of it to life. So this leads me to believe that since my body has not had its regular once-a-week dosage of ecstasy, that I am addicted to it in order to feel at peace.

For prolonged periods afterwards I would be able to get in touch with the feelings I felt while on it, and be able to link the feelings together. It would happen while hearing a song, or just on its own. Have I completely lost the serenity and peace that I once had? Is it impossible for me to feel these feelings unless on ecstasy? And if I were to be able to find some pure ecstasy, then would it harm me to take it again? There is so much I would like to find out, and I hope that you can aid me on my journey to find what I know exists inside of me by answering these few questions about my dilemma.

– From an 18 year old American girl

Reply from Dr. Karl Jansen:

A person well versed in these areas once said that E TEMPORARILY pushes the fear away so that we are able to get a glimpse of who we really are and what it is like to have our hearts open without fear, but that E does not DISSOLVE the fear permanently.

This, I feel, is what is going on with this girl and how an "addiction" to E could happen. One becomes dependent on it to evoke that state and when is not on it, our "stuff" comes creeping back in, so we do it again to return to that state. The key I feel is to combine the E experiences with other types of experiences which evoke deeper changes and transformations. Also I feel that ongoing work with a "guide" particularly when one is new to this work (and as young as this girl) is highly important, in order to INTEGRATE the experiences, to weave them in more permanently and to, strengthen one's understanding and resources to more successfully deal with the challenges of life. Also I see the "processing" in between as integrating the experiences, so they don't slip away so easily, as well as preparing the ground for future explorations.

Yes, it is not easy, it is not about recreation, that is why they call it "The Work" is what I often say.

As far as the physical "ill effects" described in the communique you sent, I feel this is part of the purification these "allies" provoke. Though many do not experience this on E, I can attest to these effects. Often it is through vomiting that we release our fears and blocks, so I, in most cases, feel it is positive. However, our organic friends can provoke even deeper purifications and releases, as we well know.

Self love

To this day I carry with me the love and realize I always bring that back to myself
The first time I tried E I was 22 and in grad school. Previously, I'd been an avid tripper via both chemicals and mushrooms and had pretty much shied away from other drugs. I'd always loved tripping and had been fortunate enough to have never had a bad trip. Then as now I considered myself an educated drug-user and always tried to find out the most thorough information beforehand.

The night I first tried E it was with a large group of friends. We were holding a rave in a cabin on a mountain, but the party started at a friend's apartment. After ingestion, a friend who'd already experienced E before couldn't stop talking about how great it was going to be and she also tried to massage me explaining this would somehow "induce" the feelings and help me relax. This only irritated me and persuaded a less than calm feeling.

When the first feelings, both emotional and physical, hit I literally felt stunned. I didn't like it at first because it made me feel "touchy-feely" and I'm not a touchy-feely person. I tensed up and felt nauseous – I wanted out. But within minutes, it was reduced to sharp flashes of light and then tender emotions and an amazingly sensual physical presence. Somehow I'd let go and really felt the full measure of the chemical/spiritual alchemy created in my being.

By the time I'd arrived at the cabin I was .... well, in ecstasy. I felt so joyful, so loving and everything was so utterly, painfully beautiful. I'd fortunately worn a green velour hooded shirt which I took great glee in touching and allowing others do as well. This simple experience was enough to create an even higher level of ecstasy and gesture of closeness with strangers. At one juncture, someone requested a simple kiss. It was the longest and most pleasurable kiss I've ever had. Exquisite.

Eventually I got around to dancing, but my dancing was more of a trance spiral in the middle of the floor – spinning, twirling gently and gazing into the mirrors with much curiosity. I think the greatest contribution I gained from the experience was to learn that truly, I love myself and that is the route to loving others.

To this day I carry with me the love I remembered because of the experience as well as the beauty and realize I can in some ways always bring that back to myself.

I have experienced E since then – to a great degree for a few years after, but for the last four years I've not been able to for a variety of reasons; dealing with moving, etc. However, nothing has ever come close to that first experience and actually I'm sorta glad. But, I'd still like to do it again someday:)

– From a 29 year old computer professional "with a penchant for poetry"

E is addictive and fucks you up

Using unnatural chemicals to find yourself is a false and nasty way to live

When I first started taking E I found a new sense of myself, and a greater feeling of spirituality for my surroundings. However, I think people should be warned of the effects that ecstasy and other such substances cause. I have been using the drug for almost four years, taking 2-3 pills, plus a bit of speed every weekend. I wish I could stop. They say E is not addictive, but I am a firm believer that it is. It is a complete escape from reality which I long for in the week. It is such a false and nasty way to live. Why should you have to drop a pill full of unnatural chemicals, in order to find yourself?

I think I'm going slightly mad. I have been going down hill ever since I did my first pill. If you have any sense you won't try E. You will find a true sense of yourself and reality through your own self and not through unnatural chemicals made in nasty backstreet alleys.

— *Email from a reader of my Internet site*

Ecstasy reveals the true self

The ecstasy state is what psychotherapy was supposed to be about

I take ecstasy about every six months. For me, that's the real bare minimum for a complete growing experience. Six months assures that you have progressed psychologically and emotionally if you're in a path of growth. I find that I can integrate the experiences and teachings perfectly to my daily life; walking in the street with a friend, listening to music, loneliness in my room, meditation, and hugging my mother and father.

LSD is really incredible, but its lessons can be pretty obscure. LSD is like a loving strict father. Ecstasy, however, is like a loving mother who gives It to you. Whether you can recognize It in both cases is up to you, and I find spacing the doses up is one of the best ways there are.

The first time we did ecstasy, it was an incredible experience, but I did not understand the possibilities. The second time around, with my best friend in the woods, it was the most amazing thing I have done in my life. Being able to sit at the table with your known problems, and other unknown ones coming up, as relaxed and objective as could be is what psychotherapy was supposed to be about. I realized my self-esteem was actually not that high at the time, and how some specific childhood problems were not completely solved.

Better yet than therapy, E is what life should be like, albeit a little less dense. My friend and I are very proud of our intelligence, though not arrogant about it. And she told me, after the experience, that if she found out that ecstasy could take away five per cent of her intelligence, she could live with that. I know this is not possible.

Overall, the E experience has made me a more serene person. Everything feels like "things work". I feel reassured that this place is pretty well organized. It makes the spiritual teachings that the material world is fantasy very tangible. I understand now how involvement with the things of the world should not proceed so far as to make you lose your wellbeing and tranquillity. My spiritual teacher once said, "you should trade nothing for your internal peace".

I now do not know how much E has done and how much I have done myself, but I can assure you that E has played a part. I am able to rest while I act, and not surrender to agitation because of activity, as well as stopping the internal dialogue for more prolonged periods.

On another front, I ask everybody to understand that for E, when it's gone, it's gone. Don't do more than a pill, or one and a half at a time. That's asking for trouble. And, when experimenting with any substance, first reach out for information. Uncensored chunks of it are available on the Internet for you to read through by the tons. Do it, and keep them uncensored. Back up the people who do research and those who make it available.

– From a 22-year old engineering student in Mexico City

Giving up coke

I'm eighteen a freshman at University of Wisconsin, and come from a well off suburban New York family . I'm a very laid back person, and like to try new things all the time. Unfortunately, I got into doing coke a few months ago, but after doing E, I haven't touched it since. I can't figure it out. Physically I felt run-down after ecstasy, my lower back was sore from all my body movements those two nights, but emotionally I was feeling great.

Cocaine to Ecstasy

How ecstasy ended cocaine addiction

This is a true story of how I kicked a Coke habit that I had for about three years. I first starting doing Cocaine about once a week. Usually on a Friday night and into Saturday. I would use it to go out to bars and go drinking. I would buy a gram, and usually there would be a little left over for Saturday morning. This went on for several months and as I came in contact with more people who liked Coke, I would start to split grams with people during the week. This increased till I was doing that everyday, this took about a year to develop. I was fixing business machines and would collect a little money everyday.

By the second year I would buy Coke at least once a day. I thought that I would try selling it, to help with the cost that were starting to add up. But, the Coke I would buy would always end up being snorted by myself and a couple close friends. By the third year nearly all of my money was going for Coke. Food became secondary to me and I would skip eating for days to be able to afford Coke. I started to hang out with a guy who shot his Coke up with needles. We became best friends, I would fix a machine and he would be waiting for me in my car, we would instantly go buy Coke with the money that I had just made.

This went on till we were homeless and living in tents in the mountains. I started to get concerned that I had a habit that I could not kick. My business was in serious trouble as I never paid my bills. Part of the problem was that Coke was really "the" thing to do in this town at the time. I stopped doing it at bars, and would go to the camp in the mountains and just lay around doing Coke all the time. My friend shot his, I snorted mine. I was doing about a gram a day, my friend doing the same in his veins. My attitude in life became one of giving up and thinking that I would die eventually, but that was OK, as long as I could do Coke till I did.

Then one day my dealer said, "Try this. It's X, it's everything you thought Coke would be before you did it." He gave me some instructions on how to do it and I bought a gram of it along with the Coke. When we got back to the mountains I tried it and the first time didn't really get much from it, and did a little more. I got hot flashes and felt uncomfortable, so put it aside and did the rest of the Coke we had bought. The next day we tried it again and only did the amount my dealer said to try, 150mg. Wow, it hit me so good. We both looked at each other, feeling the full effects of the X.

It was the best I had felt in years. Maybe ever. My friend felt the same, we were impressed. "Yes, this is what Coke was supposed to be." We both agreed. My God, it just felt so good, we couldn't believe it. Music was wonderful. Life actually felt good. We were so high, and no 'Jones'. The next day we did it again and it was the same. Wow, so good. We finished the gram and ran to Denver for more. My dealer was quite surprised that we didn't want any Coke, but said he knew we'd like the X, it had become his favourite too. We talked about how good it feels, how washing your hands on X is like the most pleasurable experience that you could imagine. We talked of how Coke is such a joke, how it does nothing but suck your money.

Now, after years of doing Coke and thinking I couldn't quit, I had lost my desire for it 100 per cent in one day. I was amazed. Because of my habit of doing something constantly, I did a dose X nearly everyday for quite a while, but it was a healthy feeling and I got my life back on track and was eating again, working normal, paying bills again. I tried to turn everyone I know onto it, but at the time there had been a bad batch of MPTP or something in Ca. and all my friends were afraid to try it, they just kept on doing Coke. I heard the story of dry spines after 50 times doing X and I had already done more than that, but with business doing good again and X being expensive too, I eventually was down to doing a dose every couple weeks or so, then my source moved and although I miss it, never had any kind of bad jones or negative withdraw symptoms.

My friend did eventually get hooked on Coke again after about six months, he was around it everyday where he worked. He died in 1989 due to Coke abuse. If X was available to us during those years I am sure he would've stayed away from Coke.

Ecstasy saved my life, that simple. To this day I stay far way from Coke, I make a point of it to stay away from people who do it too. The last few years we come across ecstasy two or three times a year, I'm married now and this stuff is great for relationships, it really gives us a breath of fresh air when we do it. To feel good is such a simple thing, but so hard to experience at times do to the daily stress that we all have. X let's us feel good, and open up.

Well, that's the story.

— From a 36 year old American man

Centrepoint

How ecstasy was used to bring closeness to a large spiritual community
For over 10 years I lived at Centrepoint, a spiritual community north of Auckland in New Zealand which, in its most prosperous years was home to some 250 people. Members tended to be white, professional, and heterosexual, with all ages up to the 60s. We were an extremely close community, we lived a way of life designed to bring closeness with each other, with, for example, regular weekend and week long encounter groups, strategies for 'clearing' difficulties between ourselves, and "longhouse" style sleeping quarters. Most members were in stable relationships although sexual promiscuity was the norm, and encouraged. In 1988 the community was introduced to ecstasy.

The setting: a small two storey house about a mile from the main community. All furniture except large cushions has been removed from the lounge. Along one wall there is a ten feet long mirror, reaching from floor level to some six feet high. Packed into this room, with places around the walls being the key positions, 50 or 60 people sitting or leaning back on the cushions, usually in a cuddle with someone. Clothing has already been removed and placed in deliberately remembered places so that it can be found again in a few hours time. (We are easy with our nakedness). We had previously been warned to do without food for a few hours beforehand.

At the appointed time, the ecstasy is quietly handed out; a ritual which has religious echoes. One person moves around the room giving out the E, followed by someone with a glass milk bottle containing water with which we wash it down. Now we wait, talking quietly, aware of beating hearts with the rise of personal excitement. Perhaps there will be music quietly playing on the stereo. Those pregnant do not indulge, but are there to join in the proceedings.

Thirty minutes. Go for a pee. Look in the mirror. Can I feel anything happening yet? Nothing. Maybe this is the time when it's not going to work. Back in the room there is the occasional loud sigh of someone "going under". Eyes are beginning to glow. I always seem to be one of the last to feel the effects, but now – yes, my ears begin to sing quietly, and a peace descends over me. There have been rare times when I must have been resisting, for then I felt very uncomfortable, frightened even. Then I sat in front of the mirror, talking to my image, and watching the changes in my appearance, until, very quickly, I could accept the loving and peace that is so natural, right and strangely familiar.

Already couples are re-forming and in deep face-to-face conversation together; there is no particular male-female grouping. Perhaps steady partnerships need to clear unfinished business with each other first, but there are no patterns to the movement. Unsaid things that prevent an open, honest relationship with anyone are now obvious and need to be said, and heard, particularly by the speaker. (It's never what we tell people but what we hear ourselves say that is the vital key). The speaker tells how he avoids closeness, and how he perceives the other person. The listener sits quietly and accepts, this is a gift that is being given. And then the other speaks, until all that is important has been said. We already practice strategies for resolving difficulties in relationships which may explain why tonight it only takes minutes to allow unhindered loving (with anyone) to occur.

Even though I have lived so closely with these people for years I am aware of a slight fear I feel before moving to another. It's safer to stay put and wait for someone to come to me. Someone comes into my mind I know I need to see. Overcoming my fear with a personal boot to get me moving I stand up. There he or she is talking with someone. I go across and sit quietly beside them. A quick acknowledgement, a touch of the hand, "Just a minute", or the message that they could be some time, see you later. If so I don't wait but get up and move to another person who has come into my mind. Now I've started moving my fear has disappeared.

Someone comes to me. "Ah, Brian." Said with such love and acceptance. I hear how some action I carried out, something I said maybe years before is still remembered and has become part of that person. We might have a short cuddle. Male, female it doesn't matter. This is someone who is as I am; he is me and I am him/her. (I must now be peaking well.) A bottle of water appears before me. Drink, pass it on. With the first few such gatherings, it was around now that clothes started coming off. Clothing got in the way of the relating and (non sexual) touching. The only trouble was finding one's gear again when it was time to leave, which explains tonight's anticipatory disrobing.

A small group is standing in front of the mirror. A person may be having a conversation with their image, or moving slowly, watching their bodies in motion. A voice speaks loudly to their reflection, "You need to get off your chuff and do it." We understand and accept. Curious to see what happens, I go to the mirror, gaze at myself for a while, tell myself something I need to hear, and laugh at my eyes which twinkle back at me, totally accepting. Although the Community is notorious for its free sexuality, at these events rarely does anyone become sexual. We have put sex aside for the evening. It has no place here.

There are a few, mostly male, with whom I do not want any contact. I should be more accepting; if I was really a loving person. But in the end it comes down to choice, nothing else. I choose not to go to some people, there is nothing there for me. After contacting my immediate circle of friends and those others who, for various reasons came to mind, I take time out to watch the overall activities. There seems to be far more space available in the once crowded lounge. Have our 'personal spaces' disappeared? We certainly take up far less room. Now contact may be with someone outside my immediate group, and we delight in finding out about each other, moving straight to the area beyond the social small talk. We share things about ourselves, our relationships, that before now we had never even admitted to ourselves.

Time had ceased to be relevant but now it does feel as if it is moving on. Another look around to see if there is anyone I have missed or am purposely avoiding through discomfort or fear and what do I want to do about it. A voice sounds. "Time to get dressed." With some reluctance, for we know the evening's magic is over, we find our clothes, dress, and in various groups walk through the warm dark back to the main Community. There are no streetlights and the city light is far enough away to enable the stars to be seen in all their glory.

Solo: various combinations of people taking E were tried. Groups of three took it together and spent the time taking each other on a tour of their favourite and most meaningful parts of the Community. One could choose a person (not our primary partner) who remained 'straight' while the other took E. I was fascinated to watch the play of blood in my (non tripping) partner's face with the change in her moods and emotions. Tears were presaged by a rush of blood all around her eyes. Normally we never notice these subtle changes. Couples of course could take it together. But my favourite was the 'Solo'.

I would always have an idea, some topic or problem which I wanted to address while on E. I would arrange a day of no work or duties (most worked on the property), and a place where I could be uninterrupted for some hours. (not as easy as it sounds.) Loose clothing, bottle of water, note pad and pen, maybe a mirror, and of course the E. Today breakfast is willingly ignored and I go to my chosen place. Check all is as required, settle down and swallow the ecstasy. While I wait, in the note pad I write a list of things that are concerning me at the time, maybe seven or eight items, covering areas of work, relationships, or life direction. Of course there is always the anticipation of opening up new areas of the self. My heart is thumping and I feel cold. I wrap a blanket about me. I feel anxious/excited. Nothing happening. Forty minutes. This definitely is the one that isn't going to work- Ah. A movement up my spine to my head, and there it is. Warmth and love. This is the real me, not that busy, careful, anxious character. I feel warm and cozy. Hello old, dear friend. How thin the veil is. I need to talk. Not to talk is like having a growing balloon in the region of my diaphragm. It's so ridiculously simple. All I have to do is talk and that provides the energy to defuse any problem. As I talk I begin to pace the room. My body responds to what I am saying, to the word pictures in my head. I also notice that when I come to something that needs to be dealt with I start to feel cold. Now this particular thought process requires that I swing my arms in a certain manner, now this bit needs my leg flexing just so. Interesting that different thought processes are connected to different parts of the body, and generate a definite movement or rhythm. All parts of our selves are inseparably linked. Acceptance needs thought, voice and body movement. I may need to repeat a word or a phrase with its associated movement over and over until it feels completed and then I can move on to the next item that presents itself. I know that something has been dealt with because it no longer has any energy. My body can't be bothered with it. In a remarkably short space of time I have dealt with all my immediate concerns. A look at my written list shows that already it is out of date. All those concerns of an hour ago are no longer relevant.

I sit quietly. Now there are actually no thoughts happening. How do I know? I am totally aware that there is just me, here and now, nothing else. Then from nowhere comes a thought. Where did that come from? No matter how much I probe I am unable to reach the origin of these things we call "thoughts" and "ideas" that pop into my conscious mind. I can only get a feeling of a vast, universe-size "something". (But even what we term 'size' has no relevance in this realm. Whatever it is there's a lot of it.).

Move on. Clothes off, (describing out loud my actions as I do it). Onto the bed. Now a survey of my body, starting at my toes. The same process as before: talking and moving any 'sticky bits' that present themselves. I've a bit of a stiff neck which has something to do with work. Let the process happen. Pictures of a small disagreement last week which I had thought not worth bothering about. Obviously my body had taken it on board. Talk and movement, unlocking the bound up energy. Now I can move on. Continue the process right through my body, externally and internally. As I complete the process I begin to feel unconditional love for this body I call me. I slide my fingertips over my skin, alternating my point of view, first through my fingers, what they are experiencing, then I become my skin, feeling my fingers' touch. I can be both lover and loved. I regard my body with loving amusement. The scars and memories, the aging and aches. My hands fascinate me for minutes. The stories that they tell.

Right, what now? Let's explore 'love'. What is its nature? Wait for the bubbles. Concepts then words come together and form into sentences. When you take all else away love is what is left. Science tells us that everything is made of atoms and energy and stuff. Science can't handle love. Atoms and energy and stuff all dance with love. The Universe is love. And that moves on to. God IS love. But how different to actually experience it. Seeing the words written down or hearing it preached means nothing compared to this. God/love. One is the other. That's it. So simple. No big deal about it. My God, when I start to open myself to the full energy of love I feel overwhelmed. (I need several really deep breaths at this point.). No wonder we hide it under all that crap. We couldn't cope if we just opened up and allowed ourselves the full experience. (I'm having to take great lung fulls of breath to cope with all this). Much easier to let love enter in little tiny doses. And we spend all of our lives looking for it. Another revelation. Love actually is an energy. Immeasurable but definite . How many people actually allow themselves to experience love as it really is?. And it needs an act of will to personally experience it. So, what do I do about it?. Accept, that that's how the world is. And me?. How about a message for myself? Be as honest to myself and others as possible. For me that is important. I am unique, the most perfect me there ever has been. That feels as if that's all I'm going to get in that direction today. I need time to assimilate all this stuff. Go for a walk. With a bit of concentration I dress. I wander along the track into the bush, talking as more thoughts come. I have my favourite spots where I can stop for a few minutes and watch the plants, birds and insects. Everything is as it should be, not the big deal that one would have on Acid, but a quiet, loving- correctness. I've had a glimpse of reality today.

One or two other observations from spending time with E: I always see a distinctive coloured halo around a candle flame. This persists even some hours after I feel I have "come down." Others have also experienced the need for deliberate deep breaths when dealing with the "energy of love", perhaps when tripping with a partner. It seems that there are times when it's the only way to cope with it.

I usually felt 'hung over' the day after, but I felt this was a small price to pay for the goodies. My body would always be totally turned off sexually for three to four days afterwards. I just wasn't interested. It would also take about this length of time to assimilate all that happened on my trip. Maybe the two were linked.

I have never been a great barefoot walker, my feet are usually very sensitive to the ground underfoot. However, this is never the case on Psychedelics, then it is natural and comfortable to be barefoot. In fact once during E I watched myself with interest as I walked along a track covered with growing and cut gorse. No pain, no splinters or discomfort afterwards.

Once on E. I was looking across a room at a man I knew, not a friend, nor was he tripping. He tended to be a rather bitter, cynical character, but in my state I saw plainly the young frightened child hidden beneath his shell. We made eye contact (no words spoken) and he immediately started crying. All he would say later was, "You got to me". What I remember of that experience was looking at him with no judgements, just 'bottom line' stuff: total love and understanding. Whatever it was carried across via eye contact. And with the gorse-walking, what would the sceptics of fire-walking say to that? All of which makes the point that E has the ability to move us into some interesting areas.

On one occasion I took E immediately followed by Ketamine. I spent a very pleasant time travelling through 'Jewelled Halls'. The next time I took K was a few days after a particularly loving solo. But on K I went in the opposite direction. I spent eternity in a place where love was totally absent; a place of bare rocks and desolation. I existed somewhere where love had been eliminated. I came round throwing up and never touched Ketamine again. I suppose I learned something of the nature of love. Or Ketamine.

At the Community we lived a life isolated from the general population of New Zealand which allowed us a degree of freedom. (It was OK to wander around the property in a blissful state of mind.).

Soon the police began taking an interest in activities, culminating in a massive police raid in 1991, during which very few drugs were actually found. However around this time some members were jailed for sexual abuse involving minors.

There were also situations involving someone in a position of power with women in which, in the name of 'opening up to one's loving', E was very much misused.

The Community's spiritual leader is at present in jail on drugs charges. Centrepoint seems to have gone the way of most communities and is at present tearing itself to bits with those who are left there split into factions, court cases, and lawyers getting very fat. One day one of those bubbles came up from nowhere, and it said 'leave.' Suddenly I could see the Centrepoint as I knew it was finished. There was no feeling of judgement, just a knowing that what was there for me had ended.

I haven't tripped at all since I left. But sometimes.

Some random notes: I do question all the above, especially as time passes and I have rejoined what we used to term the 'rat race.' I feel lucky to have had the opportunities and the safe setting for what was very much a time of self-exploration and adventure. I have a belief that we are on Earth in order to experience and learn. There were many times when I realised. 'I am having experiences unique in the world.' What If those experiences of love and loving were solely the product of ecstasy, and the discoveries and realisations and that feeling of 'this is reality' merely a drug induced delusion? As I recently read somewhere, is a religious experience just a glitch in the neurotransmitters? Well, how else are we to experience anything? We are after all bags of chemicals walking about. Ecstasy was certainly allowing some sort of human experiences to occur, even if they were out of the ordinary.

When E is used in the context described, a degree of ritual seems to be important, the preparation of the self and the setting intensifying the experience.

My use of E was predominately for 'personal exploration.' I always felt that I was using E as a tool or a key to facilitate this journey. I also see some similarity in reports of near death experiences's. Those involved repeatedly report feelings of total love and acceptance. They say, 'There is something there.' As a benefit they usually gain a release of fear of death; I can relate to much of that. And boy, was it ever Exciting.

I probably used ecstasy 10 to 15 times over two and a half years. I have also used Acid, Mushrooms and Ketamine. Acid I feel is too long and intense for me. It's like white water rafting – you never know what's around the next corner, whereas E is laying in a punt being gently poled along while someone peels you grapes. I always feel in charge with E, rarely with Acid.

– New Zealand man

Senior executive's use of ecstasy

Ecstasy could be used to improve productivity

My wife and I are both science graduates and I am a business manager with a large company. Obviously with our background we feel we are better educated than the average recreational drug user, and we both applaud your crusade against ignorance, especially with regard to non-addictive substances such as marijuana and MDMA. I have taken MDMA about 30 times over the past 2 years, after being introduced to it by a friend. Prior to that I had no experience of drugs, other than being a social drinker (I have never smoked). Although we almost exclusively use MDMA in the typical nightclub environment with friends, I am becoming more interested in alternative uses – in particular its possible role in improving performance at work.

I am absolutely convinced that if you were to take a sales team away for a weekend and gave them a couple of sessions on MDMA you would definitely see marked improvements in performance. The increased empathy with others would help them sell more effectively since they would be more aware of the customers situation (and also their personality and what matters to them), but also they would feel an enormous sense of togetherness with their other team members.

We only take MDMA in the UK, since the quality in the US is poor, and since it is much harder to find clubs which play the type of music we like (UK house), we don't want to have a disappointing experience. As I mentioned, we only take MDMA on a night out with a group of close friends. For us, the most satisfying and enjoyable aspects of MDMA use (in this setting) are:

1.   The almost childlike pleasure of being able to meet people without the usual barriers we put up to defend ourselves in normal situations. This applies (for me) to being able to meet other men for the first time without any trace of initial hostility, and being able to approach women without it being perceived as a sexual advance.

2.   Enjoyment from being able to dance with absolutely no self-consciousness, and also from feeling "at one" with the music – the ability to effortlessly dance in time with the music (whether real or perceived).

3.   Completely forgetting the outside world and the stresses associated with a very demanding job back in the US, and also for us, the relief of not having to constantly deal with the subtle differences in society encountered by expatriates abroad.

4.   Seeing others enjoy themselves so freely and completely.

I am sure MDMA use can be enjoyable and rewarding outside the nightclub setting, though we are both reluctant to try it since we feel that without the combination of light, music, surrounding and other people on MDMA, the experience will be disappointing.

Since I have taken MDMA over 30 times, I will try to describe my impression of the effectiveness of the drug with sustained use. I am fortunate in that I have a good supply of pure MDMA. I weigh 200 pounds and am physically in good shape with about 12-15% body fat. I normally take a dose of 120mg with an additional 120mg at T+90min. I have also found that a small amount of speed taken prior to the first dose prolongs the effect of the MDMA. On a longer night (we usually go until 3.30am, but sometimes we continue elsewhere until about 7 or 8am) I have found that a very small amount of speed prolongs the effect of the MDMA rather than taking another dose. One time I took 1/4 to 1/2 a dose of LSD, which was very interesting. It seemed to prolong the effect of the MDMA, and while not causing any visuals. Once I looked at a person I didn't know, and I convinced myself they were someone else – someone I knew.

More recently, we have been experimenting with GHB (sodium gamma hydroxy buterol). GHB is normally used for inducing REM sleep, but if it is taken with the MDMA, it acts to enhance the MDMA effect. A word of caution, though – taking GHB in liquid form while in a hot nightclub one can easily take to much – and an overdose will rapidly induce a coma. This is especially dangerous since hospital staff don't know how to deal with GHB overdose.

Although much has been written about the decrease in effectiveness of MDMA with use, in my experience, after the first 1 or 2 times which seemed more intense (although this was probably due more to the novelty of first experience), I have found no drop off in the intensity of the effect. What is much more important is the mood, setting, company and music. We take great care to optimize these variables, or wait for the right time. It is also true to say, however, that I generally have 3-4 months break in between doses.

I have definitely experienced small changes in my personality which I believe (hopefully) are irreversible. The main change is the feeling of empathy with others, and the ability to understand other points of view.

While I still feel stress, an experience with MDMA definitely reduces stress for a period of weeks. These points interest me most, since I work in highly competitive sales situations.

When we got home, she said she felt compelled to write down her experiences. What was interesting was that at the time she wrote it she could not communicate verbally very well, yet her handwriting was so beautiful. At first felt she would not be able to write legibly, but once she started she found it no problem at all.

I hope these random thoughts help in some way – overall I can say that MDMA has had a positive effect on both our lives and our relationship. I have no desire try harder drugs such as Cocaine and Heroin, and whenever we go out socially, my alcohol intake has dropped considerably. In fact I find it sad that people drink heavily in attempt to get to a place only MDMA can take you. Of course it can never be achieved with alcohol, and had they experienced MDMA, they would quickly realize the futility of their efforts. I think once you have used MDMA, you see the negative aspects of alcohol, and therefore tend to drink less.

The only slightly negative aspect of my experience of MDMA is that I have found it more difficult to get along with one of my closest friends – a heavy drinker who has never tried MDMA. If only he would try it we would have our close friendship back... If only we could use MDMA to treat alcoholism.

– English man living in the USA aged 40

E, tai chi and disenchantment

Ecstasy is enlightening but can lead to disappointment Tai Chi

About the same time as I started doing E I also started doing Tai Chi. After about a year I was struck by the remarkable similarity between the 'inner peace and clarity' of the state of mind attained by about an hour of focus on Tai Chi and 100mg plus of MDMA. In fact, the closest I have ever come to the euphoria I experienced initially on E was by doing Tai Chi.

The combination of E and tai chi was quite amusing, because any focus on my body or breathing in a tai chi way gave me waves of euphoria, regardless of how little or much effort I put into the exercise. Once the initial overwhelming tingles had subsided, I could also understand what my teacher was getting at. It seemed to make me far more sensitive to my own body's energy and enabled me to correct my posture to ensure more effective energy flows.

I used to do tai chi and E at raves, and it enhanced the E feelings enormously. I think the sensations enhanced by 4/4 beats and all that) can be extended to this idea about focus on breathing and 'internal' rhythms.

Disenchantment

After a couple of years, I found that the honeymoon period was drawing to a close. What was missing? After talking to lots of disenchanted clubbers I came to the conclusion that ecstasy feeds on excitement and novelty. After a while, the brain assimilates a lot of experiences, and comes up with an 'ideal' which must be met in order to have a good night: good music, friendly door staff, no queues for the toilets, room to dance – yet a feeling that the dance floor is full and intimate, cool conditions, smiles from strangers, all the people you are with having an excellent time, free water, interesting light shows etc, etc. Many now only use amphetamine because they get too disappointed compared with the euphoria of their first few times.

Alternative

I've now developed some tai chi exercises that I can do without looking too conspicuous at raves, and are quite an acceptable alternative to ecstasy. Although tai chi can never re-create the oneness and empathy of initial E experiences, no one has the crushing disappointment that a 'pear-shaped' evening on ecstasy can generate.

Ecstasy is an astounding discovery. It has helped to change the way I think, and I don't know anybody who hasn't found it fascinating and enlightening. If used intelligently I think it has tremendous potential as a therapeutic tool.

– A British university lecturer in organic chemistry

A father and daughter

We were able to feel the love that we have for each other

On the first occasion I took half a pill and was totally surprised at the emotional change that took place within me. The few visuals were highly amusing and my only period of doubt was when it became clear to me that my left eye wanted to look "inwards" and my right eye "outwards". However, without assistance from my guide, I soon discovered my "control centre" and immediately became confident that ultimately I could and would be able to control any trip when I wished to "change direction".

I truly found my feet a few months later at Glastonbury 1994. During those marvellous four days I found that I was able to trip alone and in very unusual surroundings without any paranoia. I discovered that I could "feel" music throughout my entire body, could sense the (overpowering) heat of 2,000 people in a marquee from 50 yards and could "tune in" to the mental energy of the large mass of people on the site. Finally, I discovered "my place" – the place where the "collective consciousness" appears to be most focused for me. It was there that I found that I could readily "communicate" with people who were no longer in my life – my Grandfather, for example, who had died many years ago and my former father-in-law who had passed away a year earlier.

As a parent, I know it is all too easy to miss those special opportunities where you can demonstrate how much you love your offspring – and perhaps more importantly, for them to be able to hold you and tell you that they love you. On the first trip with my 25 year old daughter we lost no time and we were able to feel the love that we have for each other. Since that night our relationship has been transformed and though we have had disagreements since, they have been quickly resolved largely because of the firm foundation we established while tripping together.

From a personal point of view, my life has changed substantially for the better since "discovering" E. I am however, still wary of the potential to become pyschologically dependant upon the drug – the urge for "more and better" is very powerful. I consider myself fortunate that I have had the years to develop a strong sense of self identity and know that I am able to more easily cope with the come down than many people younger than myself.

– From a 44 year old English Chartered Accountant

Abused and bullied

Ecstasy has helped me to come to terms with my image

I was introduced to ecstasy at university and I have enjoyed the two experiences that I have had. It has opened me up and made me think about what life can be like now.

I was abused and bullied at private school. Ecstasy has made me come to terms with my image. I now know why people have taken the piss out of me during the past and have put that right.

I am now able to openly express my views about this drug to my friends who are totally against them. I have also made a hell of a lot of new friends on the drug.

Anyway my experiences have been very limited. But I have seen the light at the end of the tunnel so to speak. Everything becomes much clearer than normal and I can look back on it as being a reversal of my whole life.

– Man, UK

Guardian Angels

I can say exactly what is on my mind to the men in my life

I have just started taking E this year. When I'm on E, the channels seem super clear and I can receive a lot of advice and insight In a very short period of time. For example, last time I felt this, I was advised by my "guardian spirits" that honesty towards men, meaning the guys I encountered, was one of my life purposes here on earth. They encouraged me to speak exactly what was on my mind to the men in my life, not to hold back for fear of hurting them or having them think poorly of me.

In the past I've had a hard time communicating exactly what's on my mind. I've tried to be nice to men who've pestered me, wanted to go out with me even though I wasn't interested. I'm finding it easier to tell them I'm not interested. And if I am interested in a man, it's easier for me to tell him that, too. On E, I feel especially open and honest, though I always try to be nice (I don't just tell guys to fuck off or anything.)

I had spent a really nice evening with this guy, all night in fact, and I thought we were getting on really well. I went to see his band play the next night and he was really cold to me. Made me feel like shit. In the past I may have just bitched about it to my girlfriends or something, but I wrote him a letter the next week with some pictures I'd taken of him and thanked him for the time we had spent the first night, but I also said I didn't understand why he'd been so cold to me after we'd had such a good time. He hasn't written me back or anything, but perhaps he'll think about the way he treats the next girl (I hope, anyway.)

At the very least, when I'm on E I experience a lot of love for my friends and for the music. The only bad experience I had was when someone sold me some shit and passed it off as E.

— From a 27 year old American woman

Deep relationship

From sweet innocence and 'thinking for both of us' to grief and pain

When it first happened, the elements making up the atmosphere of the club were almost sucked into a vacuum to one focal point. Beforehand, I was enjoying the music, the people and the vibe of the place, but when it all went into a kind of nothingness, there was no music, no light, no people near. It felt a bit like we were sitting on our own in a white room, and the only thing that mattered were Ed's eyes. My senses still registered what was going on around us, but they were happening a thousand miles away, and couldn't reach me or my thoughts.

I looked into his eyes and everything was there; his whole personality was laid out on a sheet for me to see. No words were forming in my head, just a rush of feelings. I knew what Ed was thinking, but also seemed to be able to delve into his unconscious, to parts that he didn't even know were there.

At no time did I feel scared, worried or out of control.

After what seemed like hours staring into his face, I remember starting to laugh, because all of his features were suddenly involved in the experience. They moved and moulded into different expressions, reflecting what I was seeing in his eyes, but then I looked again and my brain said 'hang on, that's not possible', and his face was normal again.

I touched his face as I saw it move, but it always stayed the same, even though I saw Ed from a toddler through to an old man. Through each change, my whole body felt the way Ed's current expression did; when he was old, the sense of calmness that overcame me had a huge effect on me afterwards.

I knew that he could not see or feel what I was going through initially, but further on in the experience, some of our thoughts and feelings were matched perfectly. It was almost like one person was thinking for both of us. If I were the kind of person who was particularly spiritually minded, I might describe it as our souls touching.

It ended as quickly as it came on. All the outside senses flooded back into our world, and he was once more the same Ed I had met a few weeks before. The experience had a profound effect on me. Perhaps it unlocked a door in my mind, allowing me to sense feelings in other people now, whereas before I would have been oblivious.

It only happened a week ago, and already people I deal with in every day life are responding to me differently. We're communicating on a different level, perhaps because I am judging them better from what I see and acting accordingly. Ed and I are close and feel very comfortable in each other's company. This closeness would normally have taken much longer or not even happened at all. All this from an experience in a breakfast club last Saturday.

A month later, we took ecstasy again. The initial effects of the second time were very similar to the first; our surroundings ceased to exist in their normal sense, and we became enveloped in a blanket of calmness and warmth.

As in the last time, I was aware only of Ed's eyes. They held everything for me, and my total attention was taken by trying to delve further, to see more. I began to feel what he did. Every emotion that was passing through his mind at that moment, passed through mine. He felt secure, happy, and very trusting towards myself. At the same time, I sensed a note of confusion, and knew that although he knew what was happening, he wasn't sharing the experience.

He became young to me once more, and the innocence that poured from him was so real I wanted to hold him close, and comfort the little boy that was opening up to me. The more I looked, the younger he became, until the point when I realised that my emotions were there for him, and his dependence on them was overwhelming.

The responsibility felt too much; I needed to look away and take a step back from it all, but the gaze was so intense I was impelled to carry on. Within a matter of seconds, the thoughts from Ed changed so abruptly that I was taken aback.

Instead of the sweet innocence of before, I felt a massive surge of distress, hurt, grief and pain. It felt like every negative emotion that had been experienced by Ed was being shared with myself. I wanted to stop it, and tried to break the gaze, but the magnetism of these feelings kept me rooted to the spot. One particular feeling shone through, a very specific mixture of everything that was buzzing through me. It had never been released, never been felt by anyone else, and was so incredibly real to me that I felt like I was experiencing whatever had caused this emotion in Ed.

Everything was swaying by this point. I felt like I was moving towards the centre of a black hole. The closer I got, the more I was pulled in. The more I was pulled in, the harder I found it to look away, and the knowledge that I was just about to go over the edge was incredibly scary. I didn't know what would happen, but knew I could not return from it and had to break the spell.

This could have taken seconds or hours; my perception of time had disappeared. I knew I should be panicking, but instead made what felt like an enormous decision at the time; I broke the intense stare and looked away.

It took more force of will to do this than I had imagined, as the vacuum I was being drawn towards felt the most natural thing in the world. Although a flood of relief washed over me, I felt incredibly drained. I was so close to reaching something, but felt utterly bereft in the knowledge that I had put a stop to it.

A while after, Ed and I discussed what had happened. My face was soaking, but I can't remember crying. I explained everything, including the mass of emotion that appeared to be linked to a particular event in his life. He told me that there was something it could have been linked to, but that he had never talked about it to anyone, and if I had tapped into it, it would be the first time anyone had shared his experience.

He didn't go into detail, but from what it felt like, I imagine it to be one of the more important events in his life. I know what he went through, and let him know that I am there if he needs me.

Immediately after this experience, our relationship began to suffer, as things were now unevenly weighted. I could look at Ed and know what he was thinking and how he was feeling, whereas my barriers had not yet come down. It has taken us a good few weeks to realise that you can't predict what happens in such powerful circumstances, and you can't always expect a happy ending.

We came very close to giving up on the situation. We even got to the stage of agreeing to avoid each other until it had all become a distant memory. Whilst up on our last pill, however, we talked openly and frankly about our relationship, and agreed to continue working through the imbalance.

We now know that these experiences are not to be taken lightly. Misguided use can result in confusion, mistrust, and most importantly loss of friendship. Used constructively, they can bring people together in a way never before imagined, to create a relationship that is unequalled both physically and mentally. It is a something that Ed and I now enjoy, and we both look forward to exploring this spiritual relationship more in the future.

– 25 year old London woman

Americans visit London

I spent the night in heaven, meeting people, hugging and dancing my brains out.
I had an experience in London while backpacking through Europe. At the end of my six week adventure, this Friday night made the entire trip worthwhile for me.

I had been given the name of a friend of friends who lived in London at the time. I called him when I got into town and we went out the following night. Lucky for us, Zete was also into techno and raving. Knowing that the scene in London is spectacular, I pressed him to find a super event for us to go to. We found out what was "on that evening. It was Absolute at the Colliseum. Sven Vath and Mr. C (two world renowned DJs) were spinning, and I was thrilled.

We arrived around 11:00pm and once inside, I could feel that it was going to be a spectacular night. The layout of the location was perfectly designed for this type of thing. One large room, another smaller room and a chill room in between. Video games. Smart bar. Unbelievable sound system, lights, lasers, the works. I spent the next half an hour casually asking around....I was looking for ecstasy. After about an hour I found what I was looking for. The music was spot on, and I began dancing. Soon after Zete and his friends arrived. We hung out and chatted until I felt myself starting to "come up".

The ecstasy was unbelievable and the music was even better. The people there were lovely, the vibe was alive and growing. I spent the night in heaven, meeting people, hugging and dancing my brains out. I had met a bunch of people who were really friendly and outgoing. I talked to one guy for awhile while we smoked a joint. After finding out that we were from the States and were new in town, he invited us to their flat for a "chill out" after the party. It was the kindest and most heartfelt gesture. Only a truly kind and generous person would invite two total strangers back to their place to share an experience after a brilliant night. And it was not like he was interested in me, we were straight.

We had an emotional night dancing. I was moved into such a deep state of trance, the music, the lights, the vibe from the beautiful girl dancing across from me. It was perfect. It was my roommate's first real experience on ecstasy and raving. He had a grin from ear to ear all night long. He felt the vibe. He told me how happy he was, how intense the vibe was, how cool everybody there was being. I felt like crying. It was a beautiful experience that culminated in us relaxing in a total strangers house in a strange city, yet we felt comfortable there. My only regret was that I would not be able to spend more time with those lovely people and get to know them better. It wasn't until 10:30 the next morning that we phoned a cab for a ride back to our hotel. For me, that night in London defined what raving is all about.

– A 23 year old American man working as a software product manager, living in California.

Schizophrenia

Ecstasy helps me to live with my schizophrenia

I cannot give you my name or even where I am from, but let me assure that everything I write here is true. I was diagnosed with schizophrenia at an early age, which is considered worse than if it develops at later. To treat this disease, I have been prescribed just about every psychotropic drug imaginable and none of them even compared to the effects that ecstasy has had on me.

Ecstasy has allowed me to see my disorder in a whole new light. I went from being an asocial, withdrawn, and somewhat paranoid zombie to a sensitive human being who experiences love and every other human emotion. I had never really felt much love in my life until I had experienced ecstasy, and I am convinced that I would have committed suicide by now without it.

You see without love a human being just withers away and dies, sometimes slowly and sometimes abruptly by suicide. You can live for a long time without love, but in the end you will die before your time. This is what many schizophrenics do everyday, they live without love. As a result, an alarming large number of people with this most tragic disease take their own life.

For me, ecstasy is not simply a party drug (although, I did use it at parties), it was much more than that. Ecstasy is the most effective medicine that I have found to date in treating my schizophrenia. It is not a cure, and it is not conventional medicine. By conventional medicine I mean a drug which directly treats the symptoms. No, ecstasy has worked for me in a different, but very equally important manner.

Ecstasy has helped me to live with schizophrenia. You see the medication that is currently given for schizophrenia helps to limit the symptoms (and it does so in some cases more than others), but you are left on your own to deal with whatever symptoms that may remain. Ecstasy helps to bridge that gap, it helps you to live with whatever symptoms you may have that the medication doesn't help with. I still live with paranoid symptoms everyday, but I am now okay with that. I accept myself for who I am, I can live with being schizophrenic. It was ecstasy that helped me come to these terms.

I came to this realization with just myself and ecstasy, I had no therapist to guide me in this area. I've had lots of therapy, but none of it really compares to what ecstasy and myself have taught me. One can only imagine how much better ecstasy therapy would be for me if I had an experienced therapist to guide me.

I continue to use ecstasy, and I will continue to use it in limited amounts until something better, or a cure for schizophrenia comes along. I do want to make it clear that ecstasy is in no way a substitution for the proper medication in dealing with schizophrenia. Medication remains essential in keeping this disease in check. Ecstasy is simply another kind of medication that should be used (infrequently) to supplement the more traditional medications.

Depression and creativity

Over the past year, I have received a series of accounts of ecstasy use from Angeline, a graphic designer who has been depressed for many years. Here is a selection of them

The best that I ever felt on ecstasy was something that was not quite happiness nor euphoria, but rather a profound and perfect sense of unity of mind, body, spirit and soul; and I understood in an instant exactly what happiness and being happy involved; and at the same time I was overwhelmed by a hope that I would someday get there.

I realised that I was looking for something that few people understand or achieve; something that I understand but haven't achieved and cannot articulate. I am searching for a state of being in which mind, body, spirit and soul are fundamentally indivisible yet each feeds the understanding of the other – a feeling that all the words in the world can only understate.

That night I almost found it. It is not something I will find alone, but rather by a dynamic combination of factors which have to be in the right place at the right time.

I personally don't believe I would have ever reached that point without the use of a psychoactive drug; which is why the "I don't need drugs to have a good time" attitude is rather puzzling to me. I suppose the question is does it matter anyway; my answer would be yes, it does matter a lot, or I wouldn't look for it, and having been made aware of the existence of such a state I don't think I will ever stop looking.

Creativity

Ecstasy breaks down mental and emotional inhibitions. Because of this I find I can think about things I wouldn't normally think about, in ways which I wouldn't normally. I write better, because I can somehow find the words. I am better able to appreciate, understand, play and create music.

I find that taking different amounts is helpful for different purposes. For my weight (90 pounds) I find that for therapeutic purposes usually half a pill (about 50-60mg) does the job; this is the dosage I find which gives minimal speed-like effects and maximal empathic effects. Between 80 to 90mg my thoughts start to become incredibly lucid and fast-moving – ideal for programming, writing and any other creative process. This is also the dose at which I start to feel jumpy and have feelings of excitement which occur in short sharp bursts. The standard dosage (about 100-135mg or a whole pill) provides a great deal of psychological and physical stimulation – I find this is not good for sit-down activities, because when I do sit down I feel a strange but very pleasant edginess in my joints. I feel the need to tense certain muscles in my arms and legs, and doing so does actually make me "feel good". It is when I get out and start dancing that I can think without trying; I become aware of and understand things I didn't before, but mostly things about myself. In this way I feel that ecstasy is an extremely selfish drug. I don't actually care any more about others; I simply feel secure and relaxed and therefore feel less threatened, and hence better about other people.

Depression

For the years I was depressed I stubbornly refused to take antidepressants on a regular basis. I didn't want to have to admit to myself that I needed a drug every day in order to feel normal. So for years and years I wandered about depressed, constantly, and one day came to the realisation that it was never going to end. There was no way out. I had waited, and waited and waited for the day when I would wake up in the morning and feel normal. I would also go to bed that night feeling normal. I had waited too long and I was tired of waiting and, I reasoned, since I haven't found it by now, I never will: loss of faith.

I also came to the conclusion that because depression is perpetuated, prolonged and amplified by a chemical imbalance in the brain (usually not enough of certain things) which in turn causes the selective shut down of certain bits of the brain which then results in a greater chemical imbalance; a cycle of despair, whatever it was that was going to take the depression away was going to have to rebalance the chemicals and wake all the hibernating parts of my brain up. I also concluded that short of a full frontal lobotomy, only a drug could help me. A drug, or suicide. Which would you prefer?

I believed, rightly or wrongly that the antidepressants on the market – MAOIs, SSRIs and tricyclic antidepressants had extremely unconvincing mechanisms. I didn't know – still don't know – how tricyclic antidepressants worked, but I was afraid that if those drugs gave my brain something to restore the chemical balance in my brain, I would need to take it every day of the rest of my life. What I needed, I thought, was for something which gives my brain a kickstart in all the right places – forcing it somehow to produce the chemicals I didn't have enough of, and also something which would go about my brain waking up all the sleeping bits. Electric shock treatments can do that, but for some reason I didn't find that a terribly attractive option.

Six months ago I discovered that E was more effective than all the different antidepressants I had been prescribed. I now take it about once a fortnight and would say that it works every time, but then again I tend to take it in controlled conditions – indoors, at home. I think I've also worked out a "maximum dosage" and have been careful not to exceed that. I take it on a need basis: half a pill lasts a couple of days at most; a whole one can last for up to a week.

The nature of my work is extremely solitary, so I am usually alone when I take E for depression. The initial rush tends to creep up on me when I least expect it. Its as though a torch is flashed around my brain, illuminating my mind's eye, and the spark of life bursts into flame. I feel an injection of tangible joy which revives my senses, fuels my pride and confirms my place and my identity. I see again, I hear again. I am alive. My head clears, and all the activities in my head are fluid, lucid, clear, concise, rational and logical. This sensation is so real I can touch it and hold it in my hands. It isn't profound or intense, it merely allows me to look at the next person and believe I am as normal as they are, and therefore have a stake in life, in this world. I am overwhelmed by the enormity of this realisation.

These positive feelings are encouraged by taking part in "normal" activities such as work. It is only afterwards that I look back on the depression and gain insights into it. I feel better able to rationalise and to face up to having been depressed. One thing it certainly has changed is that I no longer live in fear of these bouts of depression. The other way it helps is that it gives me a burst of energy to get out of bed and actually do things, and that in itself goes a very long way towards breaking the cycle of depression.

Ecstasy suits certain personalities and not others. Obviously people who have suffered from depression gain a new lease of life from the drug. It gives new hope and shows you how good you can feel, and how good life can appear to be. And this, I believe, is all it takes; external events, good or bad, don't matter, it's how you perceive them, and your attitude towards them. People can be happy with very little, and very unhappy even when they have everything. I've also found that people who are emotionally repressed feel a great affinity towards the drug because they tend to either fear or despise their emotions and find them difficult to handle, which itself can be perceived as a personal weakness.

Angeline is a 22 year old London graphic designer. More of her accounts are on her Internet site at http://www.dunvegan.demon.co.uk/angel/Exploration

Bibliography

Legal History

(This section deals largely with United States Law, and it is arranged chronologically)

1970

Sreenivasan, V.R. Problems in Identification of Methylenedioxy and Methoxy Amphetamines. *J. Crim. Law* 63 :304-312 (1972).

In a study of the spectral properties of several substituted amphetamine analogues, the properties of an unknown sample seized from an apparent drug abuser were recorded. The evidence indicated that this material was MDMA. As this report was initially presented to a group of crime laboratory chemists in August, 1970, this is probably the earliest documentation of illicit usage of ecstasy.

1972

Gaston, T.R. and Rasmussen, G.T. Identification of 3,4-Several exhibits were encountered in the Chicago area, which were identified as MDMA as the hydrochloride salt.

Chromatographic and spectrographic properties are presented.

1982

Anonymous. Request for Information. *Microgram* 15 :126 (1982).

The Drug Control Section of the DEA (Drug Enforcement Administration) has solicited information concerning the abuse potential of both MDMA and MDE. The request covered the abuse potential, the illicit trafficking and the clandestine syntheses, since 1977.

1984

Randolph, W.F. International Drug Scheduling; Convention on Psychotropic Substances; Stimulant and/or Hallucinogenic Drugs. *Federal Register* 49 :29273-29274 (1984).

A request has been made from the Food and Drug Administration for information and comments concerning the abuse potential, actual abuse, medical usefulness and trafficking of 28 stimulants and/or hallucinogenic drugs, including MDMA. International restrictions are being considered by World Health Organization.

Mullen, F.M. Schedules of Controlled Substances Proposed Placement of 3,4- Methylenedioxymethamphetamine into Schedule I. *Federal Register* 49 :30210-30211 (1984).

A request has been made for comments, objections, or requests for hearings concerning the proposal by the Drug Enforcement Administration (DEA) for the placement of MDMA into Schedule I of the Controlled Substances Act.

Cotton, R. Letter from Dewey, Ballantine, Bushby, Palmer & Wood, 1775 Pennsylvania Avenue, N.W., Washington, D.C. 20006 to F. M. Mullen, Jr., DEA. September 12, 1984.

This is a formal request for a hearing concerning the listing of MDMA as a Schedule I drug. The retaining parties are Professor Thomas B. Roberts, Ph.D., George Greer, M.D., Professor Lester Grinspoon, M.D. and Professor James Bakalar.

Mullen, F.M. Schedules of Controlled Substances. Proposed Placement of 3,4- Methylenedioxymethamphetamine into Schedule I. Hearings. *Federal Register* 49 :50732-50733 (1984).

This is a notice of an initial hearing in the matter of the placement of MDMA into Schedule I of the Controlled Substances Act. This is to be held on February 1, 1985 and is intended to identify parties, issues and positions, and to determine procedures and set dates and locations for further proceedings.

1985

Young, F.L. Memorandum and Order. Docket No. 84-48. February 8, 1985.

A formal Memorandum and Order is addressed to the Drug Enforcement Administration, laying out the ground rules for the hearings to be held in the matter of the scheduling of MDMA.

Anon : Request for Information, *Microgram* 18 :25 (1985).

A brief review is presented of the requests for hearings regarding the scheduling of MDMA. A request is made for any information that might be found concerning illicit trafficking, clandestine synthesis, and medical emergencies or deaths associated with the use of MDMA. All such information is to be sent to the Drug Control Section of the DEA.

Young, F.L. Opinion and Recommended Decision on Preliminary Issue. Docket No. 84-48. June 1, 1985.

The question of where to schedule a drug such as MDMA is considered. The Schedules have only one place for drugs without currently accepted medical use, Schedule I. But a second requirement that must be met is that the drug have a high abuse potential. There is no place for a drug without currently accepted medical use and less-than-high abuse potential.

The first opinion is that such a drug cannot be placed in any schedule. And if that is not acceptable to the administrator, then into Schedule III, IV or V, depending upon the magnitude of the less-than-high abuse potential.

Lawn, J.C. Schedules of Controlled Substances; Temporary Placement of 3,4- Methylenedioxymethamphetamine (MDMA) into Schedule I. *Federal Register* 50 :23118-23120 (1985).

The DEA invoked the Emergency Scheduling Act powers, to place MDMA into Schedule I on a temporary basis, effective July 1, 1985. This move is valid for a year, and can be extended for six months. This occurred just before the first hearing was to take place, to determine the appropriate schedule for MDMA.

[The chronology of the hearings was as follows:

June 10, 1985: Los Angeles, California
July 10,11, 1985: Kansas City, Missouri
October 8,9,10,11, Nov. 1, 1985: Washington, DC.]
February 14, 1986: (submitting briefs, findings, conclusions, and oral arguments) Washington, DC.

1986

Anon: Verordnung des BAG über die Betäubungsmittel und andere Stoffe und Präparate. March 17, 1986.

Effective April 22, 1986, MDMA has been entered into the Controlled Law structure of the Narcotics Laws of Switzerland.

Young, F.L. Opinion and Recommended Ruling, Findings of Fact, Conclusions of Law and Decision of Administrative Law Judge. Docket 84-48. May 22, 1986.

This 70 page decision was handed down as a product of the three hearings held as outlined above. A careful analysis is given of the phrase 'currently accepted medical use' and of the phrase 'accepted safety for use.' The final recommendation was that MDMA be placed in Schedule III.

Stone, S.E. and Johnson, C.A. Government's Exceptions to the Opinion and Recommended Ruling, Findings of Fact, Conclusions of Law and Decision of the Administrative Law Judge. Docket No. 84- 48. June 13, 1986.

The attorneys for the DEA reply to the decision of Judge Young with a 37 page document, including statements that he had given little if any weight to the testimony and document proffered by the DEA, and had systematically disregarded the evidence and arguments presented by the government. Their statement was a rejection of the suggestion of the Administrative Law judge, in that they maintained that MDMA is properly placed in Schedule I of the CSA because it has no currently accepted medical use, it lacks accepted safety for use under medical supervision, and it has a high potential for abuse.

Lawn, J.C. Schedules of Controlled Substances; Extension of Temporary Control of 3,4- Methylenedioxy-methamphetamine (MDMA) in Schedule I. *Federal Register* 51 :21911-21912 (1986).

The provision that allows MDMA to be placed in Schedule I on an emergency basis (due to expire on July 1, 1986) has been extended for a period of 6 months or until some final action is taken, whichever comes first. The effective date is July 1, 1986.

Anon: Zweite Verordnung zur Änderung betäubungsmittelrechticher Vorschriften. July 23, 1986.

Effective July 28, 1986, MDMA was added to the equivalent of Schedule I status, in the German Drug Law. This was in the same act that added cathenone, DMA, and DOET.

Lawn, J.C. Order. Docket 84-48 August 11, 1986.

In reply to a motion by the respondents (Grinspoon, Greer et al. to strike portions of the DEA exceptions that might allege bias on the part of the Administrative Law Judge, and to request an opportunity for oral presentation to the Administrator. The bias was apologized for, and struck. The opportunity for oral presentation was not allowed.

Kane, J. Memorandum and Opinion. Case No. 86-CR-153. In the United States District Court for the District of Colorado. Pees and McNeill, Defendants. October 1, 1986.

The is an early decision dismissing a prosecution charge for unlawful acts involving MDMA, on the basis that MDMA had been placed into

Schedule I using the Emergency Scheduling Act, and the authority to invoke this Act was invested in the Attorney General, and the Attorney General had never subdelegated that authority to the DEA. This transfer had not occurred at the time of the charges being brought against the defendants, and the charges were dismissed.

Lawn, J.C. Schedules of Controlled Substances; Scheduling of 3,4- Methylenedioxymethamphetamine (MDMA) into Schedule I of the Controlled Substances Act. *Federal Register* **51 :36552-36560 (1986).**

A complete review of the scheduling process history of MDMA, including the receipt of Administrative Law Judge Young's recommendations and a 92 point rebuttal of it, is presented. There is an equating of standards and ethical considerations concerning human research, with legal constraints. It is maintained that the original stands taken, that there is no currently accepted medical use, and there is a high abuse potential, were both correct, and this then is the final placement of MDMA into Schedule I, on a permanent basis. The effective date is November 13, 1986.

1987

Coffin, Torruella, and Pettin. United States Court of Appeals for the First Circuit. Lester Grinspoon, Petitioner, v. Drug Enforcement Administration, Respondent. September 18, 1987.

This is the opinion handed down in answer to the appeal made by Grinspoon (Petitioner) to the action of the DEA (Respondent) in placing MDMA in a permanent classification of a Schedule I drug. Most points were found for the DEA, but one specific claim of the petitioner, that MDMA has a currently accepted use in the United States, was accepted. The finding of the court was that the FDA approval was not the sole criterion for determining the acceptability of a drug for medical use. An order was issued to vacate MDMA from Schedule I.

1988

Lawn. J.C. Schedules of Controlled Substances; Deletion of 3,4- Methylene-dioxymethamphetamine (MDMA) From Schedule I of the Controlled Substances Act. *Federal Register* **53 :2225 (1988).**

Notice is posted in the Federal Register that MDMA has been vacated from Schedule I of the Controlled Substances Act and now falls under the purview of the Analogue Drug Act. It is no longer a Scheduled Drug. This ruling was effective December 22, 1987, and will be effective until such time as the Administrator reconsidered the record in the scheduling procedures, and issues another final ruling.

Lawn, J.C. Schedules of Controlled Substances; Scheduling of 3,4- Methylenedioxymethamphetamine (MDMA) into Schedule I of the Controlled Substances Act; Remand. *Federal Register* **53 :5156 (1988).**

Notice is posted in the Federal Register that MDMA has been placed again into Schedule I. The DEA has accepted the Appellate Court's instruction to develop a standard for the term 'accepted medical use,' and they have done so. The conclusion is that MDMA is properly assigned to Schedule I, and as there have already been hearings, there is no need for any further delay. Effective date, March 23, 1988.

Meyers, M.A. In the United States District Court for the Southern District of Texas, Houston Division, The United Sates of America v. A.E. Quarles, CR. No. H-88-83. Memorandum in Support

of Motion to Dismiss. March 25, 1988.

This memorandum (13 pages and attached literature) is an instructive vehicle addressing the applicability of the Analogue laws to MDMA, and the possible unconstitutional vagueness of the Act itself.

Hug, Boochever and Wiggins, Ninth Circuit Court of Appeals, California. United States, Plaintiff-Appellee v. W.W. Emerson, Defendant-Appellant.

An appeal was made, and was allowed, by three defendants, that the use of the Emergency Scheduling Act by the DEA for the placement of MDMA into Schedule I was improper, in that this power was invested specifically in the Attorney General, and that he had failed to subdelegate this authority to the DEA for its use.

Harbin, H. MDMA. Narcotics, Forfeiture, and Money-Laundering Update, U.S. Department of Justice, Criminal Division. Winter, 1988. pp. 14-19.

A brief legal history of MDMA is presented, detailing its changing status from emergency schedule, to permanent schedule, to non-schedule, to schedule again, a case against its occasional status in-between as an analogue substance. In U.S. v. Spain (10th Circuit, 1987, 825 F.2d 1426), the MDMA conviction was undermined both by the absence of sub- delegation of emergency scheduling powers by the Attorney General to the DEA, and by the failure of the DEA to publish a formal scheduling order 30 days after the publication of its 'notice-order', as required by statute. This latter failure was successful in overturning the conviction in the U.S. v. Caudel (5th Circuit, 1987, 828 F.2d 1111)

These reversals were based on the temporary scheduling status of MDMA. The vacating of the permanent scheduling Grinspoon v. DEA (1st Circuit 1987, 828 F.2d 881), coupled with these successful appeals of the temporary scheduling action, will certainly serve to allow further challenge to be made to any and all legal action that took place prior to the final and unchallenged placement of MDMA in Schedule I on March 23, 1988.

1990

Shulgin, A.T. How Similar is Substantially Similar? *J. Forensic Sciences,* **35 :8-10 (1990).**

MDMA, illegal under Federal law, can only be charged in the State of California (where it is not a Scheduled drug) as an analogue of some drug that is Scheduled. It must be shown to be substantially similar to known Scheduled drugs in structure or in activity. This similarity definition is discussed.

1991

People v. Silver. Statute Defining Controlled Substance Analogues as 'Substantially Similar' to Controlled Substance not Unconstitutionally Vague. 91 C.D.O.S. 3801., 2d App. Dist; May 21, 1991.

The question has been brought to the Appeals Court as to a possible vagueness in the wording of the California State Law concerning the definition of 'analogue'. MDMA was the focus of the appeal. The court found that there was no problem in the definition of the term 'substantially similar' but they did not, themselves, define it.

Fromberg, E. Letter to R. Doblin from the Netherlands Institute for Alcohol and Drugs. April 4, 1991.

An explanation of the Schedule I and Schedule II structure of Dutch Law is given. All new drugs must go into Schedule I, and yet MDMA was prosecuted (and defended on appeal) as a (rather minor) Schedule II drug.

Gilbert, J., Stone, P.J. and Yegan, J. Controlled Substance Analogues Law is Not Unconstitutionally Vague. Finding of the Second Appellate District Division Six. Daily Appellate Report, May 24, 1991, page 5993-5995.

The appellate Court considered an appeal concerning the classification of MDMA as an analogue of methamphetamine. This is question raised under the California Health and Safety Code section 11401, concerning analogues of scheduled drugs, as MDMA is not a scheduled drug in California. The appeal was based (in part) on the statement that 'substantially similar' was unconstitutionally vague.

It was concluded that all that was required would be that the statute be reasonably certain, so that a person of common intelligence need not guess at its meaning. They found against the appeal

1994

Argos, E. and Castello, L. El MDMA es Valioso en Medicina. El Pais, Espana, January 30, 1994 pp. 28-29.

A tribunal court in Madrid found that the material, MDMA, should be classified as a low-hazard drug akin to marijuana, rather than a high-hazard drug such as cocaine, heroin, or LSD. It has a well-defined medical value.

del Arco, M.A., La Batalla del Extasis: Su Inventor Convencio al Juez de Que es una Droga Blanda. Tiempo, Espana, February 7, 1994.

A consensus of experts presents MDMA as a drug with little hazard associated with it's use. This directly addresses the 'rave' scene (La Ruta del Bakalao) in Spain, and removes much of the judicial penalties from this social phenomenon.

Biochemistry

Elayan, I., Gibb, J.W., Hanson, G.R., Lim, H.K., Foltz, R.L. and Johnson, M., Short-term Effects of 2,4,5-Trihydroxy-amphetamine, 2,4,5-Trihydroxymeth-amphetamine and 3,4-Dihydroxy-methamphetamine on Central Tryptophan Hydroxylase Activity. *J. Pharmacol. Exptl. Ther.* :262 813-8 (1993).

The short term effects of the three title metabolites of MDMA (THA, THM and DHM) on tryptophan hydroxylase are reported. The first two metabolites were quite effective, but the third (DHM) had no effect. In vitro studies were unsuccessful in reversing these changes.

Gibb, J.W., Hanson, G.R. and Johnson, M. Effects of (+)-3,4-Methylenedioxy-methamphetamine [(+) MDMA] and (-)-3,4-Methylenedioxy-methamphetamine [(-)MDMA] on Brain Dopamine, Serotonin, and their Biosynthetic Enzymes. *Soc. Neurosciences Abstrts.* 12 169.2 (1986).

The optical isomers of MDMA were studied in rats, as to the extent of serotonin and dopamine depletion, and the changes in their respective biosynthetic enzymes TPH (tryptophane hydroxylase) and TH (tyrosine hydroxylase). The (+) was the more effective in reducing serotonin levels at several sites in the brain, and was the more effective in reducing the TPH levels at all sites. Striatal TH was not effected by either isomer.

Hanson, G.R., Hanson, G.R. and Johnson, M. Effects of (+)-3,4- Methylenedioxymethamphetamine [(+)MDMA] and (-)-3,4-Methylene-dioxymethamphetamine [(-)MDMA] on Brain Dopamine, Serotonin, and their Biosynthetic Enzymes. *Soc. Neurosciences Abstrts.* 12 169.2 (1986).

The optical isomers of MDMA were studied in rats, as to the extent of serotonin and dopamine depletion, and the changes in their respective biosynthetic enzymes TPH (tryptophane hydroxylase) and TH (tyrosine hydroxylase). The (+) isomer was the more effective in reducing serotonin levels at several sites in the brain, and was the more effective in reducing the TPH levels at all sites. Striatal TH was not effected by either isomer.

Hanson, G.R., Merchant, K.M., Johnson, M., Letter, A.A., Bush, L. and Gibb, J.W. *Effect of MDMA-like Drugs on CNS Neuropeptide Systems. The Clinical, Pharmacological and Neurotoxicological Effects of the Drug MDMA.* Kluwer, New York. (1990) Ed: S.J. Peroutka.

An increase in both neurotensin and dynorphin in selected areas of rat brain following single administrations of MDMA has been observed. The ramifications of these changes are discussed.

Johnson, M., Bush, L.G., Stone, D.M., Hanson, G.R. and Gibb, J.W. Effects of Adrenalectomy on the 3,4-Methylenedioxymethamphetamine (MDMA)-induced Decrease of Tryptophan Hydroxylase Activity in the Frontal Cortex and Hippocampus. *Soc. Neurosci. Abstr.* 13 :464.6 (1987).

The tryptophan hydroxylase (TPH) activity of rat frontal cortex and hippocampus was found to decrease seven days following an acute large dosage of MDMA. The latter area was spared enzyme loss with adrenalectomy.

Johnson, M., Hanson, G.R. and Gibb, J.W. Effect of MK-801 on the Decrease in Tryptophan Hydroxylase Induced by Methamphetamine and its Methylenedioxy Analogues. *Eur. J. Pharmacol.* 165 :315-318 (1989).

Repeated injections of methamphetamine or MDMA in rats reduced neostriatal TPH activity. If MK-801 is administered concurrently the methamphetamine depletion of enzyme is attenuated, but the MDMA induced depletion is not. There may be some involvement of NMDA receptors.

Johnson, M., Mitros, K., Stone, D.M., Zobrist, R., Hanson, G.R. and Gibb, J.W. Effect of Flunarizine and Nimodipine on the Decrease in Tryptophan Hydroxylase Activity Induced by Methamphetamine and 3,4-Methylenedioxymethamphetamine. *J. Pharmacol. Exptl. Ther.* 261: 586-591 (1992).

The effects of calcium channel blockers on the decrease of central tryptophan hydroxylase activity and serotonin concentration induced by repeated large doses of methamphetamine and MDMA were evaluated. The results suggest that calcium influx may participate in these responses.

Kelly, P.A.T., Ritchie, I.M., Sangra, M., Cursham, M.J.A., Dickson, E.M., Kelly, B., Neilson, F.P., Reidy, M.J., Stevens, M.C., Hyperaemia in Rat Neocortex Produced by Acute Exposure to Methylenedioxymethamphetamine. *Brain Res.* 665: 315-318 (1994).

Studies of cerebral blood flow and glucose utilization were measured in several areas of rat brain following the administration of MDMA. The results suggest that MDMA has the potential of disrupting cerebrovascular control.

Kumagai, Y., Lin, L.Y., Schmitz, D.A. and Cho, A.K. Hydroxyl Radical Mediated Demethylenation of (Methylene-

dioxy)phenyl Compounds. *Chem. Res. Toxicol.* 4: 330-334 (1991).

The oxidative demethylation of methylenedioxybenzene, MDA and MDMA was achieved with two hydroxy iron-containing radical systems, one with ascorbate and one with xanthine oxidase. Hydrogen peroxide alone was not effective in producing the metabolite catechols.

Kumagai, Y., Wickham, K.A., Schmitz, D.A. and Cho, A.K. Metabolism of Methylenedioxyphenyl Compounds by Rabbit Liver Preparations. *Biochem. Pharmacol.* 42: 1061-1067 (1991).

The demethyleneation of methylenedioxbenzene, MDA and MDMA is a major metabolic pathway, and is achieved in the microcome fraction by the action of P-450. Studies involving inducers and suppressors indicate that several isozymes are involved in the formation of the product catechols.

Kumagai, Y., Lin, L.Y., Hiratsuka, A., Narimatsu, S., Suzuki, T., Yamada, H., Oguri, K., Yoshimura, H., Cho, A.K. Participation of Cytochrome P450-2B and -2D Isozymes in the Demethylenation of Methylenedioxy-methamphetamine Enantiomers by Rats. *Mole. Pharmacol.* 45: 359-65 (1994).

The cytochrome P-450 isozymes in rat liver microsomes that catalyze the demethylenation of MDMA to the catechol metabolite, 3,4-dihydroxy-N-methylamphetamine, have been characterized. The two optical isomers of MDMA were studied separately.

Letter, A.A., Merchant, K., Gibb, J.W. and Hanson, G.R. Roles of D2 and 5-HT2 Receptors in Mediating the Effects of Methamphetamine, 3,4-Methylene-dioxymethamphetamine, and 3,4-Methylenedioxyamphetamine on Striato-Nigral Neurotensin Systems. *Soc. Neurosciences Abstrts.* 12: 1005 (# 277.7) 1986.

The chronic treatment of rats with methamphetamine, MDA or MDMA leads to a 2-3x increase of the neurotensin-like immunoreactivity in the striato-nigral areas of the brain. Efforts to assign neurotransmitter roles led to the simultaneous administration of serotonin and dopamine antagonists. These interrelationships are discussed.

Merchant, K., Letter, A.A., Stone, D.M., Gibb, J.W. and Hanson, G.R. Responses of Brain Neurotensin-like Immunoreactivity to 3,4-Methylene-dioxymethamphetamine (MDMA) and 3,4-Methylenedioxyamphetamine (MDA). *Fed. Proc.* 45: 1060 (# 5268) (1986).

The administration of MDA and MDMA profoundly alters the levels of neurotensin-like immunoreactivity (NTLI) concentrations in various portions of the brain of the rat. Increases of up to a factor of 3x are observed in some regions of the brain.

Nash, J.F. and Meltzer, H.Y. Neuroendocrinological Effects of MDMA in the Rat. *The Clinical, Pharmacological and Neurotoxicological Effects of the Drug MDMA.* Kluwer, New York. (1990) Ed: S.J. Peroutka.

MDMA has been observed to increase plasma ACTH and corticosterone concentrations in a dose-dependent manner. A series of pharmacological challenges suggests that serotonin release may be a responsible factor.

Poland, R.E. Diminished Corticotropin and Enhanced Prolactin Responses to 8-Hydroxy-2-(di-n-propyl-amino)tetralin in Methylenedioxy-methamphetamine Pretreated Rats. *Neuropharmacol.* 29: 1099-1101 (1990).

Pretreatment of rats with a single, modest dose of MDMA followed by a challenge with the serotonin agonist 8-OH DPAT led to a decrease corticotropin and an enhanced prolactin response. This suggests that MDMA produces abnormal serotonin receptor-coupled neuroendocrine responses.

Schmidt, C.J. and Taylor, V.L. Acute Effects of Methylenedioxymethamphetamine (MDMA) on 5-HT Synthesis in the Rat Brain. *Pharmacologist* 29: ABS-224 (1987). See also: *Biochemical Pharmacology* 36: 4095-4102 (1987).

Acute exposure of MDMA dropped the tryptophane hydroxylase activity of rats, and this persisted for several days. Subsequent administration of Fluoxetine recovered this activity, but reserpine or alpha-methyl-tyrosine did not.

Stone, D.M., Hanson, G.R. and Gibb, J.W. GABA-Transaminase Inhibitor Protects Against Methylenedioxy-methamphetamine (MDMA)-induced Neurotoxicity. *Soc. Neurosci. Abstr.* Vol. 13, Part 3 (1987). 251.3.

The neurotoxicity of MDMA (in the rat) was protected against by GABA-transaminase inhibitors.

Stone, D.M., Johnson, M., Hanson, G.R. and Gibb, J.W. A Comparison of the Neurotoxic Potential of Methylene-dioxyamphetamine (MDA) and its N-methylated and N-ethylated Derivatives. *Eur. J. Pharmacol.* 134: 245-248 (1987).

Multiple doses of MDA and MDMA decreases the level of brain tryptophan hydroxylase (TPH). The N-ethyl homologue was without effect. It is argued that although the studies here were well above human exposures, the cumulative effects of repeated exposures, the differences between rat and human metabolism, and increased human sensitivity to this drug, could present a serious threat to human abusers of this drug.

Stone, D.M., Johnson, M., Hanson, G.R. and Gibb, J.W. Acute Inactivation of Tryptophan Hydroxylase by Amphetamine Analogues Involves the Oxidation of Sulfhydryl Sites. *Eur. J. Pharmacol.* 172: 93-97 (1989).

MDMA, Fenfluramine and methamphetamine, separately, reduced the tryptophan hydroxylase activity in rat brain. The enzyme activity could be restored, in the cases of the latter two drugs, by treatment that suggested that some reversible oxidation of sulfhydryl groups was involved. With MDMA, the changes were irreversible, and serotonergic toxicity is suggested.

Stone, D.M., Stahl, D.C., Hanson, G.R. and Gibb, J.W. Effects of 3,4-methylenedioxyamphetamine (MDA) and 3,4-methylenedioxymethamphet-amine (MDMA) on Tyrosine Hydroxylase and Tryptophane Hydroxylase Activity in the Rat Brain. *Fed. Proc.* 45: 1060 (# 5267) April 13-18, 1986.

The effects of rats treated chronically with either MDA or MDMA on the enzymes involved with neurotransmitter synthesis is reported. The levels of tryptophane hydroxylase (TPH, involved with serotonin synthesis) were markedly reduced, differently in different areas of the brain. The tyrosine hydroxylase (TH, involved with dopamine synthesis) remains unchanged. This is in contrast to the documented reduction of TH that follows high dosages of methamphetamine.

Tucker, G.T., Lennard, M.S., Ellis, S.W., Woods, H.F., Cho, A.K., Lin, L.Y., Hiratsuka, A., Schmitz, D.A., Chu, Y.Y. The Demethylenation of Methylenedioxymethamphetamine

(Ecstasy) by Debrisoquine Hydroxylase (CYP2D6). *Biochem. Pharmacol.* 47: 1151-56 (1994).

The metabolism of MDMA was examined in a microsomal preparation of a yeast that expresses human debrisoquine hydroxylase. Only one product, the catechol 3,4-dihydroxy-N-methyl-amphetamine resulting from the removal of the formaldehyde carbon atom of the methylenedioxy ring, was observed.

Wilkerson, G. and London, E.D. Effects of Methylenedioxymethamphetamine on Local Cerebral Glucose Utilization in the Rat. *Neuropharmacol.* 28: 1129-1138 (1989).

MDMA was found to influence glucose utilization at some 60 different areas in the rat brain, as determined by the employment of radioactive 2-deoxyglucose. A thorough tally has been made of these areas, and the changes that follow four different dose levels of exposure.

Metabolism

Cho, A.K., Hiramatsu, M., Distefano, E.W., Chang, A.S and Jenden, D.J. Stereochemical Differences in the Metabolism of 3,4-Methylenedioxymethamphetamine in vivo and in vitro: A Pharmacokinetic Analysis. *Drug Metabol. Disposition* 18: 686-691 (1990).

The optical isomers of MDMA were demethylated to fort MDA, with the active (+)-isomer being 3x more extensively degraded. The loss of the methylenedioxy group gave N-methyl-alphamethyldopamine proved to be the major metabolite.

Fitzgerald, R.L., Blanke, R., Narasimhachari, N., Glennon, R. and Rosecrans, J. Identification of 3,4-Methylenedioxyamphetamine (MDA) as a Major Urinary Metabolite of 3,4-Methylenedioxymethamphetamine (MDMA). *NIDA Research Monograph,* **81** 321 (1988).

Rats were administered MDMA chronically and, from both the plasma and the excreta, unchanged MDMA and the demethylation product MDA were detected by GCMS as the trifluoroacetamide derivatives.

Fitzgerald, R.L., Blanke, R.V. and Poklis, A. Stereoselective Pharmacokinetics of 3,4-Methylenedioxymethamphetamine in the Rat. *Chirality* 2: 241-248 (1990).

The optical isomers of MDMA and MDA were assayed in the rat, following the administration of MDMA by two different dosages and by two different routes. The S-isomer of MDMA was found to clear more rapidly, resulting in a preferred presence of its metabolite, the S-isomer of MDA. Blood levels, isomer ratios, and half-lives are given.

Fukuto, J.M., Kumagai, Y. and Cho, A.K. Determination of the Mechanism of Demethylenation of (Methylenedioxy)phenyl Compounds by Cytochrome P450 Using Deuterium Isotope Effects. *J. Med. Chem.* 34: 2871-2876 (1991).

Kinetic studies of the demethylenation of several methylenedioxy compounds (including MDMA) have shown, by isotope effects, to be mediated by different mechanisms.

Helmlin, H.-J., Bracher, K., Salamone, S.J. and Brenneisen, R., Analysis of 3,4-Methylenedioxymethamphetamine (MDMA) and its Metabolites in Human Plasma and Urine by HPLC-DAD, GC-MS and Abuscreen-Online. Abstracts from CAT/SOFT Joint Meeting, October 10-16, 1993, Phoenix, Arizona.

Urine and plasma samples were taken from a number of patients being administered 1.5 mg/Kg MDMA for psychotherapy research purposes. Maximum plasma levels (300 ng/mL) were seen at 140 minutes. The main urinary metabolites were 4-hydroxy-3-methoxy-methamphetamine and 3,4-dihydroxy-methamphetamine, both excreted in conjugated form. The two N-demethylated homologues of these compounds were present as minor metabolites. The cross-reactivity of the Abuscreen immunoassay for both the metabolites (including MDA, another metabolite) and the parent drug were determined.

Hiramatsu, M., DiStefano, E., Chang, A.S. and Cho, A.K. A Pharmacokinetic Analysis of 3,4-Methylenedioxymethamphetamine Effects on Monoamine Concentrations in Brain Dialysates. *Eur. J. Pharmacol.* 204: 135-140 (1991).

The role of the MDMA metabolite, MDA, in the releasing of dopamine, was studied in brain dialysates. It was noted that the plasma levels of MDA were higher following the administration of (+)-MDMA as compared to (-)-MDMA, to the rat.

Hiramatsu, M., Kumagai, Y., Unger, S.E. and Cho, A.K. Metabolism of Methylenedioxymethamphetamine: Formation of Dihydroxymeth-amphetamine and a Quinone Identified as its Glutathione Adduct. *J. Pharmacol. Exptl. Ther.* 254: 521-527 (1990).

Studies were made of the in vitro metabolism of MDMA by rat liver microsomes, of the optical isomers of MDMA. A P-450 dependent hydrolysis to N,alpha-dimethyl was observed, which was further converted by superoxide oxidation to a metabolite that formed an adduct with glutathione. It is speculated that this pathway may account for some of the irreversible action on serotoninergic neurons.

Kumagai, Y., Lin, L.Y., Schmitz, D.A. and Cho, A.K. Hydroxyl Radical Mediated Demethylenation of (Methylenedioxy)phenyl Compounds, *Chem. Res. Toxicol.* 4: 330-334 (1991).

The oxidative demethylenation of several methylenedioxy compounds such as MDMA has been studied, with two hydroxyl radical generating systems. The various requirements for this metabolic transformation are defined.

Lim, H.K. and Foltz, R.L. Metabolism of 3,4-Methylenedioxymethamphetamine (MDMA) in Rat. *FASEB Abstracts.* **2** 5: A-1060. Abst: 4440.

The metabolism of MDMA in the rat is studied. Seven metabolites have been identified from urine. These are: 4-hydroxy-3-methoxymethamphetamine; 3,4-methylenedioxyamphetamine; 4-hydroxy-3-methoxyamphetamine; 4-methoxy-3-hydroxymethamphetamine; 3,4-methylenedioxyphenylacetone; 3,4-dihydroxyphenyl acetone and 4-hydroxy-3-methoxyphenylacetone

Lim, H.K. and Foltz, R.L. In Vivo and In Vitro Metabolism of 3,4-Methylenedioxymethamphetamine in the Rat: Identification of Metabolites using an Ion Trap Detector. *Chem. Res. Toxicol.* 1: 370-378 (1988).

Four metabolic pathways for MDMA metabolism in the rat have been identified. These are N-demethylation, O-dealkylation, deamination, and conjugation. A total of eight distinct metabolites have been observed and identified.

Lim, H.K. and Foltz, R.L. Identification of Metabolites of 3,4-Methylenedioxymethamphetamine in Human Urine. *Chem. Res. Toxicol.* **2: 142-143 (1989).**

The metabolites observed in the rat following MDMA administration are, to a large degree, identical to those found in man. The metabolic paths observed are N-demethylation, O-dealkylation, deamination, and conjugation. The major metabolite in this one individual (an undocumented MDMA user accident victim) is 3-methoxy-4-hydroxymeth-amphetamine.

Lim, H.K. and Foltz, R.L. Application of Ion Trap MS/MS Techniques for Identification of Potentially Neurotoxic Metabolites of 3,4- Methylene-dioxymeth-amphetamine (MDMA). Paper presented at the CAT Quarterly Meeting, February 3, 1990, San Jose, California.

The GCMS analysis of the rat liver metabolites of MDMA has given evidence of ring hydroxylation. Employing MS/MS techniques and unresolved synthetic mixtures, tentative structural assignments have been presented for the hydroxylation of MDMA at all three available ring positions. Another possible metabolite is ring-hydroxylated MDA. A possible neurotoxic role of such products is suggested by their structural relationship to 6-hydroxydopamine.

Lim, H.K. and Foltz, R.L. In vivo Formation of Aromatic Hydroxylated Metabolites of 3,4 Methylenedioxy-methamphetamine in the Rat: Identification by Ion Trap Tandem Mass Spectrometric (MS/MS and MS/MS/MS) Techniques. *Biological Mass Spectrometry* **20: 677-686 (1991).**

Metabolism studies in the rat have shown that MDMA can be hydroxylated at all three possible aromatic positions. The three corresponding compounds with N-demethylation also are formed. The 6-position is favoured. All metabolites are observed in the liver, only the 6-hydroxyl isomer in the brain, and none can be found in urine.

Lim, H.K., Zeng, S., Chei, D.M. and Foltz, R.L. Comparitive Investigation of Disposition of 3,4- (Methylenedioxy)-methamphetamine (MDMA) in the Rat and the Mouse by a Capillary Gas Chromatography-Mass Spectrometry Assay based on Perfluorotributylamine-enhanced Ammonia Positive Ion Chemical Ionization. *J. Pharmaceut. Biomed. Anal.* **10: 657-665 (1992).**

An assay is described that allows a quantitative measure of MDMA and three of its primary metabolites, methylene-dioxamphetamine, 4-hydroxy-3-methoxymethamphetamine and 4-hydroxy-3-methoxyamphetamine. The latter two metabolites were excreted mainly as the glucuronide and sulfate conjugates. The metabolic patterns of the rat and the mouse are compared.

Lin, L., Kumagai, Y., Cho, A.K. Enzymatic and Chemical Demethylenation of (Methylenedioxy)-amphetamine and (Methylenedioxy)-methamphetamine by Rat Brain Microsomes. *Chem. Res. Toxicol..* **5: 401-406 (1992)**

Metabolism of MDA and MDMA by microsomal preparation from rat brains. The products observed were the corresponding catechol derivatives. The oxidizing agents appear to involve both a cytochrome P-450 component and hydroxyl radical.

Yousif, M.Y., Fitzgerald, R.L., Narasimhachari, N., Rosecrans,

J.A., Blanke, R.V. and Glennon, R.A. Identification of Metabolites of 3,4- Methylenedioxymethamphetamine in Rats. *Drug and Alcohol Dependence.* **26: 127-135 (1990).**

Two metabolites of MDMA have been established as being present in rat urine, by both HPLC and GCMS; these were MDA and 4-hydroxy-3-methoxy-N-methylamphetamine. From HPLC alone, evidence was found for the positional isomer 3-hydroxy-4-methoxy-N-methyl-amphetamine, for 4-hydroxy-3-methoxy-amphetamine, and for 3,4- dihydroxy-amphetamine, but these were not confirmed by GCMS. MDA was identified in both plasma and brain extracts.

In vitro studies

Azmitia, E.C., Murphy, R.B. and Whitaker-Azmitia, P.M. MDMA (Ecstasy) Effects on Cultured Serotonergic Neurons: Evidence for Ca 2+ -Dependent Toxicity Linked to Release. *Brain Res.* **510: 97-103 (1990).**

The relationship of MDMA with serotonin neurons, and with calcium cation release has been determined in the foetal cells of newborn rats. Long-term serotonin changes are blocked by 5-HT re-uptake blockers, and the interactions between MDMA and caffeine have been reported. It has been suggested that Ca cation release may play a role in MDMA toxicity.

Battaglia, G., Brooks,B.P., Kulsakdinum, C. and De Souza, E.B. Pharmacologic Profile of MDMA 3,4- Methylene-dioxymethamphetamine at Various Brain Recognition Sites. *Eur.J.Pharmacol.* **149: 159-163 (1988).**

The affinity of MDMA for various neurotransmitter receptor and uptake sites was studied in vivo, using competition with various radioligands. Comparisons with MDA, MDE, amphetamine and methamphetamine are reported.

Berger, U.V., Gu, X.F. and Azmitia, E.C. The Substituted Amphetamines 3,4- Methylenedioxymethamphetamine, Methamphetamine, p-Chloroamphet-amine and Fenfluramine Induce 5-Hydroxytryptamine Release via a Common Mechanism Blocked by Fluoxetine and Cocaine. *Eur. J. Pharmacol.* **215: 153-60 (1992).**

An in vitro assay has been used to compare several drugs for their ability to induce synaptosomal serotonin release. Para-chloroamphetamine and fenfluramine were equally effective, MDMA less so, and methamphetamine very much less so still. Evidence is presented that the serotonin release produced by these drugs employs a common mechanism.

Bradberry, C.W., Sprouse,J.S., Aghajanian, G.K. and Roth, R.H. 3,4- Methylenedioxymethamphetamine (MDMA)-Induced Release of Endogenous Serotonin from the Rat Dorsal Raphe Nucleus in vitro: Effects of Fluoxetine and Tryptophan. *Neurochem. Int.* **17: 509-513 (1990).**

Brain slices of the dorsal raphe nucleus were exposed to a medium containing MDMA and the released serotonin was measured. A serotonin transport inhibitor (Fluoxetine) reduced the amount released, whereas the addition of tryptophan increased the amount released.

Bradberry, C.W., Sprouse,J.S., Sheldon, P.W., Aghajanian, G.K. and Roth, R.H. In Vitro Microdialysis: A Novel Technique for Stimulated Neurotransmitter Release Measurements. *J. Neurosci. Methods.* **36: 85-90 (1991).**

A novel technique allowing measurement of neurotransmitter release and single unit recordings from brain slices is described. The effects of MDMA on slices of dorsal raphe nucleus and frontal cortex were used to demonstrate it.

Brady, J.F., Di Stephano, E.W. and Cho, A.K. Spectral and Inhibitory Interactions of (+/-)-3,4- Methylenedioxyamphetamine (MDA) and (+/-)-3,4- Methylenedioxymethamphetamine (MDMA) with Rat Hepatic Microsomes. *Life Sci.* 39: 1457-1464 (1986).

Both MDA and MDMA were shown to form complexes with cytochrome P-450 that were inhibitory to its function as to demethylation of benzphetamine and carbon monoxide binding. Liver microsome studies showed the metabolic demethylation of MDMA and the N-hydroxylation of MDA.

Frye, G. and Matthews, R. Effect of 3,4- Methylenedioxymethamphetamine (MDMA) on Contractive Responses in the G. Pig Ileum. *The Pharmacologist* 28: 149 (1986).

Using the longitudinal muscle of the guinea pig ilium, MDMA evoked dose-related, transient contractions, but failed to reduce contractions produced by serotonin, acetylcholine, or GABA. The MDMA contractions were blocked by atropine, and do not appear to involve serotonin receptors.

Gehlert, D.R., Schmidt, C.J., Wu, L. and Lovenberg, W. Evidence for Specific Methylenedioxymethamphetamine (Ecstasy) Binding Sites in the Rat Brain. *Eur. J. Pharmacol.* 119: 135-136 (1985).

Evidence is presented from binding to rat homogenate studies. The use of the serotoninergic re-uptake inhibitor, active in vivo, does not antagonize this binding, nor in studies with uptake into striatal microsomes.

House, R.V., Thomas, P.T. and Bhargava, H.N. Selective Modulation of Immune Function Resulting from in vitro Exposure to Methylene-dioxymethamphetamine (Ecstasy). *Toxicol.* 96: 59-69 (1995).

MDMA was compared to methamphetamine for its ability to modulate the immune functional parameters. Neither B-cell proliferation nor IL-4 production was affected at any concentration. However, IL-2 production, and basal and augmented NK cell function were enhanced.

Leonardi, E.T.K., Azmitia, E.C. MDMA (Ecstasy) Inhibition of MAO Type A and Type B: Comparisons with Fenfluramine and Fluoxetine (Prozac). *Neuropsychopharmacol.* 10: 231-238 (1994).

The effects of the two optical isomers of MDMA on the monoamineoxidases in rat brain homogenates were studied. A number of other drugs pharmacologically related were also studied, and the finding related to their relative toxicities.

Levin, J.A., Schmidt, C.J. and Lovenberg, W. Release of [³H]-Monoamines from Superfused Rat Striatal Slices by Methylenedioxymethamphetamine (MDMA). *Fed. Proc.* 45: 1059 (#5265) April 13-18, 1986.

The release of tritiated serotonin and dopamine from superfused rat striatal slices was observed for three amphetamine derivatives. MDMA and p-chloroamphetamine were equivalent, and about 10x the potency of methamphetamine. This last compound was, however, some 10x more effective than MDMA in the release of dopamine.

Lyon, R.A., Glennon, R.A. and Titeler, M. 3,4- Methylenedioxy-

methamphetamine (MDMA): Stereoselective Interactions at Brain 5- HT₁ and 5-HT₂ Receptors. *Psychopharmacology* 88: 525-526 (1986).

Both MDMA and MDA, and their respective optical isomers, were assayed as to their affinity at radio-labelled serotonin (5-HT₁ and 5-HT₂) and dopamine (D₂) binding sites. The 'R' isomers of both drugs showed a moderate affinity at the 5-HT₂ receptor (labelled with ³H ketanserin), and the 'S' isomers were lower. Affinities for the 5-HT₁ site were similar, but that for D₂ sites were very low. Since the 'S' isomer of MDMA is the more potent in man, it may not work primarily through a direct interaction at 5-HT receptors.

Nichols, D.E., Lloyd, D.H., Hoffman, A.J., Nichols, M.B. and Yim, G.K.W. Effects of Certain Hallucinogenic Amphetamine Analogues on the Release of [³H] Serotonin from Rat Brain Synaptosomes. *J. Med. Chem.* 25: 530-535 (1982).

The optically active isomers of MDMA (as well as those for MDA, PMA and the corresponding phentermine analogues) have been evaluated as to their effect on the release of serotonin from rat brain synaptosomes. The (+) isomer of MDMA was the more effective (this is the active isomer in humans) suggesting that serotonin release may play some role in the psychopharmacological activity. The alpha-alpha dimethyl homologues were inactive even at the highest concentrations studied.

Rudnick, G., Wall, S.C. The Molecular Mechanism of 'Ecstasy' [3,4-Methylenedioxymethamphetamine (MDMA)]: Serotonin Transporters are Targets for MDMA-Induced Serotonin Release. *Proc. Natl. Acad. Sci USA,* 89: 1817-1821 (1992)

The mechanisms of MDMA action at serotonin transporters from plasma membranes and secretory vesicles isolated from human platelets have been studied and are reported.

Rudnick, G., and Wall, S. Non-Neurotoxic Amphetamine Derivatives Release Serotonin through Serotonin Transporters. *Molecular Pharmacology,* in press (1992).

MDMA was compared to MMA (3-methoxy-4-methylamphetamine) and MMAI (both non-neurotoxic analogues) as to their effects on several serotonin and dopamine properties in vitro studies.

Steele, T.P., Nichols, D.E. and Yim, G.K.W. Stereoselective Effects of MDMA on Inhibition of Monoamine Uptake. *Fed. Proc.* 45: 1059 (# 5262) April 13-18 1986.

In the investigation of the optical isomeric difference of activities seen for amphetamine, MDMA, and DOM (the more potent isomers being the 'S', 'S' and 'R' resp.) their abilities to inhibit the uptake of radio-labelled monoamines into synaptosomes were studied. The findings are discussed, and it is concluded that MDMA exhibits stereoselective effects similar to those of amphetamine on monoamine uptake inhibition, a parameter that is unrelated to the mechanism of action of the hallucinogen DOM.

Steele, T.D., Nichols, D.E. and Yim, G.K.W. Stereochemical Effects of 3,4- Methylenedioxymethamphetamine (MDMA) and Related Amphetamine Derivatives on Inhibition of Uptake of [³H]Monoamines into Synaptosomes from Different Regions of Rat Brain. *Biochem. Pharmacol.* 36: 2297-2303 (1987).

MDA, MDMA, and the alpha-ethyl homologue MBDB were found to inhibit serotonin uptake in brain synaptosomes. The conclusions to a broad series of studies were that MDMA and its homologues are more closely related to amphetamine than to DOM in their biochemical actions.

Wang, S.S., Ricaurte, G.A. and Peroutka, S.J. [³H]3,4 Methylene-dioxymethamphetamine (MDMA) Interactions with Brain Membranes and Glass Fiber Filter Paper. *Eur. J. Pharmacol.* 138: 439-443 (1987).

Tritiated MDMA appears to give a pharmacological 'binding profile' in rat brain homogionate studies, even in the absence of brain tissue. This appears to result from an unexpected binding of the radioligand to glass filter paper. Pretreatment with polyethylenimine eliminated this artifact.

Pharmacology

Anderson III, G.M., Braun, G., Braun, U., Nichols, D.E. and Shulgin, A.T. Absolute Configuration and Psychotomimetic Activity, *NIDA Research Monograph* 22: 8-15 (1978).

The 'R' isomer of most chiral hallucinogenics is known to be the active isomer. This generality includes LSD, DOB, DOM, DOET, and MDA. This assignment has been demonstrated both in rabbit hyperthermia studies as well as in clinical evaluations. With MDMA, however, this assignment is reversed. In both rabbit and human studies, the more potent isomer of MDMA is the 'S' form, similar to that of amphetamine and methamphetamine. The summed activity of the individual isomers did not satisfactorily reproduce the activity of the racemic mixture. Also, the addition of an N-methyl to a known hallucinogenic amphetamine routinely decreases the potency (as with DOB, DOM, TMA and TMA-2). The exception again is with MDA, which produces the equipotent MDMA. The relationship between the stimulants amphetamine and methamphetamine is similar. The two drugs MDA and MDMA appear not to be cross-tolerant in man. It is argued that the mechanisms of action of MDMA must be different from that of MDA and related hallucinogenics.

Beardsley, P.M., Balster, R.L. and Harris, L.S. Self-administration of Methylenedioxymethamphetamine (MDMA) by Rhesus Monkeys. *Drug and Alcohol Dependence* 18: 149-157 (1986)

In monkeys trained to self-administer cocaine intravenously MDMA was found, in two out of four animals, to be an effective substitute.

Beaton, J.M., Benington, F., Christian, S.T., Monti, J.A. and Morin, R.D. Analgesic Effects of MDMA and Related Compounds. *Pharmacologist* 29: ABS 281 (1987).

Analgesia of several compounds (including MDMA and several close homologues) was measured by the tail-flick response in mice. All produced analgesia, with the (+) (S) MDMA being the most potent.

Bilsky, E.J. and Reid, L.D. MDL-72222, A Serotonin 5-HT₃ Receptor Antagonist, Blocks MDMA's Ability to Establish a Conditioned Place Preference. *Pharmacol. Biochem. Behav.* 39: 509-512 (1991).

MDMA has been shown to establish conditioned place-preference in rats. An experimental 5-HT3 antagonist MDL-72222 blocked the effect, suggesting that such antagonists might be of use in the evaluation the pharmacology of self-administer drugs.

Bilsky, E.J., Hubbell, C.L., Delconte, J.D. and Reid, L.D. MDMA Produces a Conditioned Place Preference and Elicits Ejaculation in Male Rats: A Modulatory Role for the Endogenous Opioids. *Pharmacol. Biochem. Behav.* 40: 443-447 (1991).

The ability of rats to establish a conditioned place-preference was studied. This was blocked by the pre-administration of Naltrexone.

This drug interaction was studied as to ejaculatory behaviour, urination, defecation and body weight change.

Bilsky, E.J., Hui, Y., Hubbell, C.L. and Reid, L.D. Methylenedioxy-methamphet-amine's Capacity to Establish Place Preferences and Modify Intake of an Alcohol Beverage. *Pharmacol. Biochem. Behav.* 37: 633-638 (1990).

Employing behavioural studies with experimental rats, it was found that MDMA led to a dose-dependent decrease of intake of sweetened ethanol. Another study showed a positive, but not dose dependent, 'conditioned placement preference' test which, it is argued, provides further evidence for the drug's abuse liability.

Bird, M. and Kornetsky, C. Naloxone Antagonism of the Effects of MDMA 'Ecstasy' on Rewarding Brain Stimulation. *The Pharmacologist* 28: 149 (1986).

The lowering of the reward threshold (REBS, rewarding electrical brain stimulation) by the s.c. administration of MDMA to rats (as determined by implanted electrodes) was blocked by Naloxone. This suggests that MDMA affects the same dopinergic and opioid substrates involved in cocaine and d-amphetamine reward.

Braun, U., Shulgin, A.T. and Braun, G. Prufung auf zentral Aktivitat und Analgesie von N-substituierten Analogen des Amphetamin-Derivates 3,4- Methylenedioxyphenyliso-propylamin. *Arzneim.-Forsch.* 30: 825-830 (1980).

MDMA, and a large collection of N-substituted homologues, were assayed in mice for both analgesic potency and enhancement of motor activity. MDMA proved to be the most potent analgesic (compared with some 15 homologues) but was not particularly effective as a motor stimulant. The structure and pharmacological relationships to known analgesics are discussed.

Bronson, M.E., Barrios-Zambrano, L., Jiang, W., Clark, C.R., DeRuiter, J. and Newland, M.C., Behavioral and Developmental Effects of Two 3,4-Methylenedioxymethamphetamine (MDMA) Derivatives. *Drug Alc. Depend.* 36: 161-166 (1994).

Two structural homologues of MDMA, vis. N-methyl-1-(3,4-methylenedioxy-phenyl)-1-aminoethane and N-methyl-1-(3,4-methylenedioxyphenyl)-3-aminobutane, have been studied in drug discrimination in rats, and for their effects on developing chicken embryos. Some properties are shared with MDMA and may thus share its abuse liability. Both homologues appeared to develop adverse effects on the developing organism however, which MDMA did not.

Callahan, P.M. and Appel, J.B. Differences in the Stimulus Properties of 3,4- Methylenedioxyamphetamine (MDA) and N-Methyl-3,4- methylenedioxy-methamphetamine (MDMA) in Animals Trained to Discriminate Hallucinogens from Saline. *Soc. Neurosci. Abstr.* 13, Part 3, p. 1720 (1987) No. 476.2.

The stimulant properties of MDA and MDMA (including the optical isomers) were studied in rats that were trained to discriminate mescaline or (separately) LSD, from saline. 'R'-MDA appears similar to both hallucinogens, but the other isomers gave no clear-cut accord to the literature reports of behavioural activity.

Callahan, P.M. and Appel, J.B. Differences in the Stimulus Properties of 3,4- Methylenedioxyamphetamine and 3,4- Methylenedioxmethamphetamine in Animals Trained to Discriminate Hallucinogens from Saline. *J. Pharmacol. Exptl. Ther.* 246: 866-870 (1988).

In animals trained to discriminate LSD from saline, DOM, mescaline, psilocybin and (+) MDA and both (+) and (-) MDMA, responses followed the LSD cue. With animals trained to mescaline (vs. saline), both isomers of both MDA and MDMA produced mescaline-like responses, as did DOM, LSD and psilocybin.

Callaway, C.W., Wing, L.L. and Geyer, M.A. Serotonin Release Contributes to the Locomotor Stimulant Effects of 3,4-Methylenedioxyamphetamine in Rats. *J. Pharmacol. Exptl. Ther.* 254: 456-464 (1990).

The relative roles of dopamine and of serotonin have been evaluated, employing the MDMA-induced locomotor hyperactivity in the rat. It has been found that the observed activity calls upon mechanisms that depend upon the release of central serotonin, as opposed to the mechanisms believed to express amphetamine motor activity.

Callaway, C.W. and Geyer, M.A. Stimulant Effects of 3, 4-Methylene-dioxymethamphetamine in the Nucleus Accumbens of Rat. *Eur. J.. Pharmacol.* 214: 45-51 (1992)

This study examined the behavioural effects in rats of intracerebral administration of S-MDMA using an automated holeboard and open-field apparatus. Administration of S-MDMA into the nucleus accumbens septi produced locomotor hyperactivity.

Callaway, C.W. and Geyer, M.A. Tolerance and Cross-Tolerance to the Activating Effects of 3,4- Methylene-dioxymethamphetamine and a 5-Hydroxytryptamine[1B] Agonist. *J. Pharmacol. Exptl. Ther.* 263: 318-326 (1992).

Two experiments were carried out. Changes in the response of rats to MDMA were studied following chronic pretreatment with serotonin agonists responsive to different receptor subtypes. And, following chronic pretreatment with MDMA, changes in responses to these separate receptor agonists were studied. There was an acute reciprocal cross-tolerance observed between MDMA and RU-24969, a 5-HT[1b] receptor agonist, in producing activating effects in the rat. This supports the hypothesis that the release of endogenous serotonin increases locomotor activity by the stimulation of 5-HT[1b] receptors.

Cho, A.K., Hiramatsu, M., Kumagai, Y. and Patel, N. Pharmacokinetic Approaches to the Study of Drug Action and Toxicity. *NIDA Research Monograph* 136 :213-225 (1993). Ed. Linda Erinoff.

Using rats as an experimental animal, the time courses of plasma MDMA and metabolite MDA were reported following the administration of (separately) (+) and (-) MDMA. The dideutero-analogue was used as an internal standard, and the analysis was performed on the trifluoroacetamides by selected ion monitoring. Microsomal metabolic pathways were also reported.

Crisp, T., Stafinsky, J.L., Boja, J.W. and Schechter, M.D. The Antinociceptive Effects of 3,4- Methylene-dioxymethamphetamine (MDMA) in the Rat. *Pharmacol. Biochem. Behav.* 34: 497-501 (1989).

MDMA was compared to morphine as an analgesic drug in the rat, in both the tail-flick and the hot-plate tests. Both drugs were equipotent in the latter tests, but only morphine was effective in the former test. The effectiveness of MDMA was not attenuated by either the opiate antagonist naltrexone nor the adrenoreceptor antagonist Phentolamine. However, the serontin antagonist Methysergide did antagonise the MDMA effectiveness, suggesting a serotonin involvement in this action.

Dafters, R.I. Effect of Ambient Temperature on Hyperthermia and Hyperkinesis Induced by 3,4-Methylenedioxymethamphetamine (MDMA or 'Ecstasy') in Rats. *Psychopharmacol.* 114: 505-8 (1994).

An effort to understand the 'heatstroke' associated with the human use of MDMA has been made in rats studies by observing the induced toxicology of MDMA with the controlled exposed to different environmental conditions.

Davis, W.M. and Borne, R.F. Pharmacological Investigation of Compounds Related to 3,4- Methylene-dioxyamphetamine (MDA), *Subs. Alc. Act/Mis.* 5: 105-110 (1984).

MDA and MDMA, as well as the homologous 3-aminobutanes HMDA and HMDMA, were studied toxicologically in both isolated and aggregated mouse groups. Both MDA and MDMA were of similar lethality in isolated animals (ca. 100mg/Kg i.p.) which was enhanced 3 or 4 fold by aggregation. The homologues HMDA and HMDMA were approximately twice as toxic but showed no such enhancement. The prelethal behaviour characteristics and the effects of potential protective agents are described.

Dimpfel, W., Spuler, M. and Nichols, D.E. Hallucinogenic and Stimulatory Amphetamine Derivatives: Fingerprinting DOM, DOI, DOB, MDMA, and MBDB by Spectral Analysis of Brain Field Potentials in the Freely Moving Rat (Tele-Stereo-EEG). *Psychopharmacology* 98: 297-303 (1989).

Recording from several areas of the brain of freely moving rats were made following the administration of several hallucinogens and other structurally related entactogens and stimulants. The recorded results show clear regional specificity of the various classes of drugs, and suggest that serotonin receptors in the striatum might be involved with hallucinogenic action.

Dragunow, M., Logan, B. and Laverty, R. 3,4-Methylenedioxymethamphetamine Induces Fos-like Proteins in Rat Basic Ganglia: Reversal with MK-801. *Eur. J. Pharmacol.* 206: 205 (1991).

Administration of MDMA to rats leads to an accumulation of Fos proteins and Fos-related antigens. The NMDA antagonist MK-801 inhibited this induction, but Fluoxetine had no effect.

Elayan, I., Gibb, J.W., Hanson, G.R., Foltz, R.L., Lim, H.K. and Johnson, M. Long-term Alteration in the Central Monoaminergic Systems of the Rat by 2,4,5-Trihydroxyamphetamine but not by 2-Hydroxy-4,5-Methylenedioxy-methamphetamine or 2-Hydroxy-4,5-Methylenedioxyamphetamine. *Eur. J. Pharmacol.* 221: 281-288 (1992).

The effects of the i.c.v. administration of three metabolites of MDMA were studied in the rat. With 2,4,5-trihydroxyamphetamine there was a long-term decline in tryptophane hydroxylase and tyrosine hydroxylase activity, as well as a decrease in serotonin, dopamine and norepinephrin levels. This suggests that this metabolite may contribute to the neurotoxic action of MDMA on the serotonergic system.

Evans, S.M. and Johanson, C.E. Discriminative Stimulus Properties of (+/-)-3,4- Methylenedioxy-methamphetamine and (+/-)- Methylenedioxy-amphetamine in Pigeons. *Drug and Alcohol Dependence* 18: 159-164 (1986).

Pigeons were trained to discriminate (+) amphetamine from saline. Both MDA and MDMA substituted for amphetamine, and both were less potent.

Fellows, E.J. and Bernheim, F. The Effect of a Number of Aralkylamines on the Oxidation of Tyramine by Amine Oxidase. *J. Pharmacol. Exptl. Ther.* 100: 94-99 (1950).

There were animal behavioural studies made on the chain homologue of MDMA, vis., 1-(3,4- methylenedioxyphenyl)-3-methylaminobutane. This is the amine that would result from the use of the 'wrong' piperonylacetone in illicit synthesis. In the dose range 10-25 mg/Kg, toxic effects such as tremors and convulsions were seen.

Fitzgerald, J.L. and Reid, J.J. Interactions of Methylenedioxymethamphetamine with Monoamine Transmitter Release Mechanisms in the Rat Brain. *Arch. Pharmacol.* 347: 313-323 (1993).

The effects of MDMA and of amphetamine were compared as to their effectiveness in releasing the radioactivity labelled neurotransmitters serotonin, noradrenaline and dopamine from brain slices. Fitzgerald, J.L, and Reid, J.J., Sympathomimetic Actions of Methylenedioxymethamphetamine in Rat and Rabbit Isolated Cardiovascular Tissues. J. Pharmacol. Pharmacol. 46 826-832 (1994).

A series of studies of MDMA was performed on various heart tissues. MDMA appears to have sympathomimetic activity similar to amphetamine, which could account for the cardiovascular side-effects associated with its use.

Gazzara, R.A., Takeda, H., Cho, A.K. and Howard, S.G. Inhibition of Dopamine Release by Methylenedioxymethamphetamine is Mediated by Serotonin, *Eur. J. Pharmacol.* 168: 209-217 (1989).

The administration of MDMA to rats produces a long-lasting decrease in extracellular dopamine in brain tissues. To determine if the known increased release of serotonin might be the cause of this, experimental animals were pretreated with PCA which effectively decreased the serotonin content and inhibited the dopamine decrease following MDMA treatment. The serotonin release by MDMA is argued as possibly being a mediating factor in the observed dopamine release.

Glennon, R.A. and Misenheimer, B.R. Stimulus Effects of N-Monoethyl-1-(3,4- Methylenedioxyphenyl)-2-aminopropane (MDE) and N-Hydroxy-1-(3,4- Methylenedioxyphenyl)-2-aminopropane (N-OH MDA) in Rats Trained to Discriminate MDMA from Saline. *Pharmacol. Biochem. Behav.* 33: 909-912 (1989).

Both MDE and MDOH generalized to MDMA in rats trained to discriminate MDMA from saline. Amphetamine was less effective. Since MDMA substitutes for amphetamine, whereas neither MDE nor MDOH do so, these latter drugs appear to have less of an amphetamine-like component than MDMA.

Glennon, R.A. and Young, R. Further Investigation of the Discriminative Stimulus Properties of MDA. *Pharmacol. Biochem. and Behaviour* 20: 501-505 (1984).

In rats trained to distinguish between racemic MDA (and separately, 'S'-amphetamine) and saline, MDMA (as well as either optical isomer of MDA) was found to generalize to MDA. Similarly, with rats trained to distinguish between dextro-amphetamine and saline, MDMA and 'S'-MDA (but not 'R'-MDA or 'S'-DOM) produced generalization responses.

Glennon, R.A., Little, P.J., Rosecrans, J.A. and Yousif, M. The Effects of MDMA ('Ecstasy') and its Optical Isomers on Schedule-Controlled Responding in Mice. *Pharmacol. Biochem. Behav.* 26: 425-426 (1987).

The effectiveness of several analogues of MDMA were evaluated in mice trained in a reinforcement procedure. Both (+) and racemic MDMA were 4x the potency of the levo-isomer; all were less potent than amphetamine.

Glennon, R.A., Young, R., Rosecrans, J.A. and Anderson, G.M. Discriminative Stimulus Properties of MDA Analogues. *Biol. Psychiat.* 17: 807-814 (1982).

In rats trained to distinguish between the psychotomimetic DOM and saline, several compounds were found to generalize to DOM (including racemic MDA, its 'R' isomer, and MMDA-2) Others did not generalize to DOM (including MDMA, the 'S' isomer of MDA, and homopiperylamine). These results are consistent with the qualitative differences reported in man.

Glennon, R.A., Yousif, M. and Patrick, G. Stimulus Properties of 1-(3,4-Methylenedioxy)-2-Aminopropane (MDA) analogues. *Pharmacol. Biochem. Behav.* 29: 443-449 (1988).

Rats were trained to discriminate between saline and DOM or d-amphetamine. They were challenged with 'R' and 'S' MDMA, with racemic, 'R' and 'S' MDE, and with racemic MDOH (N-OH-MDA). The amphetamine-trained animals generalized to 'S' MDMA, but to neither 'R' MDMA, any of the MDE isomers, MDOH, nor to homopiperonylamine. N-substituted amphetamine derivatives (N-ethyl and N-hydroxy) also gave the amphetamine response, but none of these compounds generalized to DOM. This study supports the suggestion that MDMA represents a class of compounds apart from the stimulant or the hallucinogenic.

Glennon, R.A. MDMA-Like Stimulus Effects of Alpha-Ethyltryptamine and the Alpha-Ethyl Homolog of DOM. *Pharmacol. Biochem. Behav.* 46: 459-462 (1993).

The alpha-ethyl homologues of alpha-methyltryptamine and of DOM are a-ET and Dimoxamine. Whereas rats trained to discriminate MDMA from saline failed to generalize to DOM or alpha-methyltryptamine, they did to both of these homologues.

Glennon, R.A. and Higgs, R. Investigation of MDMA-Related Agents in Rats Trained to Discriminate MDMA from Saline. *Pharmacol. Biochem. and Behav.* 43: 759-63 (1992).

A number of MDMA metabolites and related compounds were compared to MDMA in discrimination studies in the rat. Several gave MDMA-appropriate responses, but only 4-methoxymethamphetamine showed stimulus generalization. The intact methylenedioxy ring appears unnecessary for MDMA-like action

Glennon, R.A., Higgs, R., Young, R. and Issa, H. Further Studies on N-methyl-1-(3,4- methylenedioxyphenyl)-2-aminopropane as a Discriminative Stimulus: Antagonism by 5-Hydroxytryptamine3 Antagonists. *Pharmacol. Biochem. Behavior* 43: 1099-106 (1992).

Rats were trained to discriminate MDMA from saline, and this response was evaluated with the study of antagonists of 5-HT_{1A} (NAN-190), 5-HT_2 (pirenperone), 5-HT3 (zacopride) and dopamine receptors (haloperidol). The results can give rise to several mechanistic interpretations, but it is concluded that MDMA produces it's stimulus effects via a complex mechanism involving both dopaminergic and serotonergic components.

Gold, L.H. and Koob, G.F. Methysegide Potentialtes the Hyperactivity Produced by MDMA in Rats. *Pharmacol. Biochem. Behav.* 29: 645-648 (1988).

The hyperactivity that results from MDMA administration is significantly increased by methysergide. This latter drug was itself without effect, nor did it potentiate the hyperactivity induced by amphetamine administration.

Gold, L.H. and Koob, G.F. MDMA Produces Stimulant-like Conditioned Locomotor Activity, *Psychopharmacology* 99: 352-356 (1989).

The administration of MDMA to rats concurrently with exposure to specific sensory clues (odours) produced a conditioned activity response to the clues alone. In this property, MDMA resembles other psychostimulants such as amphetamine and cocaine.

Gold, L.H., Geyer, M.A. and Koob, G.F. Psychostimulant Properties of MDMA. NIDA Monograph #95. *Problems of Drug Dependence* 345-346 (1989).

The pharmacological stimulant properties of MDMA are compared with those of amphetamine. But, as there are some hallucinogenic activity apparent as well, the overall action may be considered as unique mixture of these two properties.

Gold, L.H., Geyer, M.A. and Koob, G.F. Neurochemical Mechanisms Involved in Behavioural Effects of Amphetamines and Related Designer Drugs. NIDA Monograph #94. *Pharmacology and Toxicology of Amphetamines and Related Designer Drugs*, 101-126 (1989).

The dopaminergic aspects of the stimulatory action of MDMA, MDE and amphetamine in rats is discussed. This motor action has been evaluated in conjunction with several areas of brain neuroactivation.

Gold, L.H. , Hubner, C.B. and Koob, G.F. A Role for the Mesolimbic Dopamine System in the Psychostimulant Actions of MDMA. *Psychopharmacology* 99: 40-47 (1989).

The stimulant action produced by MDMA in rats was studied with and without the brain lesions produced by 6-hydroxydopamine. The attenuation of responses was similar to that seen with amphetamine suggests that some involvement of presynaptic release of dopamine may be involved in its action.

Gordon, C.J., Watkinson, W.P., O'Callaghan, J.P. and Miller, B.D. Effects of 3,4- Methylenedioxy-methamphetamine on Autonomic Thermoregulatory Responses of the Rat. Pharmacol. *Biochem. Behav.* 38: 339-344 (1991).

The acute s.c. administration of 30 mg/Kg MDMA to rats led to a increase in body temperature. It is concluded that MDMA stimulates the serotonin pathways that control the metabolic rate and this, accompanied by peripheral vasostriction, lead to the observed hyperthermia.

Gordon, C.J. and Fogelson, L., Metabolic and Thermoregulatory Responses of the Rat Maintained in Acrylic or Wire-Screen Cages: Implications for Pharmacological Studies. *Physiology & Behavior* 56: 73-79 (1994).

It has been observed that the nature of the holding cage can have a remarkable effect on the thermoregulatory responses of rats. The administering of MDMA to animals caged in an acrylic cage with wood-chip bedding caused a sizable temperature increase, whereas a control population in a wire-screen cage had no temperature response to MDMA at all.

Gough, B., Ali, S.F., Slikker, W. and Holson, R.R. Acute Effects of 3,4- Methylenedioxymethamphetamine (MDMA) on Monoamines in Rat Caudate. *Pharmacol. Biochem. Behav.* 39: 619-623 (1991).

A number of neurotransmitter metabolites were assayed in the rat, following the i.p. injection of MDMA. It was concluded that MDMA affects both the dopaminergic as well as the serotoninergic systems.

Griffiths, R.R., Lamb, R. and Brady, J.V. A Preliminary Report on the Reinforcing Effects of Racemic 3,4-Methylenedioxymethamphetamine in the Baboon. Document entered into evidence Re: MDMA Scheduling Docket No. 84-48, U.S. Department of Justice, Drug Enforcement Administration, October 16, 1985.

In three baboons trained to respond to cocaine, MDMA maintained self-administration at a somewhat lower level than cocaine, d-amphetamine, and phencyclidine. There was the evocation of distinct behavioural signals, which suggested that MDMA had a high abuse potential.

Harris, L.S. Preliminary Report on the Dependence Liability and Abuse Potential of Methylene-dioxy-methamphetamine (MDMA). Document entered into evidence Re: MDMA Scheduling Docket No. 84- 48, U.S. Department of Justice, Drug Enforcement Administration, October 16, 1985.

MDMA and amphetamine were compared as to locomotor activity in mice, and in reinforcing activity in monkeys as compared to cocaine. MDMA showed a fraction (20-25%) of the stimulant activity of amphetamine, and was substituted for cocaine in some of the test monkeys.

Hashimoto, K. Effects of Benzylpiperazine Derivatives on the Acute Effects of 3,4- Methylene-dioxymethamphetamine in Rat Brain. *Neurosci. Let.* 152: 17-20 (1993).

The reduction of serotonin in rat brain following exposure to MDMA was significantly attenuated with the co-administration of weak inhibitors (several benzylpiperazines) of serotonin uptake into synaptosomes. The co-administration of the more potent inhibitors (desipramine, imipramine) did not attenuate this MDMA-induced reduction of serotonin, suggesting that the effects of the piperazines may employ a different neurological pathway.

Hashimoto, K., Maeda, H., Hirai, K. and Goromaru, T. Drug Effects on Distribution of [^{3}H]3,4- Methylene-dioxymethamphetamine in Mice. *Eur. J. Pharmacol. – Environm. Toxicol.. Pharmacol. Section* 228: 247-256 (1993).

The effectiveness of a number of drugs and other compounds carrying the methylenedioxyphenyl group on the distribution of radioactive MDMA in the mouse brain was determined. It is suggested that there may exist a specific mechanism for this group which rapidly alters the disposition and metabolism of MDMA.

Hegadoren, K.M., Baker, G.B. and Coutts, R.T. The Simultaneous Separation and Quantitation of the Enantiomers of MDMA and MDA using Gas Chromatography with Nitrogen-Phosphorus Detection. *Res. Commun. Subs. Abuse* 14: 67-80 (1993).

Following the administration of racemic MDMA to the rat, the levels of both MDMA and its demethylated metabolite MDA were determined in areas of the brain. Assays were made at 1,2,4 and 8 hrs., and with a chiral derivative system that allowed the determination of the amounts of the optical isomers resulting from selective chiral metabolism. For unmetabolized MDMA, the concentrations of the (-) isomer were greater than for the (+) isomer. The reverse was true for the demethylated metabolite MDA which, although present at much lower levels, was largely the (+) isomer in all regions studied.

Hiramatsu, M., Nabeshima, T., Kameyama, T., Maeda, Y. and Cho, A.K. The Effect of Optical Isomers of 3,4-Methylenedioxymethamphetamine (MDMA) on Stereotyped Behaviour in Rats. *Pharmacol. Biochem. Behaviour* 33: 343-347 (1989).

The optical isomers of MDMA were compared as to their potencies in inducing stereotyped behaviour in rats. The 'S', or (+) isomer was the more potent, which was consistent with this isomer's increased effectiveness in the release of neurotransmitters.

Huang, X. and Nichols, D. 5-HT2 Receptor-Mediated Potentiation of Dopamine Synthesis and Central Serotonergic Deficits. *Eur. J. Pharmacol.* 238: 291-296 (1993).

Employing receptor agonists, releasing agents and enzyme inhibitors in rats, the hypothesis was tested that serotonin modulates the MDMA-induced increase in dopamine synthesis. The results indicate that the induced increases depend on both serotonin receptor stimulation and on dopamine efflux.

Hubner, C.B., Bird, M., Rassnick, S. and Lornetsky, C. The Threshold Lowering Effects of MDMA (Ecstasy) on Brain-stimulating Reward. *Psychopharm-acology* 95: 49-51 (1988).

MDMA produced a dose-related lowering of the reward threshold, as determined in rats with electrodes stereotaxically implanted in the medial forebrain bundle-lateral hypothalamic area. This procedure has been used as an animal model for drug-induced euphoria.

Huether, G., Poeggeler, B., Adler, L., Ruther, E., Effects of Indirectly Acting 5-HT Receptor Agonists on Circulating Melatonin Levels in Rats. *Eur. J. Pharmacol.* 238: 249-54 (1993).

The administration of tryptophan and serotonin-releasing drugs such as MDMA and fenfluramine, to rats, produced a dose and time dependent elevation of melatonin. This increase was enhanced by the administration of monoamineoxidase inhibitors which, when administered alone, produced no change.

Johnson, M., Bush, L.G., Gibb, J.W. and Hanson, G.R. Blockade of the 3,4- Methylenedioxymethamphetamine-induced Changes in Neurotensin and Dynorphin A Systems. *Eur. J. Pharmacol.* 193: 367-370 (1991).

The increase in immunoreactivity in the neurotensin and dynorphin systems following a single s.c. injection of MDMA in the rat has suggested that both the dopaminergic and glutamatergic systems are involved.

Johnson, M.P., Frescas, S.P., Oberlender, R. and Nichols, D.E. Synthesis and Pharmacological Examination of 1-(3-Methoxy-4-methylphenyl)-2-aminopropane and 5-Methoxy-6-methyl-2-aminoindane: Similarities to 3,4-Methylenedioxymethamphetamine (MDMA). *J. Med. Chem.* 34: 1662-1668 (1991).

The two title compounds have been viewed as analogues of DOM (missing a methoxyl group) or of alpha,4-dimethyltyramine (with O-methylation) and have been synthesized. Both compounds appear to be pharmacologically similar to MDMA, but are lacking any indications of neurotoxicity.

Johnson, M., Bush, L.G., Midgley, L., Gibb, J.W. and Hanson, G.R. MK-801 Blocks the Changes in Neurotensin Concentrations Induced by Methamphetamine, 3,4-Methylenedioxy-methamphetamine, Cocaine, and GBR 12909. *Ann. N.Y. Acad. Sci.* 668: 350-352 (1992).

A study of the neurotensin-like immunoreactivity in the rat has been shown to increase following the administration of several compounds, including MDMA. This can be blocked by the administration of a dopamine D1 receptor antagonist (SCH 23390).

Johnson, M., Bush, L.G., Hanson, G.R., Gibb, J.W. Effects of Ritanserin on the 3,4-Methylenedioxymethamphetamine-Induced Decrease in Striatal Serotonin Concentration and on the Increase in Striatal Neurotensin and Dynorphin A Concentrations. *Biochem. Pharmacol.* 46: 770-772 (1993).

The serotonin level in the striatum of the rat was reduced following the subcutaneous administration of 20 mg/Kg MDMA. Pretreatment with ritanserin prevented this decrease. Following the MDMA administration, there was a several fold increase in the concentrations of both NTLI (neurotensin-like immunoreactivity) and DLI (dynorphin A-like immunoreactivity), but the ritanserin did not block these changes.

Johnson, M., Sonsalla, P.K., Letter, A.A., Hanson, G.R., Gibb, J.W. Role of the 5-HT2 Receptor in the Methamphetamine-Induced Neurochemical Alterations. *J. Pharmacol. Exptl. Ther.* 270: 97-103 (1994).

Investigations of the action of methamphetamine at the 5-HT2 receptor have suggested that the stimulated dopamine synthesis, reported to occur also with MDMA, is regulated in a different manner for the two drugs.

Kamien, J.B., Johanson, C.E., Schuster, C.R. and Woolverton, W.L. The Effects of (+/-)-Methylenedioxymethamphetamine in Monkeys Trained to Discriminate (+)-Amphetamine from Saline. *Drug and Alcohol Dependence* 18: 139-147 (1986).

In monkeys trained to discriminate between amphetamine and saline, MDMA substituted for amphetamine suggesting that there was an amphetamine-like component to its action. This similarity suggested a dependence potential.

Kehne, J.H., McCloskey, T.C., Taylor, V.L., Black, C.K., Fadayel, G.M. and Schmidt, C.J. Effects of the Serotonin Releasers 3,4- Methylenedioxymethamphetamine (MDMA), 4-Chloroamphetamine (PCA) and Fenfluramine on Acoustic and Tactile Startle Reflexes in Rats. *J. Pharmacol. Exptl. Ther.* 260: 78-89 (1992).

The three amphetamine derivatives, MDMA, PCA and Fenfluramine share a common neurochemical action, of releasing central serotonin, but the behavioural effects they evoke are dissimilar. Use of serotonin blockers was made to study the pharmacology of these compounds.

Kasuya, Y. Chemicopharmacological Studies on Antispasmodic Action. XII. Structure-Activity Relationship on Aralkylamines. *Chem. Pharmacol. Bull.* 6: 147-154 (1958).

In vitro studies on mouse intestinal segments were carried out for the chain homologue of MDMA, vis., 1-(3,4-methylenedioxyphenyl)-3-methylaminobutane. This is the amine that would result from the use of the 'wrong' piperonylacetone in illicit synthesis. The compound shows weak atropine action.

Kramer, K., Azmitia, E.C., Whitaker-Azmitia, P.M. In Vitro Release of [3H] 5-Hydroxytryptamine from Fetal and

Maternal Brain by Drugs of Abuse. *Brain Res.* 78: 142-6 (1994).
Comparisons were made between cocaine, fenfluramine and MDMA in the foetal rats, in an effort to determine how these drugs may be damaging to the developing brain.

Krebs, K.M. and Geyer, M.A. Behavioral Characterization of Alpha-Ethyltryptamine, a Tryptamine Derivative with MDMA-like Properties in Rats. *Psychopharmacology* 113: 284-287 (1993).
There have been a number of anecdotal comparisons between MDMA and alpha-ethyl tryptamine (AET). These have supported the scheduling of the latter compound in the United States. In rat studies, AET appears to produce an MDMA-like profile of behavioural changes apparently related to serotonin release.

Kulmala, H.K., Boja, J.W. and Schechter, M.D. Behavioural Suppression Following 3,4- Methylenedioxymethamphetamine. *Life Sci.* 41: 1425-1429 (1987).
Rotation in rats was employed as an assay of the central dopaminergic activity of MDMA. At low doses it acts similarly to amphetamine, but at higher doses it appears to stimulate the dopamine receptor directly.

Lamb, R.J. and Griffiths, R.R. Self-injection of dl-3,4-Methylenedioxymethamphetamine in the Baboon. *Psychopharmacolgy* 91: 268-272 (1987).
In monkeys conditioned to the self-administration of cocaine, MDMA produced a similar but less potent response. A decrease in food intake was also reported.

LeSage, M., Clark, R. and Poling, A. MDMA and Memory: The Acute and Chronic Effects of MDMA in Pigeons Performing under a Delayed-matching-to-sample Procedure. *Psychopharmacol.* 110: 327-332 (1993).
The behaviour-disruptive effectiveness of MDMA in the conditioned behaviour of pigeons was found to be dose-dependent. Tolerance to the drug was observed, but there did not appear to be any long-lasting behavioural impairment.

Li, A., Marek, G., Vosmer, G. and Seiden, L. MDMA-induced Serotonin Depletion Potentiates the Psychomotor Stimulant Effects of MDMA on Rats Performing on the Differential-Reinforcement-of-Low-Rate (DRL) Schedule. *Society of Neurosciences Abstracts* 12: 169.7 (1986).
This is a study of Serotonin depletion and motor response. The long term depletion following both acute and chronic administration of MDMA to rats, increased activity and decreased serotonin suggests some inhibitory action of this neurotransmitter.

Li, A.A., Marek, G.J., Vosmer, G. and Seiden, L.S. Long-Term Central 5-HT Depletions Resulting from Repeated Administration of MDMA Enhances the Effects of Single Administration of MDMA on Schedule-Controlled Behaviour of Rats. *Pharmacol. Biochem. Behaviour* 33: 641-648 (1989).
Experimental rats showed an increased response in schedule-controlled behaviour studies to the effect of a single dose of MDMA if this dose was preceded by a regimen of chronic exposure to MDMA. This sensitisation was typical of amphetamine and other stimulants.

Lin, H.Q., Atrens, D.M., Christie, M.J., Jackson, D.M., McGregor I.S. Comparison of Conditioned Taste Aversions Produced by MDMA and d-Amphetamine. *Pharmacol. Biochem. Behav.* 46: 153-6 (1993).
In the experimental conditioned taste aversion paradigm, many drugs have been found to be effective. A direct comparison of MDMA with d-amphetamine showed both to be effective. The relative potency ratio was 4.5, similar to that observed in previously reported discrimination studies and for self-stimulation.

Lin, H.Q., McGregor, I.S., Atrens, D.M., Christie, M.J., Jackson, D.M. Contrasting Effects of Dopaminergic Blockade on MDMA and D-Amphetamine Conditioned Taste Aversions. *Pharmacol. Biochem. Behav.* 47: 369-374 (1994).
Employing a number of dopamine receptor ligands, a study has been made to determine the role of this transmitter in conditioned taste aversion (CTA) produced by MDMA and by d-amphetamine. It appears that dopamine plays different roles for these two drugs, and that D1 and D2 receptors independently mediate the aversive effect of amphetamine in CTA.

Marona-Lewicka, D. and Nichols, D.E. Behavioral Effects of the Highly Selective Serotonin Releasing Agent 5-Methoxy-6-methyl-2-aminoindan. *Eur. J. Pharmacol.* 258: 1-13 (1994).
Discrimination studies in rats were made to compare the title compound (MMAI) with MDMA, (+)-MBDB, (+)-amphetamine and LSD, in contrast to saline. All the compounds that mimicked MMAI were serotonin releasing agents.

Matthews, R.T., Champney, T.H. and Frye, G.D. Effects of (+/-)-Methylenedioxymethamphetamine (MDMA) on Brain Dopaminergic Activity in Rats. *Pharmacol. Biochem. Behav.* 33: 741-747 (1989).
High levels of MDMA in rats increased locomotor activity, and decreased brain dopamine turnover rate as determined by dihydroxyphenylacertic acid levels. There were some similarities to amphetamine exposure in the effects seen on dopamine neurons.

Mansbach, R.S., Braff, D.L. and Geyer, M.A. Prepulse Inhibition of the Acoustic Startle Response is Disrupted by N-Ethyl-3,4-methylenedioxyam-phetamine (MDEA) in the Rat. *Eur. J. Pharmacol.* 167: 49-55 (1989).
Both the optical isomers and the racemate of MDE, as well as racemic MDMA, were studied as to their effectiveness as prepulse inhibitors of the acoustic startle response, a measure of sensitivity to psychoactive drugs. The (+) isomer of MDE, and the racemate, and (less so) racemic MDMA were effective inhibitors, suggesting a psychostimulant component in their activities.

McKenna, D.J., Guan, X.-M. and Shulgin, A.T. 3,4-Methylenedioxyamphetamine (MDA) Analogues Exhibit Differential Effects on Synaptosomeal Release of ^{3}H-Dopamine and ^{3}H-5-Hydroxytryptamine. *Pharmacol. Biochem. Behav.* 38: 505-512 (1991).
The in vitro effectiveness of a number of MDA analogues on the release of serotonin and dopamine from synaptosomes was determined.

Miczek, K.A., Haney, M. Psychomotor Stimulant Effects of d-Amphetamine, MDMA and PCP: Aggressive and Schedule-controlled Behavior in Mice. *Psychopharmacol.* 115: 358-365 (1994).

The drugs MDMA, PCP and amphetamine were compared in a study with mice of conditioned performance and of aggressive behaviour. It was concluded that the observed properties common to all three pertained mostly to the disruption of organized behaviour patterns, but that different mechanisms may be invoked for the modulation of aggressive behaviour and conditioned performance at lower doses.

Miller, D.B. and O'Callaghan, J.P., Environment-, Drug- and Stress-induced Alteration in Body Temperature Affect the Neurotoxicity of Substituted Amphetamines in the C57Bl/6J Mouse. *J. Pharmacol. Exptl. Ther.* **270: 752-760 (1994).**
The increase in core temperature in the mouse, in response to the administration of the dextro-isomers of amphetamine, MDA and MDMA is apparently associated with the neurotoxicity produced, as measured by the levels of striatal dopamine and glial fibrillary acidic protein levels. Pretreatment with MK-801 to lower the core temperature, or simply decreasing the ambient temperature of the experimental environment, attenuated this induced neurotoxicity.

Nash, J. F. Ketanserin Pretreatment Attenuates MDMA-induced Dopamine Release in the Striatum as Measured by in vivo Microdialysis. *Life Sci.* **47: 2401-2408 (1990).**
The systemic administration of MDMA to freely moving rats produces a dose-dependent extracellular concentration of dopamine in the striatum. The effects of administering the serotonin antagonist, Ketanserin, are reported.

Nash, J.F. and Brodkin, J. Microdialysis Studies on 3,4-Methylenedioxymethamphetamine-induced Dopamine Release: Effect of Dopamine Uptake Inhibitors. *J. Pharmacol. Exptl. Ther.* **259: 820-825 (1991)**
The effects of both dopamine and serotonin uptake inhibitors on the MDMA induced increase in dopamine efflux were studied by microdialysis techniques. The dopaminergic effects are believed to be independent of those resulting from serotonin release.

Nash, J.F. and Nichols, D.E. Microdialysis Studies on 3,4-Methylenedioxyamphetamine and Structurally Related Analogues. *Eur. J. Pharmacol.* **200: 53-58 (1991).**
MDA and three analogues (MDMA, MDE and MBDB) were studied in the free-moving rat by microdialysis. The effects on dopamine were observed, and they did not correlate well with serotonin. Structural relationships are discussed.

Nash Jr., J.F., Meltzer, H.Y. and Gulesky, G.A. Elevation of Serum Prolactin and Corticosterone Concentrations in the Rat after the Administration of 3,4-Methylenedioxymethamphetamine. *J. Pharmacol. Exptl. Ther.* **245: 873-879 (1988).**
The effects of acute i.p. administrations of MDMA were seen as an elevation of prolactin and corticosterone in rats. The effects of the serotonin uptake inhibitor Fluoxetine and of p-chlorophenylalanine on MDMA-induced neuroendocrine responses are similar to those induced by p-chloroamphetamine.

Nencini, P., Woolverton, W.L. and Seidin, L.S. Enhancement of Morphine-induced Analgesia after Repeated Injections of Methylenedioxymethamphetamine. *Brain Res.* **457: 136-142 (1988).**
Chronic administration of MDMA to rats led to an enhancement of the analgesic effects of morphine administration. The changes in the serotonin and 5-hydroxytryptamine levels were confirmed.

Nichols, D.E., Hoffman, A.J., Oberlender, R.A., Jacob III, P. and Shulgin, A.T. Derivatives of 1-(1,3-Benzodioxol-5-yl-2-butanamine: Representatives of a Novel Therapeutic Class. *J. Med. Chem.* **29: 2009-2015 (1986).**
Animal discrimination studies (LSD versus saline) of the alpha-ethyl homologues of MDA and MDMA were performed. No generalization occurred with the N-methyl analogues of either group (MDMA and MBDB), and the latter compound was also found to be psychoactive but not hallucinogenic in man. It was found to be less euphoric than MDMA, but with the same sense of empathy and compassion. The term 'entactogen' is proposed for the class of drugs represented by MDMA and MBDB.

Oberlender, R. and Nichols, D.E. Drug Discrimination Studies with MDMA and Amphetamine. *Psychopharmacology.* **95: 71-76 (1988).**
Rats were trained to discriminate saline from either racemic MDMA or dextroamphetamine. The MDMA cue generalized to MDA and to all isomers of MDMA and MBDB, but not to LSD or DOM. The dextroamphetamine cue generalized to methamphetamine, but to none of the forms of either MDMA or MBDB. The 'S' isomers of both MDMA and MBDB were the more potent.

Oberlender, R. and Nichols, D.E. (+)-N-methyl-1-(1,3-benzodioxol-5-yl)-2-butanamine as a Discriminative Stimulus in Studies of 3,4-Methylenedioxymethamphetamine-Like Behavioural Activity. *J. Pharmacol. Exptl. Ther.* **255.:1098-1106 (1990).**
A number of compounds (including the racemate and the optical isomers of MBDB) were studied in rats trained to discriminate between (+)-MBDB and saline. There was generalization to both MDMA and MDA, but not to DOM, LSD or mescaline, nor for either amphetamine or methamphetamine. Several aminoindanes were also assayed.

O'Callaghan, J.P. and Miller, D.B. Neurotoxicity Profiles of Substituted Amphetamines in the C57Bl/6J Mouse. *J. Pharmacol. Exptl. Ther.* **270: 741-751 (1994).**
Whereas most of the rodent neurotoxicity has been studied in the rat, here are described studies in the mouse, with d-methamphetamine, d-DMA and d-MDMA. Astrogliosis, assessed by quantification of glial fibrillary acidic protein was used as the measure of neural damage. Fiber and terminal degeneration in the striatum was revealed by silver staining.

Park, W.K. and Azmitia, E.C. 5-HT, MDMA (Ecstasy), and Nimodipine Effects on ⁴⁵Ca-Uptake into Rat Brain Synaptosomes. *Ann. N.Y. Acad. Sci.* **635: 438-440 (1991).**
The uptake of calcium ion into the rat brain, both basal and K^+ stimulated, was increased by exposure to MDMA, a potent neuropathological drug of abuse. Interestingly, this same increase was seen with both serotonin and Fluoxetine.

Paulus, M.P. and Geyer, M.A. The Effects of MDMA and Other Methylenedioxy-substituted Phenylalkylamines on the Structure of Rat Locomotor Activity. *Neuropsychopharm.* **7: 15-31 (1992).**
The effects of acute s.c. injections of MDA, racemic, S(+) and R(-) MDMA, racemic MBDB, racemic MDEA, DOI, and methamphetamine were studied in the rat. Indirect 5-HT$_1$ effects

appear to contribute substantially to the differential changes in the amount and structure of motor behaviour induced by the phenylalkylamines. This conclusion may provide an encouraging rationale to develop postsynaptically effective 'entactogens', a potential new drug category as adjunctive psychotherapeutics.

Paulus, M.P., Geyer, M.A., Gold, L.H. and Mandell, A.J. Application of Entropy Measurements Derived from the Ergodic Theory of Dynamical Systems to Rat Locomotor Behaviour. *Proc. Natl. Acad*. 87: 723-727 (1990).

The observed activity of rats treated with MDMA followed paths with a different geometric distribution, than control animals treated with amphetamine.

Rempel, N.L., Callaway, C.W. and Geyer, M.A. Serotonin-1B Receptor Activation Mimics Behavioral Effects of Presynaptic Serotonin Release. *Neuropsychopharm*. 8: 201-11 (1993).

The locomotor hyperactivity induced by MDMA in rats appears to be due to the drug-induced release of presynaptic serotonin. It appears to act as indirect serotonin agonist, acting probably at the 5-HT$_{1B}$ receptor.

Rezvani, A.H., Garges, P.L., Miller, D.B. and Gordon, C.J. Attenuation of Alcohol Consumption by MDMA (Ecstasy) in Two Strains of Alcohol-preferring Rats. *Pharmacol. Biochem. Behav*. 43: 103-110 (1992)

The hypothesis that serotonin is involved in alcoholism has led to the design and carrying out of an experiment evaluating the action of MDMA, acutely and chronically, on the behaviour of alcohol-preferring rats. It was found to have an inhibitory action on alcohol preference, perhaps by the enhancement of serotonergic and/or dopaminergic systems in the CNS.

Ricaurte, G.A., Markowska, A.L., Wenk, G.L., Hatzidimitriou, G., Wlos, J. and Olton, D.S. 3,4-Methylenedioxymethamphetamine, Serotonin, and Memory. *J. Pharmacol. Exptl. Ther*. 266: 1097-1105 (1993).

A series of behavioural studies in the rat were conducted to assay the effect of serotonin neuron lesions on memory. MDMA was used for selective reduction of serotonin, and 5,7-dihydroxytryptamine for more extensive nerve damage than can be achieved with MDMA. The MDMA treated rats had no impairment of memory, but the more extensively damaged animals (involving both serotonin and norepinephrine systems) showed a disruption of recently aquired memory.

Robinson, T.E., Castaneda, E. and Whishaw, I.Q. Effects of Cortical Serotonin Depletion Induced by 3,4-Methylenedioxymethamphetamine (MDMA) on Behavior, Before and After Additional Cholinergic Blockade. *Neuropsychopharmacol*. 8: 77-85 (1993).

Studies in rats describe the effects of MDMA on a number of behavioural tests. The serotonergic denervation that resulted is not sufficient to produce marked and lasting behavioural deficits.

Romano, A.G. and Harvey, J.A. MDMA Enhances Associative and Nonassociative Learning in the Rabbit. *Pharmacol. Biochem. Behav*. 47: 289-93 (1994).

Conditioned response studies in rabbits have shown that MDMA, like MDA, enhances the learning process. The effects seen are not known for other psychedelic drugs, and may be unique to this chemical class.

Rosecrans, J.A. and Glennon, R.A. The Effect of MDA and MDMA ('Ecstasy') Isomers in Combination with Pirenpirone on Operant Responding in Mice. *Pharmacol. Biochem. Behav*. 28: 39-42 (1987). See also: *Soc. Neurosci. Abstr*. 13, Part 3, p. 905 (1987) No. 251.10.

The disruptive effects of the optical isomers of MDA and MDMA were studied for mice trained in a reinforcement schedule, both with and without pretreatment with Pirenpirone, a serotonin antagonist. Of the four isomers evaluated, only 'R'-MDA behaviour responses were attenuated by Pirenpirone.

Scallet, A.C., Lipe, G.W., Ali, S.F., Holson, R.R., Frith, C.H. and Slikker Jr., W. Neuropathological Evaluation by Combined Immunohistochemistry and Degeneration-Specific Methods: Application to Methylenedioxymethamphetamine. *Neurotoxicol*. 9: 529-539 (1988).

The combination of neurohistological and neurochemical evaluations suggests that the changes in serotonin levels following MDMA exposure in the rat is due to neural degeneration followed by axon loss, rather than a decrease in serotonin synthesis.

Sharkley, J., McBean, D.E. and Kelly, P.A.T. Alterations in Hippocampal Function Following Repeated Exposure to the Amphetamine Derivative Methylenedioxymethamphetamine ('Ecstasy'). *Psychopharmacology*. 105: 113-118 (1991).

Studies with labelled deoxyglucose radiography techniques demonstrate that the loss of serotonin innervation resulting from MDMA exposure in the rat resulted in lasting change in hippocampus function.

Schechter, M.D. Discriminative Profile of MDMA. *Pharmacol. Biochem. Behav*. 24: 1533-1537 (1986)

Rats trained to discriminate several psychoactive drugs (against saline) were challenged with MDMA. The findings show that MDMA may act both as a dopamine and a serotonin agonist. This property is related to its abuse potential.

Schechter, M.D. MDMA as a Discriminative Stimulus: Isomeric Comparisons. *Pharmacol. Biochem. Behav*. 27: 41-44 (1987).

Studies with rats trained to discriminate racemic MDMA from saline, showed generalization with both optical isomers of MDMA, with the 'S' isomer being more potent. The chronological observations paralleled the reported human responses.

Schechter, M.D. Advantages and Disadvantages of a Rapid Method to Train Drug Discrimination. *Pharmacol. Biochem. Behav*. 31: 239-242 (1988).

An exploration of training regimens was made for accelerating the development of discrimination protocols, using MDMA as a trial drug. The various findings are discussed.

Schechter, M.D. Effect of MDMA Neurotoxicity Upon Its Conditioned Place Preference and Discrimination. *Pharmacol. Biochem. Behav*. 38: 539-544 (1991).

Two behaviour patterns, conditioned place preference and discrimination, were used as measures of the neurotoxicity induced by MDMA in rats. Dose-dependent changes were observed. The possible involvement of both serotonin and dopamine neurons is discussed.

Schlemmer Jr., R.F., Montell, S.E. and Davis, J.M. *Fed. Proc*. 45: 1059 (1986).

The behavioural effects of MDMA have been studied in a primate colony, following multiple acute exposures. There was a decrease in activity, grooming, and food-searching, and an increase in staring. There was a disruption of social behaviour, that differed from the effects of other hallucinogens.

Schmidt, C.J. and Taylor, V.L. Reversal of the Acute Effect of 3,4- Methylenedioxymethamphetamine by 5-HT Uptake Inhibitors. *Eur. J. Pharmacol.* **181: 133-136 (1990).**

Re-uptake inhibitors of serotonin were administered at intervals following the administration of MDMA to rats. The inactivation of tryptophane hydroxylase activity that follows MDMA administration can be rapidly recovered by the early administration of such an inhibitor.

Schmidt, C.J., Fadayel, G.M., Sullivan, C.K. and Taylor, V.L. 5-HT$_2$- Receptors Exert a State-Dependent Regulation of Dopaminergic Function – Studies with MDL-100,907 and the Amphetamine Analogue, 3,4- Methylenedioxymeth-amphetamine. *Eur. J Pharmacol.* **223: 65-74 (1992).**

The role of serotonin in the stimulation of dopaminergic function as produced by MDMA, was studied by the use of a selective serotonin receptor antagonist. The interactions between these receptors and dopamine activation are discussed.

Schuldiner, S., Steiner-Mordoch, S., Yelin, R., Wall, S.C. and Rudnick, G. Amphetamine Derivatives Interact with Both Plasma Membrane and Secretory Vesicle Biogenic Amine Transporters. *Mol. Pharmacol.* **44: 1227-31 (1993).**

The interaction of fenfluramine, MDMA and p-chloroamphetamine (PCA) with brain transporter systems have been studied. The mechanisms of inhibition are discussed.

Snape, M.F., Colado, M.I., Green, A.R. Chlormethiazole and Dizocilpine Block the Behavioural, but not the Neurotoxic Effects of 5,7-Dihydroxytryptamine in Mice. *Pharmacology and Toxicology* **74: 40-2 (1994).**

Studies on the tryptamine neurotoxin 5,7-dihydroxytryptamine suggest that it is not implicated in the neurotoxicity of MDMA.

Spanos, L.J. and Yamamoto, B.K. Acute and Subchronic Effects of Methylenedioxymethamphetamine [(+/-) MDMA] on Locomotion and Serotonin Syndrome Behaviour in the Rat. *Pharmacol. Biochem. Behav.* **32: 835 (1989).**

The behavioural effects of MDMA on rats were observed. There was a 'serotonin syndrome' (low body posture, forepaw treading, headweaving) as well as autonomic signs (piloerection and salivation). These were dose-dependent, and were augmented with sub-acute exposure implying behavioural sensitisation.

Sprouse, J.S., Bradberry, C.W., Roth, R.H. and Aghajanian, G.K. MDMA 3,4- Methylenedioxymethamphetamine Inhibits the Firing of Dorsal Raphe Neurons in Brain Slices via Release of Serotonin. *Eur. J. Pharmacol.* **167: 375-383 (1989).**

Both optical isomers of MDMA as well as p-chloroamphetamine led to a reversible dose-dependant inhibition of serotonin cell firing. The (+) isomer was the more potent, and these effects were blocked by Fluoxetine. It was concluded that MDMA inhibits the raphe neurons through the release of endogenous serotonin.

Sprouse, J.S., Bradberry, C.W., Roth, R.H. and Aghajanian, G.K. 3,4- Methylenedioxymethamphetamine-induced Release of Serotonin and Inhibition of Dorsal Raphe Cell Firing:

Potentiation by L-Tryptophane. *Eur. J. Pharmacol* **178: 313-320 (1990).**

The relationship between L-tryptophan and the psychotropic and neurotoxic action of MDMA (in the rat) has been studied. A pretreatment with tryptophane appeared to increase the potency of MDMA, with the apparent release of serotonin.

Steele, T.D., Nichols, D.E. and Yim, G.K. MDMA Transiently Alters Biogenic Amines and Metabolites in Mouse Brain and Heart. *Pharmacol. Biochem. Behav.* **34: 223-227 (1989)**

The administration of MDMA to the mouse elevated the brain serotonin levels (rather than lowering them, as seen in the rat), but had little effect on the dopamine levels. The highest level depleted norepinephrine in both brain and heart. Mice appear to be resistant to the neurotoxic effects of MDMA.

Stone, D.M., Johnson, M., Hanson, G.R. and Gibb, J.W. Role of Endogenous Dopamine in the Central Serotonergic Deficits Induced by 3,4- Methylenedioxymethamphetamine. *J. Pharmacol. Exp. Ther.* **247: 79-87 (1988).**

The role of endogenous dopamine was examined in rats which had been subjected to both acute and chronic MDMA exposure. Potential mechanisms of dopamine-mediated toxicity are discussed.

Thompson, D.M., Winsauer, P.J. and Mastropaolo, J. Effects of Phencyclidine, Ketamine and MDMA on Complex Operant Behaviour in Monkeys. *Pharmacol. Biochem. Behav.* **26: 401-405 (1987).**

The loss of response to conditioned behaviour in monkeys was observed for the title drugs. All were effective i.m., with phencyclidine being the most potent, and MDMA being the least potent.

Winslow, J.T. and Insel, T.R. Serotonergic Modulation of Rat Pup Ultrasonic Vocal Development: Studies with 3,4-Methylenedioxymethamphetamine. *J. Pharmacol. Exp. Ther.* **254: 212-220 (1990).**

New-born rat pups voice a high frequency sound, an isolation call, when separated from their mothers. These calls were decreased in a dose-dependant manner following the administration of MDMA. Benzodiazepine and opioid agonists also show this response. A number of pharmacological challenges suggest that these effects may be related to serotonin changes.

Wotherspoon, G., Savery, D., Priestly, J.V., Rattray, M. Repeated Administration of MDMA Down-regulates Preprocholecystokinin mRNA Expression in Neurones of the Rat Substantia Nigra. *Mol. Brain Res.* **25: 34-40 (1994).**

Histochemical studies of rat brain tissue following MDMA administration, are reported.

Yau, J.L.W., Kelly, P., Sharkey, J., Seckl, J.R. Chronic 3,4-Methylenedioxymethamphetamine Administration Decreases Glucocorticoid and Mineralocorticoid Receptor, But Increases 5-Hydroxytryptamine (1C) Receptor Gene Expression in the Rat Hippocampus. *Neurosci.* **61: 31-40 (1994).**

The effects of short-term heavy dosings of MDMA on various receptors in several areas of the rat brain, were determined.

Yeh, S.Y. and Hsu, F-L. The Neurochemical and Stimulatory Effects of Putative Metabolites of 3,4-Methylenedioxyamphetamine and 3,4- Methylene-dioxymethamphetamine in Rats. *Pharmacol. Biochem. Behav.* **39: 787-790 (1991).**

Both MDA and MDMA, as well as their metabolites, were injected s.q. into rats. Brain analyses for serotonin and 5-hydroxyindoleacetic acid were conducted. Both MDA and MDMA appeared to have a stimulative action of the test animals.

Zacny, J.P., Virus, R.M. and Woolverton, W.L. Tolerance and Cross-Tolerance to 3,4- Methylenedioxymethamphetamine (MDMA), Methamphetamine and Methylenedioxyamphetamine. *Pharmacol. Biochem. Behav.* 35: 637-642 (1990).

Using milk intake as a titrant of behaviour, rats were evaluated for their behavioural responses to MDMA, methamphetamine (MA) and MDA. These animals were then treated chronically with either MDMA or saline, and the degree of tolerance determined by challenges with the three drugs. MDMA produced a tolerance for MDMA, there was some tolerance for these animals to MDA, depending on the schedule established, and there was no tolerance of these animals to the administration of MA.

Neurochemistry

Ali, S.F., Scallet, A.C., Holson, R.R., Newport, G.D. and Slikker Jr., W. Acute Administration of MDMA (Ecstasy): Neurochemical Changes Persist up to 120 Days in Rat Brain. *Soc. Neurosci. Abstr.* 13: 904 (1987).

Rats were given 40 mg/Kg MDMA twice daily for 4 days. After 120 days, some regions of the brain (frontal cortex, hippocampus) still had serotonin depletion. There was fighting behaviour noted between rats during the dosing and for up to two weeks following it.

Ali, S.F., Scallet, A.C., Newport, G.D., Lipe, G.W., Holson, R.R. and Slikker Jr., W. Persistent Neurochemical and Structural Changes in Rat Brain after Oral Administration of MDMA. *Res. Commun. Subst. Abuse.* 10: 225-236 (1989).

Rats were administered short-term intense levels of MDMA orally, and then assayed for neurological changes after a period of four months. Changes were seen in the levels of both serotonin and 5-hydroxyindoleacetic acid, and neurohistological changes in the brain step were observed.

Anon. Long-term Effects of 'Ecstasy': Study Finds Brain Cell Destruction. *NIDA Notes* 2 3: 7 (1987).

A short distillation of the present state of MDMA research in relationship to serotonin neurochemistry is presented.

Battaglia, G. and De Souza, E.B. Pharmacologic Profile of Amphetamine Derivatives at Various Brain Recognition Sites: Selective Effects on Serotonergic Systems. *NIDA Research Monograph Series.* 94: 240-258 (1989).

A review is presented of the affinities for a large number of substituted amphetamine derivatives for several serotonin receptors. An addition, a pharmacologic profile of binding affinities of MDMA at a number of recognition sites is tabulated.

Battaglia, G., Kuhar, M.J. and De Souza, E.B. MDA and MDMA (Ecstasy) Interactions with Brain Serotonin Receptors and Uptake Sites: In vitro Studies. *Soc. Neurosciences Abs.* 12: 336.4 (1986).

The receptor site uptake of the optical isomers, as well as the racemate, of both MDA and MDMA were measured by separate, selective labelling with appropriate radioligands. The relationships between the isomers depended on whether uptake sites or receptors were involved, and differed at different locations in the brain.

Battaglia, G., Sharkey, J., Kuhar, M.J. and De Souza, E.B. Neuroanatomic Specificity and Time Course of Alterations in Rat Brain Serotoninergic Pathways Induced by MDMA (3,4-Methylenedioxymethamphetamine): Assessment Using Quantitative Autoradiography. *Synapse* 8: 249-260 (1991).

A quantitative measure of the change in serotonin uptake sites as a consequence of MDMA exposure in rats was determined by the use of radio labelled Paroxetine. Changes as a function of time were noted in defined areas of the brain.

Battaglia, G., Yeh, S.Y. and De Souza, E.B. MDMA-Induced Neurotoxicity: Parameters of Degeneration and Recovery of Brain Serotonin Neurons. *Pharmacol. Biochem. Behav.* 29: 269-274 (1988).

A number of parameters were studied to define the nature of the neurotoxic effect on serotonin axons and terminals. Both the size and frequency of drug administration resulted in a dose-dependent response. Regeneration of these neurons was also time dependent, returning to control levels in 12 months. Pretreatment with a serotonin uptake blocker (Citalopram) prevented the neurodegenerative effects of MDMA. The rat and guinea-pig brains were affected, whereas the mouse brain was not.

Battaglia, G., Yeh, S.Y., O'Hearn, E., Molliver, M.E., Kuhar, M.J. and De Souza, E.B. 3,4- Methylenedioxymethamphetamine and 3,4- Methylenedioxyamphetamine Destroy Serotonin Terminals in Rat Brain: Quantification of Neurodegeneration by Measurements of [³H] Paroxetine-Labelled Serotonin Uptake Sites. *J. Pharmacol. Exptl. Ther.* 242: 911-916 (1987).

The effects of repeated administration of MDMA and MDA on the levels of rat brain monoamines and their metabolites are reported. Only the serotonin-related systems were found to be affected.

Battaglia, G., Zaczek, R. and De Souza, E. MDMA Effects in Brain: Pharmacologic Profile and Evidence of Neurotoxicity from Neurochemical and Autoradiographic Studies. *The Clinical, Pharmacological and Neurotoxicological Effects of the Drug MDMA.* Kluwer, New York. (1990) Ed: S.J. Peroutka.

A series of in vitro and in vivo studies of MDMA in rats has allowed a thorough mapping of the sites of MDMA-induced neurotoxicity.

Bird, M.P., Svendsen, C.N., Knapp, C., Hrbek, C.C., Bird, E.D. and Kornetsky, C. Evidence for Dopaminergic and Not Serotonergic Mediation of the Threshold Lowering Effects of MDMA on Rewarding Brain Stimulation. *Soc. Neurosci. Abstr.* 13 3: 1323 (1987) No. 365.13.

An effort was made to determine the rewarding aspect of MDMA by a combination of brain electrodes and specific neurotransmitter inhibitors. It is felt that MDMA reinforcing values may be mediated by the dopamine D_2 receptor rather than the serotonin 5-HT$_2$ receptor.

Bradberry, C.W. Microdialysis Assessment of the Impact of (+)3,4- Methylenedioxymethamphetamine, Cocaine, and Cocaethyline on Serotonergic Neurons. *Drug Devel. Res.* 33: 1-9 (1994).

The effects of MDMA were examined in brain slice preparation, with microdialysis, as to its impact on dorsal raphe serotonin neuronal firing. Serotonin release was inhibited by fluoretine, and augmented by tryptophan pretreatment.

Broening, H.W., Bacon, L., Slikker Jr., W. Age Modulates the Long-Term but Not the Acute Effects of the Serotonergic Neurotoxicant 3,4- Methylenedioxymethamphetamine. *J. Pharmacol. Exptl. Ther*. 271: 285-293 (1994).

Tissue levels of serotonin, levels of its metabolite 5-hydroxyindoleacetic acid, and populations of serotonin re-uptake sites were measured in the brains of rats exposed to MDMA at selected developmental ages. In general, there was increased changes observed when older animals were used.

Brodkin, J., Malyala, A. and Nash, J.F. Effect of Acute Monamine Depletion on 3,4- Methylenedioxymethamphet–amine-Induced Neurotoxicity. *Pharmacol. Biochem. Behav*. 45: 647-53 (1993).

The depletion of serotonin and dopamine induced by treatment of rats with acute exposure to high levels of MDMA has been explored. Several pharmacological probes have suggested that dopamine can play a major role in the neurotoxic effects of MDMA.

Callaway, C.W., Nichols, D.E., Paulus, M.P. and Geyer, M.A. Serotonin Release is Responsible for the Locomotor Hyperactivity in Rats Induced by Derivatives of Amphetamine Related to MDMA. *Serotonin: Molecular Biology, Receptors and Functional Effects*. Birkhauser Verlag, Basel. J.R. Fozard and P.R. Saxena, Eds. (1991).

In rats MDMA produces locomotor hyperactivity, but the spatial pattern of locomotion differs qualitatively from the pattern of exploration produced by other psychostimulants.

Callaway, C.W., Rempel, N., Peng, R.Y. and Geyer, M.A. Serotonin 5-HT1-Like Receptors Mediate Hyperactivity in Rats Induced by 3,4- Methylenedioxymethamphetamine. *Neuropsychopharm*. 7: 113-127 (1992).

This study was designed to evaluate the role of different serotonin (5-HT) receptor subtypes in mediating the effects of MDMA on a rat's exploration of a novel environment. This study indicates that S-MDMA produces a characteristic form of locomotor hyperactivity in rats that depends upon activation of $5-HT_1$-like receptors, possibly of the $5-HT_{1b}$ subtype.

Champney, T.H. and Matthews, R.T. Pineal Serotonin is Resistant to Depletion by Serotonergic Neurotoxins in Rats. *J. Pineal Res*. 11: 163-167 (1991).

A comparison between MDMA and p-chloroamphetamine (pCA) has been made in the rat with a view to neurotoxicity. Both compounds reduced serotonin levels in several brain areas, but neither affected the neurotransmitter levels in the pineal. This gland does not appear to have the serotonin re-uptake system that is thought to be necessary for MDMA or pCA induced neurotoxicity.

Champney, T.H., Golden, P.T. and Matthews, R.T. Reduction of Hypothalamic Serotonin Levels after Acute MDMA Administration. *Soc. Neurosciences Absts*. 12: 101.6 (1986).

Cortical, hypothalamic, and pineal levels of catecholamines, serotonin and 5-HIAA were determined shortly following an acute exposure of rats to each of several doses of MDMA. Dose-dependent decreases of serotonin and 5-HIAA were noted in some but not other areas of the brain. The catecholamine levels were unchanged.

Colado, M.J., Green, A.R., A Study of the Mechanism of MDMA

(Ecstasy)-Induced Neurotoxicity of 5-HT Neurons Using Chlormethiazole, Dizocilpine and Other Protective Compounds. *British J. of Pharmacology*.111: 131-136 (1994).

The effects of several neuroprotective compounds (chlormethiazole and dizocilpine) as well as gamma-butyrolactone, ondansetron and phenobarbitone on the neurotoxic effects of MDMA in rats. Depending upon the dosage regimen. there was some protection provided, but in general the changes were insignificant.

Commins, D.L., Vosmer, G., Virus, R.M., Woolverton, C.R., Schuster, C.R. and Seiden, L.S. Biochemical and Histological Evidence that Methylenedioxymethamphetamine (MDMA) is Toxic to Neurons in Rat Brain. *J. Pharmacol. Exptl. Ther*. 241: 338-345 (1987).

MDMA was administered chronically to rats and guinea pigs , and the neurotransmitter levels were assayed in several portions of the brain. These levels were found to be related to dosage, and to the extent of exposure. Anatomical morbidity is carefully described.

Defrese, G.D.R. *(+/-)-3,4-Methylenedioxymethamphetamine (MDMA): Extending the Debate Regarding Clinical Implications of its Neurotoxicity*. Unpublished manuscript, Department of Pharmacology, U.C. Davis, (1990).

An experimental approach is proposed, using experimental animals, to evaluate the toxicological risks to man that might result from the reintroduction of MDMA into clinical practice.

De Souza, E.B. and Battaglia, G. Effects of MDMA and MDA on Brain Serotonin Neurons: Evidence from Neurochemical and Autoradiographic Studies. *NIDA Research Monograph Series*. 94: 196-222 (1989).

A series of studies with both MDMA and MDA demonstrate dose-dependent changes in the brain serotonin neurons, which can blocked by pretreatment with a serotonin uptake blocker.

DeSouza, E.B., Battaglia, G., Shu, Y.Y. and Kuhar, M.J. In Vitro and In Vivo Effects of MDA and MDMA (Ecstasy) on Brain Receptors and Uptake Sites: Evidence for Selective Neurotoxic Actions on Serotonin Terminals. *Amer. Coll. of Neuropsychopharm*. p. 207 (Dec. 8-12, 1986).

MDA and MDMA both showed a relatively high affinity for both $5-HT_2$ serotoninergic and alpha-2 adrenergic brain receptors, but low affinities for $5-HT_1$, and for the alpha-1 and beta adrenergic receptors, as well as for dopamine, muscarinic, and opiate receptors. Chronic administration of either drug decreases the number of $5-HT_2$ receptors in various brain locations.

Dornan, W.A., Katz, J.L. and Ricaurte, G.A. The Effects of Repeated Administration of MDMA on the Expression of Sexual Behaviour in the Male Rat. *Pharmacol. Biochem. Behav*. 39: 813-816 (1991).

The repeated s.c administration of MDMA to rats produced a disruption of copulatory behaviour. These effects disappeared within a week.

Farfel, G.M., Vosmer, G.L. and Seiden, L.S. The N-Methyl-D-Aspartate Antagonist MK-801 Protects Against Serotonin Depletions Induced by Methamphetamine, 3,4-Methylenedioxymethamphetamine and p-Chloramphetamine. *Brain Res*. 595: 121-127 (1992).

The NMDA receptor antagonist MK-801 attenuates the decrease in serotonin concentration brought about by MDMA and two other amphetamine derivatives, in rats. Changes in the serotonin metabolite 5-hydroxyindoleacetic acid concentrations were similar to the serotonin in changes observed.

Farfel, G.M. and Seiden, L.S. Role of Hypothermia in the Mechanism of Protection Against Serotonergic Toxicity. 1. Experiments Using 3,4-Methylenedioxymethamphetamine, Dizocilpine, CGS 19755 and NBQX. *J. Pharmacol. Exptl. Ther.* 272: 860-867 (1995).

The interactions of these several title drugs were studied as to their relationships as seen with changes in body temperature and neurotoxicity.

Finnigan, K.T., Ricaurte, G.A., Ritchie, L.D., Irwin, I., Peroutka, S.J. and Langston, J.W. Orally Administered MDMA Causes a Long-term Depletion of Serotonin in Rat Brain. *Brain Res.* 447: 141-144 (1988).

The oral and sub-cutaneous routes of MDMA toxicity to rat serotonergic neurons are studied. Both routes lead to a dose dependent serotonin depletion.

Finnegan, K.T., Skratt, J.J., Irwin, I. and Langston, J.W. The N-Methyl-D-aspartate (NMDA) Receptor Antagonist, Dextrorphan, Prevents the Neurotoxic Effects of 3,4-Methylenedioxymethamphetamine (MDMA) in Rats. *Neurosci. Letters.* 105: 300-306 (1990).

In in vivo rat studies with various levels of MDMA and dextrorphan, the latter drug, a NMDA antagonist, completely prevented the serotonin-depleting action of MDMA.

Finnegan, K.T., Calder, L., Clikeman, J., Wei, S. and Karler, R. Effects of L-type Calcium Channel Antagonists on the Serotonin-depleting Actions of MDMA in Rats. *Brain Res.* 603: 134-138 (1993).

Of several calcium channel blockers effective at increasing the convulsion threshold induced by NMDA, only flunarizine blocked the long-term serotonin depleting effects of MDMA. It is suggested that calcium channels are not involved in the neurotoxicity of MDMA.

Gaylor, D.W. and Slikker Jr, W. Risk Assessment for Neurotoxic Effects. *Neurotoxicology.* 11: 211-218 (1990).

A mathematical basis is presented for the estimation of risk as a function of dose, with drugs that are neurotoxic. An illustration is given for MDMA, based on rat and monkey data.

Gehlert, D.R. and Schmidt, C.J. Acute Administration of Methylenedioxymethamphetamine (MDMA) Results in a Persistent and Selective Increase in 5-HT$_1$ Receptor Binding in Rat Brain. *Pharmacologist.* 29: ABS-44 (1987).

Acute administration of MDMA in the rat showed an increase in serotonin binding in 24 hours. This occurred in several parts of the brain.

Gibb, J.W., Johnson, M., Stone, D.M. and Hanson, G.R. Mechanisms Mediating Biogenic Amine Deficits Induced by Amphetamine and its Congeners. *NIDA Research Monograph.* 136: 226-241 (1993).

A large number of amphetamine-like derivatives, including MDMA, have been compared for their capacity for causing neurochemical deficits, in both the serotonin and the dopamine systems. Neurotoxicity is inferred in most cases as there is a long-term persistence of change.

Glennon, R.A., Titeler, M., Lyon, R.A. and Youssif, M. MDMA ('Ecstasy'): Drug Discrimination and Brain Binding Properties. *Soc. Neurosciences Abstracts.* 12: 250.11 (1986).

In rats treated chronically with MDMA (trained to discriminate racemic MDMA from saline), radioligand binding studies were conducted with both serotonin and dopamine sites. The Ki values for both 5-HT$_1$ and 5-HT$_2$ receptors were highest for the 'S' isomers of MDMA and MDA, with the racemate lower, and the 'R' isomer yet lower. There was no particular affinity for the dopamine receptors studied.

Gold, L.H., Hubner, C.B. and Koob, G.F. The Role of Mesolimbic Dopamine in the Stimulant Action of MDMA. *Soc. Neurosci. Abstr.*, 13, 3: 833 (1987) No. 234.13.

The administration of MDMA to rats may involve (like amphetamine) the release of dopamine. Test animals with lesions induced by 6-hydroxydopamine showed less motor activity in response to MDMA than control animals.

Gold, L.H., Hubner, C.B. and Koob, G.F. A Role for the Mesolimbic Dopamine System in the Psychostimulant Actions of MDMA. *Psychopharmacology* 99: 40-47 (1989).

MDMA was evaluated in rats as a stimulant. Lesions induced with 6-hydroxydopamine modified the amphetamine-like responses seen, suggesting that the drug's action may involve the presynaptic release of dopamine in the region of the nucleus accumbens.

Gollamudi, R., Ali, S.F., Lipe, G., Newport, G., Webb, P., Lopez, M., Leakey, J.E.A., Kolta, M. and Slikker Jr., W. Influence of Inducers and Inhibitors on the Metabolism in vitro and Neurochemical Effects in vivo of MDMA. *Neurotox.* 10: 455-466 (1989).

A number of experiments were conducted on rats, with the optical isomers of MDMA. The metabolic formation of MDA by N-demethylation, in vitro, was greater for the 'S' isomer in the female than the male. This effect was lost with prior phenobarbital induction, and may be related to P-450 isozymes. In in vivo studies, either isomer appeared to be equally effective in depleting serotonin, but pretreatment studies suggest that an active metabolite other than MDA is formed.

Gu, X.F., Azmitia, E.C. Integrative Transporter-Mediated Release from Cytoplasmic and Vesicular 5-Hydroxytryptamine Stores in Cultured Neurons. *Eur. J. Pharmacol.* 235: 51-7 (1993).

Both MDMA and PCA (p-chloroamphetamine) were found to release serotonin in microculture studies with foetal neurons. The influence of fluoxetine, deprenyl, reserpine and nimodipine on this release, were measured.

Hanson, G.R., Sonsalla, P., Letter, A., Merchant, K.M., Johnson, M., Bush, L. and Gibb, J.W. Effects of Amphetamine Analogues on Central Nervous System Neuropeptide Systems. *NIDA Research Monograph Series.* 94: 259-269 (1989).

The effects of a number of substituted amphetamines on polypeptides associated with extrapyrimidal structures, have been observed. Both MDA and MDMA are included, and a discussion is presented of their possible contribution to both motor and mood changes related to drug-exposure.

Hashimoto, K. and Goromaru, T. Reduction of [^{3}H] 6-Nitroquipazine-labelled 5-Hydroxytrypatmine Uptake Sites in Rat Brain by 3,4-Methylenedioxymethamphetamine. *Fund. Clin. Pharmacol.* 4: 635-641 (1990).

The administration of the selective serotonin uptake inhibitor 6-

nitroquipazine prevented the MDMA-induced reduction of serotonin and 5-hydroxyindoleacetic acid in rat brain. Tritiated 6-nitroquipazine was used as a probe for determining the receptor sites that recognized by MDMA.

Hashimoto, K. and Goromaru, T. Reduction of in vivo Binding of [³H]Paroxetine in Mouse Brain by 3,4-Methylenedioxymethamphetamine. *Neuropharmacol.* **29: 633-639 (1990)**

Pretreatment of a mouse with MDMA significantly modifies the radioactivity distribution of tritiated Paroxetine, a potent serotonin re-uptake inhibitor. The relative decrease of binding to hypothalimus and to cerebral cortex appears to be dose dependent.

Hashimoto, K. and Goromaru, T. Study of 3,4-Methylenedioxymethamphetamine-Induced Neurotoxicity in Rat Brain Using Specific In Vivo Binding of [³H] 6-Nitroquipazine. *Res Comm. Subst. Abuse* **13: 191-201 (1992).**

MDMA-induced neurotoxicity in the rat was studied employing 6-nitroquipazine binding. This radioligand appears to be well suited for studying neuropathology and neurochemical changes associated with brain serotonin.

Hashimoto, K., Maeda, H. and Goromaru, T. Antagonism of 3,4-Methylenedioxymethamphetamine-induced Neurotoxicity in Rat Brain by 1-Piperonylpiperazine. *Eur. J. Pharmacol. — Envir. Toxicol. and Pharmacol. Section,* **228: 171-174 (1992).**

Several serotonin uptake inhibitors were evaluated for their effects on MDMA-induced neurotoxicity. 6-Nitroquipazine, Paroxetine and 1-piperonylpiperazine were effective, but the immediate homologue of MDMA (N,alpha-dimethylpiperonylamine) was not.

Hekmatpanah, C.R., McKenna, D.J. and Peroutka, S.J. Reserpine does not Prevent 3,4-Methylenedioxyamphetamine-induced Neurotoxicity in the Rat. *Neurosci. Letters* **(in press) 1989.**

The administration of reserpine to rats, which reduces the brain monoamine stores in rats, did not prevent the degeneration of serotoninergic nerve terminals.

Hewitt, K.E. and Green, A.R. Chlormethiazole, Dizocilpine and Haloperidol Prevent the Degeneration of Serotoninergic Nerve Terminals Induced by the Administration of MDMA (Ecstasy) to Rats. *Neuropharmacol.* **33: 1589-1595 (1994).**

(no abstract available)

Hiramatsu, M. and Cho, A.K. Enantiomeric Differences in the Effects of 3,4- Methylenedioxymethamphetamine on Extracellular Monoamines and Metabolites in the Striatum of Freely-Moving Rats: An in vivo Microdialysis Study, *Neuropharmacol.* **29: 269-275 (1990).**

The effects of para-chloramphetamine and of the optical isomers of MDMA on the extracellular levels of the metabolites of dopamine and of serotonin were determined by dialysis. The level of dopamine was increased, and that of its metabolites decreased, with p-CPA, (+) MDMA and (-) MDMA showing decreased potency. The serotonin metabolite 5-HIAA was also decreased, but there was no difference between the two optical isomers of MDMA in the production of this effect.

Hoffman, B.J., Mezey, E. and Brownstein, M.J. Cloning of a Serotonin Transporter Affected by Antidepressants. *Science,* **254: 579-580 (1991).**

A DNA clone for a serotonin transporter has been isolated. The cell uptake of the complimentary DNA resembles platelet serotonin uptake, and it is sensitive to antidepressants, amphetamine derivatives and cocaine. MDMA has an exceptionally high affinity.

Insel, T.R., Battaglia, G., Johannessen, J.N., Marra, S. and De Souza, E.B. 3,4-Methylenedioxymethamphetamine Selectively Destroys Brain Serotonin Terminals in Rhesus Monkeys. *J. Pharmacol. Exptl. Ther.* **249: 713-720 (1989).**

In rhesus monkeys, the subacute administration of MDMA decreased both serotonin and 5-HIAA levels. At high levels there was also a decrease in the number of serotonin uptake sites (implying serotonin terminal destruction). There appears to be a considerable specificity as to brain region where these effects are expressed.

Jensen, K.F., Olin, J., Haykal-Coates, N., O'Callaghan, J., Miller, D.B. and de Olmos, J.S. Mapping Toxicant-Induced Nervous System Damage With Cupric Silver Stain: A Quantitative Analysis of Neural Degeneration Induced by 3,4-Methylenedioxymethamphetamine. *NIDA Research Monograph.* **136: 133-154 (1993).**

An argument is made for the quantitative potential that could be realized from the cupric silver staining of degenerating neurons. This technique was applied to rats that had been treated with MDMA and a dose-response curve of neural degeneration was obtained.

Johnson, M.P. and Nichols, D.E. Neurotoxin Effects of the Alpha-Ethyl Homologue of MDMA Following Subacute Administration. *Pharmacol. Biochem. Behav.* **33: 105-108 (1989).**

MBDB, the alpha-ethyl homologue of MDMA, was compared with MDMA in rats, as to potential neurotoxicity. There was a similar decrease in the number of observed serotonin binding sites but, unlike MDMA, there were no significant decreases in dopamine levels observed.

Johnson, M.P., and Nichols, D.E. Combined Administration of a Non-Neurotoxic 3,4-Methylenedioxymethamphetamine Analogue with Amphetamine Produces Serotonin Neurotoxicity in Rats. *Neuropharmacol.* **30: 819-822 (1991).**

Two drugs have been studied in combination, in the rat. MMAI (5-methoxy-6-methyl-2-aminoindan) and S-(+)-amphetamine by themselves do not change any serotonin parameters in the rat. However, in combination, there was a central serotonin neurotoxicity induced. It appears that dopamine release plays a critical role in the serotonin neurotoxicity expression of substituted amphetamine derivatives.

Johnson, M.P., Conarty, P.F. and Nichols, D.E. [3H]Monoamine Releasing and Uptake Inhibition Properties of 3,4-Methylenedioxymethamphetamine and p-Chloroamphetamine Analogues. *Eur. J. Pharmacol.* **200: 9-16 (1991).**

A number of analogues of MDMA and of PCA were studied to determine their effectiveness in inhibiting the uptake of serotonin into synaptosomes, with or without pretreatment with reserpine. A valid relationship between the serotonin neurotoxic potential and the dopamine releasing ability of these compounds was noted.

Johnson, M.P., Hoffman, A.J. and Nichols, D.E. Effects of the Enantiomers of MDA, MDMA, and Related Analogues on [3H]Serotonin and [3H]Dopamine Release from Superfused Rat Brain Slices. *Eur. J. Pharmacol.* **132: 269-276 (1986).**

The study of a series of MDA homologues (MDA, MDMA, MBDB) showed a dramatic dependence between chain length and dopamine release. The longer the chain, the less the release. It is concluded that dopamine release plays a minor role in the human activity of these compounds.

Johnson, M.P., Huang, X. and Nichols, D.E. Serotonin Neurotoxicity in Rats After Combined Treatment with a Dopaminergic Agent Followed by a Nonneurotoxic 3,4-Methylenedioxymethamphetamine (MDMA) Analogue. *Pharmacol. Biochem. Beh.* 40: 915-922 (1991).

Further evidence has been found linking dopamine to the long-term serotonergic neurotoxic effects of certain substituted amphetamines such as MDMA. Studies were conducted with MDAI (5,6-methylenedioxy-2-aminoindan (itself with a low neurotoxic liability) with several MAO inhibitors (clorgyline and deprenyl), with a dopamine uptake inhibitor led to no long term changes. Pretreatment with a dopamine releaser (S-amphetamine) did produce changes, however.

Johnson, M.P., Huang, X., Oberlender, R., Nash, J.F. and Nichols, D.E. Behavioural, Biochemical and Neurotoxicological Actions of the alpha-Ethyl Homologue of p-Chloroamphetamine. *Eur. J. Pharmacol.* 191: 1-10 (1990).

The alpha-ethyl homologue of PCA was studied. The relationship of this compound (CAB) to PCA is that of the non-dopamine releasing MBDB (N-methyl-1-(1,3-benzodioxol-5-yl)-2-butanamine) to MDMA. Although CAB produces less disruption of the dopamine system, its effects on the serotonin system is similar to that of PCA.

Johnson, M., Elayan, I., Hanson, G.R., Foltz, R.L., Gibbs, J.W. and Lim, H.K. Effects of 3,4- Dihydroxymethamphetamine and 2,4,5-Trihydroxymethamphetamine, Two Metabolites of 3,4- Methylenedioxymethamphetamine, on Central Serotonergic and Dopaminergic Systems. *J. Pharmacol. Exptl. Ther.* 261: 447-453 (1992).

Two metabolites of MDMA have been evaluated as to their contribution to neurotoxicity. The metabolite, 2,4,5-trihydroxymethamphetamine is toxic to both serotonin and dopamine nerve terminals, although it does not appear to explain the neurotoxic effects of MDMA.

Johnson, M., Hanson, G.R. and Gibb, J.W. Effects of Dopaminergic and Serotonergic Receptor Blockade on Neurochemical Changes Induced by Acute Administration of Methamphetamine and 3,4- Methylenedioxymethamphetamine. *Neuropharmacol.* 27: 1089-1096 (1988).

By the use of specific neurorecptor ligands, the mechanisms of acute and long-term changes in the CNS from methamphetamine and MDMA exposure, have been investigated.

Johnson, M., Letter, A.A., Merchant, K., Hanson, G.R. and Gibb, J.W. Effects of 3,4- Methylenedioxyamphetamine and 3,4- Methylenedioxymethamphetamine Isomers on Central Serotonergic, Dopaminergic and Nigral Neurotensin Systems of the Rat. *J. Pharmacol. Exptl. Ther.* 244: 977-982 (1988).

The difference of the isomers of MDA and MDMA in their ability to induce neurotransmitter changes and neurotensin immunoreactivity are reported. In general, the d-isomers of each were the more potent in affecting neurochemical systems.

Johnson, M., Stone, D.M., Bush, L.G., Hanson, G.R. and Gibb, J.W. Glucocorticoid and 3,4- Methylenedioxymethamphetamine (MDMA)-induced Neurotoxicity. *Eur. J. Pharmacol.* 161: 181 (1989).

A series of studies of the role of the glucocorticoids in the serotonin neurotoxicity of MDMA in rats has indicated some involvement in the hippocampal area.

Kalix, P. A Comparison of the Effects of Some Phenethylamines on the Release of Radioactivity from Isolated Rat Caudate Nucleus Prelabelled with ³H-Dopamine. *Arzneim. Forsch.* 36: 1019-1021 (1986).

A number of phenethylamines were found to be able to release radioactive dopamine from prelabelled caudate nuclei. MDMA was not spectacular. The simplest unsubstituted amphetamine derivatives were the most effective.

Kalix, P., Yousif, M.Y. and Glennon, R.A. Differential Effects of the Enantiomers of Methylenedioxymethamphetamine (MDMA) on the Release of Radioactivity from (³H)Dopamine-Prelabeled Rat Striatum. *Res. Commun. Subst. Abuse* 9: 45-52 (1988).

The S-isomer of MDMA (the more effective stimulant) is more effective than the R-isomer in releasing tritiated dopamine from rat striatum. It is about one sixth the potency of S-methamphetamine.

Kelland, M.D., Freeman, A.S. and Chiodo, L.A. (+/-)-3,4-Methylenedioxymethamphetamine- induced Changes in the Basal Activity and Pharmacological Responsiveness of Nigrostriatal Dopamine Neurons. *Eur. J. Pharmacol.* 169: 11-21 (1989).

Studies of acute exposure of rats to MDMA showed an inhibition of the firing of dopamine neurons, and this effect is diminished following the depletion of either serotonin or dopamine. MDMA appears to exert direct functional effects on the nigrostriatal dopamine system.

Kleven, M.S., Woolverton, W.L. and Seiden, L.S. Evidence that both Intragastric and Subcutaneous Administration of Methylenedioxmethamphetamine (MDMA) Produce Serotonin Neurotoxicity in Rhesus Monkeys. *Brain Res.* 488: 121-125 (1989).

Subacute administration of MDMA to rhesus monkeys by both intragastric and subcutaneous routes was found to lead to depletion of both serotonin and 5-HIAA in various brain regions. Serotonin uptake sites were depleted following the oral route but not the subcutaneous route.

Kopajtic, T., Battaglia, G. and De Souza, E.B. A Pharmacologic Profile of MDA and MDMA on Brain Receptors and Uptake Sites. *Soc. Neurosciences Abstrts.* 12: 336.1 (1986).

Both MDA and MDMA were studied at various brain recognition sites using radioligand binding techniques. The findings suggest that these drugs may express their effects at serotonin receptors or uptake sites and/or alpha-2 adrenergic receptors.

Logan, B.J., Laverty, R., Sanderson, W.D. and Yee, Y.B. Differences Between Rats and Mice in MDMA (Methylenedioxmethamphetamine) Neurotoxicity. *Eur. J. Pharmacol.* 152: 227-234 (1988).

A single large administration of MDMA to the rat or the mouse caused only transient changes in serotonin, norepinephrine and dopamine levels (and those of their metabolites). Repeated administrations were required to establish long-lasting changes in the rat; the mouse remained relatively insensitive. It appears that the both the nature and the degree of neurotoxicity with MDMA is species-specific.

Lowe, M.T., Nash Jr., J.F. and Meltzer, H.Y. Selective Reduction of Striatal Type-II Glucocorticoid Receptors in Rats by 3,4-Methylenedioxymethamphetamine (MDMA). *Eur. J. Pharmacol.* 163: 157-161 (1989).

A single large s.c. dose of MDMA to rats reduced, in addition to brain serotonin and 5-HIAA levels, the glucocorticoid levels in the striatum. No differences in the corticosterone levels were noted, however, suggesting that it may not play a role in the receptor reduction.

Lyon, R.A., Glennon, R.A. and Titeler, M. 3,4-Methylenedioxymethamphetamine (MDMA): Stereoselective Interactions at Brain 5-HT1 and 5-HT$_2$ Receptors. *Psychopharmacology* 88: 525-526 (1986).

The assay of the optical isomers of MDA and MDMA with isolated receptors of rat brains, suggested that MDMA does not work primarily through direct interaction with serotonin receptors.

McCann, U.D., Ricaurte, G.A., Strategies for Detecting Subclinical Monoamine Depletions in Humans. *NIDA Research Monograph* 136: 53-60, discussion 60-2 (1993).

A discussion is presented of the various strategies that might be employed to evaluate the neurotoxicity realities of MDMA in man.

Millan, M.J. and Colpaert, F.C. Methylenedioxymethamphetamine Induces Spontaneous Tail-flicks in the Rat via 5-HT$_{1a}$ Receptors. *Eur. J. Pharmacol.* 193: 145-152 (1991).

MDMA, but not amphetamine, induced dose-dependent tail-flicks in restrained rats. These effects were blocked by serotonin uptake inhibitors, implicating these receptors in this response.

Mokler, D.J., Robinson, S.E. and Rosecrans, J.A. Differential Depletion of Brain 5-Hydroxytryptamine (5-HT) by (+/-) 3,4-Methylenedioxymethamphetamine (MDMA). *Pharmacologist* 29: ABS-273 (1987).

The sensitivity of specific brain areas for the 5-HT depleting effects of MDMA may relate to the metabolic activity of 5-HT neurones in that region.

Mokler, D.J., Robinson, S.E. and Rosecrans, J.A. (+/-) 3,4-Methylenedioxymethamphetamine (MDMA) Produces Long-term Reductions in Brain 5-Hydroxytryptamine in Rats. *Eur. J. Pharmacol.* 138: 265-268 (1987).

Following chronic administration of MDMA to rats, both serotonin and 5-HIAA became depleted in the brain. It is suggested that MDMA can function as a neurotoxin.

Mokler, D.J., Robinson, S.E. and Rosecrans, J.A. A Comparison of the Effects of Repeated Doses of MDMA ('Ecstasy') on Biogenic Amine Levels in Adult and Neonate Rats. *Soc. Neurosci. Abstr.* 13. 251.9: 905 (1987).

MDMA was given to both adult and neonate rats in 10-40 mg/Kg doses over several days. The serotonin levels were decreased and the dopamine levels were significantly increased.

Molliver, M.E. Serotonergic Neural Systems: What Their

Anatomic Organization Tells Us about Function. *J. Clinical Psychopharm.* 7: 3S-23S (1987).

A review of the organization of the serotonin nervous system is presented. The findings associated with the neurotoxic effects of MDMA are used as instructive tools, and speculation is extended as to the role of these neurons in the generation of the affective state.

Molliver, M.E., Mamounas, L.A. and Wilson, M.A. Effects of Neurotoxic Amphetamines on Serotonergic Neurons: Immunocytochemical Studies. *NIDA Research Monograph Series.* 94: 270-305 (1989).

A highly detailed cytological mapping of the serotonin related structures in the rat brain, is presented. An immunocytological study, with anto-serotonin antibodies, has been made with several substituted amphetamines, including MDA and MDMA. The axon bodies are severely damaged, but the raphe cell bodies are spared. Some primate studies are discussed.

Molliver, M.E., O'Hearn, E., Battaglia, G. and De Souza, E.B. Direct Intracerebral Administration of MDA and MDMA Does Not Produce Serotonin Neurotoxicity. *Soc. Neurosciences Abstrts.* 12: 336.3 (1986).

The microinjection of either MDA or MDMA directly into the cerebral cortex resulted in no detectable cytotoxicity. This suggests that the neurotoxicity of both compounds may be due to some metabolite formed peripherally.

Monti, J.A., Beaton, J.M., Benington, F., Morin, R.D. and Christian, S.T. MDMA and MBDB Potentiate Phorbol Ester-Stimulated Catecholamine Release from PC-12 Cells. *Soc. Neurosci. Abstrt.* November: 13-18, 1988.

The 'S' isomer of both MDMA and MBDB are potent in stimulating catechol release from PC-12 cells. The norepinephrin and dopamine release was increased in the presence of phorbol dibenzoate. It is suggested that this release may be mediated by protein kinase-C.

Nader, M.A., Hoffmann, S.M. and Barrett, J.E. Behavioural Effects of (+/-) 3,4- Methylenedioxyamphetamine (MDA) and (+/-) 3,4-Methylenedioxymethamphetamine (MDMA) in the Pigeon: Interactions with Noradrenergic and Serotoninergic Systems. *Psychopharmacology* 98: 183-188 (1989).

MDA, MDMA and MDE. were studied in a conditioned behaviour involving pigeons. MDA was the most potent of the three drugs. The use of serotonin and dopamine antagonists suggested that the actions of MDA and MDMA are mediated by different neurotransmitter systems.

Nash, J.F. and Yamamoto, B.K. Methamphetamine Neurotoxicity and Striatal Glutamate Release: Comparison to 3,4- Methylenedioxymethamphet- amine. *Brain Res.* 581: 237-243 (1992).

The neurotoxicity of methamphetamine and MDMA were compared by measuring the extracellular concentrations of several compounds by microdialysis in freely moving rats. The long term dopamine neurotoxicity from repeated methamphetamine administration is mediated, in part, by a delayed increase in extracellular glutamate. Repeated MDMA administration, at a dose that produced a long-term depletion of serotonin, had no effect on glutamate release.

Nash, J.F., Meltzer, H.Y. and Gudelsky, G.A. Effect of 3,4-Methylenedioxymethamphetamine on 3,4-Dihydroxyphenylalanine Accumulation in the Striatum and Nucleus Accumbers. *J. Neurochem*. 34: 1062-1067 (1990).

The effect of MDMA on dopamine synthesis in rat brain was estimated by measuring DOPA accumulation following pretreatment with a decarboxylase inhibitor. It is suggested that dopamine plays a role in the serotonin depletion produced by MDMA.

Nash, J.F., Meltzer, H.Y. and Lowy, M.T. The Effect of Adrenalectomy on MDMA-Induced Dopamine Release in the Striatum as Measured by in vivo Microdialysis and Depletion of Serotonin. *Res. Commun. Subst. Abuse*. 13: 177-190 (1992).

The interaction of MDMA and corticosterone in neurotransmitter depletion was studied in adrenalectomized rats. There does not seem to be any significant role for corticosterone in the MDMA-induced depletion of serotonin and 5-hydroxyindoleacetic acid.

Nash, J.F., Roth, B.L., Brodkin, J.D., Nichols, D.E., Gudelsky, G.A. Effect of the R(-) and S(+) Isomers of MDA and MDMA on Phosphotidyl Inositol Turnover in Cultured Cells Expressing 5-HT2a and 5-HT2c Receptors. *Neurosci. Lett*. 177: 111-115 (1994).

The discrete optical isomers of both MDA and MDMA were studied in cells expressing serotonin receptors. The affinities were weak, but there is an intrinsic activity which may contribute to the neurotoxic effects seen at higher dosages.

Nichols, D.E., Brewster, W.K., Johnson, M.P., Oberlender, R. and Riggs, R.M. Nonneurotoxic Tetralin and Indan Analogues of 3,4-Methylenedioxyamphetamine (MDA). *J. Med. Chem*. 33: 703-710 (1990).

Four cyclic analogues of MDA were synthesized and evaluated pharmacologically. Two indanes and two tetralins were explored through discrimination studies relative to MDMA or LSD. They appear not to have serotonin neurotoxicity.

O'Hearn, E., Battaglia, G., De Souza, E.B., Kuhar, K.J. and Molliver, M.E. Systemic MDA and MDMA, Psychotropic Substituted Amphetamines, Produce Serotonin Neurotoxicity. *Soc. Neurosciences Abstrts*. 12: 336.2 (1986).

Rats exposed chronically to either MDA or MDMA were found, on sacrifice, to have a reduced number of serotonin axon terminals. This was most evident in cerebral cortex, thalamus, olfactory bulb and striatum, but also occurred in other areas. This may be due to the binding of these drugs to the uptake sites. The serotonin cell bodies and the preterminal axons are spared.

O'Hearn, E., Battaglia, G., De Souza, E.B., Kuhar, M.J. and Molliver, M.E. Methylenedioxyamphetamine (MDA) and Methylenedioxymethamphetamine (MDMA) Cause Selective Ablation of the Serotoninergic Axon Terminals in Forebrain: Immunocytochemical Evidence for Neurotoxicity. *J. Neurosci*. 8: 2788 (1988).

Following chronic administration of MDMA (or separately, MDA) to rats, there is observed a profound loss of serotoninergic neuron axons throughout the forebrain. Various regions of the brain are compared as to extent of damage. The catecholamine counterparts are not affected.

Pan, H.S. and Wang, R.Y. MDMA: Further Evidence that its Action in the Medial Prefrontal Cortex is Mediated by the Serotoninergic System. *Brain Res*. 539: 332-336 (1991).

The administration of MDMA was found to suppress the firing rates of certain brain neurons in anaesthetized rats. The (+) isomer, but not the (-) isomer, mimics the racemate. These effects are blocked by the pretreatment with a serotonin uptake inhibitor.

Pan, H.S. and Wang, R.Y. The Action of (+/-)-MDMA on Medial Prefrontal Cortical Neurons is Mediated Through the Serotoninergic System. *Brain Res*. 543: 56-60 (1991).

Rats anaesthetized with chloral hydrate were given varying amounts of MDMA intravenously. Electrodes located in the brain showed decreased neuron excitement. Studies were extended to include pretreatment with para-chlorophenylalanine and alpha-methyl-paratyrosine. The action of MDMA apparently involves some endogenous serotonin release.

Paris, J.M. and Cunningham, K.A. Lack of Serotonin Neurotoxicity after Intraraphe Microinjection of (+) 3,4-Methylenedioxymethamphetamine (MDMA). *Brain Res. Bull*. 28: 115-119 (1991).

Direct injection of MDMA into the dorsal and the median Raphe nuclei was followed, in two weeks, by assay for serotonin and catecholamine changes. No apparent neurotoxicity was found.

Peroutka, S.J. Relative Insensitivity of Mice to 3,4-Methylenedioxymethamphetamine (MDMA) Neurotoxocity. *Res. Commun. Subst. Abuse* 9: 193-206 (1988).

The effects of MDMA were determined in mouse brain serotonin uptake sites using paroxetine binding as a measure. In distinction with rats, there were no effects that could be observed at dosages of up to 30 mg/Kg, administered chronically. These findings confirm that in the mouse, MDMA is not a neurotoxic agent.

Pierce, P.A. and Peroutka, S.J. Ring-substituted Amphetamine Interactions with Neurotransmitter Receptor Binding Sites in Human Cortex. *Neurosci. Lett*. 95: 208-212 (1988).

Three psychotropic drugs, MDA, MDMA and MDE, were evaluated as to their affinities for the DOB binding site, as determined by the displacement of ^{77}Br DOB as the labelled radioligand.

Piercey, M.F., Lum, J.T. and Palmer, J.R. Effects of MDMA ('ecstasy') on Firing Rates of Serotonergic, Dopaminergic, and Noradrenergic Neurons in the Rat. *Brain Res*. 526: 203-206 (1990).

MDMA is effective in the depression of serotonin neurons in the dorsal and median raphe. Noradrenalin neurons in the locus coeruleus were also depressed at moderate dosages, but dopamine neurons were unaffected.

Ricaurte G.A. and McCann, U.D. Neurotoxic Amphetamine Analogues: Effects in Monkeys and Implications for Humans. *Ann. N. Y. Acad. Sci*. 648: 371-82 (1992)

A review is presented of the relationships between several amphetamine-related compounds (such as amphetamine, methamphetamine and MDMA) and changes in the neurotransmitter area. The changes seen in rodents are compared to those observed in non-human primates, and speculation is made concerning further extrapolation to humans. Research with these compounds should enhance our understanding of central monoaminergic systems in normal brain function, and their role in the pathophysiology of neuropsychiatric disorders

Ricaurte, G.A., Bryan, G., Strauss, L., Seiden, L. and Schuster, C. Hallucinogenic Amphetamine Selectively Destroys Brain Serotonin Nerve Terminals. *Science* 229: 986-988 (1985).

MDA was studied and found to produce long lasting reductions in the level of serotonin, the number of serotonin uptake sites, and the concentration of 5-HIAA in the rat brain. It was suggested that these deficits were due to serotonin nerve terminal degeneration. This was the research report that had been submitted for publication at the time of the MDMA hearings, and that played a focal role in the emergency scheduling of MDMA.

Ricaurte, G.A., DeLanney, L.E., Irwin, I. and Langston, J.W. Toxic Effects of MDMA on Central Serotonergic Neurons in the Primate: Importance of Route and Frequency of Drug Application. *Brain Res.* 446: 165-169 (1988).

The toxicity of MDMA was studied in primates both by the oral and the subcutaneous routes, and in single and multiple doses. Multiple doses are more effective that single doses in depleting serotonin, and the s.c route is more effective than the oral route. However, a single, oral administration of MDMA still produces a long-lived depletion

Ricaurte, G.A., DeLanney, L.E., Wiener, S.G., Irwin, I. and Langston, J.W. 5-Hydroxyindoleacetic acid in Cerebrospinal Fluid Reflects Serotonergic Damage Induced by 3,4-Methylenedioxymethamphetamine in CNS of Non-human Primates. *Brain Res.* 474: 359-363 (1988).

The usefulness of 5-hydroxyindoleacetic acid in CSF as a marker for serotonergic damage induced by MDMA was evaluated in the monkey. Following toxic doses of MDMA, there was removal of CSF for the assay of this serotonin metabolite, followed by sacrifice of the animal for direct brain measurement. The resulting positive correlation supports this technique for the eventual search for MDMA-induced damage in humans.

Ricaurte, G.A., Finnegan, K.F., Nichols, D.E., DeLanney, L.E., Irwin, I. and Langston, J.W. 3,4- Methylene-dioxymethamphetamine (MDE), a Novel Analogue of MDMA, Produces Long-lasting Depletion of Serotonin in the Rat Brain. *Eur. J. Pharmacol* 137: 265-268 (1987).

MDE was qualitatively similar to MDMA in the depletion of serotonin in rat brain, but was only one fourth as potent.

Ricaurte, G.A., Forno, L.S., Wilson, M.A., DeLanney, L.E., Irwin, I., Molliver, M.E. and Langston, J.W. (+/-) Methylenedioxymethamphetamine (MDMA) Exerts Toxic Effects on Central Serotonergic Neurons in Primates. *Soc. Neurosci. Abstr.* 13. 251.8: 905 (1987).

MDMA was given s.q. twice daily for four days to monkeys, at 2.5, 3.75 and 5 mg/Kg. Post-mortem brain analyses showed serotonin reduction (90%) and axon damage. Some was described as 'striking' and involved morphological changes.

Ricaurte, G.A., Forno, L.S., Wilson, M.A., DeLanney, L.E., Irwin, I., Moliver, M.E. and Langston, J.W. (+/-) 3,4-Methylenedioxymethamphetamine Selectively Damages Central Serotonergic Neurons in Nonhuman Primates. *J. Am. Med. Assn.* 260: 51-55 (1988).

The parenteral administration (subcutaneous, twice daily for four days) of MDMA to monkeys of three species produced both brain serotonin depletion and accompanying neuron damage upon autopsy following a two-week waiting period. Considerable microscopic detail

is given. The evidence presented could imply, but does not established, that there may be actual neuron cell death. The human pattern of use is oral rather than parenteral, but a warning for prudence is advanced for the human use of either MDMA or (the neurotoxicologically similar drug) Fenfluramine.

Ricaurte, G.A., Marletto, A.L., Katz, J.L. and Marletto, M.B. Lasting Effects of (+/-)-3,4-Methylenedioxymethamphetamine (MDMA) on Ventral Serotonergic Neurons in Nonhuman Primates: Neurochemical Observations. *J. Pharmacol. Exptl. Ther.* 261: 616-622 (1992).

A study was made of the duration of the neurotoxic effects of MDMA on squirrel monkeys (5 mg/day, twice daily, for 4 days) as a function of time, from 2 weeks to a year and a half. A control blank was used. Serotonin deficits persisted, suggesting that MDMA produces lasting effects.

Scallet, A.C., Ali, S.F., Holson, R.R., Lipe, G.W. and Slikker Jr., W. Neurohistological Effects 120 Days after Oral Ecstasy (MDMA): Multiple Antigen Immunohistochemistry and Silver Degeneration Staining. *Soc. Neurosci. Abstr.* 13. part 3 No. 251.6, p. 904 (1987).

Both silver degeneration procedures (Fink-Heimer) and immunohistochemical techniques have been applied to MDMA-treated rats long after dosing. There are indications of regional differences in recovery, and that some changes may be irreversible.

Scanzello, C.R., Hatzidimitriou, G., Martello, A.L., Katz, J.L. and Ricaurte, G.A. Serotonergic Recovery after (+/-)3,4-(Methylenedioxy)methamphetamine Injury: Observations in Rats. *J. Parmacol. Exptl. Ther.* 264: 1484-1491 (1993).

In rats, as opposed to monkeys, the damage that is done by exposure to MDMA appears to be reversable. This study explored the permanence of this recovery, and in some cases it appears to be sustained for at least a year. Some rats, however, appeared not to show this recovery.

Scheffel, U. and Ricaurte, G.A., Paroxetine as an in vivo Indicator of 3,4- Methylenedioxymethamphetamine Neurotoxicity: A Presynaptic Serotonergic Positron Emission Tomography Ligand? *Brain Res.* 527: 89-95 (1990).

The value of Paroxetine as an indicator of serotonergic nerve axon damage was demonstrated by the effectiveness of 5,7-dihydroxytryptamine in decreasing specific binding. MDMA treatment of rats gave similar reduction in labelled Paroxetine binding.

Scheffel, U., Lever, J.R., Stathis, M., Ricaurte, G.A. Repeated Administration of MDMA Causes Transient Down-regulation of Serotonin 5-HT2 Receptors. *Neuropharmacol.* 31: 881-893 (1992).

The repeated administration of MDMA to rats causes a down regulation of serotonin receptors ion the brain of the rat. N-methyl-2-iodolysergic acid diethylamide is a suitable ligand for the labelling of these receptors in vitro and in vivo..

Schlechter, M.D. Serotonergic-Dopaminergic Mediation of 3,4-Methylenedioxymethamphetamine (MDMA, 'Ecstasy'). *Pharmacol. Biochem. and Behav.* 31: 817-824 (1989).

The discriminative stimuli properties of MDMA in rats, were studied to explore the serotinergic, as contrasted to the dopaminergic, nature of the drug's action. In early part of the behavioural responses, the effects appear to be exclusively serotinergic, but in the latter period, there are some believable dominergic actions.

Schmidt, C.J. Acute Administration of Methylenedioxy-methamphetamine: Comparison with the Neurochemical Effects of its N-Desmethyl and N-Ethyl Analogues. *Eur. J. Pharmacol.* **136: 81-88 (1987).**

MDMA (and its two immediate homologues, MDMA and MDE) were studied in the serotoninergic systems in the rat brain. There was depletion of cortical serotonin which in the case of MDMA appeared to persist after at least a week.

Schmidt, C.J. Neurotoxicity of the Psychedelic Amphetamine, Methylenedioxymethamphetamine. *J. Pharmacol. Exptl. Ther.* **240: 1-7 (1987).**

Evidence is presented that MDMA has a complex effect on rat serotonergic neurons, that results in a neurotoxic change at the nerve terminals. A parallel is drawn to the neurotoxin para-chloroamphetamine.

Schmidt, C.J., Acute and Long-term Neurochemical Effects of Methylenedioxymethamphetamine in the Rat. *NIDA Research Monograph Series.* **94: 179-195 (1989).**

An analysis of short and long-term brain serotonin-related changes was made, and interpreted. Comparisons were made to PCA, methamphetamine and Fenfluramine.

Schmidt, C.J. and Kehne, J.H. Neurotoxicity of MDMA: Neurochemical Effects. *Ann. N. Y. Acad. Sci.* **600: 665-681 (1990).**

A review of the experimental findings involving both serotonin and dopamine in the neurotoxic action of MDMA. The actual mechanism of action remains unknown.

Schmidt, C.J. and Lovenberg, W. (+/-)Methylene-dioxymethamphetamine (MDMA): A Potentially Neurotoxic Amphetamine Analogue. *Fed. Proc.* **45: 1059 (5264) April 13-18, (1986). Note paper below, Schmidt** *et al.***, with this same title.**

Rats were administered MDMA s.c. at various doses and sacrificed at three hours. Brain concentrations of dopamine and serotonin, and their major metabolites were determined. The serotonin concentrations were reduced in a dose-dependent manner. Co-administration of a serotonin uptake inhibitor, Citalopram, blocked the MDMA-induced decline in striatal serotonin concentrations suggesting a mechanism similar to that of the known serotonergic neurotoxin p-chloroamphetamine.

Schmidt, C.J. and Lovenberg, W. Further Studies on the Neurochemical Effects of 4,5-Methylenedioxymethamphet-amine and Related

Analogues. *Soc. Neurosciences Abstrts.* 12: 169.5 (1986).

The racemate and optical isomers of MDMA produced depletion of cortical and striatal serotonin. The (+) isomer was the more effective material. MDA was similar to MDMA, but effects produced by the N-ethyl homologue (MDE) were reversed in a week. Whereas all three drugs caused an acute decrease in serotonin concentration, only MDA and MDMA reduced the uptake of tritiated serotonin at the dosages studied (20 mg/Kg).

Schmidt, C.J. and Taylor, V.L. Direct Central Effects of Acute Methylenedioxymethamphetamine on Serotonergic Neurons. *Eur. J. Pharmacol.* **156: 121-131 (1988).**

The optical isomers of MDMA were studied separately in the rat as to their effects on loss of brain tryptophan hydroxylase. This appeared to precede the drop of serotonin concentration in the same areas. Injections of MDMA directly into the brain had no effect on either measure.

Schmidt, C.J. and Taylor, V.L. Neurochemical Effects of Methylenedioxymethamphetamine in the Rat: Acute versus Long-term Changes. *The Clinical, Pharmacological and Neurotoxicological Effects of the Drug MDMA.* **Kluwer, New York. (1990) Ed: S.J. Peroutka**

A study is presented describing the changes in the brains of rats which had been administered MDMA. It is felt that the release of dopamine is a prerequisite for the neurotoxic effects seen.

Schmidt, C.J., Abbate, G.M., Black, C.K. and Taylor, V.L. Selective 5-Hydroxytryptamine-2 Receptor Antagonists Protect against the Neurotoxicity of Methylenedioxymethamphetamine in Rats. *J. Pharmacol. Exptl. Ther.* **255: 478-483 (1990).**

The characteristic serotonin deficits produced in rats by MDMA were prevented by the simultaneous administration of serotonin antagonists such as Ritanserin. The action of such drugs may involve dopamine.

Schmidt, C.J., Black, C.K., Abbate, G.M. and Taylor, V.L. Methylenedioxymethamphetamine-induced Hyperthermia and Neurotoxicity are Independently Mediated by 5-HT2 Receptors. *Brain Res.* **529: 85-90 (1990).**

In rats, MDMA produces a hyperthermia which can be partially antagonised, as can the induced neurotoxicity, by the administration of a serotonin antagonist.

Schmidt, C.J., Black, C.K., Abbate, G.M. and Taylor, V.L. Chloral Hydrate Anesthesia Antagonizes the Neurotoxicity of 3,4-Methylenedioxymethamphetamine. *Eur. J. Pharmacol.* **191: 213-216 (1990).**

When chloral anesthesia is administered to rats that have been administered MDMA, there is an interference with the induced neurotoxicity. This may be due to some role played by dopamine release.

Schmidt, C.J., Black, C.K. and Taylor, V.L. Antagonism of the Neurotoxicity due to a Single Administration of Methylenedioxyamphetamine. *Eur. J. Pharmacol.* **181: 59-70 (1990).**

A complex series of experiments in the rat investigating MDMA has suggested that the release of both dopamine and serotonin are implicated in the observed neurotoxicity of MDMA.

Schmidt, C.J., Black, C.K. and Taylor, V.L. L-DOPA Potentiation of the Serotoninergic Deficits Due to a Single Administration of 3,4- Methylenedioxymethamphetamine, p-Chloroamphetamine or Methamphetamine to Rats. *Eur. J. Pharmacol.* **203: 41-49 (1991).**

The role of dopamine in the serotoninergic neurotoxicity of MDMA, PCA, methamphetamine, MDE, and Fenfluramine was assessed by their co-administration with L-DOPA. The findings reported support a role for dopamine release in the toxicity of the first three of these drugs.

Schmidt, C.J., Levin, J.A. and Loverberg, W. In Vitro and In Vivo Neurochemical Effects of Methylene-dioxymethamphetamine on Striatal Monoaminergic Systems in the Rat Brain. *Biochem. Pharmacol.* **36: 747-755 (1987).**

This study compares the effects of MDMA and MDA on neurotransmitter release in vitro and the (+) isomer is the more effective. The (+) isomer is also the more effective in vivo.

Schmidt, C.J., Vicki, L., Taylor, G.M. and Nieduzak, T.R. 5-HT-2 Antagonist Stereoselectivly Prevents the Neurotoxicity of 3,4-Methylenedioxymethamphetamine by Blocking the Acute Stimulation of Dopamine Synthesis: Reversal by L-DOPA. *J. Pharmacol. Exptl. Ther.* 256: 230-235 (1991).

The effects of the optical isomers of a serotonin antagonist (one active, the other inactive) on the interaction of MDMA with both the dopaminergic and the serotoninergic systems of the male rat were studied. The protective effects against forebrain serotonin deficit that was observed, was reversed by the administration of L-DOPA.

Schmidt, C.J., Wu, L. and Lovenberg, W. Methylene-dioxymethamphetet-amine: A Potentially Neurotoxic Amphetamine Analogue. *Eur. J. Pharmacol.* 124: 175-178 (1986).

Acute administration of MDMA to rats provide selective and long lasting serotonin and 5-HIAA depletion, similar to that produced by p-chlorophenylalanine. There was an elevation of neostriatal dopamine as well as it primary metabolite homovanillic acid. A typewritten draft of this paper was presented to the DEA in conjunction with the legal hearings held concerning the scheduling of MDMA.

Schmidt, C.J., Sullivan, C.K. and Fadayel, G.M. Blockade of Striatal 5-Hydroxytryptamine(2) Receptors Reduces the Increase in Extracellular Concentrations of Dopamine Produced by the Amphetamine Analogue 3,4-Methylenedioxymethamphetamine. *J. Neurochem.* 62: 1382-89 (1994).

MDMA stimulates the synthesis and release of dopamine, and serotonin receptor antagonists interfere with this action. Studies have been made to determine which receptors are responsible.

Seiden, L.S. Report of Preliminary Results on MDMA. Document entered into evidence Re: MDMA Scheduling Docket No. 84-48, U.S. Department of Justice, Drug Enforcement Administration, October 16, 1985.

Rats were treated both acutely and chronically with MDMA, and the study of the decrease of serotonin receptors and the interpretation of neurological staining indicated a neurotoxicity similar to, but less dramatic than, that seen with MDA.

Series, H.G., Cowen, P.J. and Sharp, T. p-Chloroamphetamine (PCA), 3,4-Methylenedioxymethamphetamine (MDMA) and d-Fenfluramine Pretreatment Attenuates d-Fenfluramine-evoked Release of 5-HT in vitro. *Psychopharmacol.* 116: 508-514 (1994).

Rats were pretreated with three agents known to produce lesions in the cortex of the brain. The challenge for this destruction was through the administration of fenfluramine itself. It appears that the acute release of serotonin by fenfluramine occurs by those terminals affected by the agents used in the pretreatment regimen.

Slikker, Jr., W. and Gaylor, D.W. Biologically-Based Dose-Response Model for Neurotoxicity Risk Assessment. *Korean J. Toxicol.* 6: 205-213 (1990).

A discussion of a model of risk assessment of neurotoxicity is presented, illustrated by published experimental details from MDMA in experimental rats.

Slikker Jr., W., Ali, S.F., Scallet, A.C. and Frith, C.H. Methylenedioxymethamphetamine (MDMA) Produces Long Lasting Alterations in the Serotonergic System of Rat Brain. *Soc. Neurosciences Abstrts.* 12: 101.7 (1986).

The chronic treatment of rats with MDMA (orally) produced decreased levels of serotonin and 5-HIAA. At high dose levels there was a temporary decrease in homovanillic acid (HVA) but no change in dopamine levels.

Slikker Jr., W., Ali, S.F., Scallet, A.C., Firth, C.H., Newport, G.D. and Bailey, J.R. Neurochemical and Neurohistological Alterations in the Rat and Monkey Produced by Orally Administered Methylenedioxymethamphetamine (MDMA). *Toxicol Appl. Pharmacol.* 94: 448-457 (1988).

A complete neurohistochemical study of chronically administered MDMA, orally, to either rats of monkeys, showed extensive indications of serotonin neuron involvement, but no changes in with either dopamine or its primary metabolites.

Slikker Jr., W., Holson, R.R., Ali, S.F., Kolta, M.G., Paule, M.G., Scallet, A.C., McMillan, D.E., Bailey, J.R., Hong, J.S. and Scalzo, F.M. Behavioural and Neurochemical Effects of Orally Administered MDMA in the Rodent and Nonhuman Primate. *Neurotox.* 10: 529-542 (1989).

MDMA was compared to p-chloroamphetamine (PCA) in rats following short-term chronic oral administration. Observations were made on behavioural effects and on neurochemical changes. Both compounds showed the 'serotonin motor syndrome' but these markers were not persistent, although the brain serotonin level decreases were maintained with time. Similar decreases were seen in monkeys, but there was no behavioural modification evident.

Spanos, L.J. and Yamamoto, B.K. Methylenedioxymethamphetamine (MDMA)-induced Efflux of Dopamine and Serotonin in Rat Nucleus Accumbens. *Soc. of Neurosciences Abstr.* 12 169.6: 609 (1986).

Following MDMA administration to rats, the efflux of dopamine was decreased but then it quickly recovered. Serotonin depletion does not recover even after 2 hours, thus MDMA may be neurotoxic.

Sprague. J.E., Huang, X., Kanthasamy, A., Nichols, D.E. Attenuation of 3,4-Methylenedioxymethamphetamine (MDMA) Induced Neurotoxicity with the Serotonin Precursors Tryptophan and 5-Hydroxytryptophan. *Life Sci.* 55: 1193-1198 (1994).

Treatment of rats with serotonin precursors has been shown to attenuate MDMA-induced serotonergic neurotoxicity in the striatum, the hippocampus, and the frontal cortex of the brain. It appears that the depletion of serotonin stores is important for MDMA-induced neurotoxicity.

Steele, T.D., Brewster, W.K., Johnson, M.P., Nichols, D.E. and Yim, G.K.W. Assessment of the Role of alpha-Methylepinine in the Neurotoxicity of MDMA. *Pharmacol. Biochem. Behav.* 38: 345-351 (1991).

The catechol metabolite of MDMA, alpha-methylepinine, was evaluated as a potential contributor to the neurotoxicity of MDMA. It was formed metabolically, and also assayed directly. No relationship to biogenic amines was observed, and it appears not to be responsible for the observed MDMA effects.

Stone, D.M., Hanson, G.R. and Gibb, J.W. Does Dopamine Play a Role in the Serotonergic 'Neurotoxicity' Induced by 3,4-Methylenedioxymethamphetamine (MDMA)? *Soc. Neurosciences Abstrt.* 12 169.4 (1986).

The possibility that the negative serotonin effects of MDMA might be mediated by dopamine was investigated. Studies involving dopamine synthesis inhibitors and antagonists suggest less involvement of dopamine than is seen with methamphetamine.

Stone, D.M., Hanson, G.R. and Gibb, J.W. Differences in the Central Serotonergic Effects of Methylenedioxymethamphetamine (MDMA) in Mice and Rats. *Neuropharmacol.* 26: 1657-1661 (1987).

A number of studies as to the brain serotonin responses to MDMA (in rats) suggest that the duration of exposure might be an important factor in the estimation of toxic effects. Mice are shown to be less susceptible to MDMA, neurotoxicologically, than rats.

Stone, D.M., Merchant, K.M., Hanson, G.R. and Gibb, J.W. Immediate and Long Term Effects of 3,4- Methylenedioxymethamphetamine on Serotonin Pathways in Brain of Rat. *Neuropharmacol.* 26: 1677-1683 (1987).

The time course for the decrease of markers of central serotonin function in the rat is reported. Changes were observed at 15 minutes following a 10 mg/Kg s.c. injection, and much recovery was observed at the 2 week point. Following multiple dose administration of MDMA, significant serotonin changes were still evident after 110 days.

Stone, D.M., Stahl, D.C., Hanson, G.R. and Gibb, J.W. The Effects of 3,4- Methylenedioxymethamphetamine (MDMA) and 3,4- Methylenedioxyamphetamine (MDA) on Monoaminergic Systems in the Rat Brain. *Eur. J. Pharmacol.* 128: 41-48 (1986).

Single or multiple doses of either MDMA or MDA caused marked reduction in both serotonin and 5-HIAA, as well as in the associated enzyme tryptophane hydroxylase (TPH). Single injections elevated striatal dopamine concentrations, although after repeated injections, these values became normal. Striatal tyrosine hydroxylase (TH) was not changed.

St. Omer, V.E.V., Ali, S.F., Holson, R.R., Duhart, H.M., Scalzo, F.M. and Slikker, W. Behavioural and Neurochemical Effects of Prenatal Methylenedioxymethamphetamine (MDMA) Exposure in Rats. *Neurotox. Teratol.* 13: 13-20 (1991).

Pregnant rats were treated repeatedly with MDMA. The progeny were completely normal as to litter size, birth weight, physical appearance, maturation parameters, and other measures of behaviour. No neurological deficit could be observed, although the mother showed some decrease in weight gain, and decreases in brain levels of serotonin at selected locations.

Takeda, H., Gazzara, R.A., Howard, S.G. and Cho, A.K. Effects of Methylenedioxymethamphetamine (MDMA) on Dopamine (DA) and Serotonin (5-HT) Efflux in the Rat Neostriatum. *Fed. Proc.* 45 5266: 1059 April 13-18, 1986.

Employing electrodes implanted in the neostriatum of anaesthetized rats, the MDMA-induced efflux of dopamine and serotonin was measured. The serotonin efflux was significantly increased by MDMA, and had returned to normal by three hours. The dopamine efflux increased slightly, and then dropped below normal. MDA decreased the dopamine efflux.

Trulson, T.J. and Trulson, M.E. 3,4- Methylenedioxymethamphetamine (MDMA) Suppresses Serotonergic Dorsal Raphe Neuronal Activity in Freely Moving Cats and in Midbrain

Slices in vitro. *Soc. Neurosci. Abstr.* 13 3: 905 (1987) No. 251.7.

A study of the decrease of brain serotonin levels in cats given 0.25-5.0 mg/Kg MDMA is reported. Pretreatment with p-chloroamphetamine greatly attenuated the suppressant action of MDMA, and it is suggested that the action of the two drugs is similar.

Wagner, J. and Peroutka, S.J., Neurochemistry and Neurotoxicity of Substituted Amphetamines, *Neuropsychopharm.* 3: 219-220 (1990).

MDMA was compared with Fenfluramine as a depletor of serotonergic nerve terminals, as determined by the reduction of the density of paroxetine binding sites in rat's brains. Single dosages of 30 mg/Kg and 10 mg/Kg were required of the two drugs, respectively, to achieve significant changes.

Whitaker-Azmitia, P.M. and Azmitia, E.C. A Tissue Culture Model of MDMA Toxicity. *The Clinical, Pharmacological and Neurotoxicological Effects of the Drug MDMA.* Kluwer, New York. (1990) Ed: S.J. Peroutka

A procedure is described for studying MDMA toxicity employing tissue cultures prepared from foetal rat brains. The similarities and the differences observed between this technique and the more common in vivo techniques, are discussed.

White, S.R., Duffy, P. and Kalivas, P.W., Methylenedioxymethamphetamine Depresses Glutamate-evoked Neuronal Firing and Increases Extracellular Levels of Dopamine and Serotonin in the Nucleus Accumbens *in vivo. Neurosci..* 62: 41-50 (1994).

A series of studies in rats has shown that MDMA has inhibitory effects on the neuronal firing in the nucleus accumbens, and that this inhibition is mediated by an increase in extracellular dopamine and serotonin.

Wilson, M.A., Ricaurte, G.A. and Molliver, M.E. The Psychotropic Drug 3,4- Methylenedioxymethamphetamine (MDMA) Destroys Serotonergic Axons in Primate Forebrain: Regional and Laminar Differences in Vulnerability. *Soc. Neurosci. Abstr.* 13, part 3, No. 251.8 p. 905 (1987).

The monkey shows a striking brain loss of serotonin terminals following exposure to MDMA twice daily for 4 days at 5 mg/Kg. The distribution and extent of this damage is reported.

Wilson, M.A., Ricaurte, G.A. and Molliver, M.E. Distinct Morphologic Classes of Serotoninergic Axons in Primates Exhibit Differential Vulnerability to the Psychotropic Drug 3,4- Methylenedioxymethamphetamine. *Neurosci.* 28: 121 (1989).

An exacting study is presented describing the morphological changes seen in the serotoninergic axons in the monkey's brain following MDMA exposure.

Woolverton, W.L., Virus, R.M., Kamien, J.B., Nencini, P., Johanson, C.E., Seiden, L.S. and Schuster, C.R. Behavioural and Neurotoxic Effects of MDMA and MDA. Amer. Coll. *Neuropsychopharm. Abstrts.* p. 173 (1985).

In behavioural studies in rats and monkeys trained to distinguish amphetamine from saline, MDMA mimicked amphetamine. With chronic administration, MDMA caused a degeneration of serotonin uptake sites, but no change in affinity of the undamaged sites. These results were similar to, but greater than, those seen with MDA.

Yamamoto, B.K. and Spanos, L.J. The Acute Effects of Methylenedioxymethamphetamine on Dopamine Release in

the Awake-behaving Rat. *Eur. J. Pharmacol.* 148: 195-204 (1988).

The effects of MDMA on the caudate and nucleus accumbens dopamine release and metabolism were studied by in vivo voltammetry and HPLC with electrochemical detection. There was a dose-dependent dopamine release observed in both regions by both measures.

Yeh, S.Y. **Lack of Protective Effect of Chlorpromazine on 3,4-Methylenedioxymethamphetamine Induced Neurotoxicity on Brain Serotonin Neurons in Rats.** *Res. Commun. Subst. Abuse* 11: 167-174 (1990).

Studies involving the administration of MDMA with or without chlorpromazine suggests have suggested that chlorpromazine does not protect MDMA-induced depletion of serotonin in rats.

Yeh, S.Y. and Hsu, F-L. **Neurotoxicity of Metabolites of MDA and MDMA (Ecstasy) in the Rat.** *Soc. Neurosci. Abstr.*, Vol. 13, Part 3, p. 906 (1987) No. 251.11.

MDA, MDMA, and a number of potential metabolites (4-OH-3-OMe-amphetamine, alpha-methyldopamine, alpha-methylnorepinephrine) were studied in the rat, and the serotonin decreases measured. These metabolites have a lower neurotoxicity than the parent compound.

Zaczek, R., Culp, S. and De Souza, E.B. **Intrasynaptosomal Sequestration of [³H]Amphetamine and [³H]Methylenedioxyamphetamine: Characterization Suggests the Presence of a Factor Responsible for Maintaining Sequestration.** *J. Neurochem.* 54: 195-204 (1990).

The incorporation of tritiated amphetamine, MDA and MDMA into rat brain synaptosomes was studied. The observed dynamics is discussed in relationship to the mechanism of action of amphetamine-induced monoamine release.

Zaczek, R., Hurt, S., Culp, S. and DeSouza, E.B. **Characterization of Brain Interactions with Methylenedioxyamphetamine and Methylenedioxymethamphetamine.** *NIDA Research Monograph Series.* 94: 223-239 (1989).

Brain recognition sites have been described for labelled MDA and MDMA, and similarities between these and the corresponding amphetamine sites are noted.

Zhao, Z., Castagnoli Jr., N, Ricaurte, G.A., Steele, T. and Martello, M. **Synthesis and Neurotoxicological Evaluation of Putative Metabolites of the Serotoninergic Neurotoxin 2-(Methylamino)-1-[3,4-(methylenedioxy)phenyl]propane [(Methylenedioxy)methamphetamine].** *Chem. Res. Toxicol.* 5: 89-94 (1992).

A number of potential toxic metabolites of MDMA were synthesized and assayed as neurotoxins. One of these, 2,4,5-trihydroxymethamphetamine, was found to deplete both dopamine and serotonin.

Clinical studies

Beck, J. **The Public Health Implications of MDMA Use.** *The Clinical, Pharmacological and Neurotoxicological Effects of the Drug MDMA.* Kluwer, New York. (1990) Ed: S.J. Peroutka.

This sociological paper brings together the street acceptance of, and the pubic health rejection of, MDMA as a tool for therapy and a vehicle of simple intoxication. The part that this drug has

played in each of these roles is carefully defined.

Beck, J., Harlow, D., McDonnell, D., Morgan, P.A., Rosenbaum, M. and Watson, L. **Exploring Ecstasy: A Description of MDMA Users.** Report to NIDA, September 15, 1989. Grantee: Institute for Scientific Analysis, San Francisco, CA.

This is a 253 page report of a research project that conducted a broad and thorough analysis, through interview, of over 100 MDMA users. A fascinating picture emerges of the pros and cons of MDMA usage. This is the only analysis of this depth and candidness that has ever been done, and it is an essential reference volume for all social researchers in this area.

Buffum, J. and Moser, C. **MDMA and Human Sexual Function.** *J. Psychoactive Drugs* 18: 355-359 (1986).

A survey of some 300 MDMA users produced a response of 25%. An analysis of the presented data is offered, organized as to types of activity and performance. There was a significant increase in intimacy, and a decrease (especially for males) in performance.

Downing, J. **The Psychological and Physiological Effects of MDMA on Normal Volunteers.** *J. Psychoactive Drugs* 18: 335-340.

This is certainly the most complete clinical study on the effects of MDMA on the normal human subject. A total of 21 normal volunteers were administered known amounts of MDMA, orally. The entire group had analyses of blood chemistry, timed and frequent physiological measures, including pulse and blood pressure (for all) and as well as neurological and electrocardiographic tests (for some). The neurological and electrocardiogram evaluations were continued for 24 hours.

Physiologically, all subjects experienced an elevation in blood pressure and pulse rate, with a peaking on the average at about one hour. At the sixth hour, most subjects were at or below their pre-dose levels, and at 24 hours all were within their normal ranges. Eye dilation was seen in all subjects, more than half had jaw clench and an increased jaw reflex, which persisted in one subject to the 24 hour point. Some neurological reflexes were enhanced (deep tendon) or equivocal (planter reflex), and there were signs of incoordination (finger-nose testing, gait) in some subjects, giving a strong warning against motor vehicle operation. One subject was nauseous, with vomiting, but there were no difficulties with either urination or defecation, and there were neither headaches nor insomnia. Appetite was suppressed in all subjects to varying degrees.

At the psychological level, all subjects reported a heightened sensual awareness, and three reported sexual arousal. It is concluded that MDMA produces remarkably consistent psychological effects that are transient, and is free of clinically apparent major toxicity.

Greer, G. *MDMA: A New Psychotropic Compound and its Effects in Humans.* Privately Published, 333 Rosario Hill, Sante Fe, NM 87501. Copyright 1983. 15 pages.

The most complete study of the effects of MDMA published as of this date, describing the results of administration of MDMA to 29 human subjects (none with serious psychiatric problems) in a therapeutic setting. It is concluded that the best uses of MDMA are: facilitation of communication and intimacy between people involved in emotional relationships; as an adjunct to insight-oriented psychotherapy; and in the treatment of alcohol and drug abuse. It is explained why MDMA does not lend itself to over-use, since its most desirable effects diminish with frequency of use.

Greer, G. Recommended Protocol for MDMA Sessions. Privately Published. 333 Rosario Hill, Sante Fe, NM 87501. Copyright 1985. 6 pages.

This is a generalized protocol designed to cover the clinical use of MDMA. It reviews the issues of law, of safety, and of efficacy.

Greer, G. Using MDMA in Psychotherapy. Advances. 2: 57-57 (1985).

A conference was held at Esalen March 10-15 1985, to discuss the potential of MDMA for therapy, and to evaluate its differences from earlier therapeutic tools such as LSD. A total of 13 subjects, with the supervision of several experienced psychiatrists, participated in a experiment designed to familiarize the potential clinician with the actions of MDMA. Most of the attendees had already known of the drug in a therapeutic context, and their collected comments are presented and discussed.

Greer, G. Ecstasy and the Dance of Death. Brit. Med. J. 305: 775 (1992).

A defence of MDMA is presented, in answer to published conclusions that no clinical benefits have been observed. There is a tallying of the benefits seen amongst the author's patients, in earlier clinical studies.

Greer, G. and Tolbert, R. Subjective Reports of the Effects of MDMA in a Clinical Setting. J. Psychoactive Drugs. 18: 319-327 (1986).

This article summarizes and gives additional detail on the collection of 29 therapeutic trials discussed earlier. The protocol of drug administration, a review of both the benefits and the undesirable effects, and an outlining of the changes seen in the patients, are presented. There is a considerable body of retrospective evaluation.

Greer, G. and Tolbert, R. The Therapeutic Use of MDMA. The Clinical, Pharmacological and Neurotoxicological Effects of the Drug MDMA. Kluwer, New York. (1990) Ed: S.J. Peroutka.

A structure is provided in detail for the clinical use of MDMA in a therapeutic setting. A number of the preferred procedure d are illustrated with specific case examples.

Grob, C., Bravo, G., McQuade, J. and Doblin, R. Analgesic Efficacy of 3,4- Methylenedioxymethamphetamine (MDMA) in Modification of Pain and Distress of End-stage Cancer. Proposal submitted to the FDA for clinical approval, August 4, 1991.

A proposal has been submitted to the FDA for the evaluation of MDMA as an analgesic against clinical pain in advanced cancer patients.

Grob, C., Bravo, G., and Walsh, R., Second Thoughts on 3,4-Methylenedioxymethamphetamine (MDMA) Neurotoxicity. Arch. Gen. Psychiatry. 47: 288 (1990).

A letter to the editor presents a critique of studies done on alleged MDMA users in search for evidence of serotonin nerve damage (Price et al., Arch. Gen. Psychiatry 46 20-22 (1989). The fact that all nerve toxicity is based on animal studies, and that the long-used drug

Fenfluramine is considerably more potent a neurotoxin than MDMA, might argue that studies into the potential therapy use should be encouraged.

Grob, C.S., Bravo, G.L., Walsh, R.N. and Liester, M.B. Commentary: The MDMA-Neurotoxicity Controversy: Implications for Clinical Research with Novel Psychoactive Drugs. J. Nerv. Ment. Dis. 180: 355-356 (1992).

The points raised by Kosten and Price, in criticism to the retrospective interview paper, are answered.

Hastings, A. Some Observations on MDMA Experiences Induced Through Posthypnotic Suggestion. J. Psycho. Drugs 26: 77-83 (1994).

A study is reported with subjects who were familiar with MDMA action. The techniques of hypnosis were employed to reinstitute MDMA-like effects, and the potential for post-hypnotic suggestion in therapy is explored.

Kosten, T.R. and Price, L.H. Commentary: Phenomenology and Sequelae of 3,4- Methylenedioxymethamphetamine Use. J. Nerv. Ment. Dis. 180: 353-354 (1992).

The retrospective interview by Liester et al. is critically analysed, and found to be faulted both methodologically and as to the conclusions reached.

Liester, M.B., Grob, C.S., Bravo, G.L. and Walsh, R.N. A Study of MDMA Use Among Psychiatrists. Poster NR-62, New Research Poster Session, American Psychiatric Association, San Francisco, CA May 8, 1989.

A survey was conducted among 20 psychiatrists who had previously taken MDMA, and a tally of the various responses made. There was a discussion of both the methodological problems and the ethical considerations of this type of study.

Liester, M.B., Grob, C.S., Bravo, G.L. and Walsh, R.N. Phenomenology and Sequelae of 3,4- Methylenedioxy-methamphetamine Use. J. Nerv. Ment. Dis. 180: 345-352 (1992).

Twenty psychiatrists experienced with MDMA were retrospectively interviewed as to side effects, insight gained, pleasure experienced, and intensity of effects.

McCann, U.D. and Ricaurte, G.A. MDMA ('Ecstasy') and Panic Disorder: Induction by a Single Dose. Biol. Psychiatry, 32: 950-953 (1992).

A patient is described with a lasting panic disorder syndrome that started during the course of an alledged MDMA experience. Alprazolam improved his condition, but it was reprecipitated by OTC cold remedies, suggesting that some catecholamine function had been disturbed in the patient.

McCann, U.D. and Ricaurte, G.A. Reinforcing Subjective Effects of (+/-) 3,4- Methylenedioxymethamphetamine ('Ecstasy') May Be Separable from its Neurotoxic Actions: Clinical Evidence. J. Clin. Psychopharmacol. 13: 214-217 (1993).

Four subjects who had voluntarily, and anecdotaly, exposed themselves to MDMA, report that pretreatment with Fluoxetine found some increased somatic distress, but no attenuation of the expected responses to the drug, including enhanced awareness and ease of communication. It is implied that a pretreatment with a serotonin uptake inhibitor attenuates the neurotoxic effects of the drug MDMA, but the thrust of the report might well be to suggest that there is a neurotoxic effect in man that can indeed be attenuated.

McCann, U.D., Ridenour, A., Shaham, Y. and Ricaurte, G.A. Serotonin Neurotoxicity After (+/-)3,4- Methylene-dioxymethamphetamine (MDMA; 'Ecstasy'): A Controlled Study in Humans. *Neuropsychopharmacol.* 10: 129-138 (1994).

A group of 30 MDMA users and 28 matched controls with no history of MDMA use were studied. The MDMA subjects had lower levels of 5-hydroxyindoleacetic acid in their cerebrospinal fluid, indicating some serotonin depletion. At the psychological level, the MDMA users showed a decreased impulsivity and hostility, and increased harm avoidance and constraint.

Moody, C.P. Facsimile letter to C.S. Grob concerning FDA approval of human Phase I study application. November 4, 1992.

This is an official statement from the Pilot Drug Evaluation Section of the Food and Drug Administration, that the Phase I study submitted by Dr. Grob, has been approved.

Peroutka, S.J. Recreational Use of MDMA, Ecstasy: *The Clinical, Pharmacological and Neurotoxicological Effects of the Drug MDMA.* Kluwer, New York. (1990) Ed: S.J. Peroutka.

There is a distillation from some 300 users of MDMA as to their experiences on the drug, both as to subjective mental effects, and as to physical difficulties. Although the reports are largely favourable, there is a mention of both panic attacks and of a lethal event, and several popular myths are itemized. It is concluded that recreational use should be avoided.

Peroutka, S.J., Newman, H. and Harris, H. Subjective Effects of 3,4- Methylenedioxymethamphetamine in Recreational Users. *Neuropsychopharmacol.* 1: 273-277 (1988).

A survey has been made of about a hundred admitted MDMA users and has been organized into reports of subjective feelings such as 'closeness' (the most often reported) to 'blurred vision' (the least often reported). A brief review of the toxicological history is presented, and no unequivocal evidence of human toxicity could be concluded from this study.

Price, L.H., Krystal, J.H., Heninger, G.R. and Ricaurte, G.A., In Reply. *Arch. Gen. Psychiatry* 47: 289 (1990).

The critique of Grob et al. is responded to. The self-claimed MDMA users had been assayed by urine EMIT screening for recent drug use prior to the experiments reported (Price et al., Arch. Gen. Psychiatry 46 20-22 (1989). The justification for continued Fenfluramine use was that it had no record of abuse (as contrasted to MDMA use), and that the claims for drugs serving as psychotherapeutic adjuncts have been made for many compound for many years, and have not bourn fruit. The recommendation is strongly made that clinical studies are inappropriate at this time.

Shulgin, A.T. and Nichols, D.E. Characterization of Three New Psychotomimetics. *The Psychopharmacology of Hallucinogens,* Eds. R.C. Stillman and R.E. Willette, Pergamon Press, New York. (1978).

The psychopharmacological properties of MDMA are presented, in company with two new compounds, para-DOT (2,5-dimethoxy-4-methylthioamphetamine) and alpha,O-DMS (5-methoxy-alpha-methyltryptamine). It is described as evoking an easily controlled altered state of consciousness with emotional and sensual overtones. It appears to be with little hallucinatory component. This is the first clinical report of the effects of MDMA in man.

Siegel, R.K. MDMA: Nonmedical Use and Intoxication. *J. Psychoactive Drugs,* 18: 349-354 (1986).

From a group of 415 acknowledged MDMA users, a sub-group of 44 were chosen for examinations and tests. They were interviewed, physically examined, and tested by several of a large battery of psychological evaluation procedures. From this, patterns of use and the nature of the intoxicating effects were deduced.

The author has concluded that the visual effects of MDMA intoxication were typical of the intoxications from the classical hallucinogens such as mescaline with imagery characteristic of drug-induced hallucinations, as well as those induced by isolation and stress. These are mollified when attention is directed towards external events. There were, nonetheless, no abnormal profiles on the psychological tests. It is felt that the MDMA intoxication is neither uniformly controllable nor uniformly predictable.

Tatar, A. and Naranjo, C. MDMA in der Gruppenpsychotherapie. Symposion 'Uber den derzeitigen Stand der Forschung auf dem Gebiet der psychoaktiven Substanzen.' Nov. 29 – Dec. 12, 1985, in *Hirschborn/Neckar,* Germany.

Two independent reports of clinical utility are presented. Both investigators report MDMA use in group settings. The groups consisted mainly of psychosomatic patients involving problems such as allergies, eczema, sexual dysfunction, troublesome urination, cardiac irregularities, and cancer. There were some positive changes reported, and in some cases there were no improvements. No details are presented.

Watson, L. and Beck, J. New Age Seekers: MDMA Use as an Adjunct to Spiritual Pursuit. *J. Psychoactive Drugs,* 23: 261-270 (1991).

In an analysis of a sociological investigation into the lay use of MDMA, the quality of MDMA experiences with a sub-set of 'New Age' oriented users. As there appears to be a wide variety of motivations for MDMA use, care must be paid to the social context in evaluating drug-using behaviour.

Widmer, S. *Ins Herz der Dinge Lauschen, vom Erwachen der Liebe.* Nachtschatten Verlag, Solothurn, Switzerland, 1989.

This reference book of just over 300 pages, is a thorough collection of ideas, comments, and illustrations, of the use of MDMA and/or LSD in psychotherapy. It is in German.

Wolfson, P.E. Meetings at the Edge with Adam: A Man for All Seasons. *J. Psychoactive Drugs,* 18: 329-333 (1986).

An extensive discussion is presented listing the potential virtues and hazards of MDMA use in the psychotherapeutic setting. The roles of drugs currently used, and those of MDMA-like action that might some day be available, are reviewed. A case report of the use of MDMA in a family problem situation is presented in considerable detail.

Animal toxicology

Bronson, M.E., Jiang, W., Clark, C.R., DeRuiter, J. Effects Of Designer Drugs on the Chicken Embryo and 1-Day-Old Chicken. *Brain Res. Bull.* 34: 143-50 (1994).

The effects of MDMA and four of it homologues were compared with those of amphetamine on the chicken embryo and the young chicken. Pretreatment with the drug in ova resulted in tolerance to certain drug effects and supersensitivity to other drug effects.

Cadet, J.L. Ladenheim, B., Baum, I., Carlson, E., Epstein, C.

CuZn-Superoxide Dismutase (CuZnSOD) Transgenic Mice Show Resistance to the Lethal Effects of Methylenedioxyamphetamine (MDA) and of Methylenedioxymethamphetamine (MDMA). *Brain Res.* **655: 259-262 (1995).**

The genetic basis of the lethal effects of MDA and MDMA have been explored in transgenic mice. It has been suggested that the acute effects of these drugs might involve the intracellular overproduction of superoxide radicals secondary to hepatic injury.

Davis, W.M. and Borne, R.F. Pharmacologic Investigation of Compounds Related to 3,4- Methylenedioxyamphetamine (MDA). *Substance and Alcohol Actions/Misuse,* **5: 105-110 (1984).**

Acute toxicity studies on MDMA and several homologues, in mice, showed LD-50's of about 100 mg/Kg (i.p.) (for MDMA). In aggregate, the lethality was increased several-fold.

Frith, C.H., *28-Day Oral Toxicity of Methylenedioxymethamphetamine Hydrochloride (MDMA) in Rats.* **Project Report, Toxicology Pathology Associates, Little Rock, Arkansas (1986)**

A controlled toxicological study of some 100 rats with chronically administered MDMA (dosages up to 100 mg/Kg) showed several behavioural signs (hyperactivity, excitability, piloerection, exophthalmus, and salivation). Neither gross nor microscopic pathology was evident at necropsy.

Frith, C.H., *28-Day Oral Toxicity of Methylenedioxymethamphetamine Hydrochloride (MDMA) in Dogs.* **Project Report, Toxicology Pathology Associates, Little Rock, Arkansas (1986)**

A controlled toxicological study of some 24 dogs with chronically administered MDMA (dosages up to 15 mg/Kg) showed several behavioural signs including circling, depression, dilated pupils, hyperactivity, rapid breathing, and salivation. On necropsy, there were examples of reduced testicular size, including microscopically noted atrophy. Prostatic hyperplasia was present in two high dose males.

Frith, C.H., Chang, L.W., Lattin, D.L., Walls, R.C., Hamm, J. and Doblin, R. Toxicity of Methylenedioxy-methamphetamine (MDMA) in the Dog and the Rat. *Fundamental and Applied Toxicol.* 9: 110-119 (1987).

Toxicity studies were performed on dogs and rats and signs are described. No histopathological lesions within the CNS were observed in either species, although unusual clinical observations were recorded.

Goad, P.T. *Acute and Subacute Oral Toxicity Study of Methylenedioxymethamphetamine in Rats.* **Project Report, Intox Laboratories, Redfield, Arkansas, (1985).**

Subacute toxicity studies on rats in graded doses (25 mg/Kg/day in 25 mg increments to 300 mg) were conducted. In acute studies, the LD-50 is given as 325 mg/Kg, some six times the reported i.p. LD-50. No histological evidence of brain damage was observed.

Hardman, H.F., Haavik, C.O. and Seevers, M.H. Relationship of the Structure of Mescaline and Seven Analogues to Toxicity and Behaviour in Five Species of Laboratory Animals. *Toxicol. and Appl. Pharmacol.* **25: 299-309 (1973).**

This report describes several studies supported by the Army Chemical Centre during the period 1953-1954, and declassified in 1969. MDMA was one of eight compounds (including also mescaline, DMPEA, MDPEA, MDA, DMA, TMA and alpha-ethyl-MDPEA) studied in five animals (mouse, rat, guinea pig, dog, and monkey).

The toxicology study showed MDMA to be one of the more toxic of the drugs studied, in most animals second only to MDA. The average LD-50's given were 97, 49 and 98 mg/Kg (for the mouse, rat and guinea pig, resp. – following i.p. administration), and 16 and 26 mg/Kg (for the dog and monkey, i.v. administration).

Behavioural studies in dog and monkey were made over the dosage ranges of 5-50 and 10-75 mg/Kg respectively. These levels evoked a broad range of motor activity, autonomic activity and CNS activity in both animals (the dog more than the monkey) but the ranges studied included the lethal dose levels. Interestingly the monkey showed behaviour interpreted as hallucinations for MDMA, whereas mescaline (an acknowledged hallucinogenic compound) produced no such behaviour at doses more than two times higher (200 mg/Kg i.v.). Structure-activity relationships are discussed.

Human toxicology

Anon: Analogues, *Australian Forensic Drug Analysis Bull.* **12 14 (1990).**

Two deaths associated with a plane crash, were analysed. There was MDMA present (blood, 1.4 and 1.7 mg/L; liver, 1.5 and 6.9 mg/kg; stomach, 0.24 and 0.55 mg; urine, 48 and 44 mg/L). And also present was ethanol (blood, 0.165 and 0.145 g/100 mL) as well as the qualitative presence of cannabinoids (in both).

Allen, R.P., McCann, U.D. and Ricaurte, G.A. Persistant Effects of (+/-)3,4- Methylenedioxymethamphetamine (MDMA, 'Ecstasy') on Human Sleep. *Sleep,* **16: 560-564 (1993).**

A number of MDMA users were studied as to sleep performance. They showed a significant decrease in sleep time (19 minutes) and non-REM sleep (23.2 minutes). The authors conclude that the recreational use of MDMA may induce lasting CNS serotonergic damage.

Ames, D. and Wirshing, W.C. Ecstasy, the Serotonin Syndrome, and Neuroleptic Malignant Syndrome – A Possible Link. J. Am. Med. Assoc. 269 869 (1993).

A short review of both the 'serotonin syndrome' and the 'neuroleptic malignant syndrome' are presented, and compared to the portrait presented with MDMA overdose. A path of medical intervention is suggested based on the neurotransmitter disturbances associated with these syndromes.

Barrett, P.J. Ecstasy and Dandrolene. Brit. Med. J. 305: 1225 (1992).

An argument is made against the administration of Dandrolene in instances of hyperthermia following ecstasy intoxication. This is a muscle relaxant which may reduce thermogenesis associated with muscular activity. Rehydration seems the wiser course and supportive measures may be sufficient treatment.

Barrett, P.J. 'Ecstasy' misuse – Overdose or Normal Dose? *Anaesthesia,* **48: 83 (1993).**

The personal experiences of this physician is that there is no straightforward relationship the dose of 'ecstasy' used, and the complications that might follow this exposure. Dehydration is common, but this follows the energy expenditure in the drug use scene. Supportive therapy should be continued, but its efficacy must be continuously evaluated.

Benazzi, F., and Mazzoli, M. Psychiatric Illness Associated with 'Ecstasy'. *Lancet,* **338:** 1520 (1991).

A case of severe depression following MDMA exposure is reported. The syndrome included loss of energy, weight, and interest in all activities, decreased appetite, psychomotor retardation, hypersomnia, diminished ability to concentrate, and suicidal ideation.

Brown, C.R., McKinney, H., Osterloh, J.D., Shulgin, A.T., Jacob III P. and Olson, K.R. Severe Adverse Reaction to 3,4- Methylenedioxymethamphetamine (MDMA). *Vet. Hum. Toxicol.* **28:** 490 (1986).

A 32 year old female presumably ingested a 'standard' dose, and became comatose, but survived. Serum level was reported to be 7 micrograms/mL

Brown, C. and Osterloh, J. Multiple Severe Complications from Recreational Ingestion of MDMA (Ecstasy). *J. Am. Med. Soc.* **258:** 780-781 (1987).

A considerable body of clinical detail and selected laboratory finding is present in an apparent MDMA toxicity situation involving a 32 year old female. Serum levels of 7 mg/mL and urine levels of 410 and 816 mg/mL were reported (the latter upon admission and on the second day). An immunoenzyme assay for MDMA (using a system designed for amphetamine) reacted with MDMA at 25 mg/mL at the amphetamine cut-off point of 300 nanograms/mL. The observed complications were similar to those observed in amphetamine overdoses, and might possibly be due to an idiosyncratic reaction, an allergic reaction, or to malignant hyperthermia.

Bryden, A.A., Rothwell, P.J.N. and Oreilly, P.H. Urinary Retention with Misuse of Ecstasy. *Brit. Med. J.* **310:** 504 (1995).

(no abstract available)

Campkin, N.T.A. and Davies, U.M. Another Death from Ecstasy. *J. Royal Soc. of Med.* **85:** 61 (1992).

A young male was admitted both unconscious and convulsing following the consumption of three ecstasy tablets. Despite heroic treatment, he died some five hours later. Serum MDMA levels were measured (1.26 mg/L) although no MDA was detected. The diagnosis included disseminated intravascular coagulation with prolonged clotting times, hypofibrinogenaemia, elevated fibrin degradation products and thrombocytopaenia.

Campkin, N.T.A. and Davies, U.M. Treatment of 'Ecstasy' Overdose with Cassidy, G., Ballard, C.G. Psychiatric Sequelae of MDMA (Ecstasy) and Related Drugs. *Irish J. Psycholog. Med.* **11:** 132-133 (1994).

(no abstract available)

Daly, J.E. Commentary: 'Ecstasy' and Meningococcal Meningitus. *Infect. Dis. Med. Pract.* **3:** 123-124 (1994).

The report of meningococcal miningitis associated with MDMA use (Prasad, et al., Infect. Dis. Med. Pract. 3 122-123 (1994)) is argued as possibly being related to factors other than MDMA use.

Dandrolene. *Anaesthesia,* **48:** 82-83 (1993).

An exploration is presented for the first reported use of Dandrolene in the treatment of MDMA overdose. Its value in treatment is discussed, and remains uncertain. Nonetheless the recreational use of MDMA appears to remain a potentially lethal pastime.

Dupont, R.L. and Verebey, K., The Role of the Laboratory in the Diagnosis of LSD and Ecstasy Psychosis. *Psychiat. Ann.* **24:** 142-144 (1994).

As the usual drug-screening procedures are designed to detect only five drugs (opiates, marijuana, cocaine, amphetamines and PCP) it is argued that other abused drugs, such as MDMA, are often missed. Two reasons are advanced to support the broadening of these analyses to include both LSD and MDMA: their importance in the overall addiction problem, and their being promoted by drug sellers as being not detected in drug tests. Neither claim is documented, and the term 'psychosis' does not appear in the paper.

Chadwick, I.S., Linsley, A., Freemont, A.J. and Doran, B. Ecstasy, 3,4- Methylenedioxymethamphetamine (MDMA), a Fatality Associated With Agulopathy and Hyperthermia. *J. Royal Soc. Med.* **84:** 371 (1991).

A fatality associated with MDMA is reported. Blood and gut levels are given. Extensive morbid post mortem details are also outlined.

Cregg, M.T. and Tracey, J.A. Ecstasy Abuse in Ireland, *Irish Med. J.* **86:** 118-20 (1993).

An epidemiological study of MDMA use in Ireland is presented, based upon reports to the National Poisons Information Centre in Dublin. Most of those described were male (80%) and largely in the 16-20 year old group. The symptoms presented are described as being relatively mild.

Davis, W.M., Hatoum, H.T. and Waters, I.W. Toxicity of MDA (3,4- Methylenedioxyamphetamine) Considered for Relevancy to Hazards of MDMA (Ecstasy) Abuse. *Alcohol and Drug Abuse,* **7:** 123-134 (1987).

The toxicological literature is reviewed, and it is suggested that the toxicological data obtained from MDA be extrapolated to MDMA. A comparison of these two drug is presented.

de Man, R.A., Wilson, J.H. and Tjen, H.S. Acute Liver Failure Caused by Methylenedioxymethamphetamine ('Ecstasy'). *Nederlands Tijdschrift voor Geneeskunde.* **137:** 727-9 (1993).

An eighteen year old female who had regularly taken 1-2 tablets of MDMA every weekend, developed acute liver failure. She recovered following two months of hospitalization. It is claimed that this is the 10th published case of hepatotoxicity following MDMA use.

de Silva, R.N. and Harries, D.P. Misuse of Ecstasy. *Brit. Med. J.* **305:** 309 (1992).

This is the reinstatement of four observed cases of intracerebral haemorrhage following exposure to ecstasy or amphetamine. The original article appeared in the Scottish Medical Journal, authored by Harries and de Silva..

Dowling, G.P. Human Deaths and Toxic Reactions Attributed to MDMA and MDEA. *The Clinical, Pharmacological and Neurotoxicological Effects of the Drug MDMA.* Kluwer, New York. (1990) Ed: S.J. Peroutka.

A thorough review is presented of the case records of the reported deaths associated with MDMA use. It was concluded that such deaths are exceedingly rare, especially when considering the widespread use of this drug.

Dowling, G.P., McDonough III, E.T. and Bost, R.O. 'Eve' and 'Ecstasy' A Report of Five Deaths Associated with the Use of

MDEA and MDMA. *J. Am. Med. Assoc.* 257: 1615-1617 (1987)

Five deaths occurred in the Dallas area which have involved either MDMA or MDE. One death was stated to be due to MDMA. Two of the others had had preexisting heart conditions, one had asthma, and one was electrocuted, apparently from having climbed and fallen from a power pole. In these latter cases, MDMA was not felt to be the primary cause of death. It is suggested that a preexisting cardiac disease may predispose an individual to sudden death with MDMA. It was only with the asthma death that there was given a body level (blood) of MDMA, and it was 1.1 mg/mL.

Ellis, P. and Schimmel, P. Ecstasy Abuse. *New Zealand Med. J.* 102: 358 (1989).

A severely disturbed young woman was seen as a patient. She made frequent references to 'Ecstasy.' A urine analysis showed no evidence for the presence of MDMA, although there was observed a high level of phenothiazines. She was admitted to the psychiatric word and started on antipsychotic medication. After three days there, she committed suicide. The authors conclude, 'We are concerned that clinicians should be aware of the potentially serious medical and psychiatric consequences of the use of [MDMA] in sensitive individuals or in overdose.'

Ellis, S.J. Complications of 'Ecstasy' Misuse. *Lancet*, 340: 726 (1992).

A criticism is levelled at the medical letters published, and especially the media coverage, concerning the association of ecstasy use and human trauma. The terms used, are judgmental and scaremongering. The danger associated with MDMA use is clouded by the reports being out of context. In the absence of correlary information such as alcohol consumption, or even an estimate of MDMA use.

Fahal, I.H., Sallomi, D.F., Yaqoob, M. and Bell, G.M. Acute Renal Failure after Forrest, A.R., Galloway, J.H., Marsh, I.D., Strachan, G.A., Clark, J.C. A Fatal Overdose with 3,4-Methylenedioxyamphetamine Derivatives. *Forensic Science Int.* 64: 57-9 (1994).

An overview is presented of adverse reactions shown following exposure to drugs of the 3,4- methylenedioxy class. A fatal overdose is described, presumably following the use of one of these drugs.

Fahal et al, Ecstasy. *Brit. Med. J.* 305: 29 (1992).

A nearly lethal case of acute renal failure is reported six hours following the alleged ingestion of three 'ecstasy' tablets at a rave. It is felt that the use of the drug may have contributed to the trauma.

Friedman, R. Ecstasy, the Serotonin Syndrome, and Neuroleptic Malignant Syndrome – A Possible Link. Reply. *J. Am. Med. Assoc.* 269: 869-870 (1993).

A plan for the treatment of MDMA toxicity is presented, based on the similarity of its symptoms with the 'serotonin syndrome.'

Gledhill, J.A., Moore, D.F., Bell, D. and Henry, J.A. Subarachnoid Haemorrage Associated with MDMA Abuse. *J. Neurol. Neurosur. Psychiat.* 56: 1036-1037 (1993).

Shortly following the consumption of MDMA, a 25 year old woman presented with severe headache and vomiting. A CT scan showed subarachnoid haemorrhaging which was successfully controlled. There had apparently been a preexisting 'berry' aneurysm which may have ruptured with the surge of blood pressure from the drug. She had been a regular MDMA user for two or three years before this incident.

Glenhill, J.A., Moore, D.F., Bell, D., Hentry, J.A. Subarachnoid Haemorrhage Associated with MDMA Abuse. *J. Neurol. Neurosurgery Psychiat.* 56: 1036-1037 (1993).

Gorard, D.A., Davies, S.E. and Clark, M.L. Misuse of Ecstasy. *Brit. Med. J.* 305: 309 (1992).

A case of jaundice is reported in a young student who had been using ecstasy recreationally over a period of several months. The symptoms cleared and there were no complications.

Harries, D.P. and de Silva, R.N. 'Ecstasy' and Intracerebral Haemorrhage. *Scottish Med J.* 37: 150-152 (1992).

Four cases of intracerebral haemorrhage are reported, following exposure to amphetamine ecstasy, or mixtures thereof.

Hayner, G.N. and McKinney, H. MDMA The Dark Side of Ecstasy. *J. Psychoactive Drugs*, 18: 341-347 (1986).

The emergency treatment of two toxic episodes involving MDMA are described. One case, a 34 year old male, had a complex drug history involving mainly opiates, but the timing of the crisis suggested that MDMA injection was responsible. The other case, involving a 33 year old female, has been discussed in detail (see Brown et al., above). A listing of the side-effects that may be experienced in cases of MDMA toxicity is also presented.

Henry, J. A. Ecstasy and the Dance of Death. *Brit. Med. J.* 305: 5-6 (1992).

The positives and negatives of the drug Ecstasy (MDMA) are weighed. On the positive side, the psychotherapeutic potentials in fields as divergent and marriage guidance, alcoholism, and enhancement of perception in elderly people, have been explored, although they have been found to be without benefit. On the negative side, the adverse effects can include convulsions, collapse, hyperpyrexia, disseminated intravascular coagulation, rhabdomyolysis, acute renal failure, weight loss, exhaustion jaundice, 'flashbacks,' irritability, paranoia, depression, or psychosis. The long term effects will take time to document in detail.

Henry, J.A., Jeffreys, K.J. and Dawling, S. Toxicity and Deaths from 3,4- Methylenedioxymethamphetamine ('Ecstasy'). *Lancet*, 340: 384-387 (1992).

A report of the seven or so deaths within the United Kingdom, associated with the use of MDMA, is presented. The clinical data in these deaths, as well as in other, non-fatal, legal situations, are brought together, and discussed. Most of the lethal events involved hyperthermia, whether from the effects of the drug itself, or from circumstances associated with its use.

Hughes, J.C., McCabe, M. and Evans, R.J. Intracranial Haemorrhage Associated with Ingestion of 'Ecstasy.' *Arch. Emerg. Med.* 10: 372-374 (1993).

The summary of this report emphasizes the importance of a drug analysis in emergency medicine. The drug in this case was found to be amphetamine, not MDMA. Some mention should have been made also about the importance of not constructing a totally misleading title. Ecstasy was not involved.

Ijzermans, J.N.M., Tilanus, H.W., De Man, R.A., Metselaar, H.J. Ecstasy and Liver Transplantation. *Ann. Med. Intern.* 144: 568 (1993).

Three cases of hepatotoxic side-effects are reported following alleged exposure to MDMA, one following a single exposure. In one case, a liver transplant was performed. No clinical evidence was reported confirming the identity of the drug that was used.

Keenan, E., Gervin, M., Dorman, A. and O'Connor, J.J. Psychosis and Recreational Use of MDMA ('Ecstasy'). *Irish J. Psycholog. Med.* 10: 162-163 (1993).

A patient presented with bizarre behaviour, paranoid delusions and intermittant auditory hallucinations. He gave a history of taking MDMA weekly for a period of some five months. During his recovery period (with chlorpromazine) over the following few months, he has stopped the use of MDMA, and finds that the occasional use of cannabis does not worsen his symptoms.

Kessel, B. Hyponatraemia After Ingestion of Ecstasy. (letter). Brit. Med. J. 308: 414 (1994).

(no abstract available)

Krystal, J.H., Price, L.H., Opsahl, C., Ricaurte, G.A. and Heninger, G.R. Chronic 3,4-Methylenedioxymethamphetamine (MDMA) Use: Effects on Mood and Neuropsychological Function? Am. J. Drug Alcohol Abuse, 18: 331-341 (1992).

A group of self-acknowledged past MDMA users, participants in a tryptophan challenge test, were evaluated for a number of possible neuropsychological deficits in a battery of tests. There were no indications of deficit, although some mild memory impairment was suggested. This was felt to be inconsequential (the volunteers that just recently flown some distances to participate in the tests, and the only documented drug common to all subjects was the intentionally administered tryptophan. The conclusions, nonetheless, are framed to raise concerns about the possible detrimental effects of MDMA use.

Larner, A.J. Complications of 'Ecstasy' Misuse. Lancet, 340: 726 (1992).

An extensive discussion is presented on the mechanism of thermogenesis caused by the use of MDMA. There may indeed be a genetic predisposition to such forms of hyperthermia. Intervention with Dandrolene, although it itself is not centrally active, may be justified.

Lee, J.W.Y. Catatonic Stupor After Ecstasy. Brit. Med. J. 308: 717-18 (1994).

The author has re-evaluated the diagnosis of two patients reported to have suffered catatonia as a consequence of having taken MDMA (Maxwell et al., Brit. Med. J. 307 1399 (1993). He feels from the symptoms presented, that one was stuporous and suffered mutism, and the other, who also did not speak, had simply presented with a 'wild-eyed' look. The text-book criteria for a catonia diagnosis are reviewed.

Lee, J.W.Y. Catatonic Stupor After Ecstasy. Brit. Med. J. 308: 717-718 (1994).

A reevaluation of the symptoms observed in some patients following exposure to MDMA, has been reevaluated. The diagnosis of 'catatonic stupor' is argued as being inappropriate.

Lehmann, E., Thom, C.H. and Croft, D.N. Delayed Severe Rhabdomyolysis After Taking Ecstasy. Postgrad. Med. J. 71: 186-187 (1995).

(no abstract available)

Logan, A.S.C., Stickle, B., O'Keefe, N., Hewitson, H., Survival Following Ecstasy Ingestion with a Peak Temperature of 42-Degrees-C. Anaesthesia, 48: 1017-1018 (1993).

(no abstract available)

Manchanda, S., Connolly, M.J., Cerebral Infarction in Association with Ecstasy Abuse. Postgraduate Med. J. 69: 874-889 (1993).

A 35 year old man suffered an occlusion of a cerebral artery 36 hours following the use of MDMA. This drug exposure may be associated with the event as there were no other known risk factors.

Marsh, J.C.W., Abboudi, Z.H., Gibson, F.M., Scopes, J., Daly, S., O'Shaunnessy, D.F., Baughan, A.S.J., Gordon-Smith, E.C., Aplastic Anaemia Following Exposure to 3,4-Methylenedioxymethamphetamine ('Ecstasy'). Brit. J. Haematol. 88: 281-285 (1994).

Two cases of aplastic anemia are reported following exposure to MDMA.

Maxwell, D.L., Polkey, M.I., Henry, J.A., Hyponatraemia and Catatonic Stupor After Taking Ecstasy. Brit. Med. J. 307: 1399-1399 (1993).

(no abstract available)

McCoy, E.P., Refrew, C., Johnston, J.R., Lavery, G. Malignant Hyperpyrexia in an MDMA (Ecstasy) Abuser. Ulster Med. J. 63: 103-7 (1994).

(no abstract available)

McCann, U.D. and Ricaurte, G.A. Lasting Neuropsychiatric Sequelae of (+/-) Methylenedioxymethamphetamine ('Ecstasy') in Recreational Users. J. Clin. Psychopharm. 11: 302-305 (1991).

The prolonged responses of two patients, who had allegedly ingested large quantities of MDMA, are described. It is suggested that there may be lasting adverse functional consequences in vulnerable persons following large doses.

McGuire, P. and Fahy, T. Chronic Paranoid Psychosis after Misuse of MDMA ('Ecstasy'). Brit. Med. J. 302: 697 (1991).

Two cases are reported of chronic paranoid psychosis that followed alleged long-term self-administration of large quantities of MDMA. Other drugs had also been involved, and no toxicological evidence could confirm the drug history. Intervention treatment (Haloperidol, Sulpiride) resulted in some improvement.

McGuire, P.K., Cope, H. , Fahy, T.A. Diversity of Psychopathology Associated with Use of 3,4-Methylenedioxymethamphetamine (Ecstasy). Brit. J. Psychiat. 165: 391-395 (1994).

A retrospective evaluation was made of about a dozen psychiatric cases that had been somehow connected with the use of MDMA. It was concluded that MDMA may be associated with a broader spectrum of psychiatric morbidity than heretofore suspected.

Miller, N.S. and Gold, M.S., LSD and Ecstasy: Pharmacology, Phenomenology, and Treatment. Psychiat. Ann. 24: 131-133 (1994).

A long listings of the symptoms of effects is presented for these two drugs. It is heavily biased towards the negative and contains many errors.

O'Conner, B. Hazards Associated with the Recreational Drug Ecstasy. Brit. J. Hosp. Med. 52: 507 (1994).

A review is made of the severe reactions that have been associated with the use of MDMA. The hazardous nature of the drug is emphasized and the urgency and nature of treatment of the acutely toxic state is emphasized.

O'Neill, D. and Dart, J.K. Methylenedioxyamphetamine (Ecstasy) Associated Keratopathy. Eye 7: 805-806 (1993).

Three instances of othrwise unexplained corneal epitheliopath are described following the alledged taking of 'Ecstasy.' Although no documetation of drug exposure is mentioned, the drug has been assumed to be Methylenedioxymethamphetamine (MDMA), rather than the methylenedioxyamphetamine (MDA) mentioned in the title and the text.

Padkin, A. Treating MDMA ('Ecstasy') Toxicity. (letter). *Anaesthesia*, 49: 259 (1994).

(no abstract available)

Pallanti, S., and Mazzi, D. MDMA (Ecstasy) Precipitation of Panic Disorder. *Biol. Psychiat.* 32: 91-95 (1992).

The authors describe three patients whose panic disorder began during recreational use of MDMA (Ecstasy) and was subsequently complicated by agoraphobic avoidance that continued autonomously after cessation of the drug. Their panic disorder responded well to serotoninergic antidepressant drugs, although there was no psychotherapy done to work through the cause of the panic.

Peroutka, S.J., Pascoe, N. and Faull, K.F. Monoamine Metabolites in the Cerebrospinal Fluid of Recreational Users of 3,4-Methylenedioxymethamphetamine (MDMA, 'Ecstasy'). *Res. Commun. Subst. Abuse.* 8: 125-138 (1987).

Lumbar punctures from five MDMA users with various histories were assayed (some weeks following the last exposure) for the levels of metabolites from the three major neurotransmitters serotonin, dopamine, and norepinephrine. All assays fell within normal limits.

Poole, R.G. and Brabbins, C.J. Psychopathology and Ecstasy. *Brit. J. Psychiat.* 165: 837 (1994).

(no abstract available)

Prasad, N., Cargill, R., Wheeldon, N.M., Lang, C.C., MacDonald, T.M. 'Ecstasy' and Meningococcal Mininghitis. *Infect. Dis. Med. Pract.* 3: 122-123 (1994).

Two cases are presented wherein a diagnosis of meningococcal miningitis has been associated with an alleged use of MDMA.

Price, L.H., Ricaurte, G.A., Krystal, J.H. and Heninger, G.R. Neuroendocrine and Mood Responses to Intravenous L-Tryptophan in 3,4-Methylenedioxymethamphetamine (MDMA) Users. *Arch. Gen. Psychiat.* 46: 20-22 (1989).

Nine self-acknowledged MDMA users were used as test subjects for the determination of the ability of tryptophan to increase the serum prolactin level. This response can be used as a measure of serotonin integrity There was a statistically insignificant lessening of PRL concentrations in MDMA users.

Reynolds, P.C., Personal Communication, 1986.

A 35-years old male, who claimed to have taken MDMA, Valium, and LSD (and who died shortly after admission) had the following body levels MDMA (in mg/ml):

Blood	Urine	Bile	Gastric (total)
1.46	13.7	1.98	414 mg.

MDA .03 (present)

Neither diazepam nor nordiazepam were found.

Ricaurte, G.A. Studies of MDMA-Induced Neurotoxicity in Nonhuman Primates: A Basis for Evaluating Long-Term Effects in Humans. *NIDA Research Monograph Series.* 94: 306-322 (1989).

Dose-related serotonin depletion in experimental animals is tabulated. A comparison of primate results to those reported from rats, has allowed an extrapolation to the human MDMA-user. The conclusion drawn that, as there have been no clear indicators of problems with MDMA

users, if there is damage in man it may be very subtle in nature, possibly lying outside of our present techniques for detecting it, and possibly being very slow in onset, as compared to the rapid consequences seen from the MPTP trauma in the dopaminergic system.

Rittoo, D.B. and Rittoo, D. Complications of 'Ecstasy' Misuse. *Lancet*, 340: 725 (1992).

A cautionary note is sounded about the misinterpretation of the origins of hyperthermia as a complication in the course of anesthesia, when in fact it might be the result of prior MDMA ingestion. A serum level for MDMA is suggested as a protective manoeuvre.

Rittoo, D., Rittoo, D.B. and Rittoo, D. Misuse of Ecstasy. *Brit. Med. J.* 305: 309-310 (1992).

Three teenagers were observed with chest pains following the use of ecstasy and alcohol, and several hours of dancing. All electrocardiograms and radiographs were normal, and there were no complications.

Roberts, L., Wright, H. Survival Following Intentional Massive Overdose of 'Ecstasy.' *J. Accident Emergency Medicine*, 11: 53-54 (1994).

The symptomology of a overdose of MDMA (with 18 tablets) is described.

Rohrig, T.P. and Prouty, R.W. Tissue Distribution of Methylenedioxymethamphetamine. *J. Anal. Toxicol.* 2-53 (1992).

Two cases of death involving Methylenedioxymethamphetamine (MDMA) are reported; one case is a fatal acute overdose and the other is a drug-related death. The tissue distribution of MDMA is reported in both cases.

Rothwell, P.M., Grant, R., Cerebral Venous Sinus Thrombosis Induced by 'Ecstasy'. *J. Neurol. Neurosurgery Psychiat.* 56: 1035 (1993).

(no abstract available)

Russell, B., Schwartz, R.H. and Dawling, S. Accidental Ingestion of 'Ecstasy' (3,4-Methylenedioxymethylamphetamine). *Archiv. Dis. Childhood* 67 1114-1115 (1992).

A case is reported of a 13 month old boy who ingested one capsule of Ecstasy. Neurological and cardiovascular side effects predominated, which responded well to treatment with a Chlormethiazole infusion.

Satchell, S.C., Connaughton, M. Inappropriate Antidiuretic Hormone Secretion and Extreme Rises in Serum Creatinine Kinase Following MDMA Ingestion. *Brit. J. Hospital Medicine*, 51: 495-495 (1994).

(no abstract available)

Sawyer, J. and Stephens, W.P. Misuse of Ecstasy. *Brit. Med. J.* 305: 310 (1992).

Two cases of 'fits' are reported in young patients who had consumed Ecstasy. There were no complications or sequelae.

Schifano, F. Chronic Atypical Psychosis Associated with MDMA ('Ecstasy') Abuse. *Lancet* 338: 1335 (1991).

A psychotic state is described in a patient who had been using MDMA on occasion over the course of four years. Other drugs (cannabis, alcohol, benzodiazepines, cocaine) were also used, sporadically. Neuroleptic therapy did not appear to improve his mental state.

Schifano, F. and Magni, G. MDMA (Ecstasy) Abuse –

Psychopathological Features and Craving for Chocolate – A Case Series. *Biol. Psychiat.* 36: 763-767 (1994).

(no abstract available)

Screaton, G.R., Cairns, H.S., Sarner, M., Singer, M., Thrasher, A. and Cohen, S.L. Hyperpyrexia and Rhabdomyolysis after MDMA ('Ecstasy') Abuse. *Lancet,* 339: 677-678 (1992).

Three cases are described that alledgedly involved the use of MDMA and came to medical attention because of extreme hyperthermia. Disseminated intravascular coagulation (DIC) apparently followed as a consequence of the hyperpyrexia. Rapid cooling of the patient is recommended in such cases.

Series, H., Boeles, S., Dorkins, E., Peveler, R. Psychiatric Complications of 'Ecstasy' Use. *J. Psychopharm.* 8: 60-1 (1994).

Two case reports are presented describing significant psychiatric disorders associated with the ingestion of Ecstasy. In one case the patient developed a brief paranoid psychosis, and in the other there were experienced persistent symptoms of anxiety and depression. In both cases, the symptoms persisted for a number of weeks

Shearman, J.D., Chapman, R.W.G., Satsangi, J., Ryley, N.G. and Weatherhead, S. Misuse of Ecstasy. *Brit. Med. J.* 305: 309 (1992).

A woman experienced acute jaundice on two occasions, in from one to two weeks following the use of ecstasy, suggesting an idiosyncratic response to the drug.

Shulgin, A.T. and Jacob III, P. 1-(3,4- Methylenedioxy-phenyl)-3-aminobutane: A Potential Toxicological Problem. *J. Toxicol. – Clin. Toxicol.* 19: 109-110 (1982).

An alert is written for the toxicological community that through the ambiguity of the term 'piperonylacetone,' two different chemical precursors for both MDA and MDMA have been publicly advertised and made available. Efforts to synthesize MDMA might, through misrepresentation, yield a largely unexplored homologue.

Smilkstein, M.J., Smolinske, S.C., Kulig, K.W. and Rumack, B.H. MAO Inhibitor/MDMA Interaction: Agony after Ecstasy. *Vet. Hum. Toxicol.* 28: 490 (1986).

An abstract of a report of a 50 year old male who injected alleged MDMA while on a fixed regimen of the monoamine oxidase inhibitor phenelzine. He developed severe hypertension, diaphoresis, an altered mental status, and marked hypertonicity. With supportive care he recovered fully in some 6 hours. Caution is expressed in possible interrelations between MDMA and MAO inhibitors.

Smilkstein, M.J., Smolinske, S.C. and Rumack, B.H. A Case of MAO Inhibitor/MDMA Interaction: Agony after Ecstasy. *Clin. Toxicol.* 25: 149-159 (1987).

This is the actual published paper that appeared as an abstract under similar authorship and similar title above. There are considerable clinical details concerning the emergency room intervention.

Stone, R.J. Response to the paper of Singarah and Laviec. *Anaesthesia,* 48: 83 (1993).

Tests are suggested that might assay the hyperthermia aspects of MDMA intoxication. Those who succumb to acute toxicity may be expressing responses that are genetic mediated.

Suarez, R.V. and Riemersma, R. 'Ecstasy' and Sudden Cardiac Death. *Amer. J. Forensic Med. Pathol.* 9: 339-341 (1988).

An apparently natural death involving cardiac problems has been found to be related to MDMA use. The drug levels are given for blood and urine, but none of the metabolite MDA was identified as being present.

Tehan, B. Ecstasy and Dantrolene. *Brit. Med. J.* 306: 146 (1993).

An argument is advanced supporting the clinical intervention with Dantrolene in MDMA toxicity cases. This is supported by the successful outcome of a problem associated with MDE where body temperature responded quickly to the use of this agent.

Verebey, K., Alrazi, J. and Jaffe, J.H. The Complications of 'Ecstasy' (MDMA). *J. Am. Med. Assoc.* 259: 1649-1650 (1988). Osterloh, J. and Brown, C., In Reply. *ibid.* 259: 1650 (1988).

The body levels of MDMA and MDA following a single human trial of 50 mg are given. The peak plasma level seen (105.6 ng/Ml at 2 hrs.) decreased to 5.1 ng/Ml at 24 hrs. MDA occurred in plasma at lower levels, and both compounds appeared in urine. This suggests that the toxic incident reported by Brown and Osterloh may have followed a considerable overdose.

Walsh, T., Carmichael, R., Chestnut, J. Anaesthetic Dilemma – A Hyperthermic Reaction to 'Ecstasy.' *Brit. J. Hospital Medicine* 51: 476-476 (1994).

(no abstract available)

Whitaker-Azmitia, P.M. and Aronson, T.A. 'Ecstasy' (MDMA)-Induced Panic. *Am. J. Psychiat.* 146: 119 (1989).

Three cases are reported of transient panic attacks in individuals following the ingestion of alleged MDMA.

Williams, H., Meagher, D. and Galligan, P. M.D.M.A. ('Ecstasy'); a Case of Possible Drug-induced Psychosis. *Irish J. Med. Sci.* 162: 43-44 (1993).

A disturbed and aggressive patient was seen at the time of a police arrest, some 48 hours following the consumption of a half-tab of alledged MDMA His medical history included a skull fracture two months earlier, and his mother had a history of psychotic depression and paranoid delusions. His urine analysis showed only cannabis and benzodiazepines, the latter medically administered. His bizarre behaviour and mental disorientation was treated with Haloperidol, Diazepam, Carbamazepine, and finally with a total of 600 mg Clopenthixol which allowed an eventual resolution of his psychosis and disorientation.

Winstock, A.R. Chronic Paranoid Psychosis after Misuse of MDMA. *Brit. Med. J.* 302: 1150-1151 (1991).

A brief survey of the frequency and nature of use of MDMA is presented. A check list of reported symptoms is given, and the suggestion is offered that as it might induce psychosis more research is needed.

Wodarz, N. and Boning, J. 'Ecstasy' – Induziertes Psychotisches Depersonalisationssyndrom. *Nervenarzt,* 64: 478-80 (1993).

Following the consumption of two tablets of MDMA, a 21-year old patient exhibited a psychotic depersonalisation disorder with suicidal tendencies. With medication, the symtoms disappered over the course of six months. 'Flash-backs' occurred repeatedly.

Woods, J.D. and Henry, J.A. Hyperpyrexia Induced by 3,4-Methylenedioxyamphetamine ('Eve'). *Lancet*, **340**: 305 (1992).

A 30 year old man was admitted in convulsions, two hours after having taken six tablets of ecstasy. He recovered and was dismissed 72 hours later. Serum analysis showed the presence of 1.51 mg/L MDA and 0.2 g/L ethanol. The urine level of MDA was 48.6 mg/l but an analysis for MDMA showed only 0.5 mg/l as being present. Errors in synthesis were suspected. The original ingestion of MDMA is unlikely as MDA is only a minor metabolite of it.

Chemistry

Anon: Verfahren zur Darstellung von Alkyloxyaryl-, Dialkyloxyaryl- und Alkylendioxyarylaminopropanen bzw. deren am Stickstoff monoalkylierten Derivaten. *German Patent, 274,350*; **Filed December 24, 1912, issued May 16, 1914. Assigned to E. Merck in Darmstadt.**

A chemical process is described for the conversion of several allyl- and propenyl-aromatic compounds to the corresponding beta-or alpha-bromopropanes. These, in turn, react with ammonia or primary amines to produce the corresponding primary or secondary propylamines. Specifically, safrole was reacted with aqueous HBr, and the impure reaction product reacted with alcoholic methylamine to produce MDMA in an unstated yield. Also described and characterized are MDA and DMA, as well as the corresponding 1-phenyl-1-aminopropanes. No pharmacology is mentioned.

Anon: Formyl Derivatives of Secondary Bases. *German Patent 334,555*, **assigned to E. Merck. 1920. CA 17:1804a (1923).**

A chemical conversion of MDMA to its formyl derivative, and the properties of the latter, are described. No pharmacology is mentioned.

Biniecki, S. and Krajewski, E. Preparation of DL-1-(3,4-Methylenedioxy)-2-(methylamino)propane and DL-1-(3,4-dimethoxyphenyl)- 2-(methylamino)propane. Acta Polon. *Pharmacol.* **17**: 421-425 (1960). CA 55:14350e (1961).

A chemical procedure is given for the conversion of safrole to the beta-bromopropane with HBr, and its subsequent conversion with alcoholic methylamine to MDMA. 4-Allylveratrole was similarly converted to 3,4- dimethoxy-N-methyl- amphetamine.

Bohn, M., Bohn, G. and Blaschke, G. Synthesis Markers in Illegally Manufactured 3,4-Methylenedioxyamphetamine and 3,4-Methylenedioxymethamphetamine. *Int. J. Legal Med.* **106**: 19-23 (1993).

Some twelve impurities have been described and identified in samples of illicitly prepared MDMA and MDA. Their role as markers for the synthetic routes used, or for connercting different lots of the drugs, is discussed.

Braun, U., Shulgin, A.T. and Braun, G. Centrally Active N-Substituted Analogues of 3,4- Methylenedioxy-phenylisopropylamine (3,4-Methylenedioxyamphetamine). *J. Pharmacol. Sci.* **69**: 192-195 (1980).

Twenty two homologues and analogues of MDA were synthesized and their physical properties presented. Twelve of them were assayed in man as psychotomimetic agents. Three of them were found to be active: MDMA with a human potency of between 100 and 160 mg orally; MDE somewhat less potent with a dosage requirement of 140-200 mg orally; and MDOH, which was similar to MDMA in potency. Some animal pharmacology is reviewed, and a comparison between MDMA and MDA (toxicology, CNS pharmacology, and human effectiveness) is tabulated.

Cerveny, L., Kozel, J. and Marhoul, A. Synthesis of Heliotropin. *Perfumer and Flavorist*, **14**: 13-18 (1989).

Piperonal is a most desirable precursor to piperony methyl ketone (PMK) which can, in turn, be converted directly to either MDA or MDMA. This is a synthetic procedure for the preparation of piperonal (heliotropin) from the precursor catechol (pyrocatechol).

Fujisawa, T. and Deguchi, Y. Concerning the Commercial Utilization of Safrole. *J. Pharmacol. Soc. Japan* **74**: 975 (1954). CA 49:10958i (1955).

The conversion of safrole to piperonylacetone is described, using formic acid and hydrogen peroxide, in acetone. The yield is satisfactory, and this is probably the most direct and efficient conversion of a natural product to an immediate precursor to MDMA.

Hashimoto, K., Hirai, K. and Goromaru, T. Synthesis of Racemic, S(+)- and R(-)-N-[methyl-3H] 3,4-Methylenedioxymethamphetamine. *J. Labelled Cpds. and Radiopharmaceut.* **28**: 465-469 (1990).

Tritium-labelled MDMA was synthesized from MDA by reaction with radioactive methyl iodide in a 60% yield. The optical isomers were separated on a chiral HPLC column.

Janesko, J.L. and Dal Cason, T.A. Seizure of a Clandestine Laboratory: The N-Alkyl MDA Analogues. Paper presented at the 39th Annual Meeting of the American Academy of Forensic Sciences, San Diego, CA Feb. 16-21 (1987). See Microgram 20 52 (1987).

Several clandestine laboratories have been seized, revealing the illicit preparation of not only MDMA, but the N-ethyl (MDE), the N-propyl (MDPR), the N-isopropyl (MDIP) and the N,N-dimethyl (MDDM) homologues. These were all synthesized by the NaCNBH3 reduction method from the appropriate amine salt and piperonylacetone. Also, the N-ethyl-N-methyl, and N,N-diethyl homologues were found, prepared by catalytic hydrogenation.

Nakai, M. and Enomiya, T. Process for Producing Phenylacetones. *U.S. Patent 4,638,094*, dated January 20, 1987.

A high yield procedure is described, for the conversion of an allylbenzene to the corresponding phenylacetone. Specifically, the MDMA precursor 3,4- methylenedioxyphenylacetone is prepared in a 95% yield from safrole and butyl nitrite, in the presence of palladium bromide.

Nichols, D.E. Synthesis of 3,4- Methylenedioxy-methamphetamine Hydrochloride. FDA Master File on MDMA. 1986.

A detailed synthesis of MDMA from piperonylacetone is presented, including all the spectroscopic and physical detail, bibliographies and CVs as required to define a drug product for medical needs.

Shulgin, A.T. and Jacob III, P. Potential Misrepresentation of 3,4- Methylenedioxyamphetamine (MDA). A Toxicological Warning. *J. Anal. Toxicol.* **6**: 71-75 (1982).

The commercial availability and overt misrepresentation of 3,4-methylenedioxybenzylacetone as 3,4-methylenedioxyphenylacetone might well suggest that an unsuspecting attempt to synthesize MDMA may yield a new and unexplored base, 1-(3,4-methylenedioxyphenyl)-3-(methylamino)butane. This compound was synthesized, and characterized in comparison to MDMA. The analogous relationship between MDA and its comparable homologue, 1-(3,4-methylenedioxyphenyl)-3-aminobutane, is also explored.

Yourspigs, U.P. *The Complete Book of Ecstasy*. Synthesis Books, Birmingham, Alabama. 1992.

This is an underground press book describing, quite adequately, the equipment and the synthetic prosesses needed for the synthesis of MDMA, starting with safrole or Oil of Sassafras. The preparation of MDEA (EVE) is also offered.

Analytical methods

Anon: *Analytical Profiles of Substituted 3,4-Methylenedioxyamphetamines: Designer Drugs Related to MDA*. Published by CND Analytical, Auburn, Alabama. 109 p. (1988).

An atlas of spectra, chromatographic behaviour, outlines of chemical preparations, and a brief history of MDA, and over a score of its homologues, is presented. Spectra of the usual synthetic precursors are also given. MDMA is represented with its UV, IR (both salt and base), MS, and HPLC characteristics.

Andrey, R.E. and Moffat, A.C. Gas-Liquid Chromatographic Retention Indices of 1318 Substances of Toxicological Interest on SE-30 or OV-1 Stationary Phase. *J. Chromatog*. 220: 195-252 (1981).

The GC characteristics of many abuse drugs are presented in a review format. MDMA is included without experimental detail.

Bailey, K., By, A.W., Legault, D. and Verner, D. Identification of the N-Methylated Analogues of the Hallucinogenic Amphetamines and Some Isomers. *J.A.O.A.C.* 58: 62-69 (1975).

MDMA and four analogous methamphetamine derivatives (corresponding to 2-, 3-, and 4-methoxyamphetamine (MA) and 3-methoxy-4,5-methylenedioxyamphetamine (MMDA)) were synthesized and spectroscopically characterized. The synthesis was from the corresponding phenylacetone through the Leuckart reaction with N-methylformamide. The reported m.p. (of the hydrochloride salt) is 147-8 °C. The U.V., NMR, IR and mass spectral data are presented. Rf values (five systems) and GC retention times (four systems) are also given.

Churchill, K.T. Identification of 3,4-Methylenedioxy-methamphetamine. *Microgram*, 18: 123-132 (1985).

An analytical profile, through spectrographic tools such as UV, TLC, GC, NMR, MS, is presented for a sample of MDMA seized in Georgia. Comparisons with MDA are presented.

Clark, C.R., Noggle, F.T. and De Ruiter, J. Liquid Chromatographic and Mass Spectal Analysis of N,N-disubstituted 3,4-Methylenedioxyamphetamines. *J. Liq. Chromatog*. 13: 263-274 (1990).

The preparation of the N-methyl-N-ethyl, the N-methyl-N-propyl, and the N-methyl-N-isopropyl homologues of MDMA is described, but no physical properties are given. The route involves the reductive

methylation of the appropriate preformed N-alkyl MDA homologues. Chromatographic properties, and some mass spectroscopic data, are presented.

Clark, C.R., DeRuiter, J. and Noggle, F.T. GC-MS Identification of Amine-Solvent Condensation Products Formed During Analysis of Drugs of Abuse. *J. Chromatog. Sci*. 30: 399-404 (1992).

It is reported that during the GC-MS analysis of methanol solutions of primary amines such as MDA, amphetamine and phenethylamine, there is the formation of a small amount of the Schiff base product between the amine and formaldehyde. This product co-elutes, and is not the tetrahydroisoquinoline. Methanol solutions of MDMA result in detectable methylation, with the formation of N,N-dimethyl-MDA.

Clark, C.R., Valaer, A.K., DeRuiter, J. and Noggle, F.T. Synthesis, Stability and Analytical Profiles of 3,4-Methylenedioxyamphetamines: Derivatives of 'Ecstasy'(MDMA). *J. Alabama Acad. Sci*. 64: 34-48 (1993).

A number of the known homologues of MDMA were prepared to study their properties for eventual analytical purposes. The tools used were GCMS and HPLC using a reversed phase system.

Clark. C.R., DeRuiter, J., Noggle Jr., F.T. and Valaer, A., Identification of 1-(3,4-Methylenedioxyphenyl)-2-butanamines Related to MDMA, *Microgram*, 28: 154-168 (1995).

The alpha-ethyl homologues of MDA, MDMA and several close relatives were prepared and their spectroscopic and chromatographic properties compared. Also studied were the corresponding 1-phenylbutanes, with the amine function located at the three position.

Gudelsky, G.A., Yamamoto, B.K. and Nash, J.F. Potentiation of Cody, J.T. Cross-Reactivity of Amphetamine Analogues with Roche Abuscreen Radioimmunoassay Reagents, *J. Anal. Toxicol*. 14: 50-53 (1990).

Some 15 variously substituted amphetamine and phenethylamine derivatives, with and without N-substituents, were screened at various concentrations using the Roche Abuscreen Radioimmunoassay for amphetamines. Using amphetamine as a standard, only MDA was found to cross-react. All other compounds were negative, even at the highest concentrations. These included MDMA, MDE, MDOH, N,N-dimethyl-MDA, 2-MA, 4-hydroxyamphetamine, 2,5-DMA, TMA, methamphetamine, DOM, DOET, DOB, 2C-B and mescaline.

Gudelsky, G.A., Yamamoto, B.K. and Nash, J.F., Potentiation of 3,4-Methylenedioxymethamphetamine-induced Dopamine Release and Serotonin Neurotoxicity by 5-HT2 Receptor Agonists. *Eur. J. Pharmacol*. 264: 325-330.

Both DOI and 5-MeO-DMT, potent 5-HT2 agonists, were effective in enhancing the concentration of extracellular dopamine in the striatum of the rat brought about by the administration of MDMA. Neither of these agonists was effective in the absence of MDMA.

Cody, J.T. Detection of D,L-Amphetamine, D,L-Methamphetamine, and Illicit Amphetamine Analogues Using Diagnostic Products Corporation's Amphetamine and Methamphetamine Radioimmunoassay. *J. Anal. Toxicol.* 14: 321-324 (1990).

The commercial radioimmune assay procedures for amphetamine and methamphetamine were evaluated for a number of illicit drugs with the amphetamine backbone. MDA and MDMA gave substantial cross reactivity with both kits, but most of the others (DOM, mescaline, DOET. 2C-B, DOB, TMA) did not.

Cody, J.T and Schwartzhoff, R. Fluorescence Polarizatrion Immunoassay Detection of Amphetamine, Methamphetamine, and Illicit Amphetamine Analogues. *J. Anal. Toxicol.* 17: 26-30 (1993).

The Abbott Diagnostic Amphetamine/Methamphetamine II and Amphetamine Class Reagents were evaluated on the Abbott TDx for cross-reactivity to amphetamine and methamphetamine sterioisomers, several of their metabolites, and various illicit drugs. MDA, MDMA, MDE, as well as 4-hydroxymethamphetamine showed a cross-reactivity that would allow this procedure to be used as a screening tool.

Dal Cason, T. The Characterization of Some 3,4-Methylenedioxyphenylisopropylamine (MDA) Analogues. *J. Forensic Sci.* 34: 28-961 (1989).

The synthesis and complete spectroscopic identification of several N-alkylated homologues of MDA are presented. The compounds include MDA (and its acetyl derivative), MDMA, MDE, MDPR, MDIP, MDOH (and its acetyl derivative), MDDM, and the acetyl derivative of the oxime of MDP-2-P. Included are melting points, as well as GCMS, NMR, IR and HPLC details.

DeRuiter, J., Clark, C.R. and Noggle Jr., F.T. Liquid Chromatographic and Mass Spectral Analysis of 1-(3,4- Methylenedioxyphenyl)-1-propanamines: Regioisomers of the 3,4-Methylenedioxyamphetamines. *J. Chromatog. Sci.* 28: 129-132 (1990).

The chromatographic and spectroscopic properties, but not the synthetic details, are given for a series of alpha-ethyl benzylamines isomeric with MDA. The N-H, methyl, dimethyl, ethyl, propyl and isopropyl homologues are discussed.

Eichmeier, L.S. and Caplis, M.E. The Forensic Chemist; An 'Analytic Detective.' *Anal. Chem.* 47: 841A-844A (1975).

An analytical anecdote is presented showing the logical procedure used to distinguish MDMA from closely related drugs such as MDA in a seized sample. MDMA was acknowledged to be similar to MDA but, whereas MDA is a controlled substance, MDMA is exempt (sic) from Federal control.

Fitzgerald, R.L., Blamke, R.V., Glennon, R.A., Yousif, M.Y., Rosecrans, J.A. and Poklis, A. Determination of 3,4-Methylenedioxyamphetamine and 3,4- Methylenedioxymethamphetamine Enantiomers in Whole Blood. *J. Chromatog.* 490: 59-69 (1989).

Extracts of whole blood containing added MDA or MDMA were derivatized with N-trifluoroacetyl-L-prolyl chloride. The resulting diastereoisomers were separated by GC, allowing a sensitivity of analysis in the nanogram range.

Gan, B.K., Baugh, D., Liu, R.H. and Walia, A.S. Simultaneous Analysis of Amphetamine, Methamphetamine, and 3,4-Methylenedioxymethamphetamine (MDMA) in Urine Samples by Solid-phase Extraction, Derivatization, and Gas Chromatography/Mass Spectrometry. *J. Forensic Sci.* 36: 1331 (1991).

A method is described in which the extracts of urine are derivatized with trifluoroacetic anhydride. Deuterated amphetamine and methamphetamine were used as internal standards.

Gough, T.A. and Baker, P.B. Identification of Major Drugs of Abuse Using Chromatography. *J. Chromatog. Sci.* 20: 289-329 (1982).

An extensive review of the analytical identification of many abuse drugs is abstracted. MDMA is mentioned as one of these. There is no new experimental information presented.

Gupta, R.C. and Lundberg, G.D. Application of Gas Chromatography to Street Drug Analysis. *Clin. Toxicol.* 11: 437-442 (1977).

A gas chromatography screening procedure is described, in which the retention times of over 100 drugs are compared to those of methapyriline or codeine. MDMA is amongst them.

Hansson, R.C. Clandestine Laboratories. Production of MDMA 3,4- Methylenedioxymethamphetamine. *Analogues.* 9: 1-10 (1987).

A compilation of forensic information pertaining to MDMA is presented, including spectra (UV, MS, IR), synthetic approaches, and observations from clandestine laboratory operations (seen in Australia).

Hearn, W.L., Hime, G. and Andollo, W. Recognizing Ecstasy: Adam and Eve, the MDA Derivatives – Analytical Profiles. *Abstracts of the CAT/SOFT Meetings*, Oct. 29 – Nov. 1, 1986, Reno/Lake Tahoe, Nevada, USA.

A study is reported comparing MDA, MDMA and MDE in the EMIT immunoanalytical assay system that is designed for amphetamine. Even though they are all of decreased reactivity, there is cross-reactivity and they may be picked up as positives. Using the bottom limit cut-off of 300 nanograms/mL for amphetamine there would be a response from as little as 10-15 mg/mL of MDMA. This is a value that might be encountered in the early stages of MDMA use.

Helmlin, H., and Brenneisen, R. Determination of Psychotropic Phenylalkylamine Derivatives in Biological Matrices by High-Performance Liquid Chromatography with Photodiode-Array Detection. *J. Chromatog.* 593: 87-94 (1992)

An HPCL analysis procedure was described for the analysis of MDMA and MDA in human urine. Six hours following the administration of a 1.7 mg/kg dosage to several patients, urine concentrations ranged from 1.48 to 5.05 ug/mL. The major metabolite, MDA, showed concentrations ranging from 0.07 to 0.90 ug/ml. A separate study of the cactus Trichocereus patchanol showed a mescaline content of from 1.09 to 23.75 ug/ml

Helmlin, H-J. and Brenneisen, R. Determination of Psychotropic Phenylalkylamine Derivatives in Biological Matrices by High-performance Liquid Chromatography with Photodiode-array Detection. *J. Chromatog.* 593 87-94 (1992).

An HPLC analytical scheme has been developed for the characterization and potential quantitative measurement of some fifteen phenethylamine drugs of forensic interest. Of specific clinical interest was the urine analyses of several patients following the administration of 1.7 mg/Kg of MDMA. These values, from samples collected about six hours following drug administration, showed a range of 1.48–5.05 ug/mL for MDMA, and 0.07–0.90 ug/mL for the metabolite, MDA.

Helmlin, H. -J., Bracher, K., Salamone, S.J. and Brenneisen, R., Analysis of 3,4-Methylenedioxymethamphetamine (MDMA) and its Metabolites in Human Plasma and Urine by HPLC-DAD, GC-MS and Abuscreen-Online. *Abstracts from CAT/SOFT Joint Meeting*, October 10-16, 1993, Phoenix, Arizona.

Urine and plasma samples were taken from a number of patients being administered 1.5 mg/Kg MDMA for psychotherapy research purposes. Maximum plasma levels (300 ng/mL) were seen at 140 minutes. The main urinary metabolites were 4-hydroxy-3-methoxymethamphetamine and 3,4-dihydroxymethamphetamine, both excreted in conjugated form. The two N-demethylated homologues of these compounds were present as minor metabolites.

The cross-reactivity of the Abuscreen immunoassay for both the metabolites (including MDA, another metabolite) and the parent drug were determined.

Holsten, D.W. and Schieser, D.W. Controls over the Manufacture of MDMA. *J. Psychoactive Drugs*, 18: 371-2 (1986).

A strong argument is made for attending to the quality of manufacture, and the basic concepts of ethical principles in the exploring of drugs that have not been evaluated against the usual pharmaceutical standards. Government interference in such studies becomes necessary, to safeguard the public.

Julian, E.A. Microcrystalline Identification of Drugs of Abuse: The Psychedelic Amphetamine. *J. Forensic Sci.* 35: 821-830 (1990).

The diliturate salts (5-nitrobarbituric acid salts) of several psychedelic amphetamines have been made and observed. The amines were PA, MDA MMDA (1, not 2 as implied), DOM, DOB, TMA, Mescaline, MDMA and MDEA. Photographs of the crystals are shown.

Kunsman, G.W., Manno, J.E., Cockerham, K.R. and Manno, B.R. Application of the Syva EMIT and Abbott TDx Amphetamine Immuniassays to the Detection of 3,4-Methylenedioxmethamphetamine (MDMA) and 3,4-Methylenedioxyethamphetamine (MDEA) in Urine. *J. Anal Toxicol.* 14: 149-153 (1990).

Two popular immunological drug assays, designed for the determination of amphetamine, have been applied to urines that had been spiked with varying amounts of MDMA and MDE. The EMIT assay was insensitive except at the highest level, but there was considerable cross-reactivity with the fluorescent polarization assay.

Lim, H.K., Su, Z. and Foltz, R.L. Stereoselective Disposition: Enantioselective Quantitation of 3,4-(Methylenedioxy)Meth-amphetamine and Three of its Metabolites by Gas Chromatography/Electron Capture Negative Ion Chemical Ionization Mass Spectrometry. *Biol. Mass Spect.* 22: 403-11 (1993).

A sensitive assay for MDMA and three of its metabolites has been developed. It recognizes the optical activity of the chiral centers, and has been used to determine the degree of asymmetric metabolism of racemic MDMA in both rats and mice.

Lim, H.K., Zeng, S., Chei, D.M. and Flotz, R.L. Comparitive Investigation of Disposition of 3,4-(Methylenedioxy)meth-amphetamine (MDMA) in the Rat and the Mouse by a Capillary Gas Chromatography-Mass Spectrometry Assay Based on Perfluorotributylamine-enhanced Ammonia Positive Ion Chemical Ionization . *J. Pharmaceut. Biomed. Anal.* 10: 657-665 (1992).

An assay is described that allows a quantitative measure of MDMA and three of its primary metabolites, methylenedioxamphetamine, 4-hydroxy-3-methoxymethamphetamine and 4-hydroxy-3-methoxyamphetamine. The latter two metabolites were excreted mainly as the glucuronide and sulfate conjugates. The metabolic patterns of the rat and the mouse are compared.

Michel, R.E., Rege, A.B. and George, W.J. High-Pressure Liquid Chromatography / Electrochemical Detection Method for Monitoring MDA and MDMA in Whole Blood and Other Biological Tissues. J. Neurosci. Methods 50 61-66 (1993).

An method is described for the analysis of MDMA and MDA in biological samples. It claims a high sensitivity and a short turn-around time. MDE is used as an internal standard. Spiked blood samples, rather than actual clinical specimens, were used.

Nakahara, Y. Detection and Diagnostic Interpretation of Amphetamines in Hair. For. Sci. Intern. 70 135-153 (1995).

A review is presented of a extensive analytical literature on the incorporation and detection of amphetamine derivatives in hair. Discussed are such questions as hair pretreatment, choice of analytical instrument, animal experiments with drug incorporation rates, and the relationship between the history of drug use and detection the drug in the hair sample.

Noggle Jr., F.T., Clark, C. R. and DeRuiter, J. Gas Chromatographic and Mass Spectrometric Analysis of N-Methyl-1-aryl-2-propanamines Synthesized from the Substituted Allylbenzenes Present in Sassafras Oil. J. Chromatog. Sci. 20 267-271 (1991).

The several allylaromatic essential oils in Sassafras have been studied in the regeospecific addition of HBr to form the beta-bromopropane. The bromine atom was subsequently displace with methylamine to form the corresponding methamphetamine. Safrole gives rise to MDMA.

Noggle, F.T., Clark, C.R. and DeRuiter, J. Liquid Chromatographic and Spectral Methods for the Differentiation of 3,4-Methylenedioxymethamphetamine (MDMA) from Regioisomeric Phenethylamines. *J. Liq. Chromatog*. 14: 913-1928 (1991).

Three isomers of MDMA, with the changes restricted to the alpha-carbon and the nitrogen substituents, have been synthesized. These are the two phenethylamines N-ethyl and N,N-dimethyl-3,4-methylenedioxyphenethylamine, and 1-(3,4 methylenedioxyphenyl-2-aminobutane (BDB). Although their mass spectra are quite similar, they can be distinguished from one-another by HPLC.

Noggle, F.T., Clark, C.R. and DeRuiter, J. Liquid Chromatorgraphic and Mass Spectral Analysis of 1-(3,4-Methylenedioxyphenyl)-3-Butanamines, Homologues of 3,4-Methylenedioxyamphetamines. *J. Chromatog. Sci.* 27: 240-243 (1989).

The HPLC and GC properties of several homologues of MDA and MDMA are reported employing the homologous ketone 3,4-methylenedioxyphenyl-3-butanone are studied. These include the primary amine, and the N-methyl, ethyl, dimethyl, (n)-propyl and (i)-propyl homologues. The N-hydroxy was made, but its possible thermal instability was not discussed.

Noggle Jr., F.T., Clark, C.R. and DeRuiter, J. Identification of Safrole and Bromosafrole in Samples from the Clandestine Synthesis of MDMA from Sassafras Oil. *Microgram*, 24: 7-13 (1991).

An analysis of seized samples from an illicit MDMA laboratory showed one to be sassafras oil that contained safrole by GCMS. The other appeared to be the result of the addition of hydrobromic acid to safrole to produce two 'bromosafroles.' Addition of methylamine to this material produced some MDMA.

Noggle Jr., F.T., Clark, C.R. and DeRuiter, J. Gas Chromatographic and Mass Spectrometric Analysis of Samples from a Clandestine Laboratory Involved in the Synthesis of Ecstasy from Sassafras Oil. *J. Chromatog. Sci.* 29: 168-173 (1991).

Samples from a clandestine laboratory gave, on GC-MS analysis, evidence for the intended synthesis of MDMA from the oil of sassafras. The natural component safrole gave, with the addition of HBr, the 2-bromopropane intermediate which, on treatment with methylamine, gave MDMA.

Noggle Jr., F.T., DeRuiter, J. and Long, M.J. Spectrophotometric and Liquid Chromatographic Identification of 3,4-Methylenedioxyphenylisopropylamine and its N-Methyl and N-Ethyl Homologues are presented. *J. A. O. A. C.* 69: 681-686 (1986).

A synthesis of MDEA (the N-ethyl homolog of MDA) is reported, and the infra-red spectra of the free bases, the hydrochloride salts, and the phenylisothiocyanate adducts are recorded, as is the HPLC retention behaviour for both the bases and these derivatives.

Noggle Jr., F.T., Clark, C.R., Andurkar, S. and DeRuiter, J. Methods for the Analysis of 1-(3,4-Methylenedioxyphenyl)-2-Butanamine and N-Methyl-1-(3,4-Methylenedioxyphenyl)-2-Propanamine (MDMA). *J. Chromatog. Sci.* 29: 103-106 (1991).

The infra-red and mass spectra, and the GC and HPLC retention times, of these two known compounds, are given.

Noggle Jr., F.T., Clark, C.R., Bouhadir, K.H. and DeRuiter, J. Liquid Chromatographic and Mass Spectral Analysis of 1-(3,4-Methylenedioxyphenyl)-3-propanamines: Regioisomers of MDMA. *J. Chromatog. Sci.* 29: 78-82 (1991).

A series of N-substituted homologues of methylenedioxyphenyl-(n)-propylamine was prepared, and described by chromatographic and spectroscopic means. No melting points or other synthetic analytical detail was given.

Noggle, F.T., Clark, C.R., Pitts-Monk, P. and De Ruiter, J. Liquid Chromatographic and Mass Spectral Analysis of 1-(3,4-Dimethoxyphenyl)-2-propanamines: Analogues of MDMA. *J. Chromatog. Sci.* 29: 253-257 (1991).

A number of 3,4- dimethoxy counterparts of MDMA and its homologues have been prepared and analysed by HPLC. Described are 3,4-dimethoxyamphetamine, the N-methyl, the N- ethyl, and the N,N-dimethyl homologues.

Noggle Jr., R.T., Clark, C.R., Valaer, A.K. and DeRuiter, J. Liquid Chromatographic and Mass Spectral Analysis of N-Substituted Analogues of 3,4-Methylenedioxyamphetamine. *J. Chromatog. Sci.* 26: 410 (1988).

Several spectral properties, and the HPLC separation characteristics of MDMA and several of its homologues and analogues (MDE, MDPR, DMMA and MDOH) are described.

Noggle Jr., F.T., DeRuiter, J., McMillian, C.L. and Clark, C.R. Liquid Chromatographic Analysis of some N-Alkyl-3,4-Methylenedioxyamphetamines. *J. Liq. Chromatog.* 10: 2497-2504 (1987).

The HPLC separation characteristics of MDA, MDMA, MDE and MDDM (N,N-dimethyl-MDA) are reported on a reversed phase column.

O'Brian, B.A., Bonicamp, J.M. and Jones, D.W., Differentiation of Amphetamine and its Major Hallucinogen Derivatives using Thinlayer Chromatography. *J. Anal. Toxicol.* 6: 143-147 (1982).

Two thin-layer chromatographic systems, and several procedures for detection, are described for MDMA and 18 analogues. The retention times and the visualization colour changes are compared and described. Detection limits in urine were determined from artificially spiked samples. The reference sample of MDMA was synthesized from MDA by methylation with methyl iodide, and separation from the co-generated dimethyl and trimethylammonium homologues by liquid- liquid extraction and preparative TLC.

Poklis, A., Fitzgerald, R.L., Hall, K.V. and Saady, J.J. Emit-d.a.u. Monoclonal Amphetamine / Methamphetamine Assay. II. Detection of Methylenedioxyamphetamine (MDA) and Methylenedioxymethamphetamine (MDMA). *Foren. Sci. Intern.* 59: 63-70 (1993).

MDA and MDMA have been found to be cross-reactive in both the monoclonal and the polyclonal immunological EMIT assay. The former was much more sensitive, presumably sufficiently so for the detection of these drugs in urine following clinical intoxication.

Ramos, J.M., Johnson, S. and Poklis, A. MDMA and MDA Cross Reactivity Observed with Abbott TDx Amphetamine/Methamphetamine Reagents. *Clin. Chem.* 34: 991 (1988).

A study of the cross-reactivity of MDMA and MDA with the Abbott TDx fluorescent polarization immuno assay showed that these two drugs gave positive tests for amphetamine and methamphetamine at levels that were clinically relevant. This expands the utility of this screening procedure, but also demands additional care in the interpretation of positive results that are obtained clinically.

Renton, R.J., Cowie, J.S. and Oon, M.C. A Study of the Precursors, Intermediates and Reaction By-Products on the Synthesis of 3,4-Methylenedioxymethylamphetamine and its Application to Forensic Drug Analysis. *Foren. Sci. Intern.* 60: 189-202 (1993).

MDMA was prepared by three separate synthetic routes, and the trace byproducts and impurities were identified and presented in a way that probable synthetic method could be deduced for legal purposes.

Rizzi, A.M., Hirz, R., Cladrowa-Runge, S. and Jonsson, H. Enantiomeric Separation of Amphetamine, Methamphetamine and Ring Substituted Amphetamines by Means of a ß-Cyclodextrin-Chiral Stationary Phase. *Chromatographia*, 39: 131-137 (1994).

The separation of the enantiomers of a number of racemic amphetamine compounds, including MDMA, is described employing an optically active column. Derivatization with a chiral reagent is not required.

Ruangyuttikarn, W. and Moody, D.E. Comparison of Three Commercial Amphetamine Immunoassays for Detection of Methamphetamine, Methylenedioxyamphetamine, Methylenedioxymethamphetmaine, and Methylenedioxyethylamphetamine. *J. Anal. Toxicol.* 12: 229-233 (1988).

Three commercial immunoassays for the detection of amphetamine in urine (Abuscreen, a radioimmune assay, RIA; EMIT, a homogeneous enzyme immuno assay procedure; and TDx, a fluorescent polarization immuno assay, FPIA) have been assayed for their responses to methamphetamine, MDA, MDMA, and MDE. Some cross-reactivity to amphetamine is seen with all compounds, but the response is extremely variable depending upon the assay employed.

Ruybal, R. Microcrystalline Test for MDMA. *Microgram*, 19: 79-80 (1986).

MDMA gives a sensitive microcrystalline test with gold chloride. The crystal form is similar to that of methamphetamine.

Shaw, M.A. and Peel, H.W. Thin-layer Chromatography of 3,4- methylenedioxyamphetamine, 3,4- Methylenedioxymethamphetamine and other Phenethylamine Derivatives. *J. Chromatog.* 104: 201-204 (1975).

A broad study is presented on the TLC analyses of many phenethylamines. The compound specifically named in the title, 3,4-Methylenedioxymethamphetamine (MDMA), was a misprint that was subsequently corrected to the intended compound, MMDA. MDMA was not a part of this study.

Shimamine, M., Takahashi, K. and Nakahara, Y. Studies on the Identification of Psychotropic Substances. VII. Preparation and Various Analytical Data of Standard References of Some Hallucinogens, 3,4- Methylenedioxyamphetamine (MDA), 3,4- Methylenedioxymethamphetamine (MDMA) and 5-Methoxy-3,4- methylenedioxyamphetamine (MMDA). *Bull. Nat. Inst. Hygien. Sci.* 108: 118-125 (1990).

Reference standards of the three title compounds were prepared. Analytical data were studied with TLC, UV, IR, HPLC, GC-MS and NMR.

Simpson, B.J., Simpson, T.P. and Lui, R.H. Microcrystalline Differentiation of 3,4- Methylenedioxyamphetamine and Related Compounds. *J. Foren. Sci.* 36: 908 (1991).

Crystal gold salts can distinguish between MDA, mescaline, and DOET, whereas MDMA and MDE form crystals similar to one another and are not easily distinguished. DOM and N-hydroxy-MDA compounds were soluble in the gold chloride reagents and formed no crystals.

Sutherland, G.J. 3,4- Methylenedioxymethamphetamine (MDMA) A Basis for Quantitation by UV Spectrophotometry. *Analogues,* 10: 1-3 (1988).

Due to the absence of reference samples of MDMA (in Australia) a seized sample has been evaluated and provides a basis for quantitation employing UV.

Tedeschi, L., Frison, G., Castagna, F., Giorgetti, R. and Ferrara, S.D. Simultaneous Identification of Amphetamine and its Derivatives in Urine Using HPLC-UV. *Intern. J. Legal Med.* 105: 265-9 (1993).

Four compounds are rapidly extracted from urine, derivatized with sodium 1,2-naphthaquinone-4-sulfonate, and separated from one-another by HPLC on an ion-pair reversed phase system, using a detector at 480 nm. The compounds were amphetamine, methamphetamine, 3,4-methylenedioxyamphetamine (MDA) and 3,4- Methylenedioxymethamphetamine (MDMA).

Thompson, W.C. and Dasgupta, A. Microwave-induced Rapid Preparation of Fluoro- Derivatives of Amphetamine, Methamphetamine and 3,4- Methylenedioxymethamphetamine for GC-MS Confirmation Assays. *Clin. Chem.* 40: 1703-1706 (1994).

The use of a microwave technique allows the rapid derivitization of amphetamine-like compounds, such as MDMA, without the need of external heating.

Verweij, A. Clandestine Manufacture of 3,4- Methylenedioxymethylamphetamine (MDMA) by low pressure Reductive Amination. A Mass Sectrometric Study of some Reaction Mixtures. *Foren. Sci. Int.* 45: 91-96 (1990).

An analysis by GCMD has been made of the contaminants present in illicitly synthesized MDMA. Most of them are ascribed to impurities in the starting piperonyl acetone (piperonal, safrole, isosafrole) or in the starting methylamine (ammonia, dimethylamine, methylethylamine).

Verweij, A.M. Contamination of Illegal Amphetamine. Hydrastatinine as a Contaminant in 3,4- (Methylenedioxy)methylamphetamine. *Arch. Krim.* 188: 54-7 (1991).

The presence of hydrastatinine has been reported in the analysis of illicitly prepared MDMA. This extraordinary chemistry might involve the generation of a phenylacetaldehyde as an intermediate in the oxidation processes involving the conversion of the starting material, safrole. Structural identification depended on the comparisons of mass spectra.

Verweij, A.M.A. and Sprong, A.G.A. A Note About some Impurities in Commercially Available Piperonylmethylketone. *Microgram,* 26: 209-213 (1993).

An extensive collection of compounds, structures and IR spectra of impurities in commercial piperonylmethylketone (a precursor to MDMA) is carefully reproduced, to allow a determination to be made of the method of synthesis. The actual source of the precursor ketone that was studied here, however, was apparently not known, so no immediate application of this origin fingerprinting is obvious.

Ward, C., McNally, A.J., Rusyniak, D. and Salamone, S.J. 125-I Radioimmunoassay for the Dual Detection of Amphetamine and Methamphetamine. *J. Foren. Sci.* 39: 1486-1496 (1994).

A new radioimmunoassay has been developed that is essentially as sensitive to MDA and MDMA as it is to the primary targets amphetamine and methamphetamine. It is insensitive to the (-) isomers of amphetamine and methamphetamine.

Yamauchi, T. The Analysis of Stimulant-analogue Compounds (3,4- Methylenedioxymethamphetamine Hydrochloride). *Kagaku Keisatsu Kenkyusho Hokoku, Hokagaku Hen.* 39: 23 (1986).

People from abroad have provided samples of drugs that had been heretofore unidentified in Japan. An analytical profile of one such drug, MDMA, is provided employing most modern spectroscopic tools.

Reviews and social commentary

– including a sampling of magazine, newspaper and radio commentary

Abbott, A. and Concar, D. A Trip into the Unknown. *New Scientist,* August 29, 1992, pp. 30-34.

An overview is presented on the history of MDMA and the difficulty in determining if there is human risk paralleling the known neurotoxic effects in experimental primates. A picture is given of its extensive use in the popular party structure known popularly as 'raves,' and it has become the third most widest used drug in England, surpassed only by marijuana and amphetamine.

Abramson, D.M. Ecstasy: The New Drug Underground. *New Age,* October, 1985, pp 35-40.

This article addresses the questions that are raised by the conflict of governmental banning of drugs that are of potential value in psychotherapy, and the therapist's determination to continue exploring their use.

Adamson, S. *'Through the Gateway of the Heart: Accounts of Experiences with MDMA and other Empathogenic Substances.'* Four Trees Publications, San Francisco. Foreword by R. Metzner. 1985.

This book is a collection of some fifty personal accounts, largely involving MDMA. Some are from the notes of therapists, involving clinical usage, and others are personal accounts from self-exploration.

Adelaars, A. *Ecstasy: De opkomst van een Bewustzijnsveranderend Middel.* Published by In De Knipscheer, Amsterdam, 1991. ISBN 90 6265 342 1. 136 pp (Dutch).

This small paperback volume presents a brief history of psychedelic drugs, then the history of MDMA both in Holland and in the broader scene. The topics range from therapy to popular use.

Adler, J. Getting High on 'Ecstasy.' *Newsweek*, April 15, 1985, p. 96.

This is a short, apparently factual, overview of both the chemical and the 'street' use of MDMA. It is generally sympathetic to its medical potential.

Anon: Several reports from the *Brain/Mind Bulletin*:

(1) MDMA: Compound raises medical and legal issues. Brain/Mind Bulletin, 10, #8, April 15, 1985.

The title article is presented, and nearly the entire issue is given over to a thorough coverage of the medical and scientific aspects of MDMA.

(2) Psychiatrists, drug-abuse specialists testify in L.A. at first MDMA hearing. Brain/Mind Bulletin, 10, #12 July 8, 1985.

A news report on the first round of hearings in Los Angeles, concerning the scheduling of MDMA. An overview of the testimony is presented.

(3) Judge proposes more lenient schedule for MDMA. Brain/Mind Bulletin, 11, #11 June 16, 1986.

Administrative Law Judge Francis Young recommended, at the conclusions of the MDMA hearings, that the DEA put the drug into Schedule III, partly to ease research with the compound, and partly due to the absence of demonstrated abuse of the drug.

(4) MDMA: Federal court decides that DEA used improper criteria. Brain/Mind Bulletin, 13, #2 November, 1987.

A report is given as to the First Court of Appeals in Boston, ruling that the DEA had not sufficiently considered the arguments concerning the current medical use of MDMA.

Anon: DEA Proposal to Ban New Psychedelic Protested. *Substance Abuse Report*, December, 1984. pp 4-5.

The several letters that were addressed to the DEA in response to its announcement in the Federal Register to consider the scheduling of MDMA, are here abstracted and commented upon.

Anon: *Ecstasy: 21st Century Entheogen.* Private Tract, 28 pages.

This is an elaborate thesis that is directed totally to the promotion of the use of MDMA. There is a presumed question and answer section, that is designed for the cautiously curious.

Anon: MDMA. NIDA Capsules. Issued by the Press Office of the National Institute on Drug Abuse, Rockville, Maryland. July 1985.

A two-page precis describing the health problems encountered with MDMA use, its relationship to the neurotransmitters, and the moves being made at the Justice Department to combat 'designer drugs' such as MDMA in the future.

Anon: Designer Drugs: A New Concern for the Drug Abuse Community. *NIDA Notes*, December, 1985, pp. 2-3.

A discussion of 'designer drugs' is arranged in four groups: variations on fentanyl, on meperidine, on PCP, and on amphetamine and methamphetamine. MDMA fits this last group. The research directions of NIDA are discussed.

Anon: Ecstasy of the Eighties. *Frontline*, August 24-September 6, 1985 (page 83-85).

A review article on the emergence of MDMA, published in one of India's major national magazines. No new information, and no suggestion that there is any use in India.

Anon. The Hyping of Ecstasy. *The Illustrated London News*, October, 1988 pp. 29-32.

A developing fad is described in London, called 'Acid House' which involves loud rock music, violent dancing, and the use of MDMA. It is being largely ignored by the authorities.

Anon: Mind-bending Drug Could Leave Brains Permanently Warped. *New Scientist*, 21 January (1989) p. 30.

A short summary of the AAAS meeting in San Francisco. Peroutka is quoted as saying the consumers of MDMA should abandon its use altogether. If they continue, he said, they risk damage to their nervous systems that may take decades to manifest itself. It could emerge initially as depression or disturbance to sleep. This is the first hint as to the specific form of the down-the-road damage that is being promoted as a cost of using MDMA.

Anon: 'Ice' and 'Ecstasy' Two Dangerous Psychotropic Drugs. *Int. Criminal Police Review*. 45: 1-24 (1990).

A brief review of the dangers and health hazards of two designer drugs is presented; vis., methamphetamine and MDMA. International controls of the easily available chemical precursors should be instituted. The author is the ICPO-Interpol General Secretariat.

Anon: Deal mit Cadillac (September 4, 1989); Ecstasy und Cadillac (November 12, 1989). Der Spiegel.

Two of several news articles appearing in Germany, presenting the scandal surrounding the chemical firm Imhausen-Chemie. It had been producing, and selling, large quantities of a precursor to MDMA (piperonylacetone, which they called PMK) as well of literally millions of tablets of the final product itself (which they called 'Ecstasy,' 'XTC,' 'Adam' or 'Cadillac.'). The magnitude of operation was tons of drug, and millions of tablets. And, of course, the money volume was many millions of Deutsche Marks.

Bakalar, J.B. and Grinspoon, L. Testing Psychotherapies and Drug Therapies: The Case of Psychedelic Drugs. *The Clinical, Pharmacological and Neurotoxicological Effects of the Drug MDMA*. Kluwer, New York. (1990) Ed: S.J. Peroutka.

The problems associated with the social and medical acceptance of drugs as a valid component of the psychotherapeutic process are outlined and discussed. MDMA is used as a specific point of illustration.

Barbour, J. *Cracking Down: What You Must Know About Dangerous Drugs*. The Associated Press. 1986.

This is a 63 page illustrated essay, aimed at stopping drug use and abuse by scaring the reader. Unfortunately, the information is not completely accurate. MDMA is spun together with other designer drugs as things that destroy the brain.

Barendregt, C. Dutch Conference on MDMA. 1. 6 (1990?).

This is a summation of the January 23, 1990 conference in Amsterdam, sponsored by the Dutch Institute on Alcohol and Drugs. With the passing of legislation against MDMA in November 1988, the criminal aspect of the use of this drug has quite logically increased. Dutch drug law (of 1976) distinguishes two categories of drug; those with an unacceptable risk (Group 1, containing such drugs as cocaine and heroin) and those with less risk (Group 2, containing only marijuana and hash). Newly marketed, and illegalized, drugs such as MDMA can only be defined as Group 1 as Group 2 is closed to any new substances. It was concluded that the risks of MDMA use are to be found in its legal status, rather than in its pharmacological properties.

Barnes, D.M. New Data Intensifies the Agony over Ecstasy. *Science*, 239: 864-866 (1988).

A review and commentary is presented of the Winter Conference on Brain Res., 23-30 January, 1988, in which there was a section on MDMA. A distillation of the comments made yields the feeling that more clinical work is needed to define the value, and that there would not likely be any further clinical work done. There are extensive quotations from some of the authors of recent animal studies on serotonin toxicity.

Barnett, R. DEA: RSVP re MDMA. Editorial from *KCBS*, July 29, 1985.

With the possibility of therapeutic value seen in some psychiatric cases, KCBS felt that the action of the DEA (making MDMA illegal) short-circuited the hearings process, and was premature. A request is made to allow research on the effects and potentials of this drug to continue.

Baselt, R.C. and Cravey, R.H. Methylenedioxymeth-amphetamine. In *Disposition of Toxic Drugs and Chemicals in Man*, Third Edition. Year Book Med. Publishers, Inc., Chicago 1989. pp. 554-555.

A brief review is made of the published body levels of MDMA in reported cases of use and medical problems.

Baum, R.M. New Variety of Street Drugs Poses Growing Problem. *Chemical and Engineering News*, September 9, 1985. pp. 7-16.

A completely professional article discussing the challenges presented to law enforcement officials, legislators and scientists, by the invention of analogues of illegal drugs by underground chemists. MDMA is held out as being quite apart from the fentanyl and meperidine examples, and is analysed at some length.

Beck, J. MDMA: The Popularization and Resulting Implications of a Recently Controlled Psychoactive Substance. *Contemporary Drug Problems*, Spring, 1986. pp 23-63.

A historical analysis is made of the relationship between drug illegalization and social issues. MDMA is used as a specific example, and a considerable body of first hand observations of its use is also presented.

Beck, J. and Morgan, P.A. Designer Drug Confusion: A Focus on MDMA. *J. Drug Education*, 16 267-282 (1986).

This article discusses the competing definitions and issues surrounding the various designer drugs, but is primarily devoted to an examination of MDMA. A rationale is offered as to why interest in MDMA will continue to grow.

Beck, J. and Rosenbaum, M. 'Pursuit of Ecstasy: The MDMA Experience.' State University of New York Press, New York. 239 pp. (1994).

This book is the first complete analysis of the clinical value of MDMA, and it brings together into one place the previously scattered reports of the drug's use in therapy. The information that is compiled here, was originally the raw material for a report to the National Institute of Drug Abuse (NIDA), as the presentation of a summary of a contract awarded the authors to study MDMA. The final report was never published by NIDA, and so this book serves as a superb vehicle for making these findings available as public information.

Beebe D.K. and Walley, E. Update on Street Drugs in Mississippi. *J. Miss. State Med. Ass.* 1989 Dec,

Drug abuse is on the rise in Mississippi. Treatment centers across the state report significant increases in substance abuse cases. Consequently, family physicians must have the most current, accurate information available and the skills with which to treat either an acute crisis or the chronic problems related to drug abuse. The authors present an overview of the clinical presentations and management of some of the most widely used designer drugs: crack, ecstasy and PCP.

Beebe, D.K. and Walley, E. Update on Street Drugs in Mississippi. *J. Miss. State Med Ass.* 30 387-390 (1989).

A discussion of the drug abuse problem in Mississppi is presented. MDMA is listed with a check list of the medical compilation that can follow use.

Beebe, D.K. and Walley, E. Substance Abuse: The Designer Drugs. AFP May 1991, p. 1689.

A brief overview of the 'Designer Drug' is presented, using mescaline, the synthetic opiods, the aryehexylamines, and methaquelone as prototypes.

Bost, R.O. 3,4- Methylenedioxymethamphetamine (MDMA) and Other Amphetamine Derivatives. *J. Foren. Sci.* 33: 576-587 (1988).

A series of amphetamine derivatives are discussed as 'Designer Drugs' with structures slightly modified from explicitly named illegal drugs. A number of emergency cases are presented, which are documented with MDA, MDMA and MDE involvement. A number of analytical procedures are demonstrated.

Buchanan, J. Ecstasy in the Emergency Department. *Clinical Toxicology Update*, 7: 1-4 (1985).

A review of the history and the pharmacology of the psychoactive amphetamines is given. The overall recommendation for the emergency room is to expect an overdosed patient to present with signs similar to those with an amphetamine overdose, and to expect to treat primarily signs of anxiety and hypertension. The attending physician can expect the patient to be unaware of the actual toxin he has taken, and careful laboratory work will be needed to identify the chemical in body fluids and drug samples.

Callaway, E. The Biology of Information Processing. *J. Psychoactive Drugs* 18: 315-318 (1986).

A review is presented of the difficulties that are classically part of the communication of information, and the roles of the many psychologists and physicians who have addressed the problem. The study of neurotransmitters, and thus drugs that involve these brain chemicals, is part of the eventual understanding. The role of non-classic 'unsleepy drugs' (stimulants) such as MDMA are speculated upon as potential tools in this study.

Chaudhuri, A. Cause and Effect. *Time Out,* August 5-12 (1992).

A review of the background of MDMA and the increasing medical concern in England regarding its popularity in the rave scene. Arguments are advanced for its removal from Category A of English law, allowing its potential in therapy to be explored.

Chesher, G., Some Views on Ecstasy. *Modern Medicine of Australia* April 1990 pp. 76-85.

A brief and quite accurate review is given as to the background, therapeutic interest, legal history, and neurotoxicity of MDMA.

Climko, R.P., Roehrich, H., Sweeney, D.R. and Al-Razi, J. Ecstasy: A Review of MDMA and MDA. *Int. J. of Psychiatry in Medicine.* 16: 359-372 (1986-87).

A review of the pharmacology and toxicity of MDA is presented, with some additional data for MDMA. A balanced presentation with 75 references.

Cohen, S. They Call It Ecstasy. *Drug Abuse & Alcoholism Newsletter,* Vista Hill Foundation. 14. 6. September, 1985.

A basically negative overview of the prospects of MDMA in therapy. There is a wistful note with the 'we've been through all this before' feeling. LSD had hope, LSD failed, and this too shall fail.

Conner, M. and Sherlock, K. Attitudes and Ecstasy Use. Paper presented at the Eur. Ass. of Exp. Social Psychol. 15-20 September, 1993, Lisbon.

An anonymous questionaire was distributed amongst young people (in England) who had varying degrees of experience with MDMA. Over half the sample had tried the drug, and a substantial minority used it regularly. The results are discussed in terms of the design of literature that could be directed at changing this use pattern.

Corliss, J. Agonizing over Ecstasy. *Santa Cruz Sentinel,* Friday March 24, 1989.

An update on the controversy surrounding the use of MDMA, geared for popular consumption. Emphasis is on serotonin and damage, if not now, maybe somewhere down the road.

Cuomo, M.J., Dyment, P.G., Gammino, V.M. Increasing Use of 'Ecstasy' (MDMA) and Other Hallucinogens on a College Campus. *J. Am. College Health,* 42: 271-4 (1994).

A random survey of college students asking about their use of illicit was conducted, and the results compared with a parallel survey made four years earlier. Most drugs were used by fewer people. However, the use of marijuana and of LSD was statistically unchanged, and the use of mescaline and psilocybin had increased slightly, and the use of MDMA had increased by 50%.

Deluca, N. Closed Doors/Closed Minds. *KCBS Editorial.* July 10, 1986.

An opinion is expressed, that the easy answer to MDMA given by the federal government, illegalization by placement into Schedule I, was the wrong answer. It appears that MDMA warrants a closer look by therapists, and the DEA should not simply lock the drug away where it cannot be investigated.

De Man, R.A. Morbiditeit en Sterfte als Gevolg van Ecstacygebruik, *Ned Tijd. Gen.* 138 1850-1855 (1994).

A review is presented of the pharmacology and pharmacokinetics, the adverse effects, and the mortality that has been caused by MDMA.

Doblin, R. Murmurs in the Heart of the Beast: MDMA and the DEA, HHS, NIDA, NIMH, ADAMHA, FBI and the WHO. Privately printed. August 8, 1984.

This is a collection of many of the letters exchanged between the DEA and the FDA, that led to the decision to place MDMA in the listings of scheduled drugs. Also included are the DAWN (medical emergency) reports, and letters written in response to the proposed scheduling.

Doblin, R. The Media Does MDMA. Privately printed, August 5, 1985 -July 2, 1987.

This is a collection of articles, newspaper accounts, writings from many sources, that touch upon MDMA. It is arranged as a collage.

Doblin, R. A Proposal for Orphan Pharmaceuticals, Inc. A Division of Neurobiological Technologies, Inc. August 4, 1987.

A review of the history of MDMA and the arguments for its legitimate commercial consideration are presented. The NTI Board of Directors did not accept this proposal.

Doblin, R. Risk Assessment: The FDA and MDMA Research. *PM&E (Psychedelic Monographs and Essays)* 4: 98 (1989).

A brief review of the current status of the neurological toxicity studies, and an analysis of their extrapolation to human subjects.

Doblin, R. (1) MDMA: Risk Assessment and the FDA. April 14, 1989. (2) Regulation or Prohibition? MDMA Research in Switzerland and the United States. May 26, 1989. (3) Multidisciplinary Association for Psychedelic Studies. Summer, 1989.

These are three privately published tracts. The first reviews the present research status of MDMA, and presents an overview of the clinical experiments under way in Switzerland. The second essay lists the names and addresses of the Swiss researchers. The third entry is a continuing newsletter publication with articles and announcements concerning developments in the area of psychedelic research. News on MDMA is of the highest priority.

Dowling, C.G. The Trouble with Ecstasy. *Life Magazine,* August, 1985, pp. 88-94.

A pictorial article timed to coincide with the first of the hearings concerning the eventual fate of MDMA, and with the effective placement of it under emergency legal control.

Edwards, G. Blasted with Ennui. *Brit. Med. J.* 298: 136 (1989).

A highly critical opinion is shared with the readers concerning yet another drug being promoted as an adjunct to psychotherapy, given a appealing name, and as has happened before, eventually discovered to be highly damaging.

Ehrlich, B. Understanding Ecstasy: The MDM Story. Privately Printed Book Manuscript. About 70 pages. 1986.

This is a partial draft of a book, privately printed and circulated, covering the history and paramedical use of MDMA.

Ehrnstein, I.B., Reflections on Drug Enforcement and Drug Use. *Psychedelic Monographs and Essays,* 2: 17-24 (1987).

An instructive and favorable review of the history and the possible usefulness of MDMA is presented. There are suggestions offered as to how the inexperienced subject might approach MDMA for personal development.

Eisner, B. *ECSTASY, The MDMA Story*. Ronin Press, Berkeley 1989. 228 pages.
This book is a complete review of much of the background and history of the origin and entry of MDMA into the culture. It was in this book that an earlier edition of this bibliographic summary appeared

Farrell, M. Ecstasy and the Oxygen of Publicity. *Brit. J. Addiction,* 84: 943 (1989).
A short and appropriate review of how the furious and righteous publicity given the use of MDMA in Britain, fuelled its popularity.

Fernandez, P.L. MDMA (Extasis). Una Droga de Diseno de Alta Toxicidad Potencial. *Anal. Real Acad. Nac. Med.* 111: 485-504 (1994).
(no abstract available)

Fitzgerald, J. MDMA and Harm. *Int. J. Drug Policy,* 2, 4: Jan-Feb. (1991).
An overview of the history of MDMA use is presented, to allow the formation of opinion as to the properness of its legalization. It is concluded that no change in the legal status is warranted.

Fitzgerald, J. MDMA and Harm. *Int. J. Drug Policy,* 2: 22-24 (1993)
An analysis of the MDMA problem, vis-a-vis Australian law, is presented. There balance of the literature presentation of harm regarding the drug leans towards its being relatively safe. However, there is no evidence that the community is harmed or suffering in any way by its being maintained in an illegal status. Thus it should remain illegal.

Gallagher, W. The Looming Menace of Designer Drugs. *Discover,* 7: 24 (1986).
A long and gloomy article on the growing problems of uncontrolled analogues of heroin. There is a heavy emphasis on the medical professional's use and involvement in drug abuse. A one page side-box gives a view of MDMA, with balance between therapeutic potential and the risks of using unevaluated and unapproved new drugs.

Garfinkel, S.L. The Price of Ecstasy. *New Age Journal,* May 1989, p. 22.
This is a brief review of the current legal/clinical status of MDMA, with a note-worthy quote from the FDA spokeswoman Susan Cruzan. 'It is irrelevant to talk about clinical trials of a drug that has no legitimate medical use.'

George, S. and Braithwait, R.A, Drugs of Abuse Screening in the West Midlands: A Six Year Retrospective Survey of Results. *Ann. Clin. Biochem.* 31: 473-478 (1994).
Some 27,800 urine specimens were analyzed over a six year period. Morphine (heroin) and amphetamine were the major drugs seen, but there was very little evidence for the use of methamphetamine or MDMA.

Gertz, K.R. 'HugDrug' Alert: The Agony of Ecstasy. *Harper's Bazaar,* November 1985, p. 48.
A popular article is offered, with a balanced discussion of the case for, and the case against, the use of MDMA.

Gibb, J.W., Johnson, M. and Hanson, G.R. Neurochemical Basis of Neurotoxicity. *Neurotoxicity,* 11: 317-322 (1990).
The properties of 6-hydroxydopamine and 5,7-dihydroxytryptamine are reviewed, in a presentation of the dopaminergic and serotonergic systems. The principle drugs of discussion are methamphetamine and MDMA.

Gibb, J.W., Johnson, M., Stone, D. and Hanson. G.R. MDMA: Historical Perspectives. *Ann. N.Y. Acad. Sci.* 600: 601-612 (1990).
A review of a number of neurotoxicological aspects of MDMA is presented.

Gibb, J.W., Stone, D., Johnson, M. and Hanson, G.R. Neurochemical Effects of MDMA. *The Clinical, Pharmacological and Neurotoxicological Effects of the Drug MDMA.* Kluwer, New York. (1990) Ed: S.J. Peroutka.
An extensive review of the neurotoxicological properties of MDMA is presented. The data suggest that although MDMA perturbs both the dopaminergic and serotoninergic systems of experimental animals, it is only the serotoninergic system that is persistently altered.

Glennon, R. A. Discriminative Stimulus Properties of Phenylisopropylamine Derivatives. *Drug and Alcohol Dependence,* 17: 119-134 (1986).
A broad review of many substituted phenylisopropylamines and their responses in discriminative studies in animals trained to discriminate amphetamine (or, separately, DOM) from saline. MDMA produced no DOM-appropriate response (DOM is an hallucinogen) but did cross react with amphetamine (a stimulant).

Gold, M.S. Ecstasy, Etc. *Alcoholism and Addiction,* Sept-Oct. 1985. p. 11.
Criticism of the popular use of untested drugs such as MDMA is presented. It is argued that all new 'wonder euphorogenics' should be considered extremely dangerous until proven safe and effective for a specific condition by the FDA and the medical research community.

Goldstein, R. The Facts about 'Ecstasy' A Talk with Andrew Weil. *The Village Voice,* February 7, 1989, p. 31.
This is an overview of the present status of MDMA, followed by a careful and balanced interview with Andrew Weil on its clinical use and hazards.

Grant, A. and Wagner, J. Case Book: The Batman. Ecstasy. *Detective Comics No. 594,* published by DC Comics, Inc. 1988.
A magnificently lurid illustrated story of how the use of Ecstasy drove a sound business man and currency trader to total madness, voices in the head, urge to blow up the principals in the New York drug trade. He was the final victim.

Grinspoon, L. and Bakalar, J.B. What is MDMA? *Harvard Medical School Mental Health Letter* 2: 8 (1985).
A brief presentation of the cogent facts that define MDMA.

Grinspoon, L. and Bakalar, J.B. A Potential Psychotherapeutic Drug? *The Psychiatric Times,* January, 1986. pp 4-5, 18.
A review of the development of the use of drugs in psychotherapy, and a discussion of the role that a drug like MDMA might play in this medical area.

Grinspoon, L. and Bakalar, J.B. Can Drugs be Used to Enhance the Psychotherapeutic Process? *Am. J. Psychotherap.* 40: 393-404 (1986).
There is evidence that the psychotherapeutic process can be enhanced by the use of drugs that invite self-disclosure and self-exploration. Such drugs might help to fortify the therapeutic alliance and in other ways. One drug that may prove promising for this purpose is the psychedelic amphetamine MDMA.

Hagerty, C. 'Designer Drug' Enforcement Act Seeks to Attack

Problem at Source. *American Pharmacy* NS25: 10-11(1985).
An extensive argument is presented for the passage of the 'Designer Drug' Enforcement Act, to effectively attack the sources of new drugs.

Harris, L. S. **The Stimulants and Hallucinogens under Consideration: A Brief Overview of their Chemistry and Pharmacology.** *Drug and Alcohol Dependence*, 17: 107-118 (1986).
A literature review is made of a number of drugs that are under consideration for international control. MDMA is briefly mentioned, and described as being in man more of a stimulant than a hallucinogen.

Heilig, S. **MDMA Update: The Science and Politics of Ecstasy.** *Calif. Soc. Addic. Med. News* 20: 1-5 (1993).
A review of the recent animal studies, toxicological observations, and potential research studies with MDMA is presented.

Heilig, S. **Book Review: Jerome Beck and Marsha Rosenbaum, Pursuit of Ecstasy: The MDMA Experience. (New York: State University of New York Press, 1994)** 237 + ix pp. *J. Psychoact. Drugs,* 26: 299-300 (1994).
This book review is most favorable, and reflects the quiet move to find some public acknowledgment of the potential acknowledgment of MDMA in a research, medical or therapeutic context.

Hershkovits, D. **Ecstasy: The Truth About MDMA.** *High Times,* November, 1985. p. 33.
An interview was held with Richard Seymour, author of the book MDMA. Many good and reasonable questions, answered directly and accurately.

Hollister, L.E. **Clinical Aspects of Use of Phenylalkylamine and Indolealkylamine** Hooft, P.J. and van de Voorde, H.P.., **Reckless Behavior Related to the Use of 3,4-Methylenedioxymethamphetamine (Ecstasy): Apropos of a Fatal Accident During Car-surfing.** *Int. J. Leg. Med.* 106: 328-329 (1994).
A man suffered a lethal head injury after falling from a moving car. Both MDMA and alcohol were present, and were presumed to have contributed to his reckless behaviour.

Hollister, L. E. **Clinical Aspects of Use of Phenylalkylamine and Indolealkylamine Hallucinogens.** *Psychopharmacol. Bull.* 22: 977-979 (1986).
A generally negative evaluation of the use of hallucinogens (such as MDA, MDMA, LSD) based largely on the potential of neurotoxicity and the absence of clinical verification of value. Most of the value must be gleaned from studies of twenty years ago, and the absence of recent research is ascribed to unusually high toxicity or to the lack of interest. The legal difficulties are not addressed.

Johnson, T. **Trafic d'Extase.** *Actuel* 137. November (1990) p. 107 et seq.
This is an in-depth but reasonably current overview of the drug ecstasy and its role in the drug scene in Amsterdam, where it is apparently being synthesized for the entire continent. Comments from the as well detractors as the promoters are gathered together, with a final word on its potential legalization.

Jones, R. **Why the Thought Police Banned Ecstasy.** *Simply Living,* 2. 10. p. 91-95.
A review of the United States controversy concerning MDMA as seen through Australian eyes. There are implications of considerable use in Australia.

Kirsch, M.M. *'Designer Drugs'.* **CompCare Publications, Minneapolis. 1986.**
This book is organized into chapters that treat each of some half-dozen drugs that have been created or modified so as to circumvent explicit legal restrictions, or have recently emerged into popularity. One chapter, entitled 'Ecstasy', spins together the popular lore concerning MDMA with quotations from various writers and lecturers and several anonymous users.

Klein, J. **The New Drug They Call 'Ecstasy',** *New York* (magazine), May 20, 1985, pp 38-43.
This is a popular article that brings together quotations that express the broad range of attitudes held by both the proponents and the opponents of the current clinical employment of MDMA. Some historical background is presented, as well as an articulate description of the effect the drug produces.

Korf, D., Blanken, P. and Nabben, T. *Een Nieuwe Wonderpil? Verspreiding, effecten en risico's van ecstasygebruik in Amsterdam.* **A book in Dutch of over 150 pages. (1991)**
The origins, distribution, availability, and use of Ecstasy in The Netherlands is discussed. Since 1988, MDMA has been covered under the Opium Act, but there is little active police intervention. There appears to be extensive misrepresentation of this drug with frequent substitution of some amphetamine-like substitute. The street price remains very high.

Laverty, R. and Logan, B.J. **Ecstasy Abuse.** *New Zealand Med. J.* 102 451 (1989).
A request is extended to practitioners for information concerning possible MDMA exposure with their patients. If possible, a sample of the drug involved in any referral could be given for analysis, which would allow an accurate estimate to be made of the magnitude of this particular drug problem in New Zealand.

Leavy, J. **Ecstasy: The Lure and the Peril.** *The Washington Post* June 1, 1985. Zagoria, S. **More 'Peril' than 'Lure.'** *ibid.* July 3, 1985,
A well researched and careful article reviewing all aspects of the MDMA palavar. The reply by Mr. Zagoria expressed the thought that Ms. Leavy's presentation was too enticing, with lure outweighing peril.

Leverant, R. **MDMA Reconsidered.** *J. Psychoactive Drugs,* 18: 373-379 (1986).
A summation of thoughts and impressions gathered at the Oakland, California Conference on MDMA (May, 1986). The theme presented is the need of open-mindedness in the area of personal and well as clinical freedom of research, and MDMA was used as a focal point.

Lyttle, T. and Montagne, M. **Drugs, Music, and Ideology: A Social Pharmacological Interpretation of the Acid House Movement.** *Intern. J. Addict.* 27: 1159-1177 (1992).
The development of the 'Acid House' phenomenon from it's origin in 1988 in England, is reviewed with particular emphasis placed on the role played by music and drugs in the changing of states of consciousness.

Mandi, J. **Ecstasy.** *The Face:* 38, November, 1991. Three page article.
A rather balanced and reasonable article about some reasons for, and some difficulties associated with, the excessive use of MDMA.

McConnell, H. **MDMA.** *The Journal.* July 1, 1986 pp. 11-12.

A thorough review of the Oakland, California MDMA conference is presented, in considerable detail and with excellent balance.

McDonnell, E. One World, One Party. *S.F. Weekly*, January 29, 1992 pp 12-13.
A view of the rave scene in San Francisco, with the emphasis on MDMA (but with LSD and mushrooms also contributing) and smart drinks (vitamins, minerals, and little alcohol). and lights and music and colour. All is very expensive, and very much in style. Psychedelic drug use is taken for granted.

McDowell, M.M., Kleber, H.D. MDMA – Its History and Pharmacology. *Psychiatric Ann*. 24: 127-130 (1994).
A review of MDMA use and history is presented. Most of the emphasis is on the neurotoxic and related adverse effects of the drug, and there are few allusions to its virtues.

McGuire, P. and Fahy, T. Flashbacks following MDMA. *Brit. J. Psychiatry.* 160: 276 (1992).
A retrospective analysis of an earlier report concerning MDMA use has uncovered the fact that flashbacks had occurred. An apology is extended for the polypharmacy that was implied in that report; cannabis was present but there was no evidence for the presence of MDMA. Apparently an analysis for MDMA use was not asked for and so it was not reported as being present. More frequent urine screenings should help to implicate MDMA with medical problems, in light of the current widespread use of the drug.

McKenna, D.J. and Peroutka, S.J. The Neurochemistry and Neurotoxicity of 3,4- Methylenedioxymethamphetamine (MDMA, 'Ecstasy'), *J. Neurochem.* 54: 14-22 (1990).
A thoroughly documented review of the present state of knowledge of the effects of MDMA on animal systems.

McKenna, D.J. and Peroutka, S.J. Serotonin Neurotoxins: Focus on MDMA (3,4-Methylenedioxymethamphetamine, 'Ecstasy'). In: *Serotonin Receptor Subtypes: Basic and Clinical Aspects*, Editor, Peroutka, Wiley-Liss, New York. pp.125-146 (1991).
In a volume on serotonin receptors (part of a receptor biochemistry and methodology series) the 'halogenated amphetamine' receptor subtype is characterized in an extensive review essay of MDMA and the neurotoxicity that is ascribed to it.

McNeil, L. A Woodstock of Their Own. *Details*, Decemeber 1991 pp. 26-38.
This is a candid expose of one explicit rave weekend in Los Angeles. The picture shows that the entire structure is build about the drug MDMA which is an essential component of the event.

Millman, R.B. and Beeder, A.B., The New Psychedelic Culture: LSD, Ecstasy, 'Rave' Parties and The Grateful Dead. *Psychiat. Ann.* 24: 148-150 (1994).
A review is presented of the relationship between psychedelic drug use and social phenomena, with particular emphasis on the drug-dominated cultures such as the Grateful Dead and the rave scene. The goal for the physician who is treating these young people is to encourage the development of rewarding alternatives, including a sense of belonging in 'straight' society.

Molliver, M.E., Berger, U.V., Mamounas, L.A., Molliver, D.C., O'Hearn, E. and Wilson, M.A. Neurotoxocity of MDMA and Related Compounds: Anatomical Studies. *Ann. N. Y. Acad. Sci,* 600: 640-664 (1990).

A review and discussion is presented from a recent symposium of serotonin neuropharmacology. Comparisons of MDMA, MDA, p-chloroamphetamine and fenfluramine are made.

Nasmyth, P. The Agony and the Ecstasy. *The Face*, October, 1986 p. 52.
A popularized article from England on the properties and the uses of MDMA. It strongly suggests that the drug is already deeply instilled in British culture.

Nasmyth, P. Laing on Ecstasy. *Int. J.Drug Policy*. 1: 14-15 (1989).
A brief profile of the late controversial psychiatrist R.D.Laing, and his views of the potential of the drug MDMA in a therapy role.

Newmeyer, J.A. Some Considerations on the Prevalence of MDMA Use. *J. Psychoactive Drugs* 18: 361-362 (1986).
An epidemiology survey of MDMA use (as of 1986) from the usual information sources (Drug Abuse Warning Network, DAWN; the Community Epidemiology Work Group, CEWG; police department reports, medical examiner or coroner's office reports) gives little indications that there is a medical problem associated with its use. Epidemiologically, it can not be considered at the present time a problem. It may well be that the material currently enjoys controlled, careful use by a number of cognoscenti (as did LSD in the early 1960's) and perhaps in future years a larger number of less sophisticated individuals will be drawn into its usage, and will find ways to evince adverse reactions, police involvement, and other unpleasant consequences.

Newmeyer, J.A. X at the Crossroads. *J. Psychoactive Drugs*, 25: 341-342 (1993).
A short essay addresses the question of the eventual responses of the public to MDMA. Arguments are presented that support its gaining de facto tolerance (achieving a status akin to that of marijuana) but other observations that could lead to a hostile LSD-like rejection. He believes that the next two years will be decisive.

Nichols, D.E. MDMA Represents a New Type of Pharmacologic Agent and Cannot be Considered to be either a Hallucinogenic Agent or an Amphetamine-type Stimulant.
This is an unpublished essay submitted both to the DEA and to the WHO group, through the offices of Richard Cotton. It presents a point by point analysis from both in vitro and in vivo studies of the pharmacological properties of MDMA and its isomers, with MDA (a structurally related hallucinogenic compound) and other amphetamines. He concludes that its actions represent a new classification of pharmacology, and clinical research with it in psychotherapy would argue against placing it in Schedule I.

Nichols, D.E. Differences Between the Mechanism of Action of MDMA, MBDB, and the Classic Hallucinogens. Identification of a New Therapeutic Class: Entactogens, *J. Psychoactive Drugs*, 18: 305-313 (1986).
This article presents a review of the extensive neurological and pharmacological evidence that supports the stand that MDMA and MBDB should be classified neither as hallucinogens (psychedelic drugs) nor as simple stimulants. An argument is made for a novel classification, entactogens.

Nichols, D.E. and Oberlender, R. Structure-Activity Relationships of MDMA and Related Compounds: A New Class of Psychoactive Drugs. *Ann. N. Y. Acad. Sci.* 600: 613-625 (1990).
A review of the pharmacological and behavioural properties of MDMA

and MBDB suggests that they represent members of a new class of psychopharmacological agents. A extensive discussion is also included.

Nichols, D.E. and Oberlender, R. Structure-Activity Relationships of MDMA-Like Substances, NIDA Research Monograph Series #94 pp. 1-29 (1989).

A critical review of the structures and activities of compounds related to MDMA is presented, with particular attention directed to a somewhat less neurotoxic homolog MBDB. A considerable discussion is attached, with questions, comments, and answers, from the actual conference.

Nichols, D.E. and Oberlender, R. Structure-Activity Relationships of MDMA and Related Compounds: A New Class of Psychoactive Agents? *The Clinical, Pharmacological and Neurotoxicological Effects of the Drug MDMA.* **Kluwer, New York. (1990) Ed: S.J. Peroutka.**

An extensive analysis has been made of the structures of drugs that resemble MDMA, and the nature of their action. An argument is presented for the acceptance of a pharmacological classification of Entactogens as being distinct from the Hallucinogens, or psychedelic drugs.

O'Rourke, P.J. Tune In. Turn On. Go To The Office Late on Monday. *Rolling Stone,* **December 19, 1985 p. 109.**

The MDMA popularity craze is presented in a humorous retrospective of the drug attitudes of the 1960's.

Peroutka, S.J. Incidence of Recreational Use of 3,4-Methylenedioxymethamphetamine (MDMA, 'Ecstasy') on an Undergraduate Campus. *New England J. Med.* **317: 1542-1543 (1987).**

A random, and anonymous, poll of undergraduates at Stanford University (California) showed that some 39% of all students were experienced with MDMA (mean number of uses was 5.4, and dosage range was 60-250 mg). To date, he finds no evidence to suggest that MDMA is neurotoxic in humans.

Peroutka, S.J. 'Ecstasy': A Human Neurotoxin? *Arch. Gen. Psychiat.* **46: 191 (1989).**

A letter to the editor presents three anecdotal observations in connection with the recreational use of MDMA. (1) Frequent use decreases the favorable responses. (2) Chronic use changes the nature of the response, and (3) the material appears not to be addictive. It has been concluded that there may well be a long-term and potentially irreversible effect of MDMA on the human brain. Recreational use should be avoided.

Randall, T. Ecstasy-Fuelled 'Rave' Parties Become Dances of Death for English Youths. *J. Am. Med. Soc.* **268: 1505-1506 (1992).**

A news report and medical perspective on the problems being reported as associated with the use of ecstasy (MDMA) in the British rave scene. A brief history of ecstasy is provided.

Randall, T. 'Rave' Scene, Ecstasy Use, Leap Atlantic. *J. Am. Med. Soc.* **268: 1506 (1992).**

A brief history of the 'rave' scene in Britain is presented. The recent appearance of the phenomenon in the United States, and elsewhere around the world, is discussed.

Rattray, M. Ecstasy: Towards an Understanding of the Biochemical Basis of the Action of MDMA. *Essays in Biochemistry,* **26: 77-87 (1991).**

A review of the history, pharmacoloy and neurochemistry of MDMA is presented. Much of the presented information is factual, some of it is speculative, and several points are simply wrong.

Renfroe, C.L. MDMA on the Street: Analysis Anonymous. *J. Psychoactive Drugs,* **18: 363-369 (1986).**

In the twelve years (up to 1983) that PharmChem conducted its Analysis Anonymous service, they evaluated over 20,000 samples of street drugs. MDMA and MDA had been classified together (in some 610 examples) and of these 72 had been alleged to be MDMA. In the years 1984-1985, a cooperating reference laboratory (S.P., Miami, Florida) reported an additional 29 alleged MDMA samples. Of these 101 samples, over half proved to be, indeed, MDMA, and half of the remaining contained MDMA. This is considered a remarkably high validity rate. The origins, descriptions, and costs are discussed.

Riedlinger, J.E. The Scheduling of MDMA: A Pharmacist's Perspective. *J. Psychoactive Drugs,* **17: 167-171 (1985).**

A critical viewpoint is taken of the scheduling procedures employed with MDMA. This paper is adapted from the original letter of protest sent to the DEA, and from the written testimony presented at the hearings.

Riedlinger, T. and Riedlinger, J. The 'Seven Deadly Sins' of Media Hype in Light of the MDMA Controversy. *PM&E (Psychedelic Monographs and Essays).* **4: 22 (1989).**

This is a carefully written criticism of the uneven ways in which the popular press weighs and presents controversial issues such as the story concerning MDMA.

Riedlinger, T.J. and Riedlinger, J.E. Psychedelic and Entactogenic Drugs in the Treatment of Depression. *J. Psycho. Drugs,* **26: 41-55 (1994).**

Both the virtues of, and the problems associated with, the incorporation of psychedelic drugs into psychotherapy are discussed.

Rippchen, R. *MDMA Die Neue Sympathiedroge.* **Der Grune Zweig 103, Medieneexperiment D-6941 Lohrbach, West Germany (1986).**

A book of some 47 pages, giving an immense body of information on MDMA (in German) including translations of articles by Greer. Also included is information on other drugs such as MDE and 2CB.

Roberts, M. Drug Abuse. MDMA: 'Madness, not Ecstasy' **Crosstalk section,** *Psychology Today.* **June, 1986.**

An update of an earlier article (Psychology Today, May, 1985) which emphasizes the neurological findings, and the concept of unregulated drug synthesis. Congressional action prohibiting the manufacture and distribution of similar drugs is urged.

Roberts, T.B. The MDMA Question. Section on Social Concerns. *AHP Perspective.* **May, 1986. p. 12.**

This is a soul-searching review asking the questions as to where we must acknowledge the line between the need of drug use in therapy, and tolerating drug use in society. Provisions must be made, of course, for both.

Robins, C. The Ecstatic Cybernetic Amino Acid Test. *San Francisco Examiner* **Image, February 16, 1992 p. 6 et seq.**

A trip with the author is made through an evening, of a San Francisco rave. The noise, the excessive focus on drugs, smart drinks, energy, dance, music, cyberpunk this and virtual reality that; all make a statement of rebellion. It may all die out, but the concept is truly international in scope, and might soon require the older generation to take it seriously.

Rosenbaum, M. and Doblin, R. Why MDMA Should Not Have

Been Made Illegal, Unpublished Essay, 1990.
A brief history and analysis of the illegalization of MDMA is presented.

Saunders, N. 'E for Ecstasy,' self published, London (1993) 318 pp.
A thorough review of the medical, social and legal history of MDMA is presented, in a well documented analysis of this highly controversial drug, at the height of its popularity. The rave scene is described, as is the beginning acceptance of MDMA as a valuable therapeutic tool. An annotated bibliography, by Alexander Shulgin, is attached.

Saunders, N. MDMA – The View from England. *MAPS*, 4: 22-24 (1993).
A review is presented of the present position of MDMA in England. A critical discussion of the medical reports, the legal status, and the problems of misrepresentation which are inevitable when the streets are the only source for purchase. Speculations as to future developments are encouraging.

Sawyer, M. Ecstasy. *Select*, July 1992 pp 56-61.
A strongly written review covering all sides of the rave scene in England, and the damage that is being done by the strenuous laws against ecstasy. Emphasis is placed on the fraud that is rampant in the misrepresentation of the identities of the drugs that are being sold as MDMA.

Schuckit, M.A. MDMA (Ecstasy): An Old Drug with New Tricks. *Drug Abuse and Alcoholism Newsletter*, 23: 2 April, 1994.
A review is presented of the history, social use and dangers of MDMA use. The intended audience is the practicing physician.

Schulman, R. The Losing War Against 'Designer Drugs.' *Business Week*, June 24, 1985 pp. 101-104.
An overview of the MDMA controversy. A preview is presented, of the pharmaceutical industry's response (OK to ban it, but not with the haste that might have a chilling effect on the development of new pharmaceuticals) and local law enforcement enthusiasm (Florida has granted the State Attorney General the power to place a drug on the Controlled Drug List in as little as 24 hours).

Sedgwick, B., Lo, P. and Yee, M. Screening and Confirmation of 3,4-Methylenedioxymethamphetamine (MDMA) in Urine: Evaluation of 1000 Specimens. *Abstracts of the CAT/SOFT Meetings*, Oct. 29 -Nov. 1, 1986, Reno/Lake Tahoe, Nevada.
A sequence of 1000 'at risk' samples were screened for the presence of methamphetamine (MA) and/or MDMA (not distinguishable in the initial analysis). Of 133 presumptive positive tests, none proved to be positive for MDMA.

Seymour, R.B. *'MDMA'*, Haight-Ashbury Publications, San Francisco. 1986
This is a volume devoted entirely to the single drug MDMA. Nine chapters discuss its origins, facts that apply to it, its bright side and dark side, in a carefully balanced presentation. It was made available for the Oakland, California symposium, MDMA: A Multidisciplinary Conference, May 17-18, 1986.

Seymour, R.B. Ecstasy on Trial. *High Times*, November, 1986. p. 33.
A retrospective review article of the controversies stirred up by the publicity that followed the government hearings and the illegalization of MDMA.

Seymour, R.B., Wesson, D.R. and Smith, D.E. Editor's Introduction. *J. Psychoactive Drugs*. 18: 287 (1986).

An introduction is made to an entire issue of the Journal dedicated to the several papers presented at a two-day conference on the topic of MDMA. This was held May 17-18, 1986, at the Health Education Centre of the Merritt Peralta Medical Centre, in Oakland, California.

Shafer, J. MDMA: Psychedelic Drug Faces Regulation. *Psychology Today*, May, 1985. pp. 68-69.
This is a short overview presenting the clinical and legal views of a number of psychiatrists, administrators and researchers.

Shulgin, A.T. Twenty Years on an Ever-changing Quest, Psychedelic Reflections, Eds. L. Grinspoon and J.B. Bakalar, *Human Science Press*, New York (1983). pp. 205-212.
This is an essay on the philosophy of research associated with psychedelic drugs. MDMA is described briefly, with some of its history, pharmacology, and therapeutic potential.

Shulgin, A.T. What is MDMA? *PharmChem Newsletter* 14: 3-11 (1985).
A hypothetical interview is presented, distilling the questions fielded from many reporters, and the substance of the answers given to these questions.

Shulgin, A.T. The Background and Chemistry of MDMA. *J. Psychoactive Drugs*, 18: 291-304 (1986).
This review gathers together the physical properties of MDMA, and the published information as to toxicity and pharmacology, as of the date of the Oakland, California conference (May, 1986).

Shulgin, A.T. History of MDMA, *The Clinical, Pharmacological and Neurotoxicological Effects of the Drug MDMA*. Kluwer, New York. (1990) Ed: S.J. Peroutka.
A review, with 158 references, is presented that outlines the current (mid-1989) literature on then published literature on MDMA.

Siegel, R.K. Chemical Ecstasies. *Omni*, August 1985. p. 29.
This short essay advises caution in the immediate acceptance of drugs that are enthusiastically promoted but which have not been thoroughly researched.

Smith, D.E. and Seymour, R.B. Abuse Folio: MDMA. *High Times*, May, 1986. p. 30.
There is a continuing series of drug information sheets, one being published in each issue of High Times. This contribution is a neutral, factual presentation of the nature and use, and of the hazards and liabilities associated with the drug MDMA.

Smith, D.E., Wesson, D.R. and Buffum, J. MDMA: 'Ecstasy' as an Adjunct to Psychotherapy and a Street Drug of Abuse. *California Society for the Treatment of Alcoholism and Other Drug Dependencies News*, 12: (September) 1985 pp 1-3. A letter to the Editors in response: Holsten, D.W. and Schieser, D.W. Controls over the Manufacture of MDMA. The original authors' reply: *ibid*. 12 (December) 1985 pp 14-15.
A brief review of the therapeutic virtues and abuse risks that are associated with MDMA, and the chilling effect that illegalization of drugs has had on medical research. The authors were reminded in rebuttal (Holsten and Schieser) that the exploratory use of new drugs outside of the controls that apply to the pharmaceutical industry carry real risks as to safety and quality of product.

Solowij, N. and Lee, N. Survey of Ecstasy [MDMA] Users

in Sydney. *Drug and Alcohol Directorate NSW Health Department*, 1991 (Sydney). CEIDA, PMB No. 6, P.O. Rozelle NSW 2039 (Australia).

An extensive survey is presented of many Ecstasy users in Sydney. It has been found that the principle use of the drug has been directed towards fun, at social gatherings, and the primary effects have been the expression of a positive mood state. A secondary effect has been that of stimulation with an expression of energy and activation. Reports describe the properties of insight and of perceptual/sensual enhancement.

Solowij, N., Hall, W. and Lee, N. Recreational MDMA Use in Sydney: A Profile of 'Ecstasy' Users and their Experiences with the Drug. *Brit. J. Addictions*, 87: 1161-1172 (1992).

An anonymous survey of MDMA users involved with the social 'rave' scene showed a consensus of the users' having experienced positive mood states, and feelings of closeness with others. The stimulant effects were secondary. The usual statements of caution are attached.

Steele, T.D., McCann, U.D., Ricaurte, G.A. 3,4-Methylenedioxymethamphetamine (MDMA, Ecstasy): Pharmacology and Toxicity in Animals and Humans. *Addiction*, 89: 539-551 (1994).

A thorough and well documented review of the animal and human pharmacology and toxicology of MDMA is presented.

Sternbach, G.L. and Varon, J. Designer Drugs. *Postgraduate Medicine*, 91: 169-176 (1992).

A review is presented of several synthetic variations of known illegal drugs. The major emphasis is on the opiates (modification of demerol, i.e., MPPP and MPTP) and on the mescaline-methamphetamine analogues (namely, MDA, MDMA and MDEA).

Straus, H. From Crack to Ecstasy; Basement Chemists can Duplicate almost any Over-the-border Drug. *American Health*, June, 1987 pp. 50-54.

A brief review of the concept of special formulations or syntheses of drugs for the extra-medical market. MDMA is brought in as a minor example.

Szabo, P. MDMA Restrictions too Hasty? *The Journal*, July/August 1989, p. 4.

A brief news report describes a study reported to the American Psychiatric Association meeting (San Francisco, 1989) involving some 20 psychiatrists who were familiar with MDMA. The opinion of Dr. Liester (University of California at Irvine) sums up the consensus. There is a need for clinical research with this promising drug, and this is not likely in view of the Government's current restrictions.

Szukaj, M. MDMA (Ecstasy) – Gef hrliche Drog oder Psychotherapeutikum? *Nervenarzt*, 65: 802-805 (1994).

Both the abuse and the number of deaths associated with MDMA is increasing. A review is presented of its history, effects and side-effects. Its relevance for clinical practice is discussed.

Toufexis, A. A Crackdown on Ecstasy. *Time Magazine*, June 10, 1985. p. 64.

A news report on the placing of MDMA into emergency Schedule I status. The complement to Newsweek's positive article of about the same time.

Taylor, J.M. MDMA Frequently Asked Questions List. Internet (Usenet) Newsgroup alt.drugs, January 5, 1994

This is a review of the known facts relating to MDMA. It is balanced and fair, but it maintains the chemical errors from the Chemical Abstracts in its synthetic portion, that hydrogen peroxide is used in place of water in the final hydrolysis. Considering its very wide public distribution, this distillation of facts is of excellent quality and must be respected as a fine public service.

Taylor, J.M., MDMA Frequently Asked Questions List. USENET news group alt.drugs January 7, 1994.

This extensive summation of the chemistry, pharmacology and medical uses and problems associated with the use of MDMA is representative of the wealth of information that is available from postings on the internet. There are many FTP sites, and database collections that can be rapidly accessed, and which contain extensive information that is remarkably accurate and which is being continuously updated.

Traver, A.R., 'El Extasis.' Una n del MDMA, MDA y Dem s Feniletilaminas Psicoactias. *Premio Socidrogalcobol*, 1989.

A review is offered covering the recent appearance of a new class of drugs called 'designer drugs' or 'synthetic drugs.' The most widely used examples are MDMA and MDA.

Turkington, C. Brain Damage Found with Designer Drugs. *Amer. Psychological Assn. Monitor*, March, 1986.

A negative review of the neurotransmitter research. This is probably the source of the oft-quoted 'fact' that these drugs are the first demonstration of a neurotransmitter being modified to a neurotoxin.

von Hoyer, E. The Agony of Ecstasy; A Consumer's Guide. Dated April 20, 1988, and identified with 'WRT 404 / S. Hubbard'

The is a short essay covering the use of, the action of, and the history of MDMA. It is replete with incorrect information, and has little other value.

Weigle, C. and Rippchen, R., *MDMA: Die Psychoaktive Substanz fur Therapie, Ritual und Rekreation.* Der Grune Zweig 103, Germany. Printed in Austria about 1991. 88 pages.

A collection of essays on MDMA, some originally in German, some translated, covering the entire spectrum of clinical and social aspects of the drug.

Whitaker-Azmitia, P.M. Depression to Ecstasy. *The New Biologist*, 1: 145-148 (1989).

This is a review of a conference on the neuropharmacology of serotonin, sponsored by the New York Academy of Sciences, on July 10-13, 1989. The final session was devoted to MDMA and, involving its potential neurotoxicity, was one of the more controversial ones. It is stated that dramatic evidence was presented at the conference that a serious level of damage had occurred to the serotonin neurons of human MDMA users.

Wolfson, P.E. Letter to Richard Cotton, Dewey, Ballantine, Bushby, Palmer & Wood, Washington, D.C.

A report is made of the effective use of MDMA in conjunction with psychotherapy, in the treatment of both depressed and schizophrenic patients. The apparent anti-manic and anti-paranoia action of MDMA allowed the opening of discourse and allowed intervention with more conventional therapy. It is suggested that there is a promising potential for its use in certain psychotic situations, and a telling argument is made against its legal classification in Schedules I or II.

Woolverton, W.L. A Review of the Effects of Repeated Administration of Selected Phenethylamines. *Drug and Alcohol Dependence,* **17: 143-150 (1986)**

A review from the literature of the chronic toxicological findings regarding a number of compounds that are being proposed for international control. One reference to MDMA is cited, the Fed. Proc. note (Virus, et al. 45 1066 (1986) which has been published (see Commins, et al., 1987, section 8 above).

Wright, J.D. and Pearl, L. Knowledge and Experience of Young People Regarding Drug Misuse, 1969-94. *Brit. Med. J.* **310:** **20-24 (1995).**

A series of surveys have been made, at five year intervals, of students of the 14-15 year age. It was found that the exposure to illicit drugs has increased over the years, and within the last five years quite dramatically. Despite increased education, the level of knowledge remains limited. The primary reason for taking drugs is social pressure.

Wright, W.R. *XTC, Analyte of the Month,* **10: 3 (1989). Published by the American Association for Clinical Chemistry.**

A brief and factual review of MDMA, with a little history and some comments on the validity of immunological assays for MDMA using amphetamine assays.

Zizzo, P. MDMA – Aspects of it's Psychopharmacology. Unpublished essay written for Psych. 119, University of California at Davis, Spring 1989.

This 10 page essay briefly reviews the background and history of the therapeutic work done with MDMA.

Index

Other editions

My previous books on ecstasy were published in English as *E for Ecstasy*, *Ecstasy and the Dance Culture* and *Ecstasy, Dance Trance and Transformation* in the USA. Variations have been published in German, French, Italian, Portuguese, Czech and Hungarian with other translations in progress. Up to date details and ordering information can be found on my Internet site.

New book on the spiritual use of psychoactives

I am working on a book concerned with the spiritual effects of drugs and how they are used, based mainly on personal experiences. If you have any personal experience which may be of value to share with others, please do send me your account. More details and a progress report can be found through a link from my Internet site.

Making contact

I am always pleased to hear from readers and their feedback has helped me to make this book. But please remember that I am busy and writing letters is time consuming so I may not reply. However, I do make a point of answering any serious emails since this is very much quicker – if you don't get a reply it may be because I am away, but I also find that many of my replies are undelivered because the return address was not set up correctly. Before you ask questions, please check first to see if the answer is in this book or on my site.

> My email address is **nicholas@ecstasy.org**
> My Internet site is mirrored on both sides of the Atlantic:
> **http://ecstasy.org** in America
> **http://obsolete.com/ecstasy** in Europe

My site is regularly updated with new information. It has a section called Feedback for readers accounts and also questions with answers from experts.

Test results

I post up to date test results of ecstasy pills on my site whenever possible. I arrange for samples to be bought anonymously and sent to licensed laboratories, paying for the analysis from the proceeds of my books. My aim is that the analysis of pills sold will be so widely available and so frequently updated that those who bad quality ecstasy will go out of business. However, this is not always possible due to opposition from people who do not want results publicised.

Bookshop orders

Turnaround
Unit 3, Olympia Trading Estate
Coburg Road   tel: +44 181 829 3000
London, N22 6TZ   fax: +44 181 881 5088

Mail order

Nicholas Saunders
14 Neal's Yard
London, WC2H 9DP, UK   email: nicholas@ecstasy.org

fax: +44 171 836 3537   **single copy**   **pack of five**

			single copy	pack of five
UK	second class post	£11	£30	
Europe	surface	£12	£35	
	air	£13	not available	
Worldwide	surface	£12	£35	
	air	£16	not available	

Orders must be prepaid by Visa or Mastercard (give number, account address, name as on card, expiry date) **or** UK cheque or postal order **or** Giro or Eurocheque in pounds sterling made payable to Nicholas Saunders. No credit or other currencies.

Bulk cash on collection at less than half price

World Food Cafe
14 Neal's Yard
Covent Garden   Cash only, no cheques or credit cards
London   3pm to 5pm except Sundays
20 copies   £80   The cafe is doing me a favour by stocking these,
so please be prepared to wait and avoid lunch times. The books are supplied shrink wrapped in 20s only.

Library order details

Title: Ecstasy Reconsidered
Author: Nicholas Saunders
Publisher: Nicholas Saunders
ISBN: 0 9530065 0 6

See reverse for
Other editions
Making contact
Test results